Y0-BRL-203

ter of t...
...lirectly from the
...of its

...he subse...
t ...

THE CIVILIZATION OF THE OLD NORTHWEST

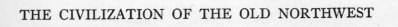

THE MACMILLAN COMPANY
NEW YORK · BOSTON · CHICAGO · DALLAS
ATLANTA · SAN FRANCISCO

MACMILLAN & CO., Limited
LONDON · BOMBAY · CALCUTTA
MELBOURNE

THE MACMILLAN COMPANY
OF CANADA, Limited
TORONTO

The Civilization
of the Old Northwest

*A Study of Political, Social, and
Economic Development,
1788 - 1812*

By

BEVERLEY W. BOND, JR.

*Professor of History
in the University of Cincinnati*

NEW YORK
THE MACMILLAN COMPANY
1934

Copyright, 1934, by
THE MACMILLAN COMPANY.

All rights reserved—no part of this book
may be reproduced in any form without
permission in writing from the publisher,
except by a reviewer who wishes to quote brief
passages in connection with a review written
for inclusion in magazine or newspaper.

Set up and printed.
Published January, 1934.

PRINTED IN THE UNITED STATES OF AMERICA

1977
B64c

To my Wife,

LOUISE WORTHINGTON BOND,

A Daughter of the Old Northwest

9769

PREFACE

As THE title implies, my aim in this volume has been to present a composite view of the civilization that arose in the formative period of the Old Northwest, between the first settlement at Marietta in 1788 and the outbreak of the War of 1812. In this quarter of a century the foundations of an American civilization were laid in this region which stretched roughly between the Ohio, the Mississippi, and the Great Lakes. At the same time an American colonial system was tested in this same area, and so successfully was it adapted to practical needs that the precedents set up in the Old Northwest, along with the distinctive civilization which developed there, were later transplanted into the Trans-Mississippi country.

In spite of its significant place in American history, the Old Northwest as a distinct section has been much neglected. Attracted by the glamour and romance of the Old South, the historian has been inclined to scorn what appears at first glance to be the rather colorless story of the Old Northwest. But a deeper survey shows that the prosaic details of a civilization founded upon corn and wheat, upon pigs and cattle, and upon hard, unremitting labor, have been ennobled by the pluck of the early settlers from so many states, who successfully set up in the wilderness a society that was patterned after their own ideals. The progress of this daring undertaking will form my main theme in this analysis of the civilization of the Old Northwest.

In the attempt to reconstruct the many-sided social, economic, and political development of the Old Northwest, I have made use of a number of collections of early Western material. Among them the library of the Historical and Philosophical Society of Ohio in Cincinnati has furnished

vii

the backbone for my research. In addition to many rare books and pamphlets, the Society's files of such important early newspapers as the *Centinel of the Northwestern Territory*, the *Western Spy*, and *Liberty Hall* have been important sources of information, while an extensive collection of early account books and other manuscripts, too numerous to mention in detail, has likewise proved useful. In Cleveland the library of the Western Reserve Historical Society yielded much valuable material, notably in the files of the *Scioto Gazette* and other early Western newspapers, and in many manuscript collections. I have made extensive use of two other important Ohio sources, the newspaper files in the Marietta College Library and the different executive journals of the Northwest Territory and the *Sargent Papers* in the Ohio State Archæological and Historical Society at Columbus. Among other collections I found important were the Indiana State Library at Indianapolis with its files of the *Indiana Gazette* and the *Western Sun*, the Pittsburgh Carnegie Library, serving as the chief depository of the *Pittsburgh Gazette*, and the Lexington, Kentucky, Public Library, containing many numbers of the *Kentucky Gazette*. In the library of the Wisconsin State Historical Society at Madison, also, I have used many newspapers and manuscripts that shed light upon early Western history.

The Library of Congress has proved to be a vast storehouse of material for this present volume. Its newspaper collections have been indispensable, including, in addition to the files of early Western gazettes, those of contemporary Eastern journals which have given a vivid background of the early Westward movement. In the manuscript division of the Library of Congress, also, I have found a wealth of material, notably in the first two volumes of the *Duncan McArthur Papers*, in the *Thomas W. Worthington Diary and Letters*, and in the *Northwest Territory MSS*. Another important collection in Washington that I have used extensively includes the transcripts of the Territorial Papers of Illinois, Indiana, Michigan, and the Northwest Territory which have been housed in the Department of State. Alongside the Library of Congress in the extent and value of its newspaper collections was the library of the American Antiquarian Society at Worcester, with files especially valuable for this present work, of the *Scioto Gazette*, the *Louisiana Gazette*, the *Missouri Gazette*, and the rare *Kentucky Almanac*. Likewise, in the Harvard University Library, I used many copies of early Western newspapers, notably *Freeman's Journal*.

In the many libraries in which I have carried on the research for this volume I have received the utmost courtesy and much intelligent aid. All of these kindly proofs of interest and friendship I hereby acknowledge, and especially my obligations to Miss L. Belle Hamlin, the former Librarian, and to Miss Eleanor Wilby, the present Librarian of the Historical and Philosophical Society of Ohio, to Mr. W. H. Cathcart, Director of the Western Reserve Historical Society Library, to Mr. V. Valta Parma, Custodian of the Rare Book Room of the Library of Congress, and to Mr. Clarence S. Brigham, Director of the American Antiquarian Society Library. Many other friends have aided with helpful suggestions, especially my colleague and former student, Mr. Charles Ray Wilson, who has carefully read and criticized the entire manuscript. Also, I wish to acknowledge my indebtedness to the Trustees of the Charles Phelps Taft Memorial Fund for the generous grant which has made possible the completion of this research and the preparation of the manuscript for publication.

BEVERLEY W. BOND, JR.

University of Cincinnati,
May 20, 1933.

CONTENTS

THE CIVILIZATION OF THE OLD NORTHWEST

Chapter I

THE BASIS FOR CIVILIZATION

LATE in 1787 an emigrant wagon left New England with the legend, "For the Ohio," painted in large white letters on its black canvas cover. This wagon was the vanguard of a migrating host which was eventually to take possession of some 248,000 square miles that lay roughly between the Ohio, the Mississippi, and the Great Lakes. The Old Northwest, as this region came to be called, had been ideally fashioned by Nature to become the home of a thriving population. A gently rolling country for the most part, it had few elevations that even approximated 1,500 feet. The eastern section and the northern tips extending along the Great Lakes were heavily forested. In what is now northern Indiana, however, in southern Michigan, and to the south in the main body of the land there were broad stretches of prairie that broadened out toward the west until they finally covered the landscape, except for a few trees along the watercourses. Usually the soil of the Old Northwest was exceedingly fertile. South of the Lakes stretched the great Corn Belt where the glaciers, as they receded, had left behind deep deposits of rich earth that was almost entirely free from stones, and once the trees had been cleared away, or the tough prairie sod had been broken up, this fertile stretch was easily cultivated by the primitive tools of the settler. Both in soil and climate this area between the Great Lakes and the Ohio was peculiarly suited to settlers from the original states. Here the Georgian or the South Carolinian, as well as the New Englander, would find a climate that was neither so warm as that of the South, nor so cold as

1

that of the North, and a soil that in general was well adapted to the varied grain and stock agriculture of the Middle States and Maryland.

After the Revolution the improvement of the different routes across the Appalachians soon made this rich region easily accessible to the people of the older states. The Wilderness Trail through Cumberland Gap came into use, roads were opened across Pennsylvania to Pittsburgh and Wheeling, and other less important routes were soon available. The extension of settlement into western New York and the opening up of the road along Lake Erie gave still another main route to the Old Northwest, one that avoided the mountain barrier in the way of the more southerly highways. Within the Old Northwest there was an excellent basis for transportation with abundant lines of communication, and no mountain ranges to be crossed. Along part of the eastern and all of the southern boundary, the Ohio River was an important avenue of transportation. On the west the Mississippi, and to the north the Great Lakes likewise made trade possible between the many little settlements, as well as with the outside world. The interior of the Old Northwest was intersected by many navigable streams, which by short portages between their headwaters also afforded easy communication between the Lakes, the Ohio, and the Mississippi. Among the most important of these cross-country water lanes were: the Cuyahoga-Muskingum, the Cuyahoga-Tuscarawas-Scioto, the Maumee-Miami, the Maumee-Wabash, the Chicago-Desplaines-Illinois, and the Fox-Wisconsin routes. There were also many smaller streams which led from the border waterways into the interior, and were navigable for a part of the year by the primitive craft of the pioneers. Among them were: the Hockhocking, the Whitewater, the Chippewa, the St. Joseph, and the Sandusky. By land there were many ancient Indian paths, on high ground out of reach of the floods, that avoided the many swamps in the valleys. Along all of these natural highways by land and by water Indians and fur traders had traveled for many years, and immigrants followed them to the fertile fields of the Old Northwest.[1]

Nominally this entire region was in possession of the United States after the peace treaty in 1783. The dramatic campaigns of George Rogers Clark, in coöperation with the scanty but hardy populations of western Pennsylvania, western Virginia, and Kentucky had won and held this vast domain for the Americans, and the peace commissioners had cannily clinched these gains. But the British still held the important trading posts on the Lakes, and from these centers, especially from Detroit, their fur traders were constantly carrying on intrigues among some 45,000 Indian inhabitants [2] who welcomed the trader, but strenuously objected to encroachments upon their hunting grounds by American settlers. Also, at Vincennes, in the Illinois settlements on the east bank of the Mississippi across from St. Louis, chiefly Cahokia and Kaskaskia, and in scattered trading posts, such as Prairie du Chien and Peoria, there were about 4,000 inhabitants, the majority of them French, but with American settlers arriving in ever-increasing numbers. At Detroit and Mackinaw, supposedly American territory, but under British control until the surrender of the Western posts in 1796, there were probably 2,000 additional inhabitants, chiefly French with a few British traders among them.[3] So far as their American allegiance was concerned these French settlers were not at all trustworthy, and, like the Indians, they were exposed to the intrigues of the British fur traders. The Spanish, too, from their posts on the west bank of the Mississippi, could be depended upon to use every opportunity to stir up the French

[1] Gephart, *Transportation and Industrial Development in the Middle West*, ch. I; Hulbert, *Historic Highways*, vol. II, chs. I and IV.

[2] This estimate is based upon approximately 15,100 Indian warriors in the Old Northwest. Obviously any attempt to give the total Indian warriors in the Old Northwest is exceedingly uncertain at best. Randall and Ryan, *History of Ohio*, vol. I, p. 170; Esarey, *History of Indiana*, vol. I, pp. 78-87; Thwaites, *Wisconsin*, p. 179.

[3] These estimates, too, are only approximate, Sargent to Secretary of State, September 30, 1796, *Journal of the Northwest Territory, 1788-1803; Census for 1800*, p. 87.

and the Indians. Under such conditions it was evident that if the United States was to continue to hold the Old Northwest, it was necessary to settle there a sufficient population of sturdy American pioneers to hold the region against Indian attacks and foreign intrigue. The opposition to such a policy from the civilized inhabitants would be negligible; but the Indians presented a much more serious problem, which was finally solved after a series of tedious campaigns.

As a precedent in the formulation of plans for the settlement of the Old Northwest, the American Congress had before it the British policy, to parcel out these Western lands in large tracts for the benefit of speculators who were organized as companies, and who would expect to realize as large a profit as possible in parceling out the land to individuals. The first of these organizations, the Ohio Company, had received a grant from Virginia in 1748 for about 200,000 acres that lay approximately between the Monongahela and the Ohio. Aside from the founding of a trading post at Will's Creek on the Potomac (Fort Cumberland) and the building of a road from there across the mountains to Brownsville on the Monongahela, this Company was of negligible importance. After the British came into undisputed possession of the Old Northwest, the Proclamation of 1763 continued a policy that forbade settlement west of the Alleghenies without specific permission; and in 1768 the Treaty of Fort Stanwix virtually recognized the Ohio as the southern boundary of the Indian country. The climax came when the Quebec Act in 1774 practically shut out American settlers from a land in which French legal procedure would rule. But though the British government plainly opposed indiscriminate settlements in the Old Northwest, it was quite evident that it had not given up the policy of extensive grants to colonizing corporations. There were numerous projects of this type, among them the ambitious plan for the colony of Charlotiana, which included approximately Illinois, Michigan, and Wisconsin. Benjamin Franklin, too, with his usual keen insight into future possibilities, proposed three new colonies, one at Detroit, another in the Illinois country, and a third on the lower Ohio. But the most important of these schemes was the Vandalia project which doubtless would have been successful under the tutelage of Benjamin Franklin, Thomas Walpole, and other astute promoters, had not the Revolution intervened.[4] All of these schemes, from the Ohio Company down, were founded upon the principle of selfish exploitation of the land for the benefit of favored individuals, the promoters of the different companies. The question arose, then: would the new American government adopt the time-honored mercantilist principles of the British colonial policy, or would it support the liberal ideas of the Revolution in a more democratic land system that recognized the interests of the individual settler?

Soon after the peace treaty was confirmed, it was apparent that some definite policy with regard to the Old Northwest was necessary. Aside from the threats from British and Spanish intrigues, there was serious danger lest the westbound tide of emigrants might turn without legal sanction into the Old Northwest, stirring up the Indians and increasing by their irresponsible conduct the complications that already existed. Scarcely had the Revolution ended when the people of the Atlantic Coast began literally to swarm and to strike out for new homes. The available lands in western Pennsylvania and western Virginia were rapidly filling up, and in spite of paper prohibitions the increasing host of emigrants threatened to force their way across the Ohio into the rich lands of the Old Northwest. Indeed, soon after the close of the Revolution, a considerable number of squatters had made clearings and built their primitive cabins on the north bank of the Ohio.[5] Therefore from every standpoint it was desirable that the Federal government should take the initiative and direct settlement in the Old Northwest, in such

[4] Howard, *Preliminaries* of the Revolution, pp. 226-233; Alvord, *Mississippi Valley in British Politics*, vol. II, ch. V, especially.

[5] Hulbert, *Ohio in the Time of the Confederation*, pp. 98-99; King, *Ohio*, pp. 191-192.

systematic fashion that retaliation on the part of the French and Indians would not be needlessly aroused, and that a population would be secured whose loyalty to hold the land against foreign intrigues could be depended upon.

Fortunately the field was soon clear for an aggressive American policy in the Old Northwest. Had the four states —Virginia, Connecticut, New York, and Massachusetts— pushed their conflicting territorial claims, so many antagonisms and perplexities would probably have arisen that any uniform plan of settlement would have been impossible. The Gordian knot was cut when New York offered to cede her claims, and the other states followed her lead until the Old Northwest became the property of the American people. Incidentally these cessions required the lands claimed by the inhabitants of the different French settlements to be confirmed, while Virginia made two reservations of land. The more important one, the Virginia Military District, extending northward from the Ohio between the Little Miami and the Scioto, was to be set aside to fulfill the land bounties for the state's Revolutionary troops which were not satisfied in Kentucky. The second reserve by Virginia, 150,000 acres opposite the Falls of the Ohio (Louisville) which was popularly known as Clark's Grant, was for the benefit of General George Rogers Clark and his veterans. Still another important reservation was the Western Reserve which Connecticut retained, a tract of approximately 3,800,000 acres that extended west about 120 miles from the Pennsylvania line in the extreme northeastern corner of the Old Northwest. While Virginia had retained only the rights in the soil, up to 1800 Connecticut held administrative jurisdiction as well over the Western Reserve.

With the title to the greater part of the soil and jurisdiction over practically the entire region vested in Congress, the Old Northwest presented a unique environment in which an American colonial policy could be worked out for the distribution of the land as well as for its political administration. This situation was in decided contrast to the one in the

Old Southwest, which stretched southward from the opposite bank of the Ohio. Here the states greatly delayed the cession of their claims, and both Kentucky and Tennessee were formed directly from counties of Virginia and North Carolina respectively, while the claims of Georgia were settled only after long delay. Thus, neither the land nor the administration of very important sections of the Old Southwest were ever under the direct control of Congress, and the Old Northwest became the one available laboratory in which an American colonial policy could be worked out that would set precedents for the organization of additional public domains as the United States slowly spread across the continent.

In the formulation of a colonial policy that would induce settlers to come into the Old Northwest, there were at least two considerations of supreme importance; the one economic, the other political. From the economic standpoint the terms under which the public land should be disposed of must meet both in price and in quantity the rather straitened financial circumstances of the majority of the immigrants. Politically it was necessary to offer these men, who came usually from the masses rather than the privileged classes, an opportunity to realize ultimately in a new environment the liberal reforms which so many of them advocated, but which the Revolutionary state constitutions had so frequently omitted. In brief, then, unless there were special inducements adapted to actual economic and political demands, there would be no particular incentive to brave the many hardships of settlement in the wilderness. This situation Congress recognized in exceptionally wise fashion. A resolution of October 10, 1780, provided that all "unappropriated" lands that were ceded by any state were to be disposed of for the "common benefit," and were to be formed into states with "the same rights of sovereignty, freedom, and independence as the other states." [6] As the ayes and noes were even, this resolution was not formally adopted, but it

[6] *Journals of the Continental Congress*, vol. XVIII, pp. 915-916.

set forth a policy to which Congress consistently adhered, and one that was in direct contrast to mercantilist principles. In place of the British policy of large grants to speculative companies, the American plan provided for the distribution of public lands in the Western country upon a democratic basis with similar terms to all applicants. Of even greater import was the promise that, in contrast to the British colonial status of perpetual dependence, the American colonies in the Old Northwest would ultimately acquire a position of equality with the original states, a rather startling change that was, in fact, the most outstanding American contribution to colonial political theory.

The first task was to fix the terms upon which the Federal government would grant the public lands. The conflict that quickly arose between the advocates of the New England system of township planting and those of the Southern system of indiscriminate location led to the triumph of the former, which meant compact settlement and a fair system of distribution. The terms that were agreed upon were embodied in the Land Ordinance of 1785 which provided for the sale of the public lands, either in townships of thirty-six square miles or in sections of 640 acres. The seven ranges of townships in the upper Ohio Valley were to be surveyed first, and sold at public auction, and this same procedure was to be followed as additional lands were opened up. The Ordinance also recognized current financial difficulties, fixing the minimum price at $1.00 per acre, which might be paid in the Continental certificates that were then so widely held. As a further incentive to take up land it stipulated that one-seventh of any payment might be made in the military land warrants that had been granted to the Revolutionary veterans. In view of the great depreciation in both Continental certificates and military warrants and their wide distribution, these concessions admirably met the limitations of the intending settler, so far as a medium of payment was concerned. This opportunity to secure fertile lands in exchange for securities that had come to be considered as almost

worthless was pleasant news indeed, and many persons proceeded to take advantage of it. But the minimum amount
available, 640 acres, was too large for the resources of the
average immigrant, and experience soon showed the necessity for a material reduction. An important clause that emphasized the democratic principles of this Land Ordinance,
reserved section sixteen in each township for the support of
public education. In brief the Ordinance of 1785 had established the principle of public sales with a fixed minimum
price, and had set up a township system which would discourage monopoly of the better lands by a favored few.

The provisions for government in the Old Northwest were
equally farsighted and democratic. In the Ordinance of 1787
Congress gave a pledge that not less than three nor more
than five states would be formed from the Old Northwest,
and confirmed it by the definite conditions under which the
advance would be made from one stage of government to
another. But with a wise recognition of conditions on the
frontier, Congress did not confer complete local autonomy
immediately. Rather the Ordinance it drew up provided that
during the early days of settlement, when there was need
for a strong authority, there would be a period of arbitrary
government under a governor and three judges selected by
the two houses. Yet these officials were held in by the restriction that the laws they adopted must come from the
codes of the original states, and that their conduct of government should always be subject to the approval of the
Federal government. The transition to the intermediate
stage, between this arbitrary government and statehood, was
obligatory when there were 5,000 free white males of voting
age in the district. In this second phase of territorial government the Ordinance gave a limited degree of self-control in
the form of a legislative assembly, the lower house to be
elected by the inhabitants of the district, the upper to be
appointed by Congress from a list that the lower house had
chosen. This assembly had full rights of legislation, subject
to the veto of the appointive governor who represented the

Federal authority. But complete local autonomy was impossible under this intermediate stage of government, and this situation was likely to cause much friction when, as was often the case, the governor tended to lean backward in the matter of democratic reforms, while the population was overwhelmingly liberal, if not radical, in its views. Yet the right of the two houses to elect a territorial delegate to represent them in Congress at least gave an opportunity to protest against injustices. The final step in the development of territorial government would come when with 60,000 free inhabitants a district must be admitted into the Union, with the same status as any of the original thirteen states. Thus, with full rights of statehood promised, emigrants to the Western lands could look forward to the time when they could put into practice their liberal ideals, once they had secured local autonomy. In addition to the frame of government, the Ordinance included a bill of rights that was comparable to the declarations of rights in most of the state constitutions of this period and guaranteed all persons who came into the Old Northwest the usual rights of habeas corpus, jury trial, and the like. An important liberal ideal was upheld in the encouragement that the Ordinance promised to public education, and last of all, it prohibited slavery or involuntary servitude except as punishment for crime. With the complementary Land Ordinance of 1785, this Government Ordinance of 1787 formed the basic structure of the distinctively American colonial policy.

The test of this American colonial policy came in the two decades and a half, approximately, between the first settlement at Marietta and the outbreak of the War of 1812. During this period a new society was taking definite shape in this Western country. As population spread along the Ohio, then into the interior and along the shores of the Great Lakes, many important problems were taken up, and many precedents were established. Especially was this true in Ohio, which was the first district in the Old Northwest to go through the successive stages of government under the Ordinance. The pattern of territorial government that was first worked out here later went through considerable modification, as the result of experience in the territories of Indiana and Illinois, before it became wholly democratic in fact as well as in theory. The land policy, too, as it was outlined in the Ordinance of 1785, was much changed, chiefly because of the inevitable conflict between those who would give first consideration to a profit for the Federal government from the sales of public lands, and those who advocated measures that were primarily in the interest of the Western settlers. In the successful solution of these problems of the land system and the territorial government was bound up in great measure the future of American expansion to the westward.

During the critical years of early settlement, the type of settlers that would be attracted to the Old Northwest was a matter of crucial importance. A group of Revolutionary veterans from New England, organized as the Ohio Company, founded the first settlement under a contract, signed October 27, 1787, which gave them a large tract, the Ohio Purchase, on the Ohio and the Muskingum. The reservation in this contract of section sixteen in each township for the support of public education and section twenty-nine for that of religion, upheld the two cornerstones of Puritan civilization. In the winter of 1787–1788 two groups of emigrants started for "Putnam's Paradise," one from Danvers, Massachusetts, the other from Hartford, Connecticut. Crossing the mountains, they embarked at Sumrill's Ferry on a small flotilla that was fittingly led by the *Mayflower*, and April 7, 1788, they landed at the mouth of the Muskingum and founded a settlement, Marietta, that became the nucleus of an extensive colony of New Englanders. Under the leadership of such men as Rufus Putnam and Ephraim Cutler the inhabitants of this settlement, many of them Revolutionary veterans, and the majority men of moderate circumstances, soon exerted an influence that was far out of proportion to their actual numbers. Moreover, even though the colony was founded by a landholding company, so strong was the spirit of democracy in this Puritan outpost in the wilderness that there was little, if any, speculation in land.[7]

The next important settlement in the Old Northwest was the one that was made by another Revolutionary veteran, Judge John Cleves Symmes, from New Jersey, who, with the backing of Elias Boudinot, Jonathan Dayton, and other influential men, secured a grant, the Miami Purchase, that ran northward from the Ohio between the Miami and the Little Miami rivers. Following the precedent of the Ohio Purchase, Symmes' contract reserved section sixteen in each township of the Miami Purchase for the support of public education, and section twenty-nine for that of religion. In July, 1788, Judge Symmes started from Morristown, New Jersey, and journeyed to Pittsburgh, then to Limestone (Maysville), the point from which the earliest settlements in the Miami Purchase were made. The first party of twenty-six, under Major Benjamin Stites, founded a settlement, November 18, 1788, at Columbia at the mouth of the Little Miami River. Forty days later another party established Losantiville, a few miles below, which, under its later name, Cincinnati, was destined to become the metropolis of the Old Northwest, and February 2, 1789, Judge Symmes founded a third settlement at North Bend. As the greater number of these pioneers in the Miami Purchase were from New Jersey and the near-by states, their gradually expanding settlements brought into the Old Northwest a broader-minded and more tolerant Middle States element, in contrast to the rather austere Puritans of Marietta.[8]

The next area of settlement, the Virginia Military Dis-

[7] Hildreth, *Pioneer History*, chs. VIII and IX; Hulbert, ed., *Records of the Ohio Company*, vols. I and II.

[8] Greve, *Centennial History of Cincinnati*, vol. I, pp. 162-169, 175-177, 184-186; Bond, ed., *Correspondence of John Cleves Symmes; Dr. Daniel Drake's Memoir of the Miami Country*, 1779–1794, in *Quarterly*, Ohio Hist. and Phil. Society, vol. XVIII, nos. 2 and 3.

trict, was distinctive in many respects from either the Ohio
Purchase or the Miami Purchase. The Revolutionary veterans who migrated from Virginia to Kentucky in such large
numbers brought military warrants with them for these
lands, and many Virginians sold their warrants to speculators, who in turn offered them to intending settlers. Under
these circumstances the greater number of the early settlers
in the Virginia Military District came from Kentucky, or else
from Virginia. For example, Nathaniel Massie, the leader of
the migration into the Virginia Military District, was a Revolutionary veteran born in Virginia who migrated to Kentucky and soon became a surveyor for holders of the military
warrants that were to be located north of the Ohio, incidentally picking up many choice bits of land on his own account.
In 1791 he founded Manchester, the first settlement in the
Virginia Military District, and settlers rapidly pushed into
the hinterland, especially after Wayne's campaign had made
the country safe from Indian attacks. Chillicothe, which was
founded in 1796, quickly became the chief center of settlement in this region.[9] In contrast to the group settlements in
the Ohio Purchase and the Miami Purchase, isolated farms
were found in the Virginia Military District from the very
first, and settlers bought lands from speculators or else from
the original claimants. The land system also was different.
In place of the township with rectangular surveys prescribed
by the Land Ordinance, the separate tracts in the Virginia
Military District were laid out under the Southern system
of indiscriminate location. As a result the early settlers gob-
bled up the choice lands, stretching out their claims in long,
narrow tracts to include rich bottoms, and leaving to the late
comer the less desirable hillsides. These settlers introduced
into the Old Northwest a Southern element that was in
strong contrast to the Puritans of the Ohio Purchase and to
the Middle State settlers of the Miami Purchase. Strongly

[9] Massie, *Nathaniel Massie*, chs. II and III; Bennett, ed., *State Centennial History of Ohio and the County of Ross*, vol. II, ch. III.

Republican in their politics, and ardent followers of Thomas Jefferson, they had the Southerner's talent for politics, and they quickly assumed the leadership in local affairs. The many native Virginians among them came chiefly from the Piedmont yeomanry rather than from the landed aristocracy of the Tidewater, an origin that easily explains their intense democracy and their religious affiliations, which were chiefly Methodist and Presbyterian. Doubtless it accounts, too, for the lack of any really strong support for slavery among these sturdy pioneers of the Virginia Military District. Much similar in its origin and development was Clark's Grant, the second military reserve by Virginia in the Old Northwest.

The Western Reserve in the extreme northeast was the scene of still another important early settlement. For the relief of its citizens who had suffered from British depredations during the Revolution, the state of Connecticut set aside a tract of 500,000 acres west of the Cuyahoga, which was known later as the Firelands. The remainder of the Reserve was sold to the Connecticut Land Company which disposed of it to speculators chiefly, and they in turn sold it to individual settlers. Like the Virginia Military District, the Western Reserve was constantly subject to Indian attacks until after Wayne's campaign, and consequently the first settlement at Cleveland was not begun until 1796. According to New England custom the land in the Reserve was surveyed in townships, five miles square, but the circumstances under which it was sold, especially the large speculative element, prevented as systematic a settlement as in the Ohio Purchase and the Miami Purchase. Like the Ohio Purchase, the Western Reserve attracted many emigrants from Connecticut, who brought with them the usual support for public education and religion, although, strange to say, there were no public reserves for these purposes in the original plans of settlement. At first New Connecticut was under the jurisdiction of the mother state, but in 1800 it was added to the Northwest Territory as Trumbull

County.[10] Still another outstanding region in the early settlement of the Old Northwest was the upper Ohio Valley where a considerable number of squatters from Virginia and western Pennsylvania had established themselves by 1785. Several of these vagabond settlements even banded together and agreed upon a primitive code, electing two justices of the peace, in spite of determined efforts to oust them. Around Fort Steuben, which was erected in 1787, a considerable settlement arose which became present-day Steubenville. Other settlements were made after the survey of the Seven Ranges under Thomas Hutchins had opened up the public lands in this region. The settlers on the spot soon peaceably adjusted their claims, and the upper Ohio Valley became another stronghold of republicanism, and the home of a population whose long experience in the backwoods made them an exceedingly practical element in the settlement of the Old Northwest.[11]

Actually in the early days of settlement the American colonial policy, as it had been formulated in the Land Ordinance of 1785 and the Government Ordinance of 1787, attracted to the Old Northwest a diverse population that well represented the chief elements of the American people at this time. The New Englanders in the Ohio Purchase and the Western Reserve, the Middle States men in the Miami Purchase, the Kentuckians and Virginians in the Virginia Military District, in Clark's Grant, and in the Illinois country, and the settlers from the backwoods of Pennsylvania and Virginia in the upper Ohio Valley brought a diversity of points of view and customs into their new homes. Other important immigrant groups entered the Old Northwest in the early period between 1788 and the outbreak of the War of 1812; the Southern Quakers fleeing from a slaveholding region, the deluded French who finally settled at Gallipolis,

[10] Alfred Mathews, *Ohio and Her Western Reserve, passim;* L. K. Mathews, *Expansion of New England,* chs. VI and VII; Whittlesey, *Early History of Cleveland, passim.*
[11] *History of Belmont and Jefferson Counties, Ohio,* pp. 154-160, 462.

and even a few Germans. From this mingling of peoples of
such different types, and from such diverse regions, there
arose a cosmopolitanism and a tolerant and democratic spirit
that has always characterized the Old Northwest. The Puritan, the Scotch-Irishman from Kentucky, Virginia, and western Pennsylvania, and other racial and sectional elements
contributed their part.[12] Politically it was significant that
these pioneers, who came for the most part from the masses
rather than the privileged classes, were liberals of a moderate
type, rather than extreme radicals. In their homes in the
Old Northwest they formed then a new society that was
much more cosmopolitan than the sectional regions that were
emerging east of the Appalachians, and one which would
take advantage of the opportunity to work out its own
ideals, practically unhampered.

Many problems, economic and social, presented themselves in the early years of settlement between 1788 and
1812. Foremost among them was the continuance or the repeal of the anti-slavery clause in the Ordinance of 1787.
Many Kentuckians and Virginians in the Virginia Military
District, in Indiana and Illinois, together with the French
inhabitants of Vincennes and the Illinois settlements, would
clamor to introduce slavery, but the anti-slavery party included many strong advocates, notably the Puritans, and
the emigrants from south of the Ohio who had come into the
Old Northwest purposely to escape from a slaveholding community. In the final decision momentous issues were involved, for already the national cleavage was beginning to
appear between the Northern system of free labor, small
farms, a varied agriculture, and comparative economic independence, and the Southern system with slave labor, large
plantations, a one-crop system, and industrial dependence.
Looming in the background was, in reality, the question
whether the Old Northwest would align itself with the North
or the South in the inevitable struggle, with all the momentous consequences that decision would involve. Still other

[12] Chaddock, *Ohio Before 1850*, ch. II.

important issues presented themselves in this early period, when the foundations of the Old Northwest were being laid, among them the establishment of a system of transportation through the wilderness, the development of trade, and the foundations of public education. The story of this early development lacks the glamour and romance of the settlement of the Old Southwest just across the Ohio. But the growth of this hard-headed, democratic, and aggressive population in the Old Northwest, and the practical sense with which they took up the many problems that confronted them, makes up the story of a distinctively American society that was destined to play an important rôle in national history. It is this development, institutional, social, and economic, of the civilization of the Old Northwest, in the basic period between the founding of the first colony at Marietta in 1788 and the outbreak of the War of 1812, which will constitute the central theme of the following pages.

Chapter II

THE LURE OF THE WESTERN LANDS

ONCE the American colonial policy was definitely outlined in the Ordinances of 1785 and 1787, immigrants came into the Old Northwest in ever-increasing numbers. In this throng there were many types—the Revolutionary veteran, the Yankee farmer weary of tilling the scanty New England soil, the young man seeking his fortune, the anti-slavery zealot from the Southern states, and the backwoodsman from Kentucky, western Pennsylvania, and western Virginia. The eager hopes that drew on this multitude may be detected in the glowing descriptions of the Western country that appear so frequently in the newspapers, in the handbills and pamphlets, and even in occasional books of this period. The newspaper columns, especially, reveal the wide range of motives that led on the pioneer, and they show, too, the keen interest of the stay-at-homes in the perils and prosperity of their more adventurous brethren.

In its bid for emigrants from the more densely populated coastal region the Old Northwest encountered a serious rivalry in the unsettled lands of New York, Pennsylvania, Kentucky, and other westward regions. The "Genesee country" in western New York attracted many inhabitants of New England, for tracts of 100,000 acres or less were available there, which could be divided as the settlers pleased, and at a price, $2.00 to $5.00 per acre, that compared favorably with the cost of Western lands. As a further inducement, the state of New York offered settlers from New England fifteen years' exemption from taxes, which was a very great attraction to these "burdened" farmers. To a much less extent, the people of New England migrated to Luzerne and Lycoming counties in Pennsylvania, to the lands of the Holland Company on the Allegheny River, to Kentucky, and a few even to the fertile lands of far-away Tennessee. In the Middle States, aside from the Miami Purchase, which at first chiefly interested the people of New Jersey, there is little evidence of any very energetic campaign to attract the population to the Western lands. Even in New York the newspapers scarcely noticed the "Genesee" lands, and the New Jersey press paid only slight attention to western Pennsylvania and Kentucky as desirable places for emigrants. In eastern Pennsylvania and in Maryland there was apparently no interest at all in the settlement of the Western lands. In the Southern states the Virginia newspapers noticed the Genesee region, but they gave much more attention to the available lands in western Virginia, in Kentucky, and in Tennessee. Thus, it is apparent that the migration to the Old Northwest was merely a phase of a general westward movement that originated chiefly in New England, New Jersey, and Virginia.

In spite of the competition from more accessible lands in western New York and Pennsylvania, or from near-by Kentucky, the Old Northwest attracted its full share of settlers, once the movement thither had begun. Even the hard-headed Yankees were aroused by the glowing reports of the Western country that were circulated among these tillers of the sterile hillsides. A typical letter from a traveler in 1786 described the Muskingum region as a veritable paradise and a particularly healthful one. Another enthusiast considered this same section "superior to anything one can conceive of," with the "deepest and richest garden mould" in the bottoms. As proof of his statements he cited a remarkable cornfield near Fort Harmar in which the stalks grew fourteen feet high.[1] The early settlers at Marietta sent back equally astounding reports, and indeed imagination ran riot throughout this earliest phase of New England settlement in the

[1] *New Haven Gazette and Connecticut Magazine*, vol. I, pp. 259, 265.

Ohio Purchase. One Marietta pioneer, in a somewhat poetic effusion, described the destiny of the new settlement as not only "the glory of America, but the envy of the world." [2] More to the point were the comments of a rather more practical individual who pointed out the possibilities of an extensive trade, as settlement increased in the Old Northwest.[3] Migration from New England to the Ohio settlements was probably stimulated, too, by the reports of many returning travelers. Among them Colonel John May of Boston returned from Marietta in 1788 with a diary stuffed full of information he had jotted down regarding this new land.[4] Upon a seven-acre farm near Little Beaver, Colonel May recorded, the owner had raised 700 bushels of corn. Nor did Marietta altogether lack the comforts of life, and as evidence he cited a dinner he enjoyed with General Harmar where there was "as elegant a table as any in Boston." Amongst the solids were "bacon gammon, venison, tongues, roast and boiled lamb, barbecued and à la mode beef, perch and catfish, lobster and oysters." . . . "For vegetables, green peas, radishes, and salads." . . . "For drink, spirits, excellent wine, brandy, and beer." Another New England traveler in the West, Thaddeus M. Harris of Dorchester, Massachusetts, was likewise impressed with the possibilities of the Marietta colony, admiring especially the full-rigged ships sailing down the Ohio, and the thrift, the neat fences, and the well-tilled farms of the New England settlers, which were in such strong contrast, Harris pointed out, to the general neglect on the Virginia side of the Ohio, where slave labor was customary.[5]

The rather exaggerated optimism of the travelers who returned to New England was somewhat counterbalanced by the homely counsel to intending emigrants, in an article in a

[2] *Providence Gazette,* July 19, 1788.

[3] *Massachusetts Spy,* June 11, 1789.

[4] Darlington, ed., *Journal and Letters of Colonel John May,* especially pp. 64-65.

[5] Harris, *Journal of a Tour into the Territory Northwest of the Allegheny Mountains* (1803) ; also in Thwaites, *Early Western Travels,* vol. III.

Providence paper that was fittingly entitled *Advice to American Farmers*. The author gave a vivid picture of the many privations as well as the rewards that came to the settler who ventured into the Western country. He advised emigrants to avoid the Niagara and Kentucky regions, and to choose lands that were directly under the control of the Federal government, especially those that were in regions free from negro slavery. They should take along apple, peach, and garden seeds, a kettle for maple sugar, and a gun with powder and shot for hunting, together with the "iron parts" of all implements. They must eschew all luxuries, but they should take with them the Bible, and those of the same faith should settle together, "in order to secure the sooner a minister and a schoolmaster." This homely advice concluded with an alluring picture of a family, "depressed by poverty," which, moving into a new country, would there replace the woods with fields, the weeds with gardens, and the beasts of prey with domestic animals, "creating new forces for independence and affluence." [6]

But the correspondents of the New England press were by no means unanimous in their praise of the Western country, and occasionally they countered the flowery statements in the letters from the settlers, or in the reports of travelers, with a derisive irony that from the very beginning of this westward migration betrayed the hostility toward this movement which later became so strong in New England. With true Yankee sarcasm, one writer, under the nom de plume of *Robinson Crusoe,* scornfully called attention to the exaggerated accounts and the pretentious names of public improvements at Marietta. In similar ironic vein a wag published "An Ohio Story of a Vermont Pumpkin," that was of marvelous length with stupendous fruit.[7] The effect of such criticisms was shown in the more moderate tone of the advertisements and other notices at the beginning of the movement to the Western Reserve, which was the second notable

[6] *Providence Gazette,* June 6, 1789.
[7] *Connecticut Courant,* October 13, 1788, and February 9, 1795.

migration from New England to the Old Northwest. The speculators in these lands extolled the fertile soil and the healthy climate of New Connecticut, but they laid greater stress upon such substantial accomplishments as the increasing settlements, the convenient mills, and the existence of churches and schools.[8] Probably, too, this change in emphasis was partly due to the disillusionment that must have come to so many pioneers of the earlier migration.

Outside of New England, the most important migration in the first few years of settlement in the Old Northwest was from New Jersey to the Miami Purchase, and in contrast to Yankee exaggeration Judge Symmes displayed great moderation in the circulars he issued in 1787 and 1788, to induce the public to come to his new colony. Calling attention to the excellent soil, he noted the abundance of navigable waterways, the accessibility of the proposed settlements to Kentucky and the Atlantic states, the mildness of the climate and the wide range of products. Yet he, too, let his imagination run riot when he included cotton and indigo among the crops that were easily grown north of the Ohio. In distinctively moderate tone, the newspapers of New Jersey also called attention to the merits of farming lands in the Miami Purchase, and one correspondent especially pointed out their great superiority to the "broken" country in the Muskingum Valley.[9] The newspapers of New York and Pennsylvania printed only a few items that were likely to attract immigrants to the Western country. But their advertising columns show how keen an interest there was in the books of travel and the like that dealt with this region. An interesting example of these publications was Thomas Hutchins' map and topographical description of the "interior parts" of North America. One advertisement called especial attention to this work upon the ground that it showed the possibilities

---

[8] *Connecticut Courant,* 1800–1810.

[9] Circular, *"To the Respectable Public,"* in *Quarterly,* Ohio Hist. and Phil. Society, vol. V, no. 3; *New Brunswick Gazette,* January 8, 1788; *New Jersey Journal,* March 11, 1789.

of the Illinois country, a land where hemp "grew spontaneously," one that abounded in varied agricultural products,
game, iron, copper, lead, and salt springs, and "in short
everything a reasonable mind can desire is to be found, or
may, with little pains, be produced there." [10] Another exceedingly popular publication was a detailed account of a
trip by John Melish to the Western country between 1806
and 1811, going down the Ohio, and returning through the
interior to the Western Reserve.[11] The notes which Melish
jotted down on this journey form a veritable Baedeker of the
country through which he passed, and, like similar publications, these *Travels* doubtless inspired many a young man to
try his fortune in the Western country. In Maryland the
newspapers printed few notices that were likely to stimulate
migration to the Western lands, but in Virginia the local
press showed considerable interest in the Old Northwest,
even during the earlier period of settlement. This contrast
was natural, in view of the many Virginians who were entitled to land bounties in the Virginia Military District which
they would be only too glad to sell to intending emigrants.
There were many statements from these eager owners that
would be worthy of a modern dealer in suburban real estate.
One Virginia writer ranked the Scioto Valley alongside of
Kentucky as the best land "in the world." Others recounted
in great detail the extensive resources of the Western country, and occasionally they indulged in flights of fancy that
were reminiscent of the early exaggerations in the New England papers. One correspondent of a Virginia newspaper, in
particular, gave a description of a marvelous sycamore tree
in the Scioto Valley, which was more than sixty feet in cir-
cumference, with a cavity so large that it sheltered thirty
persons on horseback, with room for two more.[12]

[10] *New York Journal*, April 7, 1788; Hutchins, *Topographical Description
of Virginia, Pennsylvania, etc.*, pp. 43-45.

[11] Melish, *Travels in the United States of America, in the Years 1806, 1807,
1809, 1810, and 1811.*

[12] *Virginia Independent Chronicle*, September 2, 1789; *Virginia Argus*,
September 22, 1809, and October 16, 1810.

When schemes were brought forward for actual colonization in the Old Northwest, public interest was naturally quickened. In New England the plans of the Ohio Company were received with much enthusiasm, and the newspapers of Massachusetts, especially, printed detailed reports of its proceedings. The first actual migrations to its Western lands were also given an important place in the local newspapers. Early in 1788 they recorded the departure from Providence of a wagon loaded with artificers, tools, and supplies, which was accompanied by a number of persons who proposed to settle in the Ohio country.[13] A few months later another paper announced that a second wagon had left Providence, this one carrying six gentlemen bound for the Western country, "that second land of promise where Nature smiles in all her glory, and where a most luxuriant soil and happy climate will abundantly reward the husbandman's labour." [14] About the same time the *Massachusetts Spy* noted that six wagons, holding about thirty women and children, had left Worcester for the Western lands.[15] An interesting sidelight upon this migration was an advertisement about this time in the *Providence Gazette* by Stephen Bayard of Elizabethtown on the Monongahela, who built "Kentucky boats." [16] An inkling as to the extent of this early westward movement from New England, is given by the numerous sales of land for 1788 and the next few years in Worcester and its vicinity, the home of so many of the shareholders in the Ohio Company. Among the many persons in this region who offered their farms for sale in 1788 was Rufus Putnam, who was willing to receive in exchange the military land warrants and the Federal certificates which he could use to purchase Western lands. In similar fashion Jonathan Stone, another Revolutionary veteran, sold his farm at Brookfield, and with the proceeds bought two shares of Ohio Company

[13] *Providence Gazette*, January 5, 1788.
[14] *New York Journal*, October 23, 1788.
[15] *Massachusetts Spy*, October 2, 1788.
[16] *Providence Gazette*, September 6, 1788.

stock which he used in 1789 to take up land near Belpre.[17] The list of lands for sale in and around Worcester showed a steady increase, with eight farms and two dwellings advertised in a single issue of the *Massachusetts Spy* in 1790, fourteen farms at one time in 1794, and fifteen in 1795.[18] While it would be unsafe to conclude that all these Massachusetts lands were sold in order that the owners might migrate to the Ohio Purchase, there is no doubt that a considerable number of them followed the example of Rufus Putnam and Jonathan Stone.

The second important movement from New England to the Old Northwest, which brought about the settlement of the Western Reserve, naturally aroused the greatest attention in Connecticut. Here the newspapers published frequent notices of these Ohio lands, especially after Moses Cleaveland had returned from his surveying expedition in 1796 with an exceedingly favorable report of the fertile, rolling land in New Connecticut, and of the possibilities for trade on Lake Erie, and by the Cuyahoga to the interior of Ohio. The Connecticut newspapers also paid much attention to the proceedings of the Connecticut Company, and gave occasional notices, too, of meetings of the proprietors of the Firelands west of the Cuyahoga. In contrast to the Ohio Company and John Cleves Symmes, the Connecticut Company seems to have usually disposed of its lands through speculators who dealt directly with actual settlers. The customary procedure of these speculators was to pay part of the purchase money to the state treasurer, and then to offer the lands they received, either in exchange for salable farms in Connecticut itself, or for other considerations of value. The columns of the Connecticut papers after the first settlement in the Western Reserve contain numerous advertisements of these lands. Thus, in 1801 the firm of Ephraim Root and Uriel Holmes of Hartford advertised very widely

---

[17] *Massachusetts Spy*, August 6, 1789; Hildreth, *Lives of the Early Settlers*, p. 390.
[18] *Massachusetts Spy*, 1790–1795.

their desirable lands in New Connecticut, calling the attention of all "industrious and enterprising" persons to the "pleasing prospects for the future." They must have been quite successful in disposing of their lands in the Western Reserve, in view of the long list of Connecticut farms they soon acquired and offered for sale. In a few years the firm dissolved, but Ephraim Root, on his own account, offered 100,000 acres in New Connecticut, in exchange for land in Connecticut itself, as well as nine farms which he had doubtless received in similar transactions. His former partner, Uriel Holmes, also appears to have found speculation in Western lands a profitable business.[19] Lemuel Storrs of Middletown was another large speculator in Western Reserve lands. In 1805 he offered "to the enterprising farmer" 110,-000 acres, in payment for which he was willing either to accept cash, to extend "liberal credit" with higher prices, or else to take in exchange "good farms" in Connecticut. In common with other speculators he would also take, in partial payment, security for a large part of the purchase money that was still due the state of Connecticut, a proposal that gives an illuminating sidelight into the methods of the land speculators in Connecticut. There was much competition among these different speculators and Storrs soon had his agents in Ohio to take care of settlers on the spot.[20]

Other fertile lands in the Ohio country beside those of the Western Reserve attracted the owners of the rock-strewn farms of Connecticut. Many of them joined the settlers from Massachusetts in the Ohio Purchase, and others were induced to migrate by such advertisements as that of Henry Bacon of Urbana, Ohio, who in 1807 called attention to the "superior advantages" of his lands over the "frosts and bogs" of the country bordering upon the Lake.[21] Indeed, judging from the number of farms offered for sale, from about 1800

[19] *Connecticut Courant*, October 16, 1801, April 11, 1804, April 4, 1810, and April 11, 1811.
[20] *Ibid.*, May 22, 1805.
[21] *Ibid.*, November 21, 1819.

there was a large migration from Connecticut to the Western Reserve and, to a less extent, to other sections of Ohio. An interesting bit of evidence of the popularity of the Western lands in Connecticut, as an investment, is found in the inventory in 1808 of the estate of General Joseph Williams of Norwich, which listed 16,378.09 acres lying in Geauga, Trumbull, and Portage counties, Ohio.[22] Immigrants continued to go to the Western country from Massachusetts also, some of them to the Western Reserve, others to the Ohio Purchase and to the many different settlements that began to spring up so rapidly after the Indian danger came to an end in 1795. If one may judge from the number of farms that were offered for sale, this emigration from Massachusetts greatly increased in the first decade of the nineteenth century. In 1800, for example, twelve farms or dwellings in or near Worcester were advertised for sale, and a year later twenty-four. As the Ohio country was the favorite destination of New England emigrants at this time, it is reasonable to conclude that many of these Massachusetts farmers found their way thither, especially as the *Massachusetts Spy* pointedly called attention to the amazing growth of the Ohio country, and predicted even further strides in the near future.[23]

Like the early New England schemes for colonization, the Miami Purchase attracted the greatest attention in its home state, New Jersey. Following a number of similar local projects for Western colonies which did not materialize, Judge Symmes' new settlement received considerable attention from the New Jersey papers, although he himself depended chiefly upon handbills and circulars to advertise his lands. Still another effective aid in attracting settlers was an extensive correspondence between the early pioneers in the Miami Purchase and their friends at home. From occasional advertisements it is evident also that many residents of New Jersey followed the example of the canny speculators of Con-

[22] *Connecticut Courant*, October 5, 1808.
[23] *Massachusetts Spy*, 1800–1811.

necticut and took up tracts of several thousand acres in the Miami Purchase, which they offered to settlers. From 1789 on, the newspapers of New Jersey contain notices of the considerable local migration to Judge Symmes' colony. Many advertisers offered to buy the public certificates which could be used in payment for these lands, and equally significant was the large number of farms for sale. Thus, in 1789 fourteen small farms were advertised at one time for sale in and around Elizabethtown, and in 1799 a single issue of the local paper offered thirteen tracts of agricultural land around Trenton, with fourteen separate parcels in or near New Brunswick, and five lots in near-by Princeton. These advertisements of lands for sale continued, and in 1807 one paper offered a grist and sawmill, twelve farms, and several wood lots near Trenton.[24] It is reasonable to suppose that a large percentage of the owners of these tracts migrated to the Miami Purchase. Strange to say, there were few notices of Judge Symmes' lands in either the New York or the Philadelphia papers, although there were emigrants from both these towns to the Miami Purchase. The New England papers occasionally called attention to Symmes' new colony, and in 1788, before any settlement had been made there, in a rather flamboyant advertisement in the *Connecticut Courant*, Thomas Stanley asserted that any description of this Miami country must "fall far short of its goodness." [25] A similarly glowing description in a Virginia paper showed how widespread was the interest in Judge Symmes' settlement.[26]

The lands available in the Virginia Military District aroused little interest, even in Virginia, until after the Peace of Greenville in 1795 had made settlement in the interior possible. Only occasionally had the leading Virginia papers noticed the lands between the Scioto and the Little Miami that had been allotted to the state's military bounties. But

[24] Miscellaneous New Jersey newspapers, 1789–1808, especially *New Jersey Journal*, April 8, 1789; *New Jersey Gazette*, May 27, 1799; *New Jersey Federalist*, March 30, 1807; *New Brunswick Guardian*, April 2, 1799.
[25] *Connecticut Courant*, September 22, 1788.
[26] *Virginia Independent Chronicle*, October 22, 1788.

after Wayne's campaign, this indifference vanished, and the Revolutionary veterans of Virginia began to value more highly their claims to land bounties in the Old Northwest. Many of them sold their warrants to speculators, as Hicks & Campbell, and other Virginia real-estate dealers, who offered in frequent notices to pay the highest prices for Virginia military land warrants, or else to buy "military lands" outright.[27] Like Lemuel Storrs, the Connecticut speculator in the Western Reserve, these Virginia real-estate dealers sold their lands finally to actual settlers. A typical advertisement of such land was one in 1802 by John Rose, who offered several tracts along with a number of negroes. In 1809, G. S. Stras, "advanced in years and infirm," offered for sale a long list of tracts in the West that included 248 acres in the grant to Clark's veterans.[28]

The vicissitudes of the speculator in Virginia military lands may be followed in the correspondence of General Duncan McArthur who, as agent on the spot at Chillicothe, located many land warrants for residents of Virginia, sold tracts to incoming settlers, and paid taxes for absentee landlords.[29] His clients were scattered throughout Virginia, in Richmond, Fauquier Court House (Warrenton), and other important towns. The most important speculator whom he represented was Robert Means of Richmond. This gullible individual was an excellent representative of many Eastern men who expected to realize large fortunes from Western lands, and, in the end, met the usual disappointments of the speculator. Influenced by the glowing reports from the West, Means plunged to the utmost of his ability, buying up military warrants which he sent McArthur to be located. When taxes began to accumulate on his vacant holdings, Means found it almost impossible to meet his obligations, and time and again he appealed to McArthur to send him cash in

[27] *Virginia Independent Chronicle*, November 18, 1789, January 6 and July 21, 1790; *Richmond and Manchester Advertiser*, August 6, 1795.
[28] *Virginia Herald*, September 21, 1802; *Virginia Argus*, June 2, 1809.
[29] *McArthur Papers*, vols. I and II, 1783–1812.

payment of at least a part of his lands. But he pleaded in vain, for, after the passage of the Land Act of 1800, the offer of public lands on credit, combined with the scarcity of specie in the Western country, made land sales for cash to intending settlers few and far between. Means even exchanged valuable city property for military land warrants, and for a time he seems to have enjoyed a virtual monopoly of this business in Richmond. But competition soon appeared, prices rose, and still he could not secure cash for his Western lands, although the prices he paid were low, averaging only 23 cents per acre in 1808 on one lot of warrants for 5,349 acres.[30] Means found that his immediate returns were far from satisfactory. These discouraging experiences did not end the extraordinary demand for warrants for land in the Virginia Military District, and speculators vied with one another in their offers. Among the numerous evidences of the continued interest of many inhabitants of Virginia in these lands, was an advertisement in 1810 by Carter Drew who proposed to pay a visit to the Western country, acting as general agent, exploring lands, investigating titles, and the like.[31] Another important figure in these land speculations was James Taylor, who was quite active in Kentucky in buying up land warrants, and offered 20,000 acres of "valuable military land" in Ohio to the people of New Jersey.[32]

While the Eastern newspapers paid more attention to such schemes for colonization as the Ohio Company, Judge Symmes' project, and the Virginia Military District, they did not altogether neglect the Federal lands in the Old Northwest which were gradually being opened up to settlement. A striking evidence of the general interest in these public lands was given by the numerous offers to pay cash for the Federal certificates that were at first accepted by the Land Office, and also for the Federal military warrants for which definite provision was made in the Military Reserve. Many of the

[30] Robert Means to McArthur, February 9, 1808. *McArthur Papers*, vol. II.
[31] *Virginia Argus*, September 7, 1810.
[32] *New Jersey Federalist*, September 28, 1807.

latter were used to secure lands in the Ohio and Miami purchases as well. The newspapers showed the general interest
in the public lands, in 1791, when they printed an official list
of all the tracts in the Old Northwest that were still available for settlement. Usually, too, after the passage of the
Land Act of 1796 they published notices of public land
sales.[33] The numerous claims held by residents of the older
states in these different tracts even justified the employment
of agents on the spot to manage these holdings for their absentee owners, just as in the Western Reserve and the Virginia Military District. For instance, John Matthews and
Zachariah Briggs, two experienced surveyors, offered to locate military warrants and other claims for public lands with
a fee of one-tenth of the land. For smaller tracts they proposed to accumulate warrants until they had the necessary
amount to locate an entire quarter township.[34] Other notices
show the keen interest in the public lands, but apparently it
extended chiefly to the Ohio region during the early period
of settlement up to about 1812. The available lands in Indiana were too remote and too much exposed to Indian attacks,
the areas open to settlement were comparatively small, and
the emigrants consequently preferred the nearer and safer
lands of the Ohio country. In both Illinois and Michigan the
land system was in so tangled a condition that settlers could
not be sure of their tenures, so that there, too, emigration
from the older states was discouraged.

The general interest of the inhabitants of the older states
in the Western lands was strikingly shown in the many news
items from the settlements that were given a prominent place
in the Eastern newspapers. Especially was this the case in
New England, where the stay-at-homes were alert for news
from their friends and relatives who had ventured into the
wilderness. These public news items were all the more welcome, too, in view of the uncertainties of the postal service

---

[33] *New York Daily Advertiser,* November 17, 1791; *Gazette of the United
States,* February 1, 1797; *Massachusetts Spy,* September 21, 1796.
[34] *Gazette of the United States,* January 20, 1800.

across the Appalachians. The New England papers printed many letters from the frontier settlers to their relatives and former neighbors, along with numerous communications from their own correspondents at Marietta, at Cincinnati, at Chillicothe, and later in the Western Reserve. Another source of news from the West soon became available in clippings from the many weekly newspapers that sprang up in the Old Northwest. Returned travelers, traders, and rumors that came through Pittsburgh, Buffalo, and other important stopping places on the westward routes, also added to the news items concerning the Old Northwest. In the New England newspapers much attention was paid, of course, to official news. Many items recorded the official acts of St. Clair and the judges, the general progress of the territorial government, and the important measures adopted in the state of Ohio. The adventures of Aaron Burr and the attitude toward him in the West received much attention, but true to Federalist prejudices the New England newspapers usually took a rather lenient view of his motives. Most of this news came from the Ohio country, with very rare communications in the New England papers from the distant settlements in Indiana and Illinois.

Beside news items relating to public affairs, the New England newspapers gave frequent accounts of everyday happenings in the West. The opening of a ferry across the Muskingum, or the launching of an ocean-going vessel at Marietta was a bit of news that was recorded with evident enthusiasm, and the establishment of a packet line between Cincinnati and Pittsburgh was warmly commended as an evidence of progress in this "enchanting country." Another item of a different type announced the first ball at Marietta, in December, 1788, which was attended by fifteen ladies, "as well accomplished in the manners of polite circles" . . . "as any in the old states." [35] Also, there was much favorable comment upon the superior advantages of the Ohio country, where so many New Englanders had settled, over other sections in the

[35] *Massachusetts Spy*, April 16, 1789.

Western country. As a case in point, the *Providence Gazette* cited the experiences of Colonel Shrieve of New Jersey, who proposed at first to lead a party of emigrants to New Madrid, but was discouraged by floods. Then, as he found the greater part of the desirable land in Kentucky already taken up, he finally decided upon Marietta.[36] A letter in the *Boston Gazette* called special attention to the amazing growth of the Virginia Military District, pointing out at the same time the advantages this section offered to the "middling class," and especially to "mechanics of the common trades." [37] In the columns of the popular *Massachusetts Magazine* there were many death and marriage notices from the Ohio settlements, along with much news of the campaigns against the Indians. In its monthly *Domestick Chronicle* this same periodical printed many articles upon interesting features of the West, such as the development of Marietta and the outlying districts, or the customs and manners of the Indians.[38] But none of the New England almanacs that have been examined pay the slightest attention to the Western country, the migration there, or even the Indian troubles, and this omission is all the more noticeable since these annual publications were as a second Bible in the eyes of the New England farmer. But the many and varied notices in the newspapers and magazines of New England show the close ties between this section and the Old Northwest. Incidentally they help to account for the increasing stream of migration from the former to the latter.

There is abundant evidence in the Middle States of a lively interest in the Western settlements. In contrast to the New England almanacs, those published in the Middle States contain frequent notices of the Old Northwest, notably detailed descriptions of the usual routes there from the Eastern towns. *Hutchins' Almanack*, which was published in New York, customarily printed a table of the roads with the distances between intermediate points, from Louisburg through Que-

[36] *Providence Gazette*, August 1, 1789.
[37] *Boston Gazette*, September 22, 1797.
[38] *Massachusetts Magazine or Monthly Museum*, vols. I-III, 1789-1796.

bec to Presque Isle, the Falls of the Ohio, and the mouth of the Mississippi.[39] In like fashion *Father Abraham's Almanack*, which was popular in Philadelphia and the surrounding country, gave the usual westward route from Pennsylvania, via York, Winchester, Staunton, and through the wilderness to Crab Orchard, Bard's Town, and the Falls of the Ohio. After travel down the river had become safer, this almanac gave full details of the route across Pennsylvania to Pittsburgh, and then down the Ohio and the Mississippi.[40] Likewise in the *American Museum*, which corresponded in Pennsylvania to the *Massachusetts Magazine* in New England, there were many notices of political events in the West, as well as numerous articles on the manners and customs of the Indians, with especial attention to the numerous mounds in the Muskingum Valley.[41] The newspaper files of the Middle States also printed irregular items from the Old Northwest. Even in New Jersey, the home of so many emigrants, the papers seldom had regular correspondents in the West, and aside from occasional letters from Marietta, the Miami Purchase, and the Virginia Military District, they secured their news usually by indirect channels—by traders, by returning travelers, or by expresses direct to the government in Philadelphia or Washington. Other news came secondhand to the Middle States press through Kentucky, or perhaps from Winchester, Pittsburgh, or even Albany. Coming through such mediums this information was frequently much garbled, but the very fact that it was printed at all was a proof of the widespread interest in the Western country. It included much official news regarding the movements of the governor and the judges, with occasional notices of local political controversies, such as the quarrel between Winthrop Sargent and the judges of Hamilton County.

The attention given to some more efficient means of communication to and from the Western settlements was a strik-

---

[39] *Hutchins' Improved Almanack*, 1788–1800.
[40] *Father Abraham's Almanack*, 1792–1808 (scattered numbers).
[41] *American Museum*, vols. I-XII, 1787–1792.

ing evidence of the increasing trade between the Middle
States and the Old Northwest. Among the many news items
of this type, a Philadelphia editor heralded the gathering of
a company of travelers in 1795 to go from Cincinnati to
Pittsburgh by land, as the significant start of a permanent
route. Eleven years later another Eastern newspaper man
applauded the opening of a stage line from Wheeling through
Chillicothe to Frankfort, Kentucky.[42] A significant step in
the development of Western transportation that aroused
great interest in the Eastern papers, was the movement to
construct seagoing vessels on Western waters, as a partial
solution of the problem of more convenient communication
with the Eastern seaboard. Occasionally there was a nar-
rowly provincial point of view, as the pious Quaker hope of
one correspondent from Philadelphia that the settlements
beyond Pennsylvania would free that state from all danger
of Indian attacks.[43] In strong contrast was the benevolent
spirit of a number of Pennsylvanians who organized the
"Philadelphia Society for the Information of Persons Emigrating from Foreign Countries." The avowed purpose of
this society with so formidable a name was to give information upon regions that were suitable for settlement, and to
extend pecuniary aid to emigrants when it was needed. There
were monthly meetings, and doubtless the society aided
many a poor emigrant on his way through Philadelphia to
the promised land beyond the mountains. Perhaps it was
under the inspiration of this Pennsylvania organization that
societies with similar aims were founded at Lexington and
Washington in Kentucky, and another one was proposed at
Cincinnati.[44] Such organizations were a sufficient testimony
to the needs that arose from the "almost incredible rage" for
Western settlement. In Virginia the local papers seldom contained direct communications from the West. This was to be

[42] *Gazette of the United States,* November 13, 1795; *The True American,*
July 7, 1806.
[43] *New York Daily Advertiser,* July 17, 1789.
[44] *Gazette of the United States,* October 6, 1794, and May 1, 1795; *Nor-
folk Herald,* November 6, 1797.

expected, inasmuch as emigrants from Virginia usually stopped for a time in western Virginia or else in Kentucky, and then made their way to the Old Northwest. But much Western news filtered indirectly into the Old Dominion through Kentucky, or else from Winchester, where the road to the Wilderness crossed the one up the Potomac Valley to Fort Cumberland and then across the mountains. Reports from the Old Northwest came to Virginia also through Philadelphia and Pittsburgh, but like the other usual routes there were many delays on the road, and often news was weeks old before it drifted through across the mountains. Such a situation fully explains the keen interest that the people of Virginia displayed in the different projects to improve the Wilderness Road and other direct routes to the West. But their interest in the Old Northwest was a merely general one, or else one that was due to speculative motives.

While the Eastern newspapers gave much space to items of current news from the Old Northwest, up to the Treaty of Greenville in 1795 their columns showed even greater interest in Indian relations and in the different frontier struggles. A striking example of the intense interest in these affairs was a weekly column, the *Indian Department*, which the *Boston Gazette* started in 1791, and continued later as the *Indian Chronicle*. Here accounts of Indian raids and campaigns were mingled with lengthy descriptions of quaint Indian customs and manners, with a really notable series of articles on the "Situation, Character, and Disposition of the Western Indians." [45] In like fashion other newspapers of the Atlantic states chronicled the history of Indian relations on the frontier, and from these sources an inkling may be gained as to contemporary Eastern opinion with regard to the most pressing problem of the Old Northwest. The persistence of migration, in the face of these dismal stories of the perils of the Western frontier, is specially interesting, reflecting the characteristic American determination and optimism. Less than a year after the first settlement at Marietta, the Treaty of Fort

[45] *Boston Gazette*, 1791–1798.

Harmar aroused high hopes, which were speedily dashed to the ground after the attacks upon Judge Symmes' new settlements, and the so-called massacre at Big Bottom on the Muskingum. The newspapers reported these disturbances in much detail and also the many raids upon boats descending the Ohio. They followed the progress of Harmar's and St. Clair's campaigns and showed great disappointment over the outcome of the former expedition. But when Harmar came East in 1791, the Philadelphia press highly commended his military services in the West.[46]

The news of St. Clair's defeat came as a severe shock to the inhabitants of the Atlantic states, arousing them to a full realization of the really serious situation in the Old Northwest. The delay in transmitting this news was a startling illustration of the difficulties of communication with the Ohio country. Fully six weeks passed before this important intelligence was printed in the New England papers, and even in Virginia, at the eastern terminus of the Wilderness Trail, it was not known for nearly a month.[47] The Eastern papers gave this disaster a prominent place, under such captions as a *Melancholy Account,* and the like. Later they printed numerous letters, official reports, and other material on St. Clair's ill-fated campaign, along with much caustic criticism, and one typical article bluntly laid the blame at the door of Congress, which alone, the writer considered, was responsible for the "contemptible wages paid recruits, the distances from which they were collected, and the short periods of enlistment." But the government was not altogether without support, as was evident in a Philadelphia editorial that advised a suspension of judgment until all the documents had been published.[48] The spirits of the public soon recovered from the first shock, and the press attempted to find some consolation even in defeat. There is evidence, too, that the

[46] *New Jersey Journal,* November 30, 1791.

[47] *Boston Gazette,* and *Connecticut Courant,* December 19, 1791; *Virginia Herald,* December 8, 1791.

[48] *American Museum,* vol. XI, pp. 165-169, 233-235; *Pennsylvania Gazette,* December 28, 1791.

many proprietors of Western lands, thoroughly alarmed over the probable effect of all this discouraging news upon intending emigrants, now started a counter campaign of propaganda to allay the general alarm. One Virginia editor commented upon stories of Indian triumphs with the sage remark that, "a report of this kind never *looses* by frequent repeating," and others predicted that another army would rise, phœnixlike, from the ashes of St. Clair's defeated host.[49] An outstanding example of the assurances from land speculators to soothe the fears of timid souls was the bold stand of Colonel Ward, "one of the principal settlers" on Mad River, who countered stories of Indian attacks with a statement that he considered this region a sufficiently safe place in which to leave his own family.[50]

The swift progress of events on the Western frontier, after the appointment of Anthony Wayne as commander-in-chief of the Northwestern Army, soon shifted the center of interest from recriminations over past failures to preparations for hostilities in the near future. The plans of General Wayne and the progress of his army occupied considerable space in the newspapers, and there was every indication that the general public thoroughly appreciated the critical importance of the approaching campaign on the Western frontier. Rumors of British intrigue among the Indians stirred up the people of the Atlantic Coast, and especially the report that Governor Simcoe had promised the savages a supply of arms and ammunition for their campaign against the American troops. Wayne's victory caused great relief, therefore, and the newspapers hailed it with the utmost enthusiasm, although, like the account of St. Clair's defeat, the news was greatly delayed, and reached New York, for example, almost a month after the battle.[51] From New York the news spread, notably to Baltimore where the bare report was quickly sup-

---

[49] *Virginia Herald,* January 27, 1791; *New Jersey Journal,* December 21, 1791.

[50] *New Brunswick Guardian,* September 10, 1799.

[51] *Greenleaf's New York Journal,* September 17, 1794.

plemented by a full account that two travelers from Kentucky brought to Winchester. Highly elated over such encouraging news, the leading Baltimore newspaper issued an extra edition in strictly modern fashion, and practically all the Eastern papers printed Wayne's official report under the heading, *Important and Authentic,* and similar captions that plainly showed the importance the editors attached to this victory.

Yet there was an undercurrent of alarm lest the fruits of the victory should be lost by failure to secure a satisfactory treaty from the Indians, and back of this feeling was undoubtedly a widespread distrust of British motives in the West. Consequently the newspapers followed Wayne's negotiations with the Indians in great detail, printing many communications that came direct from his headquarters. After the treaty had been negotiated, most of them printed its provisions in full, although, as was so common in these early papers, they did not give the editorial comment that would accompany a similar announcement in a twentieth-century paper. Public opinion now demanded that the final results of Wayne's victory should be realized by the surrender of the Western posts, and this attitude made itself felt in insistent fashion during the long delay before the ratification of Jay's Treaty. Some of the New England newspapers were rather pessimistic, declaring that even if the treaty were ratified, the British would probably refuse to withdraw from the Western posts, while its restrictive commercial provisions, in the eyes of many editors, overshadowed in importance the benefits that Jay's Treaty promised to the West. This opposition began to disappear after the most obnoxious provisions had been taken out of the treaty, and the Western posts had been actually surrendered. A number of editors now voiced in their comments a widespread feeling of relief that emigration to the Western lands could at length be safely undertaken.

Occasionally, alongside the many references that showed such general interest in the settlements and progress of the

Old Northwest, there were evidences of the antagonism that was gradually to develop in the Atlantic states, as the residents forsook their farms in increasing numbers in favor of the more fertile Western lands. Just before Judge Symmes headed the migration from New Jersey to the Miami Purchase, a correspondent of a Philadelphia paper called attention to the superior merits of the vacant Pennsylvania lands, as compared with those in western New York, in Kentucky, and in the Western country. In Pennsylvania, he pointed out, the roads were better, the land was more accessible to market, and a farmer was not obliged to sell his wheat for two shillings per bushel, and then pay two dollars for a pair of shoes.[52] Three years later another newspaper correspondent, this one in a New York paper, called attention to the "rage for removing into the back parts," and pointed out the advantages of a small, snug farm, well cultivated and convenient to markets, over large tracts of uncultivated lands in the "back parts." These latter, he asserted, could be regarded only as a "provision for posterity," awaiting "easy transportation and near-by markets to assure their value." [53] Much similar in its general tone was a long-winded article about this same time in a Massachusetts paper, in which the author expressed his delight over the "subsidence" of the "madness" for emigration to the Western country, and lauded the "old-fashioned industry and economy," which, he considered, "appear to be productive of more real good than building castles in the air in the regions of the Genesee and other remote uncultivated regions." [54]

This same antagonism to the Western settlements showed itself frequently in the form of caustic attacks upon the government's Indian policy up to the time of Wayne's campaign. Often in the numerous articles of this type it is almost impossible to distinguish between the really conscientious scruples against the general treatment of the Indians and the

[52] *Pennsylvania Gazette,* November 5, 1788.
[53] *New York Daily Advertiser,* June 24, 1791.
[54] *Massachusetts Spy,* August 25, 1791.

very practical opposition to Westward expansion which had either a political or an economic source. In the *Boston Gazette,* under the nom de plume a *Citizen of the United States,* one individual seriously questioned the justice of the war against the Indians, and then almost in the same breath called attention to its very serious effect upon the fur trade.[55] When criticisms of this type had become quite general, the Secretary of War prepared an official report upon the causes of the Indian wars, which was received by these critics with much sarcastic comment. Especially was this true in New England, where one editorial scored the "banditti" who first robbed the Indians of their property and then murdered them, while another newspaper called attention to the unfair methods that were employed when treaties were being negotiated with the Indians.[56] In similar fashion a Pennsylvania correspondent denounced the wars that were being waged against the Indians of the Old Northwest when so much vacant land was to be had in Pennsylvania, New York, and Kentucky,[57] and several New Englanders maintained that the Ohio River should mark the Indian boundary. Other writers, rising above such petty prejudices, maintained that it would be difficult to hold any frontier, and that to adopt the Ohio River as a boundary would mean the surrender to the Indians of the Ohio Purchase, the Miami Purchase, and the Virginia Military District. With a like appreciation of this situation, still another correspondent denounced those persons who were so exercised over the rights of the Indians, but failed to mention their crimes.[58] The Louisiana Purchase brought this latent hostility against Western expansion to the surface, and the newspapers of New England, especially, lost sight of the benefits of this measure in their animus over an act that meant additional migration and a still further decrease in the national influence of their own section. An ex-

[55] *Boston Gazette,* January 30, 1792.
[56] *Massachusetts Spy,* February 23, 1792; *Boston Gazette,* July 13, 1795.
[57] *American Museum,* vol. XI, pp. 37-38.
[58] *Gazette of the United States,* January 14, 1792.

ample of this narrow prejudice is found in an exceedingly lugubrious article in a Connecticut paper that called attention to the unpleasant and even fatal effects of the unhealthy climate of the Illinois and Louisiana country upon Northern constitutions. To point his criticisms, the author gave a long list of persons from Connecticut who had died in the Western country during the summer of 1811, including Judge Penniman and Mr. Tinker, "lately return'd from Connecticut with newly married wives." [59] In strong contrast to this dismal tale, with its petty background, was the attitude of the Virginia press, which fully appreciated the benefits to the Western country from free navigation of the Mississippi and exulted in the "glorious intelligence" of the purchase of Louisiana.

The indifference to Western problems displayed in the case of the Louisiana Purchase was also shown in the attitude of many of the New England papers toward the vital interests of the Old Northwest in the War of 1812. The dominance of local political interests had already been evident when the *Connecticut Courant* drew attention to the weak military situation at Detroit, in order to attack the Republican administration.[60] In the usual course of reporting the news, the newspapers of New England gave considerable attention to the plots of Tecumseh and the Prophet, together with Harrison's march to Tippecanoe, nor did they fail to notice the many indications of British intrigue. But these suspicions, as well as any consideration of frontier needs, were seemingly cast aside in the rage with which so many of these New England editors announced the "dreadful tidings" of the final outbreak of war with Great Britain. Of course they noted the chief military events as the war progressed, although the sectional hatred of Jefferson and his policies frequently appeared in the form of severe criticisms. Yet these same editors branded Hull's surrender as a "national disgrace," and Perry's victory as "glorious news," although they paid scant

[59] *Connecticut Courant*, November 13, 1811.
[60] *Ibid.*, September 16, 1807.

attention to the Battle of the Thames. Finally, it is quite significant that in the general rejoicing over the peace treaty many important New England papers did not mention at all its effect upon the problems of the West, and one editor even taunted the peace commissioners with their failure to hold "a foot of Canada."

The narrow New England attitude regarding the importance of the War of 1812 to the Old Northwest was not usual in other sections of the Atlantic Coast, where intense interest had been shown from the beginning of the Indian troubles. One zealous editor of a New Jersey paper actually stopped his presses in order to print the important news of the Battle of Tippecanoe,[61] and in Virginia, especially, there was much interest in a campaign in which a force of Kentucky militia was led by a native-born son of the Old Dominion. The news of the Battle of Tippecanoe aroused a spirit throughout Virginia which one editor voiced when he gloried in the heroism of the men who fell, but rejoiced still more in the "Roman spirit" in Kentucky which, instead of lamentations for the past, prepared with courage to send forth fresh forces.[62] When the Indians continued to ravage the frontier, the spirited comments of the Virginia papers aroused a popular spirit that enthusiastically welcomed the final declaration of war against Great Britain as a necessary measure for frontier well-being. Nor were these declarations of the Virginia editors mere empty words, for soon after the news came of Hull's surrender, the governor issued a stirring appeal for 1,500 patriotic young men of Virginia to volunteer, ready to march at four days' notice to the defense of the Western country.[63] The newspapers followed Harrison's movements in much detail, and the "most glorious news" of Perry's victory, quickly followed by tidings of the Battle of the Thames, raised the patriotic fervor of the Virginians to a high pitch. The morning after Richmond received the news

[61] *New Brunswick Guardian*, December 12, 1811.
[62] *Virginia Argus*, December 5, 1811.
[63] *Ibid.*, September 3, 1812.

of this victory, the *Virginia Argus* spread the tidings abroad in an extra issue which was a real achievement in an age of hand presses. That night the city was "brilliantly illuminated" in honor of the victories of Harrison and Perry.[64] This same interest in Western affairs was evident during the peace negotiations when there was a strong protest in Virginia against the British proposal for a buffer state, involving, it was pointed out, a virtual surrender of the Western settlements. [65] When news of the final peace came, the newspapers announced it to the public in another round of extra editions.

In Kentucky, whence so many emigrants crossed directly to the north bank of the Ohio, the interest in the affairs of the Old Northwest was far more general than in Virginia. Especially was this true during the first ten or twelve years of settlement. The *Kentucky Gazette,* the only newspaper in the state up to 1798, paid much attention to military news from the country north of the Ohio. Also, it occasionally printed letters from the inhabitants of the new settlements, and from 1793 on, extracts appeared from the Cincinnati newspaper, the *Centinel.* After 1795 there was practically no military news, aside from occasional Indian raids on the borders, and the *Kentucky Gazette* now gave numerous news items, notably those from the settlers who were going into the Virginia Military District in increasing numbers. From these notices it is quite evident that the many ex-Kentuckians in the Old Northwest carried on a constant intercourse with their relatives and former neighbors in their old homes. Many legal notices, also, from the Northwest Territory soon began to appear in the *Kentucky Gazette,* among them lists of the lands of non-residents who were delinquent in their taxes, and rewards offered for escaped prisoners. Among these news items were even occasional notices from Vincennes and the distant Illinois settlements. An especially interesting advertisement was one in 1797 by John Taylor, who announced that he had estab-

[64] *Virginia Argus,* October 18 and 21, 1813.
[65] *Ibid.,* October 15, 1814.

lished a ferry from Limestone across the Ohio to the terminus of the road that was being opened up from Wheeling,
and that he would attend travelers on the first and the fif-
teenth days of each month. A week or so later there was
another advertisement that a party would soon start from
Washington, Kentucky, cross the Ohio, presumably on John
Taylor's ferry, and then follow the new land route through
the Northwest Territory to Wheeling.[66]

After 1795, when settlement in the interior became possible, the *Kentucky Gazette* contained many advertisements
of lands for sale in the Virginia Military District. Of special
interest was a notice in 1796 from George Washington who
offered for sale three tracts, approximating 3,000 acres, on
the Little Miami River. With characteristic caution Washington announced that, according to the surveyor's reports,
the lands were of "first quality," and as they were near Judge
Symmes' tract and Fort Washington, they could not fail to
become valuable in the future.[67] Another advertiser in the
Kentucky Gazette, Samuel Hopkins of Mecklenburg, Virginia, wished to sell about 7,000 acres through his agent at
Lexington, Kentucky.[68] These and many similar advertisements give an excellent idea of the widespread speculation
that was being carried on at this time in Virginia military
warrants. Nor was the Virginia Military District the only
section of the Old Northwest in which inducements were
offered settlers from Kentucky. Thus, in 1800 Abraham
Freeman offered a section of first-class land in the Miami
Purchase not far from Cincinnati, on which there were "two
large improvements, excellent cabins, log barns," and other
buildings. In partial payment for this tract, which was well
fenced and was only three miles from the mill, Freeman offered to accept "breeding mares, young saddle horses, cattle,
or sheep." [69] Occasionally the *Kentucky Gazette* contained

[66] *Kentucky Gazette,* June 3 and 14, 1797.
[67] *Ibid.,* April 22, 1796.
[68] *Ibid.,* September 10, 1796.
[69] *Ibid.,* September 29, 1800.

advertisements of lands in Clark's Grant across the river from Louisville. Incidentally these offers of land in the Old Northwest do not appear to have aroused any marked resentment in Kentucky, probably because immigrants were still arriving in such large numbers that the few who migrated north of the Ohio made no particular difference.

After 1800 the notices of the Old Northwest in the *Kentucky Gazette* greatly decreased. Occasionally there were news items of unusual interest which were copied from local newspapers, as an account of the astounding migration of squirrels from Kentucky to the Northwest Territory in the fall of 1802. The bill in 1802 to move the seat of territorial government from Chillicothe to Cincinnati, and the ensuing Chillicothe riot, also aroused interest in Kentucky, and later the *Gazette* gave much space to Indian raids on the Western border, and to the Battle of Tippecanoe.[70] There were notices, too, of public and private lands for sale north of the Ohio, but they were much less frequent than in the years 1788–1800, and the tracts that were advertised were more generally distributed through the Old Northwest. But there were few, if any, of the notices of inns or ferries that would indicate a considerable travel between Kentucky and the Old Northwest. What is even more striking, the stores in such Ohio River trading centers as Cincinnati and Marietta did not find it necessary to insert advertisements of their stocks in the *Kentucky Gazette*. This same dearth of advertisements, and even of news from the Old Northwest, was true of the many newspapers, beside the *Gazette,* which were published in Kentucky from about 1800. Scattered copies of different papers issued in Lexington, in Frankfort, in Paris, in Lancaster, and in Louisville show few, if any, items relating to the Old Northwest, and consequently they strengthen the conclusion that by 1800 the Virginia Military District and other lands north of the Ohio were not attracting emi-

[70] *Kentucky Gazette,* October 16, 1801, January 1 and 8, 1802, July 2 and December 3, 1811.

grants from Kentucky in such large numbers, and that trade between the two banks of the river was quite limited.

The settlers in Tennessee showed even less interest in the Old Northwest, if the columns of their local newspapers may be taken as a criterion. In the *Knoxville Gazette*, the chief newspaper of eastern Tennessee, there were only occasional news items from the Northwest Territory, and most of them recorded the progress of Wayne's campaign. Of a somewhat different type was the toast at a Fourth of July banquet in Knoxville in 1795 to the "citizens of the Territory northwest of the Ohio—may party spirit never deprive them of the rights of freemen." [71] The important newspaper of middle Tennessee, the *Tennessee Gazette*, published at Nashville, gave occasional news from the Old Northwest, calling attention in one rather significant notice to the extensive lands which the Delawares ceded in Indiana in 1804. A later issue printed in full the Land Act of 1804 for the survey and sale of the public lands that lay west of the mouth of the Kentucky.[72] But there is no evidence in either the *Knoxville Gazette* or the *Tennessee Gazette* of any such considerable migration to the Old Northwest, as there was from Kentucky. Nor, aside from travelers who came down the Ohio, and then up the Cumberland to Tennessee, was there any considerable contact between the inhabitants of the two regions. This situation was in decided contrast to the frequent communication between the Old Northwest and the two remaining frontier centers of settlement in western Pennsylvania and western Virginia. As was to be expected, the *Pittsburgh Gazette*, which circulated extensively in these two last-named districts, devoted much space to news from the Old Northwest. Like the *Kentucky Gazette*, it gave full accounts of raids by the Indians and the campaigns against them up to the Treaty of Greenville. Also, there were many items of current news that had been picked up by travelers

[71] *Knoxville Gazette*, July 18, 1796.
[72] *Tennessee Gazette*, September 26, 1804, and April 17, 1805.

or sent in through letters, while numerous advertisements of "Kentucky boats" for sale testified to the source of a large part of the growing business of Pittsburgh. Occasionally there were advertisements in the *Pittsburgh Gazette* of lands for sale by persons who held large tracts in the Seven Ranges or in the Military Reserve. But aside from the Seven Ranges, there seems to have been no considerable migration from the Pittsburgh region into the Old Northwest during this early period.

But whatever the origin of the immigrants into the rich lands north of the Ohio, whether they came from the Eastern states or from the Kentucky settlements, their most important aim was to better their living conditions. An excellent illustration of the grievances behind this economic motive is given by the representation of a group of almost three hundred and fifty pioneers who settled between the Scioto and the Muskingum. In their old homes some of them had been men with small property and large families who hoped to make a better living in the Western country, and others had been renters, unable to pay the high prices that were charged for land in the older states, who hoped to own their farms in this new haven of refuge.[73] Judge Jacob Burnet, himself an early pioneer, has left an exceedingly enlightening analysis of the motives of these settlers in the Old Northwest. Many of them, he points out, were Revolutionary veterans who "had spent the prime of their lives in the war of independence. Many of them had exhausted their fortunes in maintaining the desperate struggle; and retired to the wilderness to conceal their poverty, and avoid companions mortifying to their pride, while struggling to maintain their families, and improve their condition. Some of them were young men, descended from Revolutionary patriots who had fallen in the contest, or become too feeble to endure the fatigue of settling a wilderness. Others were adventurous spirits, to whom

[73] Petition to Congress from John Cram and others, October 22, 1800, *Northwest Territorial Papers*, House Files.

any change might be for the better; and who, anticipating a successful rush, united in the enterprise." [74]

The number of Revolutionary veterans among these early settlers is, of course, explained to a large extent by the ease with which they could secure land in exchange for the depreciated military warrants and the Federal certificates which many of them held. The problems of the returned veteran are well pictured in the simple words of Manasseh Cutler, who had been a chaplain in the Revolution. Afterwards as the pastor of the Ipswich, Massachusetts, church he took a leading part in the organization of the Ohio Company. His interest in the Western country he explained in forcible fashion: "I had suffered exceedingly in ye war, and after it was over, by paper money and ye high price of articles of living. My salary small and family large, for several years I thought ye people had not done me justice, and I meditated leaving them. Purchasing lands in a new country appeared to be ye only thing I could do to secure a living to myself and family in that unsettled state of public affairs." [75] Another interesting example of these Revolutionary veterans who sought to better their fortunes in the Western country was William Dana, a native of Massachusetts. Unfortunately he had sold his property in exchange for the rapidly depreciating Continental currency, and in 1779 he settled upon a small farm at Amherst, attempting to eke out a precarious living for his numerous and growing family by working as a carpenter. In his poverty the fertile lands of Ohio offered a welcome relief, so that in 1789, at forty-four, he settled in Belpre, where he soon cleared his land, erected a comfortable farmhouse, and lived in plenty.[76] Manasseh Cutler and William Dana were typical of the army of Revolutionary veterans who turned to the Western lands as a place for economic betterment. At Marietta, in a list of thirty-three of the most prominent of the early settlers, twenty-three had seen active service in the Revolution, and

---

[74] Burnet, *Notes on the Northwestern Territory*, pp. 42-43.
[75] Hulbert, ed., *Records of the Ohio Company*, vol. I, p. vii.
[76] Hildreth, *Lives of the Early Settlers of Ohio*, pp. 337-340.

of the remainder all but four, and one of them a clergyman, had been too young to enlist. Ranging in rank from private to brigadier, these veterans, when they settled in the West, were usually in the prime of life, between thirty-five and fifty.[77] John Cleves Symmes led another large contingent of veterans from the Middle States into the Miami Purchase, and still others found their way from Virginia through Kentucky into the Virginia Military District.

The opportunities which the Old Northwest held for young men attracted many settlers of marked ability and varied professions, among them two journalists who came to Cincinnati. The first one, Nathaniel Maxwell, must have had an abiding faith in the future when he founded the *Centinel*, the first newspaper in the Old Northwest.[78] Another well-known Cincinnati editor, John W. Browne, was originally a Congregational minister in England. "Anxious to live" . . . "in the land of civil and religious liberty," and attracted by the promise of the Western country, he came to America in 1795 and settled at Cincinnati three years later. Beside holding many public offices, in 1804 he founded *Liberty Hall*, a weekly paper that in its editorials and general make-up was far superior to many of the contemporary Eastern journals.[79] Another hardy soul among the pioneers was the Reverend Daniel Story, who was induced to come to Marietta in 1789 from New England, in order to serve as preacher and teacher. A man in the prime of life, Story went out with high hopes, but like Roger Williams he was too outspoken for the powers that be, and he, too, suffered the poverty and disappointment destined for one who will not conform.[80]

An appointment to a Federal office was another bait that drew young men of ability to the Western country, where many of them remained as permanent settlers. However, some of them failed to appreciate the advantages of the new

[77] Hildreth, *Lives of the Early Settlers of Ohio, passim.*
[78] *Centinel*, November 23, 1793.
[79] *Liberty Hall*, January 7, 1813.
[80] *Scioto Gazette*, January 21, 1815.

settlements and instead they magnified the discomforts. A representative of this type was Stanley Griswold, the first secretary of Michigan Territory. Coming out from Connecticut, he met his first disappointment when he was obliged to pay his own traveling expenses. Detroit, he complained, was very "unpromising" socially, with exceedingly high prices, butter and cheese at fifty cents per pound, and other supplies in proportion. As his combined salary as secretary and land commissioner was only $1,700, Griswold complained that he was unable to make ends meet, and became a chronic grumbler. After he was dismissed from his Michigan office, he proposed at first to settle in the Western Reserve, but eventually he was satisfied with an appointment as one of the judges of Illinois Territory.[81] Still another important class of young men who came to the Old Northwest were the surveyors who found abundant work there, and many opportunities to pick up desirable tracts. Among the ones who remained as permanent settlers were such leading figures as Nathaniel Massie and Duncan McArthur in the Virginia Military District, and Israel Ludlow in the Miami Purchase. The popularity of this profession as an avenue to success in the West was strikingly evident in 1796, when there was keen competition for the appointment as surveyor general.[82] The army also drew young men to the West, and many of the privates and officers who came to take part in the Indian campaigns made permanent homes here, the most notable among them William Henry Harrison, who came to the Old Northwest as an aide-de-camp to Anthony Wayne. Less illustrious, but more representative of the average settler, was David Zeigler, a native of Germany, who served in the Revolutionary army, received a commission under Harmar, and ended his military career in St. Clair's ill-fated campaign.

[81] Stanley Griswold to Huntington, March 7, 1806, and June 3, 1807; R. J. Meigs to Huntington, April 15, 1810, *Huntington MSS.*

[82] Applications from: John Hall, May 23, Joseph Ellicott, May 25, and Israel Ludlow, July 9, 1796, *Northwest Territorial Papers,* B. I. A. Misc.

9769

After resigning from the army, Zeigler settled in Cincinnati, where he became a leading citizen.[83]

The courage and persistence with which these hardy pioneers surmounted their many problems are well illustrated by the experiences of Daniel Sherman, who came out to the Western Reserve from Norwalk, Connecticut, as a youth of twenty. With two other young men he traveled in a "stout" wagon, drawn by two horses, across New York State over the Genesee Trail to Buffalo, and then along the lake shore. In the Ohio country he hunted up his father's tract of 2,000 acres south of Cleveland, and camped there, ten miles away from the nearest settlement and with game as his chief dependence for food. Sherman finally fell a victim to the prevailing ague, and he set out for Lancaster on foot, meeting at every cabin on the way "a hearty welcome and kind words." Later he returned to his father's land and built a cabin. When the War of 1812 broke out there was considerable danger from stray Indians, and Sherman spent most of the winter of 1812–1813 in a blockhouse that served as a general neighborhood refuge where thirty to forty persons gathered each night. The following summer the fear of Indian attacks forced many of the settlers to go customarily in bands to plant their corn, but after Harrison's victory in the fall of 1813, this precaution was no longer necessary, and Sherman and his neighbors began to reap the fruits of their toil.[84] Occasionally the constant hardships and perils disheartened the immigrant in the Western country, and many pathetic tragedies took place in this frontier life. Among them was the story of two Dutch families who left their native land about 1787, came to Ohio, and settled close to Marietta. Finally, terrified by the frequent Indian raids, and doubtless discouraged, too, by the cold reception given them by their Puritan neighbors, these two alien families, each with three children, started on the long, weary way back to their old homes. They ascended the Ohio by boat to Pittsburgh, and

[83] *Western Spy*, September 28, 1811.
[84] *Narrative of Daniel Sherman*, April 5, 1872.

then started to walk to the seacoast at Boston, making each
day an average of not more than eight miles. One of the
women carried a pack weighing fully one hundred and forty-
six pounds on which sat her youngest offspring, and the other
two children dragged at her heels.[85] Still another typical
story was that of William Ballard, a native of New England,
who went to sea at eighteen and was held captive for eight
years by the Algerian pirates. Upon his return to Boston he
found that his parents had migrated to the Western country,
and he started out to find them, only to be drowned in the
Ohio near Wheeling.[86] Fortunately such harrowing experiences were the exception, and the vast majority of emigrants
found a new home and comparative prosperity in the Western country.

The increasing tide of immigration into the Old Northwest
may well be compared to the throng which set out from England, in the seventeenth century, to seek better conditions in
America. In much similar fashion the settlers who came into
the Old Northwest from New England, from the Middle
States, from Virginia, and from the backwoods were attracted by the many accounts of the great fertility of these
Western lands, and of the opportunity to start life afresh in
a new country. Many were induced to go, too, by such systematic schemes of colonization as the Ohio Purchase controlled by the Ohio Company, or the Miami Purchase under
John Cleves Symmes. Others were attracted by the inducements offered by land speculators of the type of Lemuel
Storrs, the hard-headed Connecticut Yankee who willingly
exchanged uncleared lands in the wilderness for the solid
values of cultivated farms in Connecticut. Or perhaps the
settler bought his lands from the speculators in the Virginia
Military District or their agents. Intensely human were the
motives of these emigrants who thronged to the Old Northwest, including in their ranks the veterans of the Revolution,
the discontented, the adventurous, the young men seeking

[85] *New York Daily Advertiser*, December 12, 1791.
[86] *The Supporter*, August 4, 1810.

their fortunes; all of them willing to brave the hardships of the long journey westward, and of a pioneer community, in order to carry out an intensely American trait, and to seek a larger and better life in a new environment. The less adventurous stay-at-homes followed with intense interest the fortunes of these wandering sons, and often the letters and other reports from the new settlements induced them to follow. In the columns of the newspapers and other publications of the Atlantic states and of the older settlements west of the Alleghenies, were mirrored then the aspirations and the gamut of human motives that inspired this great American trek across the Appalachians, toward the land of the setting sun.

Chapter III

GOVERNMENT IN THE WILDERNESS

WHEN the pioneers first settled at Marietta they found themselves, like the Plymouth colonists, outside the bounds of an organized government. Following the usual custom of American colonists under such circumstances, from the framers of the Mayflower Compact down, the directors of the Ohio Company proceeded to draw up a code of regulations which they posted upon the trunk of a large beech tree at Marietta. On July 9, 1788, a regularized administration started with the arrival of General Arthur St. Clair whom Congress had appointed governor of the Northwest Territory, comprising at that time all of the Old Northwest. The task St. Clair faced, to put into effect in this vast region the governmental provisions of the Ordinance of 1787, was indeed a momentous and a difficult one. Beside the settlers at Marietta and a few of Clark's veterans who had taken up lands across the river from Louisville, the only American inhabitants were a few straggling pioneers in Vincennes and the Illinois settlements, and the squatters in the upper Ohio Valley. The French inhabitants of Vincennes, of the Illinois settlements, and of the scattered trading posts were unacquainted with American institutions, and considerable tact would be necessary to conciliate them, in view of the Spanish intrigues which centered in St. Louis and other posts in the Louisiana district. Also, from Canada and especially from the posts at Detroit and Mackinaw which they still held, the British were constantly stirring up the Indians against the Americans. Already the Land Ordinance had created conditions under which the settlers so necessary to assert American rule were beginning to come in. The Ohio Company had founded Marietta, other colonization projects were in prospect, and the survey of the Seven Ranges had been started. It was now essential that the provisions of the Government Ordinance should be worked out in such fashion that an orderly government would be established in the Old Northwest.

During the rather arbitrary form of government which constituted the first stage under the Ordinance, the personal qualifications of the governor and the three judges were of the utmost importance. St. Clair was well fitted for his duties as the first governor of the Northwest Territory. By birth a Scotchman, a man of polish and education, in 1764 he had settled in the Ligonier Valley on the frontier of western Pennsylvania. There he had acquired considerable experience in public office, and he had served also as a distinguished officer in the American Revolution. The mature judgment of a man of fifty-four, an iron will, an imperious temper, ability much above the average, and the prestige of a former president of the Continental Congress were among St. Clair's qualifications for his new post. His two colleagues in the initial organization of the territorial government, Judge Samuel Holden Parsons and Judge James Mitchell Varnum, were New England lawyers of excellent standing, and directors in the Ohio Company. Judge Parsons, a graduate of Harvard University, had served in eighteen consecutive sessions of the Connecticut state legislature, and was an acknowledged authority on administrative and legal matters, while Judge Varnum had been at the very top of his profession in Rhode Island. Like St. Clair, both of them were Revolutionary veterans, and both were in the prime of life, Judge Varnum forty, and Judge Parsons fifty-one when they came to Marietta. As the third judge, John Cleves Symmes, did not actively take up his work for some time, to Judge Parsons and Judge Varnum fell the difficult task, along with St. Clair, of drawing up the basic code and of filling in the details of an administrative system for the Northwest Territory. All three of them were men of experience and mature judgment, who could be trusted not to adopt a radical point of view. On the other hand, as Revolutionary veterans and men in the prime of life, they were still in touch with the liberalism of the period, and would not go to the conservative extremes of older men. Their New England origin inclined the two judges to a Federalistic belief in a strongly organized government, and St. Clair was temperamentally sympathetic with this point of view. The one remaining important officer in the early years of the Northwest Territory, the secretary, Winthrop Sargent, was likewise a Revolutionary veteran, New England born and reared, and a graduate of Harvard. As he acted as governor during St. Clair's frequent absences from the territory, Sargent became an important figure in the first stage of the territorial government. With so well qualified an official personnel this initial stage in a system of colonial administration that was distinctively American, promised to be carried on with moderation and firmness, and at the same time with a very evident recognition of New England precedents and theories.

July 15, 1788, six days after he arrived in Marietta, Governor St. Clair formally inaugurated government in the Northwest Territory, in a speech that asked for the coöperation of the inhabitants, and displayed a keen appreciation of the difficulties that confronted him.[1] His first important step was to establish an administrative basis by the formation of Washington County, extending roughly from the Ohio River northward, between the line of the Scioto, the Tuscarawas, and the Cuyahoga rivers, and the western boundary of Penn-

[1] The most important source for St. Clair's administration is the *Journal of the Northwest Territory*, July 9, 1788, to January 15, 1803. This, the original record, was discovered in 1930, and has been deposited in the Ohio State Archæological and Historical Society Library. Before this MS. was found, the chief source was the *Records of the Executive Department of the Northwest Territory, 1788–1795*, in the Library of the Department of State. An officially certified transcript of this second MS. in the Ohio State Library has been used in this present narrative. Another important MS. source, the *Proceedings of the Executive of the Northwest Territory, May 16 to September 30, 1796*, is in the *Sargent Papers*, in the Ohio State Archæological and Historical Society Library.

sylvania. The next step, the adoption of a code of laws, brought out a difference of opinion between the governor and the judges that illustrated in striking fashion St. Clair's arbitrary tendencies. The judges contended that, under the Ordinance, the governor was merely coequal with themselves in legislative powers and that a bare majority could pass a law. With true Scotch pertinacity, St. Clair insisted that the governor had the absolute power of veto, criticized many of the proposals of the judges, and ultimately won his point. He was not so successful, however, in establishing his own interpretation of the clause of the Ordinance with respect to the contents of the laws that could be adopted. St. Clair held that this section of the Ordinance only gave the territorial officers authority to adopt laws of the original states, either as a whole or in part, but the judges insisted that with the governor they constituted a legislative body which had power to enact laws that even combined parts of those of the states, if necessary, and that they might also change the wording, if only they preserved the spirit of the original statute. This position the judges stoutly maintained, objecting to the restrictions upon them if they were limited to the only code, that of Pennsylvania, of which there was a complete copy in the territory. As the situation demanded quick action, St. Clair finally gave in, but unfortunately the laws that were passed in this fashion ultimately became the source of much legal uncertainty.

In drafting the new code, St. Clair insisted that the common law of England should be considered in force, except where it was superseded by statutes, and that all laws should be explicit and should apply to the entire territory. These wise limitations the governor and judges consistently adhered to in the fundamental code which they drew up at Marietta between July 25 and December 28, 1788. Although these laws were founded chiefly upon the Pennsylvania Code which Governor St. Clair had brought along with him, the original statutes were usually adapted in admirable fashion to the needs of a pioneer community. They also reflected the New

England origin of the two judges.[2] The provisions for local government were simple but effective. In each county the new code established a court of quarter sessions to hear lesser criminal cases, a court of common pleas for civil cases, and a probate court. A provision that was peculiarly adapted to the needs of a pioneer community, where settlement was widely scattered, empowered a single justice to hear petty cases. The official list for each county included a sheriff, a coroner, and the justices and clerks of the different courts. As a supreme court, the judges of the territory held three sessions annually of the general court. The great merit of this simple legal structure was the ease with which it could be expanded as additional counties were set off.

Supplementing the law setting up governmental machinery, was the one concerning crimes and their punishment, which was avowedly drawn up to meet local conditions, although it reflected in clear fashion the severity of the early New England codes. Upon conviction of murder or treason a criminal suffered the death penalty, but for the vast majority of crimes the prescribed punishment was a flogging, a fine, or exposure in the stocks. In the long list of crimes, there were interesting reminders of the problems of a frontier country, and especially those of the Old Northwest. For instance, the law met the danger from British and Spanish intrigues by a definition of treason that included any correspondence which was intended to betray the territory. Also, it forbade assemblies and riots, especially where their object was to commit an unlawful act "with violence" against an individual or the community. Such crimes as arson, robbery, and burglary it punished by a flogging of not more than thirty-nine stripes and imprisonment, and with an Old Testament sense of justice, this earliest code of the Old Northwest required a thief to make full restitution. A strong Puritan influence was shown in the numerous clauses to regulate everyday life. Thus, disobedient children or servants

[2] *Laws of the Northwest Territory,* Pease, ed., *Illinois Historical Collections,* vol. XVII, pp. 1-26.

might be committed to jail, until "they shall humble themselves to the said parent's or master's satisfaction." Again, for drunkenness there was a fine of ten dimes for the first offense, or if it were not paid, an hour in the stocks, although the law very sensibly required that such crimes should be reported "within two days next after the offense shall have been committed." The law required all responsible persons to use their influence to stop swearing or "idle, vain, and obscene conversations," and it set apart Sunday as a day of rest "from common labors and pursuits." Another important chapter in the new code, the militia law, required all men, sixteen years and upward, to enroll for service if they were needed. Each man must provide his own equipment of "a musket and bayonet or rifle, cartridge box, pouch," and other accessories, and following the customs of early New England, the militia should assemble, armed, each Sunday at the different places of public worship. A law that regulated marriage was still another important chapter in this fundamental code.

St. Clair's next important step was to appoint the necessary officials and to provide for the opening of the courts in Washington County. But he found that properly qualified appointees were scarce among these early settlers, and often he was obliged to appoint one man to several offices, as in the case of Joseph Gilman, afterward a judge of the territory, who held simultaneously the offices of justice of the peace, judge of the court of common pleas, and judge of the probate court for Washington County. St. Clair found it was equally difficult to secure efficient militia officers, and the many resignations and new appointments in this important service were a source of constant worry. Nevertheless, orderly government was soon established over the New England emigrants at Marietta, and following the example of the Pilgrims the governor set apart Thursday, December 25, 1788, as the first Thanksgiving Day in the Northwest Territory. St. Clair took no immediate steps either for the organization of the settlements that were springing up in other sections of the Old Northwest, or for the actual extension of American power over the ones that already existed. Throughout 1789 he was either busy with important Indian negotiations, or else he was absent from the territory. Meantime, the settlers in the Miami Purchase were rapidly increasing, and there was great need for orderly government here as well as at Vincennes and in the Kaskaskia region. Finally, late in 1789 St. Clair set off on the long journey down the Ohio to these different settlements. January 2, 1790, he arrived at the small settlement of Losantiville, and after changing this fanciful name to Cincinnati, he established Hamilton County, to extend northward from the Ohio, between the Miami and the Scioto. The appointment of the county officials completed the work of organization in the two basic counties of what is now Ohio, Washington County to the east of the Scioto and Hamilton County to the west.[3] With this administrative foundation completed, St. Clair left Cincinnati on his way to the Illinois country, stopping on the journey to appoint a justice of the peace and a militia officer at the pioneer settlement of Clarksville across the Ohio from Louisville.

The journey to the Illinois country was attended with many vexatious delays, and not until March 5, 1790, almost two months after he had left Louisville, did St. Clair arrive at Kaskaskia. The scanty population here, chiefly French with a hardy group of American pioneers, he found, were reduced to the "lowest ebb of poverty." The successive changes of régime since the Treaty of Paris in 1763, from French to British, and then from British to American, had wrought endless confusion. Government was a farce, and land titles were in an almost hopeless tangle. Moreover, George Rogers Clark had confiscated many supplies in the course of his campaigns, usually without compensation, the Indian trade was gone, and floods and the failure of crops, with scattering attacks by the Indians, had so disheartened

[3] *Executive Records, Northwest Territory, 1788–1795*, pp. 98, 99, 101-102; *Symmes Correspondence*, Bond, ed., p. 123 (note 150).

the French *habitants* that many of them had crossed the
Mississippi, and had settled in Spanish territory.[4] Amid such
untoward conditions, St. Clair undertook to establish at least
the semblance of orderly government, as a first step creating
St. Clair County, to stretch along the Mississippi north of
the Ohio.[5] Since the hazards of travel made it almost impossible to select a single county seat, and on the other hand
population was too scanty to support more than one county
organization, St. Clair divided this county into three districts, each with stated sessions of the local courts. With an
equally tactful recognition of local prejudices he included
among the county officials, appointees of such unmistakably
French origin as Benjamin Tardavero and Jean Baptiste Bar-
bot, and at the same time, he named Nicholas Piggott and
other American settlers to represent that element of the
population. Next the governor turned his attention to the
land titles in the Illinois country, but so great was the confusion that followed the successive régimes under which the
inhabitants had passed that the results were exceedingly disappointing. As a partial solution of this and other problems,
he suggested the voluntary removal of the inhabitants of the
low-lying districts onto higher and healthier locations, but
the lethargic French did not respond to this suggestion.

The Spanish intrigues from across the river, St. Clair discovered, were a fruitful source of unrest among these French
settlers. Especially annoying were the systematic efforts
that were being made to induce the inhabitants of the Illinois country and of Vincennes to migrate across the Mississippi, and often to go to George Morgan's new colony at
New Madrid. Many of them had already gone, and others
were preparing to do so, not knowing what might be in store
for them under American rule. An outstanding cause for this
alarm, St. Clair discovered, was the fear of the French that
their slaves would be freed immediately under the terms of

[4] Alvord, *The Illinois Country, 1673–1818*, ch. XVII; Governor St. Clair
to the President, May 1, 1790, *Northwest Territorial Papers*, B. R. L. 6098.

[5] Report of St. Clair to Thomas Jefferson, February 11, 1791, *Executive
Records, Northwest Territory, 1788–1795*, pp. 275-309.

the Ordinance. Many had left for this reason, and those that remained were apprehensive, for slavery had existed in the Illinois country ever since the French régime. To cope with this situation St. Clair issued a declaration that the Ordinance of 1787 was not, in his opinion, retroactive, and was therefore of no effect upon the slaves that were held before its passage.[6] Although this decision was a great aid in pacifying the slaveholders, it created a situation that was partially responsible for the determined efforts later on to reëstablish slavery in Illinois. Also, St. Clair attempted to adjust satisfactorily the inevitable grievances that had arisen between the peoples on either side of an international boundary, and especially one that was in the backwoods. His correspondence with the Spanish officials across the Mississippi was invariably courteous and secured results, and by such conciliatory policies he checked the migration of the inhabitants of the French settlements. But until land titles in Illinois had been adjusted in satisfactory fashion, he pointed out, it would be impossible to attract there on any large scale the emigrants who were swarming down the Ohio.

Throughout the organization of the Illinois country, St. Clair was handicapped by the absence of territorial judges. Without them legislation was impossible, yet situations constantly arose that demanded definite action. As the only possible recourse, he resorted to arbitrary government by proclamations, hoping that the judges would ultimately confirm his measures by suitable legislation. In one especially important proclamation he forbade the sale of intoxicants to the Indians, and required all retailers of liquor to take out licenses. Another decree attempted to end the intrigues of British and Spanish agents among the Indians by an order that all strangers who came to Cahokia, the chief stopping place for travelers bound for the Illinois Valley, must report promptly to the commandant. Another proclamation attempted to end a source of much annoyance from the Span-

[6] Governor St. Clair to Judge Turner, December 4, 1794, *St. Clair Papers*, Smith, ed., vol. II, pp. 330-332.

ish across the Mississippi, by refusing to foreigners the right
to hunt or cut wood on the American side of the river. Of a
similarly arbitrary type were St. Clair's instructions to Captain Jean Baptiste Mayet whom he continued as commandant at Peoria, the small but important post that commanded
trade through the Illinois and Chicago rivers to Lake Michigan. By these orders the governor hoped to restrict the trade
with the Indians to American citizens with licenses, and as
a further precaution he required every traveler through the
Illinois Valley to show a pass. As a necessary measure to
ensure the enforcement of these orders and of the laws in
general, St. Clair ordered that prisons should be built at
Cahokia and Kaskaskia. Although these decrees aroused
severe criticism, so arbitrary a policy was probably the only
one that was possible under the circumstances.

After having completed at least the forms of organization
for the Illinois country, St. Clair hastened up the Ohio for
important conferences with the Indians, leaving to Sargent
the establishment of American administration at Vincennes,
where the situation was closely parallel to the one at Kaskaskia.[7] In Vincennes and the vicinity about three hundred
families were settled, most of them French, with a few half-
breeds and Americans. The trade with the Indians had practically disappeared, the people were poor and shiftless, and
the framework of government was in so disorderly a state
that many of the inhabitants were leaving. As an initial
measure, Sargent organized Knox County, extending northward from the Ohio between the Miami River and the eastern boundary of St. Clair County. In his choice of public
officials Sargent followed the precedent which St. Clair had
set in Illinois, and appointed French settlers, among them
Antoine Gamelin, along with such decided Americans as
James Johnson. Land titles at Vincennes, Sargent discovered, were in the same confusion as in Illinois, and like St.

---

[7] Winthrop Sargent to the President, July 31, 1790, *Executive Records,
Northwest Territory, 1788–1795*, pp. 88-97; John Cleves Symmes to Robert
Morris, June 22, 1790, *Symmes Correspondence,* Bond, ed., pp. 287-292.

Clair he was unable to straighten out the situation. One bright spot in the general gloom at Vincennes should have been the presence of Judge John Cleves Symmes and Judge George Turner, two of the judges of the Northwest Territory, but these hopes were not realized, chiefly because of temperamental difficulties. Although Judge Symmes had been a justice of the superior court, and later the chief justice of New Jersey, he seems to have had little if any legal training, while Judge Turner, a native of England who, like Judge Symmes, had served in the Revolution, apparently owed his appointment to the personal friendship of Washington. The third and the least active judge of the Northwest Territory, Rufus Putnam, who was not in Vincennes at this time, was likewise a personal appointee of Washington, and one who was without any previous legal experience. All three of these judges were rather mediocre men who were inclined to be petulant, and all of them had a considerable personal interest in land speculations in the Northwest Territory. Often they were a hindrance rather than an aid to St. Clair, and this source of annoyance was, of course, aggravated during the frequent periods when Sargent, lacking the governor's prestige and himself rather irascible, took charge of affairs.

The situation at Vincennes, while the territorial government was being established there, forcibly illustrated the supreme importance of a qualified official personnel. In contrast to the excellent teamwork at Marietta between Governor St. Clair and Judges Parsons and Varnum in drawing up a code of laws, at Vincennes Sargent was unable to secure the hearty coöperation of Judge Symmes and Judge Turner. Finally the secretary and the judges did manage to agree upon three laws for which there was urgent need at Vincennes.[8] The first one strictly forbade the sale of liquor to Indians, and required every trader to take out a license. The second law prohibited the sale of liquor to the soldiers

[8] *Laws of the Northwest Territory*, Pease, ed., *Illinois Historical Collections*, vol. XVII, pp. 26-34.

of the garrison, imposed severe penalties upon private citizens who received from the troops, by purchase or gift, any "public arms, ammunition, clothing, or other accoutrements." The third measure forbade gambling in any form, declared all gambling debts void, and prohibited the indiscriminate discharge of firearms which was so often carried on in or around frontier villages, especially at night.

Sargent insisted that the three laws approved by the judges did not adequately fulfill local needs. As he could not induce his colleagues to pass the additional measures that he considered necessary, he imitated St. Clair's policy in the Illinois country and issued a number of arbitrary decrees. Perhaps the one that was most urgent, in view of the Indian peril at Vincennes, ordered the militia to be constantly ready for service, and required that no man liable for service should leave Vincennes without twenty-four hours' notice, unless he had first reported to the commanding officer. Sargent also reissued St. Clair's proclamations which forbade hunting by foreigners and required all strangers to report to the commandant of the local post. This arbitrary course was questionable policy. Even though the situation imperatively called for action, government by proclamation was a usurpation of power that was specially flagrant if it was carried on by an acting governor, when the judges, the other branch of the territorial legislature, were at hand. Indeed, this policy aroused such strong hostility that Washington found it necessary to write St. Clair a personal letter that called attention to the illegality of these decrees, and the possible dangerous consequences to the territorial government.[9]

Sargent, in fact, was temperamentally inclined to stretch his own powers, and he was altogether too headstrong and arbitrary in coming to important decisions. These characteristics were strikingly in evidence, when he undertook to organize government at Detroit upon his own initiative. Although Congress had already ignored the President's rec-

[9] Washington to St. Clair, January 2, 1791, *St. Clair Papers*, Smith, ed., vol. II, pp. 198-199.

ommendations, and had failed to provide for the civil administration of this region, Sargent apparently became worked up over idle rumors of British intentions. In the absence of St. Clair, he set out for Detroit in July, 1796, to be on the spot as soon as the British surrendered the post, even though a military force was already provided for.[10] His first official act was to create Wayne County, which included all American territory north of a line which ran up the Cuyahoga, across to the Tuscarawas, from Fort Lawrence to Fort Wayne, and then to the most southerly point of Lake Michigan. Following the usual procedure, Sargent's next step was to appoint local officials, and to provide for the different courts at Detroit. In his appointments he planned to select representatives of the French residents, as well as of the other elements in the population, in accordance with the precedents set up in the Illinois country and at Vincennes. But among the 2,165 inhabitants of Detroit and the vicinity there were few men with legal training, or even with the most elementary education. The English contingent were disqualified by their continued strong attachment to the mother country, while their alleged "tyrannical sway" before the Americans came had made them generally obnoxious. Under such circumstances the task of securing qualified officials proved to be a very difficult one. In addition Sargent found at Detroit and in the neighborhood the usual almost hopeless confusion in land titles that was characteristic of the French settlements. To add to his troubles, only a few days before his arrival the book of land records had been removed to the "British side," and he was obliged to apply to the Governor of Canada for its return. Another disturbing factor at Detroit was the constant intrigue by British traders among the Indians, under color of their claim to the privilege of "unrestrained" Indian trade under Jay's Treaty. But Sargent was unable to adjust either this situation or the tangled land system in a fashion that was at all satisfactory.

[10] *Proceedings of the Executive of the Northwest Territory, May 16 to September 30, 1796, Sargent Papers.*

Having organized government at Detroit as well as he could, Sargent next undertook a similar task at Mackinaw, the other important trading post in Michigan. He made the long journey to this distant outpost in a sailing vessel which was becalmed on the way, and indeed it is questionable whether the results justified the expense and hardships of a trip that lasted more than a month. The American garrison already stationed at Mackinaw was fully able to keep order among the twenty odd families of permanent inhabitants, without the aid of an elaborate administrative system. Moreover, the few fur traders there were so illiterate that Sargent could find only two "proper characters" among them to appoint as justices of the peace, and for the third appointee, whom the large crowds that came annually to trade made necessary, he was obliged to select the commandant of the post. Needless to say, he found the land titles at Mackinaw in the usual confusion. After he had made the few adjustments that his very limited powers permitted, Sargent returned to the Ohio Valley by way of Detroit, having completed during this trip the nominal organization of government in the existing settlements of the Old Northwest. Wayne County now included the northern region along the Great Lakes, and to the southward there stretched successively along the Ohio, Washington, Hamilton, Knox, and St. Clair counties. With these basic local units fixed, the chief problem in the future would be to subdivide them, and to elaborate the legal structure in order to meet the needs of a growing population.

Meanwhile St. Clair did not neglect the additional legislation that experience and a rapidly expanding population showed to be necessary. At two legislative sessions held at Cincinnati, November, 1790, and June–July, 1791, the governor presided, and Judge Symmes and Judge Turner were in attendance. At a third session in August, 1792, Sargent was in charge in St. Clair's absence, and was aided by Judge Symmes and Judge Putnam. Like the basic code, the laws that were adopted at these three sessions were founded upon the spirit rather than the letter of laws from the original states.[11] A pressing problem that had arisen was to provide the more elaborate system of local government which the rapid influx of settlers made necessary. Accordingly, a law that was passed in 1790 authorized the division of the counties into townships, in each of which there was to be the necessary force of local officials; a constable, one or more overseers of the poor, and a clerk, all of whom the justices of the county court of quarter sessions would appoint. Other important measures dealt with such fundamental matters as taxation, the construction and repair of highways, and the like. Of special note was the one that marked the quick transition from pioneer vigilante committees to the orderly administration of justice, by the requirement that a courthouse and a "strong and sufficient" jail should be built in each county. In the jails this act required separate apartments for debtors and for ordinary criminals, and also for the two sexes. To ensure adequate buildings, it made jailers and sheriffs liable to severe penalties, if prisoners escaped, except where it was due to the "insufficiency" of the jail. In that case the county must pay the amount owed by the escaped prisoner, in case he was a debtor. Another significant measure, and one that traced its origin to many controversies of the colonial period, carefully regulated the fees to be charged by local officials. Usually the amount ranged between 15 and 50 cents. For example, for each letter of administration he issued, a judge of the probate court received 50 cents and 30 cents for a final decree. For the publication of marriage banns, the fee was 25 cents and in addition the law allowed 110 cents to the minister or the magistrate who performed the ceremony. Payments of all these fees in the early settlements were usually in commodities, with one cent reckoned as the equivalent of a quart of Indian corn and other local products in proportion. Another act of a very practical nature required the territorial laws to be published

[11] *Laws of the Northwest Territory, Illinois Historical Collections,* Pease, ed., vol. XVII, pp. 34-116.

at least once in each county, "for the information of the citizens," and copies to be furnished to all judges and justices of the peace. Customarily the laws that had recently been passed were also posted up in public places, and there were severe penalties for "wilfully or maliciously" defacing such notices.

Unfortunately there was serious doubt as to the legal standing of the laws passed at the first legislative session in 1788, and at the three later ones, 1790–1792. In many cases the governor and the judges had not adopted laws of the original states, as the Ordinance provided, but had merely passed measures that conformed to them in spirit. Many persons held that such measures were entirely valid, and in this opinion they were apparently supported when Congress passed an act, May 8, 1792, for the publication and distribution of the laws of the Northwest Territory. This same act empowered the governor and the judges to repeal any law at their discretion, and it actually disapproved only a single chapter in the entire territorial code.[12] As the Ordinance had stipulated that the laws that were adopted should stand unless Congress rejected them, it was generally held that, with this one exception, the entire territorial code remained legally in force. While certain members of the local bar questioned this opinion, they acquiesced, and the laws were accepted without question in the different territorial courts.[13] But St. Clair with characteristic persistence still held to his original opinion that the laws must be adopted, without any essential changes, from those of the original states. Therefore he questioned the legal status of many of the laws that had been passed, and in this opinion he had strong support in Congress when the Lower House passed a resolution, February 16, 1795, that disapproved at one sweep all the laws that the governor and the judges had passed at the legislative session on August 1, 1792. Although the Senate refused to concur, the debate in the two Houses was speedily re-

12 *Annals of Congress*, Second Congress, First Session, pp. 1395-1396.
13 Burnet, *Notes on the Northwestern Territory*, pp. 3-64.

ported in the territory, to the great detriment of the laws
which were now treated with little respect.[14] In face of this
legal confusion, St. Clair decided to call a legislative session,
in order to undertake a thorough revision of the territorial
code that would have due regard to the limitations under the
Ordinance. After many delays, the session opened May 29,
1795, and sat for nearly three months.[15] In this comparatively brief period, Governor St. Clair and Judges Symmes
and Turner thoroughly overhauled the laws of the territory,
and drew up Maxwell's Code, so called from the name of
the printer, W. Maxwell, who was now established in Cincinnati.

The separate laws in Maxwell's Code were adopted from
those of the original states, with only the most necessary
alterations. In contrast to the single code that was available
to the first legislative session in 1788, there was now a sufficient variety on hand to give a wide range of choice, although, like the basic laws of 1788, the bulk of Maxwell's
Code was adopted bodily from the Pennsylvania Code,
twenty-five laws in all coming from this source. From the
Code of New Jersey, Judge Symmes' native state, only one
law was taken, but six were adopted from the Massachusetts
Code, three from the Virginia Code with which Judge Turner
was especially familiar, one from the New York Code, and
one measure combined parts of laws from both the New
York and the Pennsylvania codes.[16] The new code repealed
outright the bulk of the laws that the governor and the
judges had passed in the four legislative sessions, 1788-
1792, but unfortunately it retained either wholly or in part
a few measures that applied to such peculiarly local matters
as the militia, roads, public buildings, the safe-keeping of
prisoners, the regulations with regard to marriages, and the

---

[14] *Annals of Congress*, Third Congress, Second Session, pp. 830, 1227.

[15] Minutes, in *Quarterly*, Ohio State Archæological and Historical Society,
vol. XXX, pp. 13-53; John Cleves Symmes to Jonathan Dayton, June 17,
1795, *Symmes Correspondence*, Bond, ed., pp. 170-171.

[16] *Laws of the Northwest Territory*, Pease, ed., *Illinois Historical Collections*, vol. XVII, pp. 131-290.

penalties for various crimes. A further source of annoyance
was the failure to repeal the law that established local courts,
although another one of much similar tenor was adopted
from the Pennsylvania Code. The consequence was much
confusion in the territorial administration which lasted until
a representative assembly met in 1799, with the power to in-
itiate its own measures. Indeed it was inevitable that there
should be special needs on the Western frontier for which
the laws of the original Eastern states along the Atlantic
were wholly inadequate.

The most outstanding feature of the new code was the
elaboration of earlier territorial laws. Especially was this
true of legal procedure which was now much improved, and
was much better adapted to local conditions. Thus, a section
in Maxwell's Code that permitted justices of the peace to
hear cases of petty larceny under $1.50, and for the recovery
of debts under $5.00, with an appeal to the county courts
only, was especially fitting for a region where the settlements were often separated from the county courthouses by
long and hazardous journeys. Maxwell's Code retained the
essential features of the judiciary system, as it had already
been established, but it gave to the county court of quarter
sessions much greater importance in comparison with the
court of common pleas. The duties and powers of the general
court, too, which had before been merely outlined, this code
specified in much greater detail, requiring the judges to go
twice each year "on the circuit" to Vincennes and the Illinois
country. Another measure that promised better enforcement
of the laws was the one to regulate fees, which combined
sections from both the New York and the Pennsylvania
codes, and along with more detailed provisions, permitted
somewhat higher charges. Maxwell's Code retained the principles of taxation already laid down, but at the same time it
recognized the prejudices of a backwoods democracy by a
law that required the election rather than the appointment
of local assessors, and limited the annual rate for taxation to

not over 75 cents upon a valuation of $200.00. Still another law that recognized in striking fashion the liberal demands of a frontier people, set a fixed limit upon imprisonment for debt, although, if there were no estate, it required the debtor to make satisfaction by "personal and reasonable servitude."

Maxwell's Code also filled in many gaps in the rather skeletonlike form of the earlier code. From the Virginia Code the governor and judges adopted a statute that required the principles of the common law, as it was established in England in 1607, to be accepted in the territorial courts. This act gave legal sanction to the position which St. Clair had already taken that the common law, as it was recognized in the original states, was in force in the territory. There were other minor changes too numerous to mention. Altogether, under the leadership of the governor, the judges had revised the code in rather thorough fashion, and usually with a due regard to a strict interpretation of the legislative powers that the Ordinance conferred. The situation that made Maxwell's Code necessary, and the compromises that were adopted even then, vividly illustrate the inevitable conflict between a strict adherence to the lawmaking powers conferred by the Ordinance, and the demands of a swiftly growing population. Despite such defects, except for a few measures, notably one with regard to taxation which was adopted in 1798, Maxwell's Code held sway until 1799, when the Northwest Territory entered the second stage of government with a legislative assembly that had power to frame the necessary laws.[17]

Although the governor and the judges established at least the forms of administration in the Old Northwest during the first period of territorial government, 1788–1799, several unfortunate situations somewhat retarded the orderly progress of this American adventure in colonial administration. In a number of instances Congress was chiefly responsible. Many of the members of both houses, like the British officials who

[17] *Laws of the Northwest Territory*, Pease, ed., *Illinois Historical Collections*, vol. XVII, pp. 293-333.

were supposed to supervise the American colonies, were abysmally ignorant as to the needs of the Northwest Territory. The indifference born of this lack of understanding was chiefly responsible for the shortsighted economy which granted such inadequate salaries to the officers responsible for the territorial government. From the combined offices of governor and superintendent of Indian affairs St. Clair received a salary of only $2,000.00. To the secretary the annual compensation was only $750.00, and to each of the three judges Congress allowed $800.00. These stipends were scarcely adequate, in view of the high cost of even the bare comforts of existence in a pioneer community, and to make matters worse, there was no extra allowance for the frequent and heavy traveling expenses that the territorial officials must defray, if they carried out their official duties in proper fashion.[18] The burden was especially heavy upon the secretary, Winthrop Sargent, who so frequently acted in the place of St. Clair, and thus incurred expenses for which there was no provision aside from his meager salary. Sargent made numerous applications for relief, the first one directly to the President, while he was substituting for St. Clair in the organization of government at Vincennes.[19] As the results of this application were not at all satisfactory, Sargent journeyed to Philadelphia to present his memorial in person. As St. Clair saw fit to come East at the same time, the territory was left without a responsible executive. Sargent soon returned to the West upon the personal request of the President, but without any settlement of his application. He went to Philadelphia again in 1793, having spent a weekend at Mount Vernon on the way.[20] Still his efforts were fruitless, but he was persistent, returning to Philadelphia in August, 1796, and a year later he seems to have received

[18] Estimates for the Year 1790, *American State Papers, Finance*, vol. I, p. 34.

[19] Secretary of Northwest Territory to President, August 1, 1790, *Northwest Territorial Papers*, B. R. L. 6116.

[20] Sargent to the President, December 30, 1793, *Northwest Territorial Papers*, B. R. L. 6254.

$1000.00 in compensation for extra expenses.[21] Meantime these frequent trips to Philadelphia greatly weakened a territorial government in which such great responsibility rested upon the executive.

The administration of the Northwest Territory suffered also from too little Federal control over the officials in some instances, and too much in others. Probably this condition could not have been avoided. Important crises often arose in which the man on the spot must act at once without the delay that came from consultation with officials hundreds of miles away across the Appalachians. On the other hand, there were situations, as the adjustment of land titles in the French settlements, which demanded that the governor should have full power to act. Theoretically the Federal system of supervision over the territorial officials was an effective one. Every six months the secretary was supposed to transmit to the Secretary of State, for submission to the President, a journal of the executive proceedings of the Northwest Territory, together with the laws the governor and the judges had passed in the interim. During the ten years of Sargent's term of office, which covered the greater part of the first stage of territorial government, he regularly sent these records, except for one brief period of six months.[22] But like British attention to reports from the American colonies, Federal inspection of the proceedings of the Northwest Territory was often a mere perfunctory performance. Usually the Secretary of State made the stereotyped report that there was nothing in them which required presidential action. The one apparent exception was the advice of Edmund Randolph in 1794, that the President should submit the territorial laws to Congress for approval. As Secretary of State, Randolph summed up the general attitude of many Federal officials toward these proceedings of the Northwest Territory which he dubbed "little more than a

[21] Secretary of State to Sargent, August 13, 1796, June 30 and October 16, 1797, *Northwest Territorial Papers*, B. I. A. Domestic, 6313, 6320, 6323.
[22] *Journal of the Northwest Territory*, 1788–1803, *passim*.

history of bickerings and discontents which do not require the attention of the President." [23] Washington took great personal interest in the Northwest Territory, and during his administration the Department of State preserved the bulk of the records that Sargent sent in, but under Adams the officials in charge evidently did not consider them worth any care.

The lack of an effective system of Federal supervision was especially unfortunate, in view of the frequent absences of the governor from the territory. All too often St. Clair's attention was diverted from active participation in local affairs by Indian campaigns and negotiations, and by necessary trips East, in order to take up personally with the Federal authorities matters that were of vital importance to the territory. Scarcely nine months after his arrival at Marietta, St. Clair was back again in New York for the inauguration of his old friend, George Washington, and for a matter of much greater importance, to see that, in the organization of the new government, the interests of the Northwest Territory were not neglected. Late in the summer of 1790, conferences with the Indians took him out of the territory, although he was back in time for the legislative session at Cincinnati in November. During the following spring and summer he was often absent in Pennsylvania and Kentucky, making arrangements for the ill-fated expedition in the fall of 1791. November 9, 1791, found him back at Cincinnati with his shattered troops, but he remained less than a month, leaving again for Philadelphia, this time to defend himself successfully before an investigating committee of the Lower House. Not until about August 1, 1792, the date appointed for a conference with the judges, does St. Clair appear to have returned to the Northwest Territory, and he was absent again much of the time until April, 1795, when he returned in time to call the legislative session that drew up Maxwell's Code. A year later he was off on another exten-

[23] Edmund Randolph to the President, January 4 and 21, 1794, *Northwest Territorial Papers,* B. I. A. Misc., 6256, 6258.

sive journey, and Sargent acted as governor from early in May, 1796, until he received news at Detroit, the following September, that St. Clair had returned. In 1797 Sargent again assumed St. Clair's duties, certainly from early in July until some time in the following January.[24] The occasional absences of Sargent, too, aggravated a situation that was already a bad one, and when both the governor and the secretary were in Philadelphia in 1794, Sargent himself expected a "degree of censure." He was not mistaken, for Washington, thoroughly aroused, declared that these absences were "a great means of encouraging a spirit of riot and disorder," by relaxing the execution of the law. When Sargent did return it was in response to virtually peremptory orders from Washington, and the President treated St. Clair in similar fashion.[25]

Perhaps the most unfortunate result of St. Clair's many journeys was the responsibility that then devolved upon Sargent as acting governor. This was an especially unfortunate situation in the formative period of the government, for Sargent, who was often petulant and hasty, lacked St. Clair's prestige, although he was not inclined to recognize the obvious limitations upon his own powers. A striking illustration of this bad judgment was given when the grand jury of Hamilton County in February, 1797, turned in an indictment that accused the secretary of usurpation. This charge was based upon the official conduct of Sargent in the issue of proclamations and the administration of the government after St. Clair had arrived at Marietta. Admitting the facts in the case, Sargent declared that behind this indictment was the desire to invalidate a proclamation which forbade the sale of certain public lands. Only "powers of divination," he asserted, could have made him aware, when he himself was at Cincinnati, that St. Clair had arrived at Marietta. In

[24] Journal of the Northwest Territory, 1788–1803, passim.
[25] President to Secretary of State, March 10, 1793, and Secretary of State to St. Clair and Sargent, May 15, 1794, Northwest Territorial Papers, B. I. A. Misc. 6240, B. I. A. Domestic, 6262.

this apology, however, Sargent significantly ignored the possibility that this important measure might have been delayed until after the governor had returned. The indictment was promptly quashed in the general court to which it was referred, but the entire incident tended to shake public confidence in Sargent.[26] Another illustration of his hasty decisions was his trip in 1796 to organize government at Detroit and Mackinaw. Aside from the questionable taste in embarking upon such an enterprise without a consultation with St. Clair, especially after Congress had failed to act, Sargent showed little appreciation of the general administrative needs of the territory. This journey involved him in a predicament much similar to the one that had been the basis of the indictment from Hamilton County. Although Sargent did not learn of St. Clair's arrival at Cincinnati for nearly a month, the actual presence of the governor in the territory might readily have been interpreted to invalidate all of his proceedings at Mackinaw. However, St. Clair merely chided his over-zealous aide in gentle and courteous fashion.[27]

The embarrassing situations that were possible from an unexpected return of St. Clair were partly due to the failure to establish a definite headquarters for the régime of the governor and the judges. Usually these officials held their legislative sessions at Cincinnati, owing to its comparatively central location. St. Clair and Sargent took up executive affairs wherever they happened to be. Thus there was no fixed place of deposit for the public records, and Sargent, as secretary, did not hesitate to take any documents he considered important along with him on his travels. Finally St. Clair found it necessary to call attention to the necessity of keeping the official files at some central point, preferably Cincinnati, where they would be open to the public. The governor was compelled also to remind the secretary that the great seal of the territory should be left at some con-

---

[26] *Journal of Winthrop Sargent*, pp. 136-139.
[27] St. Clair to Sargent, August 28, and to James Ross, September 6, 1796. *St. Clair Papers*, Smith, ed., vol. II, pp. 405 and 409-411.

venient place, for Sargent, it seems, had carried it with him on the long journey to organize government at Detroit and Mackinaw, and when St. Clair arrived unexpectedly he was obliged to postpone the settlement of important matters until the arrival of the wandering secretary with the all-important insignia of territorial authority.[28] This uncertainty as to the whereabouts of the territorial records was especially inconvenient in the first few years of settlement, since Sargent, with very inadequate assistance, was unable to make sufficient copies of the laws for the local officials. For the French-speaking population of the Northwest Territory, it was necessary to translate public documents, and St. Clair testified that he was obliged to do this work himself. Yet repeated requests to have the laws printed in French were without result. Even in the English-speaking settlements the responsible officials were often altogether ignorant of the laws until the governor and the judges in 1791 required the newly appointed clerk of the legislature to send copies of all acts to the different territorial officers, and to display publicly at least one copy in each county or district. For this work and for the copies furnished to any person who applied, the clerk was to receive a fee of 8 cents per 100 words. Finally, in 1792 Congress provided for the printing and distribution of the territorial laws, and under this authority the laws of the first three legislative sessions, in 1788, 1790, and 1791, respectively, were printed in Philadelphia.[29] Soon after William Maxwell set up the first printing press in the Old Northwest Territory at Cincinnati in 1793, he was appointed public printer. Two years later, he offered Maxwell's Code to the public at 86 cents the copy, with an ample number to be distributed by direction of the government to public officials.[30] Meanwhile the apparent impossibility of securing a sufficient number of copies of the Federal laws for

[28] St. Clair to Sargent, December 1, 1796, *St. Clair Papers*, Smith, ed., vol. II, pp. 413-417.

[29] *Laws of the Northwest Territory*, vol. I. Philadelphia, 1792; *Annals of Congress*, Second Congress, First Session, pp. 1395-1396.

[30] *Centinel*, August 1, 1795.

distribution in the territory had been another source of much legal confusion.[31]

The necessity for a general circulation of the laws in force in the Old Northwest was accentuated by the difficult and dangerous journeys between small settlements which were often separated from their neighbors by miles of thick forests, swamps, or prairies. A typical official journey of pioneer days was the one that St. Clair undertook in 1790 to organize the Western settlements. Leaving Cincinnati about January 6, 1790, he was at Louisville two days later, and here he waited for days in order to secure the necessary provisions. For a time the voyage was as comfortable as a February journey in an open boat could be, but trouble started on the Mississippi. For fifteen days the governor's boat was held fast in the ice, and when it did start, the "impetuosity" of the current cast it upon a sunken log. Necessary repairs took up considerable time, and not until March 5, after a colorful if uncomfortable trip of almost two months from Cincinnati, did St. Clair arrive at Kaskaskia.[32] Journeys by land were equally uncomfortable and more dangerous. Taverns were rare and badly kept, and after leaving the outer fringe of settlement the only sources of supplies along the trail were the Indian camps and villages, from which small quantities of corn might be purchased for horse feed, if the inhabitants were peaceably inclined. Other supplies must be carried in saddlebags or on packhorses. The cost of these trips through the wilderness was so great that, without an extra allowance from the government for such purposes, St. Clair hesitated to undertake even necessary journeys. The need for a military escort, until after Wayne's victory in 1794, was a further hindrance to official trips to the more distant settlements. It frequently served also as a pretext to stir up bad feeling between the civil and the military author-

[31] Sargent to Secretary of State, September 30, 1796, and May 20, 1797, *Journal of the Northwest Territory*, 1788–1803.
[32] St. Clair's Report, February 11, 1791, *Executive Records, Northwest Territory, 1788–1795*, p. 276.

ities in the Northwest. Finally when the quartermaster at Fort Washington seized the boat that Sargent used for his journeys, in order to transport troops to Louisville, this disgruntled territorial official complained directly to the Secretary of War.[33] These different obstacles to official trips interfered especially with the personal supervision that was so necessary to establish effective government over the French settlements at Vincennes and in the Illinois country. To the latter, St. Clair accompanied by Sargent made only two trips during the eleven years of his term as governor of the Northwest Territory, one in 1790 to organize the government, and another one in 1795, to attempt to restore at least the semblance of an orderly administration. The secretary made a special trip westward in 1797 to attempt the adjustment of a critical local situation. The only recorded journey by either St. Clair or Sargent to the Michigan region was the one which the latter undertook in the summer of 1796, to organize the government, after the British surrendered Detroit and Mackinaw. As the judges likewise seldom ventured on the long journeys to the more distant settlements, there were few sessions of the general court in the very localities where it was most needed. The wonder is that American government survived at all under such conditions.

The territorial government suffered also from quarrels between the chief officials, and notably between the secretary, Winthrop Sargent, and Judges Symmes and Turner. This bad feeling almost invariably came to the surface when Sargent was acting as governor during the frequent absences of St. Clair. It first became evident at Vincennes, where the hostile attitude of the two judges practically forced Sargent to issue arbitrary decrees. It continued after the secretary and the judges returned to Cincinnati. All three of them were convinced that additional laws were needed, but they were unable to agree upon specific measures. The secretary stoutly refused either to alter or repeal laws that had been adopted

---

[33] Sargent to Secretary of War, April 10 and December 13, 1792, *Executive Records, Northwest Territory*, 1788–1795, pp. 462-464, 497-500.

with the aid of St. Clair, while the judges were unwilling to go to Marietta in order to secure the presence of their colleague, Rufus Putnam, as an arbiter.[34] The governor managed to keep on better terms with the judges, and after his return they passed several needed laws, although even then the two judges turned down fully half the important acts that St. Clair recommended. At the next legislative session, June 22–July 2, 1791, there seems to have been excellent coöperation between the two judges, Symmes and Turner, and the governor. Despite obvious needs there were no further legislative sessions for more than a year, chiefly due to the lack of a quorum, and when it was finally secured, at Cincinnati, August 1, 1792, Sargent as acting governor worked in much more harmonious fashion with Judges Symmes and Putnam. Yet the judges refused to confirm the secretary's proclamations, which required all foreigners to report to the military authorities, and forbade them to hunt in the Northwest Territory. This direct thrust greatly aroused Sargent, and in characteristic fashion he maintained that with so "materially deficient" a code of laws, the governor should have power to make "such temporary regulations as particular exigencies might require." This impossible proposal showed how greatly Sargent misunderstood the growing influences for democracy in the Old Northwest.[35]

But the judges themselves were not wholly blameless. In their extensive powers and in the organization of the general court itself, there were the germs of considerable trouble. As the supreme tribunal of the territory, the general court was a final court of appeals from all the lower courts of the Old Northwest, with no provision for an appeal from its decisions. The judges, endowed with such extensive authority, were not inclined to yield an iota of their possible powers, and at first they even denied the governor's pardoning power,

[34] Sargent to Judges Symmes and Turner, August 13, 1790, *Executive Records, Northwest Territory*, 1788–1795, pp. 234-239.
[35] Sargent to Judges Symmes and Putnam, August 5, 1792, and to Governor St. Clair, January 19, 1793, *Ibid.*, pp. 478-481, 527-542.

passing sentence in one case of murder, and issuing a warrant for execution without awaiting the pleasure of the executive. Another source of criticism was the provision that a single judge was competent to hold court. In view of the position of the general court as the final court of appeals this measure was peculiarly obnoxious to the inhabitants, since Judge Symmes and Judge Putnam were both vitally interested in two of the important land speculations in the territory, and cases were bound to arise in which they had a personal interest. Worst of all was the uncertainty and confusion that arose from the infrequent meetings of the general court. Although there were supposedly four annual sessions, at Cincinnati, at Marietta, at Detroit, and in the western counties respectively, in actual practice the judges held court in most irregular fashion, neglecting the Illinois country almost wholly. So serious did the situation become there that, at a special session of the county court of quarter sessions in 1792, the grand jury of St. Clair County complained of the failure to hold the general court in the county as "a very great grievance to its citizens." This presentment, which found its way to the President, doubtless influenced his admonitions to various members of the territorial government to spend more of their time in the Old Northwest.[36]

The many controversies between St. Clair and Sargent on the one hand, and Judges Turner and Symmes on the other, may be explained partially by the personalities and the private interests of the judges. Judge Turner was especially arrogant and insistent upon his own prerogatives, but he gave little attention to his duties as a judge, centering his interest upon land speculations in the Old Northwest. Three months after he was appointed he was still in Philadelphia, and the President, expressing his "displeasure" at such conduct, commanded him in effect to set out "immediately" for his "place of official residence." Three years later Washington again found it necessary to remind Judge Turner in po-

[36] William St. Clair to Governor St. Clair, March 13, 1792, *Northwest Territorial Papers*, B. I. A. Misc. 6191.

lite fashion that "regulations of importance" in the territory demanded his attention. Even this hint was not sufficient, and the President, thoroughly aroused, personally sent warning that he would "no longer submit to such abuses of public trust without instituting an enquiry." This vigorous language was effective, and Judge Turner returned in haste to the territory.[37] There he was often a storm center, constantly criticizing both the governor and the secretary in quite unbecoming fashion. A typical controversy with St. Clair arose when Judge Turner insisted that a prisoner from his court should be confined in the guardhouse. This order the governor refused to carry out, insisting that all civil prisoners must be cared for by the sheriff, and not committed to a military prison.[38] Judge Turner caused even greater commotion on a journey to the western counties when he arbitrarily fixed the county seat of St. Clair County at Kaskaskia, and demanded the impeachment of Henry Vanderburgh, judge of the probate court in Knox County. After careful investigation, St. Clair refused to sustain him in either case, but it is obvious that these public controversies between the governor and a judge of the territory were unseemly and detrimental to orderly government.[39]

The chief source of personal trouble with Judge Symmes arose from his position as a large landed proprietor who was in close touch with the inhabitants of the territory, and especially with those in and around Cincinnati. The trouble started when St. Clair found that Symmes had sold land at the mouth of the Little Miami, which was not included in the agreement with the Treasury Board. The governor promptly took the matter up, expressing in vigorous Scotch

[37] Tobias Lear to George Turner, September 14, 1789, and W. Jackson to the same, December 23, 1789, President to Secretary of State, April 5, 1793, Secretary of State to George Turner, November 8, 1792, *Northwest Territorial Papers*, B. I. A. Misc. 6091, 6093, 6243, B. R. L. 6219.

[38] Governor St. Clair to Judge Turner, June 19, 1791, *Executive Records, Northwest Territory*, 1788–1795, pp. 263-273.

[39] Governor St. Clair to Judge Turner, December 14, 1794, and April 28, 1795, and to Secretary Sargent, April 28, 1795, *St. Clair Papers*, vol. II, pp. 330, 342, 345-347.

fashion his astonishment that a judge of the territory had actually "published falsehoods," and was selling land of the United States which he did not own. In reply Symmes was exceedingly evasive, and attempted to justify his action by an old agreement which he had never fulfilled. Finally St. Clair issued a proclamation that called attention to the fact that the lands along the Little Miami were still the property of the United States, although he promised to protect the rights of the settlers already there.[40] As territorial governor, St. Clair had merely fulfilled his duty when he called attention to such astounding actions on the part of Judge Symmes. At the same time he had been needlessly blunt, and had failed to appreciate the peculiarities of a farsighted pioneer who was somewhat careless in details, but was not intentionally dishonest. But the incident aroused the hostility of the judge against the governor, with most unfortunate after-effects upon the territorial administration. Sargent, too, managed to incur Judge Symmes' displeasure. A typical clash between these two was the case of Thomas McCullough, a private in the Hamilton County militia, who had violated the law against indiscriminate shooting in villages while he himself was on guard. Sargent held that McCullough should be tried by a court-martial, but Judge Symmes immediately issued a sealed writ of habeas corpus upon rather untrustworthy evidence. Not to be outdone, Sargent removed the prisoner to his own house, mounted guard, and proceeded with the court-martial. Symmes, who had already been outspoken in his criticisms of Sargent's attempt to put an end to the lawlessness in Cincinnati during the Christmas holidays, carried his hostile attitude so far that, when the secretary submitted a list of the persons involved, he secretly notified them.[41]

Judge Symmes' open criticism of the governor and the

[40] Correspondence between St. Clair and Symmes, May to July, 1791, *Executive Records, Northwest Territory*, 1788–1795, pp. 385-417; *Symmes Correspondence*, Bond, ed., pp. 15-16, 25 ff, and 138 ff.

[41] Sargent to John Cleves Symmes, January 13, 1793, *Executive Records, Northwest Territory*, 1788–1795, pp. 509-519.

secretary was especially unfortunate in view of the occasional clashes between these last two officials. For example, they apparently disagreed over the enforcement of the Federal excise tax. When Sargent, as acting governor, discovered that certain residents of Cincinnati had aided David Bradford, a leader in the Whiskey Rebellion in western Pennsylvania, to escape down the Ohio, he quickly applied for a detachment of twelve soldiers from Fort Washington under a "cool, determined officer." With their aid he managed to capture two of these violators of the President's proclamation, and they were bound over for trial at the next session of the general court.[42] St. Clair's attitude toward the excise law was scarcely consistent with the secretary's vigorous measures. When an inspector's office was opened in Cincinnati the governor maintained that this tax applied only to the states, inasmuch as the inhabitants of the territory had not been represented in the Congress that put it in force. Furthermore, he pointed out, the law itself mentioned the United States, but not the Northwest Territory. In support of his stand, St. Clair cited opinions which Edmund Randolph, Thomas Jefferson, and Judge Turner had expressed to him in private conversation. But the attorney-general, William Bradford, decided positively that under the Ordinance all the laws of the United States were in force in the Northwest Territory.[43] St. Clair's rather strange attitude in this instance did not, of course, aid the Federal officers in the effort to enforce an excise tax, in face of the natural opposition of a frontier community.

Indeed, with the increasing population of the Northwest Territory, the régime of the governor and the judges was rapidly becoming out-worn, and the political controversies that arose tended to be magnified in the popular mind. An illustration was the outcry against the seemingly arbitrary action of the governor in fixing the county seat of Adams

[42] Executive Records, Northwest Territory, 1788–1795, pp. 598-601.
[43] Correspondence between St. Clair and Oliver Wolcott, 1795, St. Clair Papers, Smith, ed., vol. II, pp. 377-385.

County. As a matter of fact Sargent had organized the county in the absence of St. Clair, and had commissioned the judges of the new county court to fix the site of the courthouse. These officials changed the first location, under the influence of Nathaniel Massie, an influential speculator in land, and when St. Clair protested there was much popular clamor in which Massie doubtless had a part.[44] But there were other causes for the gradually increasing volume of complaints against the arbitrary government. In 1793 and in 1794, for example, *Manlius* and *Plebius* argued in the *Centinel* for and against the act that required all merchants and tavern keepers to take out licenses. *Philadelphensis*, entering the lists, commented upon the fact that the government of the territory was not founded upon the will of the people.[45] Equally significant was a meeting that was called at Cincinnati, February 11, 1795, by a "Citizen and Friend to the Rights of Man," to formulate a petition to the governor and judges for the redress of popular grievances.[46] But far more important was the meeting that was held at Columbia, at the mouth of the Little Miami. Early in 1796, a committee which this meeting had appointed called attention to the chief grievances of the citizens, including among them the personal interest of the judges in many of the laws they made, the political status of the inhabitants, who were being governed by laws not of their own making, and the frequent and prolonged absences of the governor and the judges. The report also objected to the condescending attitude assumed by St. Clair who, it declared, seemed to regard his own powers over officers as similar to those of the King of England. This last allusion strikingly illustrated the prejudice that the Federalist St. Clair had aroused among the republican citizens of the frontier. Yet the report did not recommend positive action, even though the governor and the

[44] Governor St. Clair to Nathaniel Massie and other Justices of Adams County, June 29, 1798, *St. Clair Papers*, Smith, ed., vol. II, pp. 425-526 (note).
[45] *Centinel*, November 30, 1796, and later.
[46] *Ibid.*, February 7, 1795.

judges should adopt laws that were "ever so ancient and obsolete," in view of "the shortness of time that our submission can be constitutionally called for." [47]

The mounting protests against the rule of the governor and the judges were inevitable. St. Clair, aided by the different judges and by the secretary, Winthrop Sargent, had achieved really remarkable results within a single decade. In spite of many obstacles, such as widespread criticism, a lack of official coöperation, and unsatisfactory means of communication, the responsible officials with the governor at their head had laid the basis of an American form of government in the Northwest Territory. This task they had accomplished in such fashion that the chief work in the future would be to extend and strengthen the foundations that had been so wisely fashioned from such of the time-honored institutions of the American people as seemed best adapted to frontier needs. This had been done, too, in spite of an Ordinance that had restricted the governor and the judges to the choice of laws from the codes of the original states that were frequently ill-adapted to the Western settlements. Yet the Federalistic point of view of Governor St. Clair and his colleagues could not long prevail after the influx of immigrants who were out-and-out Republicans. Nor was an arbitrary government suitable to the increasingly complex local conditions. The transition to the second stage of government under the Ordinance with a representative assembly became a logical and, very soon, a necessary step.

[47] *Centinel,* February 20, 1796.

Chapter IV

FROM TERRITORY TO STATE

UPON the surface there was a noticeable absence of friction in the transition in the Northwest Territory from an arbitrary government by a governor and three judges to the second stage under the Ordinance with a territorial assembly. The inhabitants, for their part, had clearly understood that with an increasing population a representative form of government would not be long delayed, while St. Clair, as the responsible executive, accepted the change without question. Once he had ascertained through a census in the fall of 1798 that the Northwest Territory contained the 5,000 white male inhabitants of voting age which the Ordinance required, he promptly ordered the election of representatives, giving a further proof of good faith in a decision that, under the "spirit and intention" of the Ordinance, the requirement that a voter must possess a freehold of fifty acres included all owners of houses and town lots of the average value of a fifty-acre tract.[1] The representatives who were elected under these conditions in December, 1798, held their first meeting in Cincinnati, February 14, 1799, and promptly adjourned after they had chosen ten persons from whom the President should appoint the five members of the legislative council. The official opening of the territorial assembly, September 24, 1799, marked the inauguration of a new era. Although the judges were now restricted to judicial functions, the governor retained powers which gave him a position in the territory much similar to that of the British execu-

[1] Proclamation, October 29, 1798. *Journal of the Northwest Territory,* 1788–1803.

tive of a royal colony. St. Clair was commander-in-chief of the territorial militia, he had the powers of appointment to the greater number of local offices and of pardon, and, most important of all, he had an unrestricted right of veto over all legislation. Like the royal governors, he soon discovered that a representative assembly constantly interfered with his authority, even though his salary did not depend upon the good will of these local legislators. Issues arose, too, that became sources of controversies, and the popular side had a mouthpiece in Congress in the person of the territorial delegate.

To add to St. Clair's troubles, his relations with the territorial secretary soon became strained. Winthrop Sargent, the somewhat overzealous New Englander with whom the governor had been rather congenial, resigned in 1798, and was succeeded by William Henry Harrison, a dashing young Virginia officer who was inclined to side with the popular party in opposition to St. Clair. In a little over a year Harrison resigned, and the new secretary, Charles William Byrd, also a native of Virginia, was closely allied by family ties and personal inclination with the Republican clique which was rapidly coming to the front in the Virginia Military District in open opposition to Governor St. Clair. Byrd soon plunged into the very thick of these intrigues, and he probably had an influential part in the final downfall of St. Clair. The gradually widening breach between the governor and the secretary naturally weakened the former's executive authority in the territory, as the scanty records from 1798 on testify. Finally, St. Clair positively refused to hold any communication whatsoever with Byrd, and the executive authority in the Northwest Territory practically broke down during the last few months of his tenure of office.[2]

At the outset, the prospect for a representative form of government was quite promising. Although the restricted franchise was a source of much injustice, especially in the Illinois

[2] *Journal of the Northwest Territory,* 1788–1803, June 28, 1798, to July 10, 1802.

district, at Vincennes, and at Detroit, where there were so many questionable land titles, the general results of the first choice of popular representatives in the Northwest Territory were excellent. Partisan spirit was noticeably absent from the elections, and the voters evidently appreciated the importance of this first legislative assembly, electing to it some of the ablest men in the territory.[3] As most of these members of the new territorial lower house had lived in the Western country for some time, they understood local needs, and were well equipped for the main task of replacing "arbitrary and unequal laws" with "those of our own choosing."[4] Notable among them was a group of native Virginians that included among its leaders Thomas Worthington, afterward governor of Ohio, Nathaniel Massie, who, in addition to his fame as a surveyor, was a business man of much ability, and William McMillan, one of the most influential pioneers in Cincinnati. In the New England born contingent were Return J. Meigs, Jr., governor of Ohio during the War of 1812, and Solomon Sibley, who played an important rôle in early Michigan. From Maryland came Shadrach Bond, the first governor of Illinois, and the speaker for this first session was Edward Tiffin, a native of England, a personal friend of Washington, and the first governor of Ohio. In the legislative council, the most outstanding member was Jacob Burnet from New Jersey, one of the ablest members of the territorial bar. General James Findlay, a native of Pennsylvania and a prominent business man in Cincinnati, was also a member of this upper house, and the president, Henry Vanderburgh, born in New York, was a Revolutionary veteran who later became one of the judges of Indiana Territory. Thus, the personnel of the two houses was made up of men of high caliber, who, like the population of the Northwest Territory, represented the ideals and customs of New England, of the Middle States, and of Virginia rather than those of any one region. Naturally the query rose, would these

[3] Burnet, *Notes on the Northwestern Territory*, chs. XIV and XV.
[4] *Western Spy*, October 8, 1799.

men of affairs work in harmony with a governor sixty-five years old, who had long been accustomed to rule in arbitrary fashion. In the background, too, were the demands of a continually increasing population for a less restricted franchise and a more representative executive. Evidently only the most consummate tact would be equal to the occasion, and that, unfortunately, was a quality in which St. Clair was sadly deficient.

The opening sessions of the territorial assembly augured well for future harmony. In his address to the two houses the governor congratulated them upon the changes in the government, and gave in clear-cut fashion his views as to the chief legislative needs of the territory. He laid special stress upon the doubtful status of many of the laws from the earlier régime, notably those relating to crimes and punishments, to the militia, and to taxation. Then, turning to an entirely different field, he noted the need for definite action to take advantage of the Federal grants for the support of schools and religion, and to secure the college township that had been promised in the Miami Purchase. Other important subjects for legislation, in his opinion, included a revision of the statute establishing the common law, a provision for jails, and certain limitations upon the powers of constables. The members of the two houses gave respectful attention to the governor's recommendations, displaying a similar spirit of courtesy in replies in which they stressed "the promotion of morality, the suppression of vice, and the encouragement of literature," as among the chief aims of government.[5] This initial harmony was soon disturbed when, by a vote of eleven to ten, a joint session elected William Henry Harrison as territorial delegate to Congress, in preference to Arthur St. Clair, Jr., who would have virtually been his father's mouthpiece. Instead, the local party in opposition to St. Clair which gradually gathered around Thomas Worthington was now assured of a representative in Congress. The businesslike methods of this assembly are illustrated by one of the

[5] St. Clair Papers, Smith, ed., vol. II, pp. 446-462.

fifty-nine rules of the lower house, which required every member present to vote, unless he was excused "for special reasons." Another excellent rule authorized the sergeant-at-arms to search for members who did not answer the roll call and to take them into custody if they came upon the floor of the house.[6]

The able personnel of this first territorial assembly showed itself in marked fashion in its deliberations. Although the members now had authority to enact laws, subject only to the governor's veto, they were quite conservative, and for the most part they retained the code which the governor and the judges had already adopted, and merely made needed modifications, or else added laws to meet situations that were not already provided for. Foremost in the ranks of these early Western lawmakers was Jacob Burnet, himself an exceedingly able lawyer, who personally drew up at least fifteen bills, most of them designed to simplify or else to confirm different phases of legal procedure.[7] The code that the territorial assembly finally drew up for the Northwest Territory under these conditions was far superior to the ill-considered jumble of laws that might have been expected on the frontier.[8] The most pressing need was to determine the status of the laws that the governor and the judges had already passed. Certain of these laws, even though they had not strictly conformed to the provisions of the Ordinance, the assembly declared still in force, including in this category such important measures as the militia act, the acts that prescribed crimes and their punishments, regulated marriages, and established townships, and others of minor importance. A number of laws they repealed outright, and still others only in part. To prevent future confusion the assembly declared finally that the laws adopted from those

[6] *Journal of the House of Representatives, Northwest Territory,* First General Assembly, First Session, p. 13; *Journal of the Legislative Council, idem.,* p. 19.

[7] Burnet, *Notes on the Northwestern Territory,* pp. 310-311.

[8] *Laws of the Northwest Territory,* Pease, ed., *Illinois Historical Collections,* vol. XVII, pp. 321-516.

of the original states were to be in force, unless there was a provision to the contrary. An important series of acts marked the transition to the second stage of territorial government. The one regulating elections provided for a census every two years of all males of voting age, as a basis upon which the governor should apportion representation among the several counties. According to this law each voter was to indicate audibly his choice for the total number of representatives to which his county was entitled, but a resort to "bribery, threats, or treating with meat or drink" debarred a candidate from either house of the territorial assembly.

The legislative assembly also provided for a territorial revenue, with a tax upon land, unimproved as well as improved, as the main dependence. The financial problem of this frontier territory was, of course, a serious one, and the auditor was given power, in cases of immediate need, to issue certificates in denominations of $1.00, $5.00, and $20.00, which could be used as a circulating medium, and were redeemable in gold or silver, with six per cent interest, upon the "faith of this territory." The total appropriations for territorial purposes by this session of the assembly were comparatively small, only $26,981.24. Among the allowances to different officials, $500.00 was to be paid the governor for "services extraordinary" during the legislative session, and $200.00 extra for his house rent. The assembly made an allowance of not more than $2,000.00 for its own members, and appropriated the same amount for printing its journals and laws. For local taxation, the law now stipulated that all houses, town lots, horses, cattle, and bond servants should be listed as taxable, and one rather unique clause required able-bodied single men, who did not own taxable property valued at $200.00 or over, to pay an annual tax of not less than 50 cents or more than $2.00. License fees on retail establishments and ferries completed the list of local taxes. This law left the appointment of three county tax commissioners and two appraisers in each township to the court of quarter sessions, which was also empowered to build or repair "necessary" . . . "county jails, courthouses, pillories, stocks, and whipping posts." A county treasurer and a force of collectors completed a well-devised system of local taxation.

Among the other laws passed by this first session of the territorial assembly was an elaborate militia act that replaced one of the earlier régime. There was a law, too, which provided that suits for small debts should be tried before the local justice of the peace, and thus put an end to the practice of sending summonses to distant sections of a county in order to collect larger fees. But these early Western legislators displayed a characteristic frontier sympathy for the debtor in an act that limited the rate of interest to six per cent, and provided drastic penalties for the usurer. The preamble of another act denounced the confinement of destitute debtors as of "no advantage," since, when these unfortunates were free, they might support themselves and their families, and "discharge their honest debts." In accordance with this very practical reasoning a prisoner for debt might be discharged if he declared upon oath that he had no estate. In any case the complaining creditor must pay 12½ cents per day for a destitute debtor's subsistence, and the prisoner was allowed the freedom of jail bounds that extended not over 200 yards from the building.

Following English and colonial precedents, the territorial assembly adopted a law that granted exemption from arrest in civil cases to all members and officers of the territorial assembly during its sessions, to judges during sittings of their courts, and to all persons on militia duty. This same law forbade arrests, in civil cases on Sunday, in places of divine worship, in the chambers of either house while the assembly was in session, or on the Fourth of July. The strong Puritan influence was evident in a number of sumptuary acts. One of them forbade all "worldly employments," hunting, fighting, etc., on the Sabbath and subjected offenders to fines of from 50 cents to $2.00, and in case of a man, two days' work, if they were not paid. This act set up similar penalties for those who "profanely curse, damn, or swear by the name of God, Christ Jesus, or the Holy Ghost." There were penalties, too, for persons found intoxicated in public places, while gambling of all types was strictly forbidden, as well as "to fight or box at fisticuffs," and dueling. The assembly also forbade the sale of intoxicants to the Christian Indians in Ohio, but with an unconscious touch of humor, this act directed that liquor which was sold contrary to its provisions should be forfeited to the very missionaries who had petitioned for such regulations. There were numerous other acts that were framed to meet the peculiar needs of the Northwest Territory, providing for roads, for the building of fences, and for other local needs. Altogether, the laws which this first legislative assembly of the Northwest Territory passed formed a code that was a notably practical and well-balanced one. The presence of able leaders in the assembly, together with the inherent American capacity for self-government, had held down the radicalism that would naturally have been expected, although it had not interfered with a sanely liberal point of view which carried out many ideals of the Revolutionary period. This happy outcome was a matter of much importance, since the body of laws which the territorial legislature of the Northwest Territory adopted in 1799 became later the basis of the state codes of Ohio, Indiana, and Illinois.

Another striking feature of this territorial assembly was the positive stand which its members took upon the slavery issue. Early in the session several officers of the Revolutionary army petitioned the local house of representatives for permission to bring their slaves into the Virginia Military District. A committee of the house promptly drew up an adverse report, upon the ground that this proposal was altogether "incompatible" with the Ordinance, even though it promised an immediate increase in the population. The lower house unanimously accepted this report, but about two months later another pro-slavery petition received stronger support, and a committee drew up a bill that would have

admitted slavery into the territory under the guise of indenture. Consideration of the proposed measure was repeatedly
postponed, until finally, after "some time spent thereon," the
house rejected it by a vote of 16 to 1.[9] This defeat of the
attempt to introduce slavery into the Northwest Territory
met the overwhelming approval of the inhabitants, to judge
by the available evidence. Only a few months before, there
had been an extended controversy in *Freeman's Journal* between *Marcus,* who favored the introduction of slaves, and
Querist, who uncompromisingly opposed the halfway type of
slavery that had been suggested. *Querist* gained the popular
support when he based his argument upon the favorite theory of the Western pioneers that the equality of all men was
a principle of "genuine republicanism." [10] Another significant
indication of the intense opposition to slavery in the Old
Northwest was the organization at Columbia in 1800 of the
Humane Society with its chief aims, the abolition of slavery,
and the overthrow of every attempt to introduce it into the
territory. The secretary of this organization exhorted "every
friend to liberty, human nature, and happiness" to rally to
its aid.[11] Nor was this admonition wholly unnecessary, for
there were occasional instances of actual slavery under the
guise of apprenticeship. But legally the Northwest Territory
continued to be free soil, except for the few slaves from the
British and French régimes, and this precedent was destined
to be of utmost importance when attempts were made later
to annul the anti-slavery clause of the Ordinance.

The first territorial assembly took up a number of other
miscellaneous matters of public interest. Especially significant were its instructions to the territorial delegate, William
Henry Harrison, to ask Congress to vest in trustees the title
to the five sections, still ungranted, of the college township
which John Cleves Symmes had promised. To complete the

[9] *Journal of the House of Representatives, Northwest Territory,* First General Assembly, First Session, pp. 6, 19, 108, 117, 121, 133, 139-140.
[10] *Freeman's Journal,* March 5, 1799.
[11] *Western Spy,* March 12, 1800.

township he was to request, further, that the remaining thirty-one sections west of the Miami should be set aside. Also, Harrison was instructed to ask Congress for legislation that would make lots 16 and 29 in the Miami Purchase actually available for the support of education and religion.[12] In a joint resolution of much similar import the two houses appointed trustees to take charge of the two townships in the Ohio Purchase that had been reserved for the use of a university.[13] This same solicitude for the reserves for public purposes was also shown in a joint address to the "citizens of the territory," which attempted to sugar-coat the unpopular land tax by roseate prophecies of future prosperity. The special grants of public lands for educational and religious purposes, this address termed "advantages superior" . . . "perhaps to those which any country can boast of." In somewhat the same strain, a resolution of the lower house, which bore the impress of the homely virtues of thrifty New England, called upon each individual to use the "utmost exertion" to build up the territory. Strict attention to business, frugality, the encouragement of home manufactures, and the retrenchment of unnecessary expenses, this resolution upheld as exceedingly desirable civic virtues. Finally, the two houses joined in an address to President Adams, the legislative council unanimously, the house of representatives by a vote of 11 to 5.[14]

The apparent harmony between the governor and the members of the assembly was rudely disturbed on the last day of the session when St. Clair announced that he had vetoed a number of bills.[15] So far as the acts to regulate marriage, taverns, and public houses, and to create the office of surveyor in each county were concerned, he gave clear and

[12] *Journal of the House of Representatives, Northwest Territory,* First General Assembly, First Session, pp. 180-181, 200-201.

[13] *Laws of the Northwest Territory,* Pease, ed., *Illinois Historical Collections,* vol. XVII, p. 519.

[14] *Journal of the House of Representatives, Northwest Territory,* First General Assembly, First Session, pp. 125-126, 183.

[15] *St. Clair Papers,* Smith, ed., vol. II, pp. 474-480.

presumably well-founded explanations for his action. But he was less successful in the attempt to justify the veto of a number of bills to create new counties, upon the ground of insufficient population. From his stand in previous issues of this same type, it was apparent that St. Clair's real motive in this instance was to uphold his contention that the governor alone could erect new counties. But the loudest popular outcry was aroused by his veto of an act to take a census which, it was understood, was to be an initial measure in a movement to secure statehood for the more populous eastern section. This veto was considered especially arbitrary, inasmuch as the need for a division of the Northwest Territory was generally conceded. The jurisdiction of the territorial government was too widely extended and the facilities for communication too primitive to make effective administration possible. Especially in the Illinois settlements and at Vincennes there was need for a strong executive to settle the many petty local quarrels, and to counteract the intrigues of the Canadian fur traders and their agents who were constantly stirring up the Indians. The most logical division was the line drawn northward from the mouth of the Miami, in accordance with the Ordinance, which would set off the eastern section with its rapidly increasing population.[16] Therefore when St. Clair used his veto power to check the proposed census, he ranged himself in direct opposition to the many inhabitants of the eastern section of the territory, who looked to statehood as the one means of securing local autonomy.

After the assembly adjourned, a dramatic battle began over the inevitable division of the Northwest Territory, with the issue of statehood rapidly forcing itself to the forefront. On the one side was St. Clair, a Federalist, arbitrary and convinced that the inhabitants of the territory were not yet prepared to undertake the obligations of statehood; fearing,

[16] Petition from the Illinois Country, February 7, 1800, *Northwest Territorial Papers*, House Files; *Annals of Congress*, Sixth Congress, First Session, pp. 1320-1321.

moreover, that a new Western state would increase Republican influence in national affairs. On the other side was the able Virginia clique, led by Thomas W. Worthington, and including incidentally the secretary, Charles Willing Byrd. This faction strongly supported speedy statehood for the eastern division of the territory, as a guarantee of a really democratic form of government, and also, it must be confessed, as a measure that would doubtless increase Republican power and their own political influence. Involved in the controversy, too, were the schemes of land speculators, for if Worthington and his followers prevailed, the capital of the new eastern division must be located at some central site, and Chillicothe in the Republican stronghold of the Virginia Military District would be the logical spot. The governor and the small party that gathered around him evidently favored Cincinnati as the capital, and proposed to prevent a division that would make necessary some other location. St. Clair made the first aggressive move when he proposed to William Henry Harrison, as territorial delegate to Congress, two dividing lines, one northward from the mouth of the Scioto, the other from opposite the mouth of the Kentucky. This plan, creating three rather than two divisions, would have divided the eastern section of the territory in such fashion that statehood would have been indefinitely postponed, and Cincinnati would have become the capital of the middle region. St. Clair evidently hoped also that, when statehood was granted, the dividing line from the mouth of the Scioto would make certain a Federalist majority, with the aid of the New England settlers in the Ohio Purchase and the Western Reserve, even though the Virginians and Kentuckians in the Virginia Military District assured Republican control of the middle region between the Scioto and the mouth of the Kentucky.[17] But St. Clair played a losing game, even while the Federalists controlled the national government. His antagonists were excellent politicians, and Worthington, their

[17] St. Clair to James Ross, December, 1799, and to William H. Harrison, February 19, 1800, *St. Clair Papers*, Smith, ed., vol. II, pp. 480-483, 489-490.

leader, hurried to Washington, in order to see that the Northwest Territory was divided by the line north from the mouth of the Miami. Harrison, too, favored this division as the one possible means of securing stable government, and of counteracting St. Clair's intrigues against statehood.[18]

Harrison displayed great tact in guiding past a Federalist majority in Congress a bill that divided the Northwest Territory according to Republican ideas.[19] As an entering wedge he proposed a revision of the judicial system in the Northwest Territory. Then, as chairman of the committee to whom this measure was referred, he manipulated matters so skillfully that their report favored a division of the territory, and the House referred the entire question of territorial needs to a committee of which Harrison again was a member. This latter committee reported in favor of the division that was favored by Worthington and the Republican element in Ohio. In the debate that followed, Harrison pointed out the unwieldiness of the present government and the "general wish" of the people for the proposed division. But St. Clair's adherents were not altogether idle, and as a result the Senate insisted upon a number of amendments. In the House there was an attempt to postpone consideration, upon the plea that many inhabitants of the territory knew nothing about this important measure. In reply, Harrison asserted that "ninetenths" of the people favored the bill, and that the chief objections had come from "interested" persons residing near Cincinnati. Throughout the struggle he had the strong support of Robert Goodloe Harper, one of the most influential Federalists in the House. The act, as it was finally approved, represented the definite triumph of Worthington and the advocates of statehood over St. Clair with his plans for an indefinite delay of this same issue. While a Senate amend-

---

[18] Thomas Worthington to Nathaniel Massie, December 27, 1799, and William H. Harrison to Nathaniel Massie, January 17, 1800, in Massie, *Life of Nathaniel Massie*, pp. 154-156; Thomas Worthington to the President, January 30, 1802, *St. Clair Papers*, Smith, ed., vol. II, p. 570.

[19] Goebel, *William Henry Harrison*, pp. 49-51; *Annals of Congress*, Sixth Congress, First Session, pp. 583, 649, 698-699.

ment provided that the Northwest Territory should be divided by a line running north from opposite the mouth of the Kentucky, this was only a Pyrrhic victory for the governor and his supporters. When the eastern division should become a state, its western boundary was to be the line north from the mouth of the Miami for which Harrison and Worthington had fought. Still another victory for the Virginia faction was a clause that made Chillicothe the capital of the Northwest Territory, after Indiana had been set off, unless the legislature directed otherwise. This entire act represented a very definite step in the direction of statehood, and Harrison pointed to it as one of his most notable triumphs in Congress, although he warily disclaimed responsibility for the clause that fixed the site of the capital.[20]

For a time the political stream seemed to run smoothly, although there were evidences of a growing determination to secure statehood for the Northwest Territory, from which Indiana Territory was set off July 4, 1800. The election, October 14, of representatives to the new assembly aroused a popular interest that showed how generally the people of the territory appreciated the issues that were involved in the struggle with St. Clair. A wag even published a list of the large number of nominations in Hamilton County, in order, as he facetiously expressed it, that the voters might decide at "one view." *Liberty* urged the citizens of Ross County to select men of temperance and judgment, and *A Farmer* pointed out to the voters of Hamilton County the small powers of the territorial legislature as compared to the "supreme powers" of the governor. They should elect therefore "good republicans," and should pass by the lawyers. *A Countryman*, too, considered that "the fewer" lawyers in the assembly "the better."[21] Occasionally some popular writer came to the defense of the much maligned lawyers, and *A*

[20] *Annals of Congress*, Sixth Congress, First Session, Appendix, pp. 1498-1500; *Western Spy*, June 11, 1800.

[21] *Ibid.*, August 27 and September 10 and 17, 1800; *Freeman's Journal*, September 26, 1800.

Candid Elector severely criticized the fashion in which the territory had been divided with little or no regard for the interests of Hamilton County.[22] But such articles were rare, in comparison with the ones that showed the rapid turn of public sentiment against St. Clair and his lawyer supporters.

When the territorial assembly first came together for its second session, November 3, 1800, there was evidently a more harmonious attitude now that Indiana had been set off, and the settlements in the Northwest Territory were more closely knit together. Unfortunately the governor was unable to appreciate public sentiment, and refused to recede from impossible positions. He addressed the two houses in a prosy speech that began with a sanctimonious recital of the Divine blessings that had been showered upon the territory, and then mentioned such innocuous subjects for legislation as equal justice to the Indians, the substitution of a ballot for viva-voce voting, changes in the militia law, and the desirability of a settlement of the controversy with Judge Symmes over a college township. So far, St. Clair was on safe ground. He ventured into controversial realms when he called attention to the failure of the local authorities in Adams County to provide for the collection of taxes, but passed by in silence his own responsibility for a situation that had arisen from his veto of the act to change the county seat. A recommendation for the resurvey of county boundaries was still more likely to stir up trouble, and to make matters worse the governor closed an address that had been quite dignified up to this point with a very unbecoming burst of wrath that castigated those persons who had circulated "the vilest calumnies and the grossest falsehoods" about himself. In reply each house sent a polite message that deprecated the criticism which the governor had mentioned, and commended his administration. But the message from the lower house was much more guarded than the one from the legislative council, and the members of the former body only agreed to insert the clause

[22] *Western Spy*, September 24, 1800.

of commendation by a significant vote of 12 to 6.[23] This hesitation was all the more noteworthy as St. Clair's commission as governor would expire in about a month, and his opponents had already launched a movement to prevent a reappointment.

The first important business that the assembly transacted during the second session was the election of William McMillan of Hamilton County and Paul Fearing of Washington County as territorial delegates to Congress, the former to complete Harrison's term to March 4, 1801, and the latter to serve the two following years. In Fearing, at least, the governor did not encounter an active opponent. Furthermore, the two houses presented an olive branch in the form of a respectful address that greatly regretted the misunderstandings that had arisen. While they insisted upon their own right to take part in the creation of counties, they suggested that the governor's claim to sole power should be referred to the territorial general court for a final decision. Moreover, the address asked the governor to return bills he did not approve within ten days, with the reasons for his disapproval, presumably so that they might be revised to meet his objections. St. Clair answered this tactful and moderate address in exceedingly opinionated fashion. Refusing to submit to the decision of a court his power to erect counties, he promised nevertheless to sign bills for that purpose when, in his opinion, the new local divisions were needed. Also, he upheld his unqualified right of veto, although he offered to join the assembly in a request to Congress to secure a modification of the provisions of the Ordinance with respect to this power.[24] The members of the assembly took St. Clair at his word, and in their instructions to William McMillan, the territorial delegate to Congress, they proposed a modified veto, much similar to the one exercised by the President. Also, they again

[23] *St. Clair Papers*, Smith, ed., vol. II, pp. 501-515; *Journal of House of Representatives, Northwest Territory*, First General Assembly, Second Session, pp. 37, 39.

[24] *St. Clair Papers*, Smith, ed., vol. II, pp. 515-523.

asked for a settlement of the controversy over the college township which Symmes had promised, and for action to make available the reserved sections sixteen and twenty-nine in his grant. St. Clair would probably not have become alarmed had the assembly confined its instructions to these matters, but it added a highly significant section, that Mc-Millan should ask for practically a manhood suffrage in the Northwest Territory.[25] This proposal was altogether contrary to St. Clair's Federalistic ideas, and in view of the Republican national victory about this same time, it must have greatly alarmed him as to the future.

In the last few days of the session the bad feeling between St. Clair and the Republican leaders came to the surface in emphatic fashion. Since his own commission as governor expired December 9, St. Clair became alarmed as to possible legislation if the secretary, Charles Willing Byrd, should become acting governor. Determined to take no chances, he gave notice, December 2, that he would prorogue the assembly six days later, and thereby he aroused his Republican opponents who had been hoping to control the territorial administration for a time at least. They now came out into the open in their opposition to St. Clair, and secured the passage in the lower house, by a vote of 9 to 8, of a resolution that ordered an address to the people upon the issue of statehood. The drawing up of this document, needless to say, was entrusted to a thoroughgoing Republican committee, and it was rushed through on the last day of the session. It drew particular attention to the population of the Northwest Territory according to the census of 1800, and it called upon the inhabitants to instruct their representatives in the assembly with regard to statehood. With a semblance of fairness the address noted the probable additional expense of a state government, and then dwelt at length upon its "superior advantages." No attempt was made to secure the approval of the legislative council, and the lower house ordered 500

[25] *Journal, House of Representatives, Northwest Territory,* First General Assembly, Second Session, pp. 53-58.

copies of the address to be printed and distributed throughout the territory. Thus Worthington and his party ensured wide publicity and seemingly official sanction for the movement in favor of the statehood that meant the complete overthrow of St. Clair. Betraying a notable lack of a sense of humor, the governor prorogued the assembly in a speech that abounded in meaningless platitudes upon the "harmony" that had prevailed, and the "zeal" with which the members had assembled.[26] Meanwhile his enemies had busily employed themselves in making representations against him to the President, which Adams in turn transmitted to the Senate with his own recommendation for a reappointment. Even though the Senate finally confirmed this nomination after about six weeks' delay,[27] the prospect of a Republican administration within a few weeks did not promise any considerable degree of peace to the harassed St. Clair.

In spite of the bad feeling between the governor and many of its members, the territorial assembly had managed to pass several acts of considerable importance during this session of scarcely five weeks.[28] One especially interesting measure, in an attempt to secure impartial justice for the red man, authorized the governor to remand all cases in which white men murdered Indians to the general court for trial. Of much practical importance in this new democracy was an act that substituted the ballot for viva-voce voting and required the presence of judges of election at each polling place. In still other measures the assembly authorized a poll tax of not over 50 cents upon each male of voting age, regulated certain details of legal procedure, and met the miscellaneous needs of a growing population by such acts as those to incorporate Marietta and to require all town plots to be recorded. These legislative accomplishments, which St. Clair had himself proposed in several instances, showed that coöperation was pos-

[26] *Journal, House of Representatives, Northwest Territory,* First General Assembly, Second Session, pp. 90, 114, 124-125, 130-131.

[27] *St. Clair Papers,* Smith, ed., vol. II, pp. 526, 529-532.

[28] *Laws of the Northwest Territory,* First General Assembly, Second Session.

sible between the governor and the assembly. Nor were the members always harmonious among themselves. For example, when an act was proposed to fix permanently the location of the territorial capital, there were so many petty quarrels between the advocates of different sites that the measure was quickly defeated in the lower house.[29]

During the eleven months' interim before the second territorial assembly met, there were many indications of the growing popular support for the Republican party, and inferentially for the local movement in favor of statehood. The *Scioto Gazette*, the organ of the Virginia clique, applauded the national election in 1800 as "a glorious victory," which once more ensured the "pure spirit of republicanism in the United States." And in Cincinnati the *Western Spy* praised Jefferson's inaugural address, and his appointments to office of men of "integrity and talent."[30] Even more significant were the many toasts at the Fourth of July celebrations in 1800 and 1801 that lauded in fulsome strains the "free government" that would come with statehood.[31] In the midst of this rising tide of Republicanism, St. Clair must have given great comfort to his opponents when he arbitrarily set off Clermont, Fairfield, and Belmont counties. His reappointment was a distinct disappointment, and Thomas Worthington probably voiced a widespread opinion when he asserted that it was "truly disagreeable to us here."[32] The Republican coterie now worked more determinedly than ever for statehood, and doubtless they inspired many of the articles bearing upon this issue which began to appear in the territorial newspapers. In a typical one in the *Scioto Gazette*, *A Countryman* called attention to the colonial status of the Northwest Territory, and denounced especially the gover-

[29] *Journal, House of Representatives, Northwest Territory,* First General Assembly, Second Session, pp. 108-109.
[30] *Scioto Gazette,* January 8, 1801; *Western Spy,* May 13, 1801.
[31] *Ibid.,* July 9, 1800, and July 8, 1801.
[32] Thomas Worthington to Abraham Baldwin, March 6, 1801, and to Albert Gallatin, August, 1801, *Worthington Letter Book,* pp. 5-7, 67-68.

nor's appointing power.[33] Other writers advanced similar arguments to stir up feeling against St. Clair, but all was not smooth sailing for the Virginians and their Republican supporters. In Federalist Marietta a public meeting strongly opposed statehood upon the score of expense, although there was a prompt reply from *A Friend of the People* who undertook to show how unsound such arguments were.[34] In Hamilton County, *A Hamilton Farmer* and *A Citizen* also opposed statehood upon the ground that it would increase taxes, and that the chief proponents of the movement were a small clique at Chillicothe who were interested for selfish reasons.[35] With so many varying opinions Worthington was somewhat apprehensive as to the attitude of the assembly, and to add to his anxiety, the census showed that the Northwest Territory did not have near the 60,000 inhabitants that would ensure statehood.[36]

When the second territorial assembly met at Chillicothe, November 23, 1801, an open conflict appeared to be inevitable between the governor and the popular party. St. Clair still had considerable influence in the legislative council, but the leaders of the opposition, Worthington and Massie, retained their seats in the lower house, where they had sufficient power to reëlect their associate, Dr. Edward Tiffin, as speaker. On the other hand, the members of the house of representatives were all property holders who had been elected by a limited franchise, and, as men of a naturally conservative tendency, they preferred peaceable relations with the executive, nor had they lost entirely their accustomed respect for St. Clair. As usual the sessions of the assembly opened in peaceful fashion. The governor made a speech that avoided controversial subjects, and called attention again to the desirability of a settlement with Symmes of the question of a college township. Legislation was desirable, too, he

[33] *Scioto Gazette*, February 12 and 19, 1801.
[34] *Western Spy*, February 11 and October 24, 1801.
[35] *Ibid.*, November 2, 1801.
[36] Thomas Worthington to John Brown, September 15, 1801, *Worthington Letter Book*, pp. 73-74.

pointed out, to revise the militia act and the criminal laws, and to relieve the critical situation in territorial finances by finding some source of revenue in addition to the land tax. The legislative council replied in happy fashion, expressing their pleasure at the opportunity "publicly" to express their "approbation" of St. Clair's reappointment, but the reply of the lower house omitted any reference to the new term of office, although it, too, was couched in polite if rather general terms.[37] Following the governor's suggestion, the two houses readily agreed to set apart a "day of public thanksgiving and prayer to Almighty God" . . . "for His numerous blessings upon the territory." Then they proceeded to draw up instructions to Paul Fearing, now the territorial delegate to Congress, which were a virtual repetition of those of the previous year, except for a clause that requested a "declaratory act" by Congress upon the "difference of opinion" that had arisen with the governor over the power to erect counties. Strong support for this particular instruction was shown in a joint resolution that declared the "firm belief" of the two houses that the power of creating counties should be exercised "jointly" with the governor. Yet the dignified fashion in which they were seeking to have this disputed question settled was an unmistakable evidence of their wish to avoid an open conflict with St. Clair.[38]

Finances proved to be the most pressing problem before the assembly, and the situation that had arisen, together with the manner in which it was met, was an interesting illustration of the happy-go-lucky methods of the frontier. Although the total estimated revenue for 1801 was only $29,114.09, the appropriations totaled $34,533.09, and the territorial treasury faced a deficit of $5,419.00. In view of the meager resources of the Northwest Territory this was a serious situation, for which the difficulties in enforcing the land tax were primarily responsible. Costs of collection were high, and

[37] *St. Clair Papers,* Smith, ed., vol. II, pp. 534-540.
[38] *Journal, House of Representatives,* Second General Assembly, First Session, pp. 24, 45-46, 49-52.

much land, especially in the Virginia Military District, was held by non-residents from whom it was difficult to secure the payment of taxes. The system of accounting, too, had been exceedingly careless, and the territorial auditor had been accustomed to issue certificates of indebtedness to meet current expenses.[39] Obviously, as St. Clair had recommended, some source of income other than the land tax was needed. But the assembly merely raised the rates slightly, and then, with a typically legislative contempt for details, proceeded to appropriate $1,000.00 from the uncollected taxes in order to open up a road from the Western Reserve to the main highway between Chillicothe and Wheeling.[40] Fortunately such careless methods did not have serious results, for with the swift spread of population there was soon an ample revenue, although the collection of taxes on lands that were held by non-residents continued to be a difficult matter.

Among the constructive measures which the assembly found time to pass at this session were those that regulated writs of attachment, executions, the partition of estates, the recording of deeds, and like features of legal procedure.[41] Specially important was a bill to prescribe fees and other allowances, which replaced the one Maxwell's Code had adopted from the New York and Pennsylvania codes. This later act by a representative assembly was well adapted in its frugal allowances to the limitations of frontier finances, as a few examples will show. For recording wills it fixed a fee of 10 cents per sheet of 100 words, and for letters of administration of $1.00 exclusive of the seal. A petit juror was to receive the large sum of 25 cents for each case, while the allowance to a grand juror was only 50 cents per diem, with a 5 cent mileage for traveling expenses. To each county clerk and sheriff for services provided for by fees, the act gave a

[39] St. Clair Papers, Smith, ed., vol, II, pp. 540-542; Journal, House of Representatives, Northwest Territory, Second General Assembly, First Session, pp. 53-54.
[40] Memorial to Territorial Assembly, December 20, 1801, Ohio Broadsides.
[41] Laws of the Northwest Territory, Second General Assembly, First Session.

munificent annual allowance of $20.00 out of the county treasury. The judges of the general court were allowed $3.00 for each twenty miles they traveled, and prosecuting attorneys were paid $20.00 for each case in Washington and Trumbull counties, and $15.00 elsewhere. The territorial treasurer received $400.00 annually, the auditor $750.00, but both these salaries were to cover stationery and other office expenses as well. Another act of special importance authorized annual township meetings, in which all taxpayers of twenty-one and over were entitled to take part in true New England fashion and to elect a long list of local officials. Other important acts for purposes of local government were those to incorporate Chillicothe, Cincinnati, and Detroit. An act of a different type, which exempted from service in the militia all Quakers and others who were "conscientiously scrupulous," provided they paid an annual tax of $1.25 each, was an indication of the large number of Quakers who were coming into the Northwest Territory.

This program of constructive legislation was soon interrupted by two bills that greatly increased the hostility to St. Clair. The less important one, to remove the territorial capital from Chillicothe to Cincinnati, failed after successive attempts to substitute Marietta, Franklinton, Steubenville, Lancaster, and even Detroit. The other one, to reopen the question of the division of the original Northwest Territory, must have stirred the wrath of the Virginia coterie. In effect it proposed to Congress a division, roughly approximating the scheme that St. Clair had already favored, which would be made by one line up the Scioto and then north, and another one northward from the intersection of the western boundary of Clark's Grant and the Ohio River to the head of the "Chickagua" River.[42] Common report had it that St. Clair himself was the author of the bill, but this accusation the governor strenuously denied, although his defense was a

[42] *Journal, House of Representatives, Northwest Territory,* Second General Assembly, First Session, pp. 65-67; *Laws of the Northwest Territory,* idem., pp. 130-132.

weak one. The bill coincided with his known views, and it originated in the legislative council under the auspices of Jacob Burnet, one of his strong supporters. Moreover, if Congress should accept the proposed change in boundaries, it would postpone statehood indefinitely by cutting off the rapidly populating Virginia Military District and the Miami Purchase from the New England settlements east of the Scioto. The real significance of the bill was generally appreciated, and when the territorial lower house passed it by a vote of 12 to 8, there were open demonstrations against St. Clair, who was supposed also to be behind the act to move the capital from Chillicothe to Cincinnati. This so-called Chillicothe riot, St. Clair and his friends greatly magnified.[43]

Although the Republican leaders did not even control a majority in the lower house of the territorial assembly, they now began agitation there with statehood as their goal. Scarcely had the act passed for a new division of the Old Northwest when the advocates of statehood, led by Nathaniel Massie and the speaker, Edward Tiffin, presented a protest to the house which was spread on the minutes. This document asserted that the proposed new division was contrary to the Ordinance and was therefore unconstitutional. Also it was inexpedient since it would delay statehood indefinitely even in the eastern division. This protest was an exceedingly clever move, since it presented the movement for statehood to the public, with the implied support of the representative branch of the assembly. The reaction of the proposed new division upon the lower house itself was soon evident, and only after much wrangling, and doubtless much wirepulling, was St. Clair able to defeat a motion to send the protest to Congress along with the obnoxious act.[44] But he could not prevent the consideration of an act to take a census of the

[43] *St. Clair Papers,* Smith, ed., vol. II, pp. 543-557, 586; *Journal, House of Representatives, Northwest Territory,* Second General Assembly, First Session, pp. 31, 62, 68; *Journal, Legislative Council, idem.,* p. 17; *Scioto Gazette,* January 2, 1802.

[44] *Journal, House of Representatives, Northwest Territory,* Second General Assembly, First Session, pp. 80-83.

Northwest Territory east of the line northward from the mouth of the Miami. This measure, which was a significant move toward statehood, was carried by the deciding vote of the speaker, Edward Tiffin. Although it failed in the legislative council,[45] doubtless the purposes of its supporters had been achieved by the favorable action in the lower house, and the battle was now on between the governor and the popular party.

The fight for statehood soon shifted to the floor of Congress, and here the odds favored Worthington and his supporters. It was fairly safe to assume that the Republican majority which had come in with the election of 1800 would favor a new state west of the Appalachians, especially if there was a strong possibility that it would add to the party's strength. Nevertheless, St. Clair promptly forwarded the act for a division of the territory, denying again that it represented a conspiracy on his part to postpone statehood. Again the old Scotchman was scarcely sincere. At home he was urging his supporters to circulate petitions in favor of the bill in such Federalist strongholds as Washington and Trumbull counties, and there were rumors that he was also using his influence over officeholders to the same effect. Meantime his opponents were sending petitions against the bill through the territory, and Worthington had gone to Washington to work against it.[46] Consequently, when Fearing presented the act, the House was fully informed with regard to its effect in delaying statehood as well as the violent opposition it had aroused in the territory, and promptly rejected it by a vote of 81 to 5. On the losing side in this vote, it may be noted, was Manasseh Cutler, the father of the Ohio Purchase, and now a Federalist congressman from Massachusetts.[47]

Having successfully defeated the move to alter the territorial boundaries, the indefatigable Worthington worked di-

[45] Journal, House of Representatives, Northwest Territory, Second General Assembly, First Session, pp. 138, 155.
[46] St. Clair Papers, Smith, ed., vol. II, pp. 543-551; Western Spy, January 16 and 30, 1802.
[47] Annals of Congress, Seventh Congress, First Session, pp. 427, 462-466.

rectly for statehood. Already he had enlisted Abraham Baldwin, a Republican senator from Georgia, in the interests of "our much neglected country." In his letter to Baldwin Worthington announced that in his opinion the most important question was, whether the territory would become an "independent state" or would remain "under the present arbitrary government, better suited for an English or Spanish colony than for citizens of the United States." After this little touch, well calculated to arouse the enthusiasm of an ardent Republican, Worthington noted in practical fashion the chief obstacles to statehood; a population somewhat short of the 60,000 required by the Ordinance, and the questionable support of the territorial assembly. Yet he was "well convinced" that "a great body" of the people would support the proposed change, and he dangled before Baldwin's eyes the probability of additional Republican votes if the Northwest Territory became a state.[48] In like astute fashion Worthington sought and gained another powerful ally in the person of William Duane, the editor of the Philadelphia *Aurora*, which was then the official organ of the Republican party. Scoring the powers of the territorial executive as thoroughly "unrepublican," Worthington gave a long recital of alleged usurpations by St. Clair, which, of course, furnished Duane with abundant material for attacks in the *Aurora* upon the governor and his administration. Worthington also offered to furnish further details if Duane desired them, and he tactfully enclosed an advance payment of $5.00 for a year's subscription to the *Aurora*.[49] From now on Duane acted upon Worthington's suggestion, and inserted subtle and correspondingly effective attacks upon St. Clair in the columns of his paper. The so-called riot at Chillicothe he characterized as a figment of the governor's imagination, and he seized the opportunity to add that the people of the territory

[48] Thomas Worthington to Abraham Baldwin, November 30, 1801, *Worthington Letter Book*, pp. 98-100.
[49] Thomas Worthington to William Duane, November 10, 1801, *Ibid.*, pp. 90-93.

were "almost universally opposed to the present form of government established there," and to St. Clair. This particular editorial was admirably timed, since it came just as Congress was about to consider the act to divide the territory, and when the House rejected this measure, Duane expatiated in his editorial column upon the lively joy with which the news had been received at Chillicothe.[50]

Worthington, who was still in Washington, working for statehood, urged upon his friend, Nathaniel Massie, the necessity for additional petitions in support of the movement.[51] William B. Giles, one of the most influential Republicans and a close friend of Jefferson, led the fight in the House. First he presented a resolution to refer the census of the Northwest Territory to a committee which would "consider whether any and what measures" were necessary to grant state government. March 30, 1802, the committee reported there were approximately 42,000 inhabitants in the area to be included, but that at the present rate of settlement, there would probably be fully 60,000 before statehood was granted. In view of these conditions, and the "great and increasing disquietude among the inhabitants," on account of the recent act to alter boundaries, the committee felt that it would be "expedient" to form a new state.[52] Any lagging interest was spurred on by one of the timely editorials in the *Aurora* that subtly appealed to good Republicans. According to Duane, the movement for statehood in the Northwest Territory was unquestionably "politic," and would destroy the "seeds of an overbearing and ambitious aristocratic influence," sown in the territory by "a few characters" who had abused the confidence reposed in them to enrich themselves and their rela-

[50] *Aurora*, January 19 and March 2, 1802.

[51] Thomas Worthington to Nathaniel Massie, February 8, 1802, in Massie, *Life of Nathaniel Massie*, p. 191.

[52] The report showed 45,365 inhabitants, altogether, in the eastern division according to the census of 1800. From this number were to be deducted the 3,400 approximately in Wayne County, north of the boundary line of the proposed state. *Annals of Congress*, Seventh Congress, First Session, pp. 470, 471, 1097-1100.

tives "from the spoils of the people." [53] On the other hand, the Federalists criticized especially the summary fashion in which the proposed enabling act ignored the existing territorial legislature. In reply, the Republicans denied that an assembly which had been elected by a limited franchise could adequately represent the inhabitants of the Northwest Territory. They betrayed their true motive in ignoring the Assembly, the fear it would not support statehood wholeheartedly, when they cited as proof of the popular attitude more than twenty petitions in favor of the change that had been signed by thousands of citizens, and none against it.[54] Such influences easily won, and within less than three weeks both Houses had passed the bill to enable Ohio to become a state, and the President had signed it. The Virginia clique had finally triumphed.

The final act in the dramatic struggle between the adherents of the Republican party in the Northwest Territory and the Federalist governor was a determined effort to oust the latter as the chief obstacle to the program of the advocates of statehood. This action, Worthington and his followers felt, was all the more necessary inasmuch as the mere passage of the enabling act by Congress did not assure statehood. Delegates in favor of the movement must be elected, the convention must then be persuaded to pass favorably upon the issue of statehood, and finally this body must accept the conditions laid down by Congress in the enabling act and adopt a constitution. Trouble might come at any one of these steps. Moreover, no chances could be taken, for if the favorable opportunity, with a Republican majority in Congress, were lost, statehood and with it popular government might be indefinitely postponed, should the Federalists return to power. With so many possibilities of failure it is no wonder that Worthington and his friends determined to oust the governor, who could be depended upon to use all his influence to

[53] *Aurora,* April 12, 1802.
[54] *Annals of Congress,* Seventh Congress, First Session, pp. 258, 294-295, 1098-1251.

oppose each necessary move toward statehood. Unfortunately for St. Clair he had made many mistakes, and had raised up numerous enemies by his arbitrary policies and his lack of tact. Consequently he was an easy mark for the campaign of ridicule and criticism that the Republican managers now waged against him. Their first open move was a letter from Nathaniel Massie to the Secretary of State, James Madison, which preferred charges against St. Clair. Thomas Worthington, then in Washington, skillfully abetted Massie by sending practically the same accusation directly to Jefferson. Among the counts in this indictment were: a free use of the veto to thwart the public will, the receipt by the governor of personal fees for marriages and commissions, and also for ferry and tavern licenses, and the appointment of his son as territorial attorney-general during good behavior, when other commissions were being issued to last during the pleasure of the executive. Very evidently St. Clair's opponents had searched his official record for material upon which to base their criticisms. These charges came to a climax with the direct accusation of what constituted his chief crime in his opponents' eyes, that he had openly avowed hostility to the substance and form of republican government, and had plotted, from partisan motives, to divide the territory in such fashion as to postpone statehood indefinitely.[55]

St. Clair promptly came to his own defense. After he had received warning of the attempt to oust him, he wrote a letter directly to the President that dwelt with a convincing note of sincerity upon the conscientious fashion in which he had attempted to carry on the government. From this letter it is clear that the old Scotchman's chief concern was for the loss of reputation that a summary dismissal would involve.[56] Early in the spring he journeyed to Washington, in order to defend himself in person from the intrigues of Worthington

[55] Thomas Worthington to Nathaniel Massie, February 9, 1802, in Massie, *Life of Nathaniel Massie*, pp. 194-196; *St. Clair Papers*, Smith, ed., vol. II, pp. 563-576.

[56] St. Clair to Jefferson, February 13, 1802, *St. Clair Papers*, vol. II, pp. 573-574.

and his other opponents. His long record of public service won him many supporters, and it was reported that even William B. Giles, who had been so influential in securing the enabling act, advised the President not to dismiss him, and Jefferson to his credit refused to shame the old veteran. Rather, in tactful fashion he conveyed to him, through the Secretary of State, his own appreciation of his services, and regretted that it was necessary to express "particular disapprobation" of his conduct in granting his son an illegal tenure of office and in exacting unjustifiable fees. Nor did the President consider that under the Ordinance the governor had the sole power to erect counties. The letter closed with the hope that St. Clair would follow "such a line of conduct as may obviate discontents among the people under your administration." To this communication St. Clair replied immediately in a letter that showed the utmost deference to the President's wishes, and acknowledged with deep appreciation the "delicate manner" in which the writer had been chided.[57]

Unfortunately St. Clair failed to appreciate the political situation either in the territory or at Washington, and continued to declaim in most unbecoming fashion against the movement for statehood. During the campaign for delegates to the state convention he made an especially ill-advised attack upon the Republican societies which were beginning to spring up in the Western country, insinuating that in reality they had been founded by the Chillicothe clique, in order to sow dissension in Hamilton County. The climax came November 3, 1802, when at his own request St. Clair appeared before the constitutional convention. First he recalled the care with which he had administered the territorial government, and then he advocated his pet scheme, the proposed division of the Old Northwest into three sections, which had aroused so much hostility. As if this tactless remark was not

[57] Secretary of State to St. Clair, June 23, 1802, *Northwest Territorial Papers*, B. I. A. Domestic, 6387; *St. Clair Papers*, Smith, ed., vol. II, pp. 570-571.

enough, he proceeded to deliver a severe criticism of the
conditions that Congress had imposed in the enabling act,
and he even went so far as to advise the convention to
delay statehood until Ohio could be admitted to the Union
without restrictions.[58] The convention did not even give the
old governor the courtesy of a reply, and scarcely waited
until he was gone to vote in favor of statehood. St. Clair's
speech was, of course, promptly reported in Washington and
it proved to be the last straw. Madison wrote a curt letter
dismissing him from his post as governor of the Northwest
Territory, because of the "intemperance and indecorum" of
his language regarding Congress. These utterances, he
pointed out, the President considered as evidence of a "dis-
organizing spirit," and they constituted a "gross violation of
the obligations of his office." This rebuke was deserved, since
St. Clair had certainly departed from the non-partisan attitude to be expected from the governor of the Northwest Territory. Yet one cannot but admire the sturdy persistence
with which he clung to his views, however unwisely. In his
farewell message to the people of the territory, he held his
head high, positively declining to stand as candidate for
Governor of Ohio, and expressing his deep concern for the
territory and its welfare.[59] The truth is, St. Clair's useful-
ness in the territorial government was at an end. He had
successfully piloted the government through its early years,
but the personal characteristics that made this work a success disqualified him for the new demands and situations
that were arising. The progress of a vigorous and expanding
frontier had pushed aside a worn-out and conservative executive, and with him passed a colonial form of government,
with an appointed executive, and a limited franchise that
checked the popular will. In its place came statehood, with
practically manhood suffrage, and local autonomy.

[58] *St. Clair Papers,* Smith, ed., vol. II, pp. 587-590, 592-597.
[59] *Ibid.,* vol. I, pp. 244-246; vol. II, pp. 597-598.

Chapter V

STATEHOOD IN OHIO

In drawing up the enabling act for Ohio which was finally approved April 30, 1802, the Republican majority in Congress did not take any chances of a possible failure, and in rather arbitrary fashion they outlined the conditions under which the inhabitants of the Northwest Territory might form a state.[1] The choice of a name they left to the convention, although they fixed the boundaries so that they corresponded roughly to those in the Ordinance, with Wayne County, which included Detroit and the region to the north, attached to Indiana Territory. This rather arbitrary arrangement, their opponents charged, the Republicans made in order to exclude the Federalists of the Michigan district from representation in the constitutional convention. Republican manipulation was to be found, too, in other important features of the measure authorizing statehood. In contrast to the Ordinance with its restricted franchise, this act gave all male citizens of voting age who were taxpayers the right to vote for delegates to the convention, thus assuring popular control. This act also included such details as the apportionment of the thirty-five delegates among the counties, and the dates for the election and the opening of the convention. The stipulation that it must meet at Chillicothe provided an environment that was favorable to Republican control, an especially important consideration, inasmuch as the members of the convention were given the right to decide whether it was "expedient" to form a state. Then, if the vote was favorable, they might proceed to draw up a constitution, with the sole

[1] *Annals of Congress*, Seventh Congress, First Session, pp. 1348-1351.

restriction that it must be "republican" and not "repugnant" to the Ordinance of 1787. The question of a popular referendum upon the completed constitution was left altogether to the judgment of the convention. Under these conditions, if a majority of the delegates were in favor of statehood, not a very difficult condition to fulfill with practically a manhood suffrage, the Republicans under the leadership of the Virginia clique would have a clear field in the convention.

After Congress had passed the enabling act, the battlefield for statehood was transferred from Washington to the Northwest Territory, and the Republicans now concentrated their efforts in order to secure delegates to the convention who would support their plans. Following the example set up in the Revolution, they had already begun to organize Republican Corresponding Societies in an attempt to mold public opinion, and thus to counter the opposition to statehood which was arising. Scarcely had the enabling act passed when *Peter Squib* started a petty squabble in the *Western Spy* over a resolution of the Republican Corresponding Society of Cincinnati, which had grandiloquently referred to "the grand day of our final emancipation." [2] Jacob Burnet was an especially active and influential enemy of immediate statehood, and he seemed to take advantage of every possible occasion to counteract Republican propaganda.[3] Intimating that only a few Chillicotheans were urging statehood, other prominent Federalists scored the "high-handed fashion" in which Wayne County had been cut off from the proposed state. At Dayton a public meeting even favored the division of the Northwest Territory that St. Clair and the assembly had proposed but Congress had rejected. In several articles in the *Western Spy*, *Frank Stubblefield* strongly voiced his objections to statehood, and accused the Republican leaders of plotting to establish slavery on the Scioto. In this same Cincinnati paper the *Friends of Humanity*, also, called attention

[2] *Western Spy*, May 1–22, 1802.
[3] Charles Willing Byrd to Nathaniel Massie, June 7 and 20, 1802, in Massie, *Life of Nathaniel Massie*, pp. 209–211.

to the danger that the convention might support a modified form of slavery as a means of increasing the population.[4] The Marietta papers, likewise, contained numerous articles against statehood, and *Mentor*, in particular, denounced the enabling act as coercive.[5] Other arguments which the opponents of statehood advanced, in order to start a backfire of popular prejudice, were: that the defects in the territorial form of government were theoretical rather than real; that the inhabitants were unable to bear the expense of statehood; and that in the course of a year or so, statehood would come as a matter of right under the Ordinance, without restrictions or conditions.[6]

All these arguments against statehood were literally overwhelmed by the popular clamor for a really democratic form of government. The columns of the local newspapers were crowded with contributions such as a *Farmer's Creed*, which called attention to the "disinterested and friendly interposition of Congress" in relieving "our oppressed people," and raising the country from its "humiliating situation to a level with the rest of the states." At the Fourth of July celebrations in 1802, ardent and perhaps somewhat bibulous patriots had visions of a territory about to emerge "from their depressed and colonial situation to that of an independent state government." Even at Marietta the Republicans proposed a toast to their town, once a hotbed of Federalism, and now on the way to a "state of Republicanism." *Plain Truth* decried the fact that the people had no voice in naming their own officers, and dubbed St. Clair a "demigod," "in his own opinion," and other writers called attention to the restricted franchise under the Ordinance, in contrast to the practically manhood suffrage which the enabling act required.[7] Virtually an official statement from the Republican supporters of statehood appeared in a pamphlet which Thomas Worth-

[4] *Western Spy*, June 12 to September 11, 1802.
[5] *Ohio Gazette*, October 19, 1802.
[6] Burnet, *Notes on the Northwestern Territory*, pp. 348-349.
[7] *Western Spy*, especially May 22, June 26, July 10 and 24, and August 7, 1802.

ington published at the height of the agitation. This clever and well-written appeal to partisan prejudice, by a man who thoroughly understood frontier psychology, called attention to the recent act for another division of the Northwest Territory as an evidence of the persistent Federalist opposition to statehood. In contrast, Worthington dwelt upon the efforts of the Republicans to deliver the inhabitants from a government that was "oppressive and unequal," and to give them one that would be "congenial to the feelings of freemen." Then, having created a favorable atmosphere for his own party, he analyzed the enabling act in detail, and called attention to the many advantages it offered. In his conclusion, Worthington displayed a keen realization of the local situation when he appealed for mutual concessions from a population that had come from many sections, and had many differences of opinion. He counseled moderation, too, in the details of the new constitution, and in the selection of "principles and regulations, which have been tried by the touchstone of experience in different states of the Union." The Federalists denounced this pamphlet as "calculated to inflame their (the people's) minds against the present government of the territory," but their attempts to answer its arguments fell rather flat.[8]

As the time approached to elect delegates to the constitutional convention, the representatives of the Republican Corresponding Societies assembled in each county to make nominations, and the Federalists followed their example in Washington County at least.[9] There were many evidences of a general appreciation of the necessity to choose the leading citizens of the territory as delegates. During the campaign a strong anti-slavery sentiment became quite noticeable, and a number of candidates issued statements pledging themselves to raise "insuperable barriers" against any attempt to

[8] *Communication to Citizens of the Northwestern Territory*, etc., by Thomas Worthington; *Ohio Gazette*, September 28, 1802, ff.
[9] *Western Spy*, August 21, 1802; Cutler, *Life and Times of Ephraim Cutler*, p. 66.

introduce slavery. A characteristic frontier prejudice was aired during this campaign in the many denunciations of lawyers, and the strong opposition to them as candidates.[10] The widespread interest that was aroused among voters who were being allowed a popular suffrage for the first time was strikingly illustrated in Hamilton County, where the ten delegates were chosen from ninety-four candidates. Twenty-six of them received from 121 to 1,635 votes apiece, and eight Republicans and two Federalists were elected. Elsewhere in the territory there was the same story of Republican victory. The people of Cincinnati had a grand celebration with a triumphal arch and a public dinner, at which they partook of an ox as an emblem of their strength, and drank many toasts to the convention and the "free and independent state." [11]

The exceptional personnel of the delegates to the constitutional convention was a further proof of the serious attitude of the voters. From Ross County came the Republican leaders, Thomas Worthington, Nathaniel Massie, and Edward Tiffin, while Washington County sent an equally strong delegation of Federalist tendencies, among them General Rufus Putnam, one of the founders of the Marietta colony, and Ephraim Cutler, a hard-headed Yankee, son of the Reverend Manasseh Cutler. The leader of the Hamilton County delegation was Charles Willing Byrd, secretary of the territory, who was hand in glove with the Worthington coterie. Another member of this group, John Reily, the first schoolmaster in Cincinnati, had been clerk for all the sessions of the territorial legislature. Other notable delegates from Hamilton County included: John W. Browne, an ardent admirer of Cobbett, first an English clergyman and later the intelligent and public-spirited editor of *Liberty Hall;* and Jeremiah Morrow, reared in Pennsylvania, who was to become Governor of Ohio, and to serve ten years as the sole repre-

10 *Western Spy,* September 25 to October 9, 1802.
11 *Ibid.,* October 20 and 27, 1802.

sentative of the state in Congress. Trumbull County in the
Western Reserve, one of the two strongholds of New England
emigrants, sent Samuel Huntington, a lawyer of great
ability who also was destined to become governor. Altogether,
the high average ability of the delegates to this constitutional
convention was a striking illustration of the splendid
type of settlers who had come to the Old Northwest from
so many different sections. Morever, such men were a sufficient
guarantee against radical action, in spite of the strong
Republican leanings of the great majority of the delegates.

The constitutional convention met at Chillicothe November
1, 1802, and promptly elected as its presiding officer
Edward Tiffin, one of the Republican leaders, who had been
speaker for all three sessions of the territorial legislature.[12]
Next, after they had listened with indifference to St. Clair's
plea to postpone statehood, they resolved that it was "expedient"
to form a state government. The one negative vote
was cast by Ephraim Cutler who, true to his Federalist principles,
refused to fall in line with the Republican majority.
Having committed itself in favor of statehood, the convention
turned to the work of drawing up a constitution, and in
the process it considered a variety of issues. In rather canny
fashion it took advantage of the very obvious eagerness of
the majority in Congress to welcome a new state that could
be counted upon to come into the Republican fold, and proceeded
to drive an excellent bargain. Alarmed over the possibilities if the new state should levy heavy taxes with undue
haste upon lands that were bought on credit from the Federal
government, Congress had requested the convention to
agree by an "ordinance irrevocable" to exempt all public
lands in Ohio from taxation for five years after they had
been purchased, which really meant until the expiration of
the time limit for payments. In return Congress offered for

12 For the details of the convention, see *Journal of the Convention of the
Northwest Territory.* For a personal narrative of the proceedings, see Cutler,
Life and Times of Ephraim Cutler, pp. 68-82; also Burnet, *Notes on the
Northwestern Territory,* pp. 350-369.

their "free acceptance or rejection" certain valuable concessions to the new state, including section sixteen in each township for the support of schools, all salt springs within Ohio for the public use, and one twentieth of the net proceeds from the sale of public lands for the building of roads, either within the state or to the Atlantic Coast. The members of the convention agreed to accept these proposals with modifications. They stipulated that Congress should set aside for the school fund public lands equivalent to one thirty-sixth of all the land that had been or would be granted in the state, and three per cent of the net proceeds of all public land sales, to build roads within Ohio alone. Also, they asked Congress to fulfill the promise of a college township in the Miami Purchase. These modifications of its original offer Congress accepted, although it passed over unnoticed the alteration the convention had made in the boundary, in order to include Maumee Bay and the lower Maumee Valley.[13]

The practical sense of the members of the convention constantly showed itself in an attitude of compromise toward the controversial issues that arose during its sessions. This was especially evident in the settlement of the status of the negro. There was considerable support for a proposal to permit slavery up to thirty-five for a male, and twenty-five for a female. Although there was a report that the original proposition came from Jefferson, and many inhabitants of the Virginia Military District brought strong pressure in its favor, this resolution failed. Instead, under the leadership of Ephraim Cutler the convention inserted a clause in the constitution that, following the Ordinance of 1787, positively prohibited slavery in the state of Ohio. The rights to be allowed free negroes under the new constitution also aroused much discussion. At first the advocates of racial equality secured the passage of a resolution to give negroes the suffrage whenever they recorded their citizenship, but the opponents of this clause secured a reconsideration and struck it out of the constitution by the deciding vote of the president

13 Patterson, *The Constitutions of Ohio*, pp. 61-65.

of the convention. Radical action against the negro was equally unsuccessful. The advocates of this latter policy secured the adoption of a clause that declared negroes ineligible to office, or to give evidence in court against a white person, only to see it lost upon reconsideration by a vote of 17 to 16. Thus, the constitutional status of the negro in Ohio was exceedingly anomalous, inasmuch as, even though he could not be held as a slave, he had no right to vote. The convention displayed a notably liberal point of view when, by an overwhelming majority of 30 to 3, it put an end to an attempt to strike out the clause that no religious test should be set up in order to hold office, and to substitute for it a requirement that no person "who denies the being of God, or a future state of rewards and punishment," should be permitted to hold office.

In the actual draft of the new constitution, the convention used as a model the Tennessee Constitution of 1796. This was a logical and in many respects a happy choice, since the constitutional convention of Tennessee, the most recent frontier state, had considered many problems that were comparable to those of Ohio. Consequently it was possible to transfer entire sections from the Tennessee to the Ohio Constitution, some verbatim, others with only slight changes.[14] For example, the constitution of Tennessee gave a precedent for the very limited powers allowed the governor in Ohio, as well as for many clauses in the bill of rights. The differences between the two constitutions strikingly illustrated the contrasts between the point of view of the rather conservative planter of Tennessee and that of the democratic small farmer of Ohio. Thus the constitutional convention of Ohio swept away the property qualifications required in Tennessee of the governor and the members of the legislature. Also, in place of a judiciary to hold office during "good behavior," it substituted a requirement that all judges should be elected

[14] For the first constitution of Ohio, see Patterson, *The Constitutions of Ohio*, pp. 73-97; for that of Tennessee, see Thorpe, *American Charters, Constitutions and Organic Law*, vol. VI, pp. 3414-3425.

for terms of seven years by joint ballot of the legislature. These democratic provisions were followed in spirit in another clause that required all local officers, sheriffs, coroners, and constables to be elected rather than appointed. The broad-minded toleration that was characteristic of early Ohio no doubt led the framers of the new constitution to reject the clause in the Tennessee constitution that prohibited ministers of the gospel from sitting in either branch of the legislature. Moreover, they recognized the militant democracy of their constituents by adopting practically manhood suffrage, in contrast to the restriction of the franchise to freeholders in the Northwest Territory and in Tennessee. This last provision completed the triumph of the Republican clique over St. Clair and his followers.

Like the Revolutionary constitutions of the older states, the Ohio constitution included an elaborate bill of rights which reflected the liberalism of the period. But unlike its Eastern prototypes it also had provisions to carry out all these theories in actual practice. Beside the usual guarantees of jury trial, the right of private property, and the like, there were sections that were clearly the outgrowth of public sentiment. Fortifying the prohibition of slavery was a clause that forbade indentures, unless they were entered upon by a mature individual in a "state of perfect freedom," and for a bona-fide consideration. With the exception of apprenticeships, all indentures that had been made outside of Ohio were to be invalid within the state if they lasted for more than a year. Another clause in the bill of rights was decidedly in agreement with frontier prejudices when it forbade imprisonment for debt, where a debtor had surrendered his estate for the benefit of his creditors. Other sections prohibited the levy of a poll tax as "grievous and oppressive," and guaranteed to "the poor" an "equal participation" in the schools and other institutions of learning that were endowed either wholly or in part by donations of public lands. To these institutions the aid of the state was pledged. In accordance with the liberal ideals of the Revolutionary era, the bill of rights upheld absolute freedom of worship, and prohibited any compulsory support of religion or forced attendance upon church services. Nor was the law to show preference to any religious society, although, consistently with the general local attitude, the constitution upheld "religion, morality, and knowledge" as "essentially necessary to good government."

Many features of the new constitution showed considerable advance over corresponding provisions in the territorial code, thus illustrating the important part that experience played in the deliberations of the convention. This was shown especially in the simplification of the judicial system. In place of the cumbersome territorial organization with local courts of common pleas, probate, and quarter sessions, and the orphans' courts, the constitutional convention provided for a court of common pleas in each county, to have general jurisdiction over all civil and criminal cases and probate business. The state was to be divided into circuits, in each of which a presiding judge would be appointed, and it would be the duty of these judges to preside over the courts of common pleas in the counties under their respective jurisdictions. For the general court, which of course was dropped with the territorial régime, the convention substituted a supreme court that would hold one session annually in each county for the convenience of the widely scattered inhabitants. Aside from these reforms, other clauses in the new constitution strikingly illustrated the practical sense of these early Western constitution makers. Thus, they fixed the seat of government at Chillicothe until 1808, but wisely postponed a final choice until the spread of population made possible a really permanent site. A clause that indicated the great advance made in general culture permitted the incorporation of "associations of persons" to hold property for the support of "schools, academies, colleges, universities, and for other purposes." Finally, in order to ensure legal stability in the transition to a state, an important provision of the constitution declared that all territorial laws then in force, except the requirements for admission to the bar, were to remain in effect until the legislature should repeal them, provided they were consistent with the fundamental law of the new state.

Even into so practical a document as the new constitution of Ohio, defects were bound to creep. The most noticeable, perhaps, arose from an excessive zeal for democracy, which was responsible, for example, for the provision that all judges should be elected for terms of seven years by a joint ballot of the state legislature. Such a provision was bound to weaken the independence of the courts, yet in view of the frontier dislike for courts and lawyers, and the general tendencies of the period, it was inevitable. The denial of the veto power to the governor and the general limitations upon his powers were other mistakes, but they were logical restrictions by a people who had been so intensely hostile to St. Clair's arbitrary government and they reflected, too, the prejudice against a strong executive which many immigrants had brought from their former homes. Unfortunately these restrictions upon the judiciary and the executive tended to elevate unduly the power of the legislative branch of the government, creating a situation that was to become a source of considerable controversy. In spite of such obvious defects, on the whole the convention drew up a fairly satisfactory and moderate constitution that was admirably adapted to the needs and ideals of the inhabitants.

By a vote of 27 to 7 the delegates refused to submit the results of their labors to a popular referendum. Nor was this an altogether mistaken policy. Federalist criticism to the contrary, a popular vote would have meant another campaign of recrimination and abuse, such as had marked the election of the delegates, and would have merely postponed the transition to the new form of government. This decision was characteristic, too, of the businesslike proceedings of the convention. In twenty-five working days the thirty-five members had completed their task, with a total expense account of only $4,556.75,[15] a record that strikingly contrasts with

[15] Randall and Ryan, History of Ohio, vol. III, p. 114.

those of more recent constitutional conventions. The peaceable fashion in which the transition was made in Ohio from a territorial status to statehood was a sufficient proof of the popularity of the new constitution. While the convention was sitting, the local newspapers had printed detailed accounts of its proceedings, and when it adjourned, they published the new constitution in full.[16] This publicity effectively answered any charges that the delegates were conspiring against the general welfare. As election day approached, the Republican societies in the different localities nominated candidates for the various state offices. The victory of the advocates of statehood was generally recognized as a distinctly Republican triumph, and even to distant Tennessee there came echoes of the rejoicing in Ohio, now that its inhabitants had "shaken off the old shackles of territorial government to become a state." [17] The local Federalists, recognizing their complete rout, made few nominations, and many of them did not vote at all, or else they cast blank ballots. The outcome of the election was Republican control of the new state government. March 1, 1802, the legislature assembled at Chillicothe, Edward Tiffin was inaugurated as governor, and statehood in Ohio had become a reality.

The dismal predictions of St. Clair and his friends were not realized, for the Republican majority in the legislature usually observed the same moderation that had marked the deliberations of the constitutional convention. During the legislative sessions begun respectively March 1 and December 5, 1803, the members of the two houses made few changes in the code that was inherited from the territorial period, confining their activities chiefly to laws that had become necessary by the change from a territorial to a state government.[18] Thus, they passed a measure that carried into effect the alterations that the constitution had made in the judicial system, especially the substitution of the court of

[16] For example, the *Western Spy*, November 10 to December 22, 1802.
[17] *Tennessee Gazette*, December 25, 1802.
[18] *Laws of Ohio*, First General Assembly, First and Second Sessions.

common pleas for the old court of quarter sessions. The legislature recognized, also, the need for a more adequate system of land records, and created the offices of surveyor and recorder in each county. Another act authorized the election of three commissioners in each county, whose duty it was to assess county taxes, and to oversee all expenditures for buildings, bridges, and other public works. Another measure, one that was reminiscent of recent contentions, created seven new counties, although it did not disturb the ten that St. Clair had already set up by proclamation. In this connection the assembly provided for the appointment of local commissioners, who should select and lay out "the most eligible place" in each county for holding court. Nor did the members of the assembly neglect other important needs for local government. They incorporated the town of Chillicothe in an elaborate act that served as a model for later measures, and in another act they set forth the duties of the constable and the justice of the peace, admonishing the latter officers to take special cognizance of persons who "fight or box at fisticuffs," or otherwise "commit an affray." This act allowed an appeal from the decision of a justice in civil suits, if $5.00 or more should be involved.

In these first two sessions the Ohio legislature left the territorial system of taxation practically unchanged, and continued also its conservative policy with regard to expenditures. The governor and the judges of the supreme court were each to receive annual salaries of only $900, for the state treasurer and the secretary of state respectively the annual stipend was $400, including office expenses, and other allowances were in proportion. This careful management made possible a total budget for the year 1803 of only $10,-950, so that, contrary to Federalist predictions, a deficit under the territorial government was avoided. An especially important act regulated elections in elaborate fashion, providing for judges, for a fixed polling place in each township, and for a single ballot, upon which the voter wrote down the names of the candidates he supported. This measure defined bribery as any act that might be interpreted to "give or propose any meat, drink, or any other reward" in return for votes, and it fixed as a penalty disqualification from office for two years and a fine of not more than $500. An additional clause, that really was a reflection upon the general lack of education in Ohio, imposed a fine upon any one who misrepresented or falsely read a ballot to an illiterate person. There were other miscellaneous acts, including one passed in order "to regulate black and mulatto persons," which required them to produce a certificate of freedom and to be registered if they wished to remain in Ohio. Also, it ordered the return of all fugitive slaves, provided the owners gave satisfactory proof of their claims.

From a legal standpoint, the third session of the Ohio assembly, beginning December 13, 1804, was the most important one in the early period of statehood up to the War of 1812, for during its progress the laws were thoroughly revised. One of the most important provisions of the new Ohio Code that was drawn up at this time removed many legal uncertainties by a summary repeal of all the laws from the territorial period, except those which were specifically reënacted. The acts of the first two sessions of the Ohio legislature were, of course, confirmed, and whatever gaps remained were filled in. Usually in this revision the legislature made use of the territorial acts as a basis for laws that were better adapted to changed conditions, or were merely simplified.[19] As an example, the several acts that dealt with crimes and punishments were founded upon the same general principles as the corresponding ones in the territorial code, but they included a much briefer list of offenses. Whipping was retained as the chief penalty for many crimes that were frequently committed in the Western country, such as counterfeiting, robbery, and horse-stealing, while for dueling with "sword, pistol, rapier, or other dangerous weapon" there were severe fines for both principals and seconds. The Puritan spirit survived in an act that prohibited all quarreling,

[19] *Laws of Ohio*, Third General Assembly.

shooting, or common labor on the Sabbath, but permitted "emigrating" families to travel, and ferrymen to ply their craft. Likewise this code put a ban upon gambling in all its forms, and imposed a 50 cent fine upon any one who "shall profanely curse, damn, or swear by the name of God, Jesus Christ, or the Holy Ghost." With the same leniency toward debtors that the territorial laws had already shown, the Ohio Code virtually abolished imprisonment for debt, and fixed the legal rate of interest at six per cent. This last clause was fortified by a provision that the penalty for usury should be forfeiture of the entire amount of the debt with one-half to the informer.

Other miscellaneous acts provided for a variety of needs for which experience showed legislation was needed. One measure defined in detail the powers of the secretary of state, the state auditor, the state treasurer, and the justices of the peace in the township. Another act, contrasting in its brevity with the elaborate one which the governor and the judges had adopted from the Virginia Code, established in Ohio the principles of the English common law prior to 1607. Still another act regulated the fees charged by public officials, following territorial precedents in its scanty allowances. Thus, county clerks received 10 cents to 12 cents per sheet of 100 words, and the pay of a juror was only 40 cents per diem. In the system of taxation the new code adhered to the general scheme of the territorial period, depending for state revenue upon the land tax with the three rates according to the value of the land, and with special provisions to ensure collections from the non-resident owners of large areas. For local purposes the assembly authorized taxes upon each head of horses, mules, and neat cattle, upon houses valued at $100 and upward, and upon all town lots. Annual license fees from ferries, retail stores, and taverns completed the sources of revenue for county needs. This law, it may be noted, required each township to care for its own indigent poor, and there were elaborate restrictions to prevent other states from dumping their pauper inhabitants in

Ohio. Altogether, the members of this third general assembly of Ohio, like those of the constitutional convention, had done a really notable piece of work, passing seventy-two acts and seventeen resolutions in a session of eighty-four days which was marked by the closest attention to business, and by a notable absence of partisanship. But even this business-like attitude was not wholly pleasing to their more radical constituents, and one ardent patriot strongly protested against the numerous statutes that had made necessary so many "judges, lawyers, clerks," and the like whom the people must support.[20]

The same moderation and recognition of local needs that marked the passage of the Ohio Code usually characterized subsequent legislation up to the outbreak of the War of 1812. This sensible legislative policy was of great importance in the progress of a population that was rapidly overflowing from the Ohio Valley and the Western Reserve into the interior.[21] The state constitution and the Ohio Code of 1805 had established the bases of the government, and the problem now was to build a legal foundation upon this structure that would keep pace with the demands of a rapidly increasing population.[22] A law of 1808, for example, added another judge to the supreme court and authorized an additional circuit for the county courts of common pleas. Another important measure for local government was the act of 1810 that permitted the incorporation of townships, and thus gave more power to the local officials in rural districts. Other acts from time to time incorporated individual towns, created additional counties in the interior and along Lake Erie, and protected the taxpayers from excessive poor relief. The members of the Ohio Legislature also made considerable changes

[20] *Scioto Gazette*, February 25 and December 26, 1805.
[21] The census of 1800 gave the population of the Northwest Territory, *i.e.*, Ohio, as 45,365, chiefly in the Ohio Valley, with about 3½ per cent in the Western Reserve. By 1810 the population was 227,843, and the entire state outside the line of the Treaty of Greenville was being rapidly settled up. *U. S. Census of 1800*, p. 85; *U. S. Census of 1810*, pp. 69-70.
[22] *Laws of Ohio*, Fourth to Eleventh General Assemblies.

in the act regarding crimes and their punishment, increasing the penalties for dueling and horsewhipping, and for aid to prisoners who escaped from the poorly constructed jails. To the usual list of crimes they added the wilful destruction of fruit trees, of trees used as landmarks in surveys, or of live stock, and by an act of 1809 they forbade the sale of spirituous liquor to Indians. A measure that drew attention to the swift progress of Ohio, fixed the permanent site of the capital in the approximate center of the state, on the left bank of the Scioto opposite Franklinton. Another important matter that needed adjustment was the final determination of the northwestern boundary, and twice the legislature petitioned Congress either to accept or reject the line which the constitutional convention had fixed to include Maumee Bay. But there was no definite settlement during this early period, up to the War of 1812.[23] In this same period, 1805–1812, the assembly passed many other acts which the rapidly increasing population made necessary. Of special interest were the measures to incorporate Baptist, Congregational, Episcopalian, and Presbyterian "societies," along with a number of academies. Usually these acts revealed a characteristic frontier dread of powerful corporations, by limitations upon the property that might be acquired, the amount varying in individual instances from $3,000 to $6,000 of annual income.

Gradually the status of the negro became a pressing problem, as intercourse increased with the slave state of Kentucky on the other side of the Ohio. Many newspaper articles show the strength of the anti-slavery sentiment in early Ohio, and there were stringent indenture laws intended to make slavery impossible under any form.[24] However, there was little good will toward the black man personally, and there is much evidence that there was a strong movement to exclude him

---

[23] *Laws of Ohio,* Fifth General Assembly, pp. 143-144, Seventh General Assembly, p. 225.

[24] Especially *Liberty Hall,* January 13 and July 14, 1806. See also a long series of essays on Slavery by W. B. in the *Western Spectator,* August 7, 1811, to February 8, 1812.

from Ohio by hostile legislation.[25] This hostility made itself felt in the anomalous position of the freed blacks under the state constitution, and in the stringent registration law in the Ohio Code of 1805. Furthermore, it tended to increase, and even the representatives in the legislature from Washington County, allowing their New England theories of equality to be overcome by the prejudices that came from actual contact with "the brother in ebony," joined the delegations from other river counties in 1807, in order to secure a more severe act. This measure went so far as to prohibit a negro from settling in Ohio, unless he produced a bond of $500 to assure his good behavior, and to guarantee he would not become a public charge. In addition to this rather drastic condition, which quite evidently the average negro could not meet, the law imposed a fine upon the employer of a negro who had not furnished the necessary bond. The climax of this act, and incidentally of the black code of Ohio, was a section that refused to allow a negro to swear or give testimony in any court of record, where either party was white, or where the prosecution had been instituted by the state or a white person. This severe measure aroused much criticism, and at Steubenville *Agricola* scored it as unconstitutional, undemocratic, and intended to prevent the migration of free blacks into a land of liberty.[26] Actually this last law, together with the restrictions in the constitution and the provisions of the code, made the position of the free negro in Ohio an impossible one, without a vote, with little chance to work, and deprived even of the means of securing justice in the courts. But public opinion reacted, and as this black code was gradually ignored negroes found their way across the Ohio in considerable numbers.

Meanwhile political dissensions began to arise in this frontier democracy. Having won their campaign for statehood, Worthington and his followers were now compelled to fight

[25] Wilson, *The Negro in Early Ohio, Ohio Archæological and Historical Quarterly*, vol. XXXIX, pp. 716-768.
[26] *Western Herald*, July 25, 1807.

in order to retain control of the new state. So far they had relied largely upon the Republican Corresponding Societies which had continued their activities after the campaign for statehood, sending delegates to the county conventions at which the various candidates were nominated, and frequently carrying on considerable correspondence among themselves.[27] Many of the old-time Federalists, now turned Republicans, had joined these societies, and were using them, so it was alleged, to gain offices, despite frenzied appeals to the public to elect "genuine independent" Americans and "democratic Republicans." With their control of the Republican Societies slipping away in this fashion, the Virginia clique began to publish innuendoes against their opponents, especially in their mouthpiece, the *Scioto Gazette*.[28] A typical editorial sarcastically commented upon the "political fishermen, old in years, but young in Republicanism." Another significant article gave great prominence to a "thoroughly Republican" Fourth of July celebration at Worthington in 1804, and still another one warned all good Republicans to be prepared for any tricks that might be attempted at the polls.[29]

The bitter hostility of the "democratic" Republicans toward the Federalists, who had so lately turned Republican, only needed a definite issue to break out into open conflict. The occasion came in 1805 when the legislature passed an act that extended the jurisdiction of justices of the peace to civil cases within their respective townships that involved not over $50.[30] When Judge Pease and his associates in Belmont and Jefferson counties declared this act unconstitutional, the "democratic" Republicans promptly introduced a resolution in the legislature that denied the right of the courts to pass upon legislative acts. It did not carry, and the

[27] *Western Spy*, March 9 and 16, and September 7, 1803, and September 19, 1804; *Scioto Gazette*, October 1, 1804.
[28] Especially *Western Spy*, May 25, 1803; *Scioto Gazette*, September 17, 1805.
[29] *Ibid.*, July 9 and 30, and October 8, 1804.
[30] *Laws of Ohio*, Third General Assembly, p. 21.

wrath of its framers increased all the more when, in another case, this time in the supreme court, Chief Justice Huntington and Judge Tod held that the justice-of-the-peace law was unconstitutional. This decision they based chiefly upon the guarantee in the constitution of Ohio that the right of trial by jury should be "inviolate," and upon the clause in the Federal Constitution that assured a jury trial in cases that involved more than $20.[31] Just at this time Chief Justice Marshall was in the very thick of his fight to assert the power of the Supreme Court in settling constitutional controversies. It was to be expected, therefore, that such ardent Jeffersonians as Worthington and his followers would seize upon a similar controversy in Ohio in order to rally popular support to their own projects.

The need of a Republican battle cry was becoming quite apparent. Before the election in the fall of 1806 there was a determined effort to oust Jeremiah Morrow, Ohio's sole congressman, and to substitute James Pritchard. Although the "democratic" Republicans won in this instance, it was evident that the "Federalist" Republicans were rapidly gaining strength.[32] In 1807, when an election became necessary for a successor to Governor Tiffin who had gone to the Senate, Nathaniel Massie, one of the Virginia clique, was the regular Republican candidate, but in several of the county conventions the delegates from the Republican Societies chose Return J. Meigs, Jr., a native New Englander of a rather conservative type. The election aroused much popular interest, fully a third of the voters turning out at the polls. Each candidate drew votes from the counties where the local organization had supported his rival, and Meigs received 5,550 votes, as compared with 4,739 for Massie. The election merely increased factional enmities, since the legislature

---

[31] For a detailed account of this attempt to override the courts, see Utter, *Judicial Review in Early Ohio, Miss. Valley Hist. Review,* vol. XIV, pp. 3-24.

[32] *Western Herald,* August 23 and 30, September 13 and 20, 1806; *Scioto Gazette,* June 5, September 4, and November 13, 1806.

later ruled out Meigs, upon the ground that he did not possess the residence qualifications required by the state constitution.[33]

At the regular election of a governor in the fall of 1808, the leading candidates were Chief Justice Huntington, a conservative, one of the judges who had declared the "justice law" unconstitutional, and Thomas Worthington, the leader of the radical Republican element. Both sides were active in the campaign. At Chillicothe, the hotbed of "democratic" Republicanism, the conservatives established a new journal, *The Supporter*, in opposition to the *Scioto Gazette*.[34] The arguments of Worthington and his followers were well represented in an article by *Plowjogger* which, after a review of the early days of the American government and the movement for statehood in Ohio, dwelt upon the struggles between the Federalists, representing privilege, and the Republicans, who were the spokesmen for the plain people.[35] At the county convention of the Republican Societies in Hamilton County there was open trouble, and a part of the delegates withdrew to nominate an opposition ticket.[36] The election of Huntington was unquestionably a victory of the more conservative Republicans, as well as of the supporters of the state judiciary in its assertion of the right to review legislation.

Worthington and his friends now increased their efforts to use the judicial decisions as an issue to secure popular support for themselves, a task that was not specially difficult in a frontier region where there was such strong opposition to courts and lawyers. Many articles against the judges began to appear in the newspapers, among them a long-winded composition by a Dr. Campbell who denied the power of the judges to declare an act unconstitutional, chiefly upon the ground that to do so would make the judiciary a superior,

[33] *Western Herald*, September 12 and 26, and October 3, 1807; *Liberty Hall*, September 14, 1807; *Western Spy*, August 17, 1807; Massie, *Life of Nathaniel Massie*, pp. 93-100.
[34] *The Supporter*, October 6 and 27, 1808.
[35] *Western Spy*, February 22 and 29, 1808.
[36] *Liberty Hall*, September 7 and 24, and October 8, 1808.

rather than a coördinate, branch of the government.[37] The legal uncertainty that came as an aftermath of the unpopular court decisions was also used as a means of arousing resentment. In Ross County, one correspondent pointed out, justices had rendered decisions for $34 and $50 which the county court of common pleas upheld, but in Jefferson County the supreme court had set aside a justice's verdict for more than $20. Very pertinently the writer inquired whether there was one law in Chillicothe and another one in Steubenville. Other correspondents hinted at collusion between the lawyers and the judiciary, or else they called attention to the "patriotism and inflexible virtue" of the legislature which had protected the people from being crushed between these two "mighty millstones." [38] In Cincinnati at a Fourth of July celebration there was a significant toast to the judiciary, "but not to remain so independent as to place it without control or responsibility, lest we be again Marshall'd." However, the judges did not lack their defenders, and *A Plain Countryman* pointed out how necessary it was to have a judicial review of the acts of the legislature.[39] By the time the legislature assembled popular feeling had been worked up to a high pitch. Worthington and his followers deemed the time now ripe to bring impeachment charges against Judge Tod and Judge Pease, upon the ground that they had declared the "justice law" unconstitutional and void. A committee of the lower house of the state legislature obligingly declared that Judge Tod's decision was contrary to the constitution and laws of Ohio, "disgraceful to his own character as a judge, and degrading to the honor and dignity" of the state.[40] The subsequent impeachment proceed-

[37] *Ohio Gazette,* March 21, 1808.
[38] *Ibid.,* March 14, 1808; *Scioto Gazette,* February 13 and 27, 1809.
[39] *Ohio Gazette,* November 3, 1808; *Western Herald,* August 12, 1808; *Liberty Hall,* July 9, 1808.
[40] For an exhaustive account of the impeachment proceedings, see Utter, *Judicial Review in Early Ohio* in *Miss. Val. Historical Review,* vol. XIV, pp. 14-19.

ings created great excitement and occupied considerable space in the Ohio newspapers.[41] The defense made by the judges created a specially favorable impression, and the senate acquitted Judge Tod by one vote, Judge Pease by a larger margin. The incident brought about a reaction in favor of the more conservative Republicans, which took the form of a protest against the high-handed methods of the "self-styled Republicans." *The Supporter* sarcastically called attention to the "glorious effects of Jacobinism in our government," and cited as an illustration the futile attempt to oust the two judges, at a cost to the state of $6,000.[42]

But the Virginia clique were resourceful. Although they had been unsuccessful in the impeachment of the two judges, they had at least secured an act by the same legislature which defied the courts and extended the jurisdiction of justices of the peace to civil cases that involved as much as $70. The climax came when at its next session, beginning December 4, 1809, the legislature passed the Sweeping Resolution, to the effect that under the state constitution the terms of all judges expired seven years after statehood was established, even including those who had been appointed after 1803.[43] This resolution, which was interpreted to vacate practically all judiciary appointments in Ohio, was clearly aimed at the judges who had assumed the right to pass upon the constitutionality of legislative acts, and the more conservative Republicans quickly took up this challenge to the freedom of the courts. An open letter from Judge Sprigg, one of the judges ousted under the Sweeping Resolution, to Judge Scott, one of the newly appointed judges, was one of the most convincing of the many communications that pointed out the real purpose and the peril involved in this new move of the radical Republicans. Judge Scott's answer, like other articles from supporters of the Sweeping Resolu-

[41] *The Supporter*, March 2, 1809; *Liberty Hall*, January 19 and February 3, 1809.
[42] *The Supporter*, February 9, 1809.
[43] Resolution, January 16, 1810, *Laws of Ohio*, Eighth General Assembly, pp. 349-350.

tion, lacked both logic and force.[44] John W. Browne, the editor of *Liberty Hall*, and a member of the constitutional convention, emphatically denounced any interpretation of the constitution that sanctioned a "general sweep" of the judges, and numerous other protests were issued.[45] In a desperate effort to curb the conservative reaction that such representations aroused, the supporters of the Virginia clique published articles that praised the judges appointed under the Sweeping Resolution, and attempted to stir up hostility toward the ones who had been retired.[46] As a last resort they turned to the Saint Tammany Society, which had been playing an important rôle in Eastern politics, and established Wigwam Number One at Chillicothe, followed by other wigwams throughout the state.[47]

The campaign preceding the election of a governor in the fall of 1810 was fought chiefly upon the issue of the Sweeping Resolution, which, it was generally understood, meant legislative coercion of the judiciary. The "democratic" Republicans nominated Thomas W. Worthington, and a communication in the *Scioto Gazette* clearly expressed their chief aims when it declaimed against the efforts of the "judge party, lawyers and Federalists," to undermine the constitution by "giving the judges power to set aside, make null and void our best laws." [48] The more conservative Republicans again nominated Return J. Meigs, Jr., chiefly through county conventions. The campaign that followed was a particularly bitter one in which the conservatives were victorious. Their next aim was to repeal the Sweeping Resolution, but this was not so easily accomplished. The veteran politicians in the ranks of their opponents turned to the Tammany Clubs for support, although the organization was gradually losing in

[44] *Liberty Hall*, May 23 and 30, 1810.

[45] *Ibid.*, August 22, 1810.

[46] *Commentator*, April 17, 1810; *Muskingum Messenger*, July 7, 1810.

[47] For the immediate effect of the Sweeping Resolution, and the rise of the Saint Tammany Societies in Ohio, see Utter, *Saint Tammany in Ohio*, in *Miss. Val. Historical Review*, vol. XV, pp. 321-340.

[48] *Scioto Gazette*, September 5, 1810.

public favor. Even after the officers had published the Saint Tammany constitution in full, so they claimed, a public meeting at Columbia passed resolutions of protest against the restricted membership, which included only "complaisant tools." In the bombastic style so often found in political documents at this time, these resolutions called upon all good citizens to aid the fight against this "mongrel brood with breech-clouts and bear-skins in their midnight wigwams." [49] The leaders of Saint Tammany, however, continued to defend their order. In a "long talk" delivered before the Cincinnati wigwam, Elias Glover in typical fashion ignored the chief criticisms that had been directed against the organization, and appealed chiefly to frontier prejudices against British oppressors.[50] These efforts succeeded in blocking temporarily the aims of the more conservative Republicans, but in the legislature that was elected in the fall of 1811, they secured an act that practically nullified the Sweeping Resolution.[51] This meant the final triumph of the more conservative element in Ohio, in its fight against the Virginia clique and an excess of democracy.

In spite of their internal dissensions the Republicans as a party dominated Ohio from the time that statehood, and manhood suffrage, became a reality. Moreover, the two factions united usually in support of Jefferson as the representative of the political ideals of the Western country. Thus, at a "large and respectable" meeting of the Republican citizens of Cincinnati to celebrate the repeal of the Alien and Sedition Acts, toasts "were drank" to Jefferson, "the mild philosopher and the man of the people," to America, an asylum ready to welcome "congenial" aliens, and to the liberty of the press.[52] Also, upon the eve of the presidential election of 1804, the voters were urged to beware of the tricks of the "monarchists" (*i.e.* the Federalists), and to vote for true

[49] *Western Spy*, April 27, 1811.
[50] *Ibid.*, May 25, 1811.
[51] *Laws of Ohio*, Tenth General Assembly, pp. 23-24.
[52] *Western Spy*, July 3, 1802.

Republican electors. Jefferson's victory was, of course, hailed with great joy.[53] This enthusiastic support for Jefferson was shown, too, in the local comments upon the purchase of Louisiana. The transfer of Louisiana to France, and the closing of the port of New Orleans had come as a veritable calamity to the people of Ohio, and there was a general feeling that this intolerable situation should be ended in short order, along with occasional intimations that, if necessary, the people of the West would take matters into their own hands. However, public opinion was probably better represented by a resolution of the legislature that expressed full confidence in the administration. When the Louisiana Purchase Treaty was finally announced, the papers gave the news much space, and strongly commended Jefferson for his action in a matter "of such infinite importance to our Western country." At Chillicothe the inhabitants held a celebration in honor of this "glorious acquisition," and the patriotic orators waxed eloquent upon this peaceful triumph of the Republicans. The legislature, too, expressed its full "approbation" of this latest addition to American territory.[54]

Jefferson's popularity in Ohio helps to explain the local attitude toward Burr and his so-called plot. The superficial details are well known.[55] In April, 1805, Burr on his way West to recoup his fortunes stopped at Marietta where he met Blennerhassett, and at Cincinnati where he became well acquainted with Senator John Smith, who was then in high esteem in the Republican councils. Burr proceeded South, then to Washington, and in August, 1806, he returned to Marietta. Meantime rumors flew thick and fast through the Western country, especially after the news spread that Burr had contracted for ten boats to be built on the Muskingum.

[53] *Scioto Gazette*, October 15 and 29, and November 5 and 12, 1804.

[54] *Western Spy*, March 9, 1803; *Scioto Gazette*, July 30 and October 8, 1803, and April 30 and June 4, 1804; *Laws of Ohio*, First General Assembly, First Session, p. 149, Second Session, p. 292.

[55] For an exhaustive account of Burr's proceedings in Ohio, see Joseph E. Holliday, *The Burr Conspiracy in Ohio*, M. A. Thesis in the Library of the University of Cincinnati.

The agitation over Louisiana was so recent that the loyal Republicans of Ohio were still on the alert for plots to separate the Western country from the Union, and strange reports had come from the East regarding Burr's plans. In this atmosphere of suspicion there appeared a series of articles in the *Ohio Gazette* signed by *A Querist,* supposedly Blennerhassett, which advocated the separation of the Western country from the Eastern states. *Regulus,* according to common report Jacob Burnet, answered in vigorous fashion, and the popular fancy was soon ready to accept any rumor, no matter how slight the foundations. Next Jefferson in characteristic fashion sent his confidential agent, John Graham, to prepare his loyal friends, Thomas Worthington, now a senator, and Edward Tiffin, the governor of Ohio, for further developments. With the local setting prepared, Jefferson issued his proclamation, November 27, 1806, against "certain persons" who were conspiring to organize a military expedition against Spain. Governor Tiffin promptly followed it with a message that warned the legislature of the dangerous situation, and four days later, in secret session, the members passed a law that forbade any proceedings that might be interpreted as hostile to the peace of the United States. A few hotheads even proposed to suspend the writ of habeas corpus, but the mere mention of such a "dangerous principle" aroused so loud a protest that the legislature did not comply.[56] Meanwhile Burr had passed down the Ohio amid great excitement, and the militia was called out at Cincinnati. The fiasco at Richmond soon followed, and later came the futile attempt to try Burr and Blennerhasset in the Ohio supreme court sitting at Chillicothe.

A careful review of the evidence regarding Burr's activities in Ohio leads to the conclusion that the Republican governor and other state officials put the worst possible interpretation upon all suspicious circumstances, and seized

[56] *Western Spy,* December 16, 1806, to January 6, 1807; *Liberty Hall,* November 25, 1806, to January 6, 1807; *Laws of Ohio,* Fifth General Assembly, pp. 45-49.

upon every pretext in order to discredit Burr personally. Jefferson himself had taken part in the general outcry through his confidential agent, nor was he probably greatly disturbed by the complete discomfiture of his greatest rival in the Republican party. Although Burr's actual designs will probably never be definitely determined, John W. Browne, the intelligent editor of *Liberty Hall*, gave a plausible explanation when he claimed that Burr was a mere land jobber who proposed to settle his lands on the Ouachita with emigrants from Ohio.[57] At least the incident had brought out the intense loyalty to Jefferson in Ohio, and at the same time it had revived the bitter feeling against the former Federalists. The sequel to this last unfortunate phase of the affair was the political persecution that drove Burr's friend, John Smith, from the Senate and eventually from Ohio.

The extreme partisanship that was displayed in the Burr episode was somewhat unusual in this early period of Ohio. There had been political dissensions, and occasionally rather extreme legislation, as in the outcry against the judges which came to a climax in the Sweeping Resolution. But once the people of Ohio had won the right to establish a state, they had carried on their government for the most part with a moderation that was indeed singular in so new a country. The constitution they adopted had included such generally accepted reforms as: virtually a manhood suffrage; the complete separation of church and state; and the removal of all property qualifications for office. True, there had been a regrettable restriction of the executive power, and a tendency to exalt unduly the legislative at the expense of the judiciary, but these features of the new constitution were readily explained by struggles of the colonial period that must still have been fresh in the minds of the Western settlers. Moreover, the members of the new state legislature did not customarily pass radical legislation, as St. Clair and his followers had predicted. Rather they accepted in its essentials the code which had been worked out in the terri-

[57] *Liberty Hall*, December 2, 1806.

torial period, and the alterations they made were chiefly intended either to simplify the processes of law, or else to meet the needs of a swiftly increasing population. By the outbreak of the War of 1812, marking the close of this early period, and less than twenty-five years after the first settlement, the political foundations of Ohio had been firmly laid, and the precedents that were set there inevitably influenced like developments in the remaining sections of the Old Northwest, as well as in the territory that lay west of the Mississippi River.

Chapter VI

INDIANA TERRITORY

THE division of the Northwest Territory in 1800 was a striking illustration of the value of that section of the Ordinance of 1787 which made possible the creation of such new administrative units as the increase in population made necessary. Indiana Territory, as it was first set off, included an extensive region that was bounded on the south by the Ohio, on the west by the Mississippi, and on the east by a line from the mouth of the Kentucky to Fort Recovery and then due north. That is, it included all of present-day Indiana, Illinois, and Wisconsin, the eastern section of Minnesota, and the western half of Michigan. In the enabling act for Ohio in 1802, Congress shifted the eastern Indiana boundary to a line running north from the mouth of the Miami, thus adding the "gore" in the southeast. The eastern section of Michigan, also, was tacked on to Indiana at this time, but in 1805 the entire Michigan region was set off as a separate territory.[1] Upper Louisiana, too, was joined to Indiana for a brief period, 1804–1805, although, like the one with Michigan, this union was so brief that it may be ignored in this survey of the development of Indiana Territory from its organization in 1800 up to the outbreak of the War of 1812. In this territory there were at first two distinct regions, with the Wabash River as the dividing line. Therefore any account of the early history of Indiana naturally falls into two divisions: first, the progress of the united territory on both sides of the Wabash, and second, the development of Indi-

[1] *Annals of Congress*, Sixth Congress, First Session, pp. 1498-1500; Eighth Congress, Second Session, pp. 1659-1660.

ana proper after the Illinois settlements were set off in 1809. When Indiana was first organized in 1800, its total white population was estimated at only 5,641. East of the Wabash, probably a fourth of the entire population was in the Vincennes district where there were chiefly French with an increasing number of Americans. In Clark's Grant north of Louisville, there were about nine hundred American settlers, and the annexation of the "gore" in 1802 added to this element which soon outnumbered the French in and around Vincennes. West of the Wabash, about two-fifths of the total population in 1800 dwelt in the Illinois settlements, which stretched along the east bank of the Mississippi for forty miles or so, from Kaskaskia to Cahokia.[2] While there were a few Americans in this distant region, the majority of its inhabitants were of French origin, and their settlements presented a peculiarly difficult problem to the new territorial government. Illiterate, usually not understanding English at all, they were a shiftless lot, unaccustomed to self-government, and chiefly concerned with the problem of securing a living. So far American rule over them had been almost a farce. Only one criminal court had been held there in five years, and land titles were in an almost hopeless confusion.[3] There were also a number of trading posts scattered through the territory, at Prairie du Chien, at Green Bay, at Peoria, and at several points on the Wabash. In spite of the comparatively few inhabitants, these posts were potential sources of danger to American control of this region. The traders, chiefly Canadian French, were hostile, and were continually intriguing among the Indians, in order to hold for Montreal the valuable fur trade of Indiana. Moreover, the Spanish in Louisiana across the Mississippi were none too friendly, and the Louisiana Purchase Treaty in 1803 ended a real threat. Altogether, it was quite obvious that if American power was to be firmly established throughout Indiana, it was neces-

[2] *Census of 1800*, pp. 1 and 87.
[3] *Annals of Congress*, Sixth Congress, First Session, pp. 1320-1321; Volney, *View of the Climate and Soil of the United States*, pp. 367-392.

sary to attract immigrants who would hold it against Indian attacks as well as foreign intrigues.

In the organization of Indiana Territory the responsible officers had before them the lessons from experience in the Northwest Territory. Their personnel, too, was exceptional from the two standpoints of personal ability and of practical training for the task before them. The governor, William Henry Harrison, a native Virginian now only twenty-seven, had already made a name for himself as aide-de-camp to Anthony Wayne, as secretary of the Northwest Territory, and then as first territorial delegate to Congress. In this last capacity he had secured the important Land Act of 1800, and had also put through the bill to create Indiana Territory. Intimately acquainted with frontier problems, young and enthusiastic, he was well fitted to govern the new territory. The secretary, John Gibson, was another well-chosen appointee. A Pennsylvanian by birth and a Revolutionary veteran, he had been an Indian trader at Fort Pitt, and had married the sister of Logan, the famous Mingo chief. Henry Vanderwigh, the most influential of the judges, after serving in the Revolution, had moved from New York to Vincennes where he had married into a prominent local family. William Clarke, another territorial judge, was a native of New York who, like Vanderburgh, had come to Vincennes after service with the Revolutionary army. As an Indian trader on a considerable scale, and the appointee to a number of local offices, he, too, had come to know frontier conditions from a practical point of view. Of the third judge, John Griffin, little is known of a definite nature, but he does not appear to have had frontier experience before his appointment in Indiana Territory. The salary allowed the governor, $2,000.00, was an ample one, but the allowance to each judge, $800.00, was altogether inadequate, and in 1807 Congress increased it to $1,200.00.[4]

[4] *Petition,* Judges of Indiana Territory, December 23, 1803, *Indiana Territorial Papers,* Senate Files, 2664; *Annals of Congress,* Ninth Congress, Second Session, p. 127.

The practical experience of the chief officers whose duty it was to organize Indiana Territory was in decided contrast to the situation in the Northwest Territory, where at the outset Governor St. Clair alone had had any actual contact with the frontier. Moreover, the task confronting the territorial officers in Indiana was a much simpler one than had been the case in the Northwest Territory. In Indiana the framework of government had been established for fully a decade, and there was an elaborate code of laws to serve as a basis for future legislation. The chief problems of the newly appointed territorial officers, then, were to secure actual enforcement of the laws, and to hold the Indians in check. For both these tasks Harrison and at least three of his colleagues possessed essential qualities coupled with much practical experience. The Territory of Indiana was formally organized July 22, 1800, when John Gibson, the secretary, took charge of affairs in the absence of Harrison, who arrived six months later. During the five years of rule by the governor and the judges, Harrison, by tactfully avoiding any appearance of arbitrary policy, managed to escape much of the unpopularity from which St. Clair had suffered. The executive proceedings for this period show the usual appointments, along with many proclamations. However, these latter items did not set up arbitrary regulations as St. Clair had done in the Illinois country, and Sargent at Vincennes, but they merely enforced existing laws, or else carried out powers that were generally conceded to be within the governor's prerogative.[5] Thus, soon after his arrival Harrison organized Clark's Grant as Clark County, and formed Dearborn County from the "gore," thus securing more effective administration in two regions which were then quite inaccessible from Vincennes. He issued a number of proclamations, also, to put an end to unlawful practices by Indian traders, to stop encroachments upon Indian lands, and to control the sale of liquor to the Indians. In other proclama-

[5] *Executive Journals of Indiana Territory*, 1800-1816, *passim*, in *Indiana Historical Society Publications*, vol. III, no. III.

tions, Harrison called attention to the territorial laws to prevent disorders among the American population, especially those against drunkenness and rioting in public places. He admonished good citizens to aid in the enforcement of the law by assisting in the arrest of the drunken and disorderly persons who "infest" the streets of Vincennes, and of those who sold liquor or otherwise violated the Sabbath.

The same sensible conservatism that was shown in administrative affairs was evident in the legislative proceedings of the governor and the judges. As the laws of the Northwest Territory at the time of division remained in force in Indiana, they merely adopted additional measures as new and urgent demands arose. During the four legislative sessions, 1800–1805, the bulk of the laws which the governor and the judges adopted came from the Code of Virginia, Harrison's native home, and that of Kentucky, from which so many of the Indiana pioneers had migrated, with only two from the Pennsylvania Code.[6] Occasionally local needs were so difficult to meet that the governor and judges interpreted quite liberally their legislative powers, and combined into a single act sections of laws from different states. They even passed one act that was taken from the codes of both Virginia and the Northwest Territory. In order to give the governor power to license ferries, they were obliged to enact an original law, although they carefully explained this disregard of the Ordinance. They passed resolutions, also, to alter minor laws, repealing especially the requirement of an examination for admission to the bar, and empowering the governor to issue licenses to all applicants. Nor did the governor and the judges make many changes in the legal and administrative system already established under the Northwest Territory, and those few were made necessary by a sparser population. Taxation was an exceedingly important and also quite a difficult problem in these early days of

[6] *Laws of Indiana*, Philbrick, ed., *Illinois Historical Collections*, vol. XXI, pp. 1-87; Howe, *The Laws and Courts of the Northwest and Indiana Territories*, in *Indiana Historical Society Publications*, vol. II, pp. 3-35.

Indiana Territory. What little property existed was chiefly of an agricultural nature, and there was real danger that an unwise system of taxation might drive settlers away. Doubtless with this consideration in mind, the governor and the judges passed an act that was admittedly based upon the tax law of 1799 for the Northwest Territory, but with modifying clauses that were adopted from the Virginia Code, and probably even with original features. So far as local taxation was concerned this new measure followed the law already in force, except that it listed slaves as well as servants, and altered the schedule of articles subject to taxation. While it retained the general land tax, it handed over to the sheriffs rather than the county treasurers the duty of collecting the taxes. The financial returns, when this measure was put in force, were not at all satisfactory, and in 1803 the governor and the judges, seemingly at their wits' end, represented to Congress the need for some additional source of territorial revenue, in order to erect much needed jails, courthouses, and other public buildings. They suggested as a solution a small tax upon Indian traders, but Congress did not see fit to grant them the necessary power. The financial situation of the territory continued to grow worse until finally Harrison could not even secure sufficient funds to publish the territorial laws, as a necessary step in their enforcement.[7]

Slavery presented an especially difficult problem in this early period. From the very beginning of territorial government, and even before, there was a determined effort to establish it throughout Indiana. Fundamentally this move arose from the existence of slavery under the French, a precedent that had been followed by the British after 1763, and by the shadowy régime which Virginia established in the Old Northwest after the Revolution. The Ordinance of 1787 with its

[7] Memorial, November 19, 1803, and Report of Committee, January 10, 1804, *Indiana Territorial Papers*, House Files, 2661 and 2671; Secretary of State to Harrison, December 21, 1803, and June 14, 1804, *Ibid.*, B. I. A. Domestic, 2669 and 2682; *Harrison's Messages and Letters*, Esarey, ed., vol. I, pp. 49-50.

prohibition of slavery in the Old Northwest had naturally stirred up the slaveholders among the inhabitants, in spite of St. Clair's assurance that the anti-slavery clause was not retroactive. Many of the French settlers in the Illinois country, thoroughly alarmed, now migrated across the Mississippi to Spanish territory, taking their slaves with them, and those that remained were anxious for a more reassuring guarantee of their rights than a mere opinion from St. Clair. Still another important source of pro-slavery agitation was the great need for settlers, and the hope that, with the complete anti-slavery triumph in the Ohio constitutional convention, settlers from Kentucky would be attracted into Indiana, if they were allowed to bring in their slaves. Nor did Harrison, who had been reared upon a slave plantation, make any attempt to discourage this movement.[8] The leaders came from the Illinois settlements where, in 1800, 107 of the 135 slaves in the territory were held. The chief support east of the Wabash came from the Vincennes district, the home of the remaining slaves.[9] In 1796 four of the most important men in the Illinois country petitioned Congress that they should be allowed to keep the slaves they already held and to bring in others, and that the status of the children of slave parents should be definitely settled. These concessions, they represented, were necessary in order to secure a supply of labor, and to prevent the removal of the Illinois settlers en masse to Spanish territory across the Mississippi. Shortly after Indiana Territory was set off, another petition of much the same tenor was presented to the Senate, and, like the first one, it was promptly tabled.[10]

The Illinois settlers were persistent, and when Harrison came to their section on official business, they seized the opportunity to urge upon him their views with regard to slavery. Upon his return to Vincennes he called for the elec-

[8] Dunn, *Indiana*, ch. VI, and especially pp. 309-314.
[9] *Census of 1800*, p. 87.
[10] Petitions from St. Clair and Randolph counties, 1796 and 1800, *Indiana Slavery Petitions and Papers*, Dunn, ed., pp. 447-455; *Indiana Territorial Papers*, Senate Files, 2646.

tion of twelve delegates to a convention that should consider the repeal of the anti-slavery clause in the Ordinance. In justification of this move, Harrison claimed he had received "proof" that "a very large majority" in the territory favored it. Some of the ablest and most influential men in the territory were members of this convention, which met at Vincennes December 20, 1802. The delegates elected Harrison president, and chose John Rice Jones, the territorial attorney-general, as the secretary. After a week's deliberation they agreed upon a memorial to Congress for a suspension for ten years of the anti-slavery clause of the Ordinance, upon the plea that it had driven from the territory many valuable citizens who owned slaves.[11] In the House a committee, of which John Randolph was chairman, strongly opposed the memorial, and cited the example of Ohio as proof that the admission of slaves was not necessary in order to induce settlers to come into the Old Northwest. The committee deemed it "highly dangerous and inexpedient to impair a provision wisely calculated to promote the happiness and prosperity of the northwestern country, and to give strength and security to that extensive frontier." The House did not pass formally upon this report, but doubtless through pro-slavery manipulation, it was referred to another committee headed by the younger Cæsar Rodney of Delaware. A year later, this second committee recommended an amendment to the Ordinance that would have permitted the introduction of slaves into Indiana Territory for the next ten years, with the limitation that the descendants of these same slaves should automatically become free, the males at twenty-five and the females at twenty-one. Action on this report was delayed, and it was finally referred to another committee, which after a long delay also favored the suspension of the anti-slavery clause as a highly desirable means to "accelerate" the population of

[11] Memorial of Convention, December 28, 1802, and Other Documents, *Indiana Territorial Papers*, House Files, 2657; *Indiana Executive Journals*, pp. 113-114.

Indiana Territory. The anti-slavery forces were sufficiently strong to table this report.[12]

Having failed to secure action through Congress, the pro-slavery party now turned to the territorial government, and induced the governor and judges to adopt an important act from the Virginia Code that compelled all negroes and mulattoes who came into the territory under contract of service to serve for the stipulated period. This law provided ample protection against the ill treatment of these persons, but it also included rather drastic provisions for dealing with those who were idle or lazy, or with runaways, and permitted the sale of slaves, subject only to the nominal restriction that it should be with the consent of the individual who was disposed of in such fashion.[13] This act, virtually establishing slavery in Indiana, represented the definite triumph of the pro-slavery party, and Harrison's rôle in the affair aroused much criticism from the anti-slavery party whose ranks were constantly increasing in the section of Indiana that lay east of the Wabash.

Meanwhile the pro-slavery party had been agitating for the second stage of territorial government with a legislative assembly. Quite evidently their purpose was to make slavery secure in Indiana by the consent of the popular representatives. The long-drawn-out effort to induce Congress to set aside the anti-slavery clause, and its final failure, doubtless strengthened their determination to settle the matter at once, and this was all the more desirable in view of the continual migration into Indiana of anti-slavery settlers. Harrison, however, opposed the transition to the second stage of government at this time, and in an open letter he pointed out the heavy taxation it would make necessary. This warn-

[12] Reports of Committees, etc., 1803-1806, *Indiana Slavery Petitions and Papers*, Dunn, ed., *Indiana Historical Society Publications*, vol. II, pp. 470-473, 476 and 494 ff; *Annals of Congress*, Ninth Congress, First Session, p. 293.

[13] Dunn, *Indiana*, pp. 299-301, 322-323; Webster, *William Henry Harrison's Administration of Indiana, Indiana Historical Society Publications*, vol. IV, no. 6, pp. 195-203.

ing effectually aroused public opinion, and the many land speculators, especially, were greatly alarmed over the prospect of an increase in their taxes. But the pro-slavery leaders continued to push their views, and Harrison found himself in a most embarrassing situation. Under the act that set off Indiana he was allowed to establish the second grade of government whenever he had "satisfactory evidence" that it was the wish of the majority of the inhabitants. After he had received a number of petitions in favor of the change he withdrew his opposition and ordered an election September 11, 1804, to ascertain the "wishes and desires of the freeholders," regarding the second grade of government.

The governor's call for an election brought forth a veritable deluge of articles in the *Indiana Gazette*.[14] *A Freeholder*, from Knox County, led the forces of opposition, and denied Harrison's right to call a special election. He charged that the governor had attempted to force the second grade of government upon the territory, just as he had worked for the slavery convention. *Gerald*, in reply, strongly defended Harrison, and other contributors, *A Citizen, A Plough Boy*, and *An Onlooker*, voiced the popular support of the change. The arguments of the advocates of the second grade of government were best summarized in the resolutions of a public meeting at Vincennes. Stressing the great difficulty to secure suitable laws under the restrictions imposed by the Ordinance, and the need for a delegate to present the needs of the territory to Congress, the resolutions pointed out that if the veto power of the governor became unbearable under the second grade of government, it was possible to seek his removal. The insinuation that there were not enough capable men in the territory to fill the additional offices they indignantly denied, and they maintained, too, that with careful economy the expenses of a territorial assembly could be met, while increasing settlement would quickly ease the general financial situation. In true frontier fashion these resolutions concluded with an appeal to democratic prin-

[14] *Indiana Gazette*, August 7–28, 1804.

ciples, asserting that their neighbors to the eastward looked "with contempt" upon their situation. Therefore "we presume that you cannot hesitate in deciding the question of either remaining in the condition of debased slaves, or assuming the dignified and independent rank of freemen." It is significant that these resolutions, as well as other pleas for the proposed change, did not display the personal antagonism toward Harrison that had been shown against St. Clair under similar circumstances. Nor did the election indicate a widespread demand for the second grade of government. Notice did not reach Wayne County, then attached to Indiana, in time, and even where the election was held, only a small proportion of the voters appeared. In Knox, Clark, and Randolph counties the advocates of the change were successful, but in Dearborn and St. Clair counties their opponents won. With a total vote of only 400 the former won by a majority of 138. The governor accepted the verdict, and called for the election, January 5, 1805, of a house of representatives.[15]

The first territorial assembly met July 29, 1805, inaugurating the second stage of government in Indiana Territory. Harrison, in his opening address to the two houses, called attention to a number of necessary reforms, including especially the control of the sale of liquor to the Indians, a codification of the laws, a revision of the militia laws, a more severe punishment for horse-stealing, and an effective revenue measure. In contrast to St. Clair in the Northwest Territory, he readily conceded the power of the assembly to create new counties, and he noted the need for a census in order to apportion representatives. In conclusion, Harrison cautioned the assembly to avoid the dissensions and jealousies that would inevitably retard the progress of the territory.[16] The members of this first territorial assembly showed a marked regard for the governor's recommendations and usually they enacted laws that met local needs much more

[15] *Indiana Executive Journals,* pp. 125-126; Dunn, *Indiana,* p. 324.
[16] *Harrison's Messages and Letters,* Esarey, ed., vol. I, pp. 152-159.

adequately than had been possible under the restrictions that the Ordinance imposed upon the governor and the judges.[17] This advantage was illustrated especially by the changes in legal procedure. In place of the expensive and complicated system of separate courts of common pleas, quarter sessions, and probate in each county, the assembly substituted a single county court of common pleas to hold six annual sessions. Over petty cases, justices of the peace continued to exercise jurisdiction, and thus saved many a long journey from the scattered settlements to the county seats. The assembly also took up such important matters in this rapidly growing frontier country as the validity of deeds, the partition of lands held in common, and the sale of land for debt. An act to permit aliens to hold land in the territory was somewhat in contrast to the usual frontier prejudice against foreigners. Another act showed considerable independence, in view of the governor's extensive powers of appointment, in provisions for the impeachment of any territorial officer, "for maladministration or corruption." Other laws regulated the elections, which the second grade of government made necessary, and required the sheriffs to take a census of all free male inhabitants, twenty-one and over, in order to apportion representation in the territorial assembly. Taxation formed another important subject of legislation, and the assembly provided for a general assessment as the basis for a sufficient tax rate to meet territorial requirements. These they kept within frugal limits, and for the year 1804–1805 the total budget was only $2,084.25, with allowances, for example, of only $250.00 to the auditor and the attorney-general respectively, $100.00 to the territorial treasurer, and a per diem of $2.00 to each member of the assembly, with a traveling allowance of $2.00 for every twenty miles.

The members of the first territorial assembly also passed

[17] *Laws of Indiana*, Philbrick, ed., *Illinois Historical Collections*, vol. XXI, pp. 91-218.

much miscellaneous legislation in their two sessions in 1805 and 1806. Determined to put a stop, if possible, to some of the more common crimes in Indiana, they made horse-stealing a capital crime for the first offense, and for the prevalent theft of hogs they prescribed imprisonment, and twenty-five to thirty-nine stripes upon the "bare back." Alterations in the branding marks of cattle and hogs that were found wandering in the woods were also to be severely punished. Nor was the welfare of the Indians neglected. The assembly prohibited the sale of liquor to them within thirty miles of the place where a council was sitting, or within forty miles of Vincennes. It even offered to put an end to all sales of liquor to the Indians, provided the neighboring states of Ohio and Kentucky, and Michigan and Upper Louisiana Territories took like action. Toward debtors the assembly showed the usual frontier leniency, permitting a bankrupt to secure his release from prison, provided he handed over all of his property to his creditors.

Other measures covered a wide range of subjects, but perhaps the most important act of this first territorial assembly in Indiana was a resolution, passed in December, 1806, for the codification of all the territorial laws. This important work was entrusted to a committee of two, John Rice Jones, a brilliant lawyer and a former attorney-general, and John Johnson, a member of the territorial lower house. The resolution directed them to bring all laws, or parts of laws on the same subject, under one head, to smooth out all discrepancies, and in general to make the laws "as complete as the nature of the case will admit." The fruit of their labors, in the form of a code of seventy-two laws, was officially approved, after careful consideration, at the next session of the assembly in 1807. Made up from laws of the Northwest Territory, from acts adopted by the governor and judges in Indiana, and from the acts of the first territorial assembly, the several sections of this code differed from the originals chiefly in a more systematic arrangement, and in a more

exact verbiage.[18] For example, the law regulating fees, which
the governor and judges had adopted from the codes of four
states, was now revised and extended to include the entire
list of officials who were compensated in this fashion. For
their laborious work, the two compilers of this Indiana code
received a joint fee of $250.00, and the assembly ordered
500 copies to be distributed through the territory. The code
of 1807, which is comparable in Indiana to the code of 1805
in Ohio, did away with misunderstandings as to the laws that
were actually in force, and it gave a definite basis for later
legislation in Indiana. Also, together with the territorial laws
passed in 1807 and 1808, it gave the separate government
established in Illinois in 1809 a code of laws that was based
upon the practical needs of frontier communities.

Finances played a leading part in the legislation passed
in 1807 and 1808 to supplement the code.[19] In opening the
assembly in 1807, Harrison called attention especially to
the very critical situation of the territorial treasury, with a
debt of $1,967.98 that was a real burden in view of the
slender financial resources. This deficit, it seems, was due
chiefly to the failure to list lands and to draw up abstracts
in the Illinois counties and in Knox County, where the land
system was still in an unsatisfactory condition. Measures
were passed to compel the collection of taxes in these counties but with little effect, to judge from the long lists of
delinquent lands that were offered for sale in Randoph
County alone.[20] To avoid such conditions in the future, the
assembly gave specific directions for listing all lands, and
for an assessment every four years, and authorized a yearly
tax for territorial purposes of 20 cents on the $100.00. They
altered, also, the act for county levies which the governor
and the judges had adopted from the Virginia Code, repeal-

[18] *Laws of Indiana*, Philbrick, ed., *Illinois Historical Collections*, vol. XXI,
pp. 223-548; Monks, *Courts and Lawyers of Indiana*, vol. I, pp. 184-185,
vol. II, p. 405.

[19] *Laws of Indiana*, Philbrick, ed., *Illinois Historical Collections*, vol.
XXI, pp. 551-674.

[20] *Harrison's Messages and Letters*, Esarey, ed., vol. I, pp. 229-236;
Western Sun, September 26, 1807, July 16 and 30, and November 12, 1808.

ing the poll tax on single men of small property and the tax on neat cattle, and authorizing, instead, a tax on "located lands" of 10 cents on the $100.00. Other acts dealt with crimes that were especially frequent in Indiana, and with a variety of local conditions, and altogether, the territorial legislature in Indiana, up to the separation from Illinois in 1809, had usually displayed much moderation and good sense.

From the beginning of the second grade of territorial government in 1805, the pro-slavery party men were exceedingly active, with their chief stronghold still in the Illinois settlements.[21] At first they were successful, securing an act in 1805 that went even further than the drastic law the governor and the judges had adopted in 1803, and practically removed all restrictions upon the introduction of slaves into the territory. The act also gave children of slaves a similar status, although it limited their term of service, the males until thirty years of age, the females until twenty-eight, and it forbade any attempt to free slaves or to remove them forcibly from the territory. The assembly completed its work by a memorial to Congress for the outright establishment of slavery in Indiana.[22] A petition from Randolph and St. Clair counties in Illinois heartily supported this pro-slavery measure. But another petition from the same locality scored the recent act for the introduction of slaves as a "violation of the Ordinance," and the Quaker inhabitants of Dearborn County in the "gore" petitioned to be joined to Ohio, professedly because of the great distance from Vincennes, but really because of their opposition to slavery.[23] These petitions were referred in the House to a committee, the chairman of which, James Mercer Garnett, was from Virginia. The committee's report, as was to be expected, opposed the petition from Dearborn County, but

[21] For a detailed account of the struggle to establish slavery in Indiana Territory, see Dunn, *Indiana*, chs. IX and X, *passim*.

[22] Memorial from Legislative Assembly of Indiana, August 19, 1805, *Indiana Territorial Papers*, House Files, 2699.

[23] Petitions, 1805, *Ibid.*, 2705, 2707, and 2715; *Indiana Slavery Petitions and Papers*, Dunn, ed., pp. 492-493.

favored the suspension of the slavery clause of the Ordinance, in order to "accelerate" the population of Indiana.[24] Congress took no immediate action, but an editorial and a number of communications in *Liberty Hall*, published in Cincinnati, took up the anti-slavery cause. In a reply in this same journal, *Eumenes*, hailing from Indiana, pictured the benefits to the slave who would be brought from the crowded fields of the South to the rich lands north of the Ohio.[25]

At the next session of the territorial assembly in the fall of 1806, the pro-slavery party strengthened its position by laws that virtually permitted the sale of slaves, or indentured servants as they were politely called, and drastically regulated their movements in the fashion of the Southern slave codes. Severe whipping was the penalty for the slaves who were found away from the homes of their masters without permission, or for those who took part in "riots, routs, unlawful assemblies, trespasses, and seditious speeches." This same session of the assembly sent resolutions to Congress for the suspension of the slavery clause in the Ordinance which, they claimed, had been passed unanimously. If Congress would adopt such a modification of the Ordinance, these resolutions represented, it would be approved by "nine-tenths of the good citizens," and some such action was necessary in order to attract slaveholders, and thus to increase the population. This memorial the House referred to a committee of which the chairman was Benjamin Parks, then territorial delegate from Indiana. Their report recommended the suspension of the slavery clause of the Ordinance, and it would probably have been adopted but for the protracted debate and the animosities that were stirred up in Congress at this time over the prohibition of the slave trade after 1808.[26]

[24] *Indiana Slavery Petitions and Papers*, Dunn, ed., pp. 494-497.
[25] *Liberty Hall*, September 17, 1805, to August 11, 1806, *passim*.
[26] Resolution, Legislative Assembly of Indiana (1806), *Indiana Territorial Papers*, Senate Files, 2728; *Annals of Congress*, Ninth Congress, Second Session, pp. 482-483; Dunn, *Indiana*, pp. 350-354.

Although the anti-slavery party had made considerable gains in the second territorial assembly which met August 17, 1807, their opponents were able to insert in the new territorial code the slavery legislation that had already been passed. They secured, too, the adoption of a memorial to Congress that strongly represented the "propriety" of admitting slaves, especially as the institution already existed in Indiana. The anti-slavery party, even if it had been outnumbered and seemingly outmaneuvered as well, was not without resources. At a public meeting in Clark County, a throng of its adherents passed resolutions that expressed "great anxiety" over the proposed introduction of slavery into the territory. They declared, also, that the people of Knox County had "decidedly opposed" the slavery convention in 1802, and that the memorial from the territorial assembly to Congress in 1805 had been forced through by "legislative legerdemain." The recent pro-slavery memorial had passed the legislative council only after much difficulty, they alleged, and had been signed by a president *pro tem*, in place of the actual president who had refused to sign it. In conclusion the resolutions proposed that, as a "vast emigration" into the territory was "decidedly" opposed to slavery, the matter should not be finally settled until Indiana was admitted as a state.[27]

The pro-slavery resolutions of the assembly and the protest from Clark County were both promptly forwarded to Congress, and there a decided change was evident in the attitude toward what was coming to be the annual pro-slavery memorial from Indiana. A committee of the Senate laconically reported that it was not "expedient" to suspend the slavery clause of the Ordinance. In the House the chairman of the committee to which these documents were referred was now Jacob Richards from a free state, Pennsylvania. In its report the committee supported the anti-slavery

[27] Resolutions, Legislative Assembly, September 19, 1807, and Petition from Inhabitants of Clark County, October, 1807, *Indiana Territorial Papers, House Files*, 2744 and 2746.

resolutions from Clark County, and recommended that, in view of the rapidly increasing population, it would be "improper" to legislate upon slavery in Indiana before the territory became a state. Doubtless the members of the committee were somewhat heartened in this report by a petition from the inhabitants of Dearborn County who again prayed to be annexed to Ohio, and this time cited openly, as justification, their strong disapproval of pro-slavery legislation in Indiana.[28] The anti-slavery faction was now making considerable gains in Indiana as well, and their supporters sent many petitions to the seventh territorial legislature which met in the fall of 1808. A typical one represented that the introduction of slavery would put an end to the large immigration into Indiana from the Eastern states, and from the anti-slavery population in the Southern states.[29]

The different petitions on slavery were referred to a committee in the Indiana lower house, the chairman of which was General Washington Johnston, a native of Virginia, a strong friend of Harrison, and one of the most influential men in the territory. The committee's report was an able document that displayed a keen insight into the situation. Pointing out that the law for the introduction of slaves had been greatly abused, and that actual slavery existed in Indiana, it stressed the far greater prosperity of the free states, and especially the tremendous development of Ohio, as an argument against a slave system which must in the end overturn the "republican virtues." If Indiana were opened up to slavery, the report pointed out, the large number of settlers who opposed it would be shut out, and the "internal tranquillity" of the Union would be proportionately threatened. Therefore, the committee deemed it inadvisable to petition Congress to modify the Ordinance. They also presented a bill to repeal the act for the introduction of slaves which the lower house passed unanimously, but the

[28] *Annals of Congress*, Tenth Congress, First Session, pp. 23-27, 816, 1331.
[29] Petition to Legislative Assembly of Indiana, October 19, 1808, *Indiana Territorial Papers*, House Files, 2761.

legislative council rejected.[30] The varying comments in the *Western Sun* on this report of General Johnston's committee reflected the divergent local views on slavery. General Johnston protested against the argument that slavery in Indiana would establish a large trade with New Orleans, and pointed out that in any case only a few persons would be benefited. But *Slim Simon* slyly recalled that Johnston himself had once advocated slavery, and *A Citizen of Vincennes* pointedly intimated that there had been much political hypocrisy in the anti-slavery statements of certain candidates in the recent elections. On the other hand, *Pop Gun* asserted that *Slim Simon* was merely trying to prove that slavery and republicanism were consistent. And so, with many long drawn out and windy articles, as was usual at the time, the debate degenerated into an acrimonious personal controversy.[31] The pro-slavery leaders still had sufficient power to win their last victory in Indiana in this session, in the form of a drastic act that forbade slaves or "servants of color" from assembling even for dancing or for reveling without their master's permission.

The struggle between the pro-slavery and the anti-slavery factions in Indiana had already become involved with the demand of the people of the Illinois settlements for a separate government. Aside from the different views regarding slavery that were held in the two sections of Indiana, on either side of the Wabash, there were other important reasons for this agitation. The difficulties of communication and the slight economic connections naturally divided the two regions, while from the administrative viewpoint the very unsatisfactory land situation and the general weakness of American control in Illinois demanded the presence and undivided attention of a strong executive.[32] One of the first

[30] Report, Committee of House of Representatives of Indiana, October 19, 1808, *Indiana Territorial Papers,* House Files, 2761; Webster, *Harrison's Administration in Indiana,* p. 221.

[31] *Western Sun,* January 28 to February 18, 1809.

[32] Volney, *View of the Climate and Soil of the United States,* pp. 331-351; Alvord, *The Illinois Country, 1673–1818,* pp. 404-427.

moves in the long-continued agitation for separation had been a petition to Congress in 1803 that, in view of the long distance from Vincennes, the Illinois settlements should be included in the proposed territory of Upper Louisiana. While a committee made an unfavorable report to the Lower House of Congress, the petition had stirred up much feeling in the territory. At its first opportunity the territorial house of representatives passed a resolution of protest against the attempts of "certain discontented, factious men" to attach the western counties to Upper Louisiana.[33] The more violent opponents of a division now took up the cudgels, and proposed that the entire Indiana Territory should be formed into a single state, to be divided later in accordance with the terms of the Ordinance. Harrison supported this proposal which favored the more populous eastern section, and purported resolutions were forwarded to Congress, with the claim that they had been signed by a "majority of the two houses respectively," although actually the house of representatives had rejected them. The inhabitants of the Illinois country continued to send Congress memorials which insisted upon a separation from Indiana. The population west of the Wabash, they claimed, numbered 4,311, but as they had been outvoted in the election upon the second grade of government, they now found themselves saddled with additional taxes. Moreover, to reach the territorial capital they must make an arduous journey across prairie lands, "which scarcely afford wood or water," and never would be settled. The petitioners scored a partial victory when a committee of the House reported that the memorial to form a single state from Indiana Territory "ought not to be granted." [34]

[33] Memorial from Illinois Settlements, 1803 and Resolution, Indiana House of Representatives, February 7, 1805, *Indiana Territorial Papers,* House Files, 2661 and 2667; *Annals of Congress,* Eighth Congress, First Session, pp. 489, 623.
[34] Petitions and other Documents, 1805, *Indiana Territorial Papers,* House Files, 2699, 2705, 2707, 2715; *Indiana Slavery Petitions and Papers,* Dunn, ed., p. 497.

The setting off of Michigan Territory in 1805 encouraged the Illinois settlers in their fight, and two years later a popular convention drew up a petition to Congress for a government like that of Michigan, "cheap, active, and liberal," since the population west of the Wabash was now supposed to number fully 5,000. A counter-petition from these same Illinois settlements scored the "machinations" of the persons who were working to divide the territory, and declared that the delegates to the "shorn" convention represented only a small faction of the inhabitants. In Congress a committee of the House, of which Benjamin Parke, the territorial delegate from Indiana, was chairman, considered these two petitions, and reported that it was "expedient" to divide Indiana Territory.[35] Petitions in favor of a division continued to pour in upon Congress. One in especial, which was openly hostile to Harrison, complained that slavery had virtually been established under his leadership, that he had carried on speculation in lands, and that he had not given Randolph County its due proportion of representation. Still another petition, signed, it was said, by ignorant French inhabitants, many of whom only made their marks, anxiously disavowed any support of the charges against Governor Harrison. All these petitions were referred in the House to a committee of which Matthew Lyon of Kentucky was chairman, and its report recited the various arguments in favor of a division. In view of the press of other business, the "unpromising aspect" of "fiscal concerns," and the "impolicy" of increasing territorial governments unless it were "manifestly necessary," the report held that it would be "inexpedient" at that time to grant Illinois a separate government.[36]

Finally, in 1808 the agitators for a division of Indiana

[35] Memorials, 1807, *Indiana Territorial Papers,* House Files, 2732 and 2733; *Annals of Congress,* Ninth Congress, Second Session, pp. 590, 624.

[36] Petitions from Inhabitants of Illinois, etc., 1807–1808, *Indiana Territorial Papers,* House Files; *Annals of Congress,* Tenth Congress, First Session, pp. 2067-2068.

assured the success of their cause when they formed an alliance with the anti-slavery party east of the Wabash, and elected Jesse B. Thomas as the territorial delegate, upon a platform that favored the setting off of Illinois. The Indiana lower house left no doubt as to the bargain that had been struck, resolving that owing to the "great and increasing discontents" west of the Wabash, separation was the "only means" . . . "of restoring harmony." Although the legislative council refused to pass this resolution, it was forwarded to Congress, and the fight over separation now became a vigorous one. Many inhabitants of Knox County, especially, strongly opposed the change, claiming that it would increase their taxes, and pointing out that Vincennes was equidistant from either boundary of the existing territory. On the other hand, Congress received a report from the grand jury of St. Clair County that set forth a long list of grievances, and prayed for relief through a separate government.[37] The battle was really won in Congress when the Lower House referred the entire matter of separation to a committee headed by Jesse B. Thomas. Their report was convincing in its arguments. Citing the provisions of the Ordinance that fixed the Wabash as a dividing line, it declared that as there were fully 11,000 inhabitants in the western section, the financial problem of the proposed territory could be taken care of. Also, the distance of the Illinois settlements from Vincennes had greatly weakened executive control, and if the division was made, government would be greatly strengthened. Moreover, a "large majority" of the inhabitants favored separation. In view of all these considerations the report recommended that it was "expedient" to form a separate territory west of the Wabash, and brought in a bill for that purpose. In the debate that followed, the opposition did not present any effective arguments, and the

[37] Petitions, Resolutions, etc., 1808, *Indiana Territorial Papers*, House Files; Dunn, *Indiana*, pp. 376-377; Webster, *Harrison's Administration in Indiana*, p. 221; *Annals of Congress*, Tenth Congress, Second Session, p. 633.

long struggle was finally ended by the act that separated the new territory of Illinois from Indiana.[38]

After March 1, 1809, when the territory of Illinois was supposed to have been formally set off, Indiana developed as a fairly homogeneous territory, until the outbreak of the War of 1812 and the accompanying troubles with the Indians temporarily halted its progress. The most pressing issue that presented itself to the inhabitants of the diminished Indiana Territory was the recognition of slavery. The outcome was certain, for by 1810, Clark, Harrison, and Dearborn counties, the strongholds of the anti-slavery faction, contained more than sixty-seven and a half per cent of the inhabitants of Indiana. In Dearborn County, too, there were many Quaker emigrants who had left Georgia and the Carolinas because of their anti-slavery views, and who had been among the aggressive leaders in the fight with the pro-slavery element of the Illinois settlements. In the opinion of these and other anti-slavery men, it was high time to take some positive action in Indiana. The twenty-eight slaves, chiefly in the Vincennes district, in 1800, had grown, according to the census of 1810, to two hundred and thirty-seven.[39] The territorial legislature put a damper upon any hope for continued increase in slaves when at its first session, after the separation from Illinois in November, 1810, it summarily repealed all the legislation that had permitted slaves to be brought into Indiana, and added severe penalties for any attempts to remove negroes from the territory without legal proceedings.[40] Gradually the slaves already in Indiana died, and as none came in to fill their places slavery disappeared. The final triumph of the anti-slavery party came in the state constitutional convention of 1816, when its members followed the example of Ohio, and adopted the anti-slavery clause of the Ordinance.

[38] *Annals of Congress,* Tenth Congress, Second Session, pp. 971-973, 1093-1094, 1808-1810.

[39] *Census for 1800,* p. 87; *Census for 1810,* p. 86; Young, *History of Wayne County, Indiana,* pp. 26-30.

[40] *Laws of Indiana,* Third General Assembly, First Session, pp. 54-55.

In the brief period between the separation from Illinois in 1809 and the outbreak of war in 1812, the Indiana territorial assembly passed much constructive legislation in addition to the anti-slavery act.[41] To provide more effective local government for the growing population, it passed acts to create additional counties, to revise the judicial system, to require the recording of town plots, and for kindred needs that arose with the increasingly complex life in a territory that a scant ten years before had been a wilderness. The public finances continued to be a source of much concern, with the taxes which were due from the Illinois counties before the separation in 1809 still unpaid, in spite of efforts to collect them by suits. Nor were collections within Indiana itself at all satisfactory, and especially was this true of the taxes upon the extensive landholdings of non-residents. Conditions became so bad that the third territorial assembly adjourned December 9, 1811, with a balance of only $3.00 in the treasury.[42] Attempts were made to relieve the situation, but the confusion that soon came with the outbreak of war prevented any really effective adjustment of finances at this time. Among the miscellaneous acts passed during the years 1809–1812, was one in response to repeated representations from Harrison as to the need for more assured compensation, for better discipline, and for more frequent drills of the militia.[43] While they ignored part of Harrison's very enlightened recommendations, the members of the assembly at least made provision for a more general understanding of militia obligations. Closely connected with this act was an attempt to improve relations with the Indians by a more careful regulation of trade, and notably of the liquor traffic. One significant clause in this act, which was doubtless aimed at the many local critics of Harrison's policies, imposed a heavy fine upon "any mischievous individuals" who went

41 Laws of Indiana, Third General Assembly, First and Second Sessions.
42 Western Sun, December 26, 1811.
43 Harrison's Messages and Letters, Esarey, ed., vol. I, pp. 380, 487-496, 547-548.

among the Indians with the deliberate intention of defeating
the aims of the United States or of Indiana Territory. Other
acts incorporated the New Hope Baptist church in Dearborn County, the "Indiana church," and the Roman Catholic church at Vincennes, this last measure a striking illustration of the broad-minded tolerance of this predominantly
American and Protestant population. Still another measure
ordered a road to be laid out on the banks of the Wabash
that would be sufficiently wide for two wagons to pass.

Although the territorial government had made steady
progress both before and after the separation from Illinois
in 1809, the Hoosier genius for politics had shown itself in
the constant factional controversy from the very organization of Indiana. The various elements in the population were
all represented in these petty squabbles, with the exception
of the French who, with characteristic indifference, usually
left the business of governing to their American neighbors.
An outstanding figure in these political quarrels in pioneer
Indiana was William McIntosh, a sturdy Scotch fighter who
was first the warm friend, and then the bitter enemy, of
Governor Harrison. John Rice Jones, the co-author of the
code of 1805, a brilliant Welsh lawyer who later moved to
the Illinois settlements, held many local offices before he,
too, quarreled with Harrison. Another picturesque politician
was Jonathan Jennings, one of the champions of the anti-
slavery cause, reared among the Scotch-Irish of the Pennsylvania frontier, who led the anti-Harrison forces, and was
elected territorial delegate to Congress at the age of twenty-
five. His chief opponent in Indiana, Thomas Randolph, was
one of a small band of Virginians, strong supporters of Harrison, which included General William Johnston, who finally
went over to the anti-slavery side, for political reasons so it
was hinted. The most important personage of them all was
William Henry Harrison, the courtly and magnetic young
governor, primarily a military man, but an able executive
who tended occasionally to depart from the impartial attitude demanded by his high office. Around these leaders cen-

tered the political controversies of the Indiana frontier, which were made the more vital by the very provincialism of the issues at stake, and the isolation of these backwoods settlements from the great centers of population. Lengthy communications in the columns of the *Western Sun* testify to the activities of these leading politicians, as well as those of lesser note.[44]

A severe handicap to political activities in early Indiana was the difficulty to secure effective organization in such widely separated settlements and with so many obstacles to communication. Usually candidates for office printed notices in the *Western Sun*, and occasionally they added statements of their platforms. They also distributed handbills, and public meetings were the chief means of naming or endorsing a candidate, as the one at Corydon in 1809 which supported Thomas Randolph as territorial delegate to Congress. The Republican Corresponding Societies spread across the border from Ohio, but difficulties of communication doubtless proved an effective barrier to this form of political organization in the early days of Indiana Territory.[45] Frequently there were prolonged and bitter controversies in the columns of the *Western Sun* before an election. Slavery was an especially fruitful source of trouble, and at one time partisan communications became so numerous and bulky that the editor was obliged to call attention to the necessity of prepaying the postage, and of sending remittances for the space they occupied in his paper. Even then they were so virulent in their personal attacks that the bewildered editor was at his wit's end, bemoaning the fact that although he wished "to act impartially" he was obliged to exercise discretion for the sake of the public interest. One peacemaker, evidently

[44] *Western Sun*, July 11, 1807, *ff.;* Goebel, *William Henry Harrison*, ch. III; Dunn, *Indiana*, chs. VIII-XI.

[45] *Western Sun*, files 1807–1812, especially April 15 and 22, 1809, and March 10, 1810, and handbills bound with these numbers; Resolution, Republican Corresponding Society of Brookville, October 26, 1811, *Indiana Territorial Papers*, Senate Files, 2802.

in ironic vein, called upon the women of Indiana, the "daughters of Fredonia," to put an end to this excessive faction. *A Citizen of Vincennes* proposed a broad political division in Indiana into Federalists and Republicans, and the editor of the *Western Sun* himself finally took a hand, pleading for independence in voting for men who were strictly republican and of unquestioned honesty.[46]

The intensity of political jealousies in Indiana was well illustrated by the Gwathmey incident in 1808. Trouble first arose over the appointment of Samuel Gwathmey, a member of the legislative council, as register of the newly opened Federal land office at Jeffersonville. As a territorial law made Federal officers ineligible to either house of the assembly, the house of representatives soon asked the governor whether Gwathmey had resigned from the council. Receiving an evasive reply, they promptly made nominations to fill the supposedly vacant place, but the legislative council rebuked such presumption, asserting that they themselves were the proper judges of the qualifications of their own members. The representatives, however, adopted a resolution of protest, which they sent to the President, and two years later Jonathan Jennings, as chairman of a committee, proposed a resolution in the House that declared all officers holding commissions under the governor to be ineligible to the territorial assembly.[47] Actually, personal hostility toward Harrison seems to have played a large part in the Gwathmey incident. Indeed the governor's vigorous policies had aroused hostility from the very start, although, in contrast to St. Clair in the Northwest Territory, he had usually paid attention to public opinion. One of his most persistent enemies, William McIntosh, who was a bitter opponent of the second grade of government, personally attacked Harrison in the

[46] *Western Sun,* November 19, 1808, January 28, March 4 and 18, 1809, and March 11 and 31, 1810.

[47] Resolutions, Indiana House of Representatives, October 6, 1808, *Indiana Territorial Papers,* B. R. L. 2755; *Annals of Congress,* Eleventh Congress, Third Session, pp. 452-453.

Indiana Gazette in a series of articles that had been inspired, it was whispered, by the land speculators and by the Indian traders who smarted under his strict regulations. Harrison's friends quickly sprang to his defense, and the quarrel came to a climax when McIntosh openly charged that Harrison had stirred up the Indians by cheating them out of their lands. The sequel was Harrison's famous suit for slander, with a verdict that was a complete vindication. Probably of a like origin were Dr. Samuel McKee's charges that Harrison had taken part in land speculations. This time Harrison publicly defended himself in a letter to the *Western Sun,* and forced McKee to retract. Still another famous attack, in the *Letters of Decius,* was published in 1805, and recounted a long list of alleged abuses. These charges, also, Harrison countered in effective fashion.[48]

Much of the hostility shown in the personal attacks upon Harrison was probably due to his tendency to take sides, notably in the controversy over slavery. But in a frontier section any action on his part to restrict the popular will, as it was expressed in legislation, would inevitably arouse antagonism. Thus, in 1808 when he vetoed two acts dealing with the judicial system, even though he carefully explained his reasons, there was much popular resentment over this assumed indication of the governor's determination to dominate the assembly. This prejudice is even supposed to have influenced somewhat the election of Jesse B. Thomas, an avowed opponent of the governor, as territorial delegate.[49] Again, in the bitter contest in 1811 for this same office between Jonathan Jennings and Thomas Randolph, Harrison was accused of attempts to influence Randolph's election, "by haranguing the electors at the polls, by riding through the country, and by writing and sending into many, if not all the

[48] Goebel, *William Henry Harrison,* pp. 63-64, 125; *Harrison's Messages and Letters,* Esarey, ed., vol. I, pp. 509-510; *Indiana Gazette,* September 11 and 18, 1804; *Western Sun,* August 15 and 22, and September 5 and 12, 1807.

[49] *Harrison's Messages and Letters,* Esarey, ed., vol. I, pp. 319 and 320; *Western Sun,* November 19, 1808.

counties in the territory, electioneering letters." [50] Soon Harrison again aroused the popular wrath, this time by his veto of an act to move the territorial capital. The supporters of the measure intimated that the veto was due to the governor's own personal interests, and they induced a "large and respectable" assembly at Madison to send a protest to Congress. The presentation of this memorial gave Jonathan Jennings a favorable opportunity to lament the "general prevalence" of party spirit in Indiana, "from the executive to the lowest—the judicial officers not excepted—insomuch as to corrupt the fountain of justice." By such representations Jennings secured a resolution for an inquiry, but Harrison's friends were sufficiently influential to have the matter dropped.

The indirect method of attack was a favorite device of the opponents of Harrison's reappointment as governor of Indiana Territory. However, at least one bitter partisan, who wrote directly to the President and the Senate, revived the McKee charges of land frauds. This letter also charged that Harrison had signed the act that permitted slavery under color of indenture, and that he had taken advantage of his position as superintendent of Indian affairs to take part in an extensive trade with the red men. These facts, the writer alleged, were common knowledge in the territory, but the *Western Sun* and the Louisville paper had refused to print any statements in detraction of Harrison. A petition from Harrison County, also, protested against a reappointment, chiefly upon the ground that as Harrison did not have the "same sentiment" as the anti-slavery party, there would be a "continual conflict" if he remained as governor. [51]

But Harrison had many warm friends who had access to the public ear through the local press. His general popularity was shown by many toasts at Fourth of July banquets, as

[50] Petitions to Congress, 1811, *Indiana Territorial Papers*, House Files, 2803.

[51] Petitions, 1809 and 1811, *Indiana Territorial Papers*, House and Senate Files; *Annals of Congress*, Twelfth Congress, First Session, pp. 1247-1248.

at Vincennes, in 1807, when a large company applauded his "approved zeal" for the interests of the Union and the prosperity of the territory. Moreover, his friends rallied to support him for reappointment.[52] In 1808 in the Illinois settlements there was a significant toast, that the governor "may continue by his upright conduct to deserve the approbation of all good men, and by his wisdom to defeat the malice of his enemies." [53] In 1809 the two houses of the territorial assembly, the lower house unanimously, the legislative council by a vote of three to one, passed a resolution that favored the reappointment of Harrison "in their names and in the names of their constituents." This should be done, since he had the good wishes of the "great majority" of the citizens, was sincerely attached to the Union, was capable of promoting the interests of the territory "in superior degree," and was to be commended especially for his "wise, disinterested" management of Indian affairs. A meeting of militia officers at Vincennes likewise favored a reappointment, in view of the effective work which Harrison had already done in the training and organization of the militia, and of the need for a military man of his superior talents at this critical juncture. Even from Harrison County there came a petition which, counteracting the anti-slavery charges from this same county, emphasized Harrison's "paternal solicitude for the peace and dignity of the community," and his consistent regard for the "true interests of his Atlantic brethren." [54] These favorable representations won, and Harrison was reappointed governor of Indiana Territory. The editor of the *Western Sun* was especially elated, since "notwithstanding all the charges which malevolence" could bring, Harrison had not lost a single vote in the Senate.[55] A "numerous meeting" of citizens, at Vincennes apparently, applauded the tranquillity they had already enjoyed, and de-

[52] *Western Sun,* July 18, 1807.
[53] *Missouri Gazette,* July 26, 1808.
[54] Memorial and Other Papers, 1809, *Indiana Territorial Papers,* Senate Files.
[55] *Western Sun,* January 20, 1810.

clared they had no desire to change from the second grade
of government, so long as Harrison remained in control.
They praised, too, his "laborious assiduity, patient investigation, and intrepid conduct," and expressed the "entire confidence" of the people of Indiana in him. In like vein late in
1811 the Indiana house of representatives resolved that it
was the "earnest desire" of their constituents that Harrison
should again be reappointed, in view of his "integrity" and
the "highly honorable and distinguished" manner in which
he had conducted the Tippecanoe campaign.[56]

Local issues, vital as they were, did not wholly absorb the
attention of the citizens of Indiana Territory, and occasionally some incident out of the ordinary brought to the surface
the sturdy support which these Hoosier pioneers, in common
with other early settlers in the Old Northwest, gave to the
Federal Union and to Jeffersonian republicanism. This attitude was especially in evidence during the agitation in Indiana over Burr's intrigues in the Western country. Public
sentiment in Indiana was especially aroused by the case of
Davis Floyd, a licensed pilot and a local politician from
Clark County who became involved in Burr's intrigues, and
was indicted jointly with him. Although Floyd was convicted of misdemeanor, and was sentenced to three days'
imprisonment, many of his friends, and even Harrison at
first, believed him innocent. But when he was elected clerk
of the Indiana house of representatives, August 17, 1807,
there was an outbreak of popular indignation against what
was felt to be mere shameless bravado. A meeting at Vincennes adopted resolutions that severely condemned the election, and asserted that it had been put through on the
opening day of the session when only a few members were
present. The inhabitants of Kaskaskia passed similar resolutions, and incidentally they took advantage of this opportunity to call attention to the unpopular connection with the

[56] Address by "a numerous Meeting of the Citizens of Indiana," November
4, 1810, *Indiana Territorial Papers*, B. R. L., 2781; Petition from Indiana
House of Representatives, December, 1811, *Ibid.*, Senate Files, 2811.

counties east of the Wabash. Both resolutions seem to have found their way to Jefferson, and Floyd resigned at the next session of the assembly.[57] Public sentiment in favor of the Union which this and other incidents of the Burr episode had aroused had been illustrated at the Fourth of July banquet at Vincennes in 1807, in a toast to the union of "Eastern and Western America—may it be perpetual." At a similar celebration a year later, the toasts displayed this same strong nationalism.[58]

Even though they were intensely loyal to the Federal Union, the inhabitants of early Indiana were persistent in their efforts to secure a greater degree of local autonomy through a modification of the restrictions the Ordinance had imposed upon popular control. With manhood suffrage and statehood established across the line in Ohio, it was but natural that the Indiana settlers would fight for a greater degree of democracy in the territorial government which, it was apparent, they must live under for some years to come. In contrast to St. Clair, Harrison appears to have encouraged this movement, and the slavery convention which he called in 1802 mentioned the restriction of the suffrage to freeholders of fifty acres as one of the chief grievances of the territory. In their memorial to Congress, they declared that this condition was "subversive of the liberties of the citizens," and placed "too great weight in the scale of wealth." Therefore, they prayed for the extension of the suffrage to all free adult males. At first a committee in Congress reported that it was inexpedient to make this change, in view of the danger from foreign intrigues. But a second report in 1804 recommended that the franchise should be extended to every white male adult who had resided in the territory for two years, and had paid the territorial tax.[59]

[57] For Burr's intrigues in Indiana, see Dunn, *Indiana*, pp. 363-365; Goebel, *William Henry Harrison*, pp. 72-74; *Harrison's Messages and Letters*, Esarey, ed., vol. I, pp. 200-202, 205-207; *Western Sun*, December 30, 1807, January 6, March 23, May 18, and November 12, 1808.

[58] *Western Sun*, July 11, 1807, and July 9, 1808.

[59] Memorial, 1802. *Indiana Territorial Papers*, House Files, 2657.

Nothing was done at this time, but the inhabitants of Indiana were insistent in their demands for reform. At the very first session of the territorial assembly the legislative council expressed the hope that the time was not "far distant" when they would have "a full participation of the rights now enjoyed by citizens of the United States." Although they had confidence in Harrison himself, they strongly protested against the principle of lodging the extensive powers of the governor in the hands of any one man. In support of this statement, both houses united in a memorial that Congress would adopt the report of its own committee, and would extend the suffrage to every free man of twenty-one or over who had resided in Indiana for a given period and had paid a territorial tax. The House accorded this memorial a favorable reception, but no definite action was taken at this time.[60]

The first concession by Congress to the inhabitants of Indiana was an act in 1808 that extended the franchise to every "free white man," twenty-one and over, who had resided in the territory for a year, and owned fifty acres, or else a town lot valued at $100.00 or more.[61] This act gave the Indiana lower house courage to ask for further favors, a limitation of the governor's veto power similar to those upon the President, and a repeal of the former's prerogative arbitrarily to dissolve or prorogue the assembly. Both houses agreed upon a petition for the popular election of the members of the legislative assembly and of the territorial delegate to Congress. This last request Congress granted in an act approved February 27, 1809, that gave all persons entitled to vote for delegates to the Indiana house of representatives the further right to choose the legislative council and the territorial delegate. This same act transferred to the

[60] Memorial, Legislative Assembly of Indiana, August 19, 1805, *Indiana Territorial Papers*, House Files, 2699; *Harrison's Messages and Letters*, Esarey, ed., vol. I, pp. 160-161; *Indiana Slavery Petitions and Papers*, Dunn, ed., p. 497.

[61] *Annals of Congress*, Tenth Congress, First Session, pp. 1434, 2834.

lower house the power of the governor to apportion the representatives among the different counties.[62]

Soon the citizens of Indiana Territory again turned their attention to the franchise, which, contrary to frontier ideals of democracy, still excluded a considerable portion of the population. Petitioners to Congress in 1809 represented that the signers paid taxes and performed militia duties, but did not possess even an indirect voice in choosing their rulers. They prayed for a manhood suffrage, and the right to elect their own civil and military officers. Sheriffs, especially, they represented, should become elective officers, as under existing conditions there was no popular control over them, a situation that was "a grievous exception" to republican principles. Part of these demands Congress conceded in 1811 in an act that extended the suffrage to "every free white male person," twenty-one and over, who paid county or territorial taxes, and had resided in the territory for a year. But the act still left the appointment of local officers in the governor's hands, with the restriction that no persons who held offices of "profit," except justices of the peace and militia officers, would be eligible to either house of the territorial assembly.[63] This act, of course, was not satisfactory, and a few months later the Indiana house of representatives petitioned that the territory should be admitted as a "free and independent state." Jonathan Jennings, the delegate to Congress, in presenting this petition recommended that Indiana should have "complete emancipation" as soon as the census showed a population of 38,000.[64] The near approach of war

[62] Resolutions of House of Representatives, and Legislative Council, October, 1808, Petition, William Pennington and others, *Indiana Territorial Papers*, House Files; *Annals of Congress*, Tenth Congress, Second Session, pp. 484, 1329, 1821-1822.

[63] Petitions, 1809, and Joint Resolutions, Legislative Assembly of Indiana, 1810, *Indiana Territorial Papers*, House Files, 2777 and 2786; *Annals of Congress*, Eleventh Congress, First and Second Sessions, p. 716, Third Session, pp. 1347-1348.

[64] Speaker, Indiana House of Representatives, to the President, December 18, 1811, *Indiana Territorial Papers*, B. R. L. 2812; *Annals of Congress*, Twelfth Congress, First Session, p. 91.

prevented final action at this time, but the entire struggle for local autonomy had been a significant one, illustrating as it did the inevitable conflict when the provisions of an Ordinance that greatly restricted popular control were enforced for a considerable length of time over an American frontier population. Moreover, the concessions won from Congress by the people of Indiana created important precedents for later territorial governments.

Though Indiana had not achieved statehood by the time the War of 1812 broke out, it had at least emerged from a wilderness into a well-established territory with a population of almost 25,000 that was concentrated in the southern and western sections. This meant that when war did finally come, the local population was sufficiently strong to resist effectively attacks either by the British or by their Indian allies. Moreover, this increasing population had finally upheld the anti-slavery clause of the Ordinance after a long and acrimonious struggle which had reached a climax in the setting up of Illinois as a separate territory. In the political development of this territory of Indiana, there had been a significant liberalization of the provisions of the Ordinance, in the direction of an increasing degree of local autonomy, and the concessions made by Congress had set precedents that would necessarily be followed as other territories were organized. In the varied development of Indiana Territory, Harrison had played a creditable part, exercising his extensive powers with tact and judgment, and usually in democratic fashion. Indeed, his career as governor was in marked contrast to that of St. Clair, and unlike the governor of the Northwest Territory, he retired amid the plaudits of a large part of the inhabitants of Indiana. Upon the foundations which he had so effectively established, it would be a comparatively easy task, once war was ended, to build the territory up to full statehood.

Chapter VII

LAW AND ORDER IN ILLINOIS

THE first few years of the new territory of Illinois, which was formally set off from Indiana March 1, 1809, tested the working value of the Ordinance of 1787. The forms of local government set up by St. Clair in 1790 still existed in 1809, with the modifications that had been made from time to time under the Northwest Territory and under Indiana Territory. But law and order had not yet been established in the remote Illinois settlements, and the chief inhabited area, stretching along the east bank of the Mississippi from Kaskaskia to Cahokia some forty miles or more, was a veritable hornets' nest of petty intrigues and quarrels. Nor did the French inhabitants give promise of any considerable development under American rule. In 1809 they were in much the same condition as St. Clair had found them in 1790, having made no perceptible advance in nearly two decades of American control. Ignorant and superstitious, they spent much of their time in hunting, neglecting the cultivation of their fields, and, ultra-conservative, they refused to adopt better agricultural methods, protesting that what was good enough for their fathers was good enough for them. Like the Indians, they fixed dates by such events as "the time of the great waters," or the period of the strawberries, the maize, or the potatoes. In American institutions of self-government, such a people, of course, took little if any interest, and the one prominent French officeholder in the early territorial period, Pierre Menard, was a native of Quebec who, coming to Kaskaskia as a trader, became an Indian agent also, and one of the most influential men in the community.[1]

Fortunately for the new territorial government, the proportion of French *habitants* in the total population of Illinois was steadily decreasing. In 1800, out of approximately 2,500 civilized inhabitants west of the Wabash, they numbered probably 2,000.[2] The balance included chiefly a hardy vanguard of American settlers, and the Canadian fur traders at Prairie du Chien, Green Bay, and Peoria. There were a few American traders, too, in these strongholds of the British fur trade, and their special post at the mouth of the Chicago River was rapidly increasing in importance, with teams constantly on hand, by 1810, to haul goods across the portage from the Illinois.[3] After 1800 the population of Illinois rapidly increased, until by 1806 it was estimated at more than 4,300, and by the census of 1810 there were 12,282 inhabitants in the newly created territory.[4] The bulk of this increase was made up of American immigrants who settled in the American Bottom opposite St. Louis and extended the old strip of inhabited area on the east bank of the Mississippi eastward, and northward toward Edwardsville. Other Americans settled in the Ohio Valley in southern Illinois, at Shawneetown, and at Fort Massac, and still others took up lands in eastern Illinois, in the Wabash valley across from Vincennes, and around Fort Dearborn.[5]

The majority of the American immigrants into Illinois in the decade, 1800–1810, came from Kentucky, although others gradually arrived from Maryland, Virginia, and other

[1] Buck, *Illinois in 1818*, pp. 90-92; Collot, *A Visit to Illinois in 1796*, *Illinois Historical Society Publications*, no. 3, p. 286; Reynolds, *Pioneer History of Illinois*, pp. 242-243.

[2] *U. S. Census for 1800*, p. 87.

[3] *Louisiana Gazette*, August 30, 1810.

[4] *Indiana Historical Society Publications*, vol. II, p. 505; *U. S. Census for 1810*, p. 86.

[5] Boggess, *Settlement of Illinois, 1774–1830*, in *Chicago Historical Society's Collection*, vol. V, especially pp. 82-83; Map of Illinois, 1812–1814, in *Illinois State Historical Library Publications*, no. 9, p. 62; Quaife, *Chicago and the Old Northwest, 1673–1835*, chs. VI, VII, XIII.

seaboard states, and even from near-by Indiana and Ohio. A very considerable number were veterans of Clark's campaign, who, having recognized the possibilities of the Illinois country, settled there permanently, and induced their relatives and friends, also, to come out from their old homes. These early American pioneers were well typified by Shadrach Bond, Sr., who came out from Maryland, and later induced his nephew, Shadrach Bond, Jr., to migrate to the Illinois settlements. The nephew, a man of much force and a successful farmer, was the first territorial delegate to Congress, and later was chosen as the first governor of the State of Illinois. Another able pioneer, one who played a somewhat different but an equally successful rôle, was William Morrison. Coming from Philadelphia to the Western country he brought Eastern business methods to his large commercial establishment at Kaskaskia, and developed a trade along the Mississippi that extended from Prairie du Chien to New Orleans. Even more striking as a personality was the brilliant Welsh lawyer and orator, John Rice Jones, who after first settling in Kaskaskia moved to Vincennes, where he held a number of important offices in the territorial government. An excellent French scholar, he was especially sympathetic with the original settlers, and was, consequently, able to render much important public service in the early years of American control.[6] The presence of such men as Shadrach Bond, Jr., and many others of a similarly desirable type among the settlers who were thronging into Illinois, gave the officers of the new territorial government a substantial basis upon which they could rely for support of the necessary measures to establish law and order. This co-operation between an exceptionally able group of territorial officers and influential settlers of judgment and ability proved so successful that, within three and a half years after the separation from Indiana, it was possible to make the transition in Illinois from the arbitrary rule of the governor

[6] Buck, *Illinois in 1818*, especially p. 95; Reynolds, *Pioneer History of Illinois*, pp. 89-90, 138-139, 272-273.

and the judges to the second grade of territorial government with a legislative assembly. This change, coming so soon after the outbreak of the War of 1812, marks the end of the first outstanding period in the history of Illinois Territory from its organization in 1809, and this chapter will be confined to these three important years.

Even with an increasing and substantial American population upon which to rely for support, the territorial officers faced a disheartening situation at the outset. By no means the least of their problems arose from the utterly inadequate means of communication between the scattered settlements in Illinois and the equally unsatisfactory situation of those with the outside world. Eastward to Indiana and Ohio and the seaboard, the usual route was up the Ohio River, then across the mountains. But at its best this journey was an exceedingly tiresome one that was impossible during the many floods, or when the river was filled with floating ice. For shipping the agricultural products of early Illinois, and even for receiving manufactured products from the Eastern states on a large scale, this route was altogether impractical. The road eastward by land to Vincennes was hazardous in the extreme, and not until 1810, a year after the territory was established, was there a regular postal service over it from Kaskaskia.[7] The one available trade route, down the Mississippi to New Orleans, was tedious and roundabout as a road to the Atlantic Coast. Thus, the development of Illinois was seriously handicapped by its inaccessibility to the chief American markets and centers of population. Internally, the situation was scarcely more satisfactory. There were trails from Shawneetown and other landing places on the Ohio across country to the American Bottom on the Mississippi, but they were destitute of bridges, and they boasted few ferries. Consequently they were really impossible for the passage of wheeled vehicles, and packhorses became the chief dependence for transportation over them. A road ran through the settlements between Kaskaskia and

[7] *Annals of Congress*, Eleventh Congress, Second Session, p. 2550.

Cahokia and there was the eastward trail, already mentioned, across the Illinois swamps and prairies to Vincennes. Navigable waterways supplemented these unsatisfactory land highways, but they, too, were subject to constant delays and dangers. The chief ones were: the Ohio on the south, the Mississippi on the west, the Wabash on the east, and several streams, notably the Illinois, that led into the interior.[8] Obviously it would be an exceedingly difficult task to establish a firm executive control over widely separated settlements that were connected by such difficult and generally unsatisfactory highways, while the isolation of the Illinois country greatly interfered with its development both in population and commerce.

The need of a better system of communication within Illinois was especially urgent, in order to control the Indians in the territory, and to curb the activities of the many Canadian fur traders. Usually the Indians of Illinois were peaceably inclined, and now that the United States had taken over the west bank of the Mississippi, they were no longer subject to continual Spanish intrigues. But the gradual spread of settlement northward toward the Illinois Valley caused occasional conflicts between the aggressive and tactless frontiersmen and the revengeful Indians. At the same time, the intrigues of Canadian fur traders who were determined to keep out their American competitors added to the perplexities of the territorial officers in their efforts to keep peace with the Indians. The situation at Prairie du Chien was typical. To ascend the river from Kaskaskia to this important post, a well-manned boat would take twenty days, a loaded boat twice as long. With such delays in communication, it was practically impossible to exercise any really effective control over the one hundred or so French Canadian families in and around this prosperous settlement. Consequently the Canadian traders dominated the post, and by 1811 they had driven away all but one of their American rivals. A

[8] Reynolds, *Pioneer History of Illinois*, pp. 131-132; Buck, *Illinois in 1818*, pp. 114-115.

strong military post at Prairie du Chien was the one possible means to assert American authority, but the officials in Washington paid little attention to repeated pleas for aid here. A similar indifference met requests for troops to be stationed at Peoria and below the mouth of the Illinois, in order to put an end to Indian depredations.[9] Thus, without an adequate military force, it became an increasingly difficult and almost impossible task to protect outlying settlements from Indian raids and to suppress the intrigues of the Canadian fur traders.

By far the most pressing and far-reaching problem that the territorial government faced was the very uncertain status of land titles in Illinois, and the many personal controversies, and the general lawlessness that had come as a result. By 1809 the greater part of the land between the Ohio and the Illinois, except for a strip north from Vincennes, was supposed to have been made available for settlement by cessions from the Indians,[10] but the land commissioners at Kaskaskia, busy with the adjustment of old claims and the award of donation tracts, did not arrange for the survey and sale of these public lands. Consequently, the alternatives presented to arriving settlers were, either to buy up old French claims and uncertain rights to donation lands, or else to take public lands without any title. As a result up to 1814 when actual sales of these Illinois public lands began, the bulk of the American settlers in the territory, especially those in the Ohio Valley, were mere squatters. The delays in confirming the old French claims and other disputed titles only added to the general confusion.[11] The situation, as a result of this anomalous land situation, was forcibly illustrated when the governor and other officers of

[9] Boilvin to Secretary of War, February 2, 1811, *Chicago Historical Society's Collection*, vol. III, pp. 59-63; Resolution of Inhabitants of St. Clair County, and Memorial to the President (1811), *Illinois Territorial Papers*, House Files.

[10] *Eighteenth Annual Report, Bureau of American Ethnology*, 1896–1897, part 2, pp. 656-657, 664-667, 672-675, and plates 17-18.

[11] Buck, *Illinois in 1818*, ch. II.

the territorial government were unable to purchase desirable lands from private persons, in order to fulfill the land-holding conditions of the Ordinance. When they asked for permission to locate and purchase land on government tracts, the Committee on Public Lands held that there was no justification for this departure "from the usual mode of land sales," and the House concurred.[12]

Even before the separation from Indiana there had been protests from the American settlers against the impossible land situation in Illinois. In 1804 a petition from 284 Illinois pioneers represented that, coming to the frontier to ransom their wives and children from the Indians, they had settled wherever they could find suitable land. Now, finding it impossible to secure titles, they prayed for relief for the "industrious poor." Another petition, a year later, from sixteen heads of families who had been induced to go to Fort Massac in order to furnish supplies to the garrison, alleged that the local commandant had promised in-lots and out-lots and a donation tract to each head of a family. Having endured many hardships and many of their number having been "called to the silent shades of death and entombed in the rubbish of the wilderness," the survivors prayed for the speedy confirmation of their lands.[13] At Shawneetown, which was rapidly becoming an important trading point for the salt produced at the near-by government saline, the territorial government of Indiana had "indulged" the settlers and they had made "many improvements." After Illinois had been organized they discovered that Governor Edwards had no authority to confirm their titles, and they feared "some monopolizing company" might secure possession of this important trading point. With a really inimitable lack of a sense of humor, one of the Shawneetown petitions to Congress declared, "we must beg leave

[12] Petition, Governor, Secretary and Judges of Illinois Territory, and Report of Committee, February, 1810, *Illinois Territorial Papers*, House Files, 2526; *Annals of Congress*, Eleventh Congress, Second Session, pp. 1378, 1427.

[13] Petitions, 1804, 1805, *Indiana Territorial Papers*, House Files.

to make mention with diffidence, lest a misconception be prepossessed from misrepresentations, that there are amongst our number both moral and religious as well as many enterprising and industrious people." Their fears with regard to their lands were partly realized in 1810 by an act which Congress passed to lay out the site of Shawneetown, and to sell the lots to the highest bidders. Thereupon the settlers on the spot petitioned to be allowed to buy in their lots at the usual price, or else to be awarded the cost of their improvements. As the journey to Kaskaskia would cost more than a single lot, they pointed out the need for a separate land office at Shawneetown. In answer to these representations, a long step forward was taken in the adjustment of the land problem in southern Illinois when a land office at Shawneetown was authorized in 1812.[14]

The confusion in land titles was an important source of the factional intrigue that was rampant in Illinois when the separation from Indiana took place. Many old claims were revived, speculation became rife, and frauds innumerable were either attempted or carried through. Standing as a bulwark against this disgraceful orgy was Michael Jones, the more influential of the two land commissioners, a man of much ability, honest but irritable. As a strong supporter of Harrison he was closely identified with an officeholding minority which had opposed the separation from Indiana, and the very necessary but unpopular measures of the land commissioners came as a welcome issue for the anti-Harrison party. Other petty grievances complicated matters until the bitter local quarrels in Illinois reached a climax when Rice Jones, one of the anti-Harrison party, was murdered on the street in Kaskaskia. Passion was now at fever heat, and the anti-Harrison men had Michael Jones indicted as accessory to this murder. At the trial a "great concourse" testified to the public excitement, and the jury promptly acquitted Jones who had been prosecuted, as one intelligent

[14] *Annals of Congress,* Eleventh Congress, Second Session, p. 2564; Petitions, 1809 and 1811, *Illinois Territorial Papers,* House Files.

observer openly asserted, from the "cool calculation of interest" to assail a public officer who was "too honest to subserve the crimes of the great land jobbers." [15] It was in such an atmosphere of political turmoil, amid a swarm of dishonest land speculators and lawbreakers in general, that the territory of Illinois was inaugurated.

Luckily for this new territorial government, faced with so many and such difficult problems, the President had been singularly fortunate in his choice of the officers who were to be in charge during the early critical years. John Boyle, his first nominee for governor, having promptly declined,[16] Madison offered the post to Ninian Edwards, the chief justice of the Kentucky court of appeals, who had been strongly recommended by Senator Pope of Kentucky, by William Wirt, and by Henry Clay. Ninian Edwards' career, up to the time he became governor of Illinois, bore a marked resemblance to that of William Henry Harrison, except that his experience was chiefly in the courts, while that of Harrison was mainly in military service. Born in Maryland in 1773, a member of a family possessing much wealth and position, Ninian Edwards had migrated when still a very young man to Nelson County, Kentucky, where he speedily established himself as a lawyer of ability, and became chief justice before he was thirty-two. Like Harrison he was appointed governor of a territory in his early manhood while his mind was still flexible, and he could adapt himself to new conditions. Indeed the successful careers of Harrison and Edwards, who both came to their respective territories as young men, were in strong contrast to the rather difficult experiences of St. Clair, who first assumed power in the Northwest Territory as a man past sixty, conservative, and too set either to gain or to comprehend new points of view. Governor Edwards was ideally

[15] Alvord, *The Illinois Country, 1673-1818*, pp. 418-427; Buck, *Illinois in 1818*, pp. 184-192; *Western Sun*, September 10 and October 22, 1808, and May 12, 1810.

[16] John Boyle to Secretary of State, April 3, 1809, *Illinois Territorial Papers*, B. R. L., 2523.

fitted for his new post. Balanced in his views, with a knowledge of men and of frontier needs that was drawn from practical experience, he possessed an ample fortune that made possible an exceedingly independent and impartial policy in the conduct of his official duties.[17]

Among the other officers who were chosen to inaugurate the separate government of Illinois, the secretary, Nathaniel Pope, born in Kentucky in 1784, a college graduate and a lawyer of experience, was a cousin of Governor Edwards. At twenty-one he had migrated to Ste. Genevieve in Upper Louisiana, and was therefore well acquainted with the problems of the Illinois country, especially as he spoke French fluently.[18] Of the three judges, the outstanding figure was Jesse B. Thomas, a native of Maryland who had come to Lawrenceburgh, Indiana, in 1803, to practice law, and had been speaker of the lower house of the Indiana territorial assembly from 1805 until 1808. In 1808 he was elected delegate to Congress and there, as has already been pointed out, he put through the bill for the division of Indiana. His appointment, therefore, was particularly acceptable to the anti-Harrison faction in Illinois. But any tendency to take part in the political turmoil of the territory was more than balanced by Judge Thomas' intimate knowledge of the Indiana Code upon which the laws of Illinois were based, and by his long experience in territorial politics.[19] The other important judge, Alexander Stuart, was a native of Virginia, a man of good education and polished manners, honest and with fine judgment.[20] The third judge, Obadiah Jones, soon resigned, and his successor, the erratic Stanley Griswold, who fortunately came to Illinois only a short time before the second grade of government was established, took

[17] Edwards, *Life and Times of Ninian Edwards*, pp. 12-28, 441-442; *Edwards Papers*, Washburne, ed., *Chicago Historical Society's Collection*, vol. III, pp. 36-41.

[18] Davidson and Stuvé, *Complete History of Illinois*, p. 244.

[19] Dunn, *Indiana*, p. 327 especially.

[20] Davidson and Stuvé. *Complete History of Illinois*, p. 243; Edwards, *Life and Times of Ninian Edwards*, p. 441.

little part in the work of the governor and the judges. In view of the strong pro-slavery agitation that had been chiefly responsible for the setting off of Illinois, it is significant that with the exception of Griswold, who may be virtually ignored as a positive force, all the important officers at first—the governor, the secretary, and the two influential judges— were natives of slave states. All of them, however, were men of practical experience and balanced judgment who would avoid the pitfalls of factional conflict, and were eminently qualified for the difficult task of establishing law and order in Illinois.

April 28, 1809, the secretary, Nathaniel Pope, inaugurated the separate territorial government of Illinois in the absence of Governor Edwards, who did not arrive until June 11. Two days later the governor held the first legislative session with Judge Stuart and Judge Thomas. These three officers made up the usual personnel of the territorial legislature for the three years of the first grade of government, since the third judge, Obadiah Jones, signed only a few laws, and Stanley Griswold, his successor, only one. Governor Edwards seldom left Illinois, and consequently took part in the passage of all but two of the early laws. This comparatively unchanged personnel of the legislative board was of great importance in this critical period of establishing American institutions in Illinois, since it assured a consistent policy. Furthermore, the extensive legal experience of the members of the board and their practical knowledge of frontier conditions ensured wise legislation that was adapted to local needs.[21] At their first session the governor and the judges removed any possible uncertainties, and gave the territory an exact legal basis by a resolution that declared the laws of Indiana of a general nature, as of March 1, 1809, in force in Illinois. In subsequent acts these experienced legislators broadly interpreted their powers to pass additional legislation, recognizing in this practical fashion

[21] *Laws of Illinois*, 1809–1811, Alvord, ed., in *Bulletin of the Illinois State Historical Library*, vol. I. no. 2.

the actual situation, for the disorders in Illinois did not admit of legalistic quibblings and long delays in consulting a far distant Federal government. Quick action was needed, and of the thirty-four laws which the governor and judges adopted in the years 1809–1811, only twelve conformed strictly to the limitations in the Ordinance upon their legislative powers. The remainder either repealed sections of the Indiana Code, or else they modified these laws with a loose adherence to the principles rather than the letter of the originals. Eleven of the twelve laws which they adopted outright, the governor and the judges took from the codes of Southern states with which they were themselves, of course, more familiar. Six of the eleven laws they adopted from the Code of Kentucky, not strictly an original state as was specified in the Ordinance, but one, the laws of which were peculiarly suited to frontier conditions and were familiar to many of the settlers in Illinois. The legislative board adopted two laws each from the Virginia and Georgia Codes, one from that of South Carolina, and in the Pennsylvania Code they found the one act they passed from a Northern state.

An important section of the laws adopted by the governor and the judges took up the revision, and incidentally the simplification of the judicial system, in order to secure more effective enforcement of the laws in Illinois. Governor Edwards seems to have had great difficulty in securing men who were qualified to act as judges of the courts of common pleas, and the legislative board summarily abolished these courts, handing over their judicial functions, both criminal and civil, to circuit courts which sat twice annually in each county, with one of the judges of the general court presiding. The administrative functions of the courts of common pleas, such as the levy of local taxes, and other local measures, the governor and the judges now assigned to the county courts, each of them presided over by three or more justices of the peace, which met six times annually. The general court, over which the territorial judges presided, they left undisturbed. Even this system was too complicated for these scattered settlements in Illinois, and the governor and the judges soon abolished the circuit courts. Henceforth the general court, which now became the one territorial trial court for more important cases, was required to hold two annual sessions at each of the county seats, Kaskaskia and Cahokia. The new law ordered all suits and processes to be tried in the county in which they originated, and it also required the clerk of the general court to open offices in each of the two villages. As population increased, however, this simplified judicial system could not carry on effectually all the business of the several former courts, and eventually the governor and judges restored the court of common pleas. For less important cases the powers conferred by the Indiana Code upon justices of the peace were left undisturbed, although appeals were allowed from their decisions, in cases where more than $4.16 2/3 was involved.

Supplementing the reforms in the judicial system were a number of measures which the governor and the judges adopted in an attempt to suppress the prevailing lawlessness in Illinois. One especially important act required the sheriffs, before each term of the circuit court, to summon as a grand jury twenty-four of the "most discreet housekeepers." By this means it would be possible to inquire into infractions of the law, and to bring presentments against notorious offenders. To put an end to the common practice of escaping into the wilderness to avoid trial, and to ensure actual punishment, another law required prisoners to be safely secured, and stipulated that whenever the county failed to provide a "sufficient" jail, the presiding judge of the general court should order the jailer to hire extra guards. Other laws were adopted of a somewhat Puritanic tinge, in order to suppress some of the more common vices in early Illinois. Adultery was severely punished, and gambling was forbidden at race tracks and in other public places. "Tables commonly called A. B. C. or E. O. or farro banks" were under a ban, and the law against private lotteries was quite severe, although, as was customary at this period, this form of gambling was openly sanctioned for public purposes. The legislative board also attempted to put an end to dueling, which was coming to be an open scandal, especially after the murder of Rice Jones, as the outcome of a duel, had aroused public opinion in Illinois. According to the law that was now adopted, a person who killed another in a duel was guilty of murder, and would be hanged if he were convicted. In any case both challenger and challenged were debarred from holding public office, and each officeholder must take an oath that he had not violated this law. Even though the duel was fought outside of Illinois, citizens were liable to these penalties when they returned to the territory. Yet such drastic measures were necessary to cope with the local conditions, and the governor and the judges managed to achieve considerable success in their attempts to establish law and order.

Among the other acts adopted by the legislative board, none was more significant than the one that repealed the Indiana law for the introduction of negroes and mulattoes, which had virtually removed all restrictions upon the entrance of slaves into Illinois. The board left undisturbed other sections of the Indiana slave code, and evidently the rights of slaveholders in the slaves they already held were not interfered with.[22] But their action in cutting off the source from which slaves were recruited was exceedingly significant in view of the Southern origin of the governor and the majority of the judges, demonstrating as it did how completely they were free from sectional prejudices. Aside from the rather lukewarm support for slavery to be expected from men who came from border states, a possible explanation of their policy was to be found in the large increase of free negroes in Illinois, from 91 in 1800 to 673 in 1810. Even though the corresponding number of slaves had only risen from 107 to 168,[23] it was apparent that the available labor supply was rapidly increasing without any need to

[22] *Louisiana Gazette*, June 27, 1811.
[23] *U. S. Census for 1800*, p. 87, and *U. S. Census for 1810*, p. 86.

introduce additional slaves. Still another possible explanation for this exclusion of slaves was the moral effect of the anti-slavery victory in Indiana, which must have greatly heartened the free-soil advocates in Illinois. Lastly, this anti-slavery faction was constantly receiving recruits by immigration from the border states, as well as from the free states and territories.

An important problem that faced the territorial government was the financial one, and it was rendered doubly vexatious by the great confusion that still existed in Illinois land titles. An act that probably helped matters required damages to be paid for the improvements upon lands which squatters were obliged to surrender. But the territorial officers were helpless, so far as the general situation was concerned, and must wait upon the slow-moving Federal officials for a final adjustment of the troublesome land situation. The governor and the judges retained the chief features of the Indiana tax law, except that they assigned to the sheriffs all the duties involved, the appraisal of property, the compilation of lists for local taxation, and collections. However, the sheriffs were not very successful, to judge from the lists of delinquent lands that they offered at public sale.[24] The legislative board also took up a number of miscellaneous matters, such as the regulation of the militia, and they adopted acts that empowered the governor to remit fines and forfeitures, and to grant pardons and reprieves. Always this legislation was marked by the moderation and practical sense which enabled the governor and the judges to deal so successfully with the discouraging problems of early Illinois. Fortunately for the very straitened territorial finances at this time, the *Missouri Gazette* established by Joseph Charless July 12, 1808, across the Mississippi at St. Louis, was an excellent medium in which to give publicity to these laws of the governor and the judges. This journal, which was published under the title, the *Louisiana Gazette*, from

[24] *Louisiana Gazette*, May 3, 1810.

November 30, 1809, to July 11, 1812, had a wide circulation in the Illinois settlements.[25]

The good judgment which the governor and judges had used in their legislative capacity during the three years of their abitrary rule, 1809–1812, was displayed as well in the details of administration.[26] For this particular department, Governor Edwards was, of course, primarily responsible, and he showed rare understanding and courage in adhering to a policy that carefully avoided any entanglements in the petty partisanship which was so prevalent in Illinois when he first arrived. Especially was this true of his appointments to office. Nathaniel Pope, the territorial secretary who inaugurated the new government, made few changes in the administrative organization as it had beeen established under Harrison as governor of Indiana Territory. Recognizing the division into Randolph and St. Clair counties, he reappointed in most instances the civil and military officers of the preceding régime. This policy stirred up a coterie of disappointed office-seekers which had so far been ignored in appointments, and they carried their grievances to Governor Edwards soon after his arrival. In an address that was really a cleverly worded invitation to join their party, they complained that though they represented a majority of the inhabitants, they had suffered many indignities in the past, and they even raked up the murder of Rice Jones as the work of the opposition party. For these "enormities," which the anti-Harrison faction, as they were dubbed, had suffered the governor could make amends by "that honorable indemnity which is in your gift," meaning, of course, by appointments to office. This address also criticized the conduct of the land commissioners at Kaskaskia, and asked for the appointment of a new board. In a courteous and dignified reply Governor Edwards showed that he under-

[25] *Louisiana Gazette*, especially March 8, 1810, April 11, July 11 and 18, and August 1, 1811.

[26] *Territorial Records of Illinois*, 1809–1812, James, ed., in *Publications of the Illinois State Historical Library*, no. III.

stood the real motives behind these overtures. Public office, he asserted, was a trust for the public good. "A partisan I can not and will not be." While he deplored the contentions which had "convulsed" the territory, he considered it his duty to guard in impartial fashion the "equal rights" of his fellow citizens. As for the land office, he pointed out, he had no power to change existing conditions.[27] True to this declaration of principles, Governor Edwards dismissed only a few officials who were notoriously incompetent, including James Gilbreath, the sheriff of Randolph County, who had been appointed by Harrison in 1806, but had been exceedingly dilatory in the collection of taxes.

Soon there were protests against Governor Edwards' general policy of retaining Harrison's appointees, most of them doubtless inspired by the disappointed anti-Harrison faction. The chief target of these disgruntled individuals seems to have been Shadrach Bond, Jr., a strong supporter of Harrison, who had been appointed, in 1808, lieutenant colonel in command of the militia of St. Clair County.[28] Finally, Governor Edwards decided to meet these criticisms by an election at which the militia would choose their own officers, subject, of course, to his confirmation. The election was held, and the governor, although somewhat reluctantly, appointed the officials that had been chosen, among them William Whiteside, who replaced Shadrach Bond, Jr., as commander of the St. Clair County militia. These militia elections inevitably aroused additional criticism from the officers who were displaced, and Governor Edwards found it necessary to explain his motives in an exceedingly frank public address. Emphasizing his belief that the will of the majority should always prevail, he called attention to the overtures that had been made to line him up with a faction. He had been unwilling to reappoint all the old officers of the militia without a careful inquiry into the

---

[27] Edwards, *Life and Times of Ninian Edwards,* pp. 28-30.
[28] Shadrach Bond, Jr., to Ninian Edwards, July 2, 1809, *Edwards Papers,* Washburne, ed., pp. 42-46.

fitness of each one, and consequently he had adopted the one course that, in his opinion, was in accord with true republican principles; that is to say, a popular election.[29] This rather idealistic statement at least served as a public announcement that the governor would not let himself become involved in the intrigues which had so far been the bane of the Illinois settlements. But even Governor Edwards soon had misgivings as to the wisdom of elections in the midst of so much local strife. His political mentor, Senator Pope, pointed out the evil effects of the militia election, unless he adopted a "uniform rule" that applied equally to all appointments. After all, Pope pointed out, under the Ordinance the responsibility for appointments must rest upon the governor, and should an improper person be elected, and then appointed, he would have difficulty in justifying himself, and if he refused to accept the popular choice, he would arouse much popular resentment.[30]

There is a tradition that throughout the three years of rule in Illinois by the governor and the judges, Governor Edwards adhered to the policy which he adopted at first in the case of the militia, and allowed the people of each county to choose their own civil and military officers.[31] The evidence in the territorial records does not justify this statement. Undoubtedly the governor was greatly disturbed over the results of the militia election, and its probable aftermath. Having learned his lesson, he probably merely consulted local opinion in making later appointments, but exercised his own discretion in the final decisions. Certainly he did not issue any further proclamations for the election of either civil or military officers, and the conclusion that he was himself responsible for appointments, except in the case of the militia, is supported by a petition from a number of the inhabitants of the Shawneetown district, when it was rumored

[29] Edwards, *Life and Times of Ninian Edwards,* pp. 31-35.
[30] John Pope to Ninian Edwards, November 9, 1809, *Edwards Papers,* Washburne, ed, pp. 37-42.
[31] Edwards, *Life and Times of Ninian Edwards,* p. 31.

that one or more new counties were to be erected in the Ohio Valley. These petitioners asked that the inhabitants should be allowed to vote for the sheriffs, and for the judges and clerks of the courts of common pleas. As a precedent they cited the concession that the governor had already made to the militia.[32] But Governor Edwards had been taught by experience that his democratic ideals did not always jibe with his personal responsibilities, and he did not see fit to grant this petition. Only five days after he had created these new counties, Madison north of Cahokia, Gallatin in the Ohio Valley with Shawneetown as its county seat, and Johnson to the east of Gallatin, he announced the appointments to the new offices. Indeed, judging from the numerous appointments he made in the course of three years, he must have had much difficulty in finding suitable men, as in the case of the attorney-general for the territory. First he appointed Benjamin Doyle, who promptly resigned, next he offered the office to John J. Crittenden of Kentucky, who also resigned in a short time, and was succeeded by his brother Thomas T. Crittenden, who held this post for a little more than six months.

In his conscientious attention to the duties of an executive, Governor Edwards was notable among the territorial governors, and certainly Illinois needed constant oversight. Only twice in the three years, 1809–1812, was he absent from the territory for any length of time. The first absence, of about four months in 1809, was necessary to wind up personal and public affairs in Kentucky, which he had left in utmost confusion when he hurried to Illinois, ten days after he received word of his appointment.[33] The second absence, for about two months in the spring of 1810, was probably for the same reason. Beside the difficult task of seeing that the laws were enforced, he found that Indian relations absorbed much of his attention, especially upon the

[32] George Robinson to Governor Edwards, June 14, 1812, with Petition, Edwards Papers, Washburne, ed., pp. 71-78.
[33] Edwards, Life and Times of Ninian Edwards, p. 31.

eve of the War of 1812. One important step to promote better relations with the red men was a proclamation that forbade any sales of intoxicating liquor to the Indians within twenty miles of Peoria. This order the governor supplemented with special instructions to Thomas Forsythe, the Indian agent at Peoria, to see that it was enforced. The unsettled land situation continued to be a source of constant worry, and Governor Edwards strongly urged upon Congress the need for a preëmption act to bring a measure of tranquillity to the territory.[34] Indeed, he was constantly at work ironing out the many difficult situations in Illinois. An example of his painstaking care was the successful management of the large saline near Shawneetown which was under his direct supervision. This source of a salt supply was of the utmost importance to the pioneers in the Lower Ohio Valley, but in characteristic fashion, the officials at Washington sent elaborate directions for the operation of these far-off salt springs. The lessees must undertake to produce at least 120,000 bushels of salt annually, and the price should be not less than 80 cents nor more than $1.00 per bushel. There were detailed requirements, too, for the saving of timber and the use of coal, as well as for various improvements and experiments. These conditions Governor Edwards promptly advertised in the leading Western papers, and he soon secured a satisfactory lease. In actual practice it became necessary to modify very considerably the government's demands, but in the end Governor Edwards secured a supply of the salt that was of such immediate importance to the Western settlers.[35]

The comparative order that Governor Edwards and the judges had established in Illinois was forcibly illustrated by the short period that elapsed before the territory was ready to enter the second stage of government with a legislative

[34] Governor Edwards to (probably) Albert Gallatin, January 26, 1812, in Edwards, *Life and Times of Ninian Edwards,* pp. 296-298.

[35] *Western Sun,* January 20, 1810; Edwards, *Life and Times of Ninian Edwards,* pp. 529-535.

assembly. Following the precedent established in Indiana, the enabling act for Illinois had given the governor power to organize a territorial assembly, whenever he had "satisfactory evidence" that a majority of the freeholders desired the change. As early as October 1, 1810, a public meeting at Kaskaskia drew up an address that favored the second grade of government.[36] The different local factions united for once in support of a movement that, aside from a greater degree of self-government, would give them a territorial delegate to present their grievances to Congress. At first the governor proposed to postpone the change, inasmuch as the number of freeholders who would be entitled to vote under the Ordinance constituted scarcely a tenth of the permanent residents of the territory. Unless the franchise were broadened, this very limited minority would control the territorial assembly, a situation especially unjust to the settlers south of Kaskaskia, where there were not more than three or four freeholders in fully a third of the population of Illinois.[37] Petitions in favor of the second grade of government continued to come in, and since any adjustment of titles, and especially the opening up of the public lands, seemed as far off as ever, March 14, 1812, Governor Edwards finally called for an election, to ascertain the wishes of those freeholders entitled to vote upon the change to the second grade of government.[38] At the same time he sought the aid of his friend, Richard M. Johnson, then a member of Congress from Kentucky, to secure an extension of the franchise to the many residents of Illinois whose titles to their lands had not been confirmed. There were then only 220 freeholders in Illinois in a total population of 12,282, Governor Edwards pointed out, and an act of Congress to extend the suffrage was necessary, if the territory was to be allowed to enter the second stage of government. This plea was supplemented by peti-

[36] Western Sun, December 8, 1810.
[37] Governor Edwards to (probably) Albert Gallatin, January 26, 1812 in Edwards, Life and Times of Ninian Edwards, p. 296.
[38] Louisiana Gazette, March 28, 1812.

tions to Congress from the many settlers in the Illinois and Ohio valleys who were without titles to their lands. These squatters pointed out their very unequal situation, if a territorial assembly was authorized, unless at the same time the suffrage was broadened.[39] Johnson acted promptly, and an act, approved May 2, 1812, followed the precedent already set up in Indiana, and extended the suffrage to every "free white male person" of twenty-one or over, who paid either county or territorial taxes, and had resided in the territory for a year. Also, this act provided that in addition to the delegates to the territorial house of representatives, the voters should choose the members of the legislative council and the delegate to Congress. Meantime a majority of the freeholders had favored the second grade of government, and an election was held under the recent suffrage act for members of the two territorial houses and for a delegate to Congress.[40]

With the opening session of the first territorial assembly, November 25, 1812, Illinois definitely entered the second grade of government. In a brief period of three years the territory had progressed from a state of governmental chaos to an orderly community that was capable of carrying on a large measure of self-government. This development had been due to the wise policies of Governor Edwards and his chief aides in the government, supported by a continually increasing number of American settlers who were determined to see law and order established in Illinois. Governor Edwards, especially, had worked conscientiously and with good judgment to secure harmony between the different factions, and he had attracted a large personal following, along with the popular confidence.[41] Moreover, under his guidance the inhabitants of Illinois had won a democratic suffrage, and the right to elect both houses of the assembly as well as

[39] Governor Edwards to Richard M. Johnson, March 14, 1812, and Petitions from Illinois (1812), *Illinois Territorial Papers*, House Files.

[40] *Annals of Congress*, Twelfth Congress, First Session, pp. 1278-1279, 2307-2308.

[41] *Louisiana Gazette*, July 18, 1811.

the territorial delegate, concessions for which a precedent had already been established in Indiana. In the future, too, these modifications of the Ordinance would necessarily be extended to the other territories that would be organized from the public domain. As for Illinois itself, the War of 1812 found the territory ready for a development that would parallel the progress of the neighboring Indiana Territory, once the Indian troubles were ended, and the bothersome land situation was finally adjusted. The one disturbing question was that of slavery, and Governor Edwards and his colleagues, by excluding additional slaves, had wisely prepared the way for the anti-slavery clause that was placed in the state constitution in 1818.

Chapter VIII

THE FIASCO IN MICHIGAN

DECIDEDLY in contrast to the notable progress that was made in the Northwest Territory, followed by Indiana and Illinois, under the Ordinance of 1787, was the fiasco that marked the attempt to establish a territorial government in Michigan between 1805, when it became a separate territory, and Hull's surrender in 1812 which temporarily put an end to American control. In many respects the situation in the Michigan region when the United States took it over in 1796 was parallel to the one St. Clair found in Illinois in 1790. The majority of the inhabitants were French, with the remainder made up of Canadian traders and a few American settlers. Like Illinois before the Louisiana Purchase, Michigan was essentially a frontier territory, and it continued to be so. Across the Detroit River were the British settlements in Upper Canada, and the fur traders of Montreal had not given up hope of renewing British control over Detroit, the key to the extensive Indian trade of the Wabash Valley and beyond. Furthermore, as it was isolated by almost two hundred miles of swamp and forest from the growing settlements in the Ohio Valley, Detroit was an exceedingly difficult post to hold in face of British designs from the east, and with a large and somewhat hostile Indian population in the hinterland. Obviously it was supremely important that a large American population, such as had come into Indiana and Illinois, should have been attracted here, and that the very unsatisfactory means of communicating with other American settlements should be replaced with an adequate system of transportation. It was also quite necessary that any plan of government should consider the long-established customs of the French population. The failure to recognize these different problems would spell the doom of territorial government in Michigan, and a study of the seven years between 1805, when Michigan was set off from Indiana, and Hull's surrender in 1812, readily shows why American rule was such a signal failure.

From 1796, when Great Britain surrendered Detroit and Mackinaw, the American policy in this region was a succession of blunders. The members of Congress, not appreciating the critical situation in Michigan, did not take adequate steps for military defense, and adopted only half-hearted and often quite tardy measures to deal with the many local problems. The officials of the Northwest Territory, to which Michigan was first annexed, showed little more understanding of the many complications in the Michigan area. After Winthrop Sargent's hasty trip in 1796 to extend territorial jurisdiction there, and to organize Wayne County, little attention was paid to a region so far away from the Ohio Valley, and in the six years that Michigan was attached to the Northwest Territory, only two sessions of the general court were held at Detroit. After 1802, when it was annexed to Indiana, there was even less governmental supervision, and indeed the territorial officers at Vincennes do not appear to have attempted the long and dangerous journey to Detroit. This impossible situation the few hardy Americans who had ventured to this region soon brought to the attention of Congress. "Sound policy," they represented, demanded the organization of a separate territory as the one possible means to secure a firm government. The Senate gave this petition sympathetic attention, promptly passing an act to organize Michigan Territory. In the House, however, a committee reported against a separate territory, and the bill passed in the Senate was rejected in February, 1804, by a vote of 58 to 59.[1] But the Americans in Michigan were per-

[1] Memorials from Michigan, 1803, *Indiana Territorial Papers,* Senate Files; *Michigan Pioneer Collections,* vol. VIII, pp. 511-513; *Annals of Congress,* Eighth Congress, First Session, pp. 16, 29-30, 78, 212, 1042.

sistent, and soon other petitions came to Congress, notably one from the "democratic republicans" of Michigan, which declared there was a "unanimous opinion" that the "good order and prosperity" of the district depended upon the grant of a separate government. Other arguments that this petition brought forward were: the close proximity of Canada; the "anti-republican notions" of many of the inhabitants of Michigan; and the general lack of "patriotic attachment" to the United States, as well as the need for an established route of communication between Detroit and Vincennes.[2] Such representations proved more successful. Once again the Senate passed an act to organize the Territory of Michigan, and this time the House concurred in a measure by which the new territorial government was to be inaugurated July 1, 1805, with Detroit as the capital.[3]

According to the act that set it off, the new territory included the vast area east of a line northward from the most southerly point of Lake Michigan, and north of a line from this same point to Lake Erie. Actually there was only a small area available for settlement. By the Treaty of Greenville, the Indians had ceded a strip six miles wide that extended along the Detroit River some forty odd miles from the River Raisin to Lake Saint Clair, the lands around Detroit, and a small area at Mackinaw. By the Treaty of Detroit in 1807, the Indians ceded an additional strip that ran inland about fifty miles, and stretched northward from the southern boundary of Michigan Territory.[4] The few civilized inhabitants of Michigan, 3,106 in 1800, with little increase by 1805,[5] dwelt chiefly along the Detroit River and on the banks of its tributary streams, with a small trading post at Mackinaw. In the rural districts the farms of the French settlers usually boasted a water front of three to five acres, and extended in

[2] Memorial October 24, 1804, and Petition of "Democratic Republicans," 1804, *Indiana Territorial Papers*, Senate Files, 2691.
[3] *Annals of Congress*, Eighth Congress, Second Session, pp. 1659-1660.
[4] *Eighteenth Report, Bureau of American Ethnology*, part 2, 1896–1897, pp. 654, 656, 676, and map no. 29.
[5] *U. S. Census*, 1800, p. 85.

long, narrow form about fifty acres to a back line, but none of them was more than 400 acres in area. Like the *habitants* of the Illinois settlements, these French farmers were exceedingly conservative, and were quite wasteful in their agricultural methods. Few of them were educated, but there were many chapels throughout the countryside, for they were a devout people. In Detroit itself, there were many fur traders, some of whom lived in great abundance, but a number of them had migrated across the river when the Americans took possession, and by 1805 this important post was far from prosperous. The houses, for the most part, were low, inelegant, and in bad repair, and even the pickets of the stockade were much decayed. For many years the inhabitants of Detroit and the near-by rural districts had been accustomed to solve their petty disputes before the commandant, and they were, of course, quite ignorant of American institutions.[6]

With so unpromising a population, much care and tact would be necessary at the outset in order to establish the territorial government. Officials experienced in frontier conditions were essential, but strange to say, Jefferson's appointments for Michigan were political in nature, and showed little, if any, appreciation of the demands of the situation. The new governor, William Hull, was a man of fifty-two, a Yale graduate who had served with distinction in the Revolution, and had won an enviable reputation in Massachusetts as a lawyer of much ability. Unfortunately, lacking the personal force so essential in the governor of a frontier region, he was easily dominated by a more masterful will, nor had he had any practical experience with Western life. Under such conditions, Augustus B. Woodward, one of the judges, easily became the controlling power in the territorial government. An exceedingly aggressive and im-

[6] Report of C. Jouett, Indian Agent at Detroit, to Secretary of War, July 25, 1803, *Michigan Territorial Papers,* Senate Files, 3501; *Michigan Pioneer Collections,* vol. I, pp. 347-371; Burnet, *Notes on the Northwestern Territory,* pp. 281-287, and note.

perious personage, he was a comparatively young man, little more than thirty-one, and was an ardent admirer of Jefferson. Selfish and quarrelsome, he constantly bullied his colleagues and concocted grandiose schemes for projects that went far beyond the slender resources of a pioneer territory, for, like the governor, he lacked practical experience on the frontier.[7] The one important officer of the new government who really understood the critical local situation was the second judge, Frederick Bates, a native of Virginia who had come to Detroit in 1795, and had built up a prosperous business. He was soon transferred to Upper Louisiana, and his successor, John Griffin, also a native Virginian who had already served as a judge of Indiana Territory, became a tool of Judge Woodward. The secretary, Stanley Griswold, was another unfortunate choice. Born in Connecticut and, like the governor, a graduate of Yale, he had served in the Revolution. After studying for the ministry he was branded as thoroughly unorthodox and a supporter of the Jeffersonian heresies, two deadly sins in conservative New England. Griswold drifted into journalism, and won his office as secretary of Michigan Territory through his political activities. Like Judge Woodward he was erratic and aggressive, and a born trouble maker. Among these territorial officers dissensions would be inevitable, while their general lack of understanding of frontier conditions, added to a weak executive, made the outlook for the new territorial government one that was far from promising.

Discouraging as the situation was in Michigan, it became far more gloomy when a fire, June 11, 1805, practically wiped out the entire town of Detroit. Hull arrived July 1, a little more than two weeks later, to find the despairing inhabitants living in temporary shelters, and everything in the utmost confusion. Although he was unable to secure suitable accommodations for nearly a week, he promptly went to work the day after his arrival. As always, he was energetic, but unfortunately he lacked an understanding of local con-

[7] *Michigan Pioneer and Historical Collections,* vol. XXIX, pp. 638-664.

ditions. In an address to the inhabitants, which the majority, not speaking English, could not understand, he carefully outlined their rights under the Ordinance and bespoke their coöperation. Next, without any consideration for the customs of the French inhabitants, he proceeded to set up the usual American local institutions, with one county that was divided into the four districts of Erie, Detroit, Huron, and Michillimackinac. This basic organization he completed by the appointment of a marshal for the territory, of justices of the peace in the districts, and of a suitable complement of militia officers.[8] Hull's next important task was to provide a legal code. Theoretically the laws of Indiana Territory were still in force here, but probably there was not a complete copy in all Michigan. An additional complication was the uncertain status of laws from the French and British régimes, but of these, too, no compilation was available. This legal uncertainty the governor and judges partially solved by the passage of a fairly complete code, but as they did not definitely repeal previous laws, much confusion arose. In characteristic fashion Judge Woodward played the leading rôle, successfully upholding his own interpretation of the Ordinance, that any three of the four chief officers, the governor and the three judges, constituted a quorum to adopt laws. This construction, of course, denied the governor's veto power, and proportionately increased Judge Woodward's own influence. He held, also, that the power to adopt laws of the original states covered those of all the states that had been formed before Michigan Territory was set off, not merely those of the original thirteen, and he cited precedents in Indiana in support of his position.[9] With this broad interpretation of their powers, the governor and the judges adopted the thirty-one laws commonly known as Woodward's Code. Four of them they took from the Code of New

[8] Hull to Secretary of State, August 3, 1805, and Executive Proceedings of Michigan Territory, July 1, 1805, to January 1, 1806, *Michigan Territorial Papers*, B. R. L.
[9] *Michigan Pioneer Collections*, vol. VIII, pp. 603-605; vol. XXXI, pp. 562-565.

York, which Hull had brought with him, four from that of
Virginia, and others from the codes of Maryland, Massachusetts, Ohio, and Pennsylvania. Seventeen of these Michigan
acts combined sections from different states, as for example
the one regulating fees which was made up from the laws of
six states. The legislative board also used much freedom
with the original laws, adopting them in principle, rather
than word for word. Professedly they adopted from the New
York Code a law that authorized a lottery of $20,000.00 for
the "encouragement of literature" and the "improvement" of
Detroit, but they made many alterations in the original law
in order to fit it to local needs. Such liberal interpretation
of the powers granted by the Ordinance was altogether necessary, and the legislative board protected itself in each instance by the saving clause, adopted from a New York law,
"as far as necessary and suitable to the circumstances of
the territory of Michigan." [10]

The new code would probably have suited a fairly populous American community, but at this time Michigan had
a very small population which was predominantly French.
This failure to recognize actual conditions is found throughout Woodward's Code. Thus, there was an elaborate judicial
system which created a supreme court presided over by the
three territorial judges, and a local court to be held twice
annually in each of the four districts which Hull had created.
In every district there was a marshal, also, whose manifold
duties corresponded to those of a sheriff, and lastly, the justices of the peace were given the usual jurisdiction over
petty criminal cases and over civil cases that did not involve
more than $20.00. This elaborate legal machinery, which
included various details of procedure, was drawn up, with
a truly New England lack of imagination, for a scant 3,000
inhabitants, of whom the greater number did not even understand the language in which these laws were written. Woodward's Code also outlined an elaborate system of taxation,
with taxes on each wheel of a pleasure vehicle, upon sleds,

[10] *Laws of the Territory of Michigan*, vol. I, pp. 2-92.

upon dogs, upon horses and upon mules, and a poll tax of $1.00 upon every inhabitant sixteen years of age and over. There were license fees, too, that varied between $10.00 and $50.00, upon ferry keepers, retailers of merchandise, tavern keepers, and auctioneers, with a tax of three per cent upon sales by auction in the district of Detroit, and two per cent elsewhere. Apparently the legislative board expected this scheme of taxation to be successful, for they made appropriations at the very outset that totaled $1,264.62½. Another important law in so exposed a region required the enrolment in the militia of all male inhabitants between fourteen and fifty, and another one outlined a rather ambitious scheme for highways that required all male inhabitants twenty-one and over, "ministers of the gospel and priests excepted," to work not more than thirty nor less than one day annually. Marriage, too, was carefully regulated, as well as a multitude of minor matters. But the Woodward Code was entirely too elaborate for so limited a population, and even graver in its consequences was the failure to make any concessions to the French law to which the inhabitants were accustomed. To add to the confusion, the greater part of the French settlers could not read it, but regardless of such imperfections a committee recommended to the Senate in 1807 "not to disapprove" it, and Congress allowed it to stand.[11]

In spite of the lack of understanding and the rather grandiose point of view found in the Woodward Code, the territorial officers might have accomplished much more in Michigan had Congress supported them whole-heartedly. Hull, aided and in fact probably led by Judge Woodward, had promptly gone to work to direct the rebuilding of Detroit. Lots were laid out and the inhabitants began to build. But the necessary confirmation of their titles by Congress became entangled in the generally unsatisfactory land situation in Michigan, which was meeting the usual delay in adjustment, and was proving to be a serious obstacle to

[11] *Annals of Congress*, Ninth Congress, Second Session, p. 29.

American immigration. Hull and Woodward went personally to Washington, after the new code had been adopted, to urge the need to approve the measures they had already passed to meet the pressing situation in Detroit, and to adjust land claims throughout the inhabited sections of Michigan. They pointed out, too, the imperative need to modify the legislative powers of the governor and the judges under the Ordinance, since it was impossible to find laws that were suited to local conditions. Consequently the legislative board, so they claimed, had tried to follow merely the "substance" of the original laws, and had made many necessary modifications in form. Even then, failing to find a "strict precedent," they had frequently neglected important matters. The only solution, Hull and Woodward intimated, was to give the board power to enact laws under the "parental control" of Congress, rather than merely to adopt them. An address to the President from the officers of the Michigan militia strongly supported these recommendations, and advocated a prompt settlement of land claims, together with the speedy extinguishment of Indian titles in order to secure lands for immigrants into Michigan.[12]

As the needs of Michigan Territory promised to meet considerable delay in Congress, Judge Woodward, in his usual energetic fashion, sent a memorial to the Senate that emphasized the necessity of immediate action, in order to adjust land titles in Michigan. "General professions of benevolence," he pointed out, no longer sufficed, and the inhabitants rightfully expected quick action. Also, Judge Woodward urged the need of some form of local representation in the government to enable the legislative board, which was acquainted with American jurisprudence alone, to make the necessary adjustments in favor of the French laws and customs. There should be a territorial delegate, too, who could present local grievances to Congress, although, in his opinion, the territory was not yet ready for the second

[12] *Annals of Congress*, Ninth Congress, First Session, pp. 42, 922-923; *Michigan Pioneer Collections*, vol. VIII, pp. 549-553.

grade of government. If only these matters were adjusted, it was Judge Woodward's optimistic belief that the rising "spirit of individual enterprise" would quickly lift the country above its present "distresses." If, however, the critical moment was lost, he feared that discord and discontent would destroy the accomplishments of years of labor.[13] Even this sane memorial did not convince Congress of the need for immediate action, and the sole legislation they adopted with regard to Michigan before the session ended was an act in April, 1806, that confirmed the steps already taken to lay out Detroit.[14] Hull, who was then in Washington, summed up in striking fashion the dismal situation of the American officials in Michigan, "surrounded by a savage foe, in the midst of a people strangers to our language, our customs and manners, without legal titles to property and no measures adopted by which they can be obtained, and not an acre of land to be offered to new settlers." [15] Still a final adjustment was delayed, and not until 1812, near the close of this early period, were the land titles in Michigan placed upon a really definite basis. Just as in Illinois, this long delay caused much local irritation and discontent, which, of course, increased the difficulties of the territorial government. Most serious of all was the retarding influence upon the American immigration which was so greatly needed.

While the governor and Judge Woodward were trying to secure coöperation from Congress, and after Hull returned to Michigan, the need for additional legislation became increasingly pressing. For some time nothing could be done. Judge Woodward and Judge Bates were both absent, and a quorum of the legislative board could not be secured.[16] The situation meanwhile became so serious that in August, 1806, the grand jury of the district court at Detroit drew up a list of the subjects upon which legislation was needed, inci-

13 *American State Papers*, Miscellaneous, vol. I, pp. 461-463.
14 *Annals of Congress*, Ninth Congress, First Session, pp. 1283-1284.
15 Hull to Secretary of State, April 30, 1806, *Michigan Territorial Papers*, B. R. L.
16 Hull to Secretary of State, August 28, 1806. *Ibid.*

dentally giving interesting sidelights upon local conditions. It was necessary, this report pointed out, to establish standard weights and measures, and to provide for the improvement of the highways and bridges, which were in "extreme bad order." There should be regulations, also, to compel the owners of stray animals to pay for the damages they committed, and to end the pernicious and slothful custom of throwing dead animals into the rivers. Other subjects for legislation, according to this report, were: the practice of racing horses along the public highways; "disorder and scandal" on the Sabbath; and "public hazard game houses." Moreover, the grand jury considered that "repeated insults" from the British across the river ought to be stopped. About a month later the territorial grand jury presented a much similar list of grievances.[17]

The legislative board finally met September 13, 1806, doubtless spurred on by the local complaints, and in the succeeding nine months they passed twenty-six additional laws, although, it must be confessed, very few of them were purposely drawn up to remedy the specific conditions of which the grand juries had complained.[18] Congress had not lightened the restrictions upon their legislative powers, as Hull and Woodward had suggested, but nevertheless the board passed at least seven laws without any pretense of adoption. As part of these acts decreased the rates upon various objects of taxation, or else reduced the salaries and fees of local officials, it would doubtless have been impossible to have found suitable measures in other codes. The remainder of these enacted laws were passed under the act of Congress which authorized the survey and the sale of the new site for Detroit, and the use of the proceeds to erect a courthouse and a jail. With this pretext, Judge Woodward now undertook to give legal sanction to his grandiose schemes for Detroit, and secured an appropriation of $20,-

17 *Michigan Pioneer Collections,* vol. XII, pp. 626-630.
18 For the laws passed September 2, 1806, to June 2, 1807, see *Laws of the Territory of Michigan,* vols. I, II, and IV, *passim.*

000.00 from the "Detroit fund" to erect an "edifice" in the public square, "for the permanent accommodation of the supreme court," and for a jail. The avenues of the new town were to be laid out in like generous fashion, with grass plots and double lines or clumps of trees on either side. The public squares were to be planted with trees, and spaces were to be reserved for public buildings, such as fire-engine houses, schools, and churches. Supplementing these "boom town" plans was an act that incorporated Detroit with an elaborate city government that was suited to a much larger population, in place of the simple organization that had been authorized under the Northwest Territory.

The remaining laws of this supplementary code were adopted from the codes of Connecticut, Maryland, Massachusetts, New York, Pennsylvania, and Virginia of the original states, and from those of Ohio and Kentucky of the later states. One of these acts needlessly elaborated the legal system by requiring the appointment of a chief judge and an associate to preside over each district court, and to have general charge of the financial affairs of the district. Another law, to prevent any unlawful expeditions against the United States, which was doubtless aimed at agitators from Canada, was copied almost literally from an Ohio act that had been adopted at the height of the agitation over Burr's schemes. Much different in type was an act to incorporate the Bank of Detroit, and another one that authorized religious societies to appoint trustees who should not hold over 2,000 acres at any one time. "The church usually denominated Catholic, Apostolic, and Roman" received special consideration in a clause that confirmed all its church property, subject only to taxation. These legislative proceedings included also numerous appropriations which the board made in haphazard fashion, probably as money became available. The numerous items for the burial of paupers are of special interest, since they doubtless reflected the widespread poverty in early Michigan. Upon the whole, barring Judge Woodward's exaggerated schemes for Detroit, these laws were somewhat of an improvement over earlier legislation in their recognition of local conditions.

The governor and the judges continued to suffer from the indifference with which Congress apparently regarded Michigan. Probably one of the explanations of this attitude was the isolation of the territory and the uncertain means of communication. A weekly mail from Detroit to Cleveland had theoretically been established by the time Michigan was set off as a separate territory. But it was not at all dependable, and there were frequent delays with many misunderstandings as a result. A striking illustration was the Federal attempt to conserve the extensive pine forests on Lake St. Clair after Gideon Granger, the postmaster-general, had complained that this timber was being wasted. August 1, 1805, the President directed Hull to issue a proclamation that forbade the cutting of governmental timber, and the governor, of course, carried out this order. At the same time he called Jefferson's attention to the acute need for timber to rebuild Detroit, and his fear that unless the government gave him discretionary power to permit the use of the pine forests, the inhabitants would be compelled to buy the necessary lumber from Canada at very high prices. Immediately upon receipt of this communication the Secretary of State empowered Hull to grant permission for cutting timber "to the poorer sufferers" by the conflagration. This permission scarcely reached Michigan before the latter part of January, 1806, and meanwhile the seeming refusal by the government to recognize a vital need must have added considerably to local discontent.[19]

Another source of much embarrassment was the lack of adequate financial support for the officers of the new territorial government. The governor's salary, $2,000.00, was am-

[19] Gideon Granger to the President, July 19, 1805, and Secretary of State to Hull, August 1 and December 13, 1805, *Michigan Territorial Papers,* B. I. A. Dom., 3508, 3509, 3512; Proclamation, September 4, 1805, and Governor Hull to Secretary of State, September 11, 1805, *Ibid.,* B. R. L., 3495.

ple, especially as Hull had a considerable private fortune. But Congress, following its usual parsimonious policy in dealing with the territories, allowed the secretary a salary of only $750.00, and the judges $800.00 each. Stanley Griswold, the secretary, complained that living expenses were higher at Detroit than in any other town in the United States. But he had not received an extra allowance for the heavy traveling expenses to his new post, nor was he given any additional compensation for the many expenditures he was obliged to make as acting governor during Hull's frequent absences from the territory. So serious did the situation become that Hull feared Griswold and the judges would all resign unless they were granted larger salaries.[20] In the secretary's case the situation was relieved temporarily by extra allowances that gave him a total income of $1,700.00, and in 1807 Congress increased his salary to $1,000.00, and that of each judge to $1,200.00.[21] Even then Reuben Atwater, who succeeded Griswold as secretary, complained that for thirteen months, beside the duties of his own office, he had acted as governor and commissioner of Indian affairs, without any extra compensation.[22] Congress was even more frugal with allowances for general expenses, and Hull arrived in Michigan to inaugurate a new government with no funds at all at his disposal to purchase stationery, or to pay for office rent and other necessary expenses. Thus, when he was obliged to secure a surveyor to lay out the town site of Detroit, there was no public fund upon which he could draw to pay for this very necessary work. This policy of Congress, to shoulder upon the territory all expenses except the salaries of the

[20] Stanley Griswold to Samuel Huntington, March 17, 1806, *Western Reserve MSS., Huntington Papers,* no. 112; Stanley Griswold to Secretary of State, December 3, 1805, and Governor Hull to Secretary of State, April 30, 1806, *Michigan Territorial Papers,* B. R. L.

[21] Stanley Griswold to Samuel Huntington, June 3, 1807, *Western Reserve MSS., Huntington Papers,* no. 113; *Annals of Congress,* Ninth Congress, Second Session, p. 1272; Tenth Congress, First Session, p. 2813.

[22] Petition of Reuben Atwater, January 4, 1813, *Michigan Territorial Papers,* Senate Files, 3570.

principal officers, worked badly in actual practice. The legislative board made appropriations and levied taxes, but the latter were probably not paid in view of the rather chaotic situation in early Michigan.[23] Even when Hull asked Congress for an appropriation to cover the very considerable expense of preparations to meet a threatened Indian attack in 1807, the Senate rejected the bill that the House had passed for this purpose.[24] So narrow a policy in Washington necessarily hampered the territorial government of Michigan in the early days of organization.

The troubles of the governor and the judges were much increased by the numerous controversies that arose with the British authorities in Upper Canada. An important source of difficulty was the British demand for the return of the slaves who escaped across the river to Michigan. Judge Woodward held that the few slaves left in Michigan in 1796, when the United States took over this region, retained their status, but that no additional slaves could legally be brought in. Basing his action upon this decision, Hull preëmptorily refused to return fugitives to their Canadian masters, and local opinion upheld him.[25] The bitter feeling that existed in Detroit was illustrated when eight slaves, the property of Matthew Elliott of Amherstburg, a former British agent among the Indians, fled to Michigan in 1807. When Elliott brought suit for the return of his slaves, "sundry disorderly persons" proposed to tar and feather him if he ventured across to Michigan, and he wisely concluded to stay at home. His agent, James Howard, who appeared in Detroit to secure the slaves, became involved in a mêlée in which he lost his wig, and received liberal decorations of tar and feathers on his hat and face. When Elliott's suit came to

[23] Various documents, *Michigan Territorial Papers*, B. I. A. Dom., 3507, 3513, 3514; Hill to Secretary of State, January 24, 1806, *Ibid.*, B. R. L.

[24] *Annals of Congress*, Ninth Congress, Second Session, pp. 88, 103, 290, 378, 622.

[25] Opinion of Judge Woodward (1807?), *Michigan Pioneer Collections*, vol. XII, pp. 517-518; Hull to Secretary of State, July 31, 1806, *Michigan Territorial Papers*, B. R. L.

trial, Judge Woodward refused to return the slaves, and he gave a similar decision in other cases.[26] Attempts to secure the return of British deserters from the army also caused much irritation. Major Campbell, the commandant at Amherstburg, complained that in one month he had lost about twenty men by desertion to the American side of the Detroit River. Finally, December 8, 1805, two British officers attempted to seize a deserter at River Rouge, but were compelled to surrender him to a mob that took him to Detroit for safe-keeping. Popular feeling against the two officers was very strong, and Stanley Griswold, who was acting governor, hysterically proclaimed that the "honor of our country" was involved. But Major Campbell was exceedingly conciliatory, disclaiming any connection with the affair, and insisting that the two officers must stand trial in an American court. There Judge Woodward, who was presiding, sentenced one officer to a fine of $40.00 and seventeen days' imprisonment, and the other one to a fine of £2,000 sterling and six months in prison. When other members of the legislative board objected to such excessive penalties, Judge Woodward in a pet reduced the fines to a few cents each, and freed the culprits. To ward off similar incidents in the future, Judge Woodward proposed to adopt an act from the Code of Virginia that provided for the return of both the deserters and the slaves, but his colleagues would not agree, and no definite action was taken.[27]

The hostility among the Michigan settlers toward the British across the river, which the attempts to take back fugitive slaves and deserters brought to the surface, was shown in many other instances. Undoubtedly one of the chief explanations of this attitude was the widespread belief that the British agents were constantly carrying on intrigues among the Indians. So far as the British officials were concerned, these charges do not appear to have been well

[26] *Michigan Pioneer Collections*, vol. XXXVI, pp. 181-189, 201.
[27] *Michigan Pioneer Collections*, vol. XII, pp. 505-507, 653-654; vol. XV, pp. 27-32, 37-38; vol. XXXI, pp. 546, 551-556.

founded, but with respect to the fur traders and their agents, there was a substantial basis, although, as always, rumors were greatly exaggerated in the popular imagination. In 1807 Hull found it necessary to call the attention of the British commandant at Amherstburg to alleged breaches of international good faith. At the same time he issued a significant proclamation that, inasmuch as "diverse persons" had habitually sent wampum, and had held councils with the Indians without the sanction of the American officers, he strictly forbade everyone, citizen or foreigner, to commit such acts in the future, and called upon the people of Michigan to be "vigalant" in apprehending offenders.[28] Another cause of prejudice was the effort on the part of former residents, who had established themselves in the British settlements after the Americans took over Detroit, to return and set up their claims to American citizenship after the land commissioners at Detroit began to award donation tracts. Rather famous cases locally were those of Robert Forsythe and John Gentle, who claimed American citizenship as a basis for establishing land claims. In each case Judge Woodward gave an adverse decision, upon the ground that neither of them had complied with the requirements for residence in the territory. These cases established a precedent which doubtless prevented many refugees from returning to Michigan, in order to set up somewhat shadowy claims to land.[29] But like the rumors of Indian intrigues, such attempts stirred up local prejudices and made all the harder the task of the responsible officials.

To make matters worse, internal dissensions soon arose over the high-handed fashion in which Judge Woodward dominated the government. This local opposition came to a climax when he arrogantly sent a bill to Congress, suggesting modifications in the territorial government which would

[28] Governor Hull to Secretary of State, September 15, 1807, *Michigan Territorial Papers*, B. R. L.
[29] *Michigan Pioneer Collections*, vol. XXXVI, pp. 199-201.

have greatly increased the powers of the governor and the judges, and his own as well. The grand jury of Michigan now drew up a protest, objecting especially to proposals to give the governor and judges power to originate laws, to make the judges the upper house of the legislature, and to substitute the chief justice—that is, Judge Woodward—for the secretary as acting governor in the governor's absence. This protest was effective in preventing the passage of Judge Woodward's bill by Congress.[30] A meeting of citizens in Detroit also protested against the "ill-intentioned" proceedings of Judge Woodward, in resolutions that were presented to the legislative board by George McDougall, Jr., a former sheriff and a delegate from Wayne County to the territorial assembly of the Northwest Territory. Calling attention to the extravagant appropriation of $20,000.00 under Judge Woodward's influence, to erect a courthouse and a jail which were not suited to the "present circumstances" of the territory, these resolutions proposed that local control should be restored over expenditures for such purposes. They complained, too, that Judge Woodward had arbitrarily kept the grand jury in session for an entire year.[31]

From his colleagues in the legislative board, also, Judge Woodward had begun to meet opposition, which, impetuous and irascible as he was, he would not endure in silence. Early in November, 1806, he wrote a letter that scathingly criticized the "injudicious conduct" of the territorial government, and cited instances of the "contempt," in his opinion with which its officers were regarded, in order to justify his own temporary withdrawal from active duties. This "extraordinary" communication the legislative board made public and forwarded to Washington, with a statement that the majority of the charges were "without semblance" of foundation, and that many persons considered the writer in a

[30] Remonstrance of Grand Jury, October 28, 1806, *Michigan Territorial Papers*, Senate Files, 3523; *Michigan Pioneer Collections*, vol. XXXI, pp. 571-572.
[31] *Michigan Pioneer Collections*, vol. VIII, pp. 579-582.

"state of unhappy lunacy."[32] Judge Woodward soon returned to his accustomed place on the board, but it was
quite apparent that he had made a grandstand play to bol-
ster up his own influence. Less than two months later, just
before he left for Washington, he sounded another note of
warning in thirteen resolutions which he submitted to the
legislative board. This time Judge Woodward caused an
open breach with the long-suffering Hull, whose official conduct this document criticized in detail. It called attention
especially to the popular criticism that had been directed
against the arbitrary employment of the militia to erect fortifications that, Woodward considered, cramped the growth
of Detroit; against certain unauthorized expenditures;
against allegedly illegal commissions to justices of the peace;
and against the arbitrary removal of officers. The resolutions also urged the need for educational facilities, for a
road between Detroit and the Maumee Rapids, and for a
complete revision of the laws.[33]

Hull countered Judge Woodward's attack in shrewd
fashion, and warded off any chance that the legislative board
might approve the latter's resolutions by managing to have
himself appointed a committee to answer them. Two years
later, in Judge Woodward's absence, he submitted a report
to the legislative board, which he also sent to Washington
as a vindication of his own official conduct. Approving the
territorial needs as they had been outlined by Woodward,
Hull answered in detail the specific criticisms of his administration, and strongly denounced the resolutions, as due
in part to Woodward's personal prejudices, as "unfortunate
in principle or in truth," and as "irrelevant" to the powers
of the legislative board, and finally, as likely to stir up trouble.[34] Meanwhile Woodward busied himself in attempts to

[32] Judge Woodward to Legislative Board, November 5, 1806, and Griswold to Secretary of State, November 12, 1806, Michigan Territorial Papers,
B. R. L.
[33] Michigan Pioneer Collections, vol. XII, pp. 462-465.
[34] Hull to Secretary of State, December 22, 1808, Michigan Territorial
Papers, B. R. L.; Michigan Pioneer Collections, vol. XII, pp. 466-472.

prejudice the Federal officials at Washington against Hull, whose commission would expire early in 1808. He laid great stress upon the discord in Michigan, and upon the popular opposition to the governor.[35] In a letter directly to the Secretary of State, he criticized severely the treaty with the Indians which Hull proposed, and finally concluded in 1807. When this letter was made public, Woodward, now openly hostile to Hull, retired to Monticello, the estate on the River Raisin which he had named in honor of his friend, Jefferson, and there he continued his intrigues, even sending to Washington the petty gossip that his henchman, Peter Audrain, retailed from Detroit. As a climax to his campaign he wrote, to the President apparently, a letter that, under pretense of revealing certain alleged French intrigues among the Indians, called attention to the "high and serious dissensions" between the governor and the secretary of Michigan Territory. For eight months, Judge Woodward declared, he himself had had no communication with Hull, who was guilty of "indiscretions", and not for sixteen months with Griswold, who was full of "malice," [36] But Woodward's charges failed in their purpose, and the President reappointed Hull April 1, 1808.

Probably the chief cause of the break between Hull and Woodward was the friction that arose between them over the Bank of Detroit.[37] At first the governor warmly supported this undertaking, which was engineered by Boston speculators, and it was through his influence that Judge Woodward's interest was enlisted. To the latter, with his visionary schemes for the development of Michigan, this speculative project for a great bank and a fur-trading company, which might be compared to the Mississippi Bubble, or the plans for the Massachusetts Land Bank, had a special

[35] *Michigan Pioneer Collections,* vol. XII, pp. 505-507.

[36] Peter Audrain to Judge Woodward, January 19, 1808, and Judge Woodward to Secretary of State, January 23, 1808, *Michigan Territorial Papers,* B. R. L.; *Michigan Pioneer Collections,* vol. XII, pp. 508-511.

[37] For a detailed account of the Bank of Detroit, see *Michigan History Magazine,* vol. I, pp. 41-62.

appeal, and he supported it with his usual impetuous zeal. Then, having secured the coöperation of the two most influential officers of Michigan Territory, these Boston promoters petitioned the legislative board to incorporate a bank with a capital of between $80,000.00 and $100,000.00. Without waiting for a charter, they put up a banking house in Detroit, elected Judge Woodward president, and opened for business, with a cashier, William Flanagan, who had been sent out from Boston.[38] Hull drew up the act of incorporation, but Judge Woodward, carried away by his visionary hopes, insisted that the authorized capital should be increased to $1,000,000.00, divided into 10,000 shares, and that the charter should run for one hundred and one years. With these conditions included, an act was passed September 19, 1806, which virtually made the notes of the bank legal tender in Michigan, by a provision that they should be accepted in all payments to the territorial treasury. There was no restriction upon these issues, except that payment in specie was binding upon the bank, and their semiofficial status was emphasized by the authority which this act gave the governor to subscribe for stock in the bank in behalf of the territory.[39]

Doubtless both Hull and Woodward were sincere but ill-advised in aiding a speculative enterprise which, in their judgment, would be of much value to the development of Michigan. But this can scarcely be said of the promoters who carried off to Boston at least $165,000.00 of the bank's notes which they promptly put into circulation. Aroused by this wildcat currency, the more conservative bankers of Boston induced Josiah Quincy to work in Congress against this Western speculative scheme, and they succeeded even in arousing the President, although Judge Woodward sent a lengthy and optimistic statement in its defense. Congress

[38] *Michigan Pioneer Collections*, vol. II, pp. 111-112; vol. VIII, pp. 571-576; vol. XXIX, pp. 643-644.

[39] *Laws of the Territory of Michigan*, vol. IV, pp. 7-9; Augustus B. Woodward to Secretary of State, January 31, 1807, *Michigan Territorial Papers*, B. R. L., 3537.

soon passed an act that "disapproved" the territorial law which had granted a charter to the Bank of Detroit.[40] The anomalous position in which the bank was now placed greatly injured the prestige of Judge Woodward as its president. Notes of the bank soon began to find their way back to Detroit, where, of course, payment was refused. Hull, who had so strongly backed the bank in the beginning, now endeavored to escape from any responsibility, and announced that he had become convinced that the promoters of the scheme had "improper views" in the beginning, and that the management was "highly reprehensible." In a public address he declared that the bank was not a public institution, and that its notes were merely promises to pay the principal out of the capital stock and other funds. He intimated, too, that control over private banks, which existed in many states, would be considered in Michigan as well.[41]

Judge Woodward was now placed in a most embarrassing position. His connection with the ill-fated Bank of Detroit made him the target of much criticism from the many persons who had suffered large losses. Even the President and the members of the Cabinet were impressed by the local hostility toward the chief justice, and there was talk of impeachment. In his own defense Woodward vehemently denied he had taken any part in land speculations at Detroit, and he probably told the truth. Also, he promised a published statement of his connection with the bank, which, of course, was not forthcoming.[42] But the entire incident, together with the reappointment of Hull, whom he had so strenuously opposed, greatly weakened his influence in Michigan, and for a time Woodward sulked on his estate

[40] Secretary of State to Hull, December 6, 1806, *Michigan Territorial Papers*, B. I. A. Dom. 3527; *Annals of Congress*, Ninth Congress, Second Session, pp. 96, 103, 482, 619, 1287.

[41] Governor Hull to Secretary of State, May 28, 1807, and Address, May 17, 1808, *Michigan Territorial Papers*, B. R. L.; *Michigan Pioneer Collections*, vol. VIII, p. 574.

[42] *Michigan Pioneer Collections*, vol. VIII, pp. 561-562; vol. XXXVI, pp. 205-206; Judge Woodward to Secretary of State, March 14, 1807, *Michigan Territorial Papers*, B. R. L.

on the River Raisin, refusing to take part in the territorial
government. His colleagues on the legislative board seized
the opportunity to complete the overthrow of the bank, by
an act that prohibited the circulation of the notes of a private
bank as general currency. At the same time they forbade the
issue of bills of credit by private institutions.[43] The officials
of the bank appealed in vain for reconsideration of this
measure, and with the departure of the cashier for his native
Boston, May 16, 1809, the Bank of Detroit collapsed. The
large issues of notes became worthless, and the entire trans-
action left an unsavory odor in Michigan which did not increase the public confidence in Hull and Woodward, the two
territorial officials who were popularly, and rightfully,
credited with lending their influence to this scheme.

Besides his quarrels with Judge Woodward, Hull was disturbed by the reported machinations of the secretary, Stanley Griswold, who appears to have been an envious and
rather malicious individual. Indeed, while no open accusations were made, Griswold seems to have fallen under suspicion during the agitation over Burr's intrigues, and he
himself complained of the failure to report to him the measure for defense that the legislative board adopted at that
time.[44] At first Griswold directed his wrath chiefly against
Judge Woodward, whom he roundly berated in private letters that scored the Bank of Detroit as an enterprise, although it is apparent that his chief objection was that he
himself had been left out in the cold so far as this scheme
was concerned. Soon he included Hull in his generously be-
stowed criticisms, scoring the governor's tactics in dealing
with the Indians, and his failure, in Griswold's eyes, to provide sufficient means of defense at Detroit in case of an
emergency. The truth probably was that Griswold was
working to secure a territorial appointment for himself,
either as governor or as a judge. Hull, who was aware of

[43] *Laws of the Territory of Michigan,* vol. IV, pp. 22-23.
[44] Stanley Griswold to Secretary of State, February 21, 1807, *Michigan
Territorial Papers,* B. R. L.

Griswold's intrigues, countered these charges by openly denouncing the "contemptible faction," including the secretary of the territory, which was "influenced by a number of British subjects," and had consistently opposed every measure of the government.[45] The limit of patience was reached when Griswold joined openly in the general criticism of Hull's action in calling out three companies of militia in December, 1807, only a short time after a treaty had been concluded with the Indians. Thoroughly exasperated, Hull now issued a proclamation that called attention to the "dangerous faction" that included certain persons "in the government" who were "inflaming the minds of the people" by the "basest falsehoods," and were encouraging desertions among the militia. This proclamation had been issued, he added, to "admonish" these persons of their duties, and to call upon all officers and citizens to discourage such "pernicious conduct." This vigorous denunciation in Michigan Hull followed with equally strong representations to Washington officials, and Griswold soon received a curt note informing him that the President "thought proper" to revoke his commission as secretary of Michigan Territory.[46] Thus Hull triumphed over the second territorial official who had come out in open opposition to him.

With Griswold dismissed, and Woodward effectually silenced, Hull was seemingly master of the situation after his reappointment, April 1, 1808. But Griswold remained in Detroit for a time, doubtless sowing dissension as usual, while Woodward, from his country residence on the River Raisin, was ever ready to seize upon any possible pretext in order to stir up trouble. However, two fellow New England-

---

[45] Stanley Griswold to Samuel Huntington, June 3 and July 10, 1807, *Western Reserve MSS. Huntington Papers*, 113 and 114; Hull to Secretary of State, July 26, 1807, *Michigan Territorial Papers*, B. R. L.

[46] *Michigan Pioneer Collections*, vol. XXXVI, p. 206; *Executive Proceedings*, December 7, 1807, and January 16, 1808, *Michigan Territorial Papers*, B. R. L.; Secretary of State to Stanley Griswold, March 16, 1808, *Ibid.*, B. I. A. Dom.

ers soon came to Hull's aid. The new secretary to succeed Griswold, Reuben Atwater, a native of Connecticut, appeared to Hull to be a "worthy, intelligent man," [47] and a third territorial judge, appointed about this time, James Witherell, was destined to exert great influence in Michigan. A native of Massachusetts, he had served in the Revolution, and had then settled in Vermont. There he was soon known as an able and experienced lawyer, and was a member of the governor's council when the President appointed him a judge of Michigan Territory. A man in the prime of life, forty-nine years old, with practical experience upon the New England frontier, Judge Witherell speedily stepped into Judge Woodward's former position as the dominating factor in the territorial government, for with so weak an executive as Hull, it was necessary that some one of the judges assume leadership. Witherell's sturdy patriotism was strikingly shown upon a well-known occasion when he appeared before the legislative board completely clothed in articles of American manufacture, and secured a resolution that after July 4, 1813, all officers of Michigan Territory, when engaged in public duties, should appear "clothed in articles the manufacture of the continent of North America." [48] With many common interests, Witherell and Hull speedily became warm friends, and the latter entered upon his second term with high hopes. In a public address he reviewed in optimistic fashion the achievements during the three years of his administration, and pledged his sincere desire to serve the public. Now that there was a quorum in the legislative board, Judge Griffin also being on hand, Hull promised that many matters which had been neglected during the past year would receive attention. As evidence of the economy with which the government had been carried on he noted the balance of $600 in the treasury, and in conclusion he ex-

[47] Hull to Secretary of State, June 2, 1808, *Michigan Territorial Papers*, B. R. L.

[48] Sheldon, *Early History of Michigan*, pp. 389-390; *Michigan Pioneer Collections*, vol. VIII, p. 616.

pressed the hope that the progress already made in the territory would continue and increase.[49]

The way was soon prepared for a legislative program, even though Judge Woodward still sulked at his country home. An act which the legislative board adopted at its first meeting, November 9, 1808, declared that three of its members constituted a quorum, and two a majority. Under these conditions, the act declared, a law could be "regularly passed," and needed only the signature of the presiding officer, rather than those of the majority of the board, as had been the usual custom. This act, which professedly had been adopted from the codes of Vermont and Connecticut, really avoided any blocking of legislation by Judge Woodward's absence, and, at the same time, it minimized the influence of Judge Griffin, his strong ally. The actual power over legislation was now lodged with Hull and Judge Witherell, and the latter's strong influence was evident in a series of forty-six acts that were popularly known as Witherell's Code.[50] Eight of these acts were not adopted from those of the original states, but were in reality enacted either to repeal former measures, notably the one that authorized aliens to hold lands in Michigan, or else to provide for local situations, for which precedents could not be found. A measure of the latter type authorized a lottery of $6,000.00, to survey and lay out a road 120 feet wide, from Detroit to the foot of Maumee Rapids, while other acts fixed license fees and the salaries of various officials, or else made minor appropriations.

Of the remaining thirty-eight laws in the new code, eight were wholly and sixteen partly from the Code of Vermont, with which Judge Witherell was so familiar. The remainder were adopted from the codes of Connecticut, Massachusetts, New York, Pennsylvania, Virginia, and Ohio. Some of them

[49] Public Address by Governor Hull, May 27, 1808, *Michigan Territorial Papers*, B. R. L.

[50] For the acts passed November 9, 1808, to May 11, 1809, see *Laws of the Territory of Michigan*, vols. II and IV, *passim*.

were copied from a single law, others included sections from different codes. Among them were detailed provisions for the organization of courts. The jurisdiction of the supreme court was precisely defined, and to meet criticisms against Judge Woodward's arbitrary methods, this law required only one regular session annually, with special sessions to hear criminal and federal cases. In each district the legislative board established a district court, with a chief justice and two assistant judges to whom were assigned many functions of the former courts of quarter sessions, including especially the oversight and collection of the taxes upon land and upon many kinds of personal property, of a poll tax upon each male inhabitant between eighteen and sixty, and of an occupational tax upon lawyers, physicians, auctioneers, peddlers, and tavern and ferry keepers. Another function of the district court was to lay out highway districts, and to provide for public education, the latter function, strange to say, with the assistance of the overseers of the poor. A probate court, also, was established in each district, and the judges were empowered to appoint guardians for children who were living "in idleness and indulgence," and even to bind them out as apprentices. For petty cases in general, the law carefully defined the duties of the justices of the peace, extending their jurisdiction to cases that involved not over $30.00, or $50.00 where a note was in question. The legislative board also adopted an elaborate schedule of fees, including 25 cents to the jailer for turning the key upon each person committed or discharged. Other laws regulated the collection of debts, the recording of deeds, limitations of suits, the forms of writs and other processes, and the like. These laws would have established an unusually enlightened and well-defined system of courts that was well suited to an American population, as in Vermont. But it was too elaborate an organization for the few inhabitants of Michigan Territory, and it failed to recognize the peculiar customs of the ultra-conservative French who constituted the bulk of the population.

A number of other measures which the legislative board adopted were much more practical in their recognition of local needs. An elaborate act on crimes and punishments, for example, fixed capital punishment as the penalty for treason or aid to the enemies of the territory, and severely punished horse-stealing, forgery, and counterfeiting, all of them crimes of common occurrence in early Michigan. Additional acts regulated ferries, taverns, and public auctions, and set up elaborate regulations for legal enclosures. The legislative board also passed detailed militia acts that gave the governor extensive discretionary power in calling out the militia, probably in the hope of meeting the criticisms that had already been directed against Hull. The hostility of the board toward Judge Woodward was plainly evident in the ban which it placed upon the notes of the Bank of Detroit, leading, as has been noted, to the downfall of that institution. Hull and Witherell even proposed to set aside Judge Woodward's pet scheme for the development of Detroit upon a grand scale, and to substitute a "plain, practical plan." But at a public meeting only one person in thirty favored the change, and the laws already passed, to lay out a great city in the wilderness, were allowed to stand. Finally, Witherell's Code attempted to end any possible legal confusion, by providing that all laws of the Northwest and Indiana territories, before Michigan was organized, would "cease to have any force or operate within this territory."

The rather high-handed control which Judge Witherell and Hull exercised over the territory soon collapsed, in face of the continual complaints aroused by the arbitrary and somewhat ill-considered measures that Hull so often adopted. At the very beginning of his administration he needlessly stirred up the militia by an order that gave exact specifications for the uniforms to be worn by the different ranks. Riflemen, for instance, must wear "short green coats, turned up with buff, buff capes, round hats, black cockades and green feathers; in the warm season white vest and pantaloons with black gaiters; in the cold season green pantaloons edged with buff." [51] So elaborate an order to a backwoods militia revealed an alarming lack of a sense of humor on the part of the responsible officer, it must be confessed. More serious was the spirit of resentment it aroused among the militia, which increased in the fall of 1807 when Hull called them out to meet an Indian attack that failed to materialize, and then put them to work to rebuild the Detroit stockade, without any allowance for pay. Another incident that caused much criticism was the arbitrary removal of James Abbott as a justice of the peace for the district of Detroit and as a lieutenant colonel, without any reasons at all that were made public. Numerous other causes of friction occurred, which a tactful and able executive, such as Harrison in Indiana Territory, or Edwards in Illinois, would have warded off. Invariably they were seized upon by Hull's enemies, who were constantly on the watch for any pretext to attack him. Judge Woodward, too, through his henchmen, was supplied with news from Detroit, which he magnified whenever there was a possibility of discrediting the governor.[52] Thus, a street brawl that took place in April, 1808, and involved only four or five men, was magnified into a riot, and Judge Woodward even called the attention of the Secretary of State to this incident.[53]

Doubtless in an effort partly to regain his own prestige, Judge Woodward now became the leader of a movement to secure a greater degree of local control over the government in Michigan. Probably with his backing a bill had been presented to the House in 1806 to admit Michigan as a state when the population should reach 40,000, and in the ensuing debate the example of Ohio had been cited to support the argument that it was inconsistent with "republican policy" to keep territories "in vassalage." Despite such argu-

[51] Executive Proceedings, September 27, 1805, *Michigan Territorial Papers,* B. R. L.
[52] Especially Peter Audrain to Judge Woodward, January 19 and April 8, 1808, *Ibid.*
[53] *Michigan Pioneer Collections,* vol. XXXVI, pp. 210-212, 220-223.

ments, the House refused to pass the bill.[54] But the supporters of a greater degree of local autonomy were persistent, and October 16, 1809, Judge Woodward presided at a public meeting in Detroit which adopted a petition to Congress for the second grade of territorial government. This petition asked, too, that Michigan should be allowed a representative in Congress at once, and that the governor should have a modified veto.[55] These advocates of a curtailment of the governor's powers were not unopposed, and a counter-petition stated that many persons had signed the first one without due consideration. The Canadian French and the majority of the Americans, it was alleged, "totally opposed" it, and the inhabitants in general had the "fullest confidence in the talents, virtues, and correct views of the governor, and the secretary (Atwater) and Judge Witherell." A third petition likewise expressed "approbation" of the existing government, but sought the right to elect a delegate to Congress.[56] With such a diversity of opinion, the movement for the second grade of government naturally made little impression upon Congress. Equally fruitless was the insistent demand that the territorial laws should be translated into French, and the report of a committee, to which this matter was referred, reflected the strong Americanism of the period. If the petition were granted, the report pointed out, there would be two separate texts of the same laws, which would lead to "different and opposite interpretations." Moreover, it would tend to "encourage and perpetuate" the dialects in other parts of the Union, which "ought rather to be discouraged." In this unfavorable report the House concurred, and the matter was dropped,[57] but such summary action did

[54] *Annals of Congress*, Ninth Congress, First Session, pp. 922-923.
[55] *Michigan Pioneer Collections*, vol. XII, pp. 544-549.
[56] *Michigan Pioneer Collections*, vol. VIII, pp. 594-596; *Annals of Congress*, Eleventh Congress, Second Session, p. 1428.
[57] Petition from Michigan, January 23, 1809, *Michigan Territorial Papers*, House Files; *Annals of Congress*, Tenth Congress, Second Session, pp. 412, 1563; Eleventh Congress, Second Session, p. 1886.

not aid the enforcement of laws among a population that did not understand them.

The seeds of dissension that had been sown by Judge Woodward and other enemies of the governor finally bore fruit when a grand jury, sitting at Detroit, September 29, 1809, drew up a long list of grievances. They presented the governor, because he had remitted a fine imposed by Judge Woodward upon John Whipple who in the supreme court had called the judge a "dam'd rascal." They presented Judge Witherell, also, for an appropriation he had put through for the survey of the road to Maumee Rapids, when the expense should have been met from the proceeds of a public lottery. Among other causes of complaints were, the penalties prescribed for traitors, which, the grand jury maintained, were already taken care of by the Federal law, and another clause in the act on crimes and punishments which, they declared, denied the constitutional right of trial by jury. This indictment also charged that there had been irregularities in the management of the Detroit fund, and it scored the enrolment of blacks and aliens in the militia. Lastly, the grand jury unanimously suggested that the territorial laws should be translated into French.[58] This presentment was spread broadcast through the territory by the printing press which Father Richard had lately brought to Detroit, and doubtless it appeared in the columns of the *Michigan Essay*, which had appeared at Detroit about two weeks earlier.[59] Thus the way was prepared for a memorial to the President for the removal of Hull. Citing many of the grievances of which the grand jury had complained, this memorial also noted Hull's arbitrary orders to the militia, and alleged that the materials for the elaborate uniforms he had prescribed were sold at a store in Detroit he himself owned. The survey of the road from Detroit to Maumee Rapids, the memorial considered a waste of public funds,

[58] Presentment of Grand Jury of the Supreme Court of Michigan, September 29, 1809, *Michigan Territorial Papers*, Senate Files.
[59] *American Antiquarian Society Proceedings*, new series, vol. XXVI, p. 82.

since the work had been done in the dead of winter, and by
the following summer the route could scarcely be located.
In short, "the constant and incorrigible versatility of this
gentleman (*i.e.* Hull), his inconsistency and his non-adher-
ence even to his own measures," had brought on great per-
plexity and confusion. Worst of all, the memorial charged,
Hull had assumed legislative, executive, and judicial powers,
and laws, or "pretended laws," had appeared under his signature alone.[60] A citizen of Michigan, who had been neutral
in the factional strife, gave a correct diagnosis when he insisted that the President should remove both Hull and
Woodward, "if it is his wish to preserve it (the territory)
from final ruin and destruction."[61]

Hull's enemies did not secure his removal from office, but
at least they ended the practically unrestricted control which
he and Judge Witherell had exercised over the territorial
government. Judge Woodward now resumed his accustomed
place at the legislative board, and he was soon back in his
old position as the dominating influence in the affairs of
Michigan, practically dictating a series of laws that the
board adopted during the remainder of this early period in
Michigan.[62] The first act after his return repealed the inno-
vations in legislative procedure that had handed over control to Hull and Witherell, and provided, instead, that all
acts must be signed by the judges, as well as the governor.
Judge Woodward's complete triumph was marked by an act
adopted two weeks later, supposedly from the codes of
Connecticut, Vermont, and Virginia, but with unmistakable
evidences of a very free use of the originals. Repealing
outright all acts of the Northwest and Indiana territories,
under which the English common law had been established
in Michigan, the legislative board declared this action was
necessary, since the various acts of Parliament involved

[60] *Michigan Pioneer Collections*, vol. VIII, pp. 589-592.
[61] Letter "from a respectable inhabitant of Michigan Territory" to Stanley
Griswold, December 1, 1809, *Huntington Papers, Western Reserve MSS.*
[62] For the acts passed September 1, 1810, to January 14, 1812, see *Laws
of the Territory of Michigan*, vols. I, II, and IV, *passim.*

were not "published among the laws of the territory." For much similar reasons it annulled the common law of France, so far as it applied to Michigan, as well as the decrees of the kings of France, the French governors of Canada and Louisiana, and the British governors of Upper Canada. Likewise, following the precedent in Witherell's Code, the board declared that the laws of the Northwest and Indiana territories before the separation of Michigan were of no force there for the future, since many of them were out of print, and were "intermingled with multiplicity of laws which do not concern or apply to this country." Thus far the board had swept away all legal uncertainties that were legacies from previous régimes. Next it proceeded to repeal all the laws that had been passed in Michigan Territory between June 2, 1807, and September 1, 1810, while Judge Woodward was absent from the legislative board. This meant the restoration of the Woodward Code and the twenty-six laws passed in 1806 and 1807, as the code of Michigan Territory.

The drastic legal changes after Judge Woodward's return to power were not universally popular. A petition to the governor and the judges alleged that the Woodward Code was "replete with imitations and inconsistencies," and that it had not observed the restricted legislative powers that the Ordinance had granted. Witherell's Code, the petitioners declared, was "more wholesome." They objected, also, to the "newfangled system" that laid out the territory in districts, and handed over the work of civil magistrates to a marshal, and they much preferred the "ordinary laws" of Ohio, with sheriffs, constables, and courts of common pleas.[63] The legislative board partially granted this petition by the abolition of the district courts. Petty cases were now heard by the justices of the peace, with a right of appeal, while more important cases came before the supreme court. This simplified legal structure was much better suited to the needs of the territory, and still another legitimate source of discontent was removed by assigning the collection of taxes, local expendi-

[63] *Michigan Pioneer Collections*, vol. VIII, pp. 617-620.

tures, and the like to five commissioners in each district who were to be elected by manhood suffrage. Other laws which the reconstituted board adopted were concerned with such legal matters as forcible entry and detainer, and the forms for warrants and other legal documents. A rather interesting act fixed the fees of an attorney in the supreme court at $5.00 if the case was settled in court, and only $2.50 if it was settled outside. This act, like the other laws adopted at this time, purported to be based upon the codes of the different states, but in customary fashion the board used great freedom in alterations of the originals, and in the combination of sections from different codes. A series of appropriation acts completed the work of the legislative board for this early period in Michigan, although the haphazard fashion in which they were passed showed how unsatisfactory was the financial situation, an impression that was confirmed by items for as much as three years' arrears of salary for different officials.

With the increase of Indian alarms and rumors of war, the situation in Michigan soon became too troubled to permit attention to legislation. Hull left Detroit in October, 1811, and Reuben Atwater, the acting governor, was busy with military preparations in the following months.[64] With Hull's surrender, August 16, 1812, the early period of Michigan Territory came to an end. In striking contrast to Ohio, Indiana, and Illinois, in Michigan the territorial government that had been set up under the terms of the Ordinance had proven a complete failure. The explanations were varied. The great majority of the local population was not sympathetic with, and did not even understand American institutions, and the hoped-for influx of the settlers who were so necessary to support the territorial government, as they had done in Illinois, did not materialize. The real root of the troubles in Michigan lay in the unfortunate appointments of men who lacked practical knowledge of frontier prob-

[64] Executive Proceedings, July 1 to December 31, 1811, *Michigan Territorial Papers*, B. R. L.

lems, and who were temperamentally ill-adapted to the responsibilities they undertook. The failure on the part of Congress to appreciate the needs of the territory, and to give the officers there adequate support, was still another important cause for the unfortunate situation that arose in Michigan. The constant quarrels, too, between the responsible officers, and the overbearing attitude of Judge Woodward, had a part in the final debacle, along with Hull's instability and general incompetence as an executive. A more positive and practical governor, as Harrison, might have done much toward the upbuilding of Michigan as an American territory. But under a weak executive, and carried on with a noteworthy disregard of the actual demands of the local situation, the territorial government failed for the time being to establish American power firmly on this distant frontier.

Chapter IX

THE CONQUEST OF THE INDIANS

THROUGHOUT the early history of the Old Northwest, from the first American settlement in 1788 to the outbreak of the War of 1812, the Indians constantly menaced the shifting outer fringe of settlement. Just as they had opposed the aggressive moves of the American colonies, and had favored the French traders up to 1763, after American settlement began in earnest the Indians turned against the pioneers whom they considered intruders upon their lands, and favored the traders from Canada. While the different tribes of the Old Northwest were comparatively few in number, probably never more than 45,000,[1] they were usually of a rather superior type, and were able to offer effective resistance, especially when they were backed by the Canadian fur traders. When American settlement first began in the Old Northwest the fierce Shawnees occupied the Scioto Valley, with the milder Delawares to the eastward, and the Wyandots and the Ottawas to the northward. To the westward the powerful Miami confederacy formed the backbone of resistance to settlement in the Miami, the upper Wabash, and the Maumee valleys. In the Wabash Valley there were a number of smaller tribes, the Piankeshaws, the Potawatomies, and the Kickapoos. Still further to the west the once powerful Illinois confederacy had almost disappeared by 1788, the Kaskaskias were a mere handful, and the Winnebagoes, the Sacs, and the other tribes north of the Illinois River had little contact with the American settlers

[1] Cf. *Ante,* ch. 1, p. 3., (note 2).

during this early period.[2] These Indian tribes commonly maintained that, by the Treaty of Fort Stanwix in 1768, the land north and west of the Ohio was theirs, and they resented any intrusions by the white man for permanent settlement. But gradually they were overawed, and the account of their conquest by the superior race logically falls into two periods: from the first American settlements in 1788 to the Battle of Fallen Timbers in 1794, followed by the Treaty of Greenville in 1795; and from the Treaty of Greenville to the Battle of the Thames in 1813 and the Peace of Ghent in 1814.

In the earlier period, up to the Treaty of Greenville, the usual American policy in dealing with the Indians was an opportunistic one that, as was so often the case in matters relating to the Western country, paid little attention to the actual situation. Congress continued the British policy of two departments to supervise Indian affairs, roughly divided by the Ohio, and St. Clair, as governor of the Northwest Territory, became superintendent of the Northern Indian Department. According to his instructions, St. Clair was to try to remove all causes of Indian discontent, and in his inaugural address at Marietta, July 15, 1788, he emphasized the necessity to cultivate good relations between the two races, and to observe strict justice toward the savages.[3] The Indians, he soon found, were greatly dissatisfied with the treaty, signed at Fort McIntosh in 1785, which had set aside lands in northwestern Ohio for the Wyandots, the Delawares, the Chippewas, and the Ottawas, and with the one negotiated at Fort Finney in 1786 that assigned to the Shawnees the land between the Miami and the Wabash. In an effort to restore good feeling, St. Clair concluded a new treaty at Fort Harmar, January 9, 1789, which was specially notable for its provisions to punish Indians and Americans

[2] Randall and Ryan, *History of Ohio*, vol. I, chs. VI and VII; Esarey, *History of Indiana*, vol. I, pp. 78-87; Alvord, *The Illinois Country*, ch. II; *Harrison's Messages and Letters*, vol. II, pp. 636-642.

[3] *American State Papers, Indian Affairs*, vol. I, pp. 9-10; *Executive Proceedings Northwest Territory*, 1788-1795, pp. 2-8.

equally if they committed crimes against one another, and also to ensure the return of horses that were stolen by either race.[4] Unfortunately neither the powerful Shawnees nor the Miamis attended these negotiations, and Indian raids continued against the scattered settlements in the Ohio Valley. In addition to the discontent caused by the treaties, St. Clair discovered that unscrupulous traders were causing much friction, and it was probably partly due to his suggestion that Congress passed acts in 1792 and 1793 to regulate the Indian trade. These laws required traders to be American citizens and to take out licenses, giving bond to observe all official regulations. Any trader found in the Indian country without a license would forfeit all his merchandise, and a special license was necessary to purchase horses there from the Indians. In order to put an end to irregular trading from unauthorized posts, Congress prohibited any purchase of land from the Indians except through a treaty, thus restricting cessions of land to those made upon official initiative. The enforcement of these regulations and the general oversight of Indian relations was entrusted to the superintendents of Indian affairs, which meant, of course, St. Clair in the Old Northwest.[5] Numerous regulations supplemented the acts by Congress on the Indian trade. Thus, St. Clair's instructions to Jean Baptiste Mayet, commandant at Peoria, emphasized the necessity of impressing upon the Indians their obligation to keep the peace, and of enforcing the law that restricted trading to the American citizens who had secured licenses. In addition, Mayet was to require all travelers through the Illinois country to show passes.[6] This last instruction was supported by an act of the governor and the judges which positively forbade all aliens to engage in the Indian trade after January 1, 1791, evidently with the hope that Canadian traders would there-

[4] *American State Papers, Indian Affairs,* vol. I, pp. 6-7 and 11.
[5] *Ibid.,* vol. I, p. 4; *Annals of Congress,* First Congress, Second Session, pp. 2301-2303; Second Congress, Appendix, pp. 1442-1443.
[6] *Executive Proceedings, Northwest Territory,* 1788–1795, pp. 124-126.

by be excluded. Another important clause of this act confirmed a proclamation that St. Clair had issued at Kaskaskia, forbidding traders to sell intoxicating liquor to Indians under heavy penalties. Unfortunately this last regulation was not always enforced, and even Winthrop Sargent as acting governor authorized at least three traders at Vincennes to sell liquor to the Indians.[7] This incident was typical of the general tendency to make regulations for the Indian trade and then proceed to break them, and indeed, with so few officials in so vast a country, effective enforcement of such measures was really an impossibility. From among the many instances of the advantage that the white men so often took over the red men, a typical one was a sale to Indians of whiskey that had been frozen in the casks, by American traders at North Bend. In exchange for a rifle these same grasping individuals exacted forty buckskins worth $1.00 each, and a horse that was valued at £15. Also, a gunsmith, apparently in league with them, demanded two buckskins before he would repair a rifle, and two more after the job was finished.[8]

The contempt with which so many of the American settlers, notably the Scotch-Irish from the western Pennsylvania border, treated the Indians, and the great injustice as a result, was another source of much friction. Frequently the settlers attacked the Indians without any discrimination between friendly and hostile tribes, and seldom could the savages secure any redress. The President himself found it necessary in 1789 to call attention to the serious consequences of these unauthorized attacks, and to forbid any expedition against the Indians that did not have official sanction.[9] Nevertheless, three years later an armed band from Kentucky entered the territory at North Bend in order

[7] *Laws of the Northwest Territory*, Pease, ed., *Illinois Historical Collections*, vol. XVII, pp. 26-28; *Executive Proceedings, Northwest Territory*, 1788–1795, pp. 561-563.

[8] *Symmes Correspondence*, Bond, ed., pp. 75-76.

[9] Secretary of War to St. Clair, December 19, 1789, *Northwest Territory MSS*.

to chastise the Indians, and even during the negotiations that led to the Treaty of Greenville a hunting party of these same hot-headed Kentuckians attacked a band of Indians in the Virginia Military District, and then openly sold the plunder at Limestone. In neither case were the offenders punished.[10] A striking illustration of the public attitude toward the Indians was given in 1794 by a number of subscriptions in Cincinnati to a common fund which, like a later act offering rewards for wolf scalps, gave from $95.00 to $136.00 for each Indian scalp that was brought in, provided the left ear was "pendant," as proof that the late owner would have no further use for it.[11]

Even parties of Indians on their way to official conferences were not always safe from attack, although the governor customarily issued a proclamation to protect them, and especially to enforce the law which restricted the sale of liquor. In September, 1794, for example, a mob in Cincinnati attacked a party of Choctaw Indians on their way from Wayne's headquarters, after an apparently false report had been spread around that they had with them a captive female white child. Although Sargent, who was acting as governor, ordered out the militia, the mob attacked the Indians again at night and the following morning. When a special court of inquiry was convened, only one of the two persons indicted by the grand jury was tried, and he was promptly acquitted. This failure showed the difficulty of securing justice when crimes were committed against Indians.[12] A much similar incident took place in 1795 in St. Clair County in the Illinois settlements, when two Indians were forcibly taken from the custody of the sheriff and murdered. Little, if any, effort was made to punish the offenders, in spite of earnest representations by the territorial

[10] *Executive Proceedings, Northwest Territory,* 1788–1795, pp. 467-468 and 619-620; *Journal of Winthrop Sargent,* p. 163.
[11] *The Centinel,* May 10, 1794.
[12] *Executive Proceedings, Northwest Territory,* 1788–1795, pp. 583-596; *Journal of Winthrop Sargent,* pp. 108-112.

officials.[13] On other occasions, too numerous to mention in detail, Indians were attacked or murdered, and the local prejudices against the redskins either prevented or greatly interfered with the punishment of the guilty white men. In view of this general situation, St. Clair proposed, with true Scotch canniness, that whenever juries failed to convict Americans who had committed crimes against Indians, the counties in which the offenses occurred should be heavily fined.[14] Occasionally, however, the pioneer sense of justice overcame innate prejudices to such an extent that Americans were adequately punished for their offenses against Indians. Thus Daniel McKean, who was convicted in Cincinnati of stealing a horse from an Indian, was sentenced to pay $1.00 to the injured savage, to receive thirty-nine lashes, and to wear a hat with the sign upon it, "I stole a horse from an Indian." [15]

With so many grievances, in addition to their strong opposition to American settlement on the north bank of the Ohio, the Indians did not respond in at all satisfactory fashion to St. Clair's efforts to establish peaceful relations with them. The friction that developed between the two races at North Bend, Judge Symmes' settlement, was typical. When the settlers first arrived the Indians were quite friendly, offering so many skins to exchange for goods of various kinds that they nearly cleaned out the supply of linen and cloth which Judge Symmes had bought for his own party. But friction soon arose, and in less than three months the Indians attacked the new settlement, many of the inhabitants fled, and Judge Symmes found it necessary to dispatch his valuable papers to Louisville, where he had already sent his daughters.[16] These experiences at North Bend were duplicated at Marietta, and at other early settlements in the Ohio Valley. Traveling through the country was unsafe, and it

[13] *Executive Proceedings, Northwest Territory,* 1788–1795, pp. 610-612, 618-619.
[14] *St. Clair Papers,* Smith, ed., vol. II, pp. 396-397.
[15] *The Centinel,* March 26, 1796.
[16] *Symmes Correspondence,* Bond, ed., pp. 75-76, 91, 286-287.

soon became clear that if American settlement was to be
made upon an extensive scale in the Old Northwest, it would
first be necessary to overawe and push back the Indians.
For the defense of the settlements that were rapidly being
made north of the Ohio, the Federal government maintained
small garrisons at Fort Harmar (Marietta), at Fort Washington (Cincinnati), at Fort Massac, at Fort Knox (Vincennes), and at a number of smaller posts in the Illinois
country. In 1789 this force, scattered through so vast a territory, numbered only 596, and the pay and allowances were
so meager that the service was far from attractive. There
were also a few scouts and rangers, but adequate expansion
of this useful branch of the service was impossible, with the
meager allowances for military expenses.[17] Consequently,
the local militia became the main dependence of the early
Western settlers for protection against the Indians, and the
first law that St. Clair and the judges adopted in 1788 provided for its organization and discipline. Later laws attempted to compel regular drill and inspection, but, as was
so often the case in this frontier country, there was a vast
difference between the making and the enforcement of laws.
Frequently St. Clair was obliged to remind the militia of
their duty, and he found it was exceedingly difficult to enforce discipline when it was necessary to depend upon local
officers to impose and to carry out penalties. When, for example, Matthew Elliott, a private in the Washington County
militia, was convicted of disobedience and neglect of duty,
he received a sentence of ten days' imprisonment, which was
remitted at the request of the regimental officers. Occasionally discipline was enforced, as in the case of another member of the Washington County militia who "wantonly" raised
a false alarm. Vincennes, where there was constant danger
from the Indians, was rather unique in the Old Northwest
at this time for the fairly good discipline that was main-

[17] Secretary of War to Chairman, Committee of House of Representatives,
February 1, 1791, *Northwest Territorial Papers*, Senate Files, 6132; American
State Papers, Military Affairs, vol. 1, p. 6.

tained over the militia under the direct supervision of Major Hamtramck, the commandant at Fort Knox.[18]

The small and scattered force of regulars, and the frequent ineffectiveness of the territorial militia, along with their comparatively limited number, made it necessary at first to devise some means of securing outside aid in a crisis, and Washington gave St. Clair permission to call for help, if necessary, from the militia of Pennsylvania and Virginia.[19] This arrangement did not work out satisfactorily. In the spring of 1791, when there were many alarms of Indian attacks upon Marietta, Sargent, as acting governor, asked for aid from Pennsylvania, issuing orders at the same time to the local militia to hold themselves ready for duty at the slightest alarm. In the end the settlers at Marietta were obliged to depend upon the local militia for protection, but there was much haggling over the expenses of this service, and finally St. Clair, who had little faith in the effectiveness of the militia, ordered them to disband, unless the people of Washington County were willing to pay for their support.[20] The situation was quite similar at Gallipolis during this same alarm. Here the commander of the militia was instructed to raise not over twenty rangers, with the same pay and rations as regular troops, but two months later the governor discharged them with the terse announcement that, if the people wanted military protection, they could pay for it. Finally Sargent asked for troops from Fort Washington to defend Gallipolis, but General Williamson did not give the necessary orders for more than two months, and meanwhile the settlement was not properly guarded. At Cincinnati two detachments were ordered out about the same time, one to go to the relief of Fort Jefferson, the other to coöperate with regular troops in erecting fortifications. Only part

[18] Executive Proceedings, Northwest Territory, 1788–1795, pp. 76, 250-252, 432-434, 440-442, and 488-489.
[19] St. Clair Papers, Smith, ed., vol. II, p. 160.
[20] Executive Proceedings, Northwest Territory, 1788–1795, pp. 247-250, 253-254, 406-407, and 436-437.

of the quota responded in either case, in spite of the alarming situation.[21]

The general ineffectiveness of the militia, and the small number of regular troops that were available, clearly showed that only by a special military force would it be possible to put an end to the continual trouble with the Indians. It became increasingly evident, too, that any American attacks should be directed against the strongholds of the hostile tribes in the upper Wabash and Maumee valleys, the regions which were particularly subject to the intrigues of traders from Canada, so long as the British held Detroit. In the spring of 1790, St. Clair called for 1,000 militia from Pennsylvania, Virginia, and Kentucky to mobilize in September, and early in October General Harmar marched from Fort Washington with 1,155 militia and 320 regulars, with the Miami village at the head of the Maumee as his destination. At this "headquarters of iniquity" Harmar destroyed the loghouses and the wigwams, but the Indians merely retreated, and the sole result was to increase their hostility toward the Americans. Any chance of a really decisive action had been lost by the quarrels between the militia and the regular troops, and the failure to execute properly the orders of the commanding officer.[22] Harmar's failure finally aroused the Federal government, especially after Colonel Thomas Proctor failed in a peace mission to the Indians, and in May, 1791, General Charles Scott was sent with a force of Kentucky militia to the mouth of Eel River in the Wabash Valley. After the usual ravaging of the Indian country this expedition returned, too, without any decisive engagement. Still another hastily arranged expedition by a small force under General Wilkinson in the following August destroyed Indian villages on the Wea plain, but without accomplishing any permanent results.[23]

[21] Executive Proceedings, Northwest Territory, 1788–1795, pp. 257, 445, 451-453, 457, and 462-464.
[22] St. Clair Papers, Smith, ed., vol. I, p. 167; American State Papers, Indian Affairs, vol. I, pp. 93-95 and 104; Military Affairs, vol. I, pp. 20-30; Albach, Western Annals, pp. 544-552.
[23] American State Papers, Indian Affairs, vol. I, pp. 129-135.

As the inadequate expedition of Harmar had failed to end the numerous raids upon the exposed frontier, Congress passed an act, March 3, 1791, to raise the necessary military force for an effective campaign, by the enrolment of an additional regiment of infantry and not over 2,000 militia. According to the instructions to St. Clair, who was put in charge of this expedition, the chief objectives were: to establish a military post at the head of the Maumee River; to inflict all possible injury upon the hostile Indians; and to secure a satisfactory boundary of the Indian country, possibly the Wabash River. To accomplish these objects 3,000 men were to be mobilized at Fort Washington by July 10, when the campaign was scheduled to start, even though the full force had not been secured.[24] St. Clair was soon busy, first at Pittsburgh, then at Fort Washington, with preparations for the campaign, but unfortunately his subordinates did not carry out his plans in satisfactory fashion. Only about three-fourths of the troops that Congress had authorized were enlisted, and of these many were unfit for active service. The contract for supplies, also, was very badly mismanaged, and at least 2,000 arms, which were forwarded to Fort Pitt without inspection, were useless. The packsaddles, too, which could have been secured in Pittsburgh, were made in Philadelphia, and the unnecessary item of transportation across the Alleghenies amounted to more than twice their value. To cap the climax, Samuel Hodgdon, the quartermaster-general, did not reach Fort Pitt until June 4, and in spite of repeated orders from St. Clair he did not arrive at the rendezvous near Fort Washington until September 10. Under such untoward conditions St. Clair started September 17, more than two months after the appointed date. Gradually his force dwindled, chiefly from desertions, until by November 3, when he encamped on a branch of the Wabash, he had only about 1,400 effective troops. The next day came the attack by the Indians, probably 1,000 strong, which

[24] *Annals of Congress*, First Congress, Third Session, Appendix, pp. 2415-2418; *American State Papers, Indian Affairs*, vol. I, pp. 171-174 and 193.

ended in a disastrous defeat that ultimately became a precipitous flight. Later, a committee of the Lower House, in exonerating St. Clair, summarized the chief causes of the disaster as: the delay in passing the enabling act; the pressure to start off the expedition before the army was properly trained; and the mismanagement in the quartermaster's department.[25]

Even after St. Clair's defeat there was strong opposition in the Eastern states to any coercion of the Indians by military force, and representatives of the Federal government continued their efforts to secure a peaceful settlement. In September, 1792, General Rufus Putnam and John Heckwelder, the Moravian missionary to the Indians, negotiated a fairly satisfactory treaty with the Wabash tribes at Vincennes, which the Senate refused to ratify upon the ground that it guaranteed the Indians their lands.[26] In the summer of 1793, there was another attempt to make peace, this time by a commission headed by Benjamin Lincoln, which went to treat with the Maumee and Wabash tribes. After the commissioners had waited for several weeks at the mouth of the Detroit River, while the Indians held a grand council at the foot of Maumee Rapids, the latter refused to negotiate, unless the American representatives conceded the Ohio River as the boundary line of the Indian country, a condition that obviously was impossible.[27] But these missions and negotiations with the Indians were proving costly to the government. The treaty negotiated at Fort Harmar, for instance, ineffective as it was, cost fully $20,000.00, and it was estimated that the Federal government was giving out annually more than 2,000 rations for conferences with the

[25] For accounts of St. Clair's defeat, see: Albach, *Western Annals,* pp. 578-581; *Memoirs of Benjamin Van Cleve,* Bond, ed., in *Quarterly,* Ohio Hist. and Phil. Soc., vol. XVII, pp. 24 ff; *Annals of Congress,* Second Congress, First Session, pp. 493, 877, and 895; *American State Papers, Military Affairs,* vol. I, pp. 36-39.

[26] Albach, *Western Annals,* pp. 604-606; *American State Papers, Indian Affairs,* vol. I, pp. 234-236, 338-340.

[27] Albach, *Western Annals,* pp. 606-631; *American State Papers, Indian Affairs,* vol. I, pp. 340-360.

Indians, in addition to a yearly expenditure of $4,700.00 for the Northern Indian Department alone.[28] As there had been no lasting results, considerable feeling developed that these expenditures should not be continued, in view of the slender resources of the Federal government. This attitude quickly gained strength, even though the only apparent alternative was a really adequate military expedition.

The many reports of Indian atrocities on the frontier also exerted a strong influence in favor of an effective expedition to put an end to such conditions. This gradually formed determination was all the stronger because of the belief that the intrigues of Alexander McKee, Matthew Elliott, Simon Girty, and other agents of the Canadian fur traders among the tribes in the upper Wabash and Maumee valleys were chiefly responsible, nor was this opinion altogether without justification. From the mass of testimony regarding these intrigues, the deposition of Thomas Rhea may be taken as typical. Captured on the western Pennsylvania border, he was taken by the Indians to Sandusky, where he saw several British officers and witnessed the distribution of quantities of arms and ammunition to the Indians. At Detroit there was abundant evidence, according to Rhea, that the British traders were supplying the Indians with the arms that were being used against American settlers, and the recital of these experiences, after he returned in about seven weeks, naturally inflamed popular opinion against the British government, and rallied support to any aggressive measures that the American authorities undertook.[29] While there is no positive proof that the British government had purposely encouraged these intrigues among the Indians, the authorities in Canada and in Detroit had, to say the least, winked at such practices. In April, 1791, Washington himself di-

[28] St. Clair to Congress, May 16, 1789, in *Force Transcripts*, pp. 1628-1631, and to the President, May 1, 1790, *Northwest Territorial Papers*, B. R. L., 6098.

[29] *American State Papers, Indian Affairs*, vol. I, pp. 196-197; *Boston Gazette*, January 9, 1792, and August 26, 1793; *American Museum*, vol. XI, pp. 163-164.

rected that Lord Dorchester, the governor of Lower Canada, should be told of the supplies of ammunition that were being given out to the Indians, and in 1794 the Secretary of State brought to the attention of the British minister in Washington a speech in which Lord Dorchester had predicted war with the United States, as well as a rumor that Governor Simcoe of Upper Canada had given orders to build a fort on the Maumee River. In each case the minister evaded the direct issue, and soon there was positive news that the fort was being erected in American territory, and that British officers were playing an important part in aiding the Indian attempts to check Wayne's advance.[30]

With the support of a gradually aroused public opinion, Washington personally took up the necessary measures to wage a really effective war against the Indians. Four months after St. Clair's defeat, Congress passed an act that gave the President authority to complete the battalions of artillery already in service, to raise two infantry regiments in the regular army, and to enlist three additional regiments for three years' service.[31] Washington promptly selected General Anthony Wayne as commander-in-chief, and by the summer of 1792 the latter was at Pittsburgh, busy in assembling his force, and later at Legionville, twenty-two miles down the Ohio, where he was equally energetic in training his troops. The following spring he moved his headquarters to Hobson's Choice near Fort Washington, where in the fall a "malady called the influenza" attacked his army, causing few fatalities, but greatly reducing the number fit for service. October 7, 1793, Wayne began his march northward, and finally went into winter quarters at Greenville. By spring he estimated his effective fighting force at

[30] President to Secretary of State, April 3, 1791, *Northwest Territorial Papers*, B. I. A. Misc., 6164; Correspondence between the Secretary of State and the British Minister (George Hammond) May 20 to June 10, 1794, *Ibid.*, B. I. A. Dom.; *American State Papers, Indian Affairs*, vol. I, p. 487.

[31] *Annals of Congress*, Second Congress, First Session, Appendix, pp. 1343-1346; Thomas Jefferson to President, December 16, 1791, *Northwest Territorial Papers*, B. I. A. Misc., 6187.

2,845, including the garrisons he had left at Fort Washington, Fort Hamilton, and other posts on his way. With so well disciplined and equipped a force the final victory at the Maumee Rapids, August 20, 1794, was a foregone conclusion, and Wayne made it all the more complete when he pursued the Indians to the very gates of the British fort, and thus made them understand that they could not depend upon their supposed friends in case of need. For a time Wayne feared that through lack of reinforcements he might lose the fruits of his victory, but he held his ground in spite of continued British intrigues.[32]

Early in June, representatives of the different tribes began to gather at Wayne's headquarters until 1,130 Indians had assembled to sign the Treaty of Greenville, August 7, 1795, which marked the first important American victory over the Indians in the Old Northwest. By its terms all of Ohio, except approximately the section west of the Cuyahoga, was opened to settlement, as well as the elongated strip in Southeastern Indiana known as the "gore." The treaty also included the cession of small strategically located areas in the Indian country for military posts, with lines of communication between them, and thus made it possible to establish such posts as Fort Wayne at the head of the Maumee, and Fort Dearborn at the mouth of the Chicago. Congress confirmed this treaty in an act that authorized the annuities, amounting altogether to $2,500.00, which had been promised to the different tribes, in addition to an appropriation of not over $1,500.00 annually, which the President was to expend upon efforts to civilize the Indians. Another act attempted to ensure lasting peace by provisions that justice should be done the Indians, that their boundary line should be respected, and that in cases of wrongdoing by Indians, the settlers should not take the law in their own hands, but should seek redress from the superintendent of Indian

[32] Albach, *Western Annals*, pp. 592-651; *American State Papers, Military Affairs*, vol. I, p. 67; *Indian Affairs*, vol. I, pp. 360-361, 491-494, 524-527, 547-548.

affairs.[33] The surrender of Detroit, the center of British influence among the Indians, in 1796 after Jay's Treaty had been ratified, rounded out the results of Wayne's victory. As an aftermath, the area in Ohio still left in possession of the Indians was gradually diminished, until by 1805, all that portion of the Western Reserve that lay west of the Cuyahoga had been ceded, along with the tract between this land and the line of the Treaty of Greenville. In 1808 the cession of a strip one hundred and twenty feet wide, with a mile on either side, from the Western Reserve to Maumee Rapids, made possible a road eastward from Detroit, while a similar strip, from the line of the Treaty of Greenville down the Sandusky Valley, joined the first one at present-day Fremont, making possible a road to southern Ohio.[34] These cessions pointedly called attention to the remorseless pushing back of the Indians, as an American population poured in after Wayne's victory had made safe the Ohio frontier.

The Treaty of Greenville, and the consequent shift of the chief theater of Indian disturbances from the Ohio region to the upper Maumee and the Wabash valleys, marked the close of the first period in the relations between the American settlers in the old Northwest and the Indians. Henceforth, and especially after the division of the Northwest Territory in 1800, Indiana Territory became the center of negotiations, until at the end of this second period came the War of 1812 and the Battle of the Thames, with the complete overthrow of Indian power. Meanwhile the Federal government continued the policy of maintaining peaceable relations, if possible, and William Henry Harrison, as governor and superintendent of Indian affairs, became the chief figure in the many parleys and treaties with the Indians. Under his leadership attempts were made to regulate, if not

[33] American State Papers, Indian Affairs, vol. I, pp. 562-564; Eighteenth Report, Bureau of American Ethnology, part 2, pp. 654-657, plates 19 and 49; Annals of Congress, Fourth Congress, Appendix, pp. 2899-2900, 2909-2916.

[34] Eighteenth Report, Bureau of American Ethnology, part 2, plate 49; American State Papers, Indian Affairs, vol. I, pp. 695-696 and 757.

to end, the liquor traffic with the Indians which was the source of so much disturbance. But little was accomplished, and so bad did the situation become that in 1808 Jefferson called Harrison's especial attention to the different Federal regulations with regard to this evil.[35] Harrison's efforts to exercise a general supervision over the Indian trade were equally fruitless. Soon after he came to Indiana he called attention to such unlawful practices by traders as following the Indians to their hunting grounds and trading without a license. He undertook, too, a more careful supervision of these traders, as in a license issued to Michael Brouillet in 1804, which gave permission to trade with the Kickapoo Indians in "all manner of goods, wares, and merchandise" under government regulations, including especially one that strictly forbade the practice of taking merchandise and spirituous liquor to the Indian camps. Harrison proposed to extend this policy of control to traders in the lands that had already been ceded by the Indians, in order to prevent "merciless rapacity." But enforcement proved to be a difficult matter, and in northern Indiana and Michigan, where the majority of the traders were Canadians, there was little pretense of even taking out licenses.[36]

In order to counteract the influence of the Canadian agents and at least to minimize the impositions practiced upon the Indians, Washington repeatedly urged the establishment of government trading posts in the Indian country. Congress adopted this suggestion, giving the President extensive powers to appoint agents and to establish trading posts under careful regulations that would eliminate personal or public profit. After a committee reported favorably in 1802 upon the two posts which had already been established in the Old Southwest, Jefferson authorized two Indian trading

[35] *Harrison's Messages and Letters,* Esarey, ed., vol. I, pp. 327-328; *Executive Journal, Indiana Territory,* p. 156.
[36] *Executive Journal, Indiana Territory,* p. 103; *Harrison's Messages and Letters,* Esarey, ed., vol. I, pp. 102-103; *American State Papers, Indian Affairs,* vol. I, p. 705; *Executive Proceedings,* October 20, 1805, *Michigan Territorial Papers,* B. R. L.; *Niles Weekly Register,* vol. III, pp. 105-107.

houses in the Old Northwest as well, one at Detroit which was closed in 1805, and one at Fort Wayne which was quite successful. In Jefferson's opinion, these trading posts would be an effective means to control and civilize the Indians, and with his approval Congress passed measures for the enlargement and general organization of this Federal enterprise.[87] Beside those at Fort Wayne and Detroit the President established three other trading posts in the Old Northwest; at Chicago in 1805, at Sandusky in 1806, and at Mackinaw in 1808. By 1809 Congress had provided, altogether, $280,000.00 for these posts, including those in the Southwest, and the government owned property valued at $37,371.28 at the four then in the Old Northwest. For the period of almost four years, December 31, 1807, to September 30, 1811, the posts at Chicago, Fort Wayne, and Mackinaw showed a profit of $17,313.79, and the only deficit in the Old Northwest, at the Sandusky trading station, which was not well located, was $3,366.50. Despite the disturbances in European trade at this time, the demand had continued for the beaver skins of the Old Northwest which were so generally used for hatter's fur. The trading posts had served, too, as centers to encourage the Indians in useful industry, and at Mackinaw they had learned to make maple sugar in large quantities. The War of 1812 and the Indian outbursts at the same time were fatal to this thriving trade, bringing losses to the government from burned and pillaged posts that were estimated at fully $37,869.61.[88] Nevertheless, the wisdom of this policy, to establish government trading posts as a means of improving relations with the Indians, had been amply demonstrated.

As still another means of settling the Indian problem in the Western country, both Washington and Jefferson strongly urged that agriculture and domestic manufactures

[87] *Annals of Congress,* Third to Seventh Congresses, *passim; American State Papers, Indian Affairs,* vol. I, pp. 583-584.

[88] *American State Papers, Indian Affairs,* vol. I, pp. 768, 784-794; Estimate of Losses of Indian Factory Department (probably 1815), *Michigan Territorial Papers,* Senate Files.

should be fostered among the tribes. Jefferson, especially, felt that this was the one permanent solution of the Indian problem, inasmuch as the increase of settlement must inevitably decrease the area suitable for hunting. Doubtless under his influence, in 1802 the Secretary of War instructed all the governors of territories to promote good feeling with the Indians of their respective districts, and to introduce husbandry and domestic manufactures among them.[39] This policy was carried out, too, in many of the treaties in which the Indians made land cessions, as in the one in 1803 that took under Federal protection the few survivors of the Kaskaskia tribe, who, finding they could no longer depend upon game, wished to learn the arts of civilization. The treaty gave them 1,630 acres and an annuity of $1,000.00, payable at their option in money, provisions, or domestic animals. In addition, the government undertook to erect a house for the chief of the tribe, to enclose not more than 100 acres with a fence, to grant an allowance of $100.00 for seven years to a priest who would teach the Indian children the rudiments of education, and lastly to make a donation of $300.00 in order to help build a church.[40] In much similar fashion a treaty with the Delawares in 1804 promised an annuity of $300.00 for five years to provide instruction in the building of fences, the cultivation of the fields, and the pursuit of the domestic arts in general. The government pledged an additional $400.00, to be spent upon horses, cattle, hogs, and agricultural implements. A treaty with the Piankeshaws at the same time likewise promised annuities that were payable in money, merchandise, provisions, domestic animals, or agricultural implements.[41] Hull's treaty in 1807 followed these precedents when it stipulated that the annuities agreed upon were to be payable in money, goods, domestic animals,

[39] American State Papers, Foreign Affairs, vol. I, pp. 18, 19, 22, 25, 28, 62, and 65; Harrison's Messages and Letters, Esarey, ed., vol. I, pp. 39-41.
[40] American State Papers, Indian Affairs, vol. I, pp. 687-688; Tennessee Gazette, September 14, 1803.
[41] American State Papers, Indian Affairs, vol. I, pp. 689-690.

or agricultural implements, and promised to furnish the Indians two blacksmiths for ten years, one to be located at Saginaw among the Chippewas, the other on the Maumee among the Ottawas. Of a much similar nature was the agreement in the Treaty of Fort Wayne in 1809 by which Harrison promised the Miamis that the government would maintain an armorer at Fort Wayne for their convenience.[42]

The desire to deal justly with the Indians was shown on many other occasions, as when Jefferson proposed that a part of the product of the Wabash Saline should be used in paying Indian annuities, in order to secure for the tribes the necessary supply of salt.[43] Also, Congress customarily paid the expenses of the Indian delegations which came in such large numbers to negotiate treaties, or to visit army posts and occasionally even Washington. The systematic efforts to secure equal justice for the Indians in the courts of the Old Northwest formed another phase of this benevolent spirit where the Indians were concerned. There was also some missionary activity among them, chiefly in the region near the Western Reserve, where there was so much similar work among the pioneers themselves. As early as 1800 the Ohio Presbytery sent Rev. Joseph Badger and Rev. Thomas Hughes on a missionary visit to the Indians near Detroit, but this expedition was not at all successful. The missionaries suffered great hardships on this trip, often through uninhabited forests, and for five days Badger lived chiefly upon chestnuts.[44] A few years later a Congregational minister, named Bacon, went up the Maumee upon a missionary visit to the Chippewas. He had a favorable reception, and the Indians expressed a strong desire to be instructed in the "arts of husbandry." Bacon, who seems to have been quite a practical individual, set to work to learn the Chippewa language, so that he might the more readily spread the gospel "among our brethren of the American

[42] *American State Papers, Indian Affairs,* vol. I, pp. 747, 761-762.
[43] *Ibid.,* p. 683.
[44] Patton, *Popular History of the Presbyterian Church in America,* p. 296.

forest." [45] While the subsequent history of this particular mission is somewhat obscure, the general missionary work among the Indians of the Old Northwest was given a fresh impetus by a resolution of the Presbyterian Synod of Pittsburgh in 1802, forming itself into the Western Missionary Society, with one of its objects "to diffuse the knowledge of the gospel" among the Indian tribes. Under these auspices two missionaries visited the Indians on the Sandusky River in the following year, and in 1806 Rev. Joseph Badger, whose trip to Detroit had made him familiar with the Sandusky region, founded a mission school there. Under Rev. Elisha McCurdy, who succeeded Badger, this Indian school was quite successful, and continued to flourish until the War of 1812 put an end to its activities. [46]

Whatever policies were adopted to pacify the Indians, there remained the basic cause of trouble, the continual encroachments upon their lands by American settlers. In spite of warnings by territorial officers, individual settlers paid little regard to Indian boundaries, and the truth was, the Federal government set them a striking precedent by the so-called treaties which in supposedly correct fashion took over enormous tracts of land from the helpless Indians, with quite inadequate returns. The gradual rolling back of the Indian boundary in Ohio after the Treaty of Greenville has already been noticed, and this same process was carried on elsewhere in the Old Northwest. In Michigan the Indians had ceded considerable tracts around Detroit and Mackinaw by this same treaty, and in 1807 Hull secured a strip along the Detroit River that ran backward into the land about fifty miles. [47] But far more important in this second period of Indian relations in the Old Northwest, from the Treaty of Greenville to the Battle of the Thames in 1813, were the cessions which Harrison secured from the Indians on both

[45] *Extracts, Minutes of the General Association of Connecticut (Congregational) for 1802,* pp. 7-8.
[46] Elliott, *Life of Rev. Elisha McCurdy,* pp. 106-107, 117, 122 *ff.*
[47] *American State Papers, Indian Affairs,* vol. I, pp. 746-747; *Eighteenth Report, Bureau of American Ethnology,* part 2, pp. 674-675, and plate no. 29.

sides of the Wabash. These successive encroachments upon Indian lands were entirely in accordance with Jefferson's policy to settle a large American population in this region, and he repeatedly urged upon Harrison the necessity of taking over additional lands.[48]

Harrison's career as governor in Indiana Territory was marked by a succession of treaties that secured large tracts from the Indians. First he made an adjustment of the uncertain boundaries of the Vincennes settlement, which was greatly to the white man's advantage. Then, in spite of Indian opposition, in 1803 he obtained the cession of a tract of about 1,152,000 acres, extending eastward from Vincennes, with a small section on the west bank of the Wabash. At the same time the Indians ceded the important saline in the Ohio Valley below the mouth of the Wabash, three tracts on the road between Vincennes and Kaskaskia, and another one on the highway between Vincennes and Clarksville. In return for these last four tracts, which were to be used as sites for inns, the Indians were to have free passage across near-by ferries. About the same time Harrison put the Kaskaskias under Federal protection, taking over for the government the rather indefinite claims of this tribe to the territory between the Ohio, the Mississippi, and the Illinois rivers. In 1804 he secured a tract in southern Indiana, between the road from Vincennes to Clarksville and the Ohio River, and a year later a large area between the White River and the Ohio, and immediately west of the line of the Treaty of Greenville. The next cession from the Indians included the Piankeshaw claims to a tract between the Wabash and the lands that the Kaskaskias had surrendered. By these different treaties, up to 1806 Harrison had extended the lands held by the Federal government over all of southern Indiana, with a rather indefinite area in Illinois

[48] *American State Papers, Indian Affairs,* vol. I, p. 688. For a detailed account of the different negotiations between Harrison and the Indians, see Goebel, *William Henry Harrison,* ch. IV; for specific cessions, see *Eighteenth Report, Bureau of American Ethnology,* part 2, pp. 662-679 and plates 17-19.

between the Wabash, the Illinois, the Ohio, and the Mississippi rivers. For a time, the threats of Tecumseh and his brother, the Shawnee Prophet, prevented any further negotiations, but Jefferson was urging that additional lands should be opened to the settlers east of the Wabash, and Harrison finally negotiated the Treaty of Fort Wayne, September 30, 1809, in the face of determined Indian opposition. This treaty ceded a large area east of the Wabash and north of Vincennes, with a tract west of the Wabash which Harrison enthusiastically described as "one of the most beautiful that can be conceived of." This time, however, he had gone too far, inasmuch as the treaty had aroused the Indian leaders to a realization of the danger from still further encroachments upon their lands, and the sequel was a gradually increasing hostility that came to a climax in the aid they gave the British in the War of 1812. At Vincennes there were plain intimations that the well-known desires of local land speculators had influenced Harrison in securing this last cession.[49]

As a matter of fact, these continued land cessions were forcing the Indians of the Wabash and Illinois valleys into an almost impossible situation. Just at this time the gradual reduction in the number of fur-bearing animals was having its effect throughout the upper Mississippi Valley, and several of the tribes found it necessary to enlarge their hunting areas. The vigorous Chippewas, the Sioux, and the Sacs, especially, were moving southward, shoving aside the weaker tribes who found themselves pushed back from the south by the advancing wave of American settlement. The only solution left them was to move to lands west of the Mississippi, but before they would consent to so momentous a step, they could be expected to resist the American settlers with all of their power.[50] This Indian unrest was increased, too, by the many violations of treaties, and by the methods commonly used to secure the cessions of land, which a group of

[49] *Western Sun*, October 14 and 21, and November 4, 1809.
[50] *Harrison's Messages and Letters*, vol. II, pp. 640-641.

Wyandots quaintly described. First, they said, the "black robes" had come to their villages, and taught the Christian principle to do unto others as you wished to be done to you, and as a practical application the Indians had asked that they should be allowed to keep the lands upon which they had made so many improvements. When the negotiations were carried on, all the Indian tribes in that particular region had been assembled, although probably nine-tenths of them were not directly interested. Yet this irresponsible majority had overawed the interested minority, in their eagerness to secure the money and the annuities that were offered, and so, the Wyandots complained, they had lost their prized lands.[51] The sense of injustice that this simple narrative revealed was often increased by the advantage that so many Federal agents took of the Indians in delivering the annuities for which they had given up their lands. The "castor" hats, fine cloth, suits, blankets, scalping knives, and other articles that made up the usual goods shipped to the Indian country were frequently received in damaged form, and there were times when a considerable part disappeared on the way.[52]

With increasing uneasiness among the Indians, Harrison sent at least two delegations to reassure them: one from Vincennes to the Indians of the upper Wabash Valley; the other from Cahokia to the Kickapoos who had been harassing the feeble remnants of the Kaskaskias. Part of the dissatisfaction among the Indians, in Harrison's opinion, was due to the influence of Americans who were opposed to his land policy. He complained especially of the intrigues by William Wells, the Indian agent at Fort Wayne and a son-in-law of Little Turtle, the Miami chief, who had aroused the Delawares and Kickapoos over cessions of their lands. Finally Harrison even considered a personal mission to Fort Wayne,

[51] American State Papers, Indian Affairs, vol. I, pp. 795-796.
[52] Harrison's Messages and Letters, Esarey, ed., vol. I, pp. 150, 167, 442-443.

in order to counteract Wells' influence.[53] The intrigues among the Indians by Americans who were unfavorable to Harrison continued, even though Congress passed an act in 1800 that strictly forbade any citizen of the United States to stir up the Indians against the government, or to act as an unofficial go-between with a foreign power.[54] Probably with this act in mind, Harrison warned the French inhabitants against any intrigues in aid of the British. The *habitants* passed strong resolutions in protest, and finally the President himself wrote, reassuring them as well as other individuals whom Harrison seems to have included in his denunciations. But rumors persisted, seemingly upon excellent foundations, that connected American citizens who were hostile to Harrison with the British intrigues among the Indians.[55]

Much more serious in its effect than the whisperings of disgruntled Americans was the continual intrigue by Canadian traders among the Indians of the Old Northwest, even after the Treaty of Greenville. Many instances might be cited of the activities of the more notorious of these agents. Thus, in 1799 the Secretary of State found it was necessary to complain to the British minister of the "reprehensible activities" of Alexander McKee who had planned, so rumor in the Western country had it, to assemble the Shawnees in order to force alterations in the Treaty of Greenville.[56] Moreover, the Canadian traders continued to send goods to the Indians in American territory, contrary to the laws of the United States. One such shipment that was seized and condemned on the Michigan border in 1802 included twelve two and a half point blankets, forty-three sheets of iron, eight copper kettles with covers, and eleven tin kettles.

[53] *Harrison's Messages and Letters*, Esarey, ed., vol. I, pp. 125-126, 141-151, 177-178, 211-212, and 221.
[54] *Annals of Congress*, Sixth Congress, Appendix, pp. 1436-1437.
[55] *Harrison's Messages and Letters*, Esarey, ed., vol. I, pp. 256-259, 282-283; *Western Sun*, August 25 and October 13, 1810.
[56] Secretary of State to British Minister, April 30, 1799, *Northwest Territorial Papers*, B. I. A. Dom.

Another shipment, seized a few months later, contained "two barrels of spirituous liquor called whiskey."[57] Later Hull made efforts to put an end to this unlawful trading, but with unsatisfactory results. The Canadian traders were also popularly held responsible for numerous disparaging reports that were circulated among the Indians, such as one in 1802 that the Americans would spread smallpox. Another widely spread rumor was that under American laws, Indians were not to be punished for crimes that they committed within their own country. These stories, going through the forest in addition to other forms of intrigue, proved a great hindrance to American efforts to gain control of the fur trade.[58] In 1810 the territorial legislature of Indiana attempted to end these constant intrigues of "mischievous individuals" by an act that positively forbade all trading within the Indian country except by licensed traders, but unfortunately this measure, which would automatically have forced out Canadian traders, was a mere gesture in the air, and British agents brazenly continued to seize upon every possible pretext to stir up the Indians against the Americans.[59]

With the constantly increasing turmoil among the Indians, frontier defense became a serious problem in the Old Northwest. In 1796, Timothy Pickering, then Secretary of War, had proposed that the numerous small posts in this region should be formed into six groups with headquarters at Pittsburgh, Cincinnati, Detroit, Fort Wayne, Greenville, and possibly Vincennes.[60] This elaborate plan was not carried out in its entirety, but the government, not altogether regardless of Western needs, stationed three of the four infantry regiments in the regular army west of the Alleghenies. By 1803 there were 705 troops at the chief posts in the Old Northwest—Detroit, Mackinaw, Fort Dearborn, Fort

[57] *Ohio Gazette*, October 19, 1802.
[58] *Harrison's Messages and Letters*, Esarey, ed., vol. I, pp. 37-39; *Western Sun*, September 12, 1807.
[59] *Laws of Indiana Territory*, Third General Assembly, First Session, pp. 66-70.
[60] *American State Papers, Military Affairs*, vol. I, pp. 112-113.

Wayne, Vincennes, Kaskaskia, and Fort Massac.[61] Regular troops were kept at these different posts down to the War of 1812, but the force was pitifully small in comparison with the needs of so extensive a region. Consequently the local militia, aided on exceptional occasions by troops from Kentucky, continued to be the chief reliance of the settlers on the frontier. The experience gained in earlier campaigns led the first legislative assembly of the Northwest Territory to enact a new militia law in 1799, which included provisions for the discipline and drill of the militia, with adequate penalties upon the officers, as well as the rank and file, for infractions of these regulations. An especially excellent feature of the act authorized the organization of volunteer companies of artillery and of horse troops. However, it was still incumbent upon the individual militiamen to furnish arms and ammunition.[62] This measure, which subsequently became the basis for militia laws in the several divisions of the Old Northwest, was fairly effective, except in its provisions for equipment. In Ohio by 1805 the total number enrolled in the militia was 15,976, but the available supply of muskets and rifles was scarcely sufficient to supply a fifth of this force.[63] Conditions were even worse in Indiana where, according to Harrison, there were "cavalry without swords, light infantry without bayonets or cartridge boxes, and battalions armed with a mixture of rifles, fowling pieces, broken muskets, and sticks." [64] Notwithstanding persistent efforts by Harrison, there was probably little improvement before the War of 1812. In Michigan, another exposed frontier, the militia was neither effectively organized nor was it well disciplined in this early period.

The need for adequate protection of the Indian frontier rapidly increased, as trouble continued between Tecumseh,

[61] *American State Papers, Military Affairs*, vol. I, pp. 139 and 175.
[62] *Laws of Northwest Territory*, Pease, ed., *Illinois Historical Collections*, vol. XVII, pp. 418-443.
[63] Blodget, *Economica*, p. 98.
[64] *Harrison's Messages and Letters*, Esarey, ed., vol. I, pp. 243-245.

who ranked with Pontiac as one of the ablest of the Indian chiefs, and his brother, the idealistic and probably cataleptic Prophet, on the one side, and the territorial government of Indiana, represented chiefly by Harrison, on the other. Harrison soon appreciated how dangerous the two brothers might become to American interests, and as early as 1807 he publicly warned the Shawnees against the Prophet, as a British agent.[65] A year later, as the Indian raids against the frontier continued, Harrison induced the Prophet to retire to Tippecanoe on the Wabash, out of reach, as he thought, of the American settlements, and gradually he came to feel that perhaps the Indian Messiah was not so dangerous after all. Certainly the Prophet was pacific in his reputed teachings, exhorting the Indians to pray to the Great Spirit who made all things, and not to lie, drink, or steal, nor to go to war, but, living peacefully with all men, to work and raise corn. But the aftermath of the Treaty of Fort Wayne convinced Harrison that both Tecumseh and the Prophet were hostile to the Americans and should be carefully watched. Early in the summer of 1810 alarms spread along the frontier, and the frightened settlers held mass meetings, in order to devise measures of defense. Harrison frankly stated the exact situation, and popular opinion rallied to support him. Events moved rapidly. In August came Harrison's dramatic interview with Tecumseh at Vincennes, when the former boldly proclaimed his unalterable resolution to prevent further intrusions upon Indian lands. It was at this interview that Tecumseh worked himself up into a savage frenzy, and Harrison, his intimate knowledge of Indian psychology coming to his rescue, boldly faced the fierce chief at the critical moment. In the end Tecumseh departed peacefully, but there was no doubt that, aided by the Prophet, he would do his utmost to arouse the Indians against the Americans.

[65] For an analysis of the motives of Tecumseh and the Prophet, and an account of the Tippecanoe campaign with the events preceding it, see: Goebel, *William Henry Harrison*, pp. 109-127; Albach, *Western Annals*, pp. 829-847; *Harrison's Messages and Letters*, Esarey, ed., vol. I, pp. 249-251 and 293; *Western Sun*, June to November, 1811, *passim*.

The Eastern newspapers printed exaggerated accounts of conditions on the frontier, reporting the settlers as already fleeing from their homes, and at Vincennes an extra edition of the *Western Sun* was necessary to reassure the anxious citizens.

Relations with the Indians in the Wabash Valley soon reached a crisis. When Tecumseh appeared at Vincennes in July, 1811, on his way to organize the Southern Indians, the citizens, thoroughly alarmed, adopted resolutions that denounced the combination he was heading as a British scheme, and asserted that, unless it were broken up, there would be no peace on the Western frontier. Incidentally the raids on the border were frightening away immigrants, and Harrison himself cited the case of a man from North Carolina who was willing to spend $20,000.00 in settling lands that had recently been acquired from the Indians, provided he were assured protection.[66] Finally, convinced that a military expedition had become the last possible recourse, Harrison left Vincennes September 26, 1811, with a force of about 1,000 which included Kentucky and Indiana militia, and a regiment of regular troops. He marched rapidly into the Indian country with the Prophet's stronghold in the upper Wabash Valley as his objective. The Battle of Tippecanoe, November 7, 1811, virtually ended the campaign, but it was by no means a decisive victory, and the sequel was a long drawn out controversy that brought to the surface the intense jealousy between the Western militia and the regulars. The *Western Sun* hailed this "glorious victory" of the militia, but a gathering at Vincennes adopted resolutions that warmly commended Colonel Boyd, in charge of the regulars, and incidentally reflected upon the conduct of the militia in the battle. In reply, officers and privates of the militia passed resolutions that indignantly resented any aspersions upon their bravery, or upon Harrison, their commander. In the

[66] *Western Sun,* July 27, 1811; Resolutions, July 31, 1811, *Indiana Territorial Papers,* House Files; *Harrison's Messages and Letters,* Esarey, ed., vol. I, pp. 547-548.

territorial legislature, resolutions passed by the Lower House thanked the Kentucky militia equally with Boyd and his regulars, while both houses joined in a congratulatory address to Harrison. President Madison, too, praised the "dauntless spirit and fortitude" of the troops, and the "collected firmness" of their commander. But local pride was again hurt when, in a letter to the Secretary of War, Colonel Boyd insisted that the regulars had borne the brunt of the fighting at Tippecanoe.[67] The most unfortunate consequence of this long-continued controversy was the prejudice it aroused, in the Eastern states especially, against Harrison upon whom the Old Northwest was fated to depend for leadership against the Indians and later the British.

Whatever the merits of the controversy between the militia and the regulars there had already been many indications that the inhabitants of the Old Northwest were becoming convinced that war with Great Britain was inevitable. Thus, after the *Chesapeake-Leopard* incident, a patriotic meeting in Cincinnati passed resolutions that strongly denounced this "late British outrage," and an enthusiastic Illinois pioneer rather bombastically asserted, with regard to the Embargo Act, that "it has dashed the philter of pillage from the lips of rapine." A more moderate Westerner considered the Embargo the one means to secure peacefully important natural rights.[68] Western public opinion was aroused, too, by the tactless diplomacy of Great Britain, and especially was the conduct of her minister, Jackson, scored by a number of correspondents. Timothy Pickering was likewise denounced as "the advocate of British politics, and the libeler of the government of the United States." This growing antagonism in the Old Northwest toward Great Britain was tersely summed up in a toast at a Fourth of July banquet in Illinois in 1808, "May American bravery ever be opposed to British

[67] *Western Sun,* November 16 and 23, and December 7 and 14, 1811, and February 8, 1812; *Harrison's Messages and Letters,* Esarey, ed., vol. I, pp. 647-648, 659, 673; *American State Papers, Indian Affairs,* vol. I, p. 776.

[68] *Liberty Hall,* August 11, 1807; *Scioto Gazette,* July 19, 1808; *Missouri Gazette,* July 26, 1808.

knavery." [69] As the election of 1810 approached, there was much impatience toward an administration which was described as a "majority without talent or energy." The hope was openly expressed that the present Federal officers would be replaced by men "whose object is the country's good," and one newspaper writer voiced a general opinion in the Old Northwest when he asserted that Congress should prefer war with honor to a "peace with disgrace." [70] The election of the War Hawks aroused much enthusiasm. There should be no submission to a foreign prince, according to one patriotic writer, and American "blood and treasure" should be drawn upon by the Twelfth Congress, if necessary, in order to uphold the national honor.[71]

But stronger than any other causes of irritation in its influence upon the Western people was the general belief that the British were encouraging the Indian raids upon the frontier. Harrison asserted that each Indian at Tippecanoe had received from British agents a gun, a scalping knife, a tomahawk, and a war club, and many of them a spear, and so recently had they been given their guns, that many of them had not even taken the trouble to remove the wrappings. One American trader testified, also, that in the baggage of an Indian on the way from the British headquarters at Malden, he had found among other articles a new rifle, eighteen pounds of powder, a quantity of lead, three blankets, and several strouds.[72] Despite these evidences of supplies from Canadian sources, the British minister at Washington strenuously denied that there had been any official aid to the Indians, and cited as proof the warning Sir James Craig, governor-general of Canada, had given in 1810 of the agitation that was going on against the United States. But with respect to unofficial British agents he was by no

[69] Liberty Hall, August 13, November 22, December 13, 1809, April 4, 1810; Ohio Gazette, July 21, 1808.
[70] The Supporter, April 1, 1810; Liberty Hall, July 11, 1810; Louisiana Gazette, July 19, 1810.
[71] Liberty Hall, July 10, 1811.
[72] Niles Weekly Register, vol. I, p. 311; Western Sun, April 18, 1812.

means so convincing. After a careful investigation, a committee of the Lower House reported that without doubt the Indians had received arms and ammunition at Malden before the Tippecanoe campaign, and that speeches had been made to them at the same time which increased the existing dissatisfaction. Although this report was laid upon the table there was an abundance of confirmatory testimony which strengthened the determination of the Western settlers to end simultaneously the Indian menace and the intrigues from Canada in the Old Northwest. Meanwhile, Indian raids on the exposed borders continued to alarm the settlers. In both Illinois and Michigan, public meetings of excited citizens drew up memorials to Congress that set forth the serious situation, and pleaded for adequate military protection.[73]

In Ohio, even, which of all the Old Northwest suffered least at this time from Indian raids, the inhabitants were wrought up over these attacks upon the frontier, and the British intrigues which were popularly supposed to be stirring them up. The determination to put an end to such a situation became much more militant after the Tippecanoe campaign, with its evidences of military aid from Canada.[74] The Ohio newspapers now began to give much space to notices of the Indian raids on the frontier,[75] and even the religious fervor of the backwoodsmen was aroused. One typically ardent patriot called upon the people to fast and pray, and to repent of their sins, so that, like the followers of Gideon, they might destroy many times their number. In Cincinnati a "great concourse" of citizens heard a sermon by the Rev. W. Burke upon the militant text, Joel III, 9, 10: "Prepare war, wake up the mighty men" . . . "Beat your plowshares into swords, and your pruning hooks into spears; let the weak say, I am strong." Other articles, upon the eve of the war, strongly

[73] Resolutions, Inhabitants of St. Clair County, 1811, *Illinois Territorial Papers*, House Files; Memorial, Inhabitants of Michigan Territory, December 10, 1811, *Michigan Territorial Papers*, Senate Files, 3564.

[74] Cady, *Western Opinion and the War of 1812*, in *Ohio Archæological and Historical Quarterly*, vol. XXXIII, pp. 427-476.

[75] *Liberty Hall*, April and May, 1812, *passim*.

supported the calls for recruits, in order to stop the increasing raids by the Indians. The extent to which popular opinion had been aroused was revealed when there was a report in Cincinnati that the Ohio recruits were almost without blankets, and that few were to be had at the stores. In this emergency the citizens gave proof of their loyalty by offering 500 blankets from their own households.

With the usual American optimism in such crises, the people of the Old Northwest enthusiastically welcomed the declaration of war, June 18, 1812, and "on to Canada" became a popular slogan, the real aim being to put an end to British intrigues among the Indians by the conquest of Canada, if necessary. An editorial in the *Muskingum Messenger*, published at Zanesville, expressed the typical exaggerated attitude of the early West, under the heading, "The die is cast —the Rubicon is passed." The editor assured his subscribers that the American government had escaped from "eternal infamy and degradation," now that war had been declared. The "genius of America" had long called for war "to revenge her wrongs, and maintain our rights," and the writer pledged the full aid of the people of Ohio to carry on the struggle. A few days later, at the Fourth of July banquet in Zanesville, there was an even more fervid toast to "the people of the United States," who would now "nobly breast the storm which had broken upon our unoffending country by the injustice and wickedness of England." [76] At Vincennes the citizens held a meeting which highly approved the declaration of war, and in Cincinnati and in other settlements the news awoke much enthusiasm. [77] Occasionally there was a discordant note, as the petulant complaint of the Federalist editor of the *Western Spectator*, published in the New England stronghold of Marietta, that Congress had held secret sessions, and that a firmer American policy might have brought both France and England to terms without the necessity of

[76] *Muskingum Messenger*, July 1 and 8, 1812.
[77] *Western Sun*, July 14, 1812; Resolutions, July 9, 1812, *Indiana Territorial Papers*, B. R. L., 2820.

war. In contrast to such querulous statements, many of the dyed-in-the-wool Federalists in Marietta, even, strongly approved the war, while the *Trump of Fame*, published at Warren in the Western Reserve, heartily joined in the general denunciation of the unpatriotic response of the governors of Massachusetts and Connecticut to the call for troops.[78]

Nor did this enthusiastic support for war decrease in Ohio after news came of Hull's surrender and the fall of Fort Dearborn. Rather, these sturdy Western settlers were spurred on to greater efforts. A typical incident was the reaction in Clermont County, near Cincinnati. Within a day after the bad news had come from Detroit, four hundred volunteers from this one county had crossed the Little Miami on the way to Cincinnati.[79] At Vincennes, while the Indians were besieging near-by Fort Harrison in the Wabash Valley, the people pursued the even tenor of their way, confident with a rare courage in their ability to defend themselves with the aid of their neighbors and the Federal government.[80] Even at Marietta, stronghold of the Federalists, the citizens "spontaneously assembled" at the courthouse, upon news of Hull's surrender, and prepared for immediate defense.[81] Lack of space forbids a detailed account of the enthusiasm with which the Western settlers supported Harrison's campaign in the Maumee Valley, through the long delay and the many crises that arose before the final victory at the Thames.[82] Without doubt one of the chief factors in this continued loyalty was the general confidence in Harrison, which was shown in so many public resolutions, as well as in other expressions of public opinion.[83]

[78] *Western Spectator*, July 11 and 18, 1812; *Trump of Fame*, July 29, 1812.
[79] *Liberty Hall*, September 1 and 22, 1812.
[80] *Western Sun*, September 1 and 8, 1812.
[81] *Western Spectator*, September 8, 1812.
[82] For accounts of Harrison's campaign, see: Goebel, *William Henry Harrison*, pp. 135-183; Bond, *William Henry Harrison in the War of 1812*, in *Miss. Valley Historical Review*, vol. XIII, pp. 499-516.
[83] See files of *Liberty Hall* and *Western Spy*, October, 1812, to April, 1813.

The general attitude of the Western people toward the War of 1812 was displayed on many occasions. For example, at the Fourth of July celebration in Cincinnati in 1813, there was a special toast to the conquest of Upper Canada.[84] Yet the chief aim in the minds of these Western patriots seems to have been to end British influence over the Indians rather than to acquire additional territory. Shortly after this anniversary affair, the people of Ohio faced with a truly courageous spirit the disheartening news of the British attack upon Fort Meigs. The stout-hearted editor of *Liberty Hall* called upon the militia to march to Harrison's aid, and there were many other evidences of the popular determination to win. The sturdy Western patriotism was shown, too, when success finally came.[85] At Cincinnati, Perry's victory at Put-in-Bay was heralded as "the most important blow" since the beginning of the war, the town was brilliantly illuminated, and there was "a continued war of cannon and small arms" until a late hour. The fall of Malden was another occasion for a procession and the firing of arms at Cincinnati, while even the little frontier town of Piqua was illuminated and held a patriotic banquet. Another grand celebration at Cincinnati took place after the arrival of news of the Battle of the Thames, in spite of the "excessive wetness" from a thirty-six hours' rain.[86] Other Western settlements celebrated the victories of Perry and Harrison, and especially was this true in Vincennes, where the *Western Sun* gave long accounts of these national successes.[87] The newspapers of the Old Northwest also followed the peace negotiations with much interest, and there was evidently a general appreciation of the results, if the British had enforced their demands for a buffer state beyond the line established by the Treaty of Greenville. Such a concession, the editor of *Liberty Hall* pointed out, would unite all parties in favor of a war which would become "not

[84] *Liberty Hall,* July 6, 1813; Pratt, *Expansionists of 1812,* ch. I, especially.
[85] *Liberty Hall,* July 27 and August 3, 1813.
[86] *Ibid.,* September 21 and October 12 to November 2, 1813.
[87] *Western Sun,* September 15 and October 30, 1813.

only just, but absolutely necessary to preserve our existence as a nation." [88] The victory at New Orleans came as "glorious news," and eventually the treaty of peace met a favorable reception.

The end of the War of 1812 and the signing of the Treaty of Ghent marked the final downfall of Indian power in the Old Northwest. After nearly a quarter of a century of strife against an ever-increasing throng of white settlers, the red men had been completely worsted. In the struggle they had suffered greatly, as an inferior culture must always do when it comes into conflict with a superior civilization. One large tract after another had been whittled away from the Indian lands, in order to provide for the expansion of American settlement. Theoretically, this had been done in conventional fashion, by treaties; but in reality these cessions had been secured by superior force, acting under such apparently peaceable forms. Signal failure had met efforts to civilize the Indians, and thus to solve the problem of supporting on a comparatively limited area a population that lived chiefly by hunting. The fur trade, too, had come into the picture, with Canadians and Americans fighting in the forests for supremacy. Perhaps the Americans had exaggerated the encouragement and actual aid which the Canadian fur traders and their agents had given the Indians, but assuredly there was a widespread belief in the Western country that only a victory over the British in Canada would end the Indian raids upon the scattered frontier settlements. Perhaps this same aim could have been secured without two costly and prolonged campaigns, had Congress provided more adequate military protection, or had there been more coöperation between the few regulars stationed at Western posts and a better organized and disciplined militia. In the end the victories of Wayne and Harrison taught the Indians that they could no longer depend upon their friends from across the border for aid, and, at the same time, these campaigns compelled the Canadians to abandon the struggle to control the fur trade

[88] *Liberty Hall,* March 1, 1814, to October 25, 1814.

of the Old Northwest. Finally, the battles of Fallen Timber and of the Thames marked the final conquest of the Indians and opened up the vast lands of the Old Northwest to the rapidly spreading settlements of the white man, as the red man was steadily pushed backward, and finally across the Mississippi.

Chapter X

THE DISTRIBUTION OF THE LAND

THE gradual conquest of the Indians in the Old Northwest and the pushing back of their boundaries made necessary a considerable revision of the system for distributing to actual settlers the lands that were being acquired. At first the policy of Congress, as it was set forth in the Ordinance of 1785, had favored the land speculators who took up large holdings in the British fashion, and thus promised immediate financial returns to an impoverished national treasury. Soon, however, it became apparent that if individual settlers were to be attracted to this Western country, they must be protected from the demands of land speculators. A conflict then arose between the farsighted advocates of terms for the distribution of the public lands that would be attractive to the multitude eager to migrate to the Western country, and the small coterie which was chiefly interested in securing financial returns for the Federal government. In the clash between these two factions the former was victorious, but only after much experimentation and controversy. In the process many difficult problems were involved, some of them of long standing. The shadowy claims of different land companies, notably those of the Wabash and Illinois Land Company, needed to be finally determined. Also, the confusion of titles among the French inhabitants of Vincennes, the Illinois settlements, and Detroit called for adjustment, and there were many Americans scattered through these French settlements, and in the upper Ohio Valley, who had established themselves merely as squatters with no legal titles to their lands.

In actual practice the Ordinance of 1785, with its mini-

278

mum of 640 acres, had not proved favorable to the average immigrant. The initial expenditure, $640.00 with fees, was prohibitive to many men of small means who wished to better their fortunes, although the provision for sales in the different states appeared to offer a general opportunity to purchase public lands. For the purposes of speculative organizations, the Ordinance was quite favorable, and for a time the motive of immediate financial gains to the government, through large-scale transactions, was in the ascendant. The first important grant under this Land Ordinance of 1785 was the one in 1787 to the Ohio Company, which was made up chiefly of Revolutionary veterans, for 1,500,000 acres, with an additional 5,000,000 acres to a group of land speculators, the Scioto Company, the two tracts to be laid out along the Ohio River east of the Scioto. Another contract was made in 1788 with John Cleves Symmes, a member of Congress, to be located between the Miami and the Little Miami rivers. These contracts promised large profits. With a one-third deduction for bad lands, the net cost, when the grants were first made, was not over 8 cents to 9 cents per acre, if payment was made in the depreciated Continental certificates. Naturally the owners of these tracts would demand as high a price as they could possibly secure from intending settlers, and there was a similar situation in the Virginia Military District, in the Western Reserve, and in Clark's Grant, the three important districts reserved in the cessions to the Federal government, and destined to fall into the hands of speculators. Under such conditions, it was quite necessary that the lands still left at the disposal of the government should be offered upon terms that would attract intending settlers, and would hold down the demands of the speculators in the extensive reserves.

Fortunately for the advocates of a policy that would favor the mass of would-be settlers, the early contracts for the sale of public lands did not realize the optimistic expectations of large financial returns. The Ohio Company met its first payment of $500,000.00 in 1787, but with the waning of the early enthusiasm for this enterprise, the directors were unable to pay the balance they owed, and they petitioned for a reduction in the nominal price of land, from $1.00 to 50 cents per acre. Although Congress did not see fit to grant this petition, in 1792 it authorized a deed to the Company for the 750,000 acres that had actually been paid for, and granted an additional 214,285 acres to cover the one-seventh of the original tract for which payment was to be made in military warrants, together with 100,000 acres to be laid out in donation lots of 100 acres each to actual male settlers. Eventually the shareholders of the Ohio Company divided the unappropriated land among themselves, and later settlers on this tract were obliged to buy from these private holders.[1] The Scioto Company made no pretense at all of meeting its payments to the government, although Joel Barlow, its agent in Paris, sold land to the gullible Frenchmen, four hundred of whom finally settled at Gallipolis in 1790.[2] The contract with Judge Symmes also proved disappointing from the financial standpoint. Symmes made initial payments of $71,428.52 in certificates and $11,904.68 in military land warrants, which gave him title to 123,397 acres. But in characteristic fashion he carelessly sold land for which he had not paid. Finally, after much wirepulling on his part, and that of friends in high official positions, in 1792 Congress authorized a patent for all the land Symmes had paid for, with an additional 106,857 acres to satisfy military warrants. Under this authority the President issued a patent to Symmes in 1794 for 311,682 acres, but the latter continued his loose methods, granting land outside of the specified boundaries.[3] This rather unsuc-

[1] Records of the Ohio Company, Hulbert, ed., vol. I, pp. xcviii-cxxxvii and 29-37; vol. II, pp. 122-124; Annals of Congress, Second Congress, First Session, Appendix, pp. 1363-1364.

[2] Executive Proceedings, Northwest Territory, 1788-1795, pp. 310-311; Petition from French Inhabitants of Gallipolis, December 22, 1792, Northwest Territorial Papers, Senate Files; Selections from Gallipolis Papers, Belote, ed., in Quarterly, Ohio Hist. and Phil. Society, vol. II, no. 2; Annals of Congress, Third Congress, Second Session, Appendix, pp. 1531-1532.

[3] Symmes Correspondence, Bond, ed., p. 32 (note 13), p. 49 (note 46); Annals of Congress, Second Congress, Appendix, pp. 1373-1374; Executive

cessful outcome of the Symmes contract, along with the parallel case of the Ohio Company and the complete collapse of the Scioto Company, naturally discouraged further grants to speculators, and helped the cause of the individual settler.

With the beginning of American settlement in the Ohio Valley in 1788, the demand for more liberal terms in the distribution of the public lands gradually became insistent, and Congress responded to the pressure that was brought upon its members, especially after the Constitution had been put into effect. While the members of Congress wished to fulfill all contracts that had been entered upon under the Confederacy, they recognized also the need for reform legislation with respect to the national land system. A proposed measure to establish a land office, and to change somewhat the method of granting lands, brought forth a debate in the Lower House that revealed the great difference of opinion between those who wished to put forward the encouragement of settlement in the Western country as the chief aim, and those who still held that the financial need of the government was the primary consideration.[4] A report from Alexander Hamilton as Secretary of the Treasury represented a compromise between these two viewpoints, with a decided leaning toward the latter one. He proposed, in brief, that the public lands should be sold for 30 cents per acre, or the equivalent in Continental certificates, with credit allowed only where tracts of at least ten miles square were involved, and then for not more than two years. Hamilton recognized a great obstacle to sales directly to the average immigrant, by a recommendation that, in place of auctions at the seat of government alone, smaller tracts might be purchased at two land offices to be located west of the Alleghenies, one in the Old Northwest, the other

---

Proceedings, Northwest Territory, 1788-1795, pp. 385-424, passim; Thomas Jefferson to St. Clair and to Judge Symmes, August 6, 1791, Northwest Territorial Papers, B. R. L., 6170, 6171.

[4] Annals of Congress, First to Fourth Congress, passim, and especially First Congress, Third Session, pp. 1880-1890; Treat, The National Land System, pp. 66-91.

one in the Old Southwest.[5] This report was given prompt consideration, and after considerable debate the House passed an act that fixed the price of land at 25 cents per acre. In the Senate the bill was postponed and the subject was finally dropped.

Several events forced action in the revision of the land policy. The outcome of the contracts with the Ohio Company, the Scioto Company, and Symmes undoubtedly strengthened the sentiment in favor of more liberal provisions for the individual settler. The exposure of a speculative scheme to secure a grant of the lower peninsula of Michigan by bribes distributed in Congress stirred up public feeling against speculative grants, and lastly the surrender of the Western posts by Jay's Treaty, along with the Treaty of Greenville which opened up the greater part of Ohio, made it imperative to take some action with regard to the public lands. The debate over a bill reported in the House January 2, 1796, plainly showed the strength of the party that favored individual settlers rather than land speculators. As it was finally passed, this Land Act of 1796 provided for a surveyor-general, under whose direction all the unappropriated public land east of the mouth of the Kentucky was to be surveyed in the usual townships of six miles square, with the reservation of salt springs, and of four sections in each township for the disposal of Congress. This act doubled the cost of public land, fixing a minimum price of $2.00 per acre for all sales. One-half was to be disposed of in quarter townships at the seat of government and the remainder in sections of 640 acres at land offices at Pittsburgh and Cincinnati. Payments were to be completed within a year, and there was a fee of $6.00 for a patent to 640 acres, and $20.00 for one to a quarter township.[6] The chief forward step in this act was the opportunity it gave to purchase land at convenient offices in the West, although the minimum amount was still out of the reach of the average settler.

[5] *American State Papers, Public Lands,* vol. I, pp. 4-5.
[6] *Annals of Congress,* Fourth Congress, Appendix, pp. 2905-2909.

The failure in the Land Act of 1796 to make provision for the sale of smaller tracts, or to fix terms of sale that suited the slender resources of the mass of immigrants, was a grave mistake. The settlers who were arriving in constantly increasing numbers were beginning to push up the tributary valleys of the Ohio, to Dayton and beyond on the Miami, and even to Franklinton on the Scioto, now that Anthony Wayne had ended the menace from the Indians. This rapidly increasing population was not satisfied to buy land upon terms that were fixed by Symmes, by the Ohio Company, or by the speculators who held warrants in the Virginia Military District, nor could they afford to take up the minimum 640 acres under the Land Act of 1796. At Vincennes and in the Illinois settlements the situation was even worse, with the available land held under questionable titles by the original French population, and no adequate provision for the incoming stream of American settlers. The inevitable result of this unsatisfactory situation was an increasing tendency on the part of immigrants into the Old Northwest to make unauthorized settlements as squatters without any legal title. Sargent issued repeated warnings against intrusions upon the public lands, but proclamations were futile in face of the oncoming tide of immigration. By 1799 St. Clair estimated that there were fully 2,000 squatters in the upper Ohio and Scioto valleys, and below the mouth of the Miami. As most of them wished to purchase their lands, but were unable to pay $2.00 per acre, he suggested that credit should be extended to them.[7] The squatters' points of view was set forth in a petition to the Senate in 1798 from 85 pioneers on the Scioto River. In order to own their homes, they represented, they had endured the hardships of settlement, and especially the dangers from Indians. But they had not been able to secure lands at reasonable rates in the Virginia Military District or from other proprietors, or to meet the terms under

[7] *Executive Proceedings, Northwest Territory, 1788–1795,* pp. 594, 604-606; St. Clair to the Senate, January 7, 1799, *Northwest Territorial Papers,* Senate Files, 6329.

the Act of 1796. Many of their "nearest friends" in "a state of despondency" had been attracted to the Spanish lands west of the Mississippi, and they themselves prayed for grants of 160 acres each at a lower price. Another petition, a year later, from the same source asked for rights of preëmption, and similar memorials came from settlers without legal titles to their lands in Jefferson County, Ohio, and in Indiana east of the mouth of the Kentucky.[8]

The disappointing sales under the Land Act of 1796 presented another argument for its revision. Finally, in 1798 a committee of the Senate headed by John Brown of Kentucky, who was well acquainted with the situation, drew up a land act that passed the Senate, but failed in the House. During the next session, St. Clair strongly urged upon Congress the necessity of some action with regard to the public lands, and the Senate again passed a bill which the House postponed after considerable discussion. After this second failure it was clear that the opposition to a revision of the Land Act centered in the Lower House, but the timely appearance of William Henry Harrison as territorial delegate gave the people of the Northwest Territory a spokesman in this same body. Under his able guidance an act was speedily drawn up that marked the final triumph of the faction that wished to consider the needs of the settlers, rather than immediate financial returns to the government. This measure established four land offices, at Cincinnati, Chillicothe, Marietta, and Steubenville respectively, at which public land would be auctioned off, with a minimum price of $2.00 per acre. East of the Muskingum it was to be sold only in sections, but between the Muskingum and a line drawn north from the mouth of the Kentucky one-half was to be offered in sections, the other half in half sections of 320 acres. The terms of sale were especially liberal, with a four years' credit from the date of purchase and an additional year to pay up all arrears. In effect this meant a five years' credit, although interest at six per cent was due on deferred payments. Also,

[8] Petitions to the Senate, 1798 and 1799, *Northwest Territorial Papers*, House and Senate Files.

this act reserved four sections in each township for future disposal by Congress.[9]

The chief advantages of the Land Act of 1800 were, the reduction of the minimum tract to 320 acres and the liberal credit allowed, two provisions that enabled even the average settler to take up public land. Yet important needs were still ignored. Except for a concession to owners of improved mill sites, this act did not give the many squatters rights of preemption, nor did it give any relief to the settlers in Indiana Territory west of the mouth of the Kentucky. Despite these omissions, the act represented an important advance from the Western point of view, and it gave a tremendous impulse to settlement in the Old Northwest. Its practical working was illustrated by a land sale at Chillicothe in 1801. For two half sections, 640 acres in all, at $2.00 per acre, the initial payment to the government was $330.00, including, beside $320.00 for the land, a surveying fee of $6.00 and a land office fee of $4.00. In addition, the patentee paid $20.00, probably to a squatter.[10] With such terms, especially as payment of the balance due could be postponed for five years, there were few settlers who could not afford to take up all the public land they could cultivate, and the demand increased so greatly that scarcely a year after the act was passed, the sales at the Chillicothe office alone totaled $220,-000.00.[11] Although the provisions for credit were a potential source of irritation, a day of reckoning five years off did not greatly trouble settlers who optimistically trusted to the future to fulfill their obligations.

The Western triumph in the passage of the Land Act of 1800, with its recognition of democratic principles in the distribution of the public lands, was the logical outcome of the

[9] *Annals of Congress,* Fifth Congress, Second Session, pp. 542-600, 1926, 2114; Third Session, pp. 2201, 2218, 2914, 2927; Sixth Congress, First Session, pp. 209-210, 650-652, 681, and Appendix, pp. 1515-1522.

[10] Thomas W. Worthington to Major H. Bedinger, June 25, 1801, *Worthington Letter Book.*

[11] Worthington to Rufus Putnam, May 16 and June 20, 1801, *Ibid.,* pp. 21 and 33-34.

rapidly increasing opposition in Congress to special grants
to favored individuals or groups. An illustration of this attitude was the indifference that met the many petitions from
Judge Symmes for a grant of the entire tract of 1,000,000
acres which his original contract had called for. Actually
Symmes had carelessly sold lands beyond the northern boundary that had been fixed by the patent from the President in
1792. With the increase in the price of public lands after
1796 to $2.00 per acre, from the 66 2/3 cents per acre which
he had expected to pay, he now found himself in the difficult
position of being obliged to establish his claim to the entire
1,000,000 acres, or else to pay the higher price for the lands
he had sold outside his patent. In this quandary he appealed to
Congress, and many claimants under him petitioned that their
lands should be confirmed, provided they paid the price
agreed upon in the original contract. In response, Congress
merely granted them preëmption rights to buy their lands at
the fixed price of $2.00 per acre, payable in three annual
installments.[12] This method of adjustment was scarcely satisfactory to settlers who in many cases had already paid
Symmes for their lands, and there were rumors of open resistance to any attempts to force them to comply. They now
besieged Congress with petitions, alleging that they could not
secure justice from Symmes, and that they faced "total stag-
nation" unless some measure was passed for their relief. The
territorial assembly, also, petitioned in 1800 for the relief of
these settlers, many of whom had already paid considerable
sums to Judge Symmes. Meanwhile Symmes, through his
son-in-law, William Henry Harrison, redoubled his efforts
to secure recognition of his claim to the entire 1,000,000
acres. But when Congress did adopt a measure in 1801, it
renewed the right to purchase land at $2.00 per acre.[13]

[12] Symmes Correspondence, Bond, ed., pp. 17-21; American State Papers,
Public Lands, vol. I, pp. 76-77: Annals of Congress, Fifth Congress, Third
Session, Appendix, pp. 3937-3938.
[13] Petitions, 1799 and 1800, Northwest Territorial Papers, House Files;
American State Papers, Public Lands, vol. I, pp. 104-106; Annals of Con-
gress, Sixth Congress, First Session, p. 167, and Appendix, pp. 1559-1563.

The relief act passed in 1801 was virtually ignored, and disgruntled persons soon began to bring suits to force Symmes to make good the titles to their lands. Scarcely knowing which way to turn, Symmes first proposed to relinquish all possible claim to land beyond the bounds of his patent, then he offered to pay the price stipulated in his original contract with the government, and finally he proposed that the entire matter should be referred either to a Federal court or to a special commissioner. The claimants to the disputed lands continued to send petitions to Congress, representing that as they had already paid Symmes considerable sums, they should be allowed further time in which to take up their preëmption rights. Evidently there was considerable sentiment in Congress in favor of these patentees under Symmes, for a committee reported to the House that all such claimants under grants prior to the settlement made in 1792 should be allowed to purchase their lands at the original price, 66 2/3 cents per acre, and that the time limit of payment should be extended. But Congress merely passed an act in 1802 that extended preëmption rights up to March 2, 1803, to all claimants under Symmes. Thoroughly alarmed as he saw his large holdings gradually crumbling away to satisfy the numerous judgments that were being secured against him, Symmes continued to petition for relief. Levi Lincoln, the attorney-general, reported that he had no claims upon the government otherwise than those founded upon justice, and he was left to face his creditors alone, when Congress finally settled the matter in 1804 by granting claimants under him preëmption rights with the privilege of completing their payments within eight years.[14] Thus in the end Symmes, who had trusted too confidingly to his influence in Congress, failed to secure any recognition of his claims to lands beyond the patent of 1792.

[14] Petitions and other documents, 1802, *Northwest Territorial Papers*, House Files; *Annals of Congress*, Seventh Congress, First Session, pp. 424, 474, and Appendix, pp. 1357-1359; Eighth Congress, First Session, Appendix, p. 1289; *American State Papers, Public Lands*, vol. I, pp. 112, 126-131.

The representations of the Illinois and Wabash Land Company met even greater opposition in Congress than did the petitions from Judge Symmes. This company, continuing the British policy of exploitation which had sanctioned the Vandalia Company, was made up of two separate organizations. The first one, the Illinois Land Company, was founded in 1773 by a group of Philadelphians who claimed, by purchase from the Indians, the title to a tract that extended, approximately, southward from the Illinois River to the Ohio and the Mississippi. The second one, the Wabash Land Company, organized in 1775, set up claims to large tracts in the Wabash Valley. After Clark's campaign the two companies were merged into the Illinois and Wabash Land Company, but the Virginia legislature refused to recognize their claims, and Congress was equally obdurate.[15] In 1791 the officers of the joint company renewed their claims, evidently hoping to find the Congress under the new Constitution more complaisant. Their offer to compromise, a committee of the Senate dismissed abruptly, upon the ground that private deeds from the Indians were valueless, but a committee from the House made a favorable report. These Illinois and Wabash Land Company claims were revived in 1797 while Sargent was in Vincennes, and he pointedly called attention to such an "extraordinary" request, and to the law that forbade private persons to negotiate with the Indians. Nevertheless these same petitioners soon urged their claims upon Congress, and this time a committee representing the Lower House agreed that their memorial should not be granted, inasmuch as the purchases from the Indians had never been confirmed by a recognized government.[16] In 1804, John Shee, who claimed to be the "sole survivor" of the Illinois and Wabash Land Com-

15 Alvord, The Illinois Country, 1673–1818, pp. 301-303, 340-341, 380-381. Originally there were twenty-two proprietors in the Illinois Land Company, and twenty in the Wabash Land Company. The joint claims of the two were estimated at 24,200,000 acres. Northwest Territory MSS.

16 Memorial, December 12, 1791, Northwest Territorial Papers, Senate Files; Journal of the Northwest Territory, 1788–1803, passim; American State Papers, Public Lands, vol. I, pp. 27, 72-75.

pany, protested against a recent government purchase of land from the Kaskaskias, and proposed to surrender his own rights, provided Congress reconveyed one-fourth of his claims. This proposal the House rejected as a "gratuity" that was altogether unjustifiable, and a second attempt to secure a compromise met a like fate, ending this land-grabbing scheme once for all, in spite of its influential backing.[17]

As a rule Congress refused its consent to the many petitions for special grants, in spite of the influence that was so frequently exerted in their favor. Thus, when Hannibal W. Dobbyn of the "Kingdom of Ireland" petitioned in 1789 for 50,000 acres upon special terms, there was an extended debate in the House, where evidently there was a strong sentiment in favor of such sales as a means of securing speedy settlement. But an even stronger faction opposed contracts with individuals for large tracts, preferring a uniform and democratic land system. There was no definite action at this time, but when Dobbyn renewed his petition in 1796, a committee definitely reported against it. A similar fate met other memorials for grants upon special terms, and the Committee on Public Lands recommended that the House should reject such petitions upon principle.[18] Occasionally Congress made exceptions to this general policy, as in the case of the Swiss emigrants at Vevay on the Ohio River. Settling first on the Kentucky River in 1796, these emigrants finally decided to secure lands north of the Ohio, and in 1802 Congress granted them four sections west of the Miami River at the usual price, but with a twelve years' limit in which to complete payments. This act, which was avowedly passed to encourage the production of wine in the Western country, laid the basis of a substantial settlement.[19] But Congress was not so favor-

[17] Memorial from John Shee, 1804, *Indiana Territorial Papers*, House Files, 2662; *American State Papers, Public Lands*, vol. I, pp. 189, 301.
[18] *Annals of Congress*, First Congress, Second Session, pp. 1104-1110; *American State Papers, Public Lands*, vol. I, pp. 71, 80, 82.
[19] Dufour, *The Swiss Settlements of Switzerland County, Indiana*, Lindley, ed., *Indiana Hist. Collections*, vol. XIII, and especially pp. xiii, xvii; *Annals of Congress*, Seventh Congress, First Session, pp. 188, 200, 1018, Appendix, p. 1355.

ably inclined toward the petition of George Rapp, representative of the German Society of Harmony, which asked for a grant of 30,000 acres in the Western country at the usual price, but with exceptional terms of credit. The Senate gave its assent, but in the House there was a prolonged debate which revealed strong opposition to special favors, and especially those to an alien population. The argument that to grant this petition would help to increase the population of the Western country met scant consideration, in face of a popular theory that the land had been ceded by Virginia for the common benefit, and should be used accordingly. Finally the House rejected the proposal by the deciding vote of the speaker, and in 1815 the Rappists purchased a tract at New Harmony upon the usual terms.[20]

The opposition to special grants did not extend to the reserves for the support of education. The precedent established in the Ordinance of 1785, to set aside section sixteen in every township in the Seven Ranges for this purpose, was followed in the grants to the Ohio Company and to Symmes. After the Land Act of 1796 had omitted this clause, the passage of the enabling act for Ohio in 1802 gave a favorable opportunity to reassert the principle of public support for education. At first Congress had made a general offer to the new state of section sixteen in each township. But the Ohio convention considered this proposal too indefinite, and stipulated that Congress should grant one thirty-sixth of all the public lands in the state for the support of education. This demand was conceded in 1803 by an act that set aside the necessary land in the Military Reserve, in the Western Reserve, and in the Virginia Military District, tracts in which such reservations had not been made so far. For the future, the act required section sixteen in every township to be reserved in all sales of public lands in Ohio, with the titles to such reserves vested in the Ohio legislature as trustees for

[20] Memorial from George Rapp and members of the Society of Harmony, January 8, 1806, *Indiana Territorial Papers*, Senate Files; *Annals of Congress*, Ninth Congress, First Session, pp. 45-477 *passim*.

the public school funds. Since the desirable land in the Virginia Military District had already been taken up, in 1807 Congress granted eighteen quarter townships and three sections elsewhere in the public lands in order to fulfill the educational reserves for this section.[21] This policy of reserves for public education was continued in 1804, when Congress provided that section sixteen in each township of the public lands in Indiana Territory, which then, of course, included Michigan, Illinois, and Wisconsin, should be set aside. This act also followed a precedent set in Ohio, by providing that an entire township in each of the three land districts that were created should be reserved for the support of a "seminary of learning." The first reservation of this latter type, in the Ohio Company Purchase, became the foundation of Ohio University, while the college township provided for in the Symmes contract was finally, after much bickering, set aside west of the Miami as the basis for Miami University.[22] The precedents established in these and similar grants for the establishment of institutions of higher learning, and for the support of public education, were of tremendous importance in the development of the Western country.

Aside from provisions for education, it was clearly the policy of Congress gradually to do away with all special reserves of the public lands. The Ordinance of 1785 had reserved four sections in each township for future disposal, but the Ohio Company and the Symmes grants had set aside only three in each township, leaving the fourth one to be used for the local support of religion. The Land Acts of 1796 and 1800 followed the Ordinance of 1785 in setting aside four sections in every township for disposal by Congress. These vacant tracts, often in favorable locations, aroused consider-

[21] *Annals of Congress*, Seventh Congress, First Session, pp. 294-295, 1098-1118, and Appendix, pp. 1349-1351, Second Session, pp. 1328, and 1588-1590; Ninth Congress, Second Session, Appendix, pp. 1264-1266; *Ohio Laws*, vol. XXI, Appendix, pp. 44-45.

[22] *Annals of Congress*, Eighth Congress, First Session, Appendix, p. 1288; *Quarterly*, Ohio Hist. and Phil. Society, vol. IV, pp. 6-9; *Symmes Correspondence*, Bond, ed., pp. 185-186 (also notes 253-255).

able feeling. Thus, in one township in Hamilton County there was no gristmill within fifteen to twenty-five miles and the only available site was in a reserved section. The inhabitants therefore petitioned Congress to be allowed the privilege of purchasing at least half this tract. Doubtless there were similar situations elsewhere, and in 1804 Congress authorized all the reserved sections still at its disposal to be sold in the usual fashion for not less than $2.00 per acre. Two years later they even ordered the sale of the site of Fort Washington, which was no longer needed as a military post.[23] But the officials of the land offices held these reserve sections at such "extraordinary" prices, $8.00 per acre, for example, in Columbiana County, that the Ohio legislature in 1804 pointed out that they were not being sold, and that they greatly retarded the settlement of the state. In response to this representation Congress fixed a price of $4.00 per acre, which probably became the usual one.[24]

Although Congress increasingly opposed special grants of land, the extensive ones already made to fulfill the land bounties offered to Revolutionary soldiers were a source of considerable irritation. Thus, an act in 1796 set off about 2,000,000 acres west of the Seven Ranges as a military reserve, for which claims must be filed by January 1, 1800. But it became necessary to extend this limit until, in 1803, Congress ordered that all land in this reserve that so far was unappropriated should be put up at public sale. However, there were later extensions of the limit in which to file claims, and not until 1832 was the residue of the unlocated lots, some 31,900 acres, sold.[25] During the interval since the first grant, many of the warrants had fallen into the hands of speculators,

[23] Petition, Citizens of Hamilton County, January, 1800, *Northwest Territorial Papers*, House Files; *Annals of Congress*, Eighth Congress, First Session, Appendix, p. 1291; Ninth Congress, First Session, Appendix, p. 1229.

[24] *American State Papers, Public Lands*, vol. I, p. 304; *Annals of Congress*, Tenth Congress, First Session, p. 2835; *Laws of Ohio*, Sixth General Assembly, pp. 175-176.

[25] *Annals of Congress*, Fourth Congress, First Session, Appendix, pp. 2935-2937; Seventh Congress, Second Session, Appendix, pp. 1602-1603; Treat, *National Land System*, pp. 242-243 and 325-340.

while the large tracts of vacant land had constituted a barrier to the development of this section of the state. The history of the extensive Virginia Military District was much similar. Reserved at first in general terms as an area between the Little Miami and the Scioto, sufficient to satisfy deficiencies in the land bounties to the Revolutionary soldiers of Virginia, the exact boundary of this tract and the time limit for the location of warrants were both left indefinite. Congress passed a number of acts to adjust these matters, but many of the warrants fell into the hands of speculators who proceeded to monopolize the best locations, creating a thoroughly unsystematic land system that was in strong contrast to the usual township scheme. The influx of settlers into the interior of Ohio after Wayne's victory made it necessary to determine the exact boundaries of this tract, and a line was run in 1802 from the source of the Little Miami to the Scioto, which Congress confirmed but which Virginia neither accepted nor rejected. The definite location of this boundary line dragged on until 1818, when the approval of Virginia was secured, and finally in 1871, the unappropriated balance of lands in the District, 76,735.44 acres, was turned over to the state of Ohio.[26] Probably this experience with the Military Reserve and the Virginia Military District accounts for the cool response to a petition from the Indiana territorial legislature and the Knox County militia, for land bounties to the troops who had fought at Tippecanoe. Congress merely allowed these Western veterans three additional years, if necessary, to complete their payments for public lands.[27]

Meanwhile Congress had not neglected the general needs of the public-land system in the Old Northwest. The clause that restricted the provisions of the Land Act of 1800 to the area east of a line northward from the Kentucky River, became an impossible condition after Harrison began to secure

[26] Annals of Congress, First Congress, Appendix, pp. 2362-2363; Third Congress, First Session, Appendix, p. 1475; Eighth Congress, First Session, Appendix, pp. 1282-1283; Treat, National Land System, pp. 325-340.

[27] Annals of Congress, Twelfth Congress, First Session, pp. 583-700, passim, Appendix, pp. 2266-2267.

from the Indians, cessions of land that lay west of this region. Congress quickly recognized this difficult situation by the passage of the Land Act of 1804, extending the provisions of the famous Act of 1800, including notably the five years' credit, to the remaining public lands in the Old Northwest, as they should be taken over from the Indians. This act undertook also to adjust long-standing grievances due to the uncertain land titles in the settlements at Vincennes, in the Illinois country, and in Michigan. It authorized land offices at Detroit, Vincennes, and Kaskaskia respectively, and it empowered the register and the receiver at each one to act as a board of commissioners which should examine all claims that were presented and should report their decisions to Congress for confirmation. An attempt was made to secure impartial officials by a clause that abolished all fees from the purchasers of public lands, and allowed a salary of $500.00 each to the two officials, with a commission of one-half of one per cent upon all sums that were actually paid in. Unfortunately the act only allowed the commissioners until January 1, 1805, scarcely nine months, as the limit within which claims must be presented.[28]

The machinery set up in the Act of 1804 for the adjustment of claims under former régimes, constituted an exceedingly significant forward step. From the very first organization of the Northwest Territory, the confusion in land titles had been the source of much discontent at Vincennes and in the Illinois settlements. In 1788, in an attempt to solve this problem Congress had passed a resolution that confirmed all claims up to 1783, and in addition donated 400 acres to each head of a family. This act did not include the American settlers, many of them veterans of Clark's campaigns, who were settling at Vincennes and in the Illinois country, but for whom no adequate provision had been made. This and other problems of the complicated land system Governor St. Clair attempted to adjust during his visit in 1790 to organize these

[28] *Annals of Congress*, Eighth Congress, First Session. Appendix, pp. 1285-1293.

frontier outposts. But he soon found that the problem was one with numerous angles.[29] Many of the inhabitants were illiterate, and often they were unable to understand English. Then, too, there were few reliable records of claims, for the common custom was to keep as proof only a scrap of paper which the owner frequently lost. Another serious complication was caused by the American settlers who had come in while the country was under the control of Virginia. They had secured from John Todd, the county lieutenant appointed by Virginia, or else from the courts, grants which they found were void under the terms offered by Congress. There were other Americans who had come in and settled as mere squatters, since they could not secure public land. Now they were greatly aroused over the danger of losing "the land we improved at the risque of our lives with a design to live on," especially as they had repeatedly been called upon to serve in the militia.

In the effort to straighten out the land tangle in the Illinois settlements, St. Clair promptly appointed a recorder of deeds and three surveyors. His instructions to Antoine Gerardin, surveyor for the district of Cahokia, show the care with which he drew up his plans. Gerardin was to lay off a tract, as near as possible to the "improvements" of Cahokia, which was to be divided into 400 acre donation lots, and he should also survey all claims held prior to 1783 that were presented for confirmation. The oath of "disinterested" persons must be considered in passing upon these claims, and all claimants must prove that they had taken up their lands before 1783 with a bona-fide intention of settlement. Lastly, not more than one tract was to be confirmed to any individual. St. Clair soon found that even these careful plans did not straighten out the land situation in the Illinois settlements. The various officers he appointed drew up lists of claims, but few of them could be confirmed, chiefly because they had not been surveyed. The poverty-stricken claimants, for their

[29] For St. Clair's proceedings at Kaskaskia, see *Executive Proceedings, Northwest Territory*, 1788-1795, pp. 78-196, 276-375, *passim*.

part, resented this stirring up of their usual lethargic existence, and they bitterly denounced the surveyor's fee that was demanded, $2.00 per lot or $2.50 per mile, as merely an addition to the "weight of misfortunes accumulated since the Virginia troops entered this country." Many persons, sensing a chance to secure extra land, presented petitions for extraordinary grants, some of them seemingly well founded, as one from the villages of Cohos and Prairie du Pont for a grant of the land along the Mississippi as a pasture and a source of firewood. Less justifiable was the claim of Father Gibault who had gone over to the Spanish side of the river for a time, but nevertheless asked for two tracts of land, as a reward for his exertions in favor of the Americans. St. Clair finally concluded that the only possible way out of the almost hopeless confusion in the Illinois country was a complete revision of the terms offered by Congress. In his opinion it was especially necessary to make some provision for granting small tracts to individuals, as a means of building up the American population.

When Sargent came to Vincennes as the personal representative of St. Clair to organize the government, he found the land situation was virtually a repetition of the one in the Illinois settlements.[30] But the problem of the American settlers was an even more serious one here, for John Todd and the local courts had given them grants estimated at fully 46,000 acres. Sargent held that all these "court" grants were without adequate authority, but that the settlers who had improved them deserved consideration from Congress, notably 131 of them who had come in since 1783, and had been called upon to do militia duty. Another difficult problem was presented by a tract of fully 150 acres in the village itself, which had been bought from the Piankeshaw Indians, and had long been settled. Also, the inhabitants of Vincennes were accustomed to use as a pasture land a tract of 5,400 acres which should be confirmed by the government. To show

[30] For Sargent's proceedings at Vincennes, see *Executive Proceedings, Northwest Territory,* 1788-1795, pp. 152-213, *passim.*

the extent of these claims, Sargent listed 143 heads of families who had settled at Vincennes before 1783, along with 15 who had left, chiefly for the Spanish settlements. One phase of the land problem at Vincennes was solved in 1791 by an act that confirmed the titles to the 150 acre tract within the village that had been bought from the Indians, and to the town commons. This same act also confirmed all grants from a court or other constituted authority, up to 400 acres, that had been actually improved, and granted 100 acres to each person who had been enrolled in the militia on August 1, 1790.[31]

But the different measures adopted by Sargent at Vincennes, and the act passed by Congress in 1791, failed to provide for the settlers who were pouring into the Old Northwest. Nor did it straighten out fully the great confusion in the land titles of the original French population, even though it was necessary to adjust these older claims before the donation tracts, sanctioned by Congress, could be laid out, or the public lands made available to incoming settlers.[32] This final adjustment was made possible by the Land Act of 1804. Just as in the Illinois settlements, official action was needed upon many excessive and questionable claims that were being put forward. As an example, when Harrison arrived in the territory, he discovered a preposterous grant which the district court, sitting at Vincennes under the authority of Virginia between 1780 and 1788, had made to its own members. Extending 120 miles eastward from the Wabash, and 90 miles to the westward, it included land around Vincennes, excepting only 20,000 to 30,000 acres in the immediate vicinity. From the claimants to this enormous holding many persons had purchased large tracts at exceedingly low rates, 1,000 acres being sold in one instance for a rifle. As Secretary of State, Madison agreed with Harrison that this preposterous

[31] *Annals of Congress*, First Congress, Third Session, Appendix, pp. 2413-2415.

[32] Reports from St. Clair and Sargent, 1794-1797, *Northwest Territorial Papers*, Senate Files, especially 6255, 6322, and 6329; *American State Papers, Public Lands*, vol. I, p. 84.

claim would present a serious problem if it were allowed, and Congress ignored a petition for confirmation.[33] Yet Harrison's activity in exposing this and other fraudulent claims in Indiana aroused much local wrath, and this hostility was probably at the bottom of the charges that Isaac Darneille and Martin McKee brought against him.

After the passage of the Act of 1804 the board of land commissioners promptly organized at Vincennes. In the *Indiana Gazette,* the one newspaper in Indiana Territory, they gave notice that they would confirm all grants under St. Clair and Harrison, provided they had not been obtained by fraud and the claimants showed some proof of title.[34] After lengthy hearings and a careful sifting of evidence the commissioners drew up an exhaustive report which included claims from the French and the British régimes, those under the district courts and the governors of the Northwest and Indiana territories, and lastly a varied list that was not covered by any act of Congress. The report was quite conservative, favoring a large number of claims, but rejecting some upon merit, and others merely upon the ground that they had been fraudulently granted by the district court. Also, the board rejected two claims that were based upon the supposed rights of the Illinois and Wabash Land Company. Several months later the commissioners presented a supplementary report, and Congress confirmed both documents in an act passed in March, 1807, that upheld all grants by the territorial governors, with the exception of those that the board had specifically rejected, and extended to July 1, 1808, the time limit for locating claims. This act was rounded out by another one which stipulated that certain tracts should be selected, in which grants of the various types authorized by Congress could be located.[35] These acts virtually settled the old claims in the Vincennes land district, and sales could now

[33] Harrison's *Messages and Letters,* Esarey, ed., vol. I, pp. 36-37, 90-91.
[34] *Indiana Gazette,* August 21, 1804.
[35] *American State Papers, Public Lands,* vol. I, pp. 289-303; *Annals of Congress,* Ninth Congress, Second Session, Appendix, pp. 1290-1292, 1295-1298.

proceed in regular fashion, as the public lands were surveyed. The opening of an additional land office at Jeffersonville in 1807 made the purchase of land still easier for the average settler in Indiana.

In the Illinois country the great confusion in land titles, which St. Clair had failed to adjust, was not settled as easily as the comparatively simple situation in Indiana. Added to the confusion among claimants under the old French titles was the dissatisfaction among the "untitled settlers," chiefly Americans. For example, lands at Peoria which had supposedly been granted by the commandant had been withdrawn from settlement by Harrison, and the settlers petitioned in vain for the confirmation of their titles.[36] At Fort Massac, also, there were a number of settlers, to each of whom in 1794 the commandant, Major Thomas Doyle, had offered an in-lot of five and a half acres, and an out-lot of five acres. They petitioned Congress that these holdings should be confirmed, and that, in addition, each head of a family should be allowed a donation lot of 400 acres.[37] These claims at Peoria and at Fort Massac were typical of many others at the isolated posts in the Illinois country. It was quite evident that until they were settled, or until at least the claimants received rights of preëmption, any sales of public land to the many incoming settlers would be impossible. Meanwhile many immigrants were forced to become mere squatters, a situation that certainly did not help the troubled political conditions in early Illinois. In 1805, a petition from at least 284 of these landless Illinois frontiersmen represented that they had settled wherever it was possible, but with an "indifferent market and little cash" they could not purchase land, and they prayed for the passage of laws that would favor the "industrious poor." [38] Meantime, another

[36] Secretary of State to Winthrop Sargent, June 30, 1797, *Northwest Territorial Papers*, B. I. A. Dom.; *Executive Journal, Indiana Territory, 1800–1816*, pp. 107-108.

[37] Petitions, January 10, 1805, *Indiana Territorial Papers*, House Files.

[38] Petitions, December 12, 1804, *Indiana Territorial Papers*, House Files, 2690.

complication had come into the land situation, in the form of a veritable orgy of land speculation which swept through the Illinois settlements about the time the land commissioners arrived at Kaskaskia. The rights to donation tracts of 400 acres and militia warrants for 100 acres were bought up, to be resold to the incoming wave of American settlers, and many fraudulent claims were advanced.

The two commissioners, Michael Jones and Elijah Backus, holding hearings at the Kaskaskia Land Office, sifted out a mass of false testimony. One man alone attempted by fraud to establish forty claims of 400 acres each, while at least 200 depositions were acknowledged to be false. As a result the board was obliged to reconsider its decisions, and its chief reliance, barring written proof, came to be the testimony of the "oldest and most respected inhabitants." Faulty surveys, with overlapping boundaries as a result, constituted still another source of much confusion.[39] So difficult did the task of investigation prove to be, that Congress granted the board an extension of time for their report to January 2, 1810, and allowed them a special agent to aid their investigations.[40] December 31, 1809, the land commissioners submitted a partial list of the claims they had confirmed in the Kaskaskia district, and Congress accepted their decisions. Two months later they drew up another and a more elaborate report, in which they distinguished four separate classes of claims. First, there were the titles under the French and the British for which the records had been in such bad condition that oral testimony had been the chief reliance. Secondly, in doubtful cases regarding the 400 acre lots to heads of families, the board had interpreted the law to provide for persons who were actual residents between 1783 and 1788. Thirdly, in rights founded upon improvements, they had held there must have been an actual planting of a crop, not a mere

---

[39] American State Papers, Public Lands, vol. I, pp. 590-591.
[40] Annals of Congress, Ninth Congress, Second Session, pp. 1291-1292; Tenth Congress, Second Session, p. 1811; Eleventh Congress, First and Second Sessions, p. 2506.

clearing of trees; and fourthly, they had been quite lenient with respect to militia rights, since the rolls were very imperfect. In making out this report the board, upon the affidavit of Robinson, the special government agent, rejected the depositions of fifteen different persons to prove numerous claims. Thus Joseph Page, a Frenchman and "a great swearer," who had made about 200 depositions, usually in favor of large land jobbers, had refused to say a word "without his book" when he was unexpectedly called upon to repeat his testimony. The commissioners closed their report with a devout acknowledgment of the Divine providence that had preserved them from "legal murder and private assassination" during these hearings so filled with perjured testimony.[41]

The perjury and fraud which now involved many of the leading citizens of the Illinois country and even government officials continued during the later proceedings of the commissioners. A claim that was typical of the many questionable ones presented was brought up by John Edgar and John Murry St. Clair, the latter said to have been a son of Governor St. Clair. This claim to 13,986 acres was based upon a grant in 1796 by the British commandant in Illinois to a Philadelphia firm, supported by a patent from Governor St. Clair which had not, however, been countersigned by the territorial secretary. Edgar and St. Clair were now using this questionable document to secure a tract of nearly 30,000 acres, and having unearthed these facts after an industrious investigation, the board summarily rejected their claim.[42] The sequel to this and other like fearless decisions was the futile attempt to convict Michael Jones of inciting the murder of Rice Jones, and it is easy to understand the former's plea that any further attacks by the land jobbers "against men who have sacrificed their peace of mind, their interests,

---

[41] Report of Land Commissioners, December 31, 1809, *Illinois Territorial Papers*, Senate Files, 2524; *Annals of Congress*, Eleventh Congress, First and Second Sessions, p. 2584; *American State Papers, Public Lands*, vol. II, pp. 123-181.

[42] *Ibid.*, vol. II, pp. 239-240.

and hazarded their lives in doing their duty," should have no weight with the government. Congress gave heed, confirming the decisions of the commissioners in most cases, but referring a few claims for further investigation.[43] When he sent the board's decisions in these deferred cases to Washington, Michael Jones pleaded for immediate action. After eight years spent in these "painful and weary" duties he was convinced that land speculators alone would want to make any further claims, and to defer to them would be unjust. The picture he painted was a dark one: "When witnesses have been suborned, when the ancient records have recently been interpolated, and when the officials who dared discharge their duty have been attempted to be made the victims of this corruption, it is time to close the doors against the admission of new frauds." [44] The report on disputed claims that accompanied this pessimistic complaint from a faithful and conscientious public servant was confirmed, but not until after the close of the War of 1812 was the land situation in Illinois finally adjusted.

In Michigan there was virtually a repetition of the confusion in land titles that existed in Indiana and Illinois. When the land commissioners first came to Detroit they found that practically no attempt to confirm titles had been made since the Americans had taken over the territory. The land claims around Detroit and the few on the river bank were based upon a wide variety of grants, some of them upon purchase from the Indians, others upon mere hearsay, and many of the surveys were far from accurate. As a "minute inquiry" would be necessary in many cases, the land commissioners at Detroit decided to send only a preliminary report in 1805.[45] Meanwhile the inhabitants were becoming

[43] Michael Jones to Jeremiah Morrow, December 1, 1810, *Illinois Territorial Papers*, House Files; *American State Papers, Public Lands*, vol. II, p. 255; *Annals of Congress*, Twelfth Congress, First Session, Appendix, pp. 2237-2238.

[44] *American State Papers, Public Lands*, vol. II, pp. 741-742.

[45] Report of C. Jouett to Secretary of War, July 25, 1803, and George Hoffman and Frederick Bates to Secretary of Treasury, December 1, 1805, *Michigan Territorial Papers*, Senate Files.

greatly alarmed, and Judge Woodward and Governor Hull impatiently protested against the delay in removing one of the chief obstacles to the economic and political development of Michigan. But Congress supported the Fabian policy of the land commissioners, and merely passed an act that confirmed the measures already taken to lay out Detroit. According to the commissioners' report, in all Michigan there were 242 claims, with about 200 more in the Indian country, aside from the posts at Mackinaw and Fort Miami. Not more than half these claims had been filed within the time limit set by Congress, and as a solution of the entire problem the board considered all claims should be allowed up to July 2, 1805, when the territorial government was established at Detroit. A year later Congress confirmed all the specific claims that the land commissioners had so far recommended. For the future it gave this board, sitting with the territorial secretary, the power to confirm tracts up to 640 acres that had been settled or improved by July 1, 1796. But only one tract was to be allowed each claimant, and all titles must be settled by January 1, 1808.[46]

The time limit for the final settlement of Michigan land claims was altogether too brief, although the commissioners asked priests to explain to their illiterate parishioners the necessity of presenting their claims. The commissioners in their report also declared that the limitation of each claimant to only one tract was unwise, since no single holding exceeded 640 acres, and most of them were under 480 acres. Lastly, they pointed out that as the soil of the front lots was rapidly becoming exhausted and there was little timber left on them, these holdings should be allowed to extend back at least 80 arpents. The inhabitants strongly supported this sympathetic and exhaustive report, and they asked, in addition, for the confirmation of claims since July 1, 1796, inasmuch as there had not heretofore been a land office at De-

[46] American State Papers, Public Lands, vol. I, pp. 263-265; Annals of Congress, Ninth Congress, Second Session, Appendix, pp. 1280-1283.

troit, and they themselves had been ignorant of the laws.[47] In 1808, Congress passed an act that granted most of these requests, and gave settlers in Michigan between July 1, 1796, and March 26, 1804, preëmption rights rather than outright confirmation of their claims. This act required all claims to be presented to the land commissioners by January 1, 1809,[48] and in order to carry out its provisions and those of previous acts of a like tenor, this board sat continuously at Detroit, June 29, 1807, to February 28, 1811, making minute examinations and passing upon 738 claims. Their decisions were confirmed in 1812 by an act that finally settled the troublesome question of the Michigan land claims,[49] but too late to allay the unrest that prevailed in the territory up to the War of 1812.

While the land systems in Indiana, Illinois, and Michigan were being adjusted, the Federal government did not ignore other needs of the public lands. The provisions for sales were becoming a source of considerable controversy between those who were inclined to put first, Western interests, and the large number who still held financial advantage to the national treasury to be the main consideration. From the Western settlers came insistent complaints of the practical working of the laws for the disposal of the public lands. For example, a petition from residents of Fairfield County in central Ohio asked that interest on land sales should be waived from the date of purchase, and that the issue of a patent should not be postponed until all payments had been made.[50] The advocates of more liberal terms secured a powerful ally in Albert Gallatin, now Secretary of the Treasury, who by his residence in Fayette County on the western bor-

[47] American State Papers, Public Lands, vol. I, p. 593; Memorial, October 26, 1807, Michigan Territorial Papers, House Files.
[48] Annals of Congress, Tenth Congress, First Session, Appendix, pp. 2874-2876.
[49] Proceedings of Commissioners at Detroit, June 29, 1807, to February 28, 1811, American State Papers, Public Lands, vol. I, pp. 305-557; Annals of Congress, Twelfth Congress, First Session, Appendix, pp. 2273-2274.
[50] Petition, 1802, Northwest Territorial Papers, House Files.

der of Pennsylvania had come into actual contact with frontier problems. Early in 1804 he submitted a report that strongly favored a reduction in the price of public lands, inasmuch as they must compete with private holdings in such large grants as the Western Reserve, the Virginia Military District and Symmes' Purchase, and with lands in Kentucky. As for the credit system, he pointed out that an initial payment of $160.00 would buy 320 acres, with a balance of $480.00 with interest due within four years. The inevitable result was to tempt settlers to buy more land than they could pay for, and already about $1,100,000.00 was due the government from nearly 2,000 individuals for public land they had purchased in the past three years. Therefore Gallatin proposed that credit should be allowed for forty days only, that the minimum price for half sections should be reduced to $1.25 per acre, and that sales should be permitted in quarter sections—*i.e.* 160 acres—with a minimum of $1.50 per acre. Congress adopted Gallatin's recommendations only in part, retaining the credit provisions and the minimum rate of $2.00 per acre in the Land Act of 1804. But this measure at least permitted the sale of quarter sections of 160 acres, and gave further relief by a clause that abolished all land-office fees, except those for survey, and at the same time allowed each of the officers a salary of $500.00, with a commission of one-half of one per cent on all receipts.[51]

The very slight modifications in the Land Act of 1804 of the terms upon which public lands would be sold caused great disappointment in the Western country, where, now that the five years' limit of credit was about to expire, many purchasers under the Land Act of 1800 found themselves facing possible forfeiture. Numerous petitions to Congress set forth the plight of these unfortunate settlers, among them one from inhabitants of Dearborn County, Indiana, and the near-by section of Ohio. They had purchased their lands, they as-

[51] *Annals of Congress*, Eighth Congress, First Session, pp. 1285-1293, *American State Papers*, vol. I, pp. 183-184.

serted, when their prospects were flattering, but misfortunes had accumulated. The large quantity of flour they raised had overstocked the market, lately the wheat crop had failed, and the fluctuating demand at New Orleans had reduced the price of beef and pork, so that freight charges in some cases had actually brought shippers into debt. To add to their troubles the abandonment of Fort Washington as an army post had "dry'd" up their source of cash, at the same time that the government was draining it away for land. Now they feared that "money'd" men who had not endured pioneer hardships would buy in their farms, and they petitioned for a reasonable extension of time in which to complete their payments.[52] Early in 1806 the newly organized standing committee on public lands made a rather dismal report to the House upon the general situation of the Western settlers. Up to October 1, 1805, the committee reported, there was due from purchasers of the public lands in Ohio alone a total of $2,094,305.00 exclusive of interest. So far, no lands had been declared forfeited, but even should these delinquent tracts be offered at public sale, there would be few if any purchasers, for no one in the neighborhood would buy, and no outsider would run the risk of coming in. As the situation was likely to grow worse, the committee concluded it would be impossible to execute the law, and they recommended that the provision for credit should be repealed. In opposition, John Randolph, chairman of the Ways and Means Committee, insisted that the existing law should be enforced, lest otherwise the public lands as a source of revenue would be "dried up and lost," and a compromise act was passed in April, 1806, that suspended sales of forfeited lands for at least five months.[53]

With the expiration of the five years' limit within which the purchasers of land under the Act of 1800 must complete

[52] Petitions, 1805, *Indiana Territorial Papers*, House Files 2701 and 2706; *Liberty Hall*, July 23, 1805.
[53] *Annals of Congress*, Ninth Congress, First Session, p. 1259, Second Session, pp. 1031-1034; *American State Papers, Public Lands*, vol. I, p. 284.

their payments, it became apparent that forfeiture was no mere idle dream. Items selected at random from contemporary newspapers give long lists of the forfeited tracts that were offered at public sale during the next few years, at the different land offices in Ohio. One long list offered at Cincinnati in 1813 included 448 separate parcels, the majority of them entire sections, and *Liberty Hall*, the local newspaper, was obliged to print what was virtually an extra edition in order to publish it.[54] This enforcement of the forfeiture clause aroused a strong protest from the West. The cash that was demanded in payments for lands was exceedingly scarce, and there were complaints that the land office took in the greater part of what was on hand, locked it up, and then sent it out of the country. Moreover, the general depression as a result of the Non-Intercourse and Embargo acts had decreased the demand for agricultural products, and had seriously affected the ability of the settlers to meet the installments due on their lands. The usual flood of petitions now descended upon Congress, and the Ohio legislature petitioned that each settler might be allowed to retain at least one section, provided he continued to pay interest upon the balance he still owed. Otherwise, they feared, the scarcity of specie must deprive "many poor but honest and industrious citizens" of their lands with the improvements.[55] As Jeremiah Morrow, the sole representative from Ohio, was chairman of the House Committee on Public Lands, these different petitions received a favorable hearing, and the committee recommended that the credit system should be abolished, upon the ground that it inevitably created hostility to the government, and would reduce the price of land. Although Edward Tiffin, one of the senators from Ohio, also used his influence

[54] See files of Ohio newspapers, 1805–1812, and especially *Scioto Gazette*, March 6, 1806; *Western Herald*, February 28, 1807; *Western Spectator*, March 11 and 19, 1811; *Western Spy*, March 12, 1808, and March 20, 1813; and *Liberty Hall*, March 25, 1813.

[55] *Annals of Congress*, Tenth Congress, First Session, pp. 1331, 1840; Second Session, pp. 500-501; *Laws of Ohio*, Sixth General Assembly, pp. 175-176, Seventh General Assembly, pp. 222-223.

and Gallatin agreed to the committee's recommendations, Congress merely passed an act in 1809 that prolonged for two years the limit of credit before lands would be forfeited.[56] But hard times still prevailed in the West, and petitions continued to pour upon Congress for relief from a really serious situation. A bill brought up in the Lower House in favor of purchasers of public lands led to an extended debate in which John Randolph, reversing his former position of making profits from the public lands, warned that the present system of sales might create a serious Western grievance. Although the entire debate showed a strong sentiment for a complete revision of the land system, the act that was finally passed merely gave another two years' extension of credit.[57]

The Western dissatisfaction over the conditions for the purchase of public lands was much increased in 1809 when the credit limit expired on lands west of the mouth of the Kentucky that had been bought under the Act of 1804. The inhabitants of Indiana now began to join the ranks of the many petitioners for modification of the terms of purchase. In December, 1810, the Indiana territorial legislature presented a memorial to Congress, which purported to give "a true and interesting picture" of the situation of many persons who had purchased public lands. Most of them, the memorial declared, were actual settlers rather than speculators, yet for a number of reasons they found themselves without the means to pay for their lands. Often the fund which they had set apart to purchase necessaries until their first crop was marketed had proved inadequate, while many persons who had expected to secure the payments of debts due them in their old homes, or to realize returns from property they left behind, had been disappointed. The Embargo, too, had interfered with their markets, and especially the low

[56] *American State Papers, Public Lands*, vol. I, p. 909; *Annals of Congress*, Tenth Congress, Second Session, Appendix, pp. 1831-1832; Edward Tiffin to Huntington, January 12, 1809, *Huntington Letters*, Western Reserve MSS. 1801–1811, no. 75.

[57] *Annals of Congress*, Eleventh Congress, Second Session, pp. 1999-2005 and 2566-2567.

price at New Orleans for pork, which was the chief export from Indiana. At the same time, small crops of corn and mast had interfered with the raising of hogs. In view of these conditions, the legislature asked for the remission of all back interest and a two years' extension of credit.[58] Without comment upon the arguments that this memorial had presented, the Committee on Public Lands reported that an extension of the time for payments upon land purchases would be a mere temporary measure that would encourage settlers to take up larger tracts than they could pay for, and that any law that placed a considerable part of the population in debt to the government was dangerous. Therefore the committee merely recommended an extension of credit for one year, and this view Congress accepted.[59]

The increasing agrarian discontent in the Western settlements finally led to the appointment of a Senate committee to consider needed revisions in the public-land laws, with Thomas Worthington of Ohio as chairman. In its report this committee recommended the abolition of the credit system, and the reduction of the cash price for public lands to $1.00 per acre. These changes the committee considered all the more necessary, since, within three land districts, Chillicothe, Zanesville, and Cincinnati, 255 forfeited tracts had been offered for sale in the last three months, and for the past six years, they estimated, settlers in Ohio had lost annually $33,000.00 which they had paid over for lands that were later declared forfeited. Notwithstanding these telling arguments, the act that was finally passed merely temporized, granting purchasers of public lands three additional years in which to pay the balances they owed.[60] But such a measure did not satisfy the settlers, especially those in Indiana, where the increasing trouble with the Indians only added to the general agricultural distress. Early in June, 1812, more

[58] Memorial, Indiana Legislative Assembly, 1810, *Indiana Territorial Papers*, House Files, 2790; *Western Sun*, December 15, 1810.

[59] *American State Papers, Public Lands*, vol. II, pp. 256-257.

[60] *Ibid.*, pp. 439-440; *Annals of Congress*, Twelfth Congress, First Session, p. 2275.

than a hundred of these Indiana pioneers petitioned for a still further indulgence, in view of the many frontier disturbances and the bad business situation, along with the great scarcity of money. Finally, Congress passed an act that gave purchasers prior to April 1, 1808, whose lands had been forfeited, the right to reënter them, and promised credit for the payments they had already made.[61] The opportunistic policy represented by this act continued after the War of 1812, and not until 1820 was a measure passed which, striking at the chief defects in the Land Laws of 1800 and 1804, abolished the credit system, reduced still further the minimum area that could be purchased, and materially cut down the price per acre.

The impatience of the Western pioneers with the land laws was doubtless responsible for a rather significant attempt at New Boston in Clermont County, Ohio, to organize a society, the *True Americans,* with its avowed purpose to see that the principle of equal rights was carried out in the distribution of the public land. The existing situation the founders of this organization denounced as "contrary to the spirit of our declaration of independence and repugnant to the principles of republican government," and drawn up "for the benefit of the wealthy and opulent," rather than that of the poor man. The socialistic doctrines of the Revolutionary period were reflected in their manifesto, "Give the poor a right to the soil, who always have to bear the heat and burthen of the day," and then the Union could defy all the intrigues of "foreign or domestic foes to destroy it." If their petition to Congress was not successful, the founders of this organization, imitating the methods of Samuel Adams and forecasting twentieth century propagandists, proposed the formation of corresponding societies as a means to ensure changes in the land system.[62] The society of the *True Americans* was merely a flash in the pan, and a small one at that, but the aims of its

[61] Petition, June 20, 1812, *Indiana Territorial Papers,* Senate Files; *Annals of Congress,* Twelfth Congress, First Session, pp. 2358-2359.
[62] *Liberty Hall,* November 14, 1810, and May 27, 1811.

founders arose from real grievances among the Western settlers.

Much more direct was the insistent demand for preëmption rights. The precedent established in the case of claimants under Symmes naturally encouraged the many squatters who had taken up lands without any title, before the Land Act of 1800 made purchase a comparatively easy matter. The general policy of Congress, however, was to discourage these illegal settlements by refusing to grant preëmption rights to such persons. As a result many memorials came to Congress, among them one from settlers between the Scioto and the Muskingum who represented that their lands were subject to public sale, and that there was danger they might be outbidden by an "unfeeling land jobber" who would take over their improvements. In view of the hardships they had suffered, they prayed therefore for preëmption rights at the usual minimum price, in the lands which they had settled. This petition the Lower House rejected in rather unceremonious fashion.[63] There was an especially insistent demand for preëmption rights from settlers in Indiana and Illinois, who, unable to purchase public lands, had often been obliged to appropriate them without any legal title whatsoever. Fearing that they would lose their lands with the improvements, they sent Congress memorials that set forth the hardships they had undergone, and their unfortunate situation. A typical petition from "Illenois" represented that the petitioners had settled there in 1790, coming from Maryland, Pennsylvania, and other seaboard states. They had worked hard and had defended the country, but as there was little or no commerce they had practically no cash to take up lands. Other petitioners represented that they had built roads across the public lands and had provided food and shelter for all travelers.[64] The situation of the Shawneetown settlers was a spe-

[63] *American State Papers, Public Lands,* vol. I, p. 111; Petition, February, 1801, *Northwest Territorial Papers,* House Files.

[64] Petitions, October 22, 1803, and September 15 and October 11, 1808, *Indiana Territorial Papers,* House Files.

cially pressing one. They had been induced to come in, they represented, by the authorities of Indiana Territory, and they feared that "some monopolizing company or set of men" might get possession of the entire settlement, for it was the natural center of the growing trade from the near-by United States Saline. In answer Congress ordered that not more than two sections of land at Shawneetown should be laid out and sold publicly, in lots not exceeding a quarter of an acre each, but this arrangement did not altogether suit the inhabitants. Soon they sent another petition, that each man already settled at Shawneetown should receive an in-lot and an out-lot near his improvements, at the usual price.[65] The failure to accede to this request was altogether consistent with the settled policy of Congress not to encourage unlawful settlements by granting preëmption rights.

Although Congress was not inclined to grant preëmption rights, it recognized Western needs by establishing land offices which were convenient to the tracts that were offered for sale. The Land Act of 1800 provided for offices at Steubenville, Marietta, and Chillicothe in addition to the one that had already been established at Cincinnati, and after the Military Reserve was thrown open to settlers, Congress established a land office at Zanesville.[66] This policy was continued in the Land Act of 1804 which authorized three new offices at Kaskaskia, at Detroit, and at Vincennes respectively. In 1807 another act provided for land offices to be opened at Canton and at Jeffersonville for the greater convenience of the purchasers of land that had lately been ceded by the Indians. This general policy to make the sales of public lands convenient to the settlers was illustrated, too, when the inhabitants of Shawneetown in southern Illinois complained that the journey to the land office at Kaskaskia was more expensive than the lots which the government had au-

[65] Petitions, November 13, 1809, and February 21, 1811, *Illinois Territorial Papers*, House Files; *Annals of Congress*, Eleventh Congress, Second Session, Appendix, pp. 2564-2566.

[66] For a complete list of land offices in the Old Northwest, with the date of establishment of each one, see Treat, *National Land System*, p. 175.

thorized to be sold. As the settlers were pouring into Illinois, and the Indian lands were being bought up, some remedy was obviously necessary, and in 1812 Congress authorized the opening of a land office at Shawneetown.[67]

The enlightened policy of Congress from 1800 on, of encouragement to individual settlers in place of large grants to speculators, had resulted in a marked increase in the sales of public lands. Up to the Land Act of 1800, sales in the Old Northwest totaled 1,334,365 acres. But in the next eleven years the sales at the different Western land offices were almost trebled, reaching 3,374,843.47½ acres, while the confirmation of numerous claims and many donation grants had taken up much additional land. Nor had the financial gains of the government been negligible. The expense of putting these lands on the market was, altogether, $503,017.71, while the corresponding receipts of the land offices in the Old Northwest totaled $5,475,229.41¼, or there had been a net gain for the government of $4,972,211.70¼, quite a tidy sum indeed. In addition there were still large amounts due upon installments,[68] so that Hamilton's hope to make the public lands yield a substantial revenue had not been altogether disappointed.

Far more important than mere temporary financial returns had been the swift increase in the population of the Old Northwest, as land became available to the individual settler.[69] In the decade, 1800–1810, the inhabitants of Ohio, where the Indian danger had been practically eliminated, and the bulk of the land was now open to settlement, had increased from 45,365 to 227,843. The opening of the land offices in the interior, the decrease in the minimum amount of land sold, and the comparatively easy terms upon which it could be secured, had been important factors in attracting

[67] Petition, February 23, 1811, *Illinois Territorial Papers*, House Files; *Annals of Congress*, Twelfth Congress, First Session, Appendix, pp. 2241-2242.

[68] *American State Papers, Public Lands*, vol. II, pp. 442, 444, and 739-740.

[69] See Census for 1800, pp. 85, 87, and for 1810, pp. 69-70, 86, 88.

this mass of settlers to Ohio. There had been a significant shift of population, too, from the Ohio Valley, where most of the large holdings of land speculators were located, to the interior counties which usually were taken up by individuals. Thus, in 1800 more than seventy-five per cent of the Ohio population had been in the belt of counties that bordered the river, but by 1810 this proportion was only about thirty-nine per cent. The interior counties which in 1800 had held about twenty-five per cent of the population, now held almost fifty-two per cent. The remaining inhabitants, about nine per cent, were found in the Western Reserve where the proportionate increase had been only five per cent. The proportionate decrease in the Virginia Military District had been an interesting illustration of the general disinclination to purchase lands that were held by speculators. In 1800 this section had held about twenty-six and two-thirds per cent of the population of Ohio, but by 1810 this percentage had decreased to nineteen and a half.

The territory of Indiana, too, had greatly benefited by the public land policy. The scant 1,523 inhabitants east of the Wabash in 1800 had increased by 1810 to 24,520 in three well-defined districts: the original area of settlement in and around Vincennes; the "gore" in southeastern Indiana; and Clark's Grant in southern Indiana, together with the public lands within the bounds of the Jeffersonville Land District. In Illinois, where there was confusion in the land system to the very end of the early period, the inhabitants had increased more slowly, from 3,347 in 1800 to 12,282 in 1810. They were found chiefly on a strip running about forty miles along the east bank of the Mississippi, from Cahokia to Kaskaskia, and in less compact settlements in the Ohio Valley in southern Illinois, chiefly at Fort Massac and Shawneetown. In Michigan there was little increase in the inhabitants up to the War of 1812, and the continued confusion in the land system had been one of the chief deterring influences. But at least the bulk of the uncertain titles in the Old Northwest had been cleared up by the end of the early period, and the situation was such that, once the war and the danger of Indian outbreaks was over, the survey and sale of public lands could be carried on in accordance with the precedents that had been established in Ohio and Indiana.

Altogether, in the brief period between the first settlement at Marietta in 1788 and the outbreak of the War of 1812, the land system which the Ordinance of 1785 inaugurated had been worked out in the Old Northwest in fairly satisfactory fashion. The British method of disposing of the land to speculators, who in turn would sell it to actual settlers, had gradually been displaced by the more democratic system of grants from the government to the individual. Thus, the advocates of the Hamiltonian theory that the public lands should be used primarily as a source of revenue, had lost in their contest with those who held to the Jeffersonian theory that the paramount consideration should be the interests of the Western settlers. In the course of the struggle between the advocates of these two theories, Congress had passed laws that fixed the price to be charged for the public land, the terms of sale, and the minimum area that could be taken up by an individual. Certain defects had appeared as this land system developed. The many forfeitures, and the large debts to the government from settlers who had taken up lands, only to find they could not pay for them, showed clearly that a further limitation was needed upon the provisions for credit. There was a well-founded demand, too, for preëmption rights in favor of individuals who had either been unable, or else had neglected, to secure titles to their lands, and, consequently, ran the risk of losing them with all their improvements. These and other problems were partly adjusted in the Land Act of 1820. But the main outlines of the national land system had been worked out in the Old Northwest before the War of 1812. The liberal policy which Congress had adopted had been an all important influence in bringing in the American population which was needed to hold this section against British and Indian attacks.

Chapter XI

PIONEER AGRICULTURE

AGRICULTURE was necessarily the main dependence of the pioneers in the Old Northwest for a livelihood. Fur-bearing animals were rapidly disappearing, and even in its palmiest days the fur trade could not have supported the thousands of immigrants who came in the first two decades of settlement. Moreover, there were practically no minerals in this region that could be profitably mined in the pioneer days, while difficulties of transportation stood in the way of industrial development upon an extensive scale. For agricultural purposes, however, the land between the Great Lakes and the Ohio was ideally adapted, with its gently rolling contour, its abundant timber and many streams, and the deep-lying deposits of rich top soil that the prehistoric glaciers had left as they receded. With such a basis, agricultural development in the Old Northwest was limited only by the number of immigrants and their aggressiveness. Once the Indians had been subdued, and the land had been made available upon reasonable terms, incoming settlers quickly transformed the tracts of public land, as they were opened up, into a countryside of well-kept farms that soon put on the usual appearance of the rural sections of the Atlantic Coast. In the early period up to 1812 this agricultural prosperity was most widely diffused in Ohio, it was found to a less extent in Indiana, and even more seldom in Illinois. The agricultural activities of Michigan up to the War of 1812 were carried on chiefly by the French settlers, although the territory was later to reproduce the American civilization of the Old Northwest. But for this present survey, agricultural con-

316

ditions in Michigan may be ignored during the brief and stormy period, 1796 to 1812.

As they spread over the Old Northwest, the pioneers naturally carried with them the customs they had known in their old homes, modifying them in many cases to meet local needs. An exceptionally interesting illustration of this transfer of long-established institutions was found in the typical form of settlement in the earliest days, which imitated the compact villages of frontier New England and other exposed communities. Clustering around a central stockade, which had been erected chiefly for protection against the Indians, were the in-lots upon which the early Western pioneers built their houses and outbuildings and where they cultivated their gardens. Beyond were the out-lots, much larger in size, and used for general agriculture. A town common for the settlers' cattle often rounded out the similarity to the early New England settlements. At Marietta, each one of the first settlers received an in-lot, 90 by 180 feet, close by the stockade of Campus Martius, and an out-lot of eight acres. Likewise at Cincinnati every pioneer householder was assigned an in-lot, 86½ by 193 feet, which was under the protection of Fort Washington, and a four acre out-lot. There was also a town common as at Marietta.[1] This compact plan of settlement was adhered to when population first began to spread up the valleys of the chief tributaries of the Ohio. Thus, in 1793 John Dunlop offered settlers above Colerain, on the Miami, out-lots of ten acres each as well as in-lots. About the same time, John Ludlow offered "good encouragement" to settlers at Mount Pleasant, about seven miles north of Cincinnati, and in the following spring John Armstrong held out inducements to families who would settle on the "fertile tract of land, bounded by the Great Miami, on which Fort Hamilton stands and including the large prairie."[2]

After Wayne's campaign and the Treaty of Greenville in

[1] *Records of the Ohio Company*, Hulbert, ed., vol. I, p. 20; Greve, *Centennial History of Cincinnati*, vol. I, pp. 186-187.
[2] *Centinel*, December 14 and 21, 1793; April 12, 1794.

1795, isolated settlement was possible, with the gradual disappearance of danger from Indian attacks, and the detached farm became common. This change from the first compact settlements appeared at an early date, even in the interior. In the spring of 1796 settlers came as far up the Miami Valley as Dayton, and, imitating the founders of earlier settlements, the proprietors laid out their town in compact form, with an in-lot 99 by 198 feet and an out-lot of ten acres for each pioneer settler. But practically immune now from Indian attacks, they made provision also for isolated settlement when they allowed each of the first settlers to purchase 160 acres at about $1.13 per acre.[3] This innovation gradually spread, and just as in the countryside east of the Appalachians, isolated farms became common in Ohio, and, to a less extent, in Indiana and Illinois. This change in the method of settlement meant that the New England system of a compact village, with its accent upon community life, was displaced to a large extent in the Old Northwest by the scattered farms of the Middle States, with the consequent development of a strong individualism. The changes in the method of settlement were illustrated by the proposals which John Cleves Symmes made in 1800 to establish a settlement in the Scioto Valley. To each head of a family he offered to donate a ten-acre home lot in his proposed village, and to sell 250 acres of farm land at $1.00 per acre on easy terms. With his usual optimism, Symmes even made preparations for the journey, but his colony did not materialize, for he had neglected the rather basic requirement to make sure of his own title to the land he proposed to settle. His offer to sell isolated tracts, however, was in strong contrast to his plans ten years before for laying out his new city in the Miami Purchase.[4]

Once he had secured his land and had built his primitive cabin, the first task of the pioneer farmer was to clear away the thick growth of trees and the dense underbrush which

[3] Steele, *Early Dayton*, pp. 21-29.
[4] *Western Spy*, February 19 and March 19, 1800; *Symmes Correspondence*, Bond, ed., pp. 68-69.

were so usual in the river valleys where the earliest settlements were made. Upon a small holding he could complete this task himself with the aid of his sturdy family. But for larger tracts outside aid was necessary; and with labor scarce, and not dependable, the owner frequently solved the problem by leases, for which the chief return was the clearing and fencing of the land. This device was favored especially by the speculators who so frequently bought up military warrants for land. In 1795, for instance, Michael Laccassagne offered to lease to families who would settle on his large tract in Clark's Grant, as much land as they would clear in five years, with 20s additional for every acre that was fenced. Furthermore, he offered 300 acres of cleared land free for three years to any one who would fence it.[5] This use of leases as a means of clearing the land was especially common in the Virginia Military District.[6] A typical agreement was the one made in February, 1801, between Thomas W. Worthington, the agent for a number of nonresident landholders, and John Downs, Jr. Downs undertook to clear by summer twenty-two acres of land, and then to raise a crop of corn, from which he would pay 100 bushels of corn as rent. Also, he was to build a good cabin, 20 by 16 feet, and to plant apple trees in the orchard. This last condition was quite common, and in another much similar agreement Worthington undertook to furnish 200 apple and 100 peach trees which the lessee agreed to plant. Duncan McArthur, also, as agent for absentee landholders of the Virginia Military District, drew up numerous agreements for clearing the land.[7] In one of the most interesting of these contracts, McArthur leased not less than fifteen nor more than thirty acres in the Round Prairie for five years to Robert Wilson, who agreed to clear the land and to fence it in ten-acre fields, as nearly square as possible. The fences must be at least eight rails high, and the tenant was not permitted

---

[5] *Centinel,* September 5, 1795.
[6] *Diary of Thomas W. Worthington, 1801–1813, passim.*
[7] *McArthur Papers,* vols. I and II, *passim.*

to cut timber except for use upon the premises. This lease was typical in its details of many others which were entered upon by McArthur and Worthington, in order to have tracts of considerable size cleared and fenced.

The settlers in the Old Northwest sensibly adopted the type of agriculture for which the climate and the soil were best suited, following in this respect the farmers of the Middle States where conditions were so similar. The chief grains they cultivated were corn and wheat, with a considerable planting of rye, oats, and barley. In the many creek and river bottoms, they secured excellent hay and pasturage, and these farmers of the Ohio Valley also cultivated hemp and flax on a rather extensive scale. The fertility of the newly cleared soil was remarkable. In the Miami Valley the corn crop, it was claimed, averaged 45 bushels, and the wheat crop ranged between 22 and 40 bushels per acre. Rye averaged 25 bushels, oats 35 bushels, and barley 30 bushels per acre.[8] These conditions were paralleled in the valleys of the Scioto and the Muskingum. In the former, one landowner on Pickaway Plains was reported to have raised 11,000 bushels of wheat, nearly 48 bushels per acre, upon a tract of 230 acres that was enclosed in a single field free from either stumps or stones, and in the Muskingum Valley corn was reported 12 to 15 feet high, and hemp of an equal height.[9] But even allowing for slight exaggerations, the average crop on the fertile lands of the Old Northwest must have appeared alluring in the eyes of the emigrant from the rocky soil of New England. Indeed, the usual expectation of the Western pioneer who purchased a quarter section, was to make a sufficient profit from his farm so that by the third year he would be able to pay back its entire cost with interest. In addition, he hoped to benefit from the rise in the value of his land. While these optimistic hopes were not always realized, the fact that

[8] Drake, *Statistical View of Cincinnati in 1815*, pp. 54-57.
[9] *Ohio Gazette*, September 7, 1802; *Cramer's Pittsburgh Almanack* for 1811, pp. 51-52.

this was held to be a normal profit was a striking proof of the remarkable fertility of these Western lands.[10]

The early settlers did not wait long to plant the fruit trees to which they had been accustomed in their old homes, and here, too, the fertile soil gave satisfactory results. Usually the vine did not flourish in the Old Northwest, although it was successfully cultivated at Vevay on the Ohio and along Lake Erie. But throughout the settlements there were orchards planted in apple and pear trees, cherries, plums, damsons, and peaches. This abundance of fruit greatly impressed John Melish when he came down the Ohio late in the summer, and he noted especially the peach orchards, which were literally loaded down with fruit from which much excellent brandy was distilled.[11] The numerous advertisements of fruit trees "of every kind" for sale, which appeared as early as 1794, testified to the popularity of orchards in Ohio. The apple trees, which were so extensively planted, were offered at very low prices, 50s per 100, or 6d each for good, thrifty stock. Many varieties were popular, one advertisement offering 1,000 "engrafted" apple trees and several seedlings, including such prime old-fashioned favorites as Harvest Apple, Pound Sweet, Golden Russet, "Spitsenburgh," Red Streak, and two varieties of Pippin.[12] Much attention was paid to the best methods of setting out and caring for the trees, and besides these cultivated orchards there were the many groves of sugar maple scattered throughout the Old Northwest, with an annual yield estimated in 1813 at 3,800,-000 pounds,[13] that supplied a real need in a region where ordinary sugar was high-priced and scarce.

Soon the settlers in the Old Northwest began to cultivate

[10] The average yield of wheat per acre in the Old Northwest was estimated at 25 to 40 bushels, rye 25 to 45, and oats 37 to 45. Indian corn averaged 30 to 50 bushels and potatoes 200 to 350 bushels per acre. Blodget, *Statistical Manual,* pp. 97 and 98.

[11] Melish, *Travels in the United States,* vol. II, pp. 85 ff.

[12] *Centinel,* February 1, 1794, and January 30, 1796; *Western Spy,* February 9, 1803, and May 6, 1806.

[13] *Cramer's Pittsburgh Almanack* for 1813, p. 41.

the vegetable gardens to which they had become accustomed in their former homes. The amazing variety and plenty of these pioneer gardens, in the first decade of settlement even, is revealed in the diary of Winthrop Sargent, the first secretary of the Northwest Territory, and an enthusiastic gardener.[14] Starting to work outside late in March, he first sowed turnip and pea seeds in the "old icehouse garden" at his home in Cincinnati. Unfortunately three inches of snow interrupted this work, but with the return of fair weather, Sargent planted many other seeds: sweet marjoram, parsley, pepper, sage, cauliflower, and twenty pecan seeds. Early potatoes he planted in beds, as well as turnips and cabbage stumps for spring greens. Corn, peas, turnips, beets, and "asperagus" were among the other vegetables that Sargent set out. Late in April when the frost was out of the ground, he sowed lima beans, "soft Indian corn," watermelon and cucumber seed, English "buck beans," and bush beans. Early in June he planted potatoes for winter use, and one or two rows of "shoots" with an equal number of "scullins," in order to determine the relative merits of these two greens. June 15 he reaped his first harvest when he cut some cucumbers, and in quick succession he gathered squash, peas, and other vegetables.

A notable factor in the agricultural progress of the Old Northwest was the interest the settlers showed in new methods and tools. Improved implements for horticultural and agricultural work were soon available in the Ohio settlements, to which transportation was comparatively cheap and easy from the rapidly growing iron manufactories at Pittsburgh. For example, Samuel Allen at his shop in Marietta offered "grass, cradle, and briar sithes and cutting knives," as well as other implements that had been fashioned by Edward Scott Degin, a craftsman of forty years' experience in Europe, Philadelphia, and Virginia. At Warren in the Western Reserve, a wide variety of the usual agricultural implements was offered the farmer in exchange for "cash, linen,

14 *Journal of Winthrop Sargent,* March 20 to August 7, 1795, pp. 141-162.

flax, rags, or sugar." There were numerous advertisements, too, of new implements for which most remarkable results were frequently claimed. Thus, a three-horse plow was offered, which, according to its inventor, would plow up three acres in one day. Another implement, which was widely advertised, was a patent boring machine, so simple in its operation, so the inventor claimed, that a boy of ten or twelve could in two minutes bore, with its aid, a hole three feet deep.[15] Whether these two remarkable inventions fulfilled in actual use all the promises of enthusiastic advertisers is not recorded. At least the very fact that they were offered for sale was a proof of the interest that the early Western farmer took in new and improved agricultural tools.

This same wide-awake spirit showed itself in the widespread interest in the Old Northwest in matters pertaining to general agricultural progress. The local newspapers printed many practical articles upon agricultural subjects, with special emphasis upon the need to diversify and rotate crops, in order to develop economic independence and to avoid the misfortunes of a one-crop system. Among the specific subjects they took up were such important ones as the proper method of cultivating hemp, cabbages, and apple trees, and the prevention of premature decay in peach trees. One article with a distinctly prophetic vision stressed the value of schools in which agriculture would be the chief subject.[16] The almanacs, also, which circulated so widely in the rural districts, contained many articles of value to the farmer. For example, the *Kentucky Almanac* for 1796 included a lengthy article on the culture of the vine, along with exceedingly useful hints to the gardener as to the proper dates on which to plant the different varieties of seeds and slips, or to set out turf. In like fashion, the early almanacs published at Cincinnati contained articles upon the destruc-

[15] *Ohio Gazette*, March 27, 1809; *Trump of Fame*, August 5, 1812; *Western Spy*, March 26, 1808, and October 13, 1810; *Pittsburgh Magazine Almanack* for 1811, and *Cramer's Pittsburgh Almanack* for 1813.
[16] See, especially, *Freeman's Journal*, August 6, 1796; *Scioto Gazette*, May 24, 1801.

tion of the Hessian fly, the shearing of sheep, the selection
of wheat for seed, and a wide variety of other topics that
were of special interest to a farmer.[17] Occasionally books
upon agricultural topics were offered for sale, as a *Treatise
on Hedging*, an "original Work" which, it was claimed, was
especially useful for the cultivation of "live fences," since its
author, Thomas Main, kept a nursery near Georgetown in
the District of Columbia.[18] Another and a very practical
evidence of the interest in agricultural improvement was the
organization in 1809 of the Vincennes Society for the Encouragement of Agriculture and the Useful Arts. Under the
leadership of General Harrison this society held semiannual
meetings, and gave a number of prizes in agricultural com-
petitions. In 1810, for example, it offered a book valued at
$5.00 upon an agricultural subject, for the largest amount of
hemp seed that was raised upon a tract of not less than a
quarter of an acre.[19]

This enlightened attitude toward advances in agriculture
was also displayed in connection with stock-raising, which
rapidly became an important phase of the varied agriculture
of the Old Northwest. At St. Clairsville, in Ohio, by 1813 one
farmer alone had built up a flock of at least 500 sheep, and
another indication of the rapid progress in sheep-raising in
Ohio was the "liberal sum" subscribed to the Canton Sheep
Company, which was organized in 1811 in Stark County in
eastern Ohio. Sheep were raised also in Indiana and in the
Illinois settlements, and one enterprising pioneer, who petitioned for two or three sections in southeastern Indiana,
promised that within four years he would put at least 500
sheep upon these lands if his petition was granted.[20] The
early Western settlers paid much attention to breeding, and
Thomas W. Worthington, an exceptionally progressive
farmer, purchased a number of pure-bred Merino ewes in

[17] *Kentucky Almanac* for 1796; *Ohio Almanac* for 1812, pp. 11, 25-26;
Browne and Company's Almanac for 1813, pp. 7-8.
[18] *Liberty Hall*, January 24, 1810.
[19] *Western Sun*, April 15, 1809, April 14, and May 5, 1810.
[20] Petition of John Allen, 1811, *Indiana Territorial Papers*, House Files.

order to improve his flock. Other sheep owners, some of them in the distant Illinois settlements, followed his example, buying Merino sheep which were imported from the Eastern states, especially from Connecticut, and occasionally from Spain. The practical results of this attention to breeding were illustrated by the prices obtained for Merino wool, $1.50 per pound in 1812, as compared with 40 cents per pound for the common type.[21] Beside their flocks of sheep, the early settlers raised many beef cattle and dairy cows. Following the time-honored custom of cattlemen in their old homes, they soon began to buy up young cattle, in order to fatten them for the Eastern markets. Thomas W. Worthington recorded in 1810 that he had bought from the Chickasaw Indians 199 head of cattle, "of good size and handsome, but thin," and many similar incidents might be cited among the owners of the rich pasture lands in the Ohio valleys. Nor was the improvement of cattle by breeding neglected, and there were many advertisements of bulls of the "English breed" and of other strains. An illustration of the results that were obtained by this careful attention to breeding was a steer which was exhibited in Cincinnati, at the March term of court in 1802. Measuring four feet four inches from horn to horn, this animal was thirteen feet six inches in length, five feet one inch in height, and weighed, dressed, between sixteen and seventeen hundred pounds.[22] Much attention was paid likewise to the breeding of horses, and there were numerous advertisements of pedigreed stallions. Hogs, too, were raised upon an extensive scale, and occasionally buffalo calves were bred.

A serious problem that continually confronted the pioneer farmer was to find some means to rid himself of the many pests, including weeds, insects, and predatory animals, which abounded in the Old Northwest, and were making heavy in-

[21] Entry, July 8, 1811, *Diary of Thomas W. Worthington; Political Observatory and Fairfield Register,* September 8, 1810; *Ohio Gazette,* October 5, 1810; *Western Spectator,* October 19, 1811, and July 11, 1812; *Louisiana Gazette,* October 24, 1810.
[22] *Western Spy,* February 27, 1802.

roads upon his crops and his domestic animals. Weeds were especially abundant in the newly cultivated soil, although they were a source of constant annoyance in established communities as well, as at Steubenville where the thorn apple became a real pest along the streets and in the gardens.[23] Insects, too, were troublesome, notably the army worms and the Hessian flies which frequently played havoc with the grain fields. But the farmer did not possess a monopoly of these insect pests, for the pioneer gardener, too, had his troubles. First in May came the cutworm, for which, according to Winthrop Sargent, there was no known "preventative." Next in succession were "numberless green worms," the size of caterpillars, grasshoppers, and yellow bugs.[24] The different Western newspapers and the almanacs published many articles, with elaborate directions for the extermination of these pests, but these remedies do not seem to have been very effective. Droughts were another frequent source of great loss to the Western farmer; but for them, of course, there was no remedy.

The smaller predatory animals, also, caused much damage, and squirrels, especially, seem to have greatly increased, along with the cultivated fields which afforded them so abundant a food supply. It is recorded that at one time they crossed the Ohio in such numbers that the boys of Cincinnati would daily "load themselves" with the carcasses. Squirrel hunts became a popular sport among the pioneers, who first fortified themselves with a barbecue and the "trimmings," and then sallied forth to shoot the squirrels, killing as many as 2,000 on one notable occasion.[25] Mice, too, were a nuisance to the farmer, and one individual claimed he had actually seen thirty-acre fields in which mice had devoured practically all the seed corn.[26] The larger wild animals, also, destroyed much agricultural property, causing especial havoc

[23] *Western Herald*, July 4, 1807.
[24] *Journal of Winthrop Sargent*, pp. 149-155.
[25] *Western Spy*, October 6, 1810; Bradbury, *Travels in America*, in Thwaites, *Early Western Travels*, vol. V, pp. 280-281.
[26] *Western Spy*, December 10, 1810.

among the flocks of sheep, and Maxwell's Code in 1795 provided bounties for the killing of wolves, foxes, and wildcats. With a delicious satire upon human honesty, this act required that the tongue and ears of each carcass, presented for a bounty, should be cut off, evidently so that it could not be brought in a second time. The legislature of the Northwest Territory renewed this act, so far as wolves were concerned, but the Ohio Code repealed it, although wolves and useless dogs continued to destroy many sheep. In Indiana, however, the legislature first repealed and then reënacted the territorial law of 1799 against wolves.[27]

Closely allied to the various acts to rid the pioneers of their losses from the larger predatory animals, were a number of measures that were passed in the attempt to protect natural resources from the careless destruction which so many irresponsible individuals committed in a frontier country. First of all, an act in Maxwell's Code forbade the willful cutting down, without express permission of the owner, of any "black walnut, whitewood, wild cherry, or blue ash trees" upon another person's land.[28] Another measure of a much similar import, which the legislative assembly of the Northwest Territory adopted later, imposed heavy penalties upon a particularly heedless class of offenders who were in the "habit of setting on fire the leaves, herbage in the woods, and other grounds, thereby producing a conflagration prejudicial to the soil (and) destructive to the timber and improvements within the territory." [29] The Indiana territorial assembly passed a much similar act that fixed heavy penalties for cutting timber, without permission, from the public lands that had been reserved for education.[30] All these con-

[27] Laws of the Northwest Territory, Illinois Historical Collections, vol. XVII, pp. 205, 503-505; Laws of Ohio, Third General Assembly, p. 295; Laws of Indiana Territory, Philbrick, ed., Illinois Historical Collections, vol. XXI, pp. 30, 562-563.
[28] Laws of the Northwest Territory, Pease, ed., Ibid., vol. XVII, p. 254.
[29] Ibid., vol. XVII, pp. 417-418.
[30] Laws of Indiana Territory, Philbrick, ed., Ibid., vol. XXI, pp. 357-361.

servation measures supplemented, of course, the numerous
Federal regulations to protect the public lands from willful
destruction.

An interesting phase of legislation in the Old Northwest
in this early period was a series of acts to protect the early
settlers from the American and Indian thieves that so often
carried off their livestock. In this connection, it became
necessary to draw up detailed regulations for the care of
"strays," so that stock, that had in reality been stolen, could
not be palmed off in this fashion. As early as 1790 the governor and the judges of the Northwest Territory adopted a
measure that, following a custom that was later to become
so common west of the Mississippi, required each owner of
stock to brand all of his "horses, cattle, and other beasts"
with a mark which he should register with the township
clerk. This same measure also contained provisions for the
care of stray animals that were picked up, and required
their prompt return, if possible, to the owner. Several months
later the governor and judges passed another act to protect
farmers against losses from the wandering stock that broke
into their fields. This act carefully defined a legal fence,
which, whether of "stone, brick, boards, rails, palisades,"
must be at least four and a half feet high. There were detailed provisions, also, regarding the construction of "worm"
and other fences, and the maintenance of boundary fences.
If a fence conformed to the legal requirements, any animal
that broke through could be held as a trespasser, and damages could be collected from the owner. But the "open woods
and uninclosed ground" were held to be the "common pasture or herbage," in which no animal might be taken up as a
stray between March 1 and December 1.[31]

The governor and the judges had used much freedom in
adapting laws of the original states with regard to strays and
fences in order to meet local conditions, and in Maxwell's
Code they replaced these very practical measures with acts

[31] *Laws of the Northwest Territory*, Pease, ed., *Illinois Historical Collections*, vol. XVII, pp. 39-40, 46-51, 84-87.

that were taken almost verbatim from the Pennsylvania Code, and consequently proved quite inadequate.[32] After the transition to the second grade of territorial government made it possible to enact rather than merely to adopt laws, it is significant that among the acts passed by the first session of the legislature of the Northwest Territory in 1799 were those regarding stray animals and enclosures. In the main they were mere expansions of the earlier ones that Maxwell's Code had repealed, and they formed the basis for similar laws in the Ohio Code of 1805. Among the important features of these last-named acts were clauses that fixed the legal height for a "worm" fence at five feet six inches, for palings at five feet, for a hedge at two feet, and required a boundary ditch to be three feet deep and three feet wide. These acts also imposed severe penalties for the alteration of a brand, and gave the owner a full year in which to redeem his property.[33] Numerous advertisements indicate that these laws were by no means a dead letter in Ohio, and that the public notice of strays or trespassing animals required by law was usually given. They show also that a pound was customarily maintained at each county seat.

The laws of the Northwest Territory regarding stray animals and fences were, of course, in force in Indiana after the separate territory was organized, and just as in Ohio, they became the basis of later legislation. The Indiana pioneers were accustomed to pick up cattle and hogs which they found in the woods, and then to slaughter them. In order to put an end to such practices a territorial act in Indiana in 1806 required that any one who brought in the carcass of a domestic animal found in the woods must show the head and ears if it were a hog, and the hide and ears if it were a cow or a steer. Thus the exact brand would appear, and if any one arbitrarily altered this mark he was fined $5.00, and was to receive not more than forty lashes. For the second

[32] *Laws of the Northwest Territory*, Pease, ed., *Illinois Historical Collections*, vol. XVII, pp. 235-242.

[33] *Ibid.*, pp. 347-350, 368-376; *Laws of Ohio*, Third General Assembly, pp. 124-128 and 215-217.

offense not more than two hours in the pillory was the penalty, and the letter T was to be branded on the left hand with a red-hot iron. At each term of court the attention of the grand jury was to be called to this law.[34] Like the Code of Ohio, the Indiana laws also defined legal enclosures, requiring "worm" fences, for example, to be at least five feet six inches high, and including provisions for the construction and upkeep of partition fences.[35] An interesting section of the Indiana laws for enclosures dealt with the extensive tract of prairie along the Wabash below Vincennes. According to French custom this land was in general charge of a syndic who was elected by the proprietors of the separate strips. It was bounded by a common fence, and the road across passed through a gate on either side. But like other customs of the French *habitants* this communal type of agriculture soon disappeared. Instead, the American system of individual holdings was introduced, after an act in 1810 ordered the removal of the gates and the erection of a fence on either side of the road, and at the same time relieved a proprietor who enclosed his own holding from all responsibility for the common fence.[36]

Beside the different measures to aid the farmer, there was much legislation in the Old Northwest which was intended to stabilize legal rights in the land. Incidentally, these latter laws were a significant indication of the solid foundations of American settlement in the Old Northwest from its very beginning. Even in the earliest régime, under St. Clair and the judges, acts were adopted in the Northwest Territory for the recording and acknowledgment of deeds, mortgages, and other legal documents. Surveys, too, were provided for, along with a careful regulation of the fees for these various services. Thus, by 1800 when Indiana Territory was set off, the basic legal structure had been created for landholding,

[34] *Laws of Indiana Territory,* Philbrick, ed., *Illinois Historical Collections,* vol. XXI, pp. 210-212.
[35] *Ibid.,* pp. 344-347.
[36] *Ibid.,* pp. 580-590, 654-656; *Laws of Indiana Territory,* Third General Assembly, First Session, pp. 36-38.

and future legislation in Ohio, Indiana, and Illinois was merely of an explanatory nature, or else it touched upon new conditions that the rapid influx of settlers created. One particularly important object of these laws was the partition of the lands which non-residents so frequently held jointly as a speculation, in the Western Reserve, in the Virginia Military District, and in the Miami Purchase. Maxwell's Code included an act for this purpose that was supposedly taken from the New York Code but was in reality freely adapted to conditions in the Old Northwest. By its provisions any proposed partition of land holdings valued at over $12,-000.00 must be extensively advertised in newspapers in the Northwest Territory, in Kentucky, and at the seat of the Federal government. For holdings of $12,000.00 and less, such extensive advertising was not required, but in either case the law carefully prescribed the procedure to be followed in the actual partition, making especial provision for ample notice to interested persons. This act was replaced by a much less complicated one which was included in the Ohio Code of 1805, and gave permission for partition under court direction, upon the suit of a joint owner. This act also made ample provision for due notice to each of the joint landholders, by advertisement in the state in which he lived in the case of a non-resident. For residents of Ohio, a personal notice must be served at least forty days before the suit for partition was heard in court.[37] Many advertisements in the local papers show that this latter law for partitioning lands was frequently put into practice in Ohio.

The laws for the partition of large holdings helped to carry out the general tendency in the Old Northwest to cut up the land into comparatively small farms rather than to create large estates. From the long lists of lands that were offered for sale for the payment of delinquent taxes, it is possible to reach some fairly definite conclusions as to the num-

[37] *Laws of the Northwest Territory*, Pease, ed., *Illinois Historical Collections*, vol. XVII, pp. 260-271; *Laws of Ohio*, Third General Assembly, First Session, pp. 378-384.

ber of acres in the average holding.[38] The largest individual tracts were in the Virginia Military District, where farms ranged between 500 and 1,000 acres each, although there were items of only 5 acres and others of 6,400 acres, with a tendency to break up holdings of the latter type. In Washington County, including chiefly the Ohio Purchase, the average farm was somewhat smaller than in the near-by Virginia Military District, ranging in 1801 between 100 and 4,000 acres. In the same year a list for Jefferson County, which was in the region of the Seven Ranges, included tracts that averaged between 160 and 640 acres. In other sections of the Old Northwest the individual farm was even smaller, including from 50 to 320 acres in the Miami Purchase in 1799, with an average of about 150 acres. A typical holding of 247 acres in the Western Reserve was offered for sale in 1812, and in the "gore" in southeastern Indiana a list of holdings in 1811 included from 10 to 958 acres each, with the average between 100 and 200 acres. At Vincennes and in the Illinois settlements, the land system was so unsettled during this early period that no general statement can be given, although there were probably few separate tracts in either district that were larger than 400 acres. From the averages of these different districts, it may safely be concluded that, for the bulk of the American settlements in the Old Northwest up to about 1812, the average farm was doubtless less than 250 acres, even though the Land Act of 1800 encouraged the settler to take up more land than he could properly cultivate. With such comparatively small holdings, the plantation system of the South was impossible, and the small farm of the Middle States, with the varied agriculture, and the democracy that inevitably attended such rural divisions became firmly established in the Old Northwest.

In a final analysis, the comparatively small area of the average farm in the Old Northwest may be considered as the result of a number of important influences that determined

[38] See Western Newspapers, 1799–1812; also, entry, October 1, 1801, McArthur Papers, vol. I.

to a large extent the peculiar social and economic development of this region. One of the most important of these forces arose from the great scarcity of labor in the pioneer days. The failure to set aside the anti-slavery clause of the Ordinance of 1787, of course, doomed slavery in the Old Northwest, although a few slaves found their way from Kentucky across the river. In Ohio negroes were occasionally held in virtual slavery as servants bound out for a limited period, and their "time" was offered for sale. But this was not a common custom, and even in Indiana and Illinois the few slaves who survived from the earliest period of American control, or who were held as servants, were of negligible importance in solving the problem of a supply of agricultural labor. Lacking sufficient negro labor, the early Western farmer was obliged to depend upon white hired men for extra help, and the result was a real problem in a country like the Old Northwest, where any able-bodied man could so easily secure land. Nor was much incentive offered by the usual low wages of an agricultural laborer, between 40 cents and 75 cents per day, and from $12.00 to $15.00 per month. For reaping and shocking wheat, the ordinary reward for a hard day's work was 66 2/3 cents, and for mowing hay, 75 cents. Generally these wages included food and lodging, but even then they were somewhat below the average wage for similar labor in the entire United States.[39] An illustration of the low wages that were paid for rural work in the Western country was an agreement in 1809 between Thomas Worthington and Martin Armstrong, in which the latter undertook to remove and cut up the timber from an acre of land, and then to grub up the tract and make it ready for the plow. As payment for this arduous job, Armstrong was to receive the munificent sum of $9.00.[40] Such small rewards for agricultural labor naturally did not prove attractive. To fill the

[39] *Smith and St. Clair Ledger, 1802–1811;* Bradbury, *Travels in America,* in Thwaites, *Early Western Travels,* vol. V, pp. 287, 306; Blodget, *Statistical Manual,* pp. 142-143.
[40] Entry, May 22, 1809, *Diary of Thomas W. Worthington.*

breach, children were occasionally bound out as apprentices, but for the most part the pioneer farmer depended upon himself and his family for the necessary labor. Occasionally, with the spirit of neighborly coöperation that was so characteristic of the early West, the near-by farmers gathered to aid in a barn-raising, a corn-husking, or in some similarly arduous task.

Another important factor in holding down the average landholding in the Old Northwest was the influence of the rapid increase in the price of the land that was in private hands. This advance was inevitable, for after choice locations in the public lands had been taken up, the newcomer must either purchase his farm from a private owner, or be content with less desirable land. The price charged by the government for unimproved land was necessarily a brake upon the demands of land speculators. At first, public land sold for 66 2/3 cents per acre, the price to John Cleves Symmes and the Ohio Company, but under the Land Acts of 1796 and 1800, $2.00 per acre became the usual rate. The credit system established by the Act of 1800, with its five years' limit in completing payments, was another restriction upon the demands of private owners, who must either reduce the cash price of unimproved lands, or else consent to deferred payments. Customarily they required a third of the selling price of their lands to be paid at once, with the remainder in two or three yearly installments. For unimproved land, however, the price rapidly rose to keep pace with an increasing population, until, for land that was convenient to an important settlement, it equaled, and at times even exceeded, the average for agricultural property near towns in the entire United States, which increased from $2.50 per acre in 1790 to $6.25 in 1805. As an example of the comparably rapid increase in the Western country, in 1789 John Cleves Symmes charged approximately 83 1/3 cents to $1.00 per acre for land near Cincinnati. By 1805, when the Cincinnati Land Office was selling unimproved public land for $2.00 per acre, a farm of "first rate" improved land at the junction of the Ohio and the Miami was offered for sale at $6.50 per acre.[41] The close connection between the terms upon which public lands were sold, and the demands of private owners of unimproved tracts, was illustrated in an offer in 1807 to sell 50,000 acres between the Miami, the Little Miami, and the Mad River for the usual purchase price of public lands, $2.00 per acre. As a special inducement, the owners of this tract agreed to accept in payment, flour, whisky, pork and beef, wheat, corn, rye, iron nails, and castings, at the market price.[42] By 1815 the average price of land in Symmes' Miami Purchase had become stabilized at $8.00 per acre for unimproved, and $12.00 per acre for improved country lands. Near the chief villages the price of the more desirable tracts had risen to $20.00 to $40.00 per acre, and even $50.00 to $150.00 in the neighborhood of Cincinnati.[43]

The influence of government terms of sale in holding down the price of private unimproved lands and the opposite effect of increasing settlement in raising the cost of improved tracts were both forcibly demonstrated in the Virginia Military District, where speculators frequently held large tracts of lands which they offered for sale, either to immigrants into Ohio, or to the speculatively inclined residents of Kentucky. In these sales they must compete with the public lands that were being opened up in near-by districts. The effect of this rivalry is shown in the sales of private lands that are recorded in the diary of Thomas W. Worthington, an agent for many land speculators, and himself a large landholder in the Virginia Military District. Five years after the Land Act of 1800 had opened up desirable tracts outside the Virginia Military District at $2.00 per acre with a five years' credit, Worthington sold an improved farm in the Scioto Valley for $4.00 per acre, but with three years in which to complete

---

[41] Blodget, *Statistical Manual*, pp. 142-143; *Symmes Correspondence*, Bond, ed., pp. 85-86; *Western Spy*, August 14, 1805.
[42] *Ibid.*, April 27, 1807.
[43] Drake, *Statistical View of Cincinnati in 1815*, pp. 53-54.

payments. The first payment of $200.00 was due a month after the sale, and was to be settled by $100.00 in cash and the remainder in wheat; a year later an additional $200.00 was due, with final payments of $100.00 each in 1807 and 1808 respectively. A purchase of land which Worthington himself made in 1810 gave a striking illustration of the rise in value of the rich Scioto Valley farming land. For a tract of 430 acres he paid $22.50 per acre for rich bottom land, $15.00 for land that was less desirable, and $12.00 for hill land, or an average price of $18.71 2/3 per acre.[44] There is abundant evidence that these large increases in land values in the Scioto Valley, together with those already cited in the Miami Valley, were paralleled in other sections of the Old Northwest. Consequently there were few settlers who could afford to buy large tracts, and those who held them for purposes of speculation were eager to sell them off.

The increasing use of the land tax in the Old Northwest was another important factor in restricting the average tract, and in forcing at the same time the break-up of the extensive holdings of unimproved land, especially in the Virginia Military District and the Western Reserve, that would otherwise doubtless have been held indefinitely for speculative purposes. The initial tax measure in the Northwest Territory, in 1792, included in the scheme for local taxation, a levy upon the annual value of improved land. This measure Maxwell's Code repealed, substituting a law that was much similar in its essential features, except that it limited the amount of the annual levy upon the land to not over 75 cents upon a valuation of $200.00.[45] Finally, in 1798 the governor and the judges adopted from the Kentucky Code the act which set a precedent for subsequent tax legislation in the Old Northwest and its subdivisions, with a classification of the unimproved land into three grades for pur-

---

[44] Entries, April 22, 1805, and August 16, 1810, *Diary of Thomas W. Worthington.*

[45] *Laws of the Northwest Territory,* Pease, ed., *Illinois Historical Collections,* vol. XVII, pp. 69-73, 201-216.

poses of taxation. This act made possible the collection of taxes upon unimproved as well as improved land, providing that, if necessary, a sufficient amount of land from any holding should be sold to satisfy taxes which were not paid within the prescribed time. The amount of this land tax was small, 30 cents per 100 acres upon land of the first, 20 cents upon land of the second, and 10 cents upon land of the third grade,[46] but it established an exceedingly important precedent.

The territorial legislature of the Northwest Territory retained the division of all land, improved and unimproved, into three grades in the tax law which they passed at their first session in 1799. Increasing the rates to 85 cents per 100 acres for first, 60 cents for second, and 25 cents for third grade land, the act gave the sheriff power, as a last resort, to sell a sufficient amount of the land to satisfy the taxes. As this provision would affect especially the numerous non-resident owners of speculative holdings in the Virginia Military District, the Western Reserve, and other large sections in private hands, the law provided that lists of lands for sale for delinquent taxes must be published in newspapers: in the Northwest Territory; at the seat of the Federal government; at Richmond, Va.; at Boston, Mass.; and at Hartford, Conn. Incidentally this was the first in a long series of regulations that were drawn up primarily to deal with the difficult problem of breaking up the large unimproved tracts that were held by non-residents. Thus, a territorial act in 1801 erected the Virginia Military District into a single tax district with a collector who was stationed at Chillicothe.[47]

The chief features of the land tax in the Northwest Territory, and particularly the provisions for its enforcement upon the lands of non-residents, were retained after Ohio became a state. The rates showed a steady increase from

[46] *Laws of the Northwest Territory*, Pease, ed., *Illinois Historical Collections*, vol. XVII, pp. 307-310.
[47] *Ibid.*, pp. 467-468.

1801, when first-quality land paid 55 cents, second quality 35 cents, and third quality 17 cents per 100 acres, to 1812 when these levies were more than doubled, with $1.25 per 100 acres for first class, $1.00 for second class, and 65 cents for third-class lands.[48] These increasing taxes upon the land naturally compelled the break-up of speculative holdings, especially after the Ohio legislature passed a series of acts to enforce the tax upon lands held by non-residents. The first one, passed in 1805, authorized the appointment of commissioners, whose duty it would be to report on the amount of land owned by non-residents in the Virginia Military District, and the taxes that were due therefrom. Next, the legislature divided Ohio into six collection districts, in order the more effectively to collect the taxes on land, and in still another act in 1810 they required the collectors to enforce the taxes due from non-residents, charging one hundred per cent interest for each year they were delinquent.[49] The effect of these different acts to enforce the land tax in Ohio was shown in the long lists of tracts that were offered at public sale in order to pay the taxes. The holdings by non-residents in the Virginia Military District formed the bulk of these delinquent tracts, but there were also scattered parcels that were offered for sale in the Ohio Purchase, in the Miami Purchase, and in the Seven Ranges, as well as in the Western Reserve after Ohio established jurisdiction there. The extent of this failure to pay taxes is illustrated by a list of delinquent tracts in 1802 in the Virginia Military District alone, which included 1,900 separate parcels, with several holdings grouped under a single name in many cases.[50] Among other items in these lists were town lots, as the many in-lots and out-lots at Chillicothe and Portsmouth which were offered for sale to pay delinquent taxes. But landowners were given ample notice of their delinquent taxes,

[48] Rate of Taxation in Ohio, 1801–1818, in *Joseph Perkins' Scrap Book*, p. 141.
[49] *Laws of Ohio*, Third General Assembly, pp. 247-248; Fourth General Assembly, pp. 74-86; Eighth General Assembly, pp. 315-342.
[50] *Western Spy*, July 17, 1802.

and there were even public warnings when taxes were about to become due upon important tracts that had been opened up under the Land Act of 1800. Again, the many non-resident owners of Ohio lands who lived in Kentucky were given sufficient warning when the Virginia Military District was formed into a separate taxing district.[51] Numerous other advertisements of a similar type warned delinquent taxpayers, and non-residents in especial, of other measures to collect the land tax.

One indication of the success of these different measures to enforce the payment of taxes was the employment of agents on the spot in Ohio, to pay taxes and to sell off lands for non-resident owners in the Virginia Military District. Cadwallader Wallace and Robert Kercheval, for example, maintained an office in Chillicothe, carrying on an extensive business as agents to pay taxes, to redeem lands that had been sold for delinquent taxes, and to attend to other business for non-resident landowners.[52] Thomas W. Worthington and Duncan McArthur were probably the two most important agents for these absentee landowners, and their accounts show the wide extent of their transactions. A typical entry in McArthur's accounts is a payment of $34.07 to cover the taxes due on 34 different tracts. Other items show that he was an astute land agent who could pick out bargains in forced sales. On one occasion, McArthur bought 40 acres which the tax collector had sold, to pay two years' taxes with interest upon a tract of 200 acres, and another time he purchased 1,000 acres on which taxes for seven years were due.[53] In similar fashion Thomas Worthington purchased delinquent tracts, intervening occasionally to save the land of a client, as when he bought in for Elias Lee, a non-resident, 200 acres in a tract of 800 acres, and 40 acres from another holding of 3,000 acres, after both these parcels had been publicly offered in

[51] *Scioto Gazette,* November 13, 1806, and January 4 and May 16, 1808; *The Palladium,* April 21, 1801.
[52] *The Supporter,* January 26, 1809.
[53] *McArthur Papers,* vol. I, *passim.*

payment of delinquent taxes.[54] Many other incidents might
be cited to show that the land tax was enforced in such fashion that the owners of large tracts were compelled to dispose
of their holdings in smaller parcels, since otherwise they
would have faced the payment of almost ruinous taxes for
their unimproved lands.

As an alternative to the sale of their holdings, the owners
of large tracts sometimes preferred to lease their lands,
usually in small parcels. With the increase in the area of improved land, this practice of tenant farming became more
general, especially in the Virginia Military District, although
there were occasional offers of land for lease in other sections
of Ohio. For example, in 1801 there was an offer to lease
3,000 acres of first-rate land in the Muskingum Valley, upon
which there were sixteen cabins, according to the advertiser,
and at least 160 acres of the tract were well fenced, and had
been planted in corn.[55] Another typical notice in 1802 offered for lease a number of out-lots near Chillicothe in the
rich Scioto Valley that had been fenced and cleared, and contained, in some instances, good cabins and productive sugar
camps.[56] In fact, maple-sugar camps were often offered for
rent, as one in the Scioto Valley which, according to the
owner, contained 500 troughs, and at least 1,000 maple trees
that were capable of producing sugar.[57] Occasionally these
early leases stipulated a cash rent, as on a tract of twenty-
five acres in Youngstown Township, improved with a dwelling and outhouses, which was offered to a prospective tenant
at an annual rental of $80.00.[58] Cash rents were rare, how-
ever, and the tenant usually settled for a part, or even all, of
his rent by a fixed proportion of his crops. Two examples in
the Scioto Valley about 1801 will illustrate this custom. In

[54] Thomas W. Worthington to Elias Lee, November 19, 1801, *Worthington
Letter Book.*
[55] *Pittsburgh Gazette,* January 16, 1801.
[56] *Scioto Gazette,* January 16, 1802.
[57] *Ibid.,* December 10, 1803.
[58] Lease, February 14, 1803, by Aaron Clark of Youngstown to Calvin
Austin of Warren, *Huntington Papers.*

one case, Duncan McArthur offered to rent 100 acres for ten bushels of corn and two pounds of maple sugar annually per acre, while in the other one, Thomas Worthington rented out a small tract which doubtless was less desirable, with an option to the tenant of three bushels of corn per acre, or else a third of the total yearly produce.[59] But these rents in produce were quite uncertain, owing to occasional crop failures, a situation that is evident in the history of a lease of 20½ acres that was made by Worthington in 1809 with a rental of fourteen bushels of corn per acre. At the end of the second year the tenant still owed 200 bushels from the first year, and the entire rent for the second year. Finally he sent eighteen and a quarter wagonloads of corn in payment, thus reducing his debt for the two years to 122 bushels.[60] Such delays in the payment of rent for agricultural land appear to have been frequent during this early period of settlement, and they doubtless influenced many owners to sell their large tracts.

The land tax that had been developed in the Northwest Territory was, of course, in force in Indiana after the separation in 1800, but the many land speculators, together with the numerous non-resident landholders in Clark's Grant, soon made their influence felt in opposition to the threefold division of the land which made possible the taxation of unimproved tracts. Consequently the territorial assembly, at its first session in 1805, substituted a measure that provided for the valuation of all privately owned land in Indiana Territory, as the basis for an annual levy to take care of territorial needs. But this law does not appear to have been satisfactory, and the legislature passed another act that ordered the sale of land belonging to delinquent owners, but with careful provisions for full publicity and the right of redemption. However, as population moved in and public expenses increased, the need for a more effective tax law became ap-

[59] *Scioto Gazette*, February 12, 1801; entry, February 26, 1801, *Diary of Thomas W. Worthington.*
[60] Entry, November 18, 1809, *Ibid.*

parent, and in 1807 the legislature passed a detailed act that imposed a land tax of not over 20 cents in the $100.00.[61] This act, too, was unsatisfactory, and notwithstanding the hostility of the speculators who held so many large unimproved tracts, in 1811 the Indian assembly returned to the division into three grades of land, with a definite tax upon each one, which had proved so effective in the Northwest Territory and later in Ohio. Upon land of the first grade the assembly now levied $1.00 per 100 acres, upon the second grade 75 cents, and upon the third grade 50 cents. The act included the usual penalties upon delinquent taxpayers, and for local needs a land tax of not more than half the levy for territorial purposes was substituted for the former ones upon cattle and other forms of personal property.[62] The long lists of lands to be sold for delinquent taxes, which had appeared in Ohio, were now published for Indiana as well. To carry the parallelism further, it is rather noteworthy that these delinquencies were most numerous in Clark's Grant where, just as in the Virginia Military District, many non-residents owned large tracts of land. But there were lengthy lists of delinquent taxpayers in Knox County also, which included Vincennes, and in Dearborn County, which chiefly covered the "gore" in southeastern Indiana.[63] In the Illinois settlements, the uncertain land situation made it practically impossible to collect taxes before the separation from Indiana, and a list of delinquents in Randolph County alone for 1808 filled a column and a half in the *Western Sun*. Nor was there any appreciable improvement before the land system was finally adjusted.[64]

From a few early financial statements of Ohio counties, it is possible to gain an insight into the important place that

[61] *Laws of Indiana Territory*, Philbrick, ed., *Illinois Historical Collections*, vol. XXI, pp. 147-153, 171-174, 592-602.

[62] *Laws of Indiana Territory*, Third General Assembly, Second Session, pp. 54-66 and 77-83.

[63] *Western Sun*, July 11, 1807, January 6, 1808, March 3, 1810, and June 2, 1812.

[64] *Ibid.*, July 16, 1808; *Louisiana Gazette*, May 3, 1810.

the land tax occupied in the general scheme of public finance in the Old Northwest. The statement of the commissioners of Hamilton County, of which Cincinnati was the county seat, for the year June 15, 1809, to June 15, 1810, showed total receipts of $4,092.08¼. Of this amount only $463.90½ had been received from fees, and the balance had been derived chiefly from the land tax and the personal property tax. The report showed that fully seventy-five per cent of the taxes due in Hamilton County were being collected, and that from the receipts for this particular year, the state of Ohio had been paid $1,009.70½, and $2,950.10 had been appropriated for county expenses. This latter item included, chiefly, the salaries of county officials, the maintenance of public buildings and prisoners, and such items as $20.00 in bounties for wolf and panther scalps, and $53.50 for allowances to the judges and clerks of elections.[65] In Butler County, just to the north of Hamilton County, and settled about a decade later, for practically the same period, August, 1809, to August, 1810, the commissioners reported expenditures of $1,761.76, with receipts for the ensuing year which they estimated at $2,814.00.[66] For Ross County in the rich Scioto Valley, with Chillicothe as its county seat, the financial statement for the year September 5, 1810, to September 4, 1811, showed total receipts of $4,331.16½. From the land tax, $1,022.00, altogether, had been collected in this important section of the Virginia Military District.[67] The thrifty Puritan settlers of Washington County to the eastward made an even better showing, with total local expenditures of $1,555.73, and a balance on hand of $1,650.36.[68] The other chief center of New England migration to Ohio, Trumbull County, which included the inhabited sections of the Western Reserve, showed an equally prosperous financial situation for the year June 14, 1811, to June 14, 1812, with total expenditures of

---

[65] *Liberty Hall,* December 26, 1810.
[66] *Ibid.,* September 17, 1810.
[67] *The Supporter,* September 14, 1811.
[68] *Ohio Gazette,* August 25, 1808.

$2,421.61, and a balance on hand at the end of the year of $1,212.37.[69] The comfortable balances and the comparatively small amount of unpaid taxes in these typical statements show how effectively the tax laws were being enforced in Ohio, and, furthermore, they are an effective testimony to the solid foundations upon which the agricultural progress of the state rested. For the few Indiana counties in this early period, no corresponding statements have been found, but there, too, local finances were being taken care of in much similar fashion.

Many concrete examples might be cited to show the amazing agricultural progress in the Western country in the early period before the War of 1812. Of a unique interest was the planting and development of the settlement at "New Swisserland," or Vevay as it was commonly called, on the Indiana bank of the Ohio. Established in 1802 by a handful of French Swiss from the canton of Vaud, the lands of this little community, about 3,700 acres, stretched along the river bank for nearly four and a half miles. By 1810 the thrifty inhabitants had brought approximately a hundred and forty acres of this tract under cultivation. Between sixteen and seventeen acres were planted in vines, and by this time these Swiss settlers were making from the grapes 2,400 gallons annually of a wine that was pronounced superior to the claret of Bordeaux, and 120 gallons of white wine. The balance of their cultivated area they had planted in the usual crops: Indian corn, wheat, hemp, flax, and the like. By 1810 there were sixty-six exceedingly industrious individuals living in this settlement, and they were citizens with much public spirit, for they offered to give slips of their vines, with full directions for planting and cultivation, to any one who was interested.[70] Gradually, other settlements in Ohio and across the river in Kentucky began to cultivate the vine, and for a

[69] *Trump of Fame,* September 16, 1812.

[70] *Liberty Hall,* October 9, 1811; *Ohio Almanac* for 1812, pp. 9-10; Dufour, *The Swiss Settlement of Switzerland County, Indiana,* in *Indiana Historical Collections,* vol. XIII.

while there were high hopes for Vevay as the center of an exceedingly flourishing industry.

The prosperity at Vevay was typical of agricultural conditions throughout the more thickly settled regions of the Old Northwest in the first decade of the nineteenth century. Thaddeus Harris, a hard-headed Massachusetts Yankee who came West in 1803, was amazed at the many small but neat houses, frequently with brick chimneys and glass window-panes, and the farms divided into fields which were enclosed with strong posts and rails. He noted, too, the thrifty apple orchards and the peach trees as further evidences of the prosperity that prevailed in Ohio, in contrast to the neglected cabins and generally run-down conditions on the Virginia bank of the river. This difference, Harris considered, was chiefly due to the dependence of the Ohio farmers upon their own labor rather than upon slavery. Loyal New Englander that he was, he added that many of these prosperous settlers had come from his own homeland, "the region of industry, economy, and steady habits." [71] John Bradbury, also, commented upon the widespread prosperity in the Western country, citing the custom of raising pumpkins in the cornfield, to be fed to the hogs in winter, as an instance of the thrift of the inhabitants. [72] Fortesque Cuming, another keen observer who traveled through the Western country, called attention to individual instances of the general advance that had been made in scarcely two decades of settlement. Especially was he struck by the success of John Bowden, who had come from Marietta to establish a tavern on the river bank below Gallipolis. By July, 1807, this pioneer had fenced and planted twenty acres, of which twelve acres had been completely cut over, grubbed, and smoothed, and eight more had been cut. Bowden also owned a natural orchard of about four hundred maple trees, from which he supplied his family with maple sugar. Another successful pioneer who attracted Cuming's

[71] Harris, *Journal of a Tour*, in Thwaites, *Early Western Travels*, vol. III, p. 357.
[72] Bradbury, *Travels in America, Ibid.*, vol. V, p. 284.

attention was a man named Wheatley, living on the Indiana side of the Ohio below the mouth of Blue River, who claimed to have raised a crop of 500 bushels of corn from six acres. A short distance below this amazingly fertile tract Cuming visited Squire Tobin who, migrating from Redstone, Pennsylvania, only three years before, now owned a fine farm.[73] The many advertisements of farms for sale, as well as miscellaneous notices in the local newspapers, support the observations of these travelers as to the quick development of agricultural lands in the Old Northwest, and especially in Ohio. Scarcely six years after the first settlers arrived, William Goforth, at his "small plantation" on the river bank near Cincinnati, had erected a dwelling house with a good stone cellar, and a frame barn, 50 by 25 feet. In addition he had set out nearly 6,000 apple and peach trees, beside a few Italian mulberry, almond, quince, cherry, and plum trees.[74] A year later at his home place at North Bend John Cleves Symmes began to build a dwelling house which ultimately cost $8,000.00, and a gristmill. During the season of 1796, the sixth after his arrival at North Bend, he harvested wheat and rye on 50 acres, planted 114 acres in corn, and had 150 head of cattle in his pastures.[75] This story of agricultural prosperity was repeated on smaller holdings, as a farm near Cincinnati which in 1800 contained 25 to 30 acres, well cleared and divided into fields by fences that were constructed from more than 10,000 rails. On this particular tract there was a small orchard of apple and peach trees that had never failed to bear, about five or six acres of "clean, timothy meadow," and about twelve acres of pasture that were partly in blue grass. Aside from the small area on the hillsides, all the land was fit for the plow, and it was free from stones, except in the "runs" where there was an ample supply of excellent building stone. There was an abundance

[73] Cuming, *Tour in the Western Country*, pp. 132-133, 237, and 239.
[74] *Centinel*, October 24, 1795.
[75] *Symmes Correspondence*, Bond, ed., pp. 179-180; *Western Spy*, March 9, 1811.

of timber, too, especially "sugar trees," and, according to the owner, the farm produced wheat, corn, and grass "equal to any." The homestead was situated in a "high and very healthy location," and there were several useful outhouses and barns.[76]

By the close of the first two decades or so of settlement, this agricultural prosperity was widespread throughout Ohio. A farm near Chillicothe, which was offered for sale in 1803, included thirty acres in cultivation, in addition to four acres in meadow and a young orchard. Upon it there was a good two-story frame house, a kitchen, a well of good water, and numerous outbuildings.[77] Out of the 143 acres in a farm near Steubenville, forty-six acres were cleared by 1807 and "under good fence," with six acres in a meadow, a large and thrifty bearing peach and apple orchard, and a sugar-maple camp. Listed among the improvements on this farm were a "good hewed log cabbin, 24 by 20 feet, a hewed shingle roof barn, 50 by 20 feet, a loom shop, with a good cabbin and stable on a different part of the place, and a horse mill lately built, and all in good repair." [78] The improvements on a farm near Hillsboro were especially elaborate, consisting of two good cabins, a "smoakhouse," a milk house and a double barn.[79] A farm of 410 acres in Columbiana County on the Ohio River contained forty acres that had been cleared and were under cultivation by 1811. Also, there was an abundance of timber on this farm, and one of the best maple-sugar camps in Ohio, together with a good mill, a dwelling house, a barn, and a still house.[80]

Occasionally in this early period fairly elaborate country seats were to be found in the Old Northwest, among them the home of John Cleves Symmes at North Bend and the famous retreat of Harman Blennerhassett near Marietta. Another noteworthy residence was the "elegant seat" of

[76] Western Spy, March 12, 1800.
[77] Scioto Gazette, September 17, 1803.
[78] Western Herald, July 4, 1807.
[79] The Supporter, March 23, 1809.
[80] Pittsburgh Gazette, October 4, 1811.

Colonel Thomas W. Worthington near Chillicothe. Patterned after the prevailing architecture in Virginia at this time, the main building of this residence was about sixty feet square, with six rooms upon each of the two floors, and cellars and vaults beneath. In the wings on either side were the kitchen, the scullery, and servants' apartments. This mansion, which was built of freestone, had been designed by two young Virginians whose work, in the opinion of Fortesque Cuming, did them great credit.[81] Such a residence indicated a very considerable accumulation of wealth for a pioneer country. An interesting example of the property that a well-to-do person might accumulate in the Old Northwest is given in an inventory in 1810 of the estate of Colonel Sproat, a prosperous resident of Marietta. Upon his home place of three and a half city lots in Marietta there was a handsome mansion, a barn, and other outhouses with a good well. There was also a garden which produced every type of fruit raised in the Western country, together with an "extensive variety" of vegetables. Colonel Sproat's agricultural holdings totaled 941½ acres, divided into four tracts, all of them improved and well situated. Included in his personal property were two or three shares in the Ohio Company, a number of shares in the Bank of Marietta, and several notes and accounts. The remainder of the personalty in this estate was made up chiefly of stocks of rum, brandy, gin, and tea, "a complete set of old bachelor's furniture," a "handsome and valuable collection of books," and one or two good horses.[82]

In Indiana, also, there was considerable agricultural prosperity in the early period up to 1812, in spite of the comparatively late settlement, and the difficulties with the Indians. A tract of 175 acres, six miles from Vincennes, that was offered for sale in 1809, contained twenty acres of cleared land with a good fence, about nine acres of timothy meadow, an orchard of 150 bearing peach trees, and a small apple orchard. On this farm the improvements included a

[81] Cuming, *Tour in the Western Country*, p. 196.
[82] *The Commentator*, March 13, 1810.

good frame house, 22 by 26 feet, with a porch on one side, and convenient outhouses.[83] Another Indiana farm, with a total area of 100 acres, that was offered for sale in 1811, included thirty acres in a "high state of cultivation," with a growing crop of corn, and nearly eight acres in an apple and peach orchard. The owner advertised that he would also sell "every kind of farming utensils, and household and kitchen furniture," and a "stock of cows, horses, and hogs." [84] Fully two-thirds of a farm of 200 acres near Vincennes was heavily timbered in walnut, locust, hickory, and ash, but the other third was described as a "handsome prairie," which was divided into one field of five or six acres of "fresh ground," and another of twelve acres laid out in a pasture and a small meadow, all of them enclosed with a good fence which was "well staked and ridered." Among the improvements were a cabin 37 by 17 feet, with two lower rooms and an entry between, which was "fit for the comfortable reception of a genteel family," a smokehouse, stables, cribs, and other outbuildings.[85] Even in distant Illinois there was agricultural prosperity among the emigrants from the East who had settled the American Bottom across the Mississippi from St. Louis. For example, in 1812 Truman Tuttle offered for sale his dwelling house and four lots in Cahokia, together with his land "in Prairie du Pont common field, 3 arpents in width from bluff to creek." He offered to sell, too, his personal property, "a gig and harness, a number of horses, neat cattle, sheep, likewise household furniture consisting of beds and bedding, table chairs, cupboards, kitchen furniture, etc." Altogether, the extensive list of property for sale indicated that the owner was in fairly prosperous circumstances.[86]

The prosperity that spread so widely during the early period, from the first settlement at Marietta to the outbreak of the War of 1812, came as a result of the swift transfer into

[83] *Western Sun,* September 2, 1809.
[84] *Ibid.,* July 28, 1810.
[85] *Ibid.,* November 9, 1811.
[86] *Missouri Gazette,* August 8, 1812.

the Old Northwest of the chief features of rural life east of the Appalachians. In the course of this movement, American immigrants, with initiative and practical sense, had demonstrated in notable fashion their ability to found a really prosperous society of small farms and a varied agriculture. A number of influences had determined the peculiar characteristics of this Western countryside. The collection of a land tax had compelled landholders to break up their large speculative holdings, while the failure of the movement to introduce slavery and the scarcity of free labor had a like influence in favor of smaller tracts. Again, the continual increase in the price of improved land and the characteristic soil and climate of the Old Northwest made a system of comparatively small farms the only really feasible one. The result was virtually a reproduction of the agricultural system of the Middle States, with a varied cultivation of grains, along with the raising of cattle, sheep, and hogs upon an extensive scale. The fertility of the land, together with the industry of the immigrants and their enlightened interest in improved implements and methods, produced really astounding results. As the Indian boundary line was pushed further westward and northward, and settlers rushed in to take up the vacant lands, the farm clearings were gradually extended, orchards and gardens were planted, comfortable dwellings replaced the primitive cabins, and barns and fences were erected. This agricultural society in the Old Northwest developed essentially as an economically self-dependent one, which, in contrast to the one-crop system of the Old Southwest, relied upon outside sources for its luxuries rather than for its necessities. With its free labor and sturdy yeomen, it became the basis of the distinctively American civilization that was destined to spread to the west bank of the Mississippi as additional land became available.

Chapter XII

OPENING UP COMMUNICATION

ONE of the most vital problems in the development of the Old Northwest was to secure an adequate system of communication. Schemes to sell public lands were futile, unless the tracts that were offered were made accessible to settlers. Also, there must be highways over which surplus products might be transported, and along which the various commodities necessary for civilized existence might be brought back in exchange. In like fashion the effective defense of the Old Northwest and the establishment of orderly government within its bounds were both largely dependent upon efficient communication. Above all other considerations, the increasing throng of immigrants into the Western country simply forced the adoption of measures to solve this ever-present problem of adequate lines of transportation. From the very first, the favorite route of travel from the seaboard was across the Appalachians to Pittsburgh, Wheeling, or some other river port, and thence down the Ohio. Eastward against the swift current of the Ohio, this route was exceedingly tedious, and during the first few years of settlement, the slow-moving boats were constantly in danger from Indian attacks. As a result, the popular road to the Atlantic Coast from the earliest settlements in the Old Northwest led southward through Kentucky, and then over the Wilderness Trail. Customarily, travelers over this route met at Crab Orchard on days that were fixed by public notice, and went through the more than two hundred miles of wilderness in large parties, the men armed for protection from the Indians.[1]

[1] *Kentucky Gazette*, July 5, 1790, January 1 and March 12, 1791, and July 6, 1795; *Knoxville Gazette*, April 24, 1795.

351

With the gradual disappearance of danger from the Indians, and the improvement in the river boats, the Ohio began to take the place of the Wilderness Trail as the usual eastward as well as the westward route for the inhabitants of the Old Northwest. However, the sparse population of the Western Reserve and the few settlers at Detroit used the water route on Lake Erie chiefly, or else the Lake Trail, and from Buffalo eastward they went overland through New York State. Gradually, the Ohio-Mississippi route, also, through New Orleans, came to be used for bulky freight. So far as transportation between the different settlements within the Old Northwest itself was concerned, there was the basis of an effective system already at hand. Three important water systems, the Great Lakes on the north, the Ohio on the south and east, and the Mississippi on the west, virtually surrounded this region with excellent waterways. In addition, many navigable streams gave easy access into the interior, and with the easy portages between them, they could be utilized as the bases for important routes through the Old Northwest. For travel by land the absence of mountains, or even high hills, made it possible to establish roads with easy grades that usually followed the time-honored Indian trails.[2] But much work was necessary before these highways on land could be used upon any extensive scale. The paths which the Indians traveled in single file must be widened for the packhorse, and very soon roadbeds, however primitive, must be constructed to take care of the wagon traffic which an increasing population made necessary. Ferries, too, must be provided across the many streams, and occasional bridges, while taverns were necessary for the slow-moving travel of the pioneer period. Most important of all for the development of both waterways and highways into the interior, it was necessary to put an end to the danger from Indian attacks. The practical fashion in which these discouraging conditions were overcome, first in Ohio, and then to a much less

[2] Gephart, *Transportation and Industrial Development in the Middle West*, pp. 24-25; Hulbert, *Historic Highways of America*, vol. II, pp. 97-115.

extent in Indiana, Illinois, and Michigan, was an important phase of the remarkable exhibition of American pluck and ingenuity that so strongly marked the early development of the Old Northwest.

For the first decade or so of settlement, the waterways were the chief avenues of communication, both internally and with the outside world. The great majority of the pioneers came down the Ohio in flatboats, 20 to 60 feet long by 10 to 20 feet wide, with hulls 3 to 4 feet above the water, which were in reality floating houses and barnyards combined. The average cost of these flatboats was $1.00 to $2.00 per foot of length, so that for a "comfortable family boat, well boarded up and roofed within seven or eight feet of the bow," the immigrant paid $35.00 with an additional $10.00 for a cable, a pump, and a fireplace.[3] The flatboat was cheap, and it was certainly the most practical boat for the pioneer who was going downstream, but it could not be navigated upstream against the current. For this latter purpose the popular craft at first was the pirogue, an open dugout, 40 to 50 feet in length by 6 to 8 feet wide, that carried a considerable cargo. With increased traffic came the need for more substantial vessels, and the Western boat yards began to build keel boats with a heavy timber, usually four inches thick, running lengthwise on the bottom to take the shock of submerged obstructions. Often, too, there were covered decks for protection from the weather and from Indians. Barges of this type carried as much as 20 tons of freight, while others were fitted with cabins and were used as passenger boats. Oars and poles were the chief means of navigating these craft upstream against the current, and many of them were schooner-rigged. Downstream, they made four to five miles per hour, but upstream, ten to fifteen miles was a good day's journey. There were boat yards at the chief settlements along

[3] For descriptions of the flatboats and other craft on these Western waters, see Dunbar, *A History of Travel in America*, vol. I, chs. XVI and XVII; Cramer, *The Navigator*, ed. 1808, pp. 19-24; *American Pioneer*, vol. I, p. 98, vol. II, p. 27.

the Ohio, but the bulk of the river craft were constructed either at Pittsburgh or at the numerous boat yards on the lower Monongahela, and an extensive and profitable business in supplying intending emigrants with boats and other necessaries developed in this district. These Western boat builders launched keel boats of considerable size at an early date, as the "Vigalant Yacht" propelled by twenty oars, on which St. Clair embarked at Marietta, December 30, 1789.[4]

In response to an insistent demand, fairly regular service was soon established on the Ohio. In January, 1791, a boat was advertised to leave Limestone for Pittsburgh, the owner of which would give "good encouragement to passengers who will come well armed," and by September, 1793, there was a weekly service on this route.[5] About two months later, a fortnightly service was inaugurated between Cincinnati and Pittsburgh. Making the round trip in four weeks, the boats of this line provided separate cabins for men and women, and supplied passengers with "provisions and liquors of the first quality at the most reasonable rates possible." For security against Indian attacks there were bullet-proof cabins, and each boat carried six pieces of artillery, numerous muskets, and a supply of ammunition. As an added precaution, shippers were given the opportunity to take out insurance upon their goods.[6] Downstream, from Cincinnati to Louisville, "boating" was offered for passengers and freight as early as 1796.[7] At its best, travel on the Ohio in pioneer times was tedious and even dangerous, as Winthrop Sargent has pointed out in his account of two typical voyages. Upon the first one, down the river, he embarked at Pittsburgh, July 3, 1794, and arrived at Cincinnati July 15, after about nine and a half days of actual travel, with a three-day stop at Marietta. The boat, he complained, had been much delayed by

[4] *Pittsburgh Gazette*, June 27, 1789, January 23, 1790, October 4, 1794, May 4, 1799, September 3, 1802, and April 29, 1803.

[5] *Kentucky Gazette*, January 29, 1791, and January 4, 1794.

[6] *Centinel*, November 23 and December 7, 1793; *Pittsburgh Gazette*, November 2, 1793.

[7] *Freeman's Journal*, July 9, 1796.

the frequent necessity of tying up at night, owing to the danger from Indian attacks and from the many obstructions to navigation. Also, the very low stage of the water had made it necessary to use oars, even downstream, in order to keep it in motion. Going upstream about a year later, Sargent left Cincinnati in a fourteen-oar barge. Often it was necessary to pull this boat against the current by means of a rope. The crew were not under good control, and the entire passage upstream, from Cincinnati to Pittsburgh, was made in twenty-eight days of actual travel.[8]

Indeed, many dangers attended a trip down the Ohio in pioneer days. Floods in the spring and fall, low water in summer, and ice in the winter seriously interfered with travel, and often held up boats for weeks at a time. In the winter of 1797, all the keel boats lying in the mouth of the Scioto were destroyed by ice, and in 1805 the ice was so thick in the Ohio that the journey from Redstone to the mouth of the Scioto took two months.[9] Many similar instances might be cited of delay and loss from the ice. Trouble arose, too, from the logs, locally known as planters, that projected perpendicularly from the river bottom, and from sawyers or floating logs. Thus, in March, 1795, a boat coming down the Ohio was wrecked by a sawyer, with the total loss of a cargo of merchandise that was valued at between $5,000.00 and $6,000.00.[10] Sand bars and rapids were still other sources of danger to the pioneer navigator. The first important rapids, the so-called Letart Falls above Gallipolis, was comparatively safe, especially after the Ohio Assembly in 1805 had authorized the appointment of a licensed pilot to guide vessels through.[11] The dangerous rapids at Louisville, commonly known as the Falls, presented a more difficult problem, and many boats descending the river were wrecked there. Kentucky provided licensed pilots at the Falls, but not until

[8] *Journal of Winthrop Sargent,* pp. 74-91, 162-169.
[9] *Kentucky Gazette,* February 11, 1797; *Scioto Gazette,* January 28, 1805.
[10] *Kentucky Gazette,* March 28, 1795.
[11] *Laws of Ohio,* Third General Assembly, pp. 249-250.

1803 did the governor and the judges adopt a similar measure for Indiana. Proposals were soon advanced to construct a canal around the Falls, but petty local squabbles interfered. Unfortunately the Indiana Canal Company, incorporated in 1805, did not function, and another effort in 1807 to build a canal failed, chiefly because of jealousy on the part of Ohio. The canal on the Kentucky side was not finally completed until 1831, in spite of the serious danger that the Falls presented to the increasing traffic on the Ohio-Mississippi route.[12]

Fortunately for the pioneer traveler on the Ohio, in 1801 Zadock Cramer, an enterprising publisher in Pittsburgh, first issued *The Navigator, or the Traders' Useful Guide in Navigating the Monongahela, Allegheny, Ohio, and Mississippi Rivers*.[13] The complete title gives an excellent clue to the contents of this little handbook, which went through twelve editions, and was a veritable Baedeker of the most important Western waterways. Describing in minute detail the main channel, and all bars and other permanent obstructions, *The Navigator* also included sectional maps that added greatly to its value, and enabled the steersman to avoid many lurking perils. In addition, it contained much information regarding the chief settlements on the banks of the Ohio and the Mississippi, as well as details regarding the navigation of the important tributaries. The frequently revised editions, which gave additional items as settlement expanded, greatly added to the value of this little volume. Indeed, without it as a guide, the enormous traffic that developed on the Ohio-Mississippi route would have been altogether impossible.

In addition to the many obstacles to navigation, the early traveler on the Ohio faced constant danger from Indian attacks, and especially was this true prior to Wayne's victory in 1794. A point of especial danger in this early period was

12 *Laws of Indiana Territory*, Philbrick, ed., *Illinois Historical Collections*, vol. XXI, pp. 63-64, 154-163, 480-481; Esarey, *History of Indiana*, vol. I, pp. 236-237; *Laws of Ohio*, Fifth General Assembly, pp. 135-136.
13 Zadock Cramer, *The Navigator*, twelve editions, Pittsburgh, 1801-1824.

a lofty rock on the Virginia bank above the mouth of the Scioto, from which the Shawnees were accustomed to attack passing boats. Finally, the exasperated local militia, aided by regular troops, cleaned up this Indian stronghold, and thus added greatly to the comfort of later voyages on the Ohio. The danger from Indian attacks explains the necessity for a "proper escort" when St. Clair was planning his trip to the Illinois country in 1790, as well as an item in 1791 of £49, 10s, Virginia currency, for an Indian escort to accompany a boat conveying public property up the Wabash to Vincennes.[14] Many instances might be cited of actual attacks by Indians upon travelers on the Ohio, a typical one occurring in 1795 when a party of savages fired upon a packet boat near Three Islands, killing one man and wounding three others. The next day these same Indians shot at a "family boat" and killed a horse.[15] But the Treaty of Greenville soon put an end to the danger from Indians on the Ohio, as far down as the mouth of the Miami. On the lower Ohio and the Mississippi, however, the Cherokees, instigated, it was believed, by the Spanish, continued to be a source of much irritation and danger. When Judge Turner wished to travel by water from Vincennes to the Illinois country in 1794, he was obliged to secure a safe-conduct from the Spanish commandant at St. Louis, and in 1799 the Indians on the lower Mississippi robbed a messenger, from Natchez to Cincinnati, of $20,000.00 in negotiable bills of exchange. There was also much trouble on the lower Ohio from river pirates. A famous band of these outlaws had its headquarters at Cave-in-the-Rock, twenty miles below Shawneetown, and here they held up and murdered many a luckless traveler on his way down the river. After the purchase of Louisiana, with the cessation of Spanish intrigues, government became more stable in these

[14] Joseph Harmar to St. Clair, November 6, 1789, *Northwest Territory MSS.;* Account, September, 1791, *Henry Vanderburgh Papers, Western Reserve MSS.* no. 732.
[15] *Kentucky Gazette,* May 30, 1795.

regions, and the dangers from Cherokees and river pirates rapidly disappeared.[16]

The perils of travel by water did not long hold back the hardy pioneers of the Old Northwest, and soon they were ascending the numerous tributaries of the Ohio which were so important a factor in the quick spread of settlement. In the upper Ohio Valley keel boats could ascend the Big Beaver and the Mahoning in "swells," as far as Youngstown and Warren. Further downstream the Muskingum was navigable for 110 miles for large bateaux, and 45 miles beyond for smaller ones. In the Scioto, boats of four feet draught could go to Chillicothe, and smaller ones at least 100 miles beyond. The Miami was navigable to the Pickaway towns 75 miles from its mouth, and 50 miles beyond for loaded canoes, while the Wabash was navigable above Vincennes. Besides these streams flowing into the Ohio, there were a number of other water routes into the interior of the Old Northwest. The Illinois-Chicago route had been an important link in the fur trade from the west bank of the Mississippi when the Americans took over the Old Northwest. Also, the Maumee, the Sandusky, and the Cuyahoga transported the furs of the interior and the agricultural products of the pioneer to the Great Lakes. From Cincinnati a thriving trade soon arose up the Licking into Kentucky, and in 1795 Elijah Craig, Jr., informed "gentlemen, merchants, and emigrants" that he would transport goods up the Kentucky to Frankfort and Dick's River.[17] But transportation on the smaller streams was difficult and expensive, aside from the danger from Indians up to 1795, and even later. The boats were usually small, a typical advertisement offering one that would carry 140 barrels of salt, and was equipped with six good "setting poles." [18] Freight charges, of course, were high. For example, in 1795 for the transportation of military stores from Fort

[16] *Kentucky Gazette*, June 14, 1794; *New Jersey Gazette*, April 29, 1799; Rothert, *The Outlaws of Cave-in-the-Rock, passim.*
[17] *The Centinel*, January 17, 1795.
[18] *Liberty Hall*, November 8, 1814.

Washington to Loramie's Store at the head of navigation on the Miami, the government paid $3.30 for each barrel of flour, 83 1/3 cents for a bushel of corn, and $1.60 per 100 pounds for miscellaneous freight. For the portage across to the St. Mary's there was an additional charge, which amounted to $2.50 for each barrel of flour in 1803.[19] In spite of such high charges the government was obliged to use these smaller streams in order to transport supplies to troops. The inhabitants, too, used them, especially in the early days of settlement. The first supplies of merchandise for the settlers around Warren in the Western Reserve, it is recorded, were brought up the Mahoning in a canoe, and the owner of this primitive store was accustomed to blow a horn as he came within sight of each settlement.[20]

The extensive use of the smaller streams made it necessary to adopt measures to keep the channels clear for the passage of boats. An illustration of the difficulties encountered by the pioneer farmer in transporting his crops to market is given by the experience of George Sample, who lived on Brush Creek five miles above its junction with the Ohio.[21] As he was unable to navigate his two boats loaded with flour through the shallows of the creek, Sample dragged them across into deep water with the aid of teams of horses, and then blithely steered them down the Ohio. The general prevalence of such conditions led the Ohio legislature to make determined efforts to open the channels of interior waterways. Twice it authorized lotteries to improve the Muskingum-Cuyahoga route, and it also sanctioned a lottery to repair the banks of the Scioto at Chillicothe. Again, in 1812 the legislature incorporated a private company to construct a canal around the falls of the Muskingum just above the mouth of the Licking. But none of these different measures to aid navigation on the smaller streams appears to have se-

[19] *The Centinel*, March 17, 1795; *Independent Gazetteer*, January 17, 1804.
[20] Notes by Leonard Case, in *Joseph Perkins' Scrap Book*, p. 186.
[21] *American Pioneer*, vol. I, p. 159.

cured satisfactory results. A series of acts that the Ohio legislature passed to protect the channels of navigable streams from artificial obstructions proved to be more effective. They required, essentially, that where mill dams were constructed across navigable streams, there must be slopes or runways for boats, or else, on the larger streams, locks of sufficient size to permit the passage of the water craft that were in common use.[22]

While trade was increasing on the streams that led into the interior, the Ohio-Mississippi waterway was likewise developing as an avenue of communication with the outside world. During the earliest years of settlement, the route up the Ohio River and then across the mountains had sufficed for the scanty trade requirements of the Old Northwest. But as settlement grew, and a considerable surplus began to accumulate, some less difficult and cheaper trade outlet became a necessity, and shipments to and from the different settlements began to follow the route already marked out by the inhabitants of Kentucky, down the Ohio and the Mississippi to New Orleans. The rise of this trade awoke the Western people to an appreciation of the need for "free navigation of the Western waters." Early in 1803, when the future of this important waterway seemed to be so uncertain, the local newspapers in the Old Northwest printed in full, with editorial comments, the debates in Congress upon the closing of the Mississippi. A petition circulated about the same time called for immediate action, with a hint that otherwise the inhabitants of the Western country might be compelled to adopt measures which "may result in consequences unfavorable to the harmony of the union." [23] The implications in this petition were emphasized, after the purchase of Louisiana, when the Ohio Assembly passed a significant resolution that strongly commended this acquisition of territory, as a

22 *Laws of Ohio*, Fifth General Assembly, pp. 74-75, 90-91; Ninth General Assembly, pp. 9, and 66-67; Tenth General Assembly, pp. 30-32, 173-178; *Western Herald*, March 21 and September 5, 1807.

23 *Western Spy*, February 16, 1803, and following issues, especially March 9, 1803.

measure that had secured to the Western country "the free and uncontrouled navigation of the Mississippi." [24] The Ohio-Mississippi route now became much more popular, larger vessels were used, and the freight rates were gradually reduced, from $6.75 per hundredweight from Pittsburgh to New Orleans, until $6.00 to $8.00 per ton became the usual charge from Cincinnati to New Orleans. Barges now came into use with a capacity of 50 or more tons.[25] One of the best of these river craft, the barge *Cincinnati,* had a 100 foot keel, a beam of 16 feet, the full rigging of a sloop, and carried 65 tons of cargo. Leaving New Orleans March 3, 1811, on her maiden voyage, she made the trip upstream to Cincinnati in eighty-six days, including a stop of nine days at Louisville, where a crew of eighteen warped her through the rapids in half a day. The voyage downstream was made in the equally fast time, for that period, of forty-two days.[26] Beside these larger vessels, the slower flatboat continued to transport much produce down the river. An interesting phase of this traffic was the development of a unique type of rivermen, especially on the route between the Illinois settlements and New Orleans. Many of them Canadian *voyageurs,* these boatmen were a rollicking lot who frequently took possession of the small river settlements at which they stopped. An interesting representative was François Menard, a Canadian who came to Kaskaskia in 1795. A famous boatman, fully equal to the emergencies that constantly arose, Menard was trustworthy yet pugnacious, ready to defend himself and his crew against any high-handed acts on the part of the Spanish authorities.

An interesting phase of the development of the Ohio-Mississippi route was an attempt to construct seagoing vessels in Ohio Valley shipyards, and thus to avoid the usual transfer of cargo at New Orleans. In 1800 a committee in Cincin-

[24] *Laws of Ohio,* Second General Assembly, p. 292.
[25] Gephart, *Transportation in the Middle West,* p. 71; *American Pioneer,* vol. I, p. 99; Hall, *Statistics of the West,* pp. 216 ff.
[26] *Liberty Hall,* May 29, 1811, and January 15, 1812.

nati received subscriptions for a shipbuilding company, and at least six gunboats were launched at the mouth of the Little Miami. At Pittsburgh, also, a number of seagoing vessels were constructed.[27] But the greatest activity was at Marietta, where shipbuilders trained in New England yards made use of the abundance of oak, pine, and locust in the near-by forests. The *St. Clair*, a square-rigged brig and the first seagoing vessel built at Marietta, left for Havana by way of New Orleans in 1800, and two years later the *Muskingum*, a vessel of 204 tons, was built. Marietta soon became a port of registry and clearance for vessels bound to foreign shores, and in 1807 its shipbuilders reached the height of their prosperity. March 3 they launched the *John Atkinson* and the *Tuscarora*, of 330 and 300 tons respectively, April 1, the *Rufus King*, and April 2 and 3 two gunboats, building altogether 1,313 tons of seagoing vessels within a year.[28] But the budding shipbuilding industry in the Ohio Valley soon decayed. The Embargo Act with its fatal effect upon shipping was a prime factor in this downfall, while the unfavorable geographic situation of the Ohio Valley ports was equally disastrous. The long journey down the Ohio and the Mississippi was exceedingly dangerous to vessels of such comparatively large tonnage, while the return voyage upstream was impracticable. The voyage of the *Nonpareil* was a striking illustration of the risks encountered by Ohio shipbuilders. This vessel, a schooner of 70 tons, left Marietta April 21, 1805, with a cargo of flour, wheat, cheese, and bacon which the owners disposed of in the Amite River. After a severe storm on Lake Pontchartrain had badly damaged the *Nonpareil*, they sold her for only $500.00. Starting home the last of August they followed the usual land route to Ohio, traveling with companies of fifteen or twenty to ensure safety, and

[27] *Western Spy*, October 1, 1800; *Liberty Hall*, March 3, 1806, and July 9, 1808; Cramer, *The Navigator*, ed. 1808, pp. 38-39.

[28] Petition, January 14, 1802, *Northwest Territorial Papers*, House Files; *First Settlement of Ohio*, MS. by Col. James Barker; *Ohio Gazette*, March 7, 1808; *Pittsburgh Magazine Almanack* for 1808, p. 59; Ambler, *History of Transportation in the Ohio Valley*, pp. 81-106.

riding "Opelousas" horses, a hardy Spanish and Indian breed. Finally, these luckless shipowners reached Marietta in October with the $500.00 received for the *Nonpareil* as their chief tangible return from this long voyage.[29] Even the hardy persistence of Yankee shipbuilders yielded in the face of such losses. But this futile attempt to found a shipbuilding industry in the Old Northwest is especially interesting as a precursor of the much later movement to secure a deep waterway from the Lakes to the Gulf.

The steamboat finally solved the problem of larger and swifter vessels for the growing traffic down the Ohio. The *New Orleans*, the first one in the Western country, passed Cincinnati "in fine stile" October 27, 1811, on her way down the river from Pittsburgh. She went as far as Louisville, and made the return trip, 185 miles upstream, in the almost unbelievable record, for the early Western settlers, of forty-five hours. At Cincinnati the excited inhabitants took short trips on the *New Orleans* while the vessel waited for a rise in the river.[30] Other steamboats followed this pioneer on the Ohio —the *Comet*, the *Vesuvius*, and the *Enterprise*, and there was great enthusiasm for the new type of vessel, which, it was confidently held, would completely revolutionize river traffic. Already the Indiana territorial assembly had incorporated the Ohio Steamboat Company, and in Cincinnati this new enterprise received much encouragement.[31] The approach of war seriously interfered with this growing interest, and until normal life was resumed, the barge, the flatboat, and the pirogue remained supreme as carriers of traffic on the inland waters of the Western country.

In this early period of the Old Northwest the Great Lakes and their tributaries were not nearly so important as routes of traffic, as was the Ohio River system which intersected the more thickly settled regions. The pioneers in the scat-

[29] *American Pioneer*, vol. I, pp. 89-105 and 128-145.
[30] *Liberty Hall*, October 30 and December 4, 1811.
[31] *Western Spy*, February 1, 1812; *Laws of Indiana Territory*, Third General Assembly, First Session, p. 61.

tered settlements of the Western Reserve used the water route on Lake Erie to Buffalo, and this was the custom of the inhabitants of early Michigan. The Cuyahoga, too, soon developed as an outlet for local produce, as well as for an extensive trade that came across the easy portages from the Scioto and the Tuscarawas. Like their fellow New Englanders at Marietta, the inhabitants of Cleveland began to build vessels of considerable size for the lake trade. More fortunate than the shipbuilders of the Ohio Valley, they possessed in Lake Erie a suitable body of water in which to navigate the vessels they constructed in their yards. The first large vessel built at Cleveland, the *Zephyr*, was launched in 1808. The *Ohio*, of 60 tons, followed in 1810, and others came in rapid succession. Boats were built at other lake ports, and the very considerable tonnage that was constructed on Lake Erie in this early period was apparent when at least sixty vessels were brought together at Cleveland in July, 1813, in order to transport Harrison's army across the lake to Canada.[32]

The waterways of the Old Northwest, numerous though they were, did not long satisfy the demand for a really dependable system of transportation. Floods in the summer and ice in the winter constantly interfered with traffic upon them, and the spread of population into the interior made it imperative to open up land routes which could be used at all seasons. The Indian trails were available for the traveler on horseback or on foot. But they were lonely in the early days of settlement, and there was constant danger of attacks by wandering bands of savages who might be lurking in the forest. For several years travelers in interior Ohio went in companies for mutual protection, just as on the Wilderness Trail. The many streams, with no ferries or bridges across them, added to the dangers of pioneer travel; and often horses and riders were drowned when they attempted to ford a swollen stream. As a matter of fact, the dexterity of a

[32] Whittlesey, *Early History of Cleveland*, p. 464; Kennedy, *History of Cleveland*, p. 139; *Western Spy*, July 7, 1813.

horse as a swimmer was an important consideration to the pioneer purchaser. Moreover, with settlements so far apart in the pioneer days, the lack of taverns on the way added to the discomforts of the traveler by land in the Old Northwest. An interesting illustration of the hardships of this pioneer travel is given by the journey of General Wilkinson in the winter of 1797 from the Wabash posts to Pittsburgh. Traveling nearly 400 miles across country through a "pathless wilderness," with snow eighteen inches deep in places and a sub-zero temperature at times, for almost two months Wilkinson was obliged to sleep in a tent.[33]

In the improvement of the land routes, Ohio, the first section of the Old Northwest to be settled, naturally led the way. The backbone of its system of highways was Zane's Trace, which, starting at Wheeling, where it connected with the road to Pittsburgh, extended through Zanesville, Lancaster, and Chillicothe to the Ohio River opposite Limestone (Maysville). It dated in reality from 1796 when Ebenezer Zane undertook to construct a wagon road on the route which he had already cleared for horseback riders. In return for his work, Congress granted him three sections of land, at the points where the new road crossed the Muskingum, the Hockhocking, and the Scioto rivers respectively. At each of these crossings Zane received exclusive right to operate a ferry and to open an inn. The highway that was thus inaugurated soon became the most important one in the Western country, opening up communication by land for 298 miles from Pittsburgh through Wheeling to Limestone.[34] Aside from the grants to Ebenezer Zane, Congress left to the pioneers of the Northwest Territory themselves the task of opening roads between the settlements. The first highway act in 1792 placed the roads in charge of local overseers, and required all males, sixteen and over, to work on them not

[33] *Gazette of the United States,* December 29, 1797.
[34] Petition of Ebenezer Zane, 1796, *Northwest Territorial Papers,* Senate Files; *Annals of Congress,* Fourth Congress, Second Session, pp. 2904-2905; *Pittsburgh Magazine Almanack* for 1804.

more than ten days annually. Under this act the construction
of necessary bridges might be included in the county levy.
A second territorial act in 1799 followed the same general
principles, and required roads to be constructed upon petitions from the inhabitants of a neighborhood. This act also
authorized ditches and drains to be cut through private property, if necessary, and empowered the builders of roads to
take the gravel, sand, wood, and other material that might be
needed from unimproved land along the right of way. Quite
a practical clause in this early road act required posts to be
set up at "forks," which would show "the most remarkable
places" to which the different roads led. Also, the act ordered
that the annual county levies should include the necessary
expenditures for laying out and maintaining roads. It remained in force in the Northwest Territory, and it was retained in Ohio throughout the early period, with only a few
amendments, the chief one transferring the supervision of
the roads to county commissioners.[35] But the road act was
not carried out in at all adequate fashion, as the budgets of
Ohio counties show. Thus, in total expenditures of $1,555.73
for the year ending June 6, 1808, the only items which the
commissioners of Washington County allowed for highways
were $150.00 expended on a bridge, and $50.00 for miscellaneous road expenses. The budget of $2,950.10 in Hamilton
County, for the year ending June 15, 1810, did not include
any expenditures at all for roads, and in Butler County, for
the year ending August, 1810, only $40.00 was allowed for
that purpose.[36]

The situation was saved by the agreement with the Federal government when Ohio was admitted into the Union,
that three per cent from the sales of public lands within the
new state should be devoted to its highways. In the first appropriation from this fund in 1804, the Ohio legislature dis-

[35] *Laws of the Northwest Territory,* Pease, ed., *Illinois Historical Collections,* vol. XVII, pp. 74-77, 452-467; *Laws of Ohio,* Second General Assembly, pp. 207-224, Seventh General Assembly, pp. 125-142.

[36] *Ohio Gazette,* August 25, 1808; *Liberty Hall,* September 17 and December 26, 1810.

tributed $17,000.00 for roads, including in the list one from Chillicothe through Cincinnati to North Bend, and another one from Cincinnati through Hamilton and Franklin to Dayton. This act also set up standards for road building, and required that a passageway of at least twenty feet should be cleared, from which stumps more than one foot high must be cut down, and that causeways of timber covered with earth should be constructed across miry spots. Lastly, the act provided that the grade of a road should never exceed fifteen per cent. Where the appropriation averaged less than $10.00 per mile, however, the act very sensibly left the specifications to the judgment of the commissioners.[37] With the aid of the three per cent fund, by 1806 all the important settlements in southern and central Ohio had been connected by roads of a more or less primitive type. In the Western Reserve, which was just beginning to be settled, a road ran from Pittsburgh through Warren to Cleveland, and along the lake shore was the Lake Trail, which had been "girdled" to a width of thirty-five feet.[38] By 1812 the legislature had appropriated, altogether, $127,105.00 from the three per cent fund, and at least three highways ran across the state from the Ohio Valley to Lake Erie, from Cleveland to Zanesville via Hudson, from Cleveland to Lancaster via Newark, and from Huron through Mansfield, Delaware, and Newark to Lancaster. Thus, there was a chain of roads, such as they were, for approximately 373 miles, from the mouth of the Miami in the southeastern corner of Ohio, through Cincinnati, Springfield, Worthington, and Cleveland to the mouth of the Conneaut in the northeast.[39] But the legislature had not made any adequate provision for the upkeep of these roads, and the general powers conferred by the highway act

[37] *Laws of Ohio*, Second General Assembly, pp. 136-146.
[38] *Map of Ohio*, by J. F. Mansfield, about 1806, in *Hist. and Phil. Soc. of Ohio Collections; Cleveland Plaindealer*, June 15, 1913; *Joseph Perkins' Scrap Book*, p. 218.
[39] Gephart, *Transportation in the Middle West*, pp. 56-57 and 134; Cramer's *Pittsburgh Magazine Almanack* for 1812, pp. 30-35; Browne's *Cincinnati Almanac* for 1811, pp. 22-23.

had not been well enforced, to judge from a bill of complaint which the grand jury of Hamilton County presented in 1809. Bridges were down, they represented, and often the roads were "mere nuisances" which were "extremely injurious" to teams. The grand jury unhesitatingly laid the blame upon the road supervisors, but probably with little effect.[40]

An important forward step in the improvement of the Ohio roads was the incorporation of the two turnpike companies in 1809, one to build an improved highway in Trumbull County, and the other one to construct the road from Zanesville to Franklinton. In their main features, these acts were identical, establishing important precedents for measures of a similar type. Upon a right of way limited to sixty feet, an "artificial" road was to be constructed, twenty-two feet broad, in accordance with detailed specifications. This roadbed, of "stone, gravel, or other proper and convenient material," the turnpike company must maintain "in perfect repair." As compensation for its expenditures the company was authorized to erect toll gates not less than eight miles apart. These acts also included clauses that recognized the right to regulate public utilities which was so generally upheld in the early West. In these particular cases the acts fixed the legal charges for toll, 6 cents for a horse and rider, for example, and 12½ cents for a two-horse wagon. Moreover, these acts looked forward to ultimate public ownership, by a provision that all profits above ten per cent must be used to buy in the stock. When all outstanding shares had been purchased in this fashion, the turnpike would become public property.[41]

Outside of Ohio, the smaller population in the early period made the problem of highways a less pressing one, although, even under these circumstances, some improvement was necessary if settlement was to be encouraged. In Indiana the territorial legislature passed several amendments to the highway act which had been adopted in the Northwest Territory

40 *Liberty Hall*, August 22, 1809.
41 *Laws of Ohio*, Seventh General Assembly, pp. 89-106, 150-152.

in 1799, the chief ones increasing the age limits for forced labor to sixteen and sixty-five, and fixing thirty-six feet as the maximum width of public roads.[42] Also, there was an attempt to secure aid from the Federal government, following the precedent in Ohio, even before Indiana became a state. Thus, in 1807 the registrar of the Vincennes land office called for bids on roads from Vincennes eastward to North Bend, and westward to Cahokia, which must be one rod wide and fit for "loaden wagons to travel on." Committees of Congress also recommended government aid for roads from Vincennes to the Indiana line on the route to Dayton, and from Jeffersonville to Detroit.[43] But few, if any, actual results came from these proposals. By 1812 there were only two main roads in Indiana. One, a fairly well-defined trail, ran from Louisville to Vincennes. The other one, from Vincennes to Kaskaskia, a contemporary described as a "straight, narrow road" which was "impossible for four-wheeled vehicles and was traveled by horsemen, packhorses, and footmen." [44]

In the Illinois settlements conditions were even worse, and the roads were so primitive that travel by water was preferable wherever it was possible. There was a fairly good highway through the main area of settlement between Kaskaskia and Cahokia, but elsewhere the roads showed little, if any, advance over the Indian pathways. Three trails, starting from Shawneetown, Golconda, and Fort Massac respectively, led from the Ohio River to Kaskaskia, and were the main routes taken by the pioneers who came to the American Bottom and near-by settlements. The most popular one, from Fort Massac, was supposedly a military road, and was marked by blazes that were painted red. A typical journey over one of these Illinois trails was made by the Reynolds family

[42] *Laws of Indiana Territory,* Philbrick, ed., *Illinois Historical Collections,* vol. XXI, pp. 108, 646-647; Third General Assembly, Second Session, pp. 46-48.

[43] *Western Sun,* September 12, 1807; Reports, January 17 and February 7, 1811, *Indiana Territorial Papers,* House Files.

[44] Cramer's *Pittsburgh Magazine Almanack* for 1812, p. 34; Reynolds, *Pioneer History of Illinois,* p. 234.

which came to Illinois from eastern Tennessee in 1800. Starting from Golconda, they made the trip through the wilderness to Kaskaskia, 110 miles away, in four wearisome weeks. First there came a tornado, which filled the roadway with fallen trees and branches. Next they were obliged to wait for days at the crossing of the Big Muddy River until the swollen waters had receded. Finally they crossed on a raft, swimming their horses, but on the way they lost one of their two precious axes. At three other creeks they were obliged to build rafts in order to cross, but they all reached Kaskaskia safely, without having passed a single habitation on the road from Golconda.[45]

In Michigan, too, the roads were in quite an unsatisfactory condition. Woodward's Code in 1805 included a road act which, following precedents elsewhere in the Northwest Territory, placed the roads in charge of local supervisors, and required forced labor from the male inhabitants of twenty-one and over. But apparently this measure remained chiefly on paper, and brought about little, if any, improvement. The main highways and bridges remained in "extreme bad order," and even the important land route to the American settlements in the Western Reserve was badly neglected.[46] In 1808 the legislative council authorized a public lottery to raise $6,000.00 for the survey and construction of a highway, a hundred and twenty feet wide, from Detroit to the Rapids of the Maumee. But this rather grandiose scheme was not effectually carried through, although the road was surveyed and cleared in a fashion. Had it been completed, it would have connected at the Rapids with a road to the Western Reserve, laid out by the Federal government, which was described in 1812 as quite passable east of Sandusky.[47] The failure of these attempts to construct a really dependable

[45] Buck, *Illinois in 1818*, pp. 114-115; Reynolds, *Pioneer History of Illinois*, pp. 249-250.

[46] *Territorial Laws of Michigan*, vol. I, pp. 75-79; *Michigan Pioneer Collections*, vol. XII, pp. 628-630.

[47] *Territorial Laws of Michigan*, vol. IV, pp. 35-36; *Trump of Fame*, October 7 and December 16, 1812.

highway from the settlements in Ohio to Detroit was, of course, one of the main causes for the collapse of American rule in Michigan in this early period.

As highways developed in the Old Northwest, ferries, and even bridges on the more traveled routes, became necessary, in order to ensure uninterrupted passage over the many streams. The fords were usually dangerous, and when there was floating ice, or a flood, they became impassable for wheeled vehicles, and often practically so to horsemen as well. The one solution was to establish ferries at important crossings, and naturally this was done first in Ohio where the larger population made highways on land a necessity. Under the first grade of government in the Northwest Territory, the governor issued licenses for ferries,[48] the first one, which was recorded December 28, 1789, authorizing Absalom Martin to keep a ferry across the Ohio from a point nearly opposite Wheeling. About two years later another license gave Robert Benham permission to establish a ferry from Cincinnati to the mouth of the Licking. This typical license recognized the principle of the regulation of public utilities, which the people of the Old Northwest had brought from their old homes on the Atlantic Coast, along with their hatred of monopolies of any sort. The exact rates to be charged were prescribed, and in addition, Benham was required to provide "good and sufficient boats." Although many other licenses were issued about this time, the rapid spread of highways evidently led to unauthorized ferries. In 1797 the legislative board found it was necessary to call attention to the power of the governor, alone, to issue ferry licenses, and to his right to revoke them where ferry keepers did not observe the prescribed conditions. Possibly it was this attempt to hold ferries so strictly under the governor's control that led the territorial assembly at its first session, in 1799, to pass an act which assumed to itself the power to issue licenses, leaving the question of rates to be

[48] *Executive Proceedings, Northwest Territory,* 1788–1795, *passim;* also *Journal of the Northwest Territory,* 1788–1803, *passim.*

determined by the county courts of quarter sessions. This act also defined the obligations of the ferryman, to keep his ferry open at night, and to take into his boat, "any passenger or passengers, carriages, wagons, horses, or cattle of any kind." [49]

The transfer to the territorial assembly of the power to issue licenses for ferries, was not at all a practical measure for so vast a country. Already the governor and the acting governor had found it necessary to delegate this power occasionally, as when Winthrop Sargent, before he departed to organize Michigan, left a dozen ferry licenses with the United States attorney in Hamilton County, to be filled out at the latter's discretion. About the same time blank licenses were sent to Vincennes for the "convenience" of the residents of Knox County. It was soon obvious that the territorial assembly alone was able to consider all the requests for ferry licenses, and in 1800 an act was passed that delegated this power to the county courts. [50] This law was retained in the state of Ohio with a few additional regulations. The ferryman was required to see that his boat was properly manned, to be in attendance whenever he should be needed, and to display publicly the charges which the local court fixed in each instance, but always within the maximum rates established by the state legislature. Other minor amendments in the state law from time to time accented the obligations of the ferryman to the public, and the care to be exercised in the issue of licenses. [51]

Apparently the several acts with respect to ferries were well enforced in early Ohio, and the records contain interesting items upon this usual means of crossing the many streams. A typical ferry of the pioneer days, the one across the mouth of the Muskingum, was propelled by a windlass attached to a rope that stretched from bank to bank. An

[49] *Laws of the Northwest Territory*, Pease, ed., *Illinois Historical Collections*, vol. XVII, pp. 357-360.
[50] *Ibid.*, First General Assembly, Second Session, pp. 19-21.
[51] *Laws of Ohio*, Third General Assembly, pp. 96-104; Eighth General Assembly, pp. 107-115.

inkling of the size and value of these early ferryboats is given by two ferry flats picked up as strays. The larger one, 40 feet long by 8 feet wide, was officially valued at $14.50, and the smaller one, 32 by 8 feet, at $12.00.[52] Public regulation and the keen competition between rival ferrymen kept the average rates on the Ohio ferries down to reasonable figures. At Cincinnati, for example, Joel Williams charged 6¼ cents for each foot passenger he ferried across the Ohio, and 50 cents for a wagon and four horses. On another important ferry, the one across the Scioto at Chillicothe, the charges were 6¼ cents each for horned cattle, 12½ cents for a man and a horse, 75 cents for a wagon and team, and other rates in proportion.[53] Occasionally there was bitter rivalry between the owners of neighboring ferries, with much price cutting as a result. An inkling as to the volume of traffic on one of these pioneer ferries is given in the report of a ferry keeper at Cincinnati that in eight months he brought 2,639 immigrants across the river, and this, of course, was only one of at least forty ferries over the Ohio.[54]

The same principle of public regulation which was applied to ferries was retained when private corporations began to build bridges on the more important Ohio highways. One of the earliest of these acts, in 1802, granted Jonathan Zane and his associates the right to build a bridge across the Muskingum at Zanesville. It required the maximum toll rates to be publicly displayed, 1 cent for each sheep or swine, 30 cents for a two-wheeled vehicle, with other charges in proportion, up to $1.50 for a four-wheeled pleasure carriage. This particular franchise was limited to ninety-nine years, but ultimate public ownership was provided for in later acts for the construction of bridges by private persons. Thus, an act that authorized a bridge across Little Beaver Creek

[52] Cramer, *The Navigator*, ed. 1808, p. 56; *Western Herald*, March 18, 1808.

[53] *Western Spy*, November 2, 1807; Gephart, *Transportation in the Middle West*, p. 48.

[54] *Liberty Hall*, January 13, 1806; *The Commonwealth*, Pittsburgh, March 12, 1806.

stipulated that at any time within fifty years, the taxpayers of Columbiana County would have the right to buy it in, provided they reimbursed the owners for their entire outlay with interest.[55] With the building of these bridges across the principal streams, and the improvement of the main highways, stagecoaches began to make their appearance in Ohio. One of the earliest lines started to run in the fall of 1805 from Cincinnati to Frankfort, Kentucky, and "during the season" a four-horse stage took passengers from Cincinnati to Yellow Springs, which became a popular watering-place at a very early date. For this latter service, which was made within two days *en route* in either direction, the fare was $5.00 one way, with a baggage allowance of forty pounds for each passenger.[56] The most important stage line in early Ohio was the one maintained by the "public carriages" which, beginning in 1805, carried mail and passengers from Pittsburgh over Zane's Trace, and then to Frankfort in Kentucky.[57] But few roads in the Old Northwest were sufficiently improved to make regular passenger lines possible, and the stagecoach, like the steamboat, did not take a really important place in the system of transportation before the War of 1812.

In Indiana, as well, the gradual increase in the population, with the accompanying demand for transportation by land, soon made ferries necessary across the principal streams. The territorial law of 1799, which gave the assembly the power of issuing licenses for ferries, was supposedly in force in Indiana after it was first set off from the Northwest Territory. But there was no territorial assembly at that time, and it was impossible, therefore, to carry out the clause giving that body the power to issue licenses. Nor could Governor Harrison and the judges find a suitable substitute in the codes of the original states. In this quandary they finally

---

55 *Laws of the Northwest Territory*, Second Assembly, First Session, pp. 209-211; *Laws of Ohio*, Seventh General Assembly, pp. 154-156.

56 *Western Spy*, August 14 and 21, 1805.

57 Gideon Granger to the President, July 19, 1805, *Michigan Territorial Papers*, Postoffice Records.

followed the usual custom in the early period of the Northwest Territory, and gave to the governor the right to license
ferries by proclamation, as they were needed. When the territorial legislature first met in Indiana, it promptly followed
the example that had been set in the Northwest Territory,
and turned over to the county courts the power to issue
licenses for ferries, imposing at the same time regulations in
the public interest that were much similar to those in force
in Ohio.[58] First by proclamation of the governor, and later
under this act of the territorial legislature, a number of ferries were established in Indiana across the Ohio, the Wabash,
and the White rivers. In the Illinois country at least two
ferries were authorized on the road between Vincennes and
Kaskaskia, one on the road from Fort Massac to Kaskaskia,
and several across the Mississippi. The ferry over the Mississippi to St. Louis proved especially profitable, with a constantly growing traffic.[59] But in this early period up to 1812,
traffic on the few primitive highways in Indiana and Illinois
did not warrant the building of expensive toll bridges.

The principle of public regulation which was carried out
with regard to ferries and bridges was applied also to the
taverns which soon began to appear in the Old Northwest.
This control was necessary, since they served the double
purpose of a stopping place for travelers and a local bar-
room. The first regulatory measure in the Northwest Territory in 1792, which required each innkeeper to take out an
annual license with a fee of $16.00, aroused so loud a pro-
test that it was repealed in Maxwell's Code. But in 1800,
the territorial legislature renewed the requirement for a license, with a fee, however, of from $6.00 to $14.00. This act
also required innkeepers to provide good entertainment
and accommodation for "man and horse," and it held them
to strict account if they permitted gambling, drunkenness,
or other disorder on their premises. Later laws in Ohio

[58] *Laws of Indiana Territory, Illinois Historical Collections,* vol. XXI, pp.
18, 352-355.
[59] *Louisiana Gazette,* May 24, 1810.

virtually repeated these provisions, and much similar acts to regulate inns were passed in Indiana and Michigan territories.[60] The license fees that these laws brought in became important items in the early county budgets, and the inns that sprang up in the various settlements soon showed great improvement in the facilities they offered travelers. At Zanesville in 1798 a log cabin sufficed as "an excuse" for a tavern, but four years later there was a really elaborate hostelry, for this period, at this important point on the road from Pittsburgh to Maysville. The inn at the sign of the Eagle and Ball was conducted in a large two-story house and was well supplied with "imported" liquors, a "number of feather beds," and other comforts too numerous to mention.[61] As an important center of travel, which soon became the territorial and later the state capital, Chillicothe boasted a number of inns, the owners of which widely advertised the merits of their establishments. By 1803 the inn at the sign of the Red Lion contained twelve rooms, which had been completely refurnished. There were also private lodging rooms apart from the tavern proper, and, according to the proprietor, the inn had "good, clean beds," and always a supply of the best liquor, with room for thirty horses in the large stable.[62] In another inn at Springfield there were seven fireplaces, a "convenient kitchen," "roomy garrets," and other attractions.[63] The traveler even found comfortable quarters in Vincennes, as in one inn where the proprietor enticingly advertised he had provided "all those things which generally afford rest to the weary—his house commodious, his bedding neat, his servants attentive, his liquors excellent and just from Baltimore, and his stabling and forage good." [64]

[60] *Laws of the Northwest Territory*, Pease, ed., *Illinois Historical Collections*, vol. XVII, pp. 61-66, 256; Laws of Indiana Territory, Philbrick, ed., *Ibid.*, vol. XXI, pp. 114-115, 284-288; *Michigan Territorial Laws*, vol. I, pp. 40-44.
[61] *American Pioneer*, vol. I, p. 75; *Ohio Gazette*, January 1, 1802.
[62] *Scioto Gazette*, December 10, 1803.
[63] *The Supporter*, May 19, 1810.
[64] *Western Sun*, September 1, 1812.

But these comparatively comfortable inns and the crude highways of this early period did not usually extend far beyond the areas of fairly close settlement. The discomforts that attended travel through the wilderness are set forth in interesting detail in an account of a journey from Cincinnati to Detroit in 1804. After passing Hamilton, this intelligent traveler found that the country was more sparsely populated, and beyond Dayton he encountered only a few scattered traders and Indians. The road, too, gradually became more difficult, until north of Stanton it was only a "tolerably clear" path. From Loramie's to St. Mary's the road which Wayne had opened for his troops had been blocked by fallen timber and undergrowth, and the bridges had rotted away, while further on, between Tawatown and Fort Defiance, there was only an "obscure trail," imperfectly blazed. There were several streams which must be crossed on rafts at high water on this part of the trip, and the traveler was obliged to spend the night in the woods. Conditions were much similar on the next lap of the journey, from Fort Defiance to the Rapids of the Maumee. This road was especially rough, and was frequently crossed by "guts" from the Maumee, across which it was necessary to swim one's horse. Beyond the Rapids there was a fairly easy road to Detroit. This same journal of an early trip from Cincinnati to Detroit gives interesting details of the traveler's expenses. Usually ferriage was 25 cents for a horse and rider, and the taverns charged: for a night's lodging, 12½ cents; for each meal, 25 cents; for a half pint of whisky, 12½ cents; for hay and stablage for one night, 25 cents; and for a gallon of grain for feed, 12½ cents. Corn, when it could be secured on the road, varied in price between $1.00 and $2.00 per bushel, and a three-pound loaf of bread sold for 25 cents. Beyond Loramie's it was necessary to provide sufficient supplies to last until the traveler reached the Rapids.[65]

The development of transportation in the Old Northwest, even though the results were crude, made possible the ex-

[65] *Independent Gazetteer,* January 17 and 24, 1804.

tension of postal service to this region. The earliest mail routes from the Eastern Seaboard were the two established in 1792, from Philadelphia through Bedford to Pittsburgh, and from Richmond by the Wilderness Trail to Danville, Kentucky. From each of these terminals, letters were sent in irregular fashion into the Old Northwest, either by military couriers or by private persons. Otherwise, they were advertised in long lists published in the Pittsburgh and Kentucky newspapers. But the swift increase of population and the need for dependable means of communicating with Wayne's army made it necessary to establish a fairly reliable mail service to this Western country. The government now decided to discard the long and dangerous route through the wilderness, and to use the safer and much more traveled one across the Alleghenies, through Pittsburgh, and then down the Ohio to Fort Washington. The direct mail service that was opened up at this time, from Baltimore through Hagerstown to Pittsburgh, made this change doubly desirable, and late in the spring of 1794 the postmaster-general drew up elaborate plans for the new route to the West, appointing Major Isaac Craig in general charge with headquarters at Pittsburgh, and General Rufus Putnam to superintend the river line from Marietta.[66] Major Craig promptly advertised for bids on the contract to transport the mails by land from Pittsburgh to Wheeling. From there he planned to convey them by three boats, running respectively between Wheeling and Marietta, Marietta and Gallipolis, and Gallipolis and Limestone (Maysville). From this last point a carrier would then take the mails by land along the Kentucky bank to Cincinnati. The government itself undertook to carry on the boat service, while the land route between Limestone and Cincinnati was to be let by contract. The keel boats which Craig secured were about 24 feet long, armed, and each one was manned by a crew of five "active young men," a boat-

66 *Annals of Congress,* Second Congress, Appendix, pp. 1333-1335; Postmaster-General to Rufus Putnam, May 24, 1794, *Northwest Territorial Papers,* Postoffice Records.

swain who received $20.00, and four hands at $15.00 per month and rations in all cases. The mail, according to Craig's plan, was to be kept in boxes, and there was to be a weekly schedule that allowed seven days from Pittsburgh to Cincinnati, and thirteen for the return trip. One boat was ready the latter part of June, 1794, and the other two were soon in service. The letting of the contracts for the postriders from Pittsburgh to Wheeling, and from Limestone to Cincinnati, and the appointment of postmasters at Marietta, Gallipolis, Limestone, and Cincinnati completed the preliminary arrangements.[67]

The plans for the new mail route did not work satisfactorily. There were constant complaints of "great delay" in the mails, although the service was carried on at "enormous" expense. One of the chief sources of trouble was the failure of the boats to wait for one another at junction points, and the constant tardiness of the boat from Gallipolis in its arrival at Limestone. As this last lap was decidedly longer than the two first ones, at General Putnam's suggestion two of the boats were ordered to alternate upon a through route from Marietta to Preston, Kentucky. A postrider was appointed to go from this point the remaining twenty-three miles by land to Limestone, thus saving much time. These changes made little improvement in the service. Often the ice in the river forced the mail boats to stop running altogether, and usually the carrier from Preston was so late that the return service from Cincinnati, where the regular schedule allowed a stop of only twenty-four hours, was unduly delayed. Moreover, the superintendent of the boat service from Marietta to Preston proved wholly unreliable, glossing over continual delays and neglects. Finally, late in 1796, as a last resort the postmaster-general let the contract for the boat service to Charles Greene, allowing him four new boats of "whaleboat" construction, valued at about $2,500.00 each. In a few months the service down the Ohio had again broken

[67] Miscellaneous Correspondence, Postmaster-General, May 24 to June 20, 1794, *Northwest Territorial Papers,* Postoffice Records. *Pittsburgh Gazette,* May 31, 1794.

down, with mails two and even three months overdue. Greene, too, had misrepresented the situation, and had been guilty of gross neglect, actually sending the mail at times in an open box, or else wrapped in a blanket which was placed in a small canoe in charge of a boy of fourteen, although the government had made a liberal allowance of $3,000.00, which should have netted nearly fifty per cent.[68] Soon Greene was forced to give up his contract, and in the fall of 1798 the postoffice department discontinued the route by water in favor of the more dependable one by "Mr. Zane's Trace," now that there was no longer such danger from Indian attacks upon travelers by land. The new mail schedule called for departure from Pittsburgh every Friday at 2 P.M. and arrival at Zane's Station (Zanesville) the following Monday morning. From Zane's a second carrier left Tuesday morning, arriving at Limestone by way of "Chillicotha" Friday morning, and a third one carried the mail over a branch route to Marietta. Zane's Trace soon became the chief mail route from Pittsburgh to the Ohio Valley, and by 1805 there were two mails weekly westward from Pittsburgh, while stagecoaches ensured dependable service all the way from Philadelphia to Frankfort.[69]

Once regular postal service had been established over Zane's Trace, it became possible to send the mails from this basic route to the principal settlements in Ohio upon a biweekly and occasionally a weekly schedule. The three earliest postoffices established in the Northwest Territory in 1794, at Marietta, Gallipolis, and Cincinnati, had increased, thirteen years later, to sixty-four in Ohio alone, with additional ones soon to be opened.[70] In 1810, an important mail

[68] Correspondence of Postmaster-General, August 23, 1794, to June 23, 1797, *Northwest Territorial Papers*, Postoffice Records; *Memoirs of Rufus Putnam*, Buell, ed., pp. 386-416.

[69] Postmaster-General to Josiah Munro, September 27, 1798, to William McCullough, March 1, 1799, and to the President, July 19, 1805, *Northwest Territorial Papers*, Postoffice Records; *Pittsburgh Gazette*, August 25, 1798; *The Commonwealth*, November 13, 1805; Boucher, *A Century and a Half of Pittsburgh*, vol. I, p. 331.

[70] *Browne's Western Calendar* for 1809.

route was established which crossed central Ohio from south to north, running from Point Pleasant via Gallipolis, Chillicothe, Franklin, Delaware, and Mansfield to Huron. Still another important post route ran from Marietta via Athens, Chillicothe, and Williamsburg to Cincinnati. By the outbreak of the War of 1812, these and other routes covered the more thickly settled sections of the state with a network of postal communication. In the Western Reserve the first mail is said to have come to Warren October 30, 1801, "safely bound up in a pocket handkerchief."[71] About three years later Congress extended this service to Cleveland and Detroit, and the postmaster-general selected as carriers on this weekly route "two enterprising, hardy young woodsmen." Also, he tried to induce "steady" persons to establish inns and ferries at important crossings, and planned to have "trees fallen" over the smaller streams, with the road blazed and the underbrush cleared out. But like the plans for the Ohio River mail route, these arrangements for an established highway through the northern Ohio wilderness were not carried out in satisfactory fashion. With practically no roads, bridges, or ferries much of the way, the mail carriers between Cleveland and Detroit were often obliged to swim their horses. In the Black Swamp the water was sometimes two to three inches deep for many miles, and the only habitations the carriers found between Cleveland and Detroit were at Huron, Sandusky, Maumee and the River Raisin.[72] In spite of these discouraging conditions they maintained with fair regularity a three days' schedule between Cleveland and Detroit.

In early Indiana and Illinois the inadequate system of transportation naturally interfered with the systematic extension of mail routes west of Ohio. Occasionally the inhabitants of these remote sections were called upon to make up

[71] *Annals of Congress,* Eleventh Congress, Second Session, Appendix, p. 2550.

[72] General Simon Perkins to Elisha Whittlesey, March 20, 1842, *Joseph Perkins' Scrap Book,* pp. 142-144; Postmaster-General to the President, July 19, 1805, *Michigan Territorial Papers,* Postoffice Records.

deficiencies in the service by private subscription.[73] For example, after much persuasion by interested settlers, the postmaster-general finally agreed to establish a postal route every four weeks from Louisville to Kaskaskia, for which the government would pay the carrier $600.00 annually, provided the citizens of Vincennes and Kaskaskia undertook to make up any deficit. This service was inaugurated February 27, 1800, with a four days' schedule from Louisville to Vincennes, and six days additional from Vincennes to Kaskaskia. After a few weeks' trial Congress was willing to take over the service from Louisville to Vincennes, and authorized weekly mails. But from Vincennes to Kaskaskia there was to be a fortnightly service, with deficiencies in receipts still to be made up by private subscriptions. By 1810 there was a weekly post from Cincinnati through Louisville and Vincennes to Kaskaskia, and thence to Cahokia and St. Louis, as well as to Fort Massac, New Madrid, and New Orleans.[74] Another interesting postal route was a "line of expresses," probably under private control, that was advertised as early as 1803 from Chillicothe to "the Natchez," and was specially equipped to carry newspapers, provided they were "fully dried and closely packed." [75] One rather unfortunate omission in this period was the failure of the government to maintain regular postal service to the important trading houses and army posts at Fort Wayne and Fort Dearborn. From Stanton, Ohio, where connection could have been made with the Eastern mails, it would have been feasible to establish fortnightly service to Fort Wayne, and from there the mail could have been forwarded by spe-

[73] First Assistant Postmaster-General to William St. Clair and others, December 14, 1797, and to George Thatcher, May 2, 1798, and Correspondence, Postmaster-General, 1799–1800, passim, Northwest Territorial Papers, Postoffice Records; Postmaster-General to Henry Vanderburgh, July 31, 1801, Indiana Territorial Papers, Postoffice Records; Annals of Congress, Sixth Congress, Appendix, p. 1499.

[74] Western Sun, May 13, 1809, and June 15, 1811; Louisiana Gazette, November 28, 1810; Annals of Congress, Eleventh Congress, Second Session, Appendix, p. 2550.

[75] Scioto Gazette, November 26, 1803.

cial messenger to Fort Dearborn.[76] Had this route been established, it would have greatly aided the defense of Fort Dearborn in the War of 1812, and it might have saved this post for the Americans.

In general the mail service in Ohio was far from satisfactory, and the editors of the local newspapers were loud in their complaints. The breakdown of the packet-boat service on the Ohio and the continual delays in the mails were especially trying to the publishers of the *Centinel* in Cincinnati and the *Kentucky Gazette* in Lexington, for in both instances they depended chiefly upon this postal route for their news items from the outside world. Nor did these delays end entirely when Zane's Trace was substituted for the water route down the Ohio. Floods and floating ice in the many streams and bad roads were constantly holding up the postriders; and the editor of the *Scioto Gazette*, in a typical complaint, asserted that this was a grievance that "calls loud" for remedy.[77] Though delays were trying to irritable newspaper editors, it was the postriders in the Old Northwest upon whom the actual discomforts and hardships of the pioneer mail service fell. Beside the physical difficulties of the early roads, there was constant danger of attacks by Indians or by highwaymen. In 1803, for instance, the mail from Chillicothe to Lexington, through a region that was comparatively thickly populated, was "forcibly taken" from the postrider by a man on foot, for whose apprehension the postoffice department offered a reward of $300.00.[78] The low pay and exacting schedules of these early Western postriders were illustrated by the experience of Asael Adams who carried the mails between Pittsburgh and Cleveland. Leaving Pittsburgh every Friday at 6 A.M. he was expected to reach Cleveland, after two overnight stops, the following Monday by 10 A.M. On the return trip his schedule called for departure from

[76] Petition from John Johnson and twenty-eight others, October 1, 1807, *Indiana Territorial Papers,* House Files.

[77] *Scioto Gazette,* July 26, 1808.

[78] *Ibid.,* November 12, 1803.

Cleveland Monday at 2 P.M., and arrival at Pittsburgh Thursday at 6 P.M. Often he was obliged to fasten the saddlebags, which held the mail, about his shoulders, and to swim his horse across swollen streams. His annual salary was only $744.00, but he was allowed to deliver newspapers and to lead a packhorse loaded with merchandise, for his own "emolument." [79] The postal authorities drew up carefully worded contracts to ensure faithful performance of their duties by these postriders. A typical one, made with John Clarke in November, 1814, to carry the mail between Pittsburgh and Warren, listed elaborate penalties for delays from any possible cause, required a bond of $200.00, and stipulated that the monthly allowance should be $12.00 and board. However, the government furnished the necessary horses,[80] and doubtless Clarke was allowed to collect the usual extra compensation for carrying packages and newspapers. Such meager compensation, along with the hardships and dangers they encountered, readily explains the frequent complaints that appear with respect to these postriders.

The mail service in Indiana and the Illinois country was equally unsatisfactory. At Vincennes the editor of the *Western Sun* was constantly citing the delayed mails as an excuse for his scanty news columns. On January 21, 1809, he complained that there had been no mail from Louisville at Vincennes for four weeks. For such delays he blamed the postrider, who on two separate occasions had refused to cross the White River for fear of the floating ice, although other persons had made the passage in safety.[81] The postal service between Vincennes and Kaskaskia was even more unsatisfactory, and several carriers were robbed and murdered on this lonely road, nor were the mail contracts carefully managed in these distant settlements. Customarily, they were awarded to men who farmed them out, and these subcon-

[79] Kennedy, *History of Cleveland*, p. 141.
[80] Contract with John Clarke, November 12, 1814, *Calvin Pease Papers*.
[81] *Western Sun*, January 21, 1809.

tractors, in turn, secured deputies, until the persons who finally did the actual work had little sense of responsibility. The results were strikingly illustrated on one occasion when a boy carrying the mail in the Illinois country spied a deer. Immediately he rode in pursuit of it, altogether disregarding in the chase the important contents of his saddlebags. Often the postriders on these Illinois routes refused to accept all the mail that was offered, upon the pretext it was too heavy for a single horse. Consequently the surplus accumulated until, on June 27, 1811, the postmaster at Vincennes reported two flour barrels full of newspapers which the postman had refused. Such delays thoroughly aroused the inhabitants of the Illinois country, as well as their neighbors across the Mississippi. On at least one occasion the citizens of St. Louis sent a private courier for the newspapers that had accumulated at the Kaskaskia postoffice, but the "public execration" of the conditions that made necessary such summary action does not seem to have had much lasting effect.[82]

The management of a frontier postoffice presented many problems. The custom of sending letters and newspapers, for which the postage was to be collected upon delivery, was generally abused. This was especially the case in Cincinnati, where the postmaster gave notice that persons who wished to receive letters or newspapers must "come prepared, with ready change cash in hand, or no letters or papers."[83] The postmaster at Vincennes gave a similar warning,[84] and even the postriders occasionally found it necessary to notify persons on their routes, who had not paid the postage upon mail they had already received, that they could not be granted "further indulgence" unless they settled up. Even when accounts were promptly paid, the receipts from an early Western postoffice were usually meager. For example, at Canfield, Ohio, probably a typical smaller postoffice, the total receipts for the year 1803 were only $100.23, much of which was not

---

[82] *Louisiana Gazette,* February 28, 1811, to May 2, 1812, *passim.*
[83] *Centinel,* April 4, 1795.
[84] *Western Sun,* December 2, 1807.

paid promptly, and the compensation allowed the postmaster was only $30.56.[85] Doubtless at Cincinnati and other larger settlements, the receipts and the compensation were greater. But they were seldom sufficient in this early period to prove attractive to qualified appointees.

In spite of many obstacles, by 1812 the inhabitants of the Old Northwest had developed a fairly effective system of communication. With indomitable courage, great persistence, and practical sense they had established routes for commerce between the different settlements and the outside world, they had opened up many interior highways, and they had made possible a rather remarkable postal service, for a pioneer country. At first when there was constant danger from the Indians and a comparatively small demand for trade routes, the many waterways had been the chief means of communication. With a growing traffic there had been considerable development in the type of boats that were used, and the water routes had been made safer. The increasing use of the Ohio-Mississippi waterway as a trade route through New Orleans was also a notable development in this period. But the growth of population, especially in the interior, made necessary a more dependable means of transportation than by the navigable streams. The result was the development, particularly in Ohio, of a rather adequate network of highways. Ferries, bridges, taverns, and turnpikes, even, had been established, and important precedents had been set for the regulation of these public utilities. Other more backward sections of the Old Northwest patterned their transportation systems after the Ohio model, and by the outbreak of the War of 1812, fairly dependable communication had been opened between all the important settlements.

[85] Report of Elijah Wadsworth, January 1 to March 31, 1803, *Western Reserve MSS.*, no. 588.

Chapter XIII

THE RISE OF TRADE AND INDUSTRY

THE commercial and industrial development of the Western country kept pace with the swift opening up of communication. The fertile soil, coupled with the tremendous energy and resourcefulness of the pioneers, soon produced a surplus, and as a result trade sprang up in the little settlements. In a short time, also, there came to be an appreciation of the possibilities for the manufacture of raw products into finished goods, in order to save the high costs of transportation, and the industrial development that followed naturally gave rise to varied occupations, as the complex demands of the community increased. All these different phases of the gradual rise of trade and industry in a primitive country are strikingly illustrated in the Old Northwest. In the early period up to the War of 1812, the greatest commercial and industrial development took place in Ohio, the most thickly settled section at this time, and the one in which the system of communication had been most widely extended. In Indiana, while the parallel movement was somewhat less in degree, it followed the same general trend as in Ohio, and this was true, too, in Illinois. There was such slight general progress in Michigan, prior to 1812, that for the present purpose this section of the Old Northwest may be ignored. Elsewhere, the remarkable rise of trade and industry within scarcely two decades, in what was at first a primitive wilderness, was one more phase of the transformation which American settlement so swiftly wrought in the Old Northwest.

Long before American immigrants began to come in, there

was a large and profitable fur trade in the Western country. Beside the furs that were collected at the scattered trading posts within this territory, there were many shipments from the Missouri Valley and from other fur-producing regions west of the Mississippi, which were conveyed up the Illinois River, then by the Chicago River and Lake Michigan, or else through Prairie du Chien up the Wisconsin, and thence to the Great Lakes. Under the British, Detroit and Mackinaw became the main receiving points for this traffic, as well as for the furs collected in the Old Northwest itself. The rival route of the American traders was up the Ohio, or else across country to Pittsburgh and then eastward. St. Clair believed it would be possible to divert the bulk of the fur trade to this latter route, if all traders within the Old Northwest were compelled to take out licenses, and if garrisons were stationed at the chief trading posts. But neither condition was fulfilled, and even after the Western posts had been surrendered, Canadian traders continued to carry on a fur trade of extensive proportions. Michael la Croix, for example, from his headquarters at Peoria traded extensively with the Indians of the Illinois Valley, down to the outbreak of the War of 1812. However, a number of American traders carried on a large and increasing business in the early period of the Old Northwest. Among them Nicholas Jarrot, who settled at Cahokia in 1794, traded with the Indians as far up the Mississippi as Prairie du Chien. In favorable years he is said to have realized two hundred to three hundred per cent upon the varied assortment of goods he offered in exchange for furs, but he constantly ran great risks from the personal enmity of the Canadian traders.[1] The fur trade over the American routes to the seaboard was greatly increased after the government established its trading posts at Fort Wayne, Mackinaw, Chicago, and Sandusky. But so far as the Old Northwest was concerned, the traffic in furs was a negligible part of

[1] Reynolds, *Pioneer History of Illinois*, pp. 175-176 and 296.

its increasing commerce, and one that was destined to
dwindle away.

The rapid development of trade in the Western settlements was illustrated by the rise of Cincinnati, their chief
commercial center. A number of factors were responsible
for the growth of the original settlement made at Losantiville, late in 1788, to the thriving metropolis of the Old
Northwest with 2,320 inhabitants in 1810.[2] The establishment of Fort Washington in 1789, and the Indian campaigns
that followed, gave rise to a lively trade, while the needs of
the ever-increasing throng of immigrants passing down the
Ohio, not to speak of those of the inhabitants of this growing settlement itself, created another demand for supplies.
In each instance these commodities were collected by the
merchants of Cincinnati from the settlers on the hinterland
between the two Miamis, and from those on the Kentucky
side of the Ohio. Again, Cincinnati quickly became the commercial center of a thriving district owing to its strategic
location, convenient to watercourses that led into the interior
lands to the northward, and opposite the mouth of the
Licking, which was a natural highway to the rich blue-grass
lands of Kentucky. Vivid pictures of the trade that sprang
up so soon in this Western settlement are given in the account books of Smith & Findlay, a leading Cincinnati firm
of the day.[3] Up to 1796 their general store did a large business with the officers at Fort Washington and with the
different quartermasters. At the same time Smith & Findlay
shipped supplies by wagon for the troops at Fort Hamilton,
and during Wayne's campaign, like other Cincinnati business houses, they carried on a thriving business at his headquarters at Greenville. Civilian customers, too, rapidly increased as settlement expanded, coming from Cincinnati,
and from the near-by settlements, Columbia, North Bend,

[2] Drake, *Cincinnati in 1810*, reprint in *Quarterly*, Ohio Hist. and Phil.
Society, vol. III, no. 2, p. 30.

[3] *Smith & Findlay Account Books and Ledgers*, 1792–1800; *Diary of
Major William Stanley*, 1790–1810, *Quarterly*, Ohio Hist. and Phil. Society,
vol. XIV, nos. 2 and 3, pp. 19-32.

White's Station, from "up Miami," from "up Licking," and from Fort Hamilton. Much of this trade was wholesale, and the different Cincinnati houses were soon making shipments to retailers in Bardstown, Frankfort, and other settlements in the interior of Kentucky, and occasionally even to such distant points as Vincennes.

The variety of the goods offered by representative Cincinnati firms constantly increased, thus keeping pace with the rapidly growing prosperity of the settlers, and their correspondingly greater demands. Of home products, Smith & Findlay by 1795 sold whisky and brandy in large quantities, along with imported gin, Lisbon and Madeira wines, coffee, lump sugar, Bohea tea, and chocolate. In their stock of hardware they included cups and saucers, looking-glasses, china plates, "pains" of glass, spoons and tableware. In the list of "dry goods" were shawls, pocket handkerchiefs, combs, Nankeen linen, coating, and corduroy. Rival firms offered much similar stocks, one Cincinnati merchant calling especial attention to his "excellent bitters" made according to the "London dispensatory," and equal, if not superior, to any made by Stoughton.[4] Actually the stocks of merchandise offered by the average general store in Cincinnati soon compared favorably with those of similar establishments east of the Alleghenies. Thus, in 1799, William & M. Jones at their newly opened store advertised goods that ranged from queensware and hair powder to scythes and bar iron, and, as a sideline, this establishment sold "superfine and fine flour, bread, sea and butter biscuits, and light cakes."[5] In 1805 another typical Cincinnati firm offered for sale, ladies' and men's stockings and gloves, prints, "elastic spring and patent braces," morocco and kid shoes, and umbrellas and parasols, decanters, schoolbooks, and novels, with other goods too varied to mention. This firm, like other Cincinnati merchants, also advertised large stocks of Monon-

---

[4] *Centinel,* February 23, April 19, and July 12, 1794, and November 7, 1795.
[5] *Western Spy,* August 13, 1799.

gahela and Kentucky whisky, the two brands that appear
to have been most popular in the Western country at this
time.[6]

Marietta was secondary to Cincinnati alone as a trade
center in early Ohio, supplying the rich Muskingum Valley,
the settlers across the Ohio in Virginia, and many travelers
up and down the Ohio. Its general stores offered stocks similar to those in Cincinnati with many luxuries available by
1807—almonds, raisins, figs, port wine, old claret, and "cordial of Martinique," perfumes for ladies, silk umbrellas and
Madras handkerchiefs.[7] Chillicothe developed rapidly as
the trade center for the Scioto Valley. Beside the usual
assortment of merchandise its stores sold "velvet thick-set,
corduroy, and other fashionable Manchester goods," together with glassware and tools of various kinds. In the invariable stock of drinkables one Chillicothe merchant included cordials of seven different flavors, and another firm
advertised such luxuries for these Western settlements as
"pickled and spiced oysters, shad, mackerel, and herring."
In contrast to these last tidbits for the epicure, Overstreet's
Chewing Tobacco, sold by the keg, revealed the taste of
the everyday pioneer, and an extensive assortment of Pennsylvania tanned leather, and "Spanish soal leather" for sale,
showed how quickly civilized footgear had replaced the deer-
skin moccasins of the earliest settlers. The intense rivalry
between the merchants of Chillicothe was shown in the numerous advertisements of "fresh" and "cheap" goods which
were purportedly sold at the "most reduced prices."[8] A
number of other trading centers sprang up in Ohio as population grew, among them Steubenville in the upper Ohio
Valley and Warren in the Western Reserve. In Cleveland
with its few settlers there was comparatively little local

[6] *Western Spy*, September 4, 1805; *Liberty Hall*, August 27, 1808.
[7] *Ohio Gazette*, September 9, 1807.
[8] *Scioto Gazette*, June 4, 1801; *The Supporter*, December 30, 1809, March
17 and August 4, 1810, and August 11, 1811.

trade during this early period, and the first general store appears to have been opened in 1801.[9]

West of Ohio the chief commercial centers in the Old Northwest were Vincennes, Kaskaskia, and Cahokia. In Indiana, Louisville became the commercial center for the rapidly increasing population across the river in Clark's Grant, and Vincennes, as the territorial capital, soon boasted stores that advertised a really remarkable variety of goods, in view of the difficulties of transportation from the chief sources of supply. Their advertisements called attention to "handsome assortments" of dry goods, along with complete stocks of potter's ware and saddles, and many other articles that were in general use in regions that were much further developed.[10] In the Illinois country, probably the most successful merchant was William Morrison, who, coming from Philadelphia in 1790, established his main store at Kaskaskia with a branch at Cahokia. Beside a large retail trade in furs and agricultural products which he exchanged for a wide variety of goods, Morrison carried on an extensive wholesale business with merchants in St. Louis, Ste. Genevieve, and New Madrid. Another important mercantile business in this frontier country was carried on by William Bullitt & C. Smith, with stores at Vincennes, Kaskaskia, Cahokia, and Ste. Genevieve.[11]

The progress of trade in the Western country was nowhere more strikingly shown than in the rapid advance in the methods of carrying on sales. The earliest known type of mercantile establishment among the pioneers was the floating store, usually a large flatboat that had been roofed over and furnished with shelves and a counter. In its progress downstream this novel store offered its customers a varied assortment of goods, as they thronged to the different land-

[9] Whittlesey, *Early History of Cleveland,* p. 381.

[10] *Indiana Gazette,* September 11, 1804; *Western Sun,* April 20 and June 8, 1808, October 6, 1810.

[11] Reynolds, *Pioneer History of Illinois,* pp. 129-132; *Indiana Gazette,* September 25, 1804.

ing places.[12] Later, as settlement crept up the smaller streams, keel boats that could be navigated upstream against the current were utilized for this same purpose. With a larger population the general store situated in some convenient center of settlement was established, and with still more extensive trade, auction and market houses were opened. These establishments, which were owned and controlled by the respective communities in which they were erected, were a natural outcome of the strong opposition to monopoly which showed itself so forcibly in the Old Northwest in the many attempts to regulate utilities and business in the general public interest. As early as 1795 there was an auction house in Cincinnati for the sale of dry goods and other imported articles. In 1801 a public market house, also, was built in this same little frontier town, with the lower story of stone and the upper one of wood. This venture proved so successful that a second market house was erected in a short time. Markets were held four days in each week, and a town ordinance forbade purchases elsewhere of small quantities of flour, beef, pork, and vegetables while these public market houses were open. By 1815 there were three market houses altogether in Cincinnati, which offered the housewife at very reasonable prices a tempting array of poultry, meats, fish, vegetables, and fruits, along with such staples as butter, eggs, and cheese.[13] In this early period markets were established, also, at Vincennes, Chillicothe, and Steubenville. At Steubenville an especially interesting regulation undertook to ensure honest measurement of the wagonloads of "stone coal" that came to market in such large numbers.[14]

The bulk of the goods sold in the Old Northwest, espe-

[12] Cuming, *Sketch of a Tour to the Western Country*, p. 98.
[13] *Centinel*, November 21, 1795, and February 13, 1796; *Western Spy*, November 6, 1805; Greve, *Centennial History of Cincinnati*, vol. I, pp. 427 and 502; *Ohio Almanac* for 1810; Drake, *Statistical View of Cincinnati in 1815*, pp. 137, 140-141.
[14] *Western Herald*, September 26, 1807.

cially in the first decade of settlement, came from Philadelphia and Baltimore. The Western merchants made business trips to these Eastern cities, usually twice a year, returning with the extensive assortments of goods that so strikingly reflected the rapidly increasing purchasing power of these frontiersmen. An illustration of these purchasing expeditions was a journey eastward in August, 1797, of a representative of Riddle & Woodson who kept a large general store in Cincinnati. [15] Going first to Philadelphia, this merchant purchased a varied stock there that included, among other items, clothing, hardware, books, combs, scissors, razors, various tools, tableware, soap and other toilet articles, tin, and fourpenny nails "from the prison factory." From Philadelphia he went to Baltimore where he bought "James River Tobacco," Scotch snuff, wines, sugar, spices, chocolate, and raisins. Altogether, his purchases in the two cities totaled £2,051, 11s, 5d, and as the firm's stock on hand when he left Cincinnati was valued at only £518, 19s, 5d, evidently Riddle & Woodson counted upon a quick turnover in their merchandise.

The improvements in transportation soon lowered the excessive freight charges from Pittsburgh across the Alleghenies, and this route continued to be the chief one over which merchandise of high value was imported into the Western country as far west as Vincennes. The industrial development in the Pittsburgh district was of especial importance, since by saving high freight charges across the mountains, it greatly reduced the wholesale prices of glassware, window glass, and iron manufactures in the Western country. Merchants were now able to purchase in Pittsburgh "Juniatta" and "Monongahela" iron, slit iron and nails, which they sold to their customers, and by 1808 they could secure from these same Pittsburgh manufacturers such comparative luxuries for those times as woven wire screens to clean grain, fenders for fireplaces, sifters for bricklayers

[15] *Riddle & Woodson, Account Books,* 1797.

and plasterers, and screens for cellar windows and skylights.[16] In exchange for the manufactured goods and the luxuries imported from the Atlantic Coast, the chief shipments eastward from the Old Northwest up the Ohio and across the mountains were necessarily articles small in bulk and high in value, such as whisky, linen, hemp, maple sugar, and potash. An important trade soon developed, however, in cattle and hogs on the hoof which drovers collected and took east across the mountains. In the year 1810, it was estimated, fully 40,000 hogs alone were driven from Ohio to the Eastern markets, more than forty per cent of them from the Scioto Valley. The trade in cattle was equally extensive.[17]

But with the primitive means of transportation that were available, the Alleghenies stood in the way of trade upon any considerable scale up the Ohio and then east, and the inhabitants of the Western country soon turned to the Ohio-Mississippi route as an outlet for their bulky products. Already the French residents, and later the American inhabitants of Vincennes and the Illinois country, had pointed the way.[18] Thus, William Morrison was accustomed to ship furs, lead, flour, horses, and other products from the Illinois country down the Mississippi in barges that sometimes required 40 to 50 boatmen for the return trip. Gradually, too, as the Illinois settlers gave up hunting as a livelihood in favor of the more dependable agriculture, there was a marked increase in their trade down the Mississippi. But this traffic was soon completely overshadowed by the increasing shipments from Kentucky and Ohio, and to a less extent

[16] *Western Spy,* March 12, 1800; *Ohio Gazette,* March 7, 1808; *The Supporter,* October 20, 1809; *Liberty Hall,* June 16, 1812.

[17] Gephart, *Transportation in the Middle West,* pp. 92-93 and 103; *Scioto Gazette,* July 26, 1808, and November 29, 1809; *The Supporter,* October 27, 1810; Cramer's *Magazine Almanack* for 1812; *Niles Weekly Register,* vol. VI, p. 210.

[18] Reynolds, *Pioneer History of Illinois,* p. 131; *Western Spy,* June 18, 1799, August 19, 1801, and April 10, 1802; Galpin, *The Grain Trade of New Orleans, Miss. Valley Hist. Review,* vol. XIV, pp. 496-507.

by those from Indiana. Especially after the Spanish Treaty in 1795, which guaranteed free navigation of the Mississippi, the Ohio-Mississippi trade route made great strides, and the merchants of Cincinnati and other river settlements now advertised for flour, pork, and other products to be shipped to New Orleans. After the purchase of Louisiana there was much optimism in the Western country over the possibilities of the Ohio-Mississippi route. Under the nom de plume *Aristides*, a correspondent of the *Scioto Gazette* pointed out the inevitable flow of exports from the Old Northwest through New Orleans. The farmers, he considered, should form a closer union with the merchants, in order to secure their full share of the profits from this trade, for the latter were in a far better position to gather the products of the country and to export them.[19] This same optimistic viewpoint was an important influence in the movement in the Ohio Valley to build seagoing vessels that would convey Western products directly to foreign ports. While this particular undertaking was not a success, the flow of products down the Ohio-Mississippi route constantly increased. Thus, during the first six months of 1811, fifty-three boats left the Scioto Valley alone with cargoes valued at $83,900.00. About eighty per cent of this freight was made up of flour, pork, and wheat, while buckwheat, meal, lard, corn, horses, hogs, plank, Windsor chairs, nails, and an occasional wagon were in the remaining twenty per cent.[20] For the same year, 1811, the cargoes of the barges and flatboats, the majority of them probably having originated in the Old Northwest, that passed Louisville in less than two months bound down the river were valued at $223,660.50.[21]

The uncertainties of the Ohio-Mississippi trade were discouraging. Often the barges engaged in this traffic were wrecked on the way, or else they were captured by robbers.

[19] *Scioto Gazette*, October 1 and 29, 1803.
[20] *The Supporter*, July 20, 1811.
[21] *Ohio Gazette*, November 25, 1811.

Even when the cargoes reached New Orleans in safety, markets were uncertain, and selling agencies were at first badly organized. Altogether, these risks were too great for the individual shipper to assume, and the one possible solution was the organization of trading companies with adequate resources for such contingencies. The Ohio Company, founded at Pittsburgh in October, 1802, set an example which business men of Cincinnati followed a year later in the organization of the Miami Exporting Company, with a capital of $100,000.00, to do a general banking and exporting business.[22] This latter company promptly advertised for agricultural products to be shipped to New Orleans. Among the commodities which it offered to accept at first in payment of shares and later to buy for cash, were beef "on the foot," corn-fed hogs, flour, hemp, lard, meat, kiln-dried cornmeal, cordage, and barrels.[23] A number of similar organizations soon sprang up. In 1810 the Farmers Exporting Company, with headquarters in the Little Miami Valley, offered to accept for export, cornmeal, pork, flour, "inspected lard in ten-gallon cans of white walnut," whisky, hemp, and "good merchantable butter." The Cincinnati Exporting and Importing Company and the Farmers and Mechanics Exporting Company of Hamilton, also, were at least projected.[24] Soon the bulk of the trade from the Old Northwest down the Ohio-Mississippi route was being carried on through these corporations, or else through well-established firms, such as Smith & Findlay. Cincinnati, the chief port for this traffic, shipped bacon, pork, lard, flour, whisky, pot and pearl ashes, lumber and kiln-dried cornmeal. In return, its merchants received from New Orleans coffee, salt fish, claret, wines, mahogany, sugar, molasses and rice, lead and

22 *Pittsburgh Gazette,* October 8, 1802; *Laws of Ohio,* First General Assembly, pp. 126-136; Gephart, *Transportation in the Middle West,* pp. 99-100.

23 *Western Spy,* July 13, 1803, and October 10, 1804.

24 *Browne's Cincinnati Almanac* for 1811, p. 22; *Liberty Hall,* August 29, October 10 and 31, 1810, and January 18, 1814.

furs from Missouri, and tobacco and cotton from Kentucky
and Tennessee.[25]

With the growth of trade there came a noticeable tendency
toward the same governmental regulation that was exercised over transportation. The law adopted in 1792 by the
governor and judges, which required every storekeeper in
the Northwest Territory who sold articles not produced in
the United States, to take out an annual license with a fee
of $16.00, was exceedingly unpopular among a pioneer popu-
lation with its individualistic theories, and frequently it was
ignored.[26] The revised code of Ohio in 1805 required a similar license, with a fee of $10.00, and apparently this last
measure directed against the Canadian traders among the
Indians, was enforced. A law adopted in Indiana about this
time required, in similar fashion, an annual license, with a
fee of $15.00, to be taken out by any one who sold mer-
chandise "other than the produce or manufacture" of the
territory. This act must have proved difficult to enforce, for
it affected every owner of a general store, and in 1813 it
was repealed.[27] Another phase of this public regulation of
trade was marked by an act passed in 1802 in the Northwest Territory for the appointment of official inspectors to
test the quality and to examine the packing of all "wheat
or rye flour, Indian corn, or buckwheat, meal, biscuit, butter,
hog's lard, pork and beef" shipped to "any other state or
country." The safeguards provided against frauds were
quite practical, one clause in especial stipulating that an
inspector must use "a proper instrument" to see that flour
was well packed and of the standard indicated by the miller.
In a later act, the Ohio legislature added "post ashes or
pearl ashes" to the list of exports that must be carefully inspected. The members of the Indiana territorial legislature

[25] Drake, *Statistical View of Cincinnati in 1815*, p. 148.

[26] *Laws of the Northwest Territory*, Pease, ed., *Illinois Historical Collections*, vol. XVII, pp. 61-66; *Centinel*, February 7, March 28 and May 3, 1795.

[27] *Laws of Ohio*, Third General Assembly, pp. 96-104; *Laws of Indiana
Territory*, Fourth General Assembly, pp. 16-17, and Philbrick, ed., *Illinois
Historical Collections*, vol. XXI, pp. 75-76.

passed a much similar act, but they repealed it within a year, probably because of the opposition it had aroused.[28] Another measure to regulate business, which was passed in 1805 by the Ohio legislature, established standard measures for a foot, a yard, a bushel, and a gallon, with duplicates for each county in the state. Two years later this law, too, was repealed, although a much similar act in Indiana seems to have remained in force.[29]

One of the most serious obstacles to commercial development was the great scarcity of specie in the Old Northwest, especially in the first decade of settlement. This situation created the problem of finding an acceptable medium of exchange, and it was solved, in a fashion, by the universal custom of barter in both retail and wholesale trade. The account books of Smith & Findlay show how generally this Cincinnati firm accepted payments for their goods in this form.[30] The bulk of the commodities they received in trade were, of course, local agricultural products—butter, cheese, eggs, lard, ham, bacon, potatoes, cabbages, rye, and tobacco. Among the articles of local manufacture which were customarily traded in were: flour, buckwheat meal, Indian meal, cider, beer, brandy, salt, and in one three months' period, 3,095 gallons of whisky. Other articles in the long list which Smith & Findlay accepted on account were: "country" linen, rope, wool hats, candles, leather, deerskins, and even feather beds. A part of these varied commodities they absorbed in their local trade, but by far the greater portion they used in their extensive export business. Many unusual forms of payment in these same account books illustrate the scarcity of ready money in early Ohio. Occasionally,

[28] *Laws of the Northwest Territory,* Second General Assembly, First Session, pp. 92-100; *Laws of Ohio,* Tenth General Assembly, pp. 32-35; *Laws of Indiana Territory,* Fourth General Assembly, First Session, pp. 58-61, Second Session, pp. 90-91.

[29] *Laws of Ohio,* Fourth General Assembly, pp. 10-12; Sixth General Assembly, p. 166; *Laws of Indiana Territory,* Philbrick, ed., *Illinois Historical Collections,* vol. XXI, pp. 102-103.

[30] *Smith & Findlay, Ledgers,* 1793-1799.

horses were offered in payment, and Griffin Yeatman, a well-known tavern keeper in Cincinnati, partially settled his account with a yoke of oxen. Another account was credited with £19, 12s, 6d, for "22 sheep and a bell," others with a keel boat, a Kentucky boat, or a "periogg," and there was a credit item of £700 in 1796 for houses and lots in Hamilton. Smith & Findlay gave credit, too, for ordinary labor, listing such items as the repair of the firm's boat, labor in the garden, or work in making caps and "callicoe" shirts. Most unusual of all was the account of a Cincinnati clergyman for £6, 15s which included items of whisky that totaled four and a half gallons in less than three months. This account the firm settled by "our subscription for preaching."

That the custom of settling accounts by barter prevailed throughout the Old Northwest is shown by numerous advertisements and account books of this early period. The general stores in Chillicothe, Marietta, Steubenville, Warren, Vincennes, Kaskaskia, and other early settlements were accustomed to exchange their stocks for a long list of local products. Occasionally they accepted rather unusual commodities, as when a Marietta firm offered to receive in trade "hemp seed, tar, ginseng, snakeroot, or hog's lard," and a merchant in Chillicothe announced that he would accept beef cattle on the hoof in exchange for his entire stock.[31] The publishers of the local newspapers, also, were willing to receive payments in commodities from their many delinquent subscribers and advertisers. Thus, the publisher of the *Scioto Gazette* announced that he would accept cash, but in quite practical fashion he conceded an option in "wheat, flour, corn, sugar, beef, pork, flax, or country-made linen" for the benefit of all persons who owed him on account. At Vincennes the editor of the *Indiana Gazette,* likewise, was willing to receive payments in kind.[32] In truth, the list of commodities that were accepted in payment of these and other accounts really constituted a roll of the chief prod-

[31] *Ohio Gazette,* August 31, 1802.
[32] *Scioto Gazette,* October 15, 1804; *Indiana Gazette,* August 7, 1805.

ucts of the Old Northwest. Public opinion strongly supported this system of barter, chiefly upon the ground that it developed local economic independence. But with the increase in general business, the lack of a standard medium of exchange greatly interfered with many routine transactions, notably legal executions upon property. Yet the difficulties of early transportation alone were sufficient to prevent the accumulation of specie in the Western country upon any extended scale. As an illustration, during the War of 1812 the government shipped between $300,000.00 and $400,-000.00 in specie from Philadelphia to the Miami Exporting Company in Cincinnati, in order to pay for supplies for the troops, but the eight wagonloads into which this important shipment was divided were more than seven months on the way.[33] With specie so difficult to secure, the inhabitants of the Old Northwest were obliged to resort to such devices as "store checks" in payment of wages.

To meet the needs of an expanding commerce, the notes of Eastern banks soon began to be used as a common medium of exchange. This practice caused endless confusion from the many variations in the value of this paper money and the difficulty, at such a distance, to distinguish between the good and the bad notes. There were frequent public warnings, however, regarding the notes of unsound banks, and in 1807, Henry Clay, for example, called attention to certain questionable issues by banks in Maine and Massachusetts. An example of the losses that might come to holders of the obligations of distant banks was given by the notes of the Farmer's Exchange Bank of Gloucester, Rhode Island, which were widely circulated in the Northwest Territory, even after the bank had been closed and its paper was being accepted in Boston with a discount of ninety-five per cent.[34] The use of these notes of distant banks also became unsafe, because of the extensive operations of gangs

[33] *Western Spy*, November 7, 1812; *Liberty Hall*, June 8, 1813.
[34] *Western Spy*, June 11, 1807; *Liberty Hall*, July 12, 1809; *Commentator*, July 1, 1809.

of counterfeiters in the early West. The rather careless methods of printing banknotes and the distance of these settlements from the banks of issue made this practice a comparatively easy one, and counterfeit bills of the Bank of North America and of the United States Bank appeared as early as 1794. The occasional appearance of counterfeit silver dollars, and of forgeries of the personal notes which often circulated as cash, added to the general monetary confusion.[35] Cincinnati, as the chief commercial center, suffered especially. A particularly active gang of counterfeiters had its headquarters in the near-by settlement of Columbia at the mouth of the Little Miami. In 1805 the local officers seized an elaborate apparatus there for the manufacture of counterfeit paper dollars, and made a number of arrests. Upon another occasion, three members of a band which was rounded up in Columbia were committed to prison, two were bound over for appearance in court, and the remaining four escaped. In Cincinnati proper, there were also frequent arrests, as that of Ebenezer Case, who, arriving in September, 1810, supposedly on a business trip, was arrested when he attempted to pass a counterfeit $20.00 bill. After a jury had found him guilty, Case was sentenced to suffer twenty-five lashes, to go to prison for thirty days, and to pay a fine of $40.00, with the costs of prosecution.[36] Such severe sentences did not end the activities of these "banknote bootleggers," nor did they confine their activities to the Cincinnati area. In Washington County counterfeiting operations that were being carried on near Marietta were broken up in 1799, and even in the distant Illinois settlements counterfeit notes circulated in such large quantities that systematic and persistent measures were necessary to suppress them.[37]

[35] *Centinel,* August 2, 1794; *Freeman's Journal,* August 13 and October 22, 1796.
[36] *Western Spy,* April 17 and September 4, 1805, and December 29, 1810; *The Supporter,* July 28, 1809.
[37] Secretary of State to President of Bank of U. S., May 6, 1799, *Northwest Territorial Papers,* B. I. A. Dom.; *Louisiana Gazette,* January 11, 1812.

The one possible solution of the difficult problem of exchange for the Western country, lacking a sufficient supply of specie, was to establish local banks with power to issue secured notes which would be generally accepted. Ohio, with its growing trade, led the way, and the first bank, the Miami Exporting Company, organized at Cincinnati in 1803, soon gave up its commercial activities in order to engage in banking alone. It issued at least $100,000.00 in notes, which were well secured, and proved a great aid in supplying the need of the Western country for a medium of exchange. The Miami Exporting Company was quite prosperous, paying by 1810 an annual dividend of nine per cent which was soon increased to ten, and later to fifteen per cent. Among the other banks which were incorporated in Ohio in this early period were the Bank of Marietta and the Bank of Chillicothe, both chartered in 1808, to be followed a year later by the Bank of Steubenville. By 1814 the Ohio legislature had granted charters, also, to the Bank of Muskingum at Zanesville, to the Western Reserve Bank at Warren, and to the Farmers and Mechanics Bank and the Bank of Cincinnati at Cincinnati, while plans were on foot to organize banks at such interior trading points as Lebanon, Dayton, and Urbana.[38] The charter granted the Bank of Muskingum in 1812 illustrates the care with which the acts to incorporate these Ohio banks were drawn up. The capital stock was limited to $100,000.00, and the entire debt of the bank, including notes and bonds, could not exceed three times the capital that had actually been paid in. For any excess obligations the directors were to be held personally liable, a provision that should have ensured a sound paper money. Also, the charter restricted real-estate holdings to the banking house, or else to property taken over in satisfaction of a debt, and it prohibited any trading activ-

[38] Drake, *Statistical View of Cincinnati in 1815*, pp. 150-151; *Liberty Hall*, July 5, 1810; *Western Spy*, December 7, 1811; *Laws of Ohio*, Sixth to Twelfth General Assemblies, *passim*.

ities.[39] Under such careful regulations the early Ohio banks quickly acquired high standing both at home and abroad. Only two years after the Bank of Chillicothe was organized, its directors were able to purchase all of its shares that were held east of Philadelphia, and to offer them to, presumably, local persons who were specially interested. At the same time, they declared a semiannual dividend of five per cent, which they raised later to six per cent. Like other banks in Ohio, the Bank of Chillicothe constantly kept on hand a large stock of Eastern banknotes. Another proof of the general standing of the Ohio banks was the offer of a bank at Washington, Pennsylvania, to give silver in exchange for the notes of the Bank of Marietta and of other good Western banks. Also, in 1812 subscription books were opened in Pittsburgh for the shares of the newly organized Bank of Muskingum, an enterprise which, it was believed, would promote industry in Ohio and would greatly increase real-estate values there.[40]

In Indiana in the early days of settlement, would-be bankers undertook to meet the demand for a medium of exchange by setting up "wildcat" banks, in which the chief stock in trade was a supply of nicely engraved banknotes. If business prospered the banker might redeem all, or at least a part of these notes. If not, as more frequently happened, he left the country, leaving his late neighbors a legacy of worthless paper. In Madison the local merchants issued "shinplaster" notes of 6¼ cents, 12½ cents, and 50 cents respectively, in order to provide some sort of monetary standard. But barter continued as the chief means of carrying on business throughout this early period, and the first two Indiana banks were chartered in 1814, one at Vincennes, the other one at Madison.[41] In Illinois there was a much similar situation, and barter sufficed for the limited amount

[39] *Laws of Ohio,* Tenth General Assembly, pp. 40-51.

[40] *The Supporter,* August 11, 1809, January 13, 1810, and July 6, 1811; *Scioto Gazette,* July 17, 1809; *Pittsburgh Gazette,* March 27, 1812.

[41] Esarey, *History of Indiana,* vol. I, pp. 264-265.

of trading until 1816, when the log-cabin bank at Shawneetown was granted the first banking charter that was issued
in the territory.[42]

The lack of specie and the generally unsettled monetary
situation, even after the establishment of banks, was largely
responsible for the unsatisfactory business conditions in the
Old Northwest. Other important factors were the uncertainties of trade, and the excessive optimism of a pioneer community. In any case there were frequent bankruptcies, and
in Ohio many insolvent debtors applied for the benefit of
the bankruptcy law, with nine such notices in a single issue
of *The Supporter* which was published at Chillicothe. There
were also occasional applications in Indiana for the relief
of bankrupt individuals or firms.[43] The invariable complaint
in these applications was that the collection of accounts was
almost impossible, and this statement is borne out by the
many and varied appeals to hard-hearted debtors. Some
creditors urged their claims in rather gentle terms; others,
exasperated almost to the breaking point, threatened re-
calcitrant debtors with the law, and a druggist in Cincinnati complained that he would be unable to send for a fresh
supply of medicine unless his customers settled their accounts. The printer of the *Scioto Gazette* announced that
as he had contracted for new type, to be paid for in cash,
he must ask subscribers to settle all their arrears. A Chillicothe merchant first offered to extend a month's credit to
his customers, and then, after many losses, he refused to
allow any credit whatsoever.[44] Many similar incidents might
be cited of frantic appeals by creditors throughout the Old
Northwest for the settlement of accounts. But many of
them were in vain, and as a result many pioneer business
and professional men, thoroughly disgusted with their tardy

[42] Buck, *Illinois in 1818*, pp. 69, 148.
[43] *The Supporter*, March 17, 1810; *Western Sun*, August 11, 1810.
[44] *Centinel*, August 9, 1794; *Scioto Gazette*, January 2, 1802, and August
27, 1803; *The Supporter*, March 17, 1810; *Indiana Gazette*, September 11,
1804; *Louisiana Gazette*, December 7, 1811.

and unsatisfactory collections, forsook the Western settlements to return to their old homes in the East.

The many financial difficulties of the early settlers, added to the high costs of transportation, resulted in a significant movement in the Old Northwest in favor of local economic independence. A correspondent of the *Scioto Gazette* pointed out that the purchase of goods from distant sources of supply used up the money in circulation, drawing it away from the West, and that, at the same time, it took away the agricultural products without making any adequate return to the soil. In like fashion, the Vincennes paper, the *Western Sun*, in an especially able series of articles, strongly favored domestic manufactures.[45] Besides these articles, and numerous newspaper comments of a similar nature, many toasts at Fourth of July banquets and other celebrations were of the same tenor, and in 1809 the Ohio legislature passed a joint resolution that the members of the two houses should appear at the opening of the next session clad in "home manufactures." As a further means of stimulating this domestic industry, a contributor to a Cincinnati newspaper advocated an increase in the flocks of sheep, another one urged the ladies to save the high prices they paid for imported goods by spinning at home, and still other writers strongly urged the establishment of factories in the Western country.[46]

One of the first practical evidences of the movement in the Old Northwest in favor of home manufactures was the attempt to develop the local salt wells. Although an abundant and a cheap supply of salt was a matter of vital importance, it proved to be a difficult problem for the pioneers of the early West. At first they were obliged to pay from $6.00 to $10.00 per bushel for the salt which was brought over the mountains on packhorses. Later they secured a supply from Kentucky at $2.00 to $2.50, but it was not

[45] *Scioto Gazette,* October 1, 1803; *Western Sun,* May 19, 1810, and *ff.*
[46] *Laws of Ohio,* Seventh General Assembly, p. 230; *Liberty Hall,* July 12, 1809, and May 16 and August 29, 1810; *Western Spy,* February 5, 1814.

sufficiently large to satisfy the demands of a rapidly increasing population.[47] Fortunately there were a number of salt springs on the public lands in the Old Northwest, and they were soon made available for general use. In the enabling act of 1803, the Federal government handed over all these wells within Ohio to the new state, and beginning with its first session the legislature passed a long series of acts to utilize them. At first it attempted to make the large wells in the Scioto Valley a source of profit, but when scheme after scheme of this type had failed, the legislature in desperation offered lessees sites that were practically free of all charges for rent. But the results were not at all satisfactory, and persistent efforts to develop salt wells on the Muskingum above Marietta and at Delaware in central Ohio were scarcely more successful.[48] For the settlers in Ohio the chief source of their salt supply continued to be western New York and Kentucky, although, about 1810, "Kenhawa" salt began to come in. Customarily the salt from western New York was transported by Lake Erie to Cleveland, and from there packhorses or oxteams hauled it overland to the head of navigation on the Tuscarawas, or else to Worthington near the Scioto, and from these points it was distributed in central and southern Ohio. At Springfield in the interior, "lake" salt was offered in 1810 at $2.50 per bushel, and at Steubenville in southern Ohio in 1806 the price was $3.00 per 56 pounds.[49]

The one salt spring that was of real value to the inhabitants of the Old Northwest was the Wabash Saline in southern Illinois, about thirty miles west of the Wabash. Here the Federal government reserved a rectangular area, ten by

[47] *Centinel,* April 19, 1794; *Freeman's Journal,* March 18, 1797; *Western Spy,* October 8, 1800, and April 15, 1801; Gephart, *Transportation in the Middle West,* pp. 85-86.

[48] *Laws of Ohio,* First to Twelfth General Assemblies, *passim;* Cramer, *The Navigator,* ed. 1808, p. 50; *Ohio Gazette,* September 7, 1802.

[49] *The Supporter,* January 26, 1811; *Scioto Gazette,* March 21, 1810; *Ohio Almanac* for 1810; *Browne's Cincinnati Almanac* for 1811, p. 31; *Western Herald,* December 20, 1806; *Muskingum Messenger,* March 31, 1810.

thirteen miles, which was the site of extensive salt springs, and placed it under the management of the territorial authorities. While Harrison was in control, his avowed policy was to consider the pressing need of the pioneers for a supply of salt at a low price, as superior to any consideration of profit to the government.[50] After Illinois was set off from Indiana, the Wabash Saline was included in the new territory, and its management devolved upon Governor Edwards, who continued Harrison's general policy. Under his supervision, the wells proved quite productive and were well managed, but it was impossible to meet the large and increasing demand for salt when it was offered at so reasonable a rate. Finally the government agent at the Wabash Saline announced in 1808 that he could only fill applications when they were accompanied with the cash for payment, and even then, he warned, the supply might prove insufficient. Very soon he found it was necessary to limit the salt sold to any one individual to $325.00 in value. The Wabash Saline continued to prosper, producing annually, by 1811, 150,000 bushels, which sold at 70 cents per bushel on the spot. Shawneetown soon became the main shipping point for this salt, and these wells assured an abundant supply throughout the Indiana and Illinois settlements, as well as in the near-by regions.[51]

Still another practical evidence of the movement for local economic independence was the establishment of mills, at which the farmer could convert his grain into flour or meal for his own use or else for exchange for the commodities he needed. At first the pioneers used hand mills, crude contrivances that were little better than Indian mortars. Another early device was the floating mill, which consisted of two flatboats to hold the machinery, with a wheel between

---

[50] Harrison's *Messages and Letters*, Esarey, ed., vol. I, pp. 157-158.
[51] *Western Sun*, August 13, 1808, and April 22, 1809; *Louisiana Gazette*, July 12 and 19, 1810; Cramer, *The Navigator*, ed., 1808, p. 50; ed., 1811, p. 136 (note).

them that was turned by the river current. A mill of this type possessed a twofold advantage: it was easily moved, and when it was anchored off shore it was safe from Indian attacks. But horse mills and water mills gradually replaced these primitive contrivances, until the gristmill became a familiar object in the early Ohio landscape. Usually the same plant included a sawmill also, and thus provided the cornmeal, flour, and lumber for export as well as for local use.

In the early period many inducements were offered to settlers who would found mills. Thus, in 1798, the Connecticut Land Company promised a bounty of $200.00, or else a loan of $500.00 on easy terms, to those persons who would erect certain badly needed mills in the Western Reserve. About a year later the first mill in this region was opened at Warren as a combined grist and sawmill, and there is contemporary testimony that it "ground tolerably well," although each customer was obliged to bolt his own flour.[52] A typical mill property of the early West was one in Jefferson County, Ohio, which boasted two grindstones and two bolting cloths, with a horse mill near by that was especially useful during the frequent droughts, and a sawmill.[53] As population moved westward, mills of this type also began to appear in Indiana and Illinois. A famous mill in Illinois was the one Henry Levens erected in the American settlement at New Design. Here much flour was ground for export, and here, too, the lumber was sawed, so it was claimed, for almost all the flatboats that were built in the early Illinois settlements.[54] Incidentally, the principle of public regulation was applied to mills, also, in the Old Northwest, the law fixing the charges to be made by the miller, and providing severe penalties for such petty crimes

[52] *Resolution, Connecticut Land Company,* December 4, 1798; *Notes by Leonard Case,* in *James Perkins' Scrap Book,* p. 186.
[53] *Western Herald,* February 7, 1807.
[54] Reynolds, *Pioneer History of Illinois,* pp. 127-128, 143-144.

as false measures, or the theft of any grain that had been brought to a mill to be ground.[55]

The distillery was almost as important as the mill to the inhabitants of the Old Northwest, inasmuch as whisky was a well-nigh universal pioneer remedy for real or imaginary ills, and it soon became an important article of export as well. No doubt making use of experience already acquired in western Pennsylvania and Kentucky, the pioneers soon began to use their corn and rye in the distillery. As a result, distilling developed so rapidly that by 1795 a Federal inspector was stationed in the Ohio district to enforce the internal revenue laws.[56] Breweries, too, were soon started, among them the Cincinnati Brewery, opened in 1812, which supplied merchants, innkeepers, the "river trade," and citizens in general with draft beer, and with bottled ale and porter that had been made "in the best Philadelphia manner." These breweries, like the distilleries, occupied an important position in early Western economy, absorbing as they did a large part of the crops. Thus, one Cincinnati brewer offered to contract for 20,000 bushels of barley for the coming season, and his rival wanted 12,000 bushels.[57] Beside supplying the local demand, the breweries followed the example of the distilleries, and shipped part of their product down the Ohio-Mississippi route. The initial expenditure of the Western distiller was not large. An ordinary still sold, complete, for $45.00 and up, and the capacity usually varied between 50 and 150 gallons. But workmen with experience in distilling were scarce, and distillers were constantly on the lookout for labor-saving devices, and were, consequently, probably a little gullible. In 1802 a patented still was offered for sale that was warranted to work off "spirits" of the standard quality with a fifth of

[55] *Laws of the Northwest Territory*, Pease, ed., *Illinois Historical Collections*, vol. XVII, pp. 366-368; *Laws of Ohio*, Third General Assembly, pp. 154-155; *Laws of Indiana Territory*, Philbrick, ed., *Illinois Historical Collections*, vol. XXI, pp. 361-366.

[56] *Centinel*, March 28, 1795.

[57] *American Statesman*, March 10, 1812; *Centinel*, September 12, 1795; *Liberty Hall*, April 13, 1813; *Western Spy*, June 12 and 26, 1813.

the labor, a tenth of the fuel, and not more than a tenth of the operating cost of the old-time still. Rights were offered for sale, also, to use in the Western country a new method of distilling which, it was claimed, would require one-half the fuel, and one-half the copper in the usual distillery.[58]

The desire for local economic independence in Ohio soon showed itself in a miscellaneous list of manufactures that were intended primarily to meet the demands of the home market, although, as the country developed, there came to be a surplus for export as well. Foremost among these products was maple sugar which was made upon an extensive scale, and potash, or "pearl ash," a product of the many ashes that accumulated when the backwoodsmen cleared the land, or when they kindled the universal wood fire. In Cincinnati the owners of a "pot and pearl ash factory" offered 6 cents for a quarter bushel of wood ashes, and they were willing to collect them from the doorsteps.[59] Tanneries, also, were soon established, and journeyman tanners came to be in great demand. A type of manufacture that was quite in line with the movement for local economic independence was the production of grindstones for mills. The prices of grindstones imported over the mountains were almost prohibitive in view of the high freight charges on such bulky articles, yet they were essential to the pioneer. In their usual practical fashion the early settlers in Ohio proceeded to utilize an important quarry near Chillicothe, which, it was claimed, produced grindstones, selling at $80.00 to $120.00, that were superior to French "burrs" and ground a "nicer" flour.[60] Another important local industry that circumstances practically compelled the inhabitants of the Old Northwest to undertake was the manufacture of paper. In winter especially, before there was a local source of supply, the early Western newspapers were often compelled to suspend for weeks for want of the paper

[58] *Western Spy*, September 3, 1800, and March 13, 1802; *Scioto Gazette*, November 5, 1803; *The Supporter*, June 29, 1811.
[59] *Liberty Hall*, January 10, 1810.
[60] *Niles Weekly Register*, vol. III, p. 320.

that was held up by ice on the waterways, or else by impassable highways. The first recorded paper mill in the Old Northwest was the one established on Little Beaver Creek in eastern Ohio in 1808. Two years later there was a second one at Lancaster, and in 1811 one was established at Cincinnati. The proprietors of this latest establishment offered to buy rags from the thrifty housewives at 3 cents per pound, and they seem to have furnished the local newspapers with a steady supply of paper.[61] But the most extensive local manufactures in this early period, both in value and in output, were the household products, especially woolen goods and linens, which were made by the thrifty pioneer women. Spinning wheels and looms were important articles of commerce, and as the volume of household manufactures grew, machines were set up in the settlements to prepare and card the wool for the spinner, while dyeing establishments, also, soon appeared. One of the latter at Chillicothe offered to dye woolen goods blue, China blue, purple, slate, chocolate, Turkey red, and many other shades.[62] Rope, too, was made from home-grown hemp, and there were other miscellaneous household manufactures too numerous to mention in detail.

By 1812, the astounding increase in production and the improvements in communication had made possible at least the beginning of modern industrialism in Ohio, with cotton or woolen factories at such important centers as Cincinnati, Marietta, and Chillicothe. At Zanesville and Steubenville the inhabitants were beginning to make use in their iron furnaces of the near-by deposits of iron ore and "stone coal." [63] The use of steam as a motive power came across the Alleghenies to the Old Northwest as early as the fall of 1809, when a cotton factory in Cincinnati was "formed upon the English

[61] *Western Herald,* July 15, 1808; *Scioto Gazette,* May 16, 1810; *Western Spy,* January 26, 1811.

[62] *Western Herald,* July 19, 1807; *Trump of Fame,* December 10, 1812; *The Supporter,* February 17, 1810.

[63] *Pittsburgh Gazette,* December 21, 1804; *Pittsburgh Magazine Almanack* for 1811 and for 1813; Melish, *Travels,* pp. 240-241; *Niles Weekly Register,* vol. II, p. 31; vol. VI, pp. 209-210.

Manchester plan." About the same time a steam mill established at Marietta operated "fully to the satisfaction of the engineers and proprietors," grinding a bushel of grain in three minutes, and at Chillicothe, under the leadership of Thomas W. Worthington, the citizens organized the Chillicothe Manufacturing Society to utilize local products and thus save a part of the large sums that were being sent away for outside manufactures. Other modern factories were proposed at Springfield and at Dayton.[64] The extent of these industrial strides in early Ohio was forcibly shown in the Census for 1810 which gave the annual value of the state's manufactured products as $2,894,290.00.[65] This estimate, however, was too low, since it did not include flour, meal, and the various other products of the numerous mills, and it omitted many household manufactures in regions that were too remote to be reported to the census taker. In the separate items, household manufactures included 1,943,333 yards of woven goods alone valued at $999,538.00, and among the industrial establishments distilleries came first in the value of their product, with tanneries second. Already iron furnaces showed considerable activity, and naileries supplied an especially important local need. Cotton and woolen factories, fulling mills and salt works were found in the long list of manufacturing plants that reflected the progress the inhabitants of Ohio had made toward local economic independence.

In Indiana and Illinois there was a much similar story, although industrial development in these more sparsely settled regions was much smaller in volume and variety. In Indiana, the annual value of all manufactures in 1810 was given as approximately $300,000.00, undoubtedly a very low estimate, in view of the difficulties in securing information from so

[64] *Ohio Almanack* for 1810; *Liberty Hall*, October 17, 1810; *Western Spectator*, December 14, 1811, and January 18, 1812; *Scioto Gazette*, March 7, 1810; *The Commentator*, October 14, 1807; Drake, *Statistical View of Cincinnati in 1815*, p. 47.

[65] *Arts and Manufactures of the United States for the Year 1810*, prepared by Tench Coxe, pp. 38 and 115-120.

many scattered settlements.[66] Household manufactures, valued at $159,051.63, made up more than half of this total, and included woolen, linen, and cotton goods. For this last-named domestic product the housewife was offered "Tennessee cotton" of good quality, to be had in Vincennes. The development of household manufactures created also a demand for wool carding and dyeing, and John Bruner of Vincennes announced he would dye cotton and wool either pale or deep blue, accepting in payment "good ashes," tow thread, and flax. The Agricultural Society of Vincennes greatly encouraged these home manufactures by its annual offer of prizes for the best woven cotton, woolen, and linen goods.[67] Other types of domestic manufactures were not neglected, and by 1810 Indiana boasted a number of distilleries, tanneries, grist and sawmills, naileries and even one small cotton factory. In the few settlements in Illinois the annual value of manufactures was estimated in 1810 as $120,000.00, and here, too, household manufactures headed a list that included the products of distilleries, tanneries, five grist and sawmills combined, and at least one large brickyard.[68] These beginnings of industrialism in the distant Illinois settlements reflected the strides that had been made by the movement for economic independence throughout the Old Northwest. For the entire region, by 1810 the total annual value of all manufactures was $3,314,290.00, an estimate that would doubtless have been larger had a more thorough survey been possible.[69]

One of the chief obstacles to industrial development in the Old Northwest was the same scarcity of labor that had been so effective in limiting the size of agricultural holdings. When varied industries began to develop in the settlements, the custom of taking on apprentices helped to solve somewhat the problem of a sufficient and a dependable supply of labor. But they were often hard to hold, as many advertisements for the

[66] *Arts and Manufactures of the United States for the Year 1810,* prepared by Tench Coxe, pp. 38 and 162 *ff.*
[67] *Western Sun,* July 1, 1809, February 18, and May 26, 1810.
[68] *Arts and Manufactures of the United States for the Year 1810,* prepared by Tench Coxe, pp. 38 and 164-165.
[69] *Ibid.,* p. 38.

return of runaways testified, and judging by the rewards offered, the masters often considered their apprentices of little value. One irate master offered a reward of 6 cents for the return of an apprentice but "not thanks," and another one sarcastically advertised he would give "one chew" of tobacco immediately upon the return of his runaway apprentice, and a half bushel of potatoes the following fall.[70] This general scarcity of labor was felt especially in the larger settlements. In the more remote regions the storekeeper, the blacksmith, the gunsmith, and the miller supplied the chief needs of the backwoods farmers. But the growth of the small towns created a lively demand for the brickmakers, the bricklayers, the stonemasons, and the carpenters who were needed to erect the more elaborate buildings that so quickly replaced the pioneer cabins. A growing export trade, too, called for coopers to fashion the barrels that held flour, corn, and pork. Likewise, increasing luxury made a place for watch and clock makers, and even the eternal housekeeping problem arose, with advertisements, familiar to modern ears, for a "girl" to do the general housework. In response to the demand for greater specialization, butchers, tailors, and other tradesmen appeared, and certainly at Chillicothe there was a tombstone maker. Barbers, too, came in, notably one individual of an enterprising nature who heartily congratulated the citizens of Marietta upon his arrival, promising "the most exquisite satisfaction to all who may need his services."[71] John Martin, who came from Baltimore in 1806, opened an up-to-date establishment in Cincinnati, where gentlemen could have their hair dressed "in the most fashionable mode." Those who wished to appear well on Sunday night might call on Saturday, and Martin would arrange their hair so that, "by merely combing it out it will look as well as if dressed that morning." Martin also sold a variety of perfumes, cosmetics, and toilet articles that appealed to the feminine taste.[72]

[70] Scioto Gazette, January 31, 1810; Western Spy, March 9, 1811.
[71] The Commentator, October 29, 1807.
[72] Western Spy, June 24, 1806.

Many evidences show that this scarcity of labor in the Old Northwest persisted. Thus, in 1799 there was not a single blacksmith within twenty miles of Dayton, and at Vincennes, in 1811, the publisher of the *Western Sun,* unable to secure qualified assistance, was obliged to issue his paper for a time as a biweekly sheet.[73] With so great a demand and such a comparatively small supply, labor became quite independent, and in Cincinnati the carpenters and the shoemakers organized in order to regulate wages in their respective trades.[74] Naturally this scarcity of workingmen in the growing settlements of the Old Northwest led to comparatively high wages. Stonemasons, for instance, received $1.00 to $1.50 per day, and other handicraftsmen were paid on about the same scale. At Vincennes, the publisher of the *Western Sun* offered to pay $30.00 per month and "boarding found" to a good journeyman printer.[75] Such wages were sufficient to provide a comfortable living, in view of the low cost of local products and the constantly decreasing prices of supplies from the outside. In 1810, prices at Marietta and Cincinnati were fully ten per cent less than at Pittsburgh, with flour selling at $4.00 per barrel, beef, mutton, and veal at 4 cents to 5 cents per pound, fowls at $1.00 per dozen, eggs at 6 cents to 10 cents per dozen, and whisky at 37½ cents to 40 cents per gallon. House rent, too, was reasonable, varying, as an average, between $30.00 per annum at Zanesville and $60.00 at Cincinnati. Customarily there was a garden on each house lot, so that the tenant could supplement the supplies he bought at the general store with an abundance of vegetables and small fruits.[76]

The swift development of the Old Northwest soon attracted an influx of professional men, teachers, ministers, physicians, and lawyers. At that time, teaching was not re-

[73] *Western Spy,* September 10, 1799; *Western Sun,* January 5, 1811.
[74] *Western Spy,* February 5, 1800, and September 26, 1812.
[75] Bradbury, *Travels in America,* in Thwaites, *Early Western Travels,* vol. V. pp. 287, 306; *Smith & St. Clair Ledger, 1802–1811; Western Sun,* February 9, 1808.
[76] Melish, *Travels,* vol. II, pp. 53-268, *passim.*

garded as a profession that required special preparation, and certainly there were no general professional standards for the frontier minister. As between the doctors and the lawyers, the former should logically have been in much greater demand in a region where ague and rheumatic complaints abounded, and where sanitation and hygienic principles in general were so commonly disregarded. Nevertheless, physicians met scanty financial encouragement, and the first one who appeared at Marietta soon found that his stock of medicines was exhausted, although few actual patients had appeared. Since collections were correspondingly meager he returned, thoroughly disgusted, to his native Massachusetts.[77] Dr. Drake, even, conceded to be the most eminent physician in the Western country, found it necessary to announce that he was "open for practice at the usual place," and was especially "anxious" to see all persons who were indebted to him. Moreover, he followed the usual custom of pioneer physicians, and supplemented his fees by the profits from a "medical shop," in which he kept an "extensive assortment of genuine medicines," and of medical books, Cooper's *Surgical Dictionary*, the *Massachusetts Pharmacopœia* and the like. All sales, according to his advertisement, would be on a strictly cash basis; but like other business and professional men in the Old Northwest, Dr. Drake was obliged to accept corn, rye, pork, and other commodities from his customers and patients.[78]

With the increase in population, apothecaries started "medicine stores," where they sold a wide variety of drugs and toilet supplies, salnitre, salts, toothache drops that gave "immediate relief," along with toothbrushes, lotions for the face and skin, and damask lip salve. Stocks of surgical supplies and instruments met the need for home treatment in many remote settlements, and a Dr. Sellman, who claimed to be the first person engaged in "the business of an apothecary regularly" in Cincinnati, offered as early as 1812 to put

[77] *Barker Diary*, p. 23.
[78] *Liberty Hall*, May 9, 1810, and May 8, 1811.

up "assortments of medecine suitable for private families,"
with "plain and obvious directions." Like his contemporaries,
he also sold dyes, paints, and varnishes. A rival Cincinnati
apothecary, at the sign of the Pestle and Mortar, proposed
to carry on a wholesale as well as a retail trade, selling country physicians and merchants a wide variety of medical supplies.[79] An interesting local touch was given by the earnest
request of many of these early drug stores that their customers would return all empty bottles. The "apothecary"
shops, and the general stores as well, especially in the smaller
towns, also sold the patent medicines which enjoyed a wide
popularity in this pioneer country. Among these supposedly
infallible remedies, most of them imported from the Atlantic
seaboard, were Bateman's drops, Godfrey's cordial, Dr.
Steers' "chymical Opodellock," Anderson's pills, Church's
cough drops, "tasteless" ague pills, and Hamilton's worm-
destroying lozenges. The various remedies prepared by
Samuel H. P. Lee, widely proclaimed as a member of the
Connecticut Medical Society, were also advertised upon an
extensive scale, and they included anti-bilious pills, worm-
destroying lozenges, an elixir, ague and fever drops, a restor-
ative, and an ointment that, it was claimed, had cured 20,000
cases of the itch. A pamphlet with testimonials was quite
similar in its make-up to such publications of the present day,
especially in the claim that Lee's remedies would be effica-
cious in virtually all the diseases to which mankind is heir.
In like fashion there were widespread advertisements of
Paul's Columbian Oil as a cure for rheumatism, consumption,
pains in any part of the body, colds, toothache, croup, pleu-
risy, bloody flux, mumps, and lastly as a "bracer to the re-
laxed fiber" that would "restore it to its proper tone." Most
astounding of all, however, in their appeal to the credulous
were the advertisements which ascribed most remarkable
qualities to the Elixir of Longevity. According to flamboyant
public notices, the inventor of this magic preparation, Dr.
Yement of Sweden, had lived to the ripe age of 104, his

[79] *Western Spy*, April 3, 1802, and May 21, 1808.

mother to 107, his father to 112, and his grandfather to 114 years. Fortunately this long-lived mixer of patent medicines was safely out of the reach of any inquisitive Westerner, or rather his heirs, who might have tested the Elixir.[80]

The general human gullibility of these pioneers was doubtless responsible for the equally extravagant claims put forth by many of the "tooth doctors" who found their way into the Old Northwest. A typical representative of this gentry announced that he would take care of all diseases of the mouth, and of premature decay and deficiencies of the teeth. He would set artificial teeth, so that they would be "useful and highly ornamental," and would use "tenderness and care in the different operations," ensuring "beauty and elegance," and observing the "utmost candor" in his advice. Also, he had on sale a remarkable oil that would cure toothache without any need for extraction, and a like effective liquid that would fasten the teeth to the gums. In contrast to this advertisement, a much more conservative "surgeon dentist" merely advised parents to see that their children's teeth were properly cared for, and offered, like most of his confreres, to return the fee to any patient who was not satisfied with his "performance." [81]

Beside the vendors of patent medicines and the charlatan "tooth doctors," a flock of medical quacks, which descended upon the Old Northwest, were a veritable plague to the really qualified physicians. The unsatisfactory standards of the medical profession in the early days of settlement were strikingly illustrated by the record of one enterprising settler who first practiced law, then "physick," and wound up as a tanner and a parson. Another individual, somewhat more aggressive, advertised that his "electric and galvanic medical apparatus" would cure sufferers from "bruises, ulcers, headaches, lockjaw, palsy, gout, rheumatic pains, toothache occasioned by colds," and many other afflictions, and that "deranged" per-

[80] See especially, *Liberty Hall*, October 29, 1808, and May 11, 1813; *The Supporter*, July 7, 1810, and August 24, 1811.
[81] *Western Spy*, March 12, 1808, and November 9, 1811.

sons would receive much benefit from this same treatment. Other so-called medical men offered to cure cancers, cataracts, and other surgical cases without fail, usually upon a basis of "no cure, no pay." [82] In the face of such extravagant claims, the really qualified practitioners took up the cudgels against the quacks. Frequently there were wordy battles that crowded newspaper columns with the rival claims of the qualified physicians, and the quacks who were found even in the distant Illinois settlements. Under the leadership of Dr. Daniel Drake, in 1811 the more reputable physicians of Ohio secured a law that required all practitioners to take out a license which was based upon "good moral character," and at least three years' training in the theory and practice of medicine, or else they must present a certificate from a recognized medical society. In addition, candidates must answer satisfactorily questions put by an examining board, in "anatomy, surgery, materia medica, chymistry, and the theory and practice of medecine." [83]

During the régime of the governor and judges in the Northwest Territory, there were no formal restrictions upon the legal fraternity, and lawyers practiced in the early territorial courts with no apparent standards for admission to the bar. Nevertheless, there was an exceptionally able group of lawyers in the territory in these early days. In 1799, Jacob Burnet, whose standing among the lawyers was comparable to that of Dr. Daniel Drake among the physicians, induced the first territorial assembly to pass an act that set up standards, of a kind, for admission to the territorial bar. By this measure, the governor was to issue a license, upon a certificate from the general court that the applicant was of "good, moral character," and had studied law for four years in the territory. A lawyer who moved into the Northwest Territory

[82] Cuming, *Sketches of a Tour to the Western Country*, p. 92; *Liberty Hall*, June 16, 1812; *Scioto Gazette*, January 30 and February 20, 1804, and August 7, 1806; *Western Spectator*, August 1, 1812; *Louisiana Gazette*, May 24, 1810, February 14, March 14, and April 18, 1811.
[83] *Laws of Ohio*, Ninth General Assembly, pp. 19-23; *Liberty Hall*, January 16, 1811.

might be admitted to an examination for a license after twelve months' residence, provided he produced a certificate from an outside court of record, while residents of any state might practice, provided they presented satisfactory evidence of their competence. The Ohio legislature partially altered these requirements in 1804, by an act that recognized the need for less centralized authority in this respect, and transferred the power to issue licenses from the governor to any two judges of the supreme court of the state.[84] In Indiana, in 1803, the governor and the judges delegated to any judge of the general court the power to examine applicants and to issue licenses to practice law in the territory. But by the code of 1807, the territorial legislature required licenses to be issued by at least two judges of the general court, and, following a rather noticeable tendency toward provincialism, it forbade non-residents to practice in the Indiana courts.[85] The need for these different laws to raise the standards of the early Western bar was all the greater, in view of the natural prejudice of a community that was chronically in debt against all courts and lawyers.

The advent of professional men was a striking illustration of the increase in occupations that accompanied the rapid development of the Old Northwest, and especially that of Ohio during the early period to 1812. By 1811, Gallipolis, a village of only 300 inhabitants, boasted one tavern keeper, two blacksmiths, two tanners, three storekeepers, three master masons, and six or seven carpenters.[86] The census taken in 1810 showed that Cincinnati, the most important commercial center, contained then a population of 2,320 which was engaged in a wide variety of occupations. Beside a bank and two printing establishments there were two wool-carding machines in this thriving river town, a cotton factory, twenty-

[84] *Laws of the Northwest Territory*, Pease, ed., *Illinois Historical Collections*, vol. XVII, pp. 340-347; *Laws of Ohio*, Second General Assembly, pp. 124-127.

[85] *Laws of Indiana Territory*, Philbrick, ed., *Illinois Historical Collections*, vol. XXI, pp. 86, 340-344.

[86] Melish, *Travels*, vol. II, p. 116.

four stores, and twenty-three licensed taverns. In the long list of artisans there were: two printers, one bookbinder, three gold- and silversmiths, and clock, watch, and mathematical instrument makers, one jeweler, twenty-five cabinetmakers and carpenters, six carriage makers and wheelwrights, six turners and chair and spinning-wheel makers, two plane makers, two boatbuilders, four coopers, one combmaker, one brushmaker, three potters, fifteen brickmakers, sixteen stone cutters, masons, and bricklayers, one limner and stucco worker, seven plasterers, four house painters and glaziers, three tobacconists, six bakers, two brewers, four butchers, one tallow chandler, four hatters, three tanners and curriers, thirteen boot and shoe makers, one saddle-tree maker, nine saddlers, one upholsterer and harness maker, two gunsmiths, nine blacksmiths, two coppersmiths, two tinmen, one rope and seine maker, two reed makers, twelve weavers, two blue dyers, eight tailors, and five wagoners, carters, and draymen. Beside this wide variety of industrial occupations in a town that had been founded in the wilderness only two decades before, an abundant supply of professional men was listed that included nine attorneys, eight physicians, surgeons, and apothecaries, and one notary public.[87]

The varied occupations in Cincinnati were an index to the industrial advance that was taking place throughout the Old Northwest. Nevertheless, by 1820, eight years after the close of the early period, and after the tremendous increase in immigration that followed the War of 1812 had already begun, agriculture was still in the lead. In Ohio, the most thickly populated section, about seventeen per cent of the inhabitants were engaged in industrial or professional pursuits, scarcely one per cent in trade, and the remainder, some eighty-two per cent, in agriculture. In Indiana and Illinois, just emerging from the pioneer stage, the proportions of the population working in agriculture were even greater, ninety and ninety-two per cent respectively.[88] Alongside this agricul-

[87] *Ohio Almanac for 1810.*
[88] *U. S. Census for 1820*, pp. 39, 40.

tural development, there had arisen a very considerable trade between the different settlements of the old Northwest, as well as an expanding commerce through which the increasing surplus products were exported, and the commodities that advancing civilization demanded were brought back in return. Also, by 1812, with the end of the early period, the foundations had been laid of an industrialism which, corresponding to the varied agriculture which also was developed, determined the ultimate destiny of the Old Northwest as a section that was economically independent in most of its essential supplies. Its chief dependence upon outside sources was to market its surplus products, and to secure commodities, luxuries for the most part, which it did not itself produce. The progress that had been made in trade and industry in scarcely two decades of settlement was almost unbelievable, but it was no less substantial and enduring.

Chapter XIV

CULTURAL AND SOCIAL FOUNDATIONS

THE swift political and economic advance in the Old Northwest was paralleled by an increasing realization of cultural and social ideals. The settlers had brought with them the tastes and habits of their old homes, and with economic stabilization and the accumulation of wealth, they found leisure in which to indulge their tastes for cultural pleasures and for recreation in general. In their strongholds, Pittsburgh and Lexington, the Scotch-Irish settlers west of the Alleghenies had already made a beginning in the reproduction of the cultural and social life of the older sections of the United States. At Pittsburgh, the first newspaper west of the Appalachians, the *Pittsburgh Gazette,* appeared July 26, 1786, and in a few years Zadock Cramer began his energetic career as a publisher. At Lexington the *Kentucky Gazette* was first published August 11, 1787, and John Bradford's press was soon busy, issuing pamphlets and books. These two centers of a budding culture set before the settlers in the Old Northwest striking examples of the possibilities of the Western country, granted there was sufficient initiative, and the seed fell upon fruitful soil.

From the very beginning, the immigrants into the Old Northwest, with their intense belief in democracy, supported the principle of public education as it had been set forth in the Ordinances of 1785 and 1787. True to their traditions, the Puritan settlers in the Ohio Purchase, as one of their first and most important measures, engaged Reverend Daniel Story as their minister and teacher. For the support of the local school, provision was made to lease the reserved section of land in Marietta, and the Ohio Company added an appropriation of $150.00. The first school, opened at Marietta in 1789, was held in a blockhouse of the Campus Martius, and by 1800 the determination to secure better educational facilities led to the opening of the Muskingum Academy, in a building that had been erected by public subscriptions. These New England settlers opened other schools, as their settlements spread, locating the first one outside of Marietta at Belpre.[1] There was a much similar progress in education among the settlers from New Jersey in the Miami Purchase. The first school in this region was started in 1790 at Columbia, and two years later another one was being held at the near-by settlement of Cincinnati.[2] The rapid growth of this latter town encouraged the establishment of additional local schools, and this regard for education quickly spread to still other sections of the Old Northwest. At Manchester in the Virginia Military District the pioneers opened a school in 1796, and at Chillicothe bids were called for in 1809, for a two-story brick academy, 36 by 46 feet, to be erected by public subscriptions.[3] In the Western Reserve a school was soon started at Warren, and the first one in Cleveland was opened in 1802 in Major Carter's "front room." Asael Adams, who was teaching in this pioneer Cleveland school in 1806, received the scanty salary of $10.00 per month and board.[4] The strides that education made in early Ohio were illustrated by the incorporation of academies in 1808 at Dayton, Chillicothe, and Worthington, and at Steubenville and Gallipolis in 1811.[5] In Indiana with its smaller

---

[1] *Ohio Company Records,* Hulbert, ed., vol. I, pp. 39-40, 102 (note); vol. II, pp. 50, 65, 121; Dunn, *Education in Territorial Ohio, Ohio Archæological and Historical Quarterly,* vol. XXXV, no. 2, pp. 322-379; Venable, *Literary Culture in the Ohio Valley,* pp. 182-183.

[2] Greve, *Centennial History of Cincinnati,* vol. I, pp. 180 and 362.

[3] *Scioto Gazette,* March 27, 1809.

[4] Upton, *History of the Western Reserve,* vol. I, p. 186; Kennedy, *History of Cleveland,* pp. 112, 115.

[5] *Laws of Ohio,* Sixth General Assembly, pp. 17-21, 51-54, 156-158; Ninth General Assembly, pp. 39-42 and 57-63.

population public education was apparently not regarded with the same popular interest, if one may judge from the experience of William F. Thompson, a doctor, a minister, and a would-be pedagogue, who proposed to open a school near Vincennes.[6] In the Illinois settlements, however, the American immigrants at New Design started a school in 1783, and in 1806 another one at Belleville taught surveying, mathematics, and science.[7]

There was a notable development in the curricula of these schools in the Old Northwest that kept pace with contemporary educational progress in the older states. Especially was this true of the Cincinnati schools, which made rapid strides forward in the first two decades or so of settlement. A school founded in Cincinnati in 1794 specialized in courses that were fundamental to the popular occupation of surveying, offering instruction in "reading, writing, arithmetic, bookkeeping, trigonometry, mensuration, gauging, surveying, navigation, the elements of geometry, and algebra." Intending patrons were warned that "moderate correction" would be used "when necessity required." [8] Nor were the classics entirely neglected in early Cincinnati, for a school opened in 1801 proposed to instruct boys in "the Latin and Greek languages, and some other parts of literature connected with them, if required." Other schools stressed the English language, "grammatically taught," geography with the use of maps and globes, moral science, natural philosophy, history, especially American, and *"belles lettres."* A "School for Young Ladies," opened in 1802, was followed by other institutions in early Cincinnati for female education with curricula, drawn up especially to meet the needs of the fair sex, that, besides the usual subjects, included elocution, "mantua-making in the newest fashion," plain sewing, embroidery, tam-

[6] *Western Sun,* December 2, 1809, August 1, 1810, and November 9, 1811; Dillon, *History of Indiana,* pp. 566-568.
[7] Reynolds, *Pioneer History of Illinois,* p. 122; Reynolds, *My Own Times,* pp. 92-95.
[8] *Centinel,* December 27, 1794, and December 12, 1795.

bouring, lace-work, drawing, and painting.[9] Schools were also soon established for special purposes, as an evening school opened in 1799 which charged $2.00 for three months' tuition, the "scholars to find firewood and candles." Three years later, Robert Stubbs, a well-known local astronomer, opened another evening school, this one for instruction in science and the languages. Every Friday evening he proposed to devote to the study of geography, and of the "cause of that pleasing variety of the seasons of the year, and why the days increase by months within the limits of the Polar Circle." In 1808, Stephen Benton started a prototype of the modern technical school as a day school in Cincinnati which specialized in surveying, navigation, plain trigonometry, "and application," and in 1799 Francis Menessier was conducting classes in French in connection with his coffeehouse.[10] In the smaller settlements the schools were neither so numerous nor did they, as those of Cincinnati, teach such varied subjects, but they, too, showed much progress.

Usually the early schools in the Old Northwest were supported almost wholly by tuition fees, but frontier democracy soon made itself felt in the attempt to secure free public education. The reservation of section sixteen of the public lands for purposes of education had given an initial impetus to this movement, and steps were soon taken to translate it into practice. First, in 1801 the territorial legislature made provision for the lease of the sections in the Ohio Purchase and in the Miami Purchase that had been reserved for the benefit of public education. Next, the school lands in Ross County in the Virginia Military District were offered for lease upon terms which, it was hoped, would provide an ample school fund. Finally, in 1805 the Ohio legislature passed an act that set up a board of trustees in each township to lease the school lands, using the proceeds so that all citizens "may be equal

[9] *Western Spy,* October 31, 1801, July 31, 1802, March 27 and October 9, 1805; *Liberty Hall,* April 10, 1811.
[10] *Western Spy,* September 17 and November 5, 1799, November 10, 1802, and January 11, 1808; *Liberty Hall,* October 1, 1808.

partakers of the benefits thereof, agreeably to the true intent of the donation." [11] Likewise in 1810 the territorial legislature of Indiana made provision for the lease of school lands.[12]

The zeal for public education in the Old Northwest also showed itself in the founding of universities which were supported chiefly from the townships reserved for this purpose in the Ohio Purchase and the Miami Purchase, and in Indiana, Illinois, and Michigan by the Land Law of 1804. The first concrete step to take advantage of these reserves was the charter which the legislative assembly of the Northwest Territory granted in 1802 to establish the "American Union University" at the little settlement fittingly named Athens in the Ohio Purchase. This charter gave the trustees full power to lease the two townships that had been reserved for this purpose, to choose the faculty, and to exert general control over the university. The chief aims of the proposed institution, according to the charter, were, "the instruction of youth in all the various branches of the liberal arts and sciences," for "the promotion of good education, virtue, religion, and morality." Later the Ohio legislature provided for the appraisal and lease of the two college townships, including especially lots in the town of Athens, and changed the name of the new institution to Ohio University.[13] But not until the late summer of 1808 did the trustees definitely announce their intention to open a university where the usual collegiate branches would be taught. A year later, a "commodious brick building" had been completed two stories high, and Reverend Jacob Linley, a graduate of Princeton who had been elected "presiding instructor," reported a number of students already under his care. The range of subjects in this backwoods uni-

[11] Laws of the Northwest Territory, First General Assembly, Second Session, pp. 8-19; Laws of Ohio, Third General Assembly, pp. 230-231; Scioto Gazette, October 1, 1803.
[12] Laws of Indiana Territory, Third General Assembly, First Session, pp. 46-47.
[13] Venable, Literary Culture in the Ohio Valley, pp. 173-174; Laws of the Northwest Territory, Second General Assembly, First Session, pp. 161-171; Laws of Ohio, First General Assembly, pp. 147-148; Second General Assembly, pp. 193-206; Third General Assembly, pp. 79-80.

versity, as they were advertised, was quite ambitious, including the "Latin and Greek languages, natural and moral philosophy, logic, geography, rhetoric, history, mathematics, navigation, surveying, arithmetic, and English grammar." The expenses of the students were unbelievably small, according to modern standards. As the funds from the university lands were more than sufficient to pay the salaries of the professors, there was no charge for tuition. Firewood and "other necessary contingencies" cost $2.00 per quarter, and good board was to be had for $1.50 per week, with rooms in the dormitory rent free. The institution rapidly progressed. The trustees purchased globes, and "such classical books as may be necessary in the pursuit of science," and they gave their "unanimous approbation" to an examination of the students upon Homer, Cicero, Ovid, Blair's Lectures, geography, English grammar, and other less important subjects.[14]

The proposed university in the Miami Purchase did not materialize so soon, for the controversy with Judge Symmes over the particular township that was to be reserved for this purpose caused a long delay. Finally Congress proposed a substitute, and a township was set aside west of the Miami River, upon which Miami University was founded in 1824.[15] The inhabitants of Cincinnati, much disgruntled over the loss of their college township, started an independent movement to establish a university, which led to the incorporation of Cincinnati University in 1809, to be supported by funds from a public lottery.[16] Unfortunately the "extreme scarcity of money" and strong public opposition interfered with the sale of the lottery tickets. The building that was erected from the meager proceeds blew down, and the Cincinnati University was allowed to lapse, only to be revived in later years in the form of a great municipal university. In the Western Reserve, also, plans to found a university were fruitless at first, chiefly

[14] *Ohio Gazette,* August 11, 1808; *Scioto Gazette,* June 5, 1809.

[15] *Quarterly,* Ohio Hist. and Phil. Society, vol. IV, pp. 3-5, and nos. I and II; *Laws of Ohio,* First General Assembly, pp. 62-68; Seventh General Assembly, pp. 184-192.

[16] *Western Spy,* April 27, 1807; *Liberty Hall,* August 27, 1808.

because its proponents failed to secure a grant of land from the Connecticut Land Company. Later, under a charter granted in 1803 to the Erie Literary Seminary, an academy was established at Burton that developed into the Western Reserve University.[17]

In Indiana the township which the Land Act of 1804 set aside in the Vincennes Land District for the support of a university was utilized in 1806, when the territorial legislature appointed a board of trustees, which included Governor Harrison, to establish Vincennes University. This act strongly reflected Western ideals of democracy, especially in its preamble, which declared that knowledge should be "widely diffused" in a "commonwealth where the humblest citizen may be elected to the highest public office," and where "the heaven-born prerogative" of the right of election belongs to all citizens. The act required that Indians be admitted to the proposed university, and that the trustees should establish a separate institution for the education of "females" as soon as there were sufficient funds. The chief source of income was, of course, the revenue from the reserved township, but in addition, the legislature authorized the trustees to raise by a public lottery not over $20,000.00 for a library and for "necessary philosophical and experimental apparatus." This rather detailed act also provided for the appointment at first of four professors who would give courses in the "Latin, Greek, French, and English languages, mathematics, natural philosophy, ancient and modern history, moral philosophy, logic, rhetoric, and the law of nature and nations." Later the trustees might appoint professors of law, of physics, and of divinity, but "no particular tenets of religion" were to be taught. Arrangements were soon made to secure the necessary funds, and Vincennes University was

[17] *Connecticut Courant,* September 22, 1800; Webb, *Connecticut Land Company,* in *Historical Collections of the Mahoning Valley,* vol. I, pp. 142-165; Kennedy, *History of the City of Cleveland,* p. 447 (note 38); *Laws of Ohio,* First General Assembly, pp. 117-121.

open for students in 1810.[18] The townships reserved for universities in the Kaskaskia and Detroit land districts were not taken advantage of in the early period up to 1812, but they were destined to become the bases of the great state universities in Illinois and Michigan.

The pioneers of the Old Northwest were not satisfied with schools alone. They recognized the need for books as well, and in their usual practical fashion they founded subscription libraries which were the beginning of a widespread system in a later period. The first one recorded in the Old Northwest was established in 1796 in the New England settlement at Belpre, with a list of eighty books that included such substantial works as Locke's *Essays on the Human Understanding*, Hume's *History of England*, Gibbon's *Decline and Fall of the Roman Empire*, and Thomas Jefferson's *Practical Farmer*. The famous "coon-skin" library founded in 1803 in Ames Township in the New England colony of the Ohio Purchase was made up of a varied collection of essays, history, and poetry that was purchased in Boston for $73.50.[19] At Cincinnati in 1802 a number of citizens subscribed $340.00 for a library, but the first practical results of the movement came in 1813 when a library was opened with subscriptions that totaled $1,500.00, and a collection of books that numbered a year later more than 300 volumes.[20] At Dayton, a much smaller and more remote settlement, the Dayton Library Society, incorporated in 1805, first established its headquarters in the town postoffice. The eagerness of the backwoods readers to have a "first look" at a new book led to an interesting rule of this early library that this lucky person would be determined by drawing lots.

[18] *Laws of Indiana Territory*, Philbrick, ed., *Illinois Historical Collections*, vol. XXI, pp. 178-184; Petition from Trustees of Vincennes University, November 20, 1807, *Indiana Territorial Papers*, House Files, no. 2748; *Western Sun*, March 25, 1809.
[19] Venable, *Literary Culture in the Ohio Valley*, pp. 135-142.
[20] *Western Spy*, February 18, 1806, May 8, 1813, and March 12, 1814; Venable, *Literary Culture in the Ohio Valley*, pp. 139, 141.

Another rule read that, if a drop of tallow was spilt on a book from the candles which were in such general use, or if a leaf was folded over, there would be a fine of three cents.[21] By 1812 other libraries had been incorporated in Ohio, at New Town, at Wooster, at Poland in the Western Reserve, and in Washington County, and at Zanesville the Muskingum Literary Society first met in July, 1810, in order to purchase books. [22] Outside of Ohio, the only known public library in the Old Northwest, up to 1812, was the one that the Vincennes Library Company founded about 1808. This library, when it was first opened, contained 210 volumes, chiefly of biography, geography, history, and poetry. The absence of theological works is probably explained by the fine collection that had been made by the Catholic bishops of Vincennes. The Vincennes Historical and Antiquarian Society, organized in 1808, also accumulated many books.[23]

The few subscription libraries did not satisfy the large and increasing demand for books among the early settlers. Occasionally there were public auctions. A long list that was offered in this fashion at Cincinnati in 1794 included, among others, *Paradise Lost*, Dr. Johnson's *Idler*, H. H. Brackenridge's *Modern Chivalry*, and Carr's *Sermons*.[24] But the general store was the chief source for books, and the shoppers from the outlying districts, as well as the residents of the different settlements, could soon buy them along with their usual supplies. In Cincinnati, the general stores sold many books. A typical list advertised in 1799 was made up of *Pilgrim's Progress*, the *Common Prayer Book*, the *Schoolmaster's Assistant*, the *Laws of the United States*, music books, and biographical, historical, and romantic works too

[21] *Laws of Ohio*, Third General Assembly, pp. 288-290; Steele, *Early Dayton*, pp. 84-85.

[22] *Laws of Ohio*, Sixth General Assembly, pp. 127-129; Eighth General Assembly, pp. 197-199, 251-253; Tenth General Assembly, pp. 5-7; *Muskingum Messenger*, July 7, 1810.

[23] *Laws of Indiana Territory*, Philbrick, ed., *Illinois Historical Collections*, vol. XXI, pp. 202-203, 547-548; Venable, *Literary Culture in the Ohio Valley*, pp. 262-264; *Western Sun*, March 23, 1808.

[24] *Centinel*, May 24, 1794.

numerous to mention separately. In the same newspaper a rival merchant also advertised a long list of books for sale. The tastes of Cincinnati readers gradually broadened, as is evident from a list of books offered by a general store in 1802 which included *Abelard and Heloise,* the *Vicar of Wakefield,* the *Sorrows of Werther,* a *Dictionary of Love,* the *Redemption of Women* in two volumes, Euclid's *Elements,* and *Domestic Medicine.* For the poetry lover this same list offered many volumes, especially Young's *Night Thoughts* and Milton's *Works.* For the reader of biography, it presented the *Life of Voltaire,* and it recognized a widespread interest in geography by including Carey's *American Atlas,* as well as "Maps of the United States, of Kentucky, of the North Western Territory, of the Seven Ranges of Townships, and of the Countries through which the twelve apostles travelled in propagating the Christian religion." In 1805, Thomas Dugan, at his general store in Cincinnati, sold spelling books, arithmetics, a *Complete Letter Writer,* slates, pencils, wafers, and sealing wax, *Family Bibles, Testaments,* and a *Dictionary of the Bible,* in addition to many other books. Occasionally there was an appeal to the credulous to buy such books as the *Easy Instructor* which, it was claimed, would make study "much easier for the learner than any hitherto known." Another loudly heralded work was a chart that gave "a chronological view of the most remarkable events of all the principal nations of the world from the earliest to the present days, as far as they are recorded in History." [25]

The offices of the local newspapers in Cincinnati were active rivals of the general stores in their bid for the book trade, offering many volumes of geography, history, biography, and theology. They also sold novels and schoolbooks. Among the many books which they made available to the people of Cincinnati were: *Gil Blas* in four volumes "elegantly bound," Plutarch's *Lives,* Æsop's *Fables,* Thompson's

[25] *Western Spy,* August 20, 1799, January 23, 1802, February 13, 1805, and January 3, 1806.

Seasons, the *Life of Dr. Johnson, Robinson Crusoe, Arabian Nights,* Watt's *Psalms,* the *History of Charles XII of Sweden,* the *Philadelphia Almanac,* Cramer's *Ohio Navigator,* and books "for the children." "A concise statement of the Trial and Confession of William Clutter," who was executed in Kentucky in 1810, catered to the frontier fondness for the morbid and the gruesome. These printing offices also received subscriptions for works that were published outside of Cincinnati, notably a journal, "from St. Louis in Louisiana to the Pacific Ocean," by Robert Frazier, an account of Lewis and Clark's expedition, and the history of Burr's trial. Often the publishers of books advertised that they would receive subscriptions for works they were printing, or else they employed the postmaster as an agent. Among the many works that were offered the people of Cincinnati in this fashion was *A Universal Dictionary of Arts and Sciences,* in twenty volumes, quarto with plates, which was scheduled to appear, a half volume that cost $3.00 every two months. The *Poetical Works of Edward Young,* in four volumes, cost 62 cents each "in boards," and 87 cents in "elegant binding." A two volume *Compendious History of the World from the Creation to the Peace of Amiens,* with a continuation to the Coronation of Napoleon, was priced to subscribers at 75 cents a volume, and Goldsmith's *Geography,* advertised as "a new plan for the use of the schools," also sold for 75 cents. These varied representatives of the books sold by subscription through the Cincinnati postoffice may fittingly be closed with a two-volume work entitled, "Nature displayed in her Mode of teaching Language to Man, or a New and Infallible Method of acquiring language in the analyses of the human mind, and consequently suited to every capacity." This rather amazing and professedly inclusive text had been "adapted to the French (language)".[26]

Occasionally the local presses in Cincinnati printed fairly

[26] *Western Spy,* May 8, 1805, February 18, 1806, January 12 and April 27, 1807; *Liberty Hall,* November 26 and December 29, 1808, December 20, 1809, and July 3, 1810.

elaborate books. The first one, the territorial code commonly known as Maxwell's Code, from the printer, William Maxwell, was issued in 1795 under official patronage. For distribution by the territorial government there were 200 copies, and the printer offered 800 additional ones to subscribers at 19 cents for every fifty pages, and 30 cents for nonsubscribers, although sales were evidently not satisfactory.[27] The Cincinnati publishers continued to issue the acts of the territorial assembly, along with other official documents. The few additional works they printed were chiefly of a theological nature, and their rather heavy contents may be illustrated by a pamphlet published in 1801 upon "the Arcanum opened, containing the fundamentals of the pure and most ancient Theology—The Urim, or Halcyon Cibola, containing the platform of the spiritual tabernacle rebuilt, composed of one grand substantive and seven excellent tables, in opposition to spurious Christianity." In contrast to this heavy essay, there was an occasional publication in lighter vein, the most important one, Daniel Drake's *Notices Concerning Cincinnati*, which was first printed in 1810, and was reissued in 1815 in much expanded form.[28]

But Cincinnati did not have a monopoly of the book trade in the Old Northwest, and long lists of volumes for sale were advertised in all the important commercial centers. At Marietta, especially, the general stores and the local printing presses advertised many of the titles that were to be had in Cincinnati also. "Poetical works" were quite popular in this Puritan settlement, especially those of Addison, Young, Pope, Burns, Thompson, and Milton. Other noteworthy books that were sold at Marietta were Johnson's *Dictionary*, 500 copies of Steuben's *Military Exercise*, the *Works* of Sir Walter Scott, and a *History of the American Revolution* "in Scripture style." By 1810 the demand for books in Marietta

[27] *Centinel*, August 1, 1795, and March 12, 1796.
[28] Reprint in *Quarterly*, Ohio Hist. and Phil. Society, vol. III, nos. 1 and 2; Venable, *Literary Culture in the Ohio Valley*, pp. 304-305; *Western Spy*, August 19, 1801.

justified the opening of a book and stationery store that, so far as available records show, was the first one in the Old Northwest. This establishment offered a wide range of books on "history, biography, geography, philosophy, theology, politicks, law, logic, agriculture, medecine, musick, astronomy, surveying, mathematicks, and metaphysicks." Schoolbooks, Bibles, hymnbooks, and Greek, Latin, and English classical works, also, were found in the seven hundred volumes that had been imported from Baltimore, and would be sold at "Philadelphia retail rates," with only the freight charges added. This same bookstore received subscriptions, too, for "an elegant edition" of *Orlando Furioso* translated from the Italian, and for an "American Review of History and Politicks, and General Repository of Literature and State Papers," which it was proposed to publish in Baltimore.[29]

At Chillicothe, for so long the territorial capital, there was a considerable demand for the books that the general stores and the printing offices sold. The local presses printed a number of official publications, and in 1809 a particularly enterprising individual opened a bookbindery. At Warren in the Western Reserve in 1812 a long list of books was offered for sale at the office of the *Trump of Fame,* the local newspaper, and likewise at Steubenville, books were sold and subscriptions were solicited for proposed works, one of them *A History of the Life and Misfortunes of Charlotte Temple,* by Mrs. Rawson.[30] Books even found their way to Vincennes, in spite of the difficulties of transportation, and in addition to the lists advertised by the stores, the postmaster, General Johnston, offered a number of volumes for sale as early as 1807. A book at Vincennes that was of special interest in view of the local religious situation was a revised edition of the *Real Principles of Roman Catholics,* by a

---

[29] *Ohio Gazette,* January 1, 1802, and March 7, 1808; *Western Spectator,* November 27, 1810, and March 14, 1812; *Commentator,* June 5, 1810.

[30] *Scioto Gazette,* April 4 and May 23, 1808, and October 2, 1809; *The Supporter,* May 18, 1809; *Trump of Fame,* July 22, 1812; *Western Herald,* January 10, 1807.

French clergyman. Goldsmith's *Essays*, Lowe's *Poems*, and the *Knickerbocker History of New York* were among the other books sold in this frontier town, together with Cuming's *Notes on a Tour Through the Western Country, 1807–1809*. This last work sold for $1.25 with a free copy for every nine subscribers, and a discount of five per cent to merchants.[31] In many of the other settlements in the Old Northwest, books were invariably included in the stocks of goods which the ubiquitous general store offered its customers.

Books alone did not satisfy the keen, practical minds of settlers who demanded some knowledge of contemporary affairs. For a time the *Pittsburgh Gazette* and the *Kentucky Gazette* enjoyed a wide circulation. But there was need for local mediums in which to publish advertisements, the news, and political items, and as an outlet for Western literary offerings. The realization of these needs was made possible by the steady income which a local newspaper would secure from legal notices, and as usual, Cincinnati led the way.[32] The first newspaper, the *Centinel of the North-Western Territory*, was a small weekly sheet of four pages which appeared at Cincinnati November 9, 1793. According to the publisher, William Maxwell, its chief aims were: to give the news; to serve as an advertising medium; and to publish local—*i.e.*—territorial grievances. At the top of the first page Maxwell printed as the apt motto of this frontier newspaper: "Open to all parties—but influenced by none." In June, 1796, the *Centinel* was discontinued, to be succeeded by *Freeman's Journal* with its succinct motto: "Free, but not licentious." This latter newspaper followed the territorial capital to Chillicothe in 1800, but a year later another weekly sheet, the *Western Spy and Hamilton Gazette*, had appeared in Cincinnati. Joseph Carpenter, the editor of the

[31] *Western Sun*, December 9, 1807, December 24, 1808, April 15, 1809, January 20, February 18, and April 7, 1810.
[32] For a list of Cincinnati newspapers, see *Am. Antiquarian Society Proceedings*, New Series, vol. XXIX, pp. 141-150; also, Greve, *Centennial History of Cincinnati*, vol. I, ch. 24.

latter, inclined toward Federalism, but he adhered consistently to his promise to be "strictly impartial," and open to all communications that were not scurrilous. A rival paper, *Liberty Hall*, which was much more partisan in its strong Republicanism, was first issued in Cincinnati December 4, 1804. The other two newspapers that were started at Cincinnati prior to 1812, the *Whig* and the *Cincinnati Observer*, did not flourish. The editor of the *Observer* was at the same time the proprietor of a coffee shop, where he kept on hand "the most approved newspapers from the seat of government for the perusal of his customers." [33]

Chillicothe was, of course, an important newspaper center after the territorial capital was moved there from Cincinnati.[34] The *Scioto Gazette*, first issued in 1800, speedily became the mouthpiece of the Virginia clique in their fight against St. Clair, and after 1803 it was the official organ of the Republican party in Ohio. Representing a somewhat opposing view politically, *The Supporter* was started in 1808 as "an honest, candid, and independent federal paper," which, so the editor claimed, was governed by the principles of Washington's administration. Up to 1812 at least three additional newspapers were launched at Chillicothe upon more or less stormy careers, the *Ohio Herald* in 1805, the *Fredonian* in 1807, and the *Independent Republican* in 1809. At Marietta, also, a number of newspapers were published in this early period.[35] The *Ohio Gazette*, which first appeared December 18, 1801, was markedly Jeffersonian in its sympathies. On the other hand, the editor of the *Commentator*, established September 16, 1807, was supported by many New England settlers in the Ohio Purchase, since he was strongly inclined to Federalism, appealing to the "hundred per cent" Americans, and maintaining that the Constitution

[33] *Western Spy*, May 28, 1799, July 23, 1800, November 6, 1811, and April 2, 1814; *Liberty Hall*, March 20, 1811.

[34] For a list of Chillicothe papers, see *American Antiquarian Society Proceedings*, New Series, vol. XXIX, pp. 131-140.

[35] For a list of Marietta papers, see *American Antiquarian Society Proceedings*, New Series, vol. XXIX, pp. 164-168.

of the United States was his "political creed" and "invaluable criterion." The *Commentator* expired soon after the advent of the *Western Spectator* at Marietta in October, 1810. Avowing himself "a Federal Republican," the editor of this last-named sheet acknowledged his attachment to "our free constitution," and adopted the motto: "Be just and fear not." Even more strongly Federalist in its politics was the *American Friend,* first published April 24, 1813, by David Everett, an experienced editor and well-known orator who had come to Marietta from Massachusetts.[36]

During the second decade or so of settlement, a veritable flock of newspapers sprang up in the different Ohio settlements. At Steubenville in 1806 the *Western Herald* entered upon a long and prosperous career, and about a year later the *Western Star* was founded in Lebanon by an editor who stoutly maintained his belief in a "republican form of government," and his fear of the "characters" who wished to dismember the Union. Another famous Ohio newspaper, the *Muskingum Messenger,* was founded at Zanesville in 1809, after the state capital had been moved there. At Warren in the Western Reserve, the first issue of the *Trump of Fame* appeared June 16, 1812, the publisher frankly acknowledging that his object was first "to benefit himself," and then "to profit society." The *Western Intelligencer,* printed at Worthington, and the *Ohio Centinel* at Dayton were also included in the total of thirty-one newspapers that were published in Ohio in the early period.[37] For Indiana Territory, legal notices were printed in the Ohio or Kentucky papers until July, 1804, when Elihu Stout from Lexington, Kentucky, started the *Indiana Gazette,* shipping his printing press and type from Frankfort in a small boat that was nearly three months on the tedious water route to Vincennes. Two years later his printing office burned with all its contents, but the cou-

---

[36] *Commentator,* September 18, 1807; *American Friend,* April 24, 1813; *Proposals to publish the Western Spectator,* 1810.

[37] *Western Star,* February 13, 1807; *Trump of Fame,* June 16, 1812; *American Antiquarian Society Proceedings,* New Series, vol. XXIX, pp. 129-180.

rageous printer soon revived his newspaper under a new title, the *Western Sun*. For his motto he printed, under a rising sun, the caption: "Each Century has its own peculiar mode of doing business, and men, guided more by custom than by reason, follow without enquiry the manners which are prevalent in their own time." [38] In Illinois, the *Missouri Gazette*, later the *Louisiana Gazette*, printed in St. Louis, published official notices, and otherwise met the needs of the comparatively few settlers.

In their general make-up these early Western newspapers were much similar to the contemporary weekly gazettes that were published east of the Alleghenies. Reflecting the tastes of their subscribers, they gave the greatest attention in their news columns to political and governmental affairs. Customarily they printed the laws and proceedings of the local legislatures, official proclamations by the governors, and a variety of legal notices. Nor did their publishers ignore local political issues. Thus, the struggle for statehood in Ohio, and the attempt, later on, of the Tammany Societies to dominate politics, aroused a veritable whirlwind of long-winded partisan communications. Often these compositions were exceedingly personal and quite bitter, but the authors usually hid under fanciful nom de plumes. Similar outbreaks attended the elections, for which the local politicians usually nominated candidates through the newspapers. The leaning toward politics was noticeable even in the news items. The local news in these early journals was almost wholly confined to Indian relations or unusual occurrences, and from outside the Old Northwest, there were few items from Kentucky or Tennessee, in comparison with those from the Atlantic states, and especially from Washington. Federal laws that were of especial interest to the Western people, presidential messages, occasional excerpts from the proceedings of Congress, and bits of political gossip found their way into the columns of these Western newspapers. In the foreign

[38] Law, *Colonial History of Vincennes*, p. 138; *Western Sun*, especially July 11, 1807.

news, accounts of the Napoleonic campaigns occupied much space, and in spite of upstanding assertions of Western democracy, the doings of royalty were by no means ignored. As practically all these items of outside news, both domestic and foreign, were copied from Eastern newspapers, it is evident that they were weeks and sometimes even months old by the time they reached the newspaper columns of the Old Northwest. Yet even with such delays, the local newspapers kept the inhabitants in touch with important events in the world that lay beyond the mountains.

Usually the early Western newspapers were edited in an impersonal fashion, but at least two of them, *Liberty Hall*, published at Cincinnati, and the *Western Spectator*, at Marietta, were quite remarkable, in a newly settled region, for their excellent editorials and their generally high standards. Rev. John W. Browne, the founder of *Liberty Hall*, was an English Congregational minister of decidedly liberal views who, by his able editorials and the dignified tone of his paper, attained to a unique place among his contemporaries. The broad scope of his paper is shown by his request for contributions on "agriculture and commerce, the biographical memoirs of persons notable for their patriotism, philosophy, poetry, science, and piety," and for "moral and instructive essays." In his editorials Browne was fearless and caustic, clearly showing the influence of Cobbett and other English Liberals. An example of his clear-cut style was a keen analysis and comparison of speeches by the President of the United States, the King of Great Britain, and the Emperor of France, very much in favor of the first-named. Yet intensely as he supported Republican views, Browne was no mere partisan. While he refused to allow his paper to become a "vehicle to disseminate scandal or slander," he vigorously fought for freedom of speech, and gave each side in a controversy the opportunity to present its arguments.[39] In contrast to Browne, the editor of the *Western Spectator*

[39] *Liberty Hall*, December 4, 1804, January 22 and April 16, 1805, October 28, 1806, and December 8, 1807.

was inclined toward Federalism, yet he, too, was fair-minded. In his prospectus he appealed for patronage to "farmers and mechanics, to the yeomanry of our country, on whom its safety depends—to men unbiased by the cravings of ambition, who desire not either to deceive or to be deceived." His paper met the varied tastes of a wide constituency in excellent fashion, with one of its most striking features a weekly column that was headed "State of the Union." Under this heading there was much pertinent information, with caustic criticisms of public affairs and men. Especially during the War of 1812, the editor boldly stood for the freedom of the press, not hesitating to criticize the Federal Administration in its conduct of the war. Yet like his colleague of *Liberty Hall,* the editor of the *Western Spectator* opened his columns to both sides, and published many communications from "democratic Republicans." [40]

Bitter fights between the editors of rival newspapers frequently enlivened the daily grind of life in the small Western settlements. In Cincinnati, for example, the publishers of the *Western Spy* and *Liberty Hall* were often at sword's points, with many innuendoes in each paper that were directed against its rival. The editor of *Liberty Hall,* it must be confessed, was much the cleverer, and eventually he refused to notice the violent attacks of his less subtle rival.[41] In Chillicothe there was a similar rivalry between the editors of the *Scioto Gazette* and *The Supporter.* One especially choice bit from the latter, under the nom de plume, "A Brother," begins a lengthy criticism with the caustic comment: "Stolen or strayed—(but most probably the latter on account of its inconsiderable value)—the last remaining atom of intellect belonging to the editor of the *Scioto Gazette.*" [42] At Marietta, also, there was keen rivalry, this time between the printers of the *Ohio Gazette* and those of the

[40] *Proposals to publish the Western Spectator,* 1810; *Western Spectator,* especially November 13, 1810, June 27, July 4, and September 22, 1812.
[41] *Liberty Hall,* August 27, 1805.
[42] *The Supporter,* February 2, 1809.

Commentator, and occasionally the two editors descended to such personal accusations as quite open hints regarding the failure to pay board bills.[43] But personal comments were characteristic of the American press during this period, and they were probably not taken very seriously.

Politics and news items were not allowed to crowd out of these Western newspapers the time-honored *Poets' Corner* which the publishers inherited from the colonial gazette of the Atlantic Coast. Beginning in the *Centinel* and continued in *Freeman's Journal,* the "Seat of the Muses" became an accepted feature. With a delicious, but perhaps an unconscious, irony the *Western Sun* followed the *Indiana Gazette* in heading this column, the "Poetical Asylum." The printer of the *Western Spy,* more flattering, adopted the caption, "Parnassiad Column," with the motto:

> "With sweetest flowers enrich'd,
> From various gardens cull'd with care." [44]

Although many poems were copied from the standard collections that were on hand in the newspaper offices, the effusions of home authors were more popular, and at least these Western poets were assiduous. Frequently they wrote upon patriotic themes, as a long and stupid ode on the birthday of President Adams. The Battle of Tippecanoe aroused a female patriot to burst forth in stanzas that began:

> "O dark and dreary was the night,
> While chill November blew,
> When on the Wabash's distant bank,
> Encamped our gallant crew."

This same poetaster celebrated the Fourth of July in similarly heavy lines:

[43] *Ohio Gazette,* May 4, 1808.
[44] *Western Spy,* November 13, 1805.

"All hail! celestial happy day,
That brings to our rejoicing hearts
The birthday of America,
When she defied all tyrant's arts." [45]

Other poets of the Old Northwest composed even heavier lines, if that were possible, choosing for their compositions such awesome titles as, "the Poet's objection to smoking, pernicious weed; whose scent the fair annoys"; "To an Old Fruit Woman"; and lines, "from a Mother to her Infant Daughter" on the "Villain Man." Also, they attempted sonnets with fearful results, and one gentleman of the bar, evidently not heavily endowed with a sense of humor, indited lines upon "The Lawyer's Farewell to his Muse," which purported to have been copied from Blackstone. The *Poets' Corner* was even used to remind delinquent subscribers of the accounts they owed the newsboy.

Alongside the *Poets' Corner* these early newspapers often printed one or more columns of essays and other literary compositions which were copied from standard authors or else from current periodicals. The resourceful printer of the *Indiana Gazette,* upon one occasion, filled up columns, which otherwise would have been blank as a result of delayed mails, with extracts from Goldsmith's *Essays.* But the home-grown product was more popular, and the editor of the *Gazette,* himself, claimed that one of his chief aims was to publish "original essays, political, moral, literary, agricultural," and on "domestic economics." The editor of the *Western Star* asked outright for the "literary productions of gentlemen of information." [46] The returns from this and similar requests were disappointing, including heavy essays on such subjects as, *Masonry, Morals,* the *Death and Burial of Saul, Adolescentia,* and the *Destructive Tendency of Spirituous Liquors. A Comparison between the Sexes,* and a *Parable against Per-*

---

[45] *Western Spy,* November 28 and December 5, 1812.

[46] *Indiana Gazette,* August 7 and 21, 1804; *Western Star,* February 13, 1807.

secution give further hints as to the usual dreary subjects of the literary contributions to these local papers, although there were occasional articles in a lighter vein. A continued novel, *Edwina and Edelia*, ran for four months in *Liberty Hall*, in the form of a series of very stupid letters. Rather clever ironical articles also appeared occasionally, as one on the *Sympathy between the Breeches Pocket and the Animal Spirits*, and an oration in *Praise of Rum*. But the usual homemade offerings of pioneer humor were heavy and even grotesque.

The literary columns of the early Western newspapers frequently contained items of scientific interest. The discovery in Cincinnati of the supposed tooth of a mastodon brought forth a lengthy communication in *Liberty Hall* from "a Lover of Nature." Again, in 1807 the Cincinnati papers gave much space to accounts of a comet that was visible for two hours on September 30. But without a telescope, scientific observations were practically impossible, and there were many sanctimonious reflections upon the works of God.[47] During the winter of 1811–1812, the different newspapers gave much attention to the earthquake shocks that alarmed the Mississippi Valley, and occasionally they noted varied topics of current scientific interest, as a new machine for weaving by hand, the many mammoth bones in Kentucky, and the effect of nitrous and "oxigenated muriatic" acid in "destroying infection."[48] Evidently the people of the Old Northwest were also keenly interested in explorations, and in geographical information in general, for practically all the local newspapers printed elaborate accounts of the resources and topography of the territory that was acquired by the Louisiana Purchase Treaty, and most of them contained full accounts of the Lewis and Clark Expedition.

To the present-day reader, the advertising columns of these early Western newspapers present their most characteristic feature. It is impossible even to enumerate the manifold

[47] *Liberty Hall,* December 30, 1805, and December 21, 1807; *Western Spy,* October 12, 1807.
[48] *Ibid.,* September 15 and 22, 1810, January 11 and 18, 1812.

aspects of social, economic, and political life that are mirrored in these columns, but they are indispensable, if one is to gain any real insight into the everyday life of the Old Northwest. A notable and at times a somewhat humorous touch was given by the use of captions for advertisements that show a considerable resemblance to the modern headline. Thus, an advertisement that called for the payment of delinquent accounts was aptly headed, "Be Punctual," and the notice of a butcher that he would sell "low for cash" was under the equally fitting caption, "Something Strange." Another advertisement, under the heading, "Better late than never," appropriately called attention to Browne's *Cincinnati Almanac* for 1806. Of quite another type was a notice from an irate husband who repudiated all the debts of his absconding wife. The printer naughtily labeled this notice, "O! O! O! Woman." Another advertisement of a similar type was ironically headed, "Something Wonderful." [49] Rival merchants frequently employed unique devices in their advertisements in order to catch the eye. In Cincinnati, John O'Ferrall advertised a large stock of goods from Baltimore under the heading, "Look Here," with the notice itself upside down. A rival, John H. Piatt, quickly stole the headline, "Look Here," adding another line, "New Store," to call attention to his own varied stock from Philadelphia. Piatt does not seem to have prospered, for under the heading, "20,000 Dollars Worth of Goods," he soon offered to sell his entire stock, so that he might return eastward. For a later advertisement he chose an equally appropriate heading, "Just a Going." [50]

In most cases the newspapers of the Old Northwest appeared weekly, barring delays in the mails or interference from lack of paper, and they usually included only four pages. In the first newspaper, the *Centinel*, each page of the early issues measured 8½ by 10 inches, and those of later numbers, 9 by 15 inches. The *Western Spy* was somewhat

---

[49] Especially files of *Western Spy* and *Liberty Hall*, 1801–1810.
[50] *Western Spy*, December 2 and 30, 1806, January 6, 1807.

larger, 11 by 18 inches, and this was about the average size of the more important of the local newspapers. The prices charged by the publishers were moderate. A subscription to the *Centinel* cost "250 cents" per annum, and a single copy 7 cents. For advertisements, the rate was $1.00 per square for the first three weeks and 25 cents for each later insertion. Subscriptions to the *Centinel* were received at the printing office in Cincinnati, and by agents in the near-by settlements, Columbia, North Bend, Colerain, and Newport on the south bank of the Ohio. The publishers of *Freeman's Journal*, the *Centinel's* successor, continued this scale of charges for subscriptions and for advertising.[51] The printers of the *Western Spy*, the third paper founded in Cincinnati, fixed $2.50 as the price for town subscriptions, but they charged country subscribers $3.00. Later they reduced the subscription to $2.00 if it were paid in advance, and to any one who obtained six subscribers they offered a year's subscription free of charge. For advertisements "making no more in length than breadth," the *Spy* charged 50 cents for the first, and 25 cents for each succeeding insertion. In distributing their paper, these printers at first employed special agents to serve country subscribers, but as it was almost impossible to secure reliable persons, they finally used the rather unsatisfactory post routes.[52]

The rates for subscription and advertisement adopted by the *Western Spy* and other Cincinnati papers became the usual ones for newspapers in the Old Northwest. For the *Ohio Gazette* and the *Commentator* in Marietta, and for the *Scioto Gazette* and *The Supporter* in Chillicothe, the annual subscription was $2.00 in advance, and $2.50 if it were paid at the end of the year. The printer of the *Commentator*, who was an especially aggressive man, employed agents to receive subscriptions at Chillicothe, Lancaster, Zanesville, Cincin-

[51] *Centinel*, December 7, 1793, March 7 and September 19, 1795; *Freeman's Journal*, July 9, 1796.
[52] *Western Spy*, May 28 and December 3, 1799, February 20 and 27, 1805, and April 1 and September 23, 1806.

nati, Athens, Steubenville, Warren, Gallipolis, Bainbridge, and Dayton in Ohio, and at certain towns in Virginia, Kentucky, Massachusetts, New York, Pennsylvania, and the District of Columbia.[53] In Indiana, the circulation of the local paper was necessarily smaller, and the publishers' expenses heavier, as a result of the high freight on paper and other supplies. Consequently, the *Indiana Gazette*, which was published at Vincennes, cost $2.50 in advance and $3.00 at the end of six months. For advertisements of the usual square type this gazette charged $1.50 for the first insertion, and 25 cents for "each continuance." Postage was extra, and no subscription was received for less than six months. The successor of the *Indiana Gazette*, the *Western Sun*, reduced these charges to the ones usual in Ohio, probably because with an increased population had come the possibility of larger profits.[54]

Like the merchants and professional men, the early Western publishers found it was difficult to collect the accounts due from either subscribers or advertisers. William Maxwell, publisher of the *Centinel*, complained he could not collect enough money to buy necessary supplies of paper, and since fully half of the advertisements sent him were not accompanied by the necessary cash, he committed such communications "to the book," unless they were prepaid.[55] Equally trying were the experiences of the publishers of *Liberty Hall* and the *Western Spy*. Neither gentle reminders, threats to suspend publication, nor warnings that legal measures would be invoked, if necessary, secured adequate results. Other printers had similar experiences. Eight years after the first issue of the *Scioto Gazette*, the publisher announced that many of the original subscribers had not paid a cent, and two years later he threatened to discontinue delivery to the worst delinquents, and to use "compulsory measures" to collect

[53] *Commentator,* September 16, 1807.
[54] *Indiana Gazette,* August 7, 1804; *Western Sun,* July 11, 1807.
[55] *Centinel,* especially September 27 and December 20, 1794, March 26 and April 9, 1796.

what was due. In contrast, the printer of the *Western Spectator* announced that he would not discontinue subscriptions until all "arrearages" were paid, and that he would insert advertisements "till forbid." [56] Apparently he was no more successful than his brother printers, as judged by actual results. This uncertainty of collections probably accounts for the numerous proposals to issue newspapers that did not materialize. For example, in 1805 elaborate plans were made to publish the *Whig* at Franklin, Ohio, but evidently the three hundred advance subscribers that were required were not secured, for the paper did not appear. Some publishers, discouraged, simply gave up, as William Maxwell, who, preferring the postoffice in Cincinnati to the very uncertain returns from the *Centinel*, "declined the printing business." [57] At Marietta the *Ohio Gazette* managed to exist for seven years, and then, in 1808, Samuel Fairlamb, the publisher, found it was necessary to put delinquent accounts into the hands of an attorney. As the sheriff offered Fairlamb's house lot and printing press at public sale about this time, it is evident that the *Ohio Gazette* had not been a profitable venture, although it continued to appear at irregular intervals for three more years. [58]

A shortage of paper often hampered the Western printers, and sometimes they were obliged to suspend their newspapers temporarily for this reason. Occasionally they printed the weekly issue on ordinary gray wrapping paper, and more frequently they reduced the size of the page. The opening of local paper mills greatly helped this situation, but supplies of printer's ink were still difficult to secure. On one occasion the publishers of *Liberty Hall* loaned their rivals of the *Western Spy* a supply of ink, and the *Ohio Centinel* at Dayton was even suspended temporarily for want of this necessity. [59] But the lot of the publisher of an early Western news-

[56] *Scioto Gazette*, May 30, 1808, and November 7, 1810; *Western Spectator*, October 17, 1812.
[57] *Western Spy*, October 9, 1805; *Freeman's Journal*, July 9, 1796.
[58] *Ohio Gazette*, July 7, 1808.
[59] *Liberty Hall*, October 30, 1811.

paper was not one of continual discouragement. Six months after he started *Liberty Hall* "with every difficulty and obstacle" in his way, Rev. John W. Browne reported a wide circulation in Cincinnati and near-by counties, with copies that were distributed regularly along the post roads into the interior districts. The circulation of the rival paper, the *Western Spy,* gradually declined until 1809, when a new management started with a list of about one hundred subscribers which was increased in a little over two years to more than thirteen hundred. *The Supporter,* one of the few Federalist newspapers in the Old Northwest, was also quite prosperous, with agents, two years after it was started, to receive subscriptions in Chillicothe, Cincinnati, Marietta, Zanesville, and Pittsburgh.[60] The *Scioto Gazette* and the *Western Sun* also enjoyed wide circulations.

A number of newspapers from outside circulated in the Old Northwest. One of the most important, the *Louisiana Gazette,* became, from its origin at St. Louis in 1808 as the *Missouri Gazette,* the official gazette and the chief local newspaper for the inhabitants of the Illinois settlements. The publisher employed at least five agents on the east bank of the Mississippi, and on one route alone in this region there were upwards of sixty subscribers in 1809. Incidentally, the publishers of the *Louisiana Gazette* threatened in the usual fashion to bring suits unless their Illinois subscribers paid up.[61] Many of the Kentucky papers, too, circulated north of the Ohio. The *Independent Gazetteer,* published in Lexington, had agents at Cincinnati and Vincennes, and another Lexington paper, the *American Statesman,* received subscriptions at Cincinnati, Kaskaskia, and Fort Massac, while the *Western World,* issued in Frankfort, employed agents at Chillicothe, Franklinton, Kaskaskia, and Vincennes.[62] Of especial inter-

[60] *Liberty Hall,* June 18, 1805; *Western Spy,* September 12, 1812; *The Supporter,* September 29, 1810.

[61] *Missouri Gazette,* November 23, 1809; *Louisiana Gazette,* March 8 and April 12, 1810, July 18 and November 30, 1811.

[62] *Independent Gazetteer,* September 6, 1803; *American Statesman,* November 2, 1811; *Western World,* December 18, 1806.

est, in their appeal to certain racial elements that were even then coming into the Old Northwest, were notices for subscribers to the *Virginia German Eagle*, to be published at Staunton, Virginia, and to the *Hibernian Chronicle* and the *Harp of Erin*, printed in New York. The inhabitants of the Old Northwest were also invited to subscribe to the *Washington Gazette*, which it was proposed to publish at the national capital as a weekly journal, with "accurate" news upon public affairs.[63]

The circulation of almanacs was probably even wider than that of newspapers. The pioneer farmers followed the custom of the rural districts in their old homes east of the Appalachians, in regarding the almanac as a veritable gospel of the weather and a compendium of useful information of a varied character. The *Kentucky Almanac*, published at Lexington, was the first one to be distributed widely in the settlements north of the Ohio, and beginning in 1794, its astronomical calculations were made for Vincennes and the "territory northwest of the Ohio," as well as for Kentucky. In addition to the phases of the moon, predictions regarding the weather and the like, this almanac contained much general information for the pioneer reader.[64] The *Western Almanac* of Washington, Pennsylvania, and the *Pittsburgh Magazine Almanack*, put out by Zadock Cramer, were also popular in eastern Ohio. In 1806, two local almanacs made their appearance in Cincinnati, the *Ohio Almanac* which was issued from the press of the *Western Spy*, and *Browne's Cincinnati Almanac* which the rival publisher of *Liberty Hall* brought out. These two almanacs soon enjoyed a wide circulation in the Old Northwest, and their contents give hints as to the tastes of the average rural settler. Joseph Carpenter, the printer of the *Ohio Almanac*, rather cleverly appealed for patronage, upon the ground that the purchase of a local almanac would keep money in circulation at home, and for a

[63] *Scioto Gazette*, January 11, 1808; *Western Spectator*, February 8 and May 9, 1812.
[64] *Kentucky Almanac*, 1794–1808.

"reasonable consideration" he offered to take back copies at the end of the year. The contents of his first issue were varied. Beside the usual calendar, with detailed astronomical information, there was a list of the principal roads, with the distances between Cincinnati and Pittsburgh, Detroit, Lexington, and Lawrenceburgh, respectively. This almanac gave, too, the personnel and the calendar of the different Ohio courts, and tables of the usual coins in circulation with the rates of exchange. Beside recipes for various home remedies, there were "curious and useful" articles, upon the *Folly of Disputes on Religious Subjects,* upon *Comparisons of Drunkenness,* and upon the *Condor.* The romantic story of *Damon and Pythias* was in strong contrast to practical directions for the care of turkeys. The success of this first issue of the *Ohio Almanac* induced the printer to enlarge later editions, and to add much information of local value. In 1808 he published a long and especially valuable account of religious organizations in Ohio, and in 1810, another article of much importance, this one upon the resources, the settlement, and the general development of the state.[65]

The rival almanac, *Browne's Western Calendar* or the *Cincinnati Almanac,* was equally successful. The first issue was somewhat delayed while the attention of William McFarland, who made the astronomical calculations, was fully occupied in his "necessary avocations" as sheriff. When the *Cincinnati Almanac* did appear, the demand for it was so extensive that the publisher could scarcely print a sufficient supply. The price, the same as that of the *Ohio Almanac,* was low, $6.00 per gross, or $1.00 per dozen, and 12½ cents for a single copy. The table of contents of the 1810 edition gives an adequate idea of this really excellent almanac. In addition to the usual astronomical calculations, it contained sketches on the settlement and improvement of Chillicothe, and "Instances of Longevity—Account of a remarkable tree—Salaries of the Officers of the United States Government—Account of Zanesville—Journal of a Tour through the State of Ohio, in

[65] *Ohio Almanac,* 1806, and 1808–1810.

the summer of 1809—Religious Intelligence—a long list of roads thro' the State of Ohio—Account of the Cincinnati Cotton Manufactory, etc." The *Liberty Hall* printing office, it may be noted, also offered German almanacs for sale "by any quantity." [66]

The broad-mindedness and the comparatively high cultural standards of the early settlers in the Old Northwest were strikingly shown in the amusements of their leisure hours, as well as in the books they read. Here, too, the customs of the older sections of the United States were quickly introduced, and a varied social life speedily arose in the larger settlements. One of its most interesting features was the widespread popularity of amateur theatricals, given, as befitted so modest a period, by young men only with occasional professional aid. The "Cincinnati Theatre" opened October 1, 1801, with the *Poor Soldier* as the play. There was an "original" prologue and an epilogue, both of them, needless to say, quite stupid. But the audience was gratified when the curtain rose with a display of "excellent scenery," and "the whole piece went off, not only to the satisfaction, but the admiration of a crowded meeting of spectators." Next, this same amateur organization attempted a more ambitious play, *She Stoops to Conquer*. Another performance of the *Poor Soldier*, with *Peeping Tom of Coventry* added to the program, was followed by a double bill which presented the *Agreeable Surprise* and the *Dumb Doctor, or the Dumb Lady Cured*, which closed this season of amateur theatricals. Although tickets had sold at only 50 cents for each performance, the financial returns had not been altogether satisfactory. Dramatic entertainments continued to be given in Cincinnati, with a professional performance in 1805. A few months later the Thespian Society announced performances of the *Poor Gentleman* and other plays. Probably from this same society came the "Gentlemen of Cincinnati" who in the fall of 1806

[66] *Liberty Hall,* October 15, 1805, April 14, 1807, and November 15, 1809; *Browne's Cincinnati Almanac,* 1809, 1811.

gave a comedy, *Secrets Worth Knowing,* to which they added the intriguing farce, *Love à la Mode.*[67]

For a time the drama seems to have been neglected in Cincinnati, but in 1811 the revived Cincinnati Theatre inaugurated a notable season with a comedy, the *Farm House or the Female Duellist.* There were two performances of this play each week, and tickets sold for 75 cents, with children at half price. Next in the season's dramatic offerings was a bill of frontier vaudeville. The program opened with a comic song, followed by the "celebrated Polish minuet" as danced in London, New York, and elsewhere. The next number was the "grand pantomimic spectacle," *Cinderella,* and a musical farce, the *Spoiled Child,* closed the evening's entertainment. The last recorded performance of this unusual dramatic season of 1811 in Cincinnati was a play, *Douglas or the Noble Shepherd,* followed by a farce, the *Padlock.* During this season professional actors seem to have taken the leading rôles, with the young men of Cincinnati in the minor parts.[68] All of the inhabitants were not so broad-minded in their tastes, and these theatrical performances aroused the ire of one of Cincinnati's leading divines. His stern denunciations were ably answered by *Theatricus* in an article that warmly defended the organization of the young men of the city to improve themselves, "exhilirate" the public, and devote the proceeds to the poor.[69] The vogue of amateur theatricals was not confined to Cincinnati, but it soon spread to other settlements. July 4, 1808, the youths of Lebanon in Ohio gave a performance at the courthouse of the *Traveller Returned* for which they charged only 25 cents, with children at half price. At Chillicothe the Thespian Society, organized in 1811, gave a tragedy, the *Revenge,* followed by the "much admired" farce, the *Hotel.* This double bill they presented in an im-

[67] *Western Spy,* October 10 and December 5 and 26, 1801, February 20, 1802, July 7 and November 20, 1805, and September 23, 1806.
[68] *Liberty Hall,* June 6 and 12, 1811; *Western Spy,* June 22, 1811.
[69] *Liberty Hall,* January 11 and 23, 1815.

provised theater in Keys Tavern. At Vincennes, too, the young men of the town organized a Thespian Society in 1806 which enjoyed a prosperous career.[70]

The popularity of amusements of a cultural type took still another direction when a "drawing and painting academy" was opened in Cincinnati in 1812, where "portrait, miniature, landscape, and ornamental painting" were taught for an entrance fee of $2.00, with $6.00 per quarter tuition. The instructor, however, did not ignore the uncertainties of his artistic venture, for in quite practical fashion he indicated he would paint signs "in a neat and durable manner," and would "prepare cloth for wagon covers, awnings, and boat curtains."[71] Much more frivolous as a recreation was the dancing school which was opened in Cincinnati in 1799. Beside morning classes, there was an evening session for the gentlemen who could not attend during the day. The dancing master, claiming to have taught "with great reputation in different parts of Maryland and Virginia," offered instruction in the "minuet, cotillion, French and English sets," the "most fashionable" "country dances, and the city cotillion," as it was taught in New York, Philadelphia, and Baltimore. For such up-to-date instruction his terms were an entrance fee of $3.00 with tuition of $5.00 per quarter. Like the amateur theatricals, the dancing schools stirred up the strictly religious element, and a contributor in the *Western Spy* roundly condemned them as "nurseries of idleness, frippery, and folly," which were rapidly becoming the "prevailing rage." "Versatility of mind, hatred for study or sober reflections," according to this author, were the "inseparable companions" of such institutions.[72] In spite of this and other like severe denunciations, the dancing schools flourished in Cincinnati and spread to other early settlements. One was even

[70] *Western Star*, June 30, 1808; *The Supporter*, April 6 and 13 and May 11, 1811; *Western Sun*, January 7, 1815; Venable, *Literary Culture in the Ohio Valley*, pp. 260-261.

[71] *Liberty Hall*, September 1, 1812.

[72] *Western Spy*, November 19, 1799, and April 22, 1801.

started in 1809 at Chillicothe, which was a center of strong Methodist influence.[73]

Singing schools, also, were popular among the Western people, with the first one on record meeting Monday evenings at the courthouse in Cincinnati as early as December, 1796. By 1801 a singing school for ladies and gentlemen was meeting in Cincinnati two nights in each week, with tuition of $1.00 for thirteen nights, and $2.00 for a quarter, subscribers "to find their own wood and candles." In 1810 the Harmonical Society of Cincinnati announced that it would "gratify the public with an evening of pleasurable entertainment," and in the following year, the Euphonical Society was founded in the same town.[74] At Marietta there was a singing school by 1802 which met three days weekly in the academy building,[75] and others were organized in the different settlements. An inkling of their popularity was given by an advertisement in a Chillicothe paper that called the attention of singing masters, as well as of booksellers, to the new edition of Smith & Little's *Patent Note Book*, with additional tunes which were "much approved of in Kentucky and Ohio." [76] Debating societies, also, were popular and served as training places for many early Western politicians. Among them was the Athenian Adelphian Society, organized by a few of the New Englanders in Athens County, Ohio, which celebrated the Fourth of July in 1808 with a debate at the local schoolhouse upon the question whether public festivals were for the benefit of mankind.[77] Still another popular form of entertainment was the school "exhibition," at which male students often spoke, but young ladies as a rule modestly confined their activities to proofs of their progress in reading, writing, geography, needlework, and kindred subjects. On one such occasion, thirty young ladies rendered "musical

[73] *Scioto Gazette,* March 20, 1809.
[74] *Freeman's Journal,* December 17, 1796; *Western Spy,* October 31, 1801; *Liberty Hall,* April 18, 1810, and June 6, 1811.
[75] *Ohio Gazette,* January 1, 1802.
[76] *The Supporter,* May 25, 1811.
[77] *Ohio Gazette,* July 21, 1808.

compositions," including *Moses in the Bulrushes,* "to the satisfaction" of an audience of Cincinnatians.[78]

The social instincts of the inhabitants of the Old Northwest found another outlet in the various organizations which they brought with them from their old homes. First, of course, came the churches, which were equally important as social and religious centers, serving in the rural districts especially as common meeting places. For the male inhabitants there were also political organizations which usually recognized social needs as well, the most notable the Republican and the Tammany Societies. In addition, Masonic lodges were soon founded. The first one in the Old Northwest, established at Marietta June 28, 1790, under the leadership of Rufus Putnam, was practically a reorganization of the well-known American Union Lodge of the Revolutionary army. The Grand Lodge of Massachusetts promptly recognized this Marietta lodge, and soon there was another one in Cincinnati. Other lodges were founded at Chillicothe, in the Western Reserve, and in other settlements, and in 1808 the Grand Lodge of Ohio was organized at Chillicothe.[79] In Vincennes, the first Masonic lodge seems to have been organized in 1809.[80] The many Revolutionary officers in the Old Northwest made possible the organization of the "Society of the Cincinnati North West of the Ohio" at Marietta October 22, 1800. Somewhat in contrast was a "Society of Mechanics" that was founded in Cincinnati in 1808. [81]

With their strong social instincts, the Western pioneers naturally supported public celebrations of various kinds. One of the first important occasions of this type was the formal entrance of St. Clair into Marietta July 9, 1788, as governor of the Northwest Territory. Escorted by officers from Fort Harmar, St. Clair crossed the Muskingum in a government

[78] *Western Spy,* January 1, 1806; *Liberty Hall,* July 9, 1808.
[79] *History of Washington County, Ohio,* pp. 416-420; Drake, *Picture of Cincinnati in 1815,* pp. 165-166; *Resolution, New England Lodge, no. 48,* in *Huntington Papers.*
[80] Cauthorn, *History of Vincennes,* p. 148.
[81] *Western Spy,* December 10, 1800, and February 1, 1808.

barge, and was then conducted to a "bower" that had been erected especially for the occasion. Much speechmaking and general rejoicing followed. An excellent illustration of the pomp that attended territorial officialdom, even in these primitive settlements, was the opening of the general court at Cincinnati, April 12, 1794. The constables, with "battoons," led the procession from the chambers of the judge to the "public ground." There followed in order: the sheriff and the coroner with white wands, the "gaoler," the "honorable judge," the clerk with a green bag, the judges of the county court of pleas, the justices of the peace of Hamilton County, attorneys, messengers, and other attendants. Four days later the sheriff, the coroner, and the gentlemen of the bar gave a dinner in honor of the judge, to which they invited the grand jury. It is recorded in all seriousness that this latter day was spent "with perfect harmony and decorum." [82] Occasionally there were grand official balls, as the one in December, 1790, which the inhabitants of Marietta gave in honor of Governor St. Clair and his family. This assembly, so one account reads, "was numerous and brilliant, consisting of several dancing couples, besides several others." [83]

The Fourth of July was by far the most important public festival in the minds of the fervently patriotic inhabitants of the Old Northwest. The pioneers of Marietta set a precedent, July 4, 1788, scarcely three months after the first settlement. In celebration of the day they first listened to a flowery oration by Judge Varnum, and then they feasted upon venison, bear's meat, buffalo, roast pig, and various kinds of fish, including a 100 pound pike that had been caught in the Muskingum.[84] In the Western Reserve, the other chief settlement by New Englanders, the earliest pioneers celebrated the Fourth of July in 1796 at Conneaut Creek, with about fifty men, women, and children present. After a Federal salute of fifteen rounds, with a sixteenth in

[82] *Centinel,* April 12 and 19, 1794.
[83] *Pittsburgh Gazette,* January 23, 1790.
[84] Hildreth, *Pioneer History,* pp. 214-215.

honor of New Connecticut, it is recorded that the company "drank several pails of grog, supped, and retired in remarkable good order." Another interesting pioneer celebration in this same region was the one at Warren in 1800. On this particular occasion, the settlers displayed great ingenuity in improvising musical instruments without which the Fourth would have been altogether incomplete. A large elder was fashioned into a fife, a section of a hollow tree served as a drum hoop, the skin of a fawn furnished excellent drum heads, and a pair of leading lines were utilized as cords. Thus equipped, the fife and drum crops, according to a contemporary report, "gave forth most patriotic music." [85]

As the settlements increased in population, the celebrations of the Fourth of July in the Old Northwest became more elaborate. In the towns there was usually a parade, led by a liberty cap on a pole. After this the ardent Republicans, doubtless somewhat exhausted by their outbursts of joy, were willing to listen quietly to an oration and the reading of the Declaration of Independence. Last of all came the climax of the day, a dinner in a specially constructed "bower," with numerous toasts and flowing spirits of every variety, and here patriotism reached a grand crescendo. The many details of these celebrations of the Fourth of July which have been recorded give interesting sidelights upon early Western customs and manners. At Chillicothe in 1804 the ladies gathered on the town green to enjoy an "elegant collation," and at the same time the "gentlemen" celebrated the Fourth on the banks of the Scioto, with the "mechanics" in a specially constructed arbor. Again at Chillicothe, in 1809, there was a specially grand celebration, and the Republicans took advantage of the occasion to elect delegates to a county convention. After this essential duty had been performed, General Worthington delivered an oration that began with the discovery of America, touched upon Luther's Reformation, and came down to the events of 1776 in the United

[85] Whittlesey, *Early History of Cleveland*, pp. 181-182; *Leonard Case's Notes*, in *Joseph Perkins' Scrap Book*.

States. After a disquisition upon the mission of America as an asylum for the "distressed" and "persecuted," the orator closed this typically Fourth of July speech by reading the Declaration of Independence. General McArthur then proposed a long list of toasts, and each one of them was followed by music and the firing of musketry.[86] Another popular Fourth of July orator, David Everett, the editor of the *American Friend,* found in the Book of Daniel and the Revelations of St. John guarantees of the independence and prosperity of the United States.[87] At Zanesville in 1811, the ladies were invited to hear the oration and the reading of the Declaration of Independence, but not to attend the dinner, and a year later a subscription of 75 cents was solicited from "each man" in this same town, for the dinner and drink which the local innkeeper was to furnish. The dinner, according to contemporary accounts, was an exceedingly enthusiastic one, with toasts that strongly supported the war against the hated British. The company showed remarkable self-control, dispersing at an early hour "without a solitary circumstance of insobriety or ill conduct to mar the beauty of the occasion." [88]

In the sparser settlements of Indiana the Fourth of July was celebrated with even more enthusiasm, perhaps, than in the more sophisticated towns of Ohio. At Vincennes the ladies were customarily invited to these entertainments, as in 1807 when the entire company sat down to dinner under a "bower" near Colonel Vigo's spring, with John Gibson, secretary of the territory, presiding. After a bountiful repast there were eighteen patriotic toasts, which must have tested the capacity even of the seasoned pioneers. At Corydon in 1810, there was a parade of the militia, followed by a dinner in a grove with seventy ladies and about two hundred men present.[89] The American settlers in Illinois were not a whit

---

[86] *Scioto Gazette,* July 9, 1804, and July 10, 1809.
[87] *American Friend,* July 17, 1813.
[88] *Muskingum Messenger,* July 1, 1811, July 1 and 8, 1812.
[89] *Western Sun,* July 11, 1807, and August 25, 1810.

behind in their observance of the nation's birthday. At Kaskaskia in 1810, the celebration of the Fourth closed with an elegant ball, which "a brilliant circle of ladies attended, whose smiles seemed to speak the language of their hearts." Another celebration, this same year, was conducted in a setting of rural plenty that was typical of these early Illinois settlements. The company gathered in a grove of large walnut trees at the home of Colonel Shadrach Bond, Jr., and after an American flag had been hoisted, they sat down to an excellent dinner, "prepared and given by Colonel Bond." The Declaration of Independence was read, there were discharges of artillery, and the diners drank numerous toasts. Throughout the proceedings there was the usual "harmony and universal rejoicing." [90] Even the citizens of Shawneetown, far off from the other American settlements in Illinois, gathered on the bank of the Ohio in 1812 to celebrate the Fourth. A "large concourse" of ladies and gentlemen enjoyed an "elegant barbecue," and "harmony and good order" again prevailed.[91]

The pioneer love for amusement and for social gatherings, added to the traditions of settlers who came from Kentucky and Virginia, accounts for the rise of horse-racing as a popular sport. The first race recorded, at Cincinnati, lasted for two days in October, 1801, with a tidy purse of $50.00, and in succeeding years these Cincinnati races became an annual event. In 1805 they were combined with a fair and lasted three days. For the first day, the purse was $80.00, for the second day $60.00, and on the last day the sweepstakes were run, with a subscription of $500.00, to be settled "on the ground." Although great crowds attended each day, like the theater and the dancing school, horse races did not always meet the approval of the more religiously inclined portion of the population. These latter, a correspondent of the *Western Spy* ironically asserted, "slyly swig'd it by themselves until their faces were in a blaze, and themselves in a delicious

[90] *Louisiana Gazette*, July 19 and August 2, 1810.
[91] *Missouri Gazette*, July 25, 1812.

state of intoxication." But the opponents of the sport had their inning, for the scaffold upon which a number of ladies stood watching the races fell, and they "in every position" took "speedy flight" to the ground.[92] Such was the dire fate of women who ventured to unhallowed amusements, but, like the criticisms of the piously minded, it had little effect. The racing fever spread to Hamilton, Canton, and Pickaway Plains in Ohio, to Whitewater, Indiana, to Newport, Kentucky, and doubtless to other settlements. At the races on Pickaway Plains the crowds were so large that booths were set up at which "beer, cakes, liquors, victuals" were sold.[93]

The limitations of this present volume will not permit a detailed description of the husking bee, the barn-raising, the jamboree, and other familiar forms of diversion among the Western pioneers. But one or two examples of less familiar and typical sports may be noted. Hunting was especially popular with the male inhabitants, and there were numerous public hunts. E. Hutchinson, living on Mill Creek near Cincinnati, conducted three-day hunts, starting a fresh and "active" fox each morning, with a pack of thirty hounds. At the end of the day's sport, he offered a "sumptuous dinner," evidently with "trimmings," to his patrons.[94] Another interesting example of pioneer sport was a hunt which about three hundred inhabitants of Warren and of the surrounding townships in the Western Reserve enjoyed on Christmas Day, 1812. Forming in a widespread circle at nine o'clock in the morning, the hunters began to move toward the center, blowing their horns every fifteen minutes in order to keep their lines in regular formation. About twelve o'clock the entire party closed in, and divided the game they had rounded up, eight deer and about a hundred wild turkeys. Fortunately no accidents marred the day, in spite of the

[92] *Western Spy,* September 30, 1801, September 26, 1804, September 11 and October 30, 1805; *Liberty Hall,* October 29, 1805.
[93] *Western Spy,* October 12, 1807, and February 1, 1808; *Liberty Hall,* November 12, 1808; *Western Herald,* September 6, 1806; *The Supporter,* March 31, 1810; *Scioto Gazette,* May 15, 1811.
[94] *Liberty Hall,* February 27, 1811.

almost constant discharge of rifles as the lines became closer.[95]

The Western settlers were exceedingly fond of exhibitions of real or supposed marvels of all types, and in this respect, it must be confessed, they had their full share of the general credulity of their age. At Chillicothe, for example, in 1805 a learned pig was shown which was guaranteed to write, print, and spell ordinary Christian names. Admittance to this remarkable performance was 25 cents, with children half price, and the company was promised additional entertainment, with a "variety of music." In Cincinnati a living elephant was shown in 1809, "the only one in the United States," according to the exhibitor, and an opportunity to gaze upon this marvel cost only 25 cents.[96] Equally strong in its appeal to public curiosity was the Museum of Wax Works which was opened in Cincinnati in 1815. The "elegant wax figures as large as life" represented a wide range of historical and romantic personages, among them: George Washington, Aaron Burr, the Bashaw of Tripoli, a Sleeping Beauty, a scriptural group representing Elijah raising the widow's son, a scene from Hamlet, "representing the Prince of Denmark and the beautiful Ophelia," and Mrs. Clark, the London beauty. The cost of admission to this varied display was 50 cents, with half price for children. Like the twentieth-century movie, this pioneer exhibition was accompanied by music "on a large and elegant organ." Still another modern touch was given by notices that requested gentlemen to refrain from smoking in the Museum, and offered for sale the profiles of the characters represented, "elegantly fram'd." [97]

The popular enthusiasm in Cincinnati for the exhibition of wax figures was an indication of the extent to which the culture of the older sections of the country was being reproduced in the Old Northwest. The long lists of books that were available, at the general store and in the increasing num-

[95] *Trump of Fame,* December 30, 1812.
[96] *Scioto Gazette,* December 26, 1805; *Liberty Hall,* February 9, 1809.
[97] *Western Spy,* June 5, 1813.

ber of libraries, were partly responsible for a background of general information that enabled the early settlers to recognize the different historical personages and the literary characters that were represented by the wax figures. The quick development of schools had contributed to the same result. Secondary education, of a sort, had spread through the settlements, and with the aid of the reserved section in each township, a really effective public-school system had been at least inaugurated. A parallel movement had taken place in the rise of the publicly supported university, which, from the small beginning made in this early period, was to become one of the most significant features of American education. The newspapers, likewise, that sprang up so quickly in the little Western settlements, had done their part in keeping the inhabitants abreast of the times, and in creating a medium for the appearance of political and literary outbursts. Even in their amusements the early settlers in the Old Northwest had often displayed the finer tastes of their old homes in their support of amateur theatricals, musical organizations, and the like. Moreover, they had found time for lighter amusements, some of them imported from the Atlantic Coast, others characteristic of the Western country. Among public anniversaries, the Fourth of July had called forth a significant expression of intense patriotism and Republicanism. In short, cultural and social development in the Old Northwest had kept pace with economic progress, in laying the foundations of a civilization west of the Appalachians that was destined to reach high levels from these humble beginnings.

Chapter XV

RELIGION AND ORDER

AN IMPORTANT phase of the distinctive civilization that was developed in the Old Northwest was the strength of religious influences. This was not surprising, however, in view of the background of the early settlers. The inhabitants of the American colonies were an essentially religious people, although the Revolutionary liberals, from whom the vast majority of the emigrants into the Old Northwest were drawn, insisted upon the complete separation of Church and State. Yet they did not abandon their religious faith, and the very intensity of their belief, which had been strengthened by the revivals conducted by Jonathan Edwards and George White-field, had led to a multiplicity of creeds, with a rapid disintegration of the established churches. In the Western settlements, with complete religious freedom, this tendency would naturally be accentuated, and it was reasonable to presume that the Methodist and Baptist churches, which were rapidly winning the approval of the masses, along with the Presbyterian faith of the many Scotch-Irish, would appeal much more strongly to the people of the frontier than the Congregational Church, the time-honored official ecclesiastical organization of New England, or the Episcopal Church which had occupied a similar position in the Southern colonies. Experience had already shown, too, how closely the spread of religion was bound up with the cause of law and order. The mere establishment of political institutions and the passage of laws would not suffice in carrying out successfully the American colonial policy, unless there was strong popular support of the government. This necessary condition was secured to a marked degree when the settlers brought with them, along with other long-cherished traditions, their strong religious belief and their respect for its outward observance. Therefore, aside from its mere intrinsic interest, the progress of religion in the early settlements of the Old Northwest was of very great importance, as the development of one of the chief influences that upheld law and order.

Before the American settlers came into the Old Northwest, there had been little aggressive religious influence upon the Indians and the few supposedly civilized inhabitants. Aside from the Moravian missions to the Indians, the first religious organization to secure a foothold was the Roman Catholic Church of the early French settlers. When the Northwest Territory was first organized, there was a Catholic church at Detroit, another one at the River Raisin, and a mission at Mackinaw. In the other French settlements, the adherence of the inhabitants to the Church was really nominal, and the parishes were badly run down. At Vincennes there was a parish without a priest, the church itself a "very poor log building, open to the weather, neglected and almost tottering." Father Rivet, who came in 1796, greatly strengthened the parish, and did much missionary work among the near-by Indians. The Catholic churches at Kaskaskia and Cahokia were likewise badly neglected until the Olivier brothers came in 1799, John to go to Cahokia and Donatien to Kaskaskia. At Gallipolis, the remaining important French settlement in the Old Northwest, a priest arrived soon after the unfortunate French immigrants, but as he met little encouragement he soon left. Outside these French settlements there were few adherents of the Catholic Church in the Old Northwest, and there was little likelihood that it would spread among the prejudiced Americans who soon settled there. An attempt to organize a congregation in Cincinnati in 1811 failed, and the great development of the Church in this region under Father Fenwick and Bishop Faget came in a later period.[1]

[1] Shea, *History of the Catholic Church,* vol. II, pp. 481-491; vol. III, p. 334; *Western Spy,* December 7, 1811.

In the new American settlements, the religious situation reflected the diversity of faiths at this time on the Atlantic Coast and in the backwoods. The men from New England and the Scotch-Irish, who took so prominent a part in the settlement of the Old Northwest, brought with them their Calvinistic beliefs and their characteristic church organization. The immigrants at Marietta, true to Puritan tradition, founded a Congregational church in the first few months of their settlement. Rev. Daniel Breck of Tapsfield, according to tradition, preached the first sermon July 20, 1788, in the "bower" that the Marietta settlers had prepared for their Fourth of July banquet. For a time Rev. Manasseh Cutler served as minister at Marietta, and Rev. Daniel Story of Boston, the first regular minister, who was also the village teacher, took charge of the services March 22, 1789. Soon he also had regular appointments at Belpre and Waterford. In 1796 the congregation at Marietta, made up of thirty-one New England Congregationalists and one Scotch Presbyterian, was formally organized as a church, and two years later they began to hold services in the Muskingum Academy, in preference to a blockhouse in the stockade which had so far served them as a meeting house. In 1809 they moved again, this time into a building of their own.[2] The Congregational Church was organized also in the Western Reserve, the other New England stronghold in the Old Northwest. Missionaries sent by the Connecticut Missionary Society laid the foundations. The first one, Rev. Joseph Badger who arrived in 1800, founded a church at Austinburgh a year later. The only other minister he encountered in all the Western Reserve was Rev. William Wick, a Presbyterian missionary from the Synod of Pittsburgh. The two became fast friends, and Wick was soon receiving an allowance from the Connecticut Missionary Society, which meantime had sent an additional missionary to New Connecticut.[3] But the financial

[2] Dickinson, *First Church Organization in Marietta, passim;* Hildreth, *Pioneer History*, p. 259.
[3] Walker, *History of the Congregational Churches of the United States,*

resources of the Connecticut Missionary Society were small, while the Presbyterians, intrenched among the Scotch-Irish of western Pennsylvania, had ample funds and were quite aggressive. The upshot was a close alliance between the Congregational and the Presbyterian churches in the Western Reserve, where these two Calvinistic faiths pooled their missions. The plan of union they adopted, dubbed the "Presbygational" system, sanctioned the interchange of ministers and the union of communicants of the two denominations into single congregations. Gradually the Presbyterians, backed by the Erie Presbytery, assumed the lead, and by 1806 there were five Congregational and seven Presbyterian missionaries in the Western Reserve with a corresponding increase in the number of congregations. In 1803 there were at least two churches with pastors, one at Hopewell and the other at Youngstown, and two congregations, at Warren and at Concord, without ministers. By 1808 there were nearly twenty organized congregations in this region as a result of the united efforts of the Congregational and Presbyterian churches.[4]

In their main strongholds in the Ohio Valley, the Scotch-Irish settlers who came from the Atlantic Coast, from Kentucky, and from western Pennsylvania soon established Presbyterian congregations. Their first church building, the one at Cincinnati, was located upon half a square which the Presbyterian proprietors of the town site had set aside for this purpose. During the summer of 1789 this pioneer congregation worshipped beneath the trees, but in 1792, under the leadership of their first pastor, Rev. James Kemper, they

---

pp. 312, 313; *Narrative of the Missions to the New Settlements, Congregational Assembly of Connecticut, passim;* Kennedy, *History of the Presbyterian and Congregational Churches of the Western Reserve,* pp. 18, 19; Extracts, *Minutes of General Association of Connecticut for 1802* (Congregational), pp. 7-9.

[4] Kennedy, *History of the Presbyterian and Congregational Churches of the Western Reserve,* pp. 150-153; Walker, *History of the Congregational Churches of the U. S.,* pp. 314-319; Extracts, *Minutes of the General Association of Connecticut* (Congregational) for 1805, pp. 3 and 30; Patton, *Popular History of the Presbyterian Church in America,* p. 299.

raised $300.00 in subscriptions for a church building. By 1812 the congregation had far outgrown this early structure, and they were able to subscribe $16,000.00 for a new one.[5] From Cincinnati, Presbyterianism spread up the Miami Valley, with a congregation at Dayton by 1800. In the Scioto Valley, and especially at Chillicothe, immigrants from Kentucky founded a number of Presbyterian congregations, and, in like fashion, settlers from western Pennsylvania brought Presbyterianism to the upper Ohio Valley. A Presbyterian minister preached in Steubenville in 1798, and a church was organized there in 1801. At Marietta, Rev. Stephen Lindley arrived in 1803 to take charge of the Presbyterian church. This progress of Presbyterianism in these early settlements was greatly aided by the custom of appointing licentiates who took charge of congregations that could not support a regular minister. The denomination spread so fast that by 1803 there were three presbyteries in the Old Northwest. The Presbytery of Ohio, covering the upper Ohio Valley on both banks of the river, included fifteen charges that were supplied with ministers, three that had vacant pulpits, although they could support a minister, and six "destitute" congregations. Seven ministers were listed in the Presbytery of Washington, which embraced the Miami and Scioto valleys and a few churches across the Ohio in Kentucky, while the Presbytery of Erie included among its churches four congregations in the Western Reserve. With the continued growth of the Presbyterian Church, especially in the little towns, the territory west of the Virginia Military District was set off in 1811 as the Miami Presbytery, and further to the eastward the Presbytery of New Lancaster was formed.[6]

The Presbyterian Church soon spread to Indiana, first into the "gore" in the southeast, which was included in the Miami Presbytery, with a minister in charge of Lawrence-

[5] Montfort, *First Presbyterian Church* (Cincinnati) in *One Hundred Years of Presbyterianism in the Ohio Valley, passim.*

[6] Galbraith, *History of Chillicothe Presbytery*, pp. 30-68, *passim; History of Belmont and Jefferson Counties, Ohio*, p. 500; Extract, *Minutes of Presbyterian General Assembly for 1803*, pp. 15 and 29-32.

burgh and the Whitewater region. In Clark's Grant ministers from Kentucky frequently held services while they were visiting their old friends. "Supplies," too, came to preach, and there was an organized church at Palmyra in 1807. At Vincennes the first sermon by a Presbyterian minister is said to have been preached at the home of Governor Harrison. Soon a church was organized, and Rev. Samuel T. Scott, who became pastor in 1808, frequently preached from the "Presbyterian pulpit" in a grove near Vincennes.[7] In 1810, the territorial legislature incorporated the Presbyterian Church at Vincennes, in an act that lauded the "propagation of the gospel," inasmuch as it contributed to civilization. Therefore "republican legislatures" should extend their "constitutional aid to every institution whose basis is religion, and whose object is general philanthropy and the improvement of the human species."[8] In Illinois, the Presbyterian Church does not appear to have secured a permanent foothold during this early period, although a number of missionaries preached in these settlements, the first one probably Rev. John Finley of Chester, Pennsylvania, who came to Kaskaskia in 1797, but soon returned to Kentucky.[9]

But neither the Congregational nor the Presbyterian churches appealed strongly to the masses of the backwoodsmen, and their congregations increased chiefly from their adherents among the emigrants from the Atlantic Coast who moved into the Old Northwest. Of the Calvinistic churches, the most popular by far was the Baptist faith, which had strongly intrenched itself in Kentucky before settlement began in the Northwest Territory. Its extremely democratic organization suited the settlers, and the Baptists soon spread north of the Ohio. The first known Baptist congregation in the Old Northwest was organized under the leadership of Rev. Stephen Gano, from Providence, Rhode Island, in Co-

[7] Esarey, *History of Indiana*, vol. I, pp. 321, 322.
[8] *Laws of Indiana Territory*, Third General Assembly, First Session, pp. 116-118.
[9] Norton, *History of the Presbyterian Church in Illinois*, vol. I, pp. 11-14.

lumbia at the mouth of the Little Miami, March 10, 1790, only fourteen months after the arrival of the first settlers. This pioneer congregation included thirty members, comprising the bulk of the adult population of the little settlement, and by 1793 its numbers had so greatly increased that a meetinghouse was built. From this nucleus other Baptist congregations were sent out, as the settlers penetrated the Miami Valley, until the Miami Baptist Association was organized in 1798 from the parent church at Columbia and four of its offsprings. By 1805 this association had increased to twenty-one churches and 656 members. The many Baptists from Kentucky who settled north of the Ohio soon made necessary the formation of the Scioto Association in 1805, and of the Mad River Association in 1811, the latter including six churches in the interior of Ohio.[10] The Baptists expanded into the Western Reserve as well, and it has been claimed that the first sermon ever preached in Warren was delivered by a Baptist minister before a congregation of about fifty persons who had gathered in a clearing in the woods.[11] By 1808, the six Baptist churches in the Western Reserve and the upper Ohio Valley formed the Beaver Association. Indeed, by 1809 the Baptists had become the second leading denomination in Ohio, and included sixty congregations and approximately 2,500 members, with four associations that covered the settled parts of the state.[12]

An interesting feature of the Baptist immigration into Ohio was the large anti-slavery element it included, notably among the immigrants from New Jersey and the other Middle States. Their influence was shown when the Miami Association refused to correspond with the neighboring associations in Kentucky, or with the Redstone Association, because all these congregations included many slaveholding members. This prejudice was carried to such extremes that one congre-

[10] Asplund, *Annual Register of the Baptist Denomination in North America for 1791*, p. 34; Dunlevy, *History of the Miami Baptist Association*, pp. 17-52, *passim*.
[11] *Notes by Leonard Case*, in *Joseph Perkins' Scrap Book*, p. 184.
[12] Benedict, *History of the Baptists in America*, vol. II, pp. 258 and 262.

gation actually withdrew from the Miami Association because it corresponded with the Philadelphia Association, which in turn recognized the Charleston (S. C.) Association. Even more strongly anti-slavery in their views were the members of a German Baptist church at Pleasant Run near Lancaster, Ohio. Originally this congregation was composed of fifteen members, who, refusing to have "any communion or visible fellowship" with slaveholders, had left their homes in Rockingham County, Virginia, and had sought "an asylum in the wilderness, where they might enjoy, unembarrassed and unreproached, the free exercise of principles which they held most dear." By 1809 this little church numbered seventy members, to whom the ministers preached in English or German, according to the make-up of the congregation.[13]

The Baptist Church spread also among the frontiersmen of Indiana and Illinois. The Whitewater Association, organized in the "gore" in 1809, included nine churches. There was much progress in Clark's Grant also. The Kentuckians who had moved there decided to erect a meetinghouse, in which they authorized their trustees to place glass sashes and shutters, and "to bring in the bill." Meanwhile, other Baptist congregations were being organized in Clark's Grant, so that by 1812 it was possible to form the Silver Creek Association with ten churches. In 1809 the five Baptist churches in and around Vincennes had formed the Wabash Association which soon had more than 800 members, scattered along both banks of the Wabash.[14] In the Illinois settlements probably the first Baptist preacher was Rev. James Smith, a "separate" Baptist who came from Kentucky in 1787, and was captured by the Indians. Rev. Josiah Dodge, who came a little later, found that the Baptists and the Methodists among the settlers, lacking a minister of either denomination, were accustomed to hold joint services. Although he preached

[13] Benedict, *History of the Baptists in America,* vol. II, pp. 257-258 and 261.
[14] *Ibid.,* pp. 263-264; Stitt, *Indiana Baptist History,* 1798–1808, pp. 37-43; Esarey, *History of Indiana,* vol. I, p. 320.

frequently and made a good impression, the joint meetings continued. Finally Rev. David Badgely, who arrived about 1796, organized at least two Baptist churches among the American settlers. The increase in members was so rapid that the Baptists in these distant settlements on the Mississippi formed an association in 1809 which included ten congregations, three of them across the river in Missouri, eight ordained ministers, and about 400 members. Unfortunately disputes over slavery soon broke up this organization,[15] but just as in Ohio and Indiana, the Baptists made great gains in early Illinois, in spite of their lack of aggressive methods.

Of the non-Calvinistic denominations that were organized among the early settlers, the Episcopal Church made the least progress. This was to be expected, for it had been the privileged church of the Southern colonies, and its ritualism was not likely to appeal to the democratic Westerners who had sprung so largely from the masses. The first recorded Episcopalian activity in Ohio started in 1792, when Dr. Joseph Doddridge, from across the Ohio in Virginia, began to hold services in eastern Ohio, officiating monthly at the courthouse in Steubenville from 1798 on. A second Episcopal congregation was organized at Worthington, the settlement north of Franklinton which a group of New Englanders, organized as the Scioto Company, founded in 1803. Their leader, Rev. James Kilborn, was an Episcopal minister, and the company set aside eighty acres for the benefit of St. John's Episcopal Church. This congregation was quite prosperous, worshiping in an academy building that was erected in 1807. In addition there were many scattered communicants of the Episcopal Church in early Ohio, notable among them being William Henry Harrison, and they formed the nuclei of the congregations which Bishop Philander Chase organized in 1818 into the Diocese of Ohio.[16]

[15] Reynolds, *Pioneer History of Illinois*, pp. 216-218, 226-227; Benedict, *History of the Baptists in America*, vol. II, p. 264.

[16] Doddridge, *Notes*, ed. 1876, pp. 10-11, 15; *History of Franklin and Pickaway Counties (Ohio)*, pp. 419, 429; *Journals of Annual Conventions of the Protestant Episcopal Church of Ohio*, vol. I, pp. 5-6.

The Quakers, though they were not so small in numbers as the Episcopalians, were neither so numerous nor even so widespread as the Presbyterians, but they exerted an influence in the Old Northwest that was far out of proportion to their actual membership. The bulk of them came from the Carolinas and Georgia, entire meetings at times moving north of the Ohio because of their anti-slavery views. One of the most important of these Quaker immigrations moved from Trent River, North Carolina, into eastern Ohio, and settled a short distance west of Wheeling in September, 1800. Other Quakers, originally from New Jersey and eastern Pennsylvania, drifted across Pennsylvania until the rich lands of the Old Northwest drew them across the Ohio. At first these Quaker pioneers worshiped in the woods, but they soon built a meetinghouse, and organized the Concord Meeting. Other Friends settled in the neighborhood, and ultimately they established an important center of Quaker influence in eastern Ohio. In western Ohio the first important Quaker settlement was on a tract of some 3,000 acres near Waynesville, in Warren County, where practically the entire Bush River meeting from South Carolina settled. Other Quakers came into the neighborhood in such numbers that in four years, 1803–1807, the Miami Monthly Meeting received 1,826 of them. More than 800 of these Quaker immigrants came from South Carolina and Georgia, 45 from Pennsylvania and 69 from New Jersey. Quaker immigrants also found their way into other sections of Ohio, in such numbers that the Ohio Yearly Meeting was organized in 1813 to include Ohio, Indiana, and the adjacent sections of Pennsylvania and Virginia.[17]

From their settlements in Ohio many Quakers went into Indiana, among them David Hoover who came from North Carolina in 1802 and settled north of Dayton. In 1806 Hoover with four companions explored the Whitewater region to the westward, and a number of Friends soon migrated there, settling especially in and around Richmond.

[17] Jones, The Later Periods of Quakerism, vol. I, p. 11, ch. 11.

In September, 1807, an "indulged" meeting that was held in the Whitewater settlement included about eighty Friends. Two years later there were at least 265 persons in this settlement, and others were coming in, most of them Southern Quakers who were leaving their former homes because of their anti-slavery views. From these Whitewater settlements Quaker emigrants went westward, notably to Lick Creek, where they organized a monthly meeting in 1812. These Indiana Quakers had an important part in the struggle to keep slavery out of the territory, and, in spite of their anti-militaristic views, they lived on excellent terms with their neighbors.[18]

The Methodists, however, were by far the most popular and influential denomination in the Old Northwest. Their Arminian appeal to free will, in contrast to Baptist Calvinism, was peculiarly acceptable to a frontier people, and their doctrine of conversion met a ready response from an emotional and somewhat unanalytical population. Moreover, the organization of this church was well suited to the peculiar needs of an expanding frontier. The bishops presided over the annual conferences, each of which was divided into districts in charge of presiding elders, and these latter, in turn, into the circuits that were under the charge of the ministers. Thus, from the circuit and its pastor up, there was an effective system of supervision, while each division was quite elastic, and in actual practice both district and circuit were expanded or divided to meet the demands of a growing population. Lastly, there were local preachers who organized congregations in sparsely settled communities, and by officiating until a regularly ordained minister arrived, gave important aid to the spread of the church. The wisdom of this ecclesiastical organization was demonstrated by the quick expansion of the Methodist Church as it followed closely the progress of settlement in the Old Northwest.

Kentucky emigrants first brought Methodism north of the Ohio. Francis Clark, a Kentucky preacher, appeared in the

[18] Jones, *The Later Periods of Quakerism*, vol. I, pp. 420-423.

Cincinnati region at an early date, and in 1798 another Kentucky minister organized the Miami Circuit, extending along the Miami and the Little Miami valleys north from the Ohio to the Dayton neighborhood. A second circuit was established in 1800 in the Scioto Valley, and in this same year these two pioneer circuits reported 255 white and 2 colored members. There were also a few Methodists at this time in eastern Ohio, notably at Steubenville, where there were regular services "in the midst of much opposition." [19] With the rapid increase of population the Methodist Church made large gains. The Ohio District, formed in 1803, included three circuits in Ohio alone, one extending across the river in both Ohio and Virginia, and one in Virginia. In 1806 the Whitewater Circuit in southeastern Indiana was set off, and two years later the Ohio District, which now numbered 3,885 white and 29 black persons, was divided into the Miami and the Muskingum Districts. Methodism continued to grow in Ohio, until by 1810 the Miami District reported 4,756 white and 28 colored members, the Muskingum District 2,271 and 15 respectively.[20] The advance into Indiana and Illinois was equally swift. The Whitewater circuit, the first one in Indiana, extended down the Whitewater Valley from about the present site of Richmond to the Ohio, and then up the Miami Valley, thus including the chief settlements in the "gore." The early itinerant on this circuit made his rounds with characteristic aggressiveness, gathering into the different "classes" the Methodist families which had settled among the Baptists and Quakers of the region. In Clark's Grant, Methodist activity seems to have started with a two days' meeting which two Methodist preachers held at Springville in 1801. From time to time, other Methodist ministers from Ken-

---

[19] *Minutes of the Annual Conference of the Methodist Episcopal Churches for the Years 1773–1813*, p. 243; Chaddock, *Ohio before 1850*, pp. 112-113; Sweet, *Rise of Methodism in the West*, pp. 16-17; *History of Belmont and Jefferson Counties* (Ohio), p. 503.

[20] Sweet, *Rise of Methodism in the West*, p. 91; *Ohio Almanac* for 1808; *Minutes of the Annual Conferences of the Methodist Episcopal Church, for the Years 1773–1813*, p. 480.

tucky crossed the Ohio to preach in the pioneer cabins, and in 1808 the Silver Creek Circuit was formed, embracing the chief settlements in Clark's Grant. In the Vincennes region one of the earliest Methodist services was conducted in the old fort by the light of tallow candles, one of which, according to tradition, Governor William Henry Harrison held.[21] In the Illinois settlements Rev. Joseph Lillard from Kentucky organized a Methodist class which soon dissolved, but was reorganized in 1796 by Rev. Hosea Riggs, a local preacher, and in 1803 the Methodist settlers in the American Bottoms petitioned the Western Conference to send them a regular preacher. Benjamin Young came out a year later as the missionary pastor of the Illinois Circuit, which in three years had 218 white and 2 colored members. In 1808 the different circuits in Indiana and Illinois and at least two others in Missouri were organized as the Indiana District, which by 1810 had 1,692 white and 9 colored members.[22] This swift progress was typical of the rise of the Methodist Church in the Old Northwest, and it soon became an important influence for law and order, as well as a spiritual organization.

An important factor in the swift spread of religion in the Old Northwest was the practical sense and aggressiveness of the ministers in the early years of settlement. Not particular about the place of worship, they frequently held services in groves, with congregations sitting around on logs, or else they officiated in the cabins of the pioneers. Often they made use of public buildings, schoolhouses, or courthouses. In Steubenville, an upper room of the courthouse was free to all denominations, and here for years Dr. Joseph Doddridge conducted Episcopalian worship. At Cross Creek, Jefferson County, every third Saturday this same indefatigable minister preached at the "house of the Widow McGuire." When

[21] Sweet, *Rise of Methodism in the West*, pp. 26-28; Sweet, *Circuit Rider Days in Indiana*, pp. 4-5 and 9.

[22] Reynolds, *Pioneer History of Illinois*, pp. 214-218; Sweet, *Rise of Methodism in the West*, pp. 33 and 152; *Minutes of the Annual Conferences of the Methodist Episcopal Churches for the Years 1773-1813*, p. 480.

church buildings were erected they were at first quite primitive, many of them mere log houses. The Presbyterian Church in Cincinnati was considered one of the best in the Northwest Territory. The stout frame building, thirty by forty feet, was "inclosed with clapboards, but neither lathed, plastered, nor ceiled." The floor, of boat plank, was loosely laid on sleepers, and planks that rested on blocks of wood served as seats. The pulpit was fashioned from a "breastwork of unplaned cherry boards," behind which the preacher stood upon a boat plank supported by two blocks of wood. As wealth increased, the church buildings became more pretentious, and by 1812 the Presbyterian congregation in Cincinnati was able to raise $16,000.00 in subscriptions for a new church. At Chillicothe, in 1809, the new Presbyterian church impressed a traveler as a fine building, with a congregation that "would do credit to some of the first churches" in seaboard towns.[23]

Generally the preacher could be sure of a receptive hearing from the frontiersmen, who were inclined to be superstitious, and were essentially fundamentalists. From an early religious training, they had imbibed a deep respect for spiritual matters which made their settlements a fruitful field for the early minister. Especially did the tide of religious enthusiasm run high among these Western settlers at times of public excitement. Thus, "a great concourse" of the inhabitants of Cincinnati assembled at the stone meetinghouse in May, 1812, to hear a sermon that was preached to the Cincinnati Troop before it left for active service. The sermon bristled with patriotic militarism, the minister choosing the text, "Prepare war, wake up the mighty men, let all the men of war draw near; let them come up; beat your ploughshares into swords and your pruning-hooks into spears; let the weak say I am strong." In contrast to this militant and evidently popular sermon, a lengthy article appeared about the same

[23] Doddridge, *Notes*, ed. 1876, pp. 15-16; Finley, *Sketches of Western Methodism*, pp. 102, 193; Montfort, *One Hundred Years of Presbyterianism in the Ohio Valley*, p. 12; *Scioto Gazette*, April 24, 1809.

time in a Marietta paper that was headed: "Hear ye, Hear ye, The Word of the Lord." The author, evidently a pacifist, proposed that the next three weeks should be observed as a solemn fast, during which no one should partake of either flesh or strong drink. At the end of this period of religious fervor he would have the entire village assemble together, "and on whom the spirit of the Lord has come, let him or her boldly declare the Word of the Lord." [24] Even in ordinary times, the attendance upon religious meetings was excellent. Rev. John W. Browne, the Congregational minister who edited *Liberty Hall*, on a tour through the Western Reserve in the summer of 1809, preached at Warren two evenings, with a "considerable number" in attendance. In the village of Burton, he noted about seventy or eighty persons, including twenty to thirty men, who had met for worship on the Sabbath.[25]

There were many unattached ministers who wandered through the Old Northwest, preaching wherever they could find an audience. One of these itinerant parsons, Rev. Casper Voorhes, advertised a sermon "in the German language," to be delivered at the courthouse in Cincinnati, Sunday, September 15, 1811, an evidence of the presence of a considerable German element in the settlement at this early time.[26] Many other footloose ministers preached from time to time in the different settlements, some of them evangelists and others fanatical cranks. Thus, Rev. Samuel F. Council, D.D., of Virginia, who was advertised to preach at Cincinnati in 1806, did not acknowledge a connection with any particular denomination, but claimed rather to be "a reasoner," and preached "upon the belief in God and no more," denying the Westminster Confession of Faith, and in particular the articles upon the Trinity.[27] Doubtless with a much stronger appeal to Western orthodoxy was a sermon upon the Devil,

[24] *Western Spy*, May 23, 1812; *Western Spectator*, May 23, 1812.
[25] Browne's *Cincinnati Almanac* for 1812, pp. 27-28.
[26] *Western Spy*, September 14, 1811.
[27] *Liberty Hall*, September 1, 1806.

which the Rev. William O. Thompson proposed to preach at the courthouse in Vincennes, in September, 1810. The reverend gentleman promised to answer "unscriptural and irrational errors concerning that mighty potentate," with "clear, rational, and scriptural discovery and refutation." For the sake of the "honest, naked truth," he asked for a hearing, although there is no record as to whether this request was granted. In strong contrast to this rather erratic parson was Lorenzo Dow, the famous evangelist, who preached merely "for the purpose of spreading the gospel," and who, according to one Western enthusiast, "for his zeal and industry in inculcating the doctrines of morality and religion, has rarely been excelled." [28]

One of the difficult problems of the pioneer ministers was to supply the early settlers with the Bibles and the religious literature which were so welcome, but for which many backwoods households could not pay. In the earliest years of settlement piously-minded persons in the Eastern states helped to supply this need. Among the subscriptions to establish the first colony of the Ohio Company at Marietta was one for a Bible "of the first quality" to be placed in the church, and the Connecticut Missionary Society appropriated $200.00 in 1802 for Bibles and religious literature to be distributed by the missionaries in the Western Reserve. Through this same medium this society distributed also a *Summary of Christian Duties and Doctrines,* which had been compiled under its direction. The Methodist circuit riders, always practical, used their saddlebags to bring religious as well as secular books to their members.[29] The development of the book trade in the Old Northwest was a great aid to the ministers and their congregations. Many Bibles of the old-fashioned family type, and also ordinary ones, were offered for sale, along with dictionaries of the Bible, the latter including

[28] *Western Sun,* September 15, 1810; *Scioto Gazette,* September 24, 1804.
[29] *Subscription List, 1788, Western Reserve MSS.* no. 607; *Extracts, Minutes of Congregational Association for 1802,* p. 9, and *Ibid. for 1805,* p. 3; Sweet, *Rise of Methodism in the West,* pp. 68–69.

especially the one that was published by Zadock Cramer, and was advertised at Vincennes in 1805. Another popular book, *The Easy Instructor, or A New Method of Teaching Sacred Harmony,* included the rudiments of music and a number of "Psalm Tunes." [30] But many settlers were so far off from the towns, or else so poverty-stricken, that some systematic means of distributing Bibles seemed necessary. At Cincinnati in 1811 a number of persons of all denominations formed the Miami Bible Society, the first of a number of similar organizations, in order to distribute Bibles to the poor and to frontier churches. Dues were $1.00 annually, or $15.00 for a life membership. The Ohio Bible Society which was founded at Marietta in 1802, with Rufus Putnam at its head, received 481 Bibles and 67 Testaments in the first year of its existence, as a donation from sister societies, presumably in the Eastern states. In addition, the Scioto Bible Society and the Connecticut Reserve Bible Society were soon engaged in the work of distributing Bibles to the inhabitants of the Old Northwest. This movement spread, and even at New Design in the Illinois settlements, a group of American settlers subscribed $100.00 for a Bible Society, although none of them, it must be confessed, ever paid up.[31] Another closely related phase of religious activity in the Old Northwest was the gradual spread of Sunday schools. The first one, it is claimed, was started at Marietta in the early summer of 1791 by Mrs. Mary Lake, who at first collected a group of four or five children, which gradually increased to twenty, in the stockade of Campus Martius.[32] Other Sunday schools followed in the different settlements.

The ministers in the early Western settlements were usually men of fine moral fiber and great courage, qualities that were highly necessary in view of the inadequate financial

[30] *Western Sun,* April 20, 1808; *The Supporter,* March 16, 1809.

[31] Drake, *Picture of Cincinnati in 1815,* pp. 164-165; *Reynolds, Pioneer History of Illinois,* p. 227; *Western Spectator,* October 31, 1812; *Western Spy,* October 9, 1813; *Weekly Recorder,* October 25 and November 1, 1814.

[32] *The First Sabbath School in Marietta, Western Reserve MSS.* no. 613, p. 17.

support they received, and the many hardships they were called upon to undergo. Rev. Daniel Story, the first minister in Marietta, was supposed to have an allowance of $15.00 per week and his board. But a large part of his salary depended upon the contributions of parishioners, which did not seem to come up to expectations, and the remainder, which the Ohio Company had subscribed, was paid at irregular intervals. In 1798 the young minister's prospects brightened when he became pastor of the combined Congregational and Presbyterian church at Marietta, with a salary of $300.00 which was increased to $450.00 when the congregation took over the local "ministerial section" of reserved land. Soon dissensions arose in this mixed congregation, a number of members withdrew, and Story voluntarily gave up half his salary. He resigned in 1804 and died a few months later, worn out by the difficulties and prejudices he had encountered.[33] The hardships he suffered were duplicated and even exceeded by the early missionaries to the Western Reserve. Rev. Joseph Badger, whom the Connecticut Missionary Society sent out in 1800, returned to his old home in 1802, and brought his wife and six children back to the Western settlements. After he had built a cabin for them at Austinburgh, and had secured a cow and necessary provisions, he departed upon a missionary tour. But when the Society cut down his meager allowance from $7.00 per week to $6.00, even this heroic minister resigned. Rev. Thomas Barr, another missionary in the Western Reserve, came to Euclid in 1809, with a salary of only $380.00, upon which he expected to support a family of nine. Although three cows and a horse helped somewhat, he found many supplies were very expensive: $2.00 per bushel for wheat, 75 cents for corn, and $8.00 to $10.00 per hundredweight for fresh pork. For several years Mr. Barr averaged five or six sermons each week,

[33] *Ohio Company Records,* Hulbert, ed., vol. I, pp. 40, 102 (note); vol. II, pp. 90, 156, 224-225; Dickinson, *First Church Organization in Marietta,* pp. 9 (note), 12, 13, 16; *Scioto Gazette,* January 21, 1805.

in addition to numerous funerals and visits.[34] Often these pioneer ministers engaged in secular occupations, also, in order to increase their scanty allowances. Isaac McCoy, whom the Baptist Church at Silver Creek, Indiana, licensed to preach in 1808, was an excellent wheelwright, and he continued to ply his trade, even after he moved to Vincennes as pastor of the Maria Creek Baptist Church. In like fashion, Dr. Joseph Doddridge, the pioneer Episcopalian minister in the upper Ohio Valley, practiced medicine in order to make ends meet. Still another notable example of the Western settlers who combined secular occupations with clerical duties was Edward Tiffin, the first governor of Ohio. On weekdays he carried on the exacting routine of a country doctor, and on Sundays he preached regularly at his appointments in the neighborhood of Chillicothe.[35] It was devotion to duty, such as this, on the part of the pioneer ministers that made possible the quick spread of religious organizations through the Western settlements.

The typical minister of the Old Northwest was the Methodist circuit rider who carried his message through the forests, across swamps, and through dangerous fords to the settlers on the frontier. Aggressive, usually not overly educated, he thoroughly understood the frontier masses with whom he dealt, and he exerted a very real influence over them. The length of the average circuit over which he traveled is almost unbelievable. Whitewater Circuit extended from Hamilton across country to the Whitewater, down that stream to Lawrenceburgh, and then up the Miami back to Hamilton. This circuit the preacher was expected to make every four weeks, stopping at many regular appointments on the way. Will's Creek Circuit was even longer, extending from Zanesville, as a center, for 475 miles over rough trails, and at times the minister was compelled to strike through

[34] Kennedy, *Plan of Union*, pp. 20, 21, 47; Extracts, *Minutes of the General Association for Connecticut* (Congregational) *for 1806*, pp. 2-4.

[35] Stewart, *Early Baptist Missionaries and Pioneers*, vol. I, pp. 201-228; Doddridge, *Notes*, pp. 11-12; Finley, *Sketches of Western Methodism*, pp. 264-265.

the wilderness in order to make his round within the expected four weeks. The compensation which the circuit rider received for such arduous work was pathetically small, at first an annual allowance of only $64.00, and traveling expenses that included board, such as it was, at the homes of his members. In 1800 this pittance was increased to $80.00 and traveling expenses for the circuit rider himself, a similar allowance for a wife, $16.00 for each child up to seven, and $24.00 for those between seven and fourteen. Even these meager sums were seldom paid in full. In the Miami District in 1809, apparently only one preacher received his entire allowance, and ten circuits reported deficiencies that ranged between $4.55 and $67.00 each.[36] With such meager support the life of a circuit rider usually became a struggle for the bare necessities of life. When Rev. James B. Finley went to the Will's Creek Circuit with its round of 475 miles, his first occupation was to build a cabin, twelve by fourteen feet, in which the chief articles were a bed and some wearing apparel. When his funds were practically exhausted, he sold the very boots off his feet in order to purchase provisions for his family. Another famous Methodist preacher, Peter Cartwright, after working for three years on the Marietta Circuit of about three hundred miles along both banks of the Ohio, decided to return to his home in southern Kentucky for a new outfit. As he has himself forcibly pointed out, "my horse had gone blind; my saddle was worn out; my bridle reins had been eaten up and replaced—after a sort—at least a dozen times; and my clothes had been patched until it was difficult to detect the original." With only seventy-five cents in his pocket, Cartwright set out on horseback, upon the long journey of nearly five hundred miles. Aided by the generally kind attitude toward the circuit rider, he reached his home with six and a quarter cents in his pocket. His father gave him a fresh horse, a bridle and saddle, some new clothes, and forty dol-

[36] Sweet, *Rise of Methodism in the West*, pp. 27, 46-47, 165; Finley, *Autobiography*, p. 194.

lars in cash, and he left, "equipped" for another three years of service.[37]

The very difficulties he encountered strengthened the determination of the circuit rider to carry out his mission. This is well illustrated in the career of Peter Cartwright, who was a militant Christian, ready to hold his own, when necessary, against frontier rowdies. When a band armed with knives, clubs, and whips swore they would break up a camp meeting which was being held in the Scioto Valley, and continually interrupted the preachers, Cartwright called upon the magistrates to enforce the law. In the mêlée that ensued, he knocked down the leader of the mob, and when all the ministers, from the presiding elder down, refused to preach, he ascended the pulpit and held his congregation. Next day he was on hand at the magistrate's court to see that about thirty disturbers of the peace received adequate punishment. Upon another occasion, two young men threatened to horsewhip Cartwright because, they claimed, he had administered a liquid that gave their sisters the "jerks." Cartwright instantly pulled out a bottle, which, he relates, was quite formidable in appearance, but actually it was filled with innocent peppermints. Advancing toward the belligerent brothers, he shouted, "yes; if I gave your sisters the jerks, I will give them to you too." Badly frightened, the men backed off, and the quick-witted preacher escaped, unharmed. Ready wit of this sort was frequently a great aid, as the Methodists, especially, suffered from attempts by rowdies to interrupt their meetings. Indeed, disturbances of an annoying type frequently occurred at religious meetings on the frontier. At Chillicothe, during a season of "extreme hot weather," it became necessary to appeal to the sense of justice of men "of decent manners and respectability," who were accustomed to crowd the windows and doors of the meetinghouse, thus "pre-

[37] Finley, *Autobiography*, pp. 193-195; Cartwright, *Autobiography*, pp. 102-106.

venting the circulation of fresh air to the weaker sex," who were inside.[38]

Through their readiness to take up the cudgels in a religious controversy, the Methodist circuit riders became the heroes of many a wordy contest with their more modest Baptist brethren over Calvinism and immersion. The Universalists, who were scattered throughout the Old Northwest, were the special objects of Methodist wrath, along with the Deists, with whom they were frequently confused. There were many ecclesiastical denunciations of the Shakers also, and occasionally there were actual encounters with them. Thus, Peter Cartwright once invited the Shaker elders from the settlement at West Union, Indiana, to take part in a debate in the neighborhood. But the elders, after indulging in much personal abuse of Cartwright, departed without giving him a chance to reply. Undaunted, the courageous circuit rider openly denounced the "dreadful delusion," and visited many members of the Shaker community in their cabins. He "rescued" eighty-seven individuals, and formed them immediately into a Methodist congregation. This persistent aggressiveness of the circuit rider was illustrated also at Marietta, where the Calvinistic Puritans who had founded the settlement strongly opposed the establishment of a Methodist congregation. After persistent efforts a Methodist church was organized here in 1804, but the congregation rarely assembled without a shower of stones from a mob, or some other evidence of hostility.[39] Doubtless a partial explanation of this violent prejudice was to be found in the legal requirements that the income from the lands reserved for ministerial support must be apportioned among the different religious organizations.[40] But this opposition was in vain when it confronted the aggressive Methodist circuit rider.

[38] Cartwright, *Autobiography*, pp. 49-50, 91-92; *Scioto Gazette*, July 9, 1804.

[39] Sweet, *Rise of Methodism in the West*, pp. 52-54; Cartwright, *Autobiography*, pp. 53-55; Finley, *Sketches of Western Methodism*, pp. 454-459.

[40] *Laws of Ohio*, Third General Assembly, pp. 200-207; Fourth General Assembly, pp. 33-34; *Commentator*, June 5, 1810.

Just as the circuit rider was the typical preacher, so the camp meeting was the characteristic form of worship in the Old Northwest. Starting among the Presbyterians of eastern Kentucky, the camp meeting with its accompanying revival reached a climax in the great meeting at Cane Ridge in Kentucky in August, 1801, with some 25,000 persons attending these services.[41] The revival of religion and the doctrine of conversion that accompanied it met a quick response from the Western people. Its central idea of the need for personal salvation, and for some outward manifestation of the change from a state of sin to one of righteousness, was peculiarly suited to frontier psychology with its impulsiveness, its lack of restraint, and its credulity. The camp meeting, too, served as a convenient excuse to bring the settlers together in the social gatherings which were so popular among them. One of the most interesting features of this spiritual movement was the physical exertion that so frequently accompanied periods of religious exaltation, the falling exercise, the "jerks" which spread like a contagion, dancing, shouting, and many other forms of hysterical excess. The camp meeting, with its attendant revival, spread like wildfire across the Ohio, even penetrating as far as the Western Reserve. The inhabitants of the Old Northwest, like the people of Kentucky, thronged these meetings, and there were the usual accompaniments of spiritual fervor which was so often expressed in bodily exercise. The reactions of the different denominations were, of course, chiefly determined by their own peculiar doctrines and methods. Although individual ministers attempted to tone down the most violent features, the Methodists usually accepted the camp meeting and the revival, since the doctrine of repentance was a cardinal principle of their own creed. The Calvinistic Baptists, however, rather discouraged such methods, and the Presbyterians split into two camps: the conservatives who held to the old accepted doctrines, and the less orthodox who supported the camp meeting and

[41] Cleveland, *The Great Revival in the West*, 1797–1805, *passim*.

its methods, and preached the doctrine of an inner light in each soul.

One of the obvious results of the camp meetings was the impetus they gave to new and radical religious movements.[42] The New Lights, as the more liberal division in the Presbyterian Church was soon called, separated from the parent church, entire congregations under the leadership of their pastors going over to this new organization. Claiming that the Bible was their sole guide, these "schismatics" fully accepted the camp meeting and the revival, along with their religious excesses. They were especially strong in southern Ohio, and from their ranks the Shakers, a much more radical sect from New York State, secured many recruits. The Shakers, or "The United Brethren of Believers in Christ's Second Appearing," as they called themselves, indulged in strange physical contortions that resembled the hysterical excesses at revivals. Their societies were organized upon a communistic basis, and they refused to recognize marriage as a Christian institution. The first important Shaker community in southern Ohio was founded in 1805, with 370 members, at Union Village three miles west of Lebanon, under the leadership of Rev. Richard McNemar who had become an influential figure in the New Light secession from the Presbyterian Church. This community became quite prosperous, farming an extensive tract and producing a large part of their own supplies. They soon had a lively trade with their neighbors, and their careful workmanship and general reliability secured high prices and ready sales. But the peculiar Shaker views upon marriage, added to the refusal to bear arms, and the natural antagonism of the New Lights, aroused intense hostility, and three times between 1810 and 1813 infuriated mobs attacked Union Village, and small groups horsewhipped individual Shakers.

In spite of persecution, the Shakers were quite aggressive. Missionaries from Union Village established other Shaker

[42] For the New Light and the Shaker movements, see McLean, *Shakers of Ohio*, pp. 28-40, 59 *ff.*, 190 *ff.*, and 276 *ff.*

communities, one of them at Watervleit. This settlement, which held title to at least 800 acres, was exceedingly prosperous, but it, too, was attacked by a mob. Shaker missionaries also managed to convert two settlements on Eagle Creek and Straight Creek in Adams County, Ohio, which, under the leadership of their pastor, Rev. John Dunlavy, had forsaken the Presbyterian Church to join the New Lights. Probably because of the usual antagonism of their neighbors, the people of these two communities left their homes, a part of them to settle at Union Village, the others to take the long journey by water to West Union, on Busseron Creek, in Knox County, Indiana, where the Shakers, in their usual fashion, had converted to their faith other New Lights. There the Shakers established a flourishing settlement, although they often suffered from Indian attacks and from much plundering under the polite name of requisitions by the militia. The strong hostility to Shakerism brought about a war of pamphlets pro and con, and numerous wordy articles in the newspapers of Ohio and Indiana continued the controversy.[43] In Ohio, where the Shaker doctrine of celibacy led many men to abandon their wives and their children, leaving them "destitute of the means of support," popular indignation soon found expression in an act of the state legislature in 1811. This measure provided that, upon a petition from a woman that her husband had left her to join the Shakers, the court of common pleas should award her a "just and equitable" portion of the family property. The court was also to set aside property for the support of minor children, who were to be under the mother's care. Furthermore, the law provided a fine of $500.00 for any one who enticed a man from his wife and family to join the Shaker faith, although this penalty did not extend to sermons or public addresses.[44] In spite of such regulations, the Shakers continued to flourish.

Psychologically, the camp meetings aroused a religious

---

[43] *Liberty Hall,* July 11 and 25, 1810; *Western Sun,* October 6, 1810.
[44] *Laws of Ohio,* Ninth General Assembly, pp. 13-16.

emotionalism among the inhabitants of the Old Northwest, which frequently showed itself in crises. Thus, during the Indian raids upon the border settlers, just before the War of 1812, there was much popular excitement and even superstitious exaggeration. This attitude was even more pointedly shown during the series of earthquakes, beginning December 16, 1811, that centered in the Mississippi Valley. While they were in progress, furniture was thrown about in the Ohio Valley even, doors flew open, and bricks fell from the tops of chimneys. Many of the settlers interpreted these physical phenomena as manifestations of Divine wrath, and they flocked to the churches to pray and repent of their sins, with a considerable addition to the ranks of church members, Whitewater Circuit in southeastern Indiana increasing from 567 to 843.[45] This disposition to find a supernatural interpretation for important happenings was widespread, with a striking example in Deacon Enoch Shepard of the First Presbyterian Church of Marietta, who wrote an essay entitled, "Thoughts on the Prophecies applicable to the Times." The deacon's chief theory was that the French Revolution, in the light of the Prophecies, really forecast the fall of the Papacy. Other essays of a much similar character bore such weighty titles as: *The Probability of Revelation, The Tests of Revelation,* and *The Impression of the Divine Character in the Energy of the Christian Religion.* The prevailing orthodoxy also appeared in the form of many theological controversies. A battle of this type in Cincinnati in 1808 was opened with a pamphlet entitled, *The Dagon of Calvinism, or The Moloch of Decrees, a Poem in Three Cantoes.* The author of this vitriolic publication, which attacked both the Baptists and the Presbyterians, was, it was claimed, protected by the Methodist Church. Rev. Joshua L. Wilson, pastor of the Presbyterian church in Cincinnati, answered with a counter blast, *Episcopal Methodism or Dagon Exhibited,* which he

[45] Drake, *Picture of Cincinnati in 1815,* pp. 233-240; Sweet, *Rise of Methodism in the West,* pp. 28-29; *Western Spy,* December 28, 1811, and January 18, 1812.

offered to the faithful at 25 cents the copy. A solemn ecclesiastical war now arose, in which the *Western Spy* printed the thunderbolts launched by Rev. Mr. Wilson, the champion of the Calvinists, and the rival newspaper, *Liberty Hall*, published the equally pungent attacks of Rev. Solomon Langdon, the defender of the Arminians. Other controversialists entered the field, until the dispute finally died down for want of public interest.[46]

Radical theology and the rise of new sects were not the sole results of the camp meetings and the accompanying revivals. The regularly established congregations had large accessions as well. Thus, the combined Congregational and Presbyterian church in the tiny hamlet of Austinburgh in the Western Reserve added forty members after the revival, probably more than a hundred per cent of its previous entire membership.[47] The Baptists, too, profited, in spite of their rather indifferent attitude toward camp meetings, and their mother church at Columbia, alone, received ninety members in the course of one year.[48] By 1810 the region covered by the original Miami and Scioto circuits combined, had a total membership of 7,070, for whom two districts, the Miami and the Muskingum,[49] had been formed, and undoubtedly the camp meetings and the revivals had been an influence in this notable increase. But the actual church membership in the Old Northwest was never large in proportion to the total population. In 1810 the Methodists, by far the strongest denomination, had a membership of approximately 8,750. If all the other denominations combined had an equal number of members, a very liberal estimate indeed, the entire church membership at this time in the Old Northwest was scarcely

[46] *Western Spectator*, September 7, November 23 and 30, 1811; Files of *Western Spy* and *Liberty Hall*, November, 1811–March, 1812, and especially *Western Spy*, January 11 and April 11, 1812; Sweet, *Rise of Methodism in the West*, pp. 50-51.
[47] Kennedy, *Plan of Union*, p. 29.
[48] Benedict, *History of the Baptists in America*, vol. II, p. 260.
[49] *Minutes of the Annual Conferences of the Methodist Episcopal Churches for the Years 1773–1813*, p. 480.

seven per cent of the population.[50] But the influence of religion was not to be measured by the mere numbers of church members, for the camp meetings, the circuit riders, and the many devoted preachers and missionaries who traveled through the wilderness, spread religion as a civilizing and moderating influence, even to the outlying habitations of the backwoods.

One of the outward evidences of the far-reaching and vital influence of religion upon the inhabitants of the Old Northwest, was the passage of legislation that regulated minute details of moral conduct and the observance of the Sabbath, in the Northwest Territory, in Ohio, and in Indiana. The marked religious bent shown in such legislation also found expression in the observance of public fast or thanksgiving days, a custom that bore testimony also to the strong Puritan influence in the Old Northwest. Scarcely eight months after the first settlement at Marietta, in true New England fashion St. Clair proclaimed December 25, 1788, as a day of "solemn thanksgiving and praise" when all the people should "acknowledge with gratitude their infinite obligations to Almighty God for benefits received" and should "implore His superintending care and Providence for future blessings." [51] This precedent was followed later, and at critical times, especially, the hold of religion was shown in outward observance. In 1793 the governor set apart a day of fasting and prayer, this time Wednesday, September 25, for the success of Wayne's army. The next summer, when the troops were on the march to the Indian country, another proclamation set apart August 14 as a day of public "fasting, humiliation, and prayer to solicit at the throne of Grace for mercy and protection," and for the Divine blessing upon all civil and military officers.[52] At Marietta, as befitted a community of New

[50] *Minutes of the Annual Conferences of the Methodist Episcopal Churches for the Years 1773–1813*, p. 480; *U. S. Census for 1810*, pp. 69 *ff.*

[51] Proclamation of Governor St. Clair, December 17, 1788, *Executive Proceedings Northwest Territory, 1788–1795*, pp. 66–67.

[52] Proclamation of Governor St. Clair, September 21, 1793, and Proclamation of Winthrop Sargent, July 31, 1794, *Ibid.*, pp. 567, 577–579.

Englanders, the custom seems gradually to have been established of observing an annual Thanksgiving Day without even waiting for official proclamations.[53]

The strong influence of religion as it was carried to the masses by the early preachers, and especially the circuit riders, was an important factor in the unusual orderliness, for a frontier region, that was found in the Old Northwest. This was notably true in the realm of morals. Although the constant shifting of population was bound to cause much confusion in the relations between the sexes, there was no uncertainty regarding the public attitude, as it was expressed in the law codes. St. Clair and the judges had adopted an excellent law that gave the ministers the power to perform the marriage ceremony, or if the contracting parties preferred, the judges of the general court and those of the courts of common pleas were permitted to act in this capacity. This measure contained clauses, also, to guard against hasty or ill-advised action, requiring the banns to be published at least fifteen days before the ceremony, and the marriage to be properly registered. Seventeen for the man and fourteen for the woman were the minimum ages, and the parents' consent must always be secured in the case of minors. The territorial legislature retained this law, but the Ohio Code of 1805 included clauses that were better adapted to the needs of a larger population. A license was now required from the clerk of the county court of common pleas, and either an ordained minister or a justice of the peace could perform the ceremony. There were ample fines, too, for violations of the marriage laws. In 1810 this act was slightly altered to permit "the society of people called Quakers and Mennonites" to perform the ceremony according to their peculiar rites. The marriage laws of Ohio were closely followed by the Indiana Code of 1807.[54] There were also ample divorce laws.

[53] *Ohio Gazette,* November 24, 1808; *Commentator,* November 25, 1809.
[54] *Laws of the Northwest Territory,* Pease, ed., *Illinois Historical Collections,* vol. XVII, pp. 22-23, 338; *Laws of Ohio,* Third General Assembly, pp. 312-315; Eighth General Assembly, pp. 119-122; *Laws of Indiana Ter-*

· The first one, in Maxwell's Code, handed over this power to
the general court, and required the ample notice to the other
party in a suit which was necessary in a frontier country.
The revised code of Ohio repealed this law, putting all di-
vorces under the jurisdiction of the supreme court. But it
opened an easy means of escape from a frequent marital
problem of the frontier when it made a divorce automatic,
if it was proved that a previous marriage had not been dissolved at the time of the second ceremony, or when either
husband or wife had been "wilfully" absent for five years.
In Indiana the governor and judges first repealed and then
reënacted the law of Maxwell's Code on divorce. However,
they attempted to strengthen the moral code by a law that
prescribed the death penalty for bigamy, and imposed heavy
penalties for such offenses as compelling a woman to marry
against her will, or for an attack upon an "unmarried female" under sixteen.[55]

Despite law codes, there is much evidence that human
nature was as frail in the Old Northwest as it has always
been elsewhere. Irate husbands advertised they would not be
responsible for the debts of the wives who had deserted
them, and the newspapers printed many summonses to erring
spouses to appear in court to answer suits for divorce. While
notices of this type appeared in the newspapers printed in
all sections of the Old Northwest, they were especially numerous, in proportion to the population, in the Illinois country. Such names as Therese Amoux, Victoire Aurel, Celeste
Champaign, and Sarah Masterson show that erring wives
were found among both French and American inhabitants.[56]
Occasionally these newspaper notices give glimpses of the

ritory, 1801–1809, Philbrick, ed., *Illinois Historical Collections*, vol. XXI,
pp. 251-252.

[55] *Laws of the Northwest Territory*, Pease, ed., *Illinois Historical Collections*, vol. XVII, pp. 258-260; *Laws of Ohio*, Third General Assembly, pp.
177-179; *Laws of Indiana Territory*, Philbrick, ed., *Illinois Historical Collections*, vol. XXI, pp. 15, 66-68.

[56] *Western Sun*, July 25, 1807; *Louisiana Gazette*, March 8, 1810, September 12 and October 19, 1811.

tragedies that arose in the domestic life of these early set-tlers. Uriah Gates, for example, gave notice that his wife, Rebecca, had stolen his money, meal, flour, and meat, and had gone to another man's home. Uriah plaintively added, "she threatens to peel every apple tree in my orchard, and to close the scene, poison me." [57] Another erring wife had run away from Greenville with a discharged soldier, and at Columbia this precious pair had sold all of the husband's wearing apparel, his farming tools, his feather beds, and his household furniture, and had stolen two deeds to lots.[58] But the woman was not always to blame, as was evident from the many appeals of wives for freedom from the husbands who had deserted them. For example, Silence Gardner asked for a divorce from Benoni Gardner of Washington County, who had deserted her after twenty years of married life.[59] Elias Thompson, who had deserted his wife and two children in New York State, came to Ohio to find that the frontier, even, did not afford a safe refuge from matrimonial bonds. His family followed him, and by a public notice his wife, who was evidently a woman of determination, left him without any excuse, if he failed to support her and their children.[60] In Indiana with its more scattered and primitive population, the aid of the legislature was occasionally necessary, in order to straighten out matrimonial tangles. A typical case was that of Catharine Moore, who, first marrying John Prince, had been promptly deserted by her spouse. Understanding by hearsay that Prince had embarked upon a second matrimonial adventure, the lady soon consoled herself by marrying Robert Moore, without taking the trouble to secure a divorce, and the Indiana legislature legalized this second marriage. Another case that was settled in similar fashion arose when Elizabeth Richardson discovered, "to her great mortification," that her husband was a member of a notori-

[57] *Western Spy*, October 26, 1807.
[58] *Freeman's Journal*, August 27, 1796.
[59] *Ohio Gazette*, February 5, 1802.
[60] *Liberty Hall*, January 23, 1811.

ous band of thieves. As he had been drummed out of Indiana, the legislature obligingly dissolved this marriage, too.[61]

In addition to the restraining influence of religion, the enforcement of law by an able and conscientious group of judges and lawyers must not be overlooked, in any attempt to account for the comparatively good order that prevailed among the frontiersmen of the Old Northwest. The requirements for admission to the bar, set up under the leadership of Judge Burnet, had their effect in the Northwest Territory, and later in Ohio and in Indiana. The life of these early Western lawyers was by no means an easy one, with settlements that were so far apart. Because of their small number, the members of the bar of the Northwest Territory were accustomed to accompany the judges on their circuits, and Judge Burnet has given an interesting description of a typical journey from Cincinnati to Vincennes in 1799. Descending the Ohio to the Falls at Louisville, this party of legal luminaries struck across country from this point, and not until the seventh day of this journey through the wilderness did they arrive at their destination.[62] With journeys of this type in prospect, it is no wonder that the judges and the lawyers objected so strenuously to sessions of courts in distant counties. The results are illustrated by a complaint from Sargent in 1798 that in four of the new counties which the growing population of the Old Northwest had made necessary, no sessions of the general court had been held for the past three years.[63] Nor was the situation much improved after the division of the Northwest Territory. In 1802 the Hamilton County court was obliged to adjourn, because the "gentlemen of the bar" had not returned from Marietta, where doubtless they had been attending the sessions of the superior court. The judges of Indiana Territory, also, complained that they were obliged to hold court once a year in

[61] *Laws of Indiana Territory*, Philbrick, ed., *Illinois Historical Collections*, vol. XXI, p. 648; Third General Assembly, Second Session, pp. 4-5.
[62] Burnet, *Notes*, pp. 64-65 and 72-73.
[63] Sargent to Judges of the Territory, April 5, 1798, *Journal, Northwest Territory*, 1788–1803.

each county, which created "a circuit of fifteen hundred miles of wilderness intersected with many large streams difficult of passage." [64] The evil consequences of this situation were felt especially in the distant Illinois settlements, and were an important factor in the early disorders there.

In spite of the arduous character of their duties, the judges in the Northwest Territory were usually men of a high type who were fearless in searching out violations of the law, even though such action might be highly unpopular. Thus, Judge Turner, in opening the general court at Cincinnati in 1794, called especial attention to the law against gambling, and insisted that he was determined to enforce it. A few months later, Oliver Spencer, a judge of the probate court in Hamilton County, denounced the frequent failure to account in his court for the estates of deceased persons. Altogether fearless in its denunciation of crime was Judge Goforth's charge to the grand jury, in opening the court of quarter sessions at Cincinnati in March, 1795. This document, which was printed in the *Centinel* in response to a special request from the grand jury, insisted that this body should inquire into the observance of the law against gambling.[65] In the rural districts, court procedure in the early days was often primitive, and at the same time quite effective. An eyewitness has described the trial, at the mouth of the Ashtabula River, of a young man who was accused of injuring his neighbor's property and stealing his horse. On one side was a young lawyer, lately from Connecticut, and the legal representative of the opposing side was a bricklayer. Another observer has left a sketch of the monthly court held at Letart Falls on the Ohio, when that small settlement became the rendezvous of some sixty or seventy men. Part of them were interested in trials for small debts, defamation, assaults, and the like, and the remainder came to wrestle, fight, shoot at a mark for wagers, gamble, or drink whisky. This same traveler has also given

[64] *Western Spy*, November 3, 1802; Petition to Congress from Judges of Indiana Territory, November 1, 1803, *Vanderburgh Papers*, no. 732.
[65] *Centinel*, April 19 and November 22, 1794, March 7, 1795.

an interesting description of the primitive court that was held by Squire Ellis on the bank of the Ohio opposite Maysville. Seated on a bench under two locust trees, the squire had a table before him with pen and ink, and several men sat on the same bench awaiting his decisions. When he had finished, the entire company adjourned to a near-by tavern where they drank a toast to peace and good order.[66]

But crime was inevitable in a newly settled section, and robbery was perhaps the most common offense, as was to be expected where settlement was so scattered. An incident that attracted much local attention happened in 1809, when a gang of twelve men attacked a house east of Dayton, and carried away $400.00, two guns, and some clothing. Going to another house in the neighborhood these same marauders stole $333.00, one or two silver watches, a piece of broadcloth, and sundry other articles. Other robbers stole $200.00 from an aged couple in Madison County, Ohio, and in still another robbery the thieves broke into a house near Portsmouth in the absence of the owner and his family, and stole two guns and a large quantity of clothing. Although the owner offered a considerable reward, none of this property seems to have been returned.[67] Occasionally thieves broke into shops, and John Cellars of Chillicothe complained that he had been robbed of sixteen gold and silver watches, two pairs of silver sugar tongs, and one set of spoons. At Steubenville Thomas Gray offered a reward of $15.00 for the apprehension of the individual who broke into his pattern shop, stole two bars of lead weighing about 50 pounds each, and broke a number of articles.[68] The very attention that these incidents attracted showed how rarely really serious robberies were committed.

Occasionally, in the more remote districts, bands of robbers held up travelers on the waterways as well as on the

[66] Melish, *Travels*, vol. II, pp. 283-284; Cuming, *Sketches of a Tour in the Western Country*, pp. 16, 180.

[67] *The Farmer's Friend*, October 2, 1809; *The Supporter*, June 23, 1810; *Scioto Gazette*, July 10, 1806.

[68] *Ibid.*, November 20, 1806; *Western Herald*, May 20, 1808.

land routes. One gang, which had its headquarters on the White River in Indiana, was a real menace to voyagers down the Ohio, seizing boats with their cargoes, and often murdering the occupants, while other bands of outlaws had their strongholds on the Ohio, notably the one at Cave-in-the-Rock, but they soon disappeared as more settlers came in. There was also much trouble from irresponsible wanderers on the highways, the hitch hikers of the Old Northwest. Upon one occasion, two of them stopped at Belpre and stole several trunks filled with cash, jewelry, and other articles valued at $2,000.00 to $3,000.00. Seizing a skiff, they escaped to the Virginia bank where they were soon captured and the stolen property was recovered. The Washington County court sentenced one of them to receive 39 lashes with a fine of $250.00, and the other one to be given 15 lashes and to pay a fine of $50.00. An incident that was much like modern happenings of a similar nature occurred near Poland in the Western Reserve. A man came to the store of James Hazlep with a considerable quantity of clothing, linen, and other articles for sale, but this pioneer storekeeper forced him to confess he had stolen these goods from washtubs and hedges along the road, and would have taken him to prison had he not escaped, leaving behind him the goods, and a horse that he had also doubtless stolen. Again, a probable thieves' cache was found under the roots of a tree near Cincinnati, which contained four coats, five vests, six shirts, nine pairs of stockings, and numerous other articles of apparel.[69] But such incidents were comparatively rare, and the vast majority of travelers in the Old Northwest made their journeys in perfect safety.

The swift punishment that was usually dealt out was another deterrent from crime. The common penalty for petty crimes was a fine or a whipping, and often both. Among the many records of the just but severe fashion in which this frontier justice was administered, was that of the three in-

[69] *Western Spectator*, May 2, 1812; *Trump of Fame*, July 1, 1812; *Centinel*, February 7, 1795.

dictments that were filed at the April term of the general court, in Cincinnati, in 1794. The first offender, Thomas Cochran, an innkeeper who was convicted of violating the law against gambling in public places, was sentenced to pay a fine of $100.00, with all the costs of the prosecution, and to forfeit his license. The other two accused persons, one a free negro accused of larceny, the other a runaway, were given 31 and 29 lashes apiece.[70] Occasionally penalties were much more severe. Edward Stalcup was executed at Chillicothe for the murder of Asa Mounts, and a man convicted of manslaughter at Cincinnati in 1812 was fined $1,000.00 and condemned to not more than two years' imprisonment.[71] There were numerous convictions of horse thieves, too, with hanging as the usual penalty, although occasionally the offender was let off with a fine and a whipping. Fugitives from justice were pursued, often for long distances. Thus, Robert Slaughter, a notorious horse thief, escaped to the Spanish territories, only to be seized and returned to Indiana. On the way back, he managed to shoot his captor, Joshua Harbin, but he was finally brought to trial, and in spite of strenuous objections to various points of court procedure, he was convicted.[72] Another fugitive from the Old Northwest who was caught after a long pursuit was Obadiah Wilson, a noted swindler and horse thief who had a habit of marrying women of means, and then vanishing after he had secured their property. Although he escaped from the jail at Chillicothe, Wilson was captured in Baltimore, and brought back to Ohio for trial.[73] A notorious case in Indiana was that of Abraham Hiler, accused of the murder of John Coffman of Wayne County, Indiana, who escaped to Kentucky. Governor Harrison secured his extradition and a jury convicted him, but later Hiler was pardoned.[74] On still another occasion, two

[70] *Centinel*, April 19, 1794.
[71] *Western Spy*, December 19, 1812.
[72] *Indiana Gazette*, October 16, 1804.
[73] *Massachusetts Spy*, October 9, 1805.
[74] *Executive Journal, Indiana Territory*, pp. 148-150.

horse thieves, fleeing from Urbana toward Detroit, were finally caught by Indians, who returned them with the three horses with bridles and saddles which they had stolen, and received a reward of $60.00. The thieves were put in prison in Urbana, but unfortunately some one, probably a confederate, released them during the night.[75] One of the chief means to secure the return of escaped criminals was illustrated by the reward of $20.00 that was offered for Peter Green, who "ran away from his bail." The notice described Green in rather detailed fashion as a tallow chandler, "a slave to a pipe, a German born—but can speak tolerable English." He was supposed to be on his way toward Detroit, carrying with him a quantity of "chintse and callico, etc.," which he intended trading with the Indians.[76] Other rewards were offered in Western newspapers for the return of runaway slaves and deserters from the army, and invariably these notices gave detailed descriptions.

One great obstacle to the effective punishment of the more serious crimes was the general insecurity of the early Western jails. In 1792 the governor and judges adopted an act for the Northwest Territory that required each county to provide an adequate jail, and attempted to hold either the sheriff or the jailer responsible for prisoners that escaped through their negligence. It also declared that the county would be liable when a prisoner in a civil suit broke away, owing to the "insufficiency" of the jail, and it imposed heavy penalties for an attempt to aid a prisoner to escape.[77] In spite of these rather severe provisions, there were many escapes, if the record of the Hamilton County jail was typical. In October, 1794, Daniel Symmes, the sheriff of Hamilton County, offered $10.00 reward for the return of each one of the three prisoners who had escaped from jail, and five

[75] *The Supporter*, September 7, 1811.
[76] *Freeman's Journal*, July 2, 1796.
[77] *Laws of the Northwest Territory*, Pease, ed., *Illinois Historical Collections*, vol. XVII, pp. 80-84.

months later he offered a "handsome allowance" for the return of four white men who had been confined for debt, and $10.00 for a runaway negro. The five of them had stolen a "flatt," and gone down the river. Many similar notices from Symmes show that the Hamilton County jail continued to be by no means a secure place for the confinement of prisoners.[78] A hint as to the responsibility for this situation is given by an advance of $100.00, which the territorial government made, August 24, 1795, to Nathan Barnes, the jailer, who was "ill able" to wait until the justices had inspected his accounts for firewood and the "sustenance" of prisoners. For the future, the governor and judges stipulated, the sheriff, and not the jailer, should keep these accounts.[79] Symmes continued to offer rewards for escaped prisoners, and eventually the Hamilton County jail was set on fire, supposedly by six debtors who had been confined in an upper room. Although the fire was put out, one of the prisoners managed to escape. At length the sheriff decided to place prisoners accused of serious crimes in Fort Washington for safe-keeping, but they still managed to escape.[80] It was quite clear that the attempt to fix upon the sheriff, the jailer, or the county the responsibility for escaped prisoners had failed, and the first territorial legislature in 1799 repealed these provisions of what must have been a most unpopular law.[81] Conditions in the Hamilton County jail continued to be unsatisfactory, and this same situation seems to have been general throughout Ohio and Indiana.

Aside from the Illinois settlements, there was usually good order and respect for law in the Old Northwest. But there were a few outstanding sources of trouble that were pecu-

[78] *Kentucky Gazette,* October 11, 1794; *Centinel,* March 7 and 28, and July 11, 1795.
[79] Minutes, Executive Session of Governor and Judges, August 24, 1795, *Sargent Papers.*
[80] *Centinel,* October 31, 1795, and February 27, 1796; *Freeman's Journal,* March 11, 1797.
[81] *Laws of the Northwest Territory,* Pease, ed., *Illinois Historical Collections,* vol. XVII, p. 515.

liarly typical of the frontier. Among them was the custom of settling disputes by duels. At first the men of the North-west Territory crossed the Ohio in order to fight their duels in Kentucky, but this custom aroused a strong protest, and the legislative assembly, at its first session, included dueling in the list of crimes, with heavy penalties upon seconds as well as principals.[82] In spite of this law, dueling was a common custom, until public opinion was aroused by the murder of Rice Jones on the public street in Kaskaskia in 1808, as the sequel of a duel between the murdered man and Shadrach Bond, Jr. The immediate result was the adoption by the governor and judges of Illinois Territory of an act that debarred from public office any person who participated in a duel, and required that if either principal were killed, his opponent should be tried for murder. As an alternative to the duel, this measure provided that any person who considered himself insulted should take the matter before a jury, which would have the power to award damages.[83] Still another cause of disorder came from the occasional clashes between civil and military authorities at the different army posts. In Cincinnati, especially, the citizens complained at times of the arbitrary conduct of the regular army officers at Fort Washington, and there were similar criticisms in the little town of Hamilton concerning Captain John Armstrong at Fort Hamilton.[84] Much annoyance also arose in the early Western settlements from the custom of firing arms upon the slightest pretext, and invariably as a feature of public holidays. Aside from the actual danger to the inhabitants, this practice was likely to arouse false alarms of an attack by Indians. The governor and judges of the Northwest Territory adopted an act against such offenders, but it had little effect, to judge by the "abominable practice of discharging firearms" which ushered in Christmas at Cincinnati in

[82] *Centinel,* January 9, 1796; *Laws of the Northwest Territory,* Pease, ed., *Illinois Historical Collections,* vol. XVII, p. 382.
[83] *Laws of Illinois Territory,* 1809–1811, pp. 25-27.
[84] *Symmes Correspondence,* Bond, ed., pp. 148-149, 161.

1794.[85] Such practices, however, were typical of a frontier region, and they gradually disappeared before the onmarch of civilization.

For the greater part of the early period the disorders in the Illinois settlements were an exception to the general orderliness in the Old Northwest. This situation arose chiefly from the long delay in settling land titles and the great distance from the seat of government. Especially injurious in its effects upon local order was the failure to hold regular sessions of the general court either at Kaskaskia or at Cahokia. When Judge George Turner did come to Kaskaskia in 1794, he stirred up so much trouble by his arbitrary methods that St. Clair, accompanied by Judge Symmes, was obliged to follow him a year later in order to straighten out affairs. But local dissatisfaction and disorders continued. Sargent, who went out to Kaskaskia in the fall of 1797, reported that an association, "not inconsiderable," had been formed there to support French intrigues. After a careful investigation, and personal interviews with many of the settlers, he believed he had intimidated the many "bad" men in the settlement, but he was uncertain how long any semblance of order would continue. Nor were the local officials always free from blame for conditions in early Illinois, although it is virtually impossible to form a just estimate of the maze of petty intrigues that prevailed. A typical incident was the presentation of John Dumolin, judge of the court of quarter sessions, by the grand jury at Cahokia in 1801 for having acted "tyrannically, corruptedly, and illegally." [86] After a separate territorial government was established in Illinois, the local situation greatly improved. The new territorial offi-

[85] *Laws of the Northwest Territory*, Pease, ed., *Illinois Historical Collections*, vol. XVII, pp. 32-33; *Executive Proceedings, Northwest Territory, 1788–1795*, p. 458; *Journal of Winthrop Sargent*, p. 129.

[86] Sargent to Judge Symmes, February 6, 1793, *Executive Proceedings, Northwest Territory, 1788–1795*, pp. 547-548; Alvord, *The Illinois Country*, ch. 19; James McHenry to St. Clair, May, 1796, *St. Clair Papers*, Smith, ed., vol. II, pp. 395-396; Sargent to Secretary of State (?), October 2, 1797, *Northwest Territorial Papers*, Senate Files, 6322; *Executive Journal, Indiana Territory*, p. 105.

cers received strong support, as when the grand jury unanimously thanked Judge Alexander Stuart for his charge in October, 1809, which had emphasized the necessity, if the law was to be enforced, that good citizens would come out openly as witnesses against crimes. Moreover, Judge Stuart had denounced the general disposition to help runaway slaves, and to aid prisoners to escape from jail, and in his conclusion he had summed up the entire matter when he asserted: "The crimes that have been committed within the last nine months call aloud for the efforts of all honest men to bring the guilty to punishment, and thereby set an example which will deter others from committing like offenses." By special request of the grand jury this charge was printed in the *Missouri Gazette* which circulated through the Illinois settlements.[87] Judge Stuart's vigorous denunciation of lawless conditions was supported in vigorous fashion, and many offenders in Illinois felt the authority of the courts. Two notorious ones, James Gilbraith, a former sheriff, and Jacob Funk, a justice of the peace, were each fined $25.00 for violations of the law against gambling, in spite of their very considerable influence.[88] Governor Edwards remitted both fines, but these examples, and others of a similar character, showed that the courts did not lack backbone, and that the laws would be administered impartially.

The final establishment of order in the Illinois settlements was typical of the progress that was made throughout the Old Northwest, in this early period, in enforcing the law. The American settlers who thronged into these rich lands had, for the most part, been trained in law observance, while the quick spread of religion, and its strong hold upon them, had been a steadying influence. At times this frontier religion had tended to go to radical extremes in the camp meetings and the attendant revivals. Radical sects, as the Shakers, the New Lights, and the Deists, had secured large followings, but such excesses of zeal are readily explained

[87] *Missouri Gazette,* October 26, 1809.
[88] *Illinois Territorial Records,* p. 18.

by the introspection and the impulsiveness of frontier psychology. Notwithstanding bizarre manifestations of this type, the influence of the circuit rider, and of the other heroic ministers of the Old Northwest, had been ranged alongside the fearless onslaughts upon crime by judges and other officers, in order to secure a remarkable degree of law and order among the settlers in the Old Northwest.

Chapter XVI

THE AMERICAN COLONIAL POLICY VINDICATED

IN THE twenty-four years between the first settlement at Marietta in 1788 and the outbreak of war with Great Britain in 1812, the newly formulated American colonial policy had gone through a searching test in the Old Northwest. At the close of these two and a half decades or so of settlement, the chief aims of its proponents had been achieved, and a sufficiently large American population had been induced to come in, to meet successfully British intrigues and to hold the Indians in check. The approximately 6,000 white inhabitants when the Americans first began to arrive had now increased to almost 300,000, and the Spanish danger had been ended by the quick growth of the Indiana and Illinois settlements, even before the United States had secured the left bank of the Mississippi through the Louisiana Purchase Treaty. Yet the danger from the British in Canada, in alliance with the Indians, was still to be reckoned with, although there were hopeful signs of a final victory in a critical struggle. Already the settlers in the Old Northwest, aided by their neighbors from Kentucky, had proved their military worth in several campaigns against the Indians, in spite of the temporary setback in St. Clair's defeat. Moreover, the progress of the varied forms of transportation in the Old Northwest had now made it possible to use the growing settlements as a basis for supplies as well as man power. Thus, Anthony Wayne had depended chiefly upon the Ohio Valley for the food and the horses needed for his campaign, and in like fashion the troops for the Tippecanoe expedition had been fitted out by the Western settlements. When the War of 1812 came, the population in the Old Northwest had increased so rapidly that, with the aid of their neighbors in Kentucky, they could raise and equip, except for purely military supplies, the forces that eventually met and overthrew the British and their Indian allies, thus finally saving the Old Northwest for the American nation.

The American colonial policy, as it was worked out in the Old Northwest, had also been successful in attracting a virile population, and one that, in contrast to the settlers across the Ohio in Kentucky, did not represent merely a single state, or only one distinctive section. Under the national land policy, supplemented by equally enlightened provisions for a territorial government, a stream of immigrants had been attracted into the Old Northwest which had its origin in the New England, in the Middle, and in the Southern states, and in the backwoods of western Pennsylvania, western Virginia, and Kentucky. These representatives of diverse populations had mingled in the Old Northwest to found a civilization that combined in a notable degree the ideals and the points of view of the various elements of population from which these immigrants had sprung. Moreover, the great majority of the settlers in the Old Northwest came from the masses of the older states, and many of them were Revolutionary veterans who hoped to find better living conditions for themselves and their families in the land beyond the mountains. They represented, too, the liberal party in the Revolutionary period, and they naturally expected to throw aside the outworn conservatism of colonial days, and to put into effect their democratic ideals. The civilization that they established was, therefore, one with a distinctively modern and progressive point of view.

The foundation stones of this American colonial venture were the Land Ordinance of 1785 and the Government Ordinance of 1787, and the practical sense that was displayed in modifying these terms to meet actual conditions was mainly responsible for the success of the experiment. The Land Ordinance of 1785, in the form in which it had been passed, originally represented a compromise between those who would use the public lands merely as a financial asset, and those who would put foremost Western interests and the needs of the would-be emigrant of small means. In the end the two last-named considerations triumphed, and the Land Act of 1800 modified the terms of the Ordinance in such fashion that it ensured the sale of the public lands to individual settlers rather than to speculators. Defects soon appeared in the provisions for public sales, even though the average immigrant could now take up his own land. The credit system, especially, caused trouble, and the many squatters upon the public lands made it necessary to adopt some system of preemption. These difficulties the Land Act of 1820 and the Preëmption Act of 1841 finally adjusted. But in the early period up to 1812, while the Old Northwest was being established, the land policy of the Federal government had been definitely modified in the interest of the Western country, and of the individual small landholder. Thus, precedents were set for the distribution of the Trans-Mississippi public lands, as well as of those in the Old Northwest.

In similar fashion, the Government Ordinance of 1787 was modified in the light of actual experience. Although the Ordinance had, for the most part, worked successfully in the Northwest Territory where it was first put into effect, it had certain obvious defects. The restricted suffrage it provided and its generally autocratic provisions had their roots in colonial conservatism. When settlers who usually supported the new Revolutionary liberalism were allowed a representative assembly they naturally opposed a franchise that was restricted to property holders, and thus made possible continued control by a governor who represented the old Federalism. The strength of this opposition came to the surface when the transition was made to statehood in Ohio in 1803, and the Republican cohorts established universal male suffrage along with other liberal reforms. This example naturally influenced the inhabitants of neighboring Indiana to demand a more democratic form of territorial government.

In response Congress first gave them the right to vote
directly for the legislative council and for the territorial
delegate, and then, in 1811, it passed the act that conferred
popular suffrage. Following these precedents it became necessary to allow the same privileges in Illinois, and these reforms in the territories of the Old Northwest inevitably led
to similar modifications in the provisions for the government
of later territories.

Aside from the slight changes that experience showed to
be necessary, the provisions of the Government Ordinance
were successfully put into practice, and Governor St. Clair,
an able though somewhat arbitrary administrator, firmly laid
the foundations of government in the Old Northwest, with
the aid of officers of judgment and experience. The substantial fashion in which this work was done, and the extent to
which it met the wishes of the inhabitants, was illustrated
when the territorial assemblies, and even the legislature of
the state of Ohio, based their codes upon the work of St.
Clair and his aides. In the territories of Indiana and Illinois
the Ordinance was carried out with perhaps somewhat less
friction than in the Northwest Territory, for Governor Harrison and Governor Edwards were younger men, and were,
therefore, more adaptable than St. Clair, and both of them
had acquired an extensive practical knowledge of Western
problems before they assumed power in their respective territories. The one instance in the Old Northwest where the
Ordinance failed was Michigan. Here Hull, who was utterly
unfit for his duties, and Judge Woodward, a man of irascible
temper who planned grandiose but impossible schemes, were
in power, and they proved to be most unfortunate appointees. Perhaps no one could have succeeded in Michigan, in
view of the land situation and the generally feeble policy of
Congress. But elsewhere in the Old Northwest experience
demonstrated the practical nature of the Ordinance of 1787,
especially if the modifications of the provision for suffrage
were made which were necessary to meet the demands of a
growing democracy.

Like the political organization, the economic system that was established by the American settlers in the Old Northwest set up precedents that were followed in later Trans-Mississippi settlements. The Land Ordinance of 1787 and the Land Laws that followed exerted much influence in restricting the size of the average landholding, thus ensuring a rural population made up chiefly of small farm yeomen. The dramatic fight to uphold the anti-slavery clause of the Ordinance of 1787 had a similar effect in the end. From the early days of settlement many owners of land in the Virginia Military District, together with other Southern emigrants and numerous inhabitants of the French settlements, had clamored for the admission of slaves into the Northwest Territory. They dangled before the settlers the promise of a greatly increased population if such action were taken, but the strong Puritan and Middle States contingent, with the aid of the anti-slavery element among the Southern settlers, effectively blocked such maneuvers in the legislative assembly of the Northwest Territory, and later in the Ohio State Convention. In Indiana the struggle was more bitter and prolonged under a territorial governor who was supposed to favor slavery, and was backed by influential sections of the population. Finally the anti-slavery party was successful here also, even though the scantier settlements, and the ever-present danger from the Indians, made doubly attractive the possibility of an increased population, if only slavery were permitted. In Illinois the battle raged with even more intensity between the anti-slavery and the pro-slavery forces, but with a similar outcome. This thoroughgoing victory of the anti-slavery forces was a momentous one in its effect upon the social and economic life of the Old Northwest. Lacking a dependable supply of labor, the farmer north of the Ohio, in contrast to his neighbor south of the river, was obliged to depend chiefly upon himself and his family to clear and till his farm. This limited supply of labor, added to the restrictions under the Land Laws, had its effect. Small farms, rather than large plantations, became the usual custom, and the early settlers adopted the varied agriculture to which the soil and climate were better suited, in preference to some one general crop as tobacco. In their grain fields and herds of stock, in their orchards and their fine vegetable gardens, these farms of the Old Northwest reproduced the chief features of the varied agriculture of the Middle States, and thus laid the basis of the very considerable agricultural self-sufficiency that is still characteristic of the Middle West.

Along with the agriculture of the Middle States, it was fitting that the Old Northwest should at least partially adopt the industrialism and the large degree of local economic independence of this same region. This phase of early Western civilization was made possible by the swift progress in opening up avenues of communication, to keep pace with the demands of an increasing commerce. Internally, the merchants and traders used at first the many waterways that marked the boundaries of the Old Northwest, or else opened up access into the interior. Later they took advantage of a network of highways that gradually extended between the different settlements, and that made possible, aside from trade routes, the beginnings of a postal system. External trade routes, also, were soon available, and it became possible to send out the cattle and hogs "on the hoof," the whisky, the flour, the lumber, and the other products of which the West had a surplus, in exchange for the manufactured articles, the wines, and the other luxuries which an increasingly prosperous population demanded. The general store quickly arose as the center of this early trade, with stocks, in the larger settlements, that compared favorably with those of similar establishments in the Atlantic states. Occasionally specialized stores were opened for the sale of drugs, stationery, and the like. The high prices of imported commodities and the many difficulties of transportation developed a strong movement for local economic independence, which took a number of forms. The gristmills that were quickly established ground out flour and meal, and the sawmills turned out lumber, while the distilleries produced the whisky which the inhabitants of the Old Northwest considered so necessary for their comfort. The pioneer housewife, also, produced household manufactures upon a large scale, chiefly linens and woolens. Before long the Western settlers began to utilize local deposits of coal and iron, and to manufacture cotton and woolen goods in small factories that occasionally used steam as a motive power. With this increasing commercialism and industrialism specialized occupations arose. In place of merely unskilled laborers, carpenters and bricklayers came in, barbers began to open their shops, watchmakers were in demand, and professional men, lawyers, doctors, teachers, and ministers, helped make up the panorama of industrial life in the settlements of the Old Northwest. Luxuries, too, were in demand, and in twenty-four short years the basis of a modern economic life had been laid.

Nor did the pioneers of the Old Northwest found a civilization that was wholly materialistic, for they brought with them the cultural tastes and the educational ideals of the older settlements along the Atlantic Coast. The very origin of the Western immigrants, from the masses, and their chief purpose, to find better living conditions, made them determined to secure for their children the opportunities which in many cases they had not enjoyed themselves. The settlers from New England, especially, were foremost in upholding their traditions of popular education, and the reservation of section sixteen of the public lands enabled them to put their ideals into practice. It was fitting that Marietta, a distinctly New England settlement, should lead the way in establishing a school scarcely a year after the first settlers landed. Other settlements followed this example, until by the close of the early period in 1812, there were few, if any, centers of population in the Old Northwest that lacked schools. In Cincinnati and some of the larger settlements, there were even schools of special types, such as those which were founded for female education, night schools, and the prototype of the modern technical school. Nor had higher learning been neglected, and here again the New England emigrants were the leaders when they established Ohio University at Athens, upon the basis of two townships of public lands that had been set aside for this purpose in the grant to the Ohio Company. Vincennes University was the only other institution, founded in similar fashion, which was actually opened in the Old Northwest in this early period, but the New Englanders of the Ohio Purchase and the early inhabitants of Vincennes had set an important precedent that other Western communities followed, by establishing institutions of higher learning that were supported by public funds.

Closely connected with the support of public education in the Old Northwest was a considerable demand for books, which was all the more remarkable in view of the many hardships of pioneer life, and the small individual incomes. Books of current interest as well as standard authors were brought across the mountains for these Western readers, their titles covering a wide range that met the tastes of the lovers of poetry, romance, biography, travel, and adventure, of the student of theology, or of the historically minded reader. In most cases the general store supplied these needs, but in at least one instance a book and stationery store bore witness to the extensive demand that had sprung up for such wares, while another source of supply was afforded by the subscription libraries that were started in most of the larger settlements, as the humble predecessors of the Carnegie Library of modern fame. Occasionally, too, the local presses printed books that were chiefly legal or theological in nature. The weekly gazette of the Atlantic Coast also spread to the Old Northwest. Following the *Centinel,* first established in Cincinnati in 1793, these journals were soon being published in all the important settlements. Founded primarily to publish legal notices, like their Eastern prototypes they included much political news which was often several weeks late, owing to vexatious delays in the mails. Practically all of them imitated, likewise, the gazettes of the seaboard in their *Poets' Corner* and in their miscellaneous *Literary Of-*

ferings. These last two types of columns usually afforded a resting place for the compositions of many local aspirants for literary fame, or for the extracts from other periodicals that at least revealed to the inhabitants of the Old Northwest the existence of an important outside world. Almanacs, too, were published, which followed a time-honored custom in the Eastern states, and even in New England, by printing an almost laughable jumble of calendars, weather predictions, useful information, political news, essays, and anecdotes.

Even in their recreations the early settlers in the Old Northwest frequently preserved the traditions of their old homes, and in spite of their arduous labors, the pioneers in Cincinnati soon found time to indulge their taste for amateur dramatics, and this form of amusement spread to other settlements. Singing schools and debating societies, also, became popular among the Western settlers, who were accustomed to gather by candlelight for their evening recreations, or perhaps in the glow of a blazing hearth. Yet organizations of this type were merely the surface indications of the cultural standards which were being established in the Old Northwest in the brief period between 1788 and 1812. In the typically American civilization that thus arose were mingled: the educational ideals of New England and the Middle States; the love of good reading which was so widespread among the Southern planters; and the general regard for the finer things of life which these emigrants brought across the mountains. Thus, the cultural foundations were laid of the civilization of the Middle West, with its public schools and libraries, its state universities, its love of music, and its literary clubs and similar organizations.

But the picture would not be complete without an attempt to explain the strong Puritanical spirit of the Old Northwest which has shown itself in such decided fashion throughout the Middle West. The Puritan settlers from New England were, of course, primarily responsible for a rather strict attitude toward life in general, and the intolerance that occasionally became evident in this early period up to 1812. But their number was comparatively small, and, without adequate support, their influence could never have been so great, in spite of their rugged perseverance and their sturdy characteristics. Therefore, in any attempt to account for the strength of Puritan ideals, it is necessary to bear in mind the effective aid which certain other denominations in the Old Northwest gave the Congregationalists from New England. The conscientious Quakers, small in numbers but strong in influence, the Presbyterians, and even the Baptists doubtless aided in support of the Puritan ideals. But most important of all were the Methodists, who were the most numerous of all the denominations that found a foothold in these Western settlements. With their basic doctrine that church members should separate themselves from the worldly-minded, and with their rigid church discipline over their flocks, the Methodists readily fell in line with the Puritan point of view, and their large numbers, together with the energetic work of their circuit riders, made them invaluable allies in giving the initial impulse to the Middle West conscience which has become so important a factor in American history. In the early period this Puritan influence showed itself in sumptuary legislation, such as laws against Sabbath breaking and swearing, against gambling, and for the control of poolrooms and barrooms, which were the natural outcome of a strong religious consciousness. Later on, it was to find an outlet in this same region in a militant anti-slavery movement, and still later in the anti-saloon crusade. The same Puritan influence of the New England conscience, combined with the militant social consciousness of the Quaker, the Presbyterian, and the Methodist gave to this Western frontier a strong moral fiber that accounts to a large extent for the unusual orderliness that was another of its leading characteristics. But colonial examples of a stern justice and a quick punishment, using the pillory, the whipping post, and, in extreme cases, the gallows, must also be taken into account. The backwoodsman, likewise, firmly believed in ready justice, and an exceptionally able bar helped to enforce the laws, and to establish an unusual degree of orderliness in the Old Northwest. Still another striking feature of this Puritanic spirit was the strong sense of social obligations, which was later to be emphasized so markedly in the community point of view of the Middle West.

The ideals of public education, the demand for books of a more serious nature, and the popularity of the numerous mediums for the expression of public opinion were all outward evidences of the democracy that was so ingrained in the Old Northwest. The economic system that was soon established, with its small farms and free labor and its varied agriculture, also developed this spirit, while the very origin of the majority of the pioneers, from the middle and the lower classes of the older states, made inevitable the development of a thoroughgoing democracy whose supporters tended to become somewhat vociferous at times in their public statements. These Western patriots gave utterance to abstract principles of democracy in varied fashion: in the toasts at Fourth of July banquets; in editorial columns; in frequent communications from the correspondents of the local newspapers; and in other mediums of public expression. At times they lauded the United States as the one true citadel of democracy, plainly showing the strong influence of the French philosophers in their frequent allusions to the "Rights of Man." By a strict adherence to this and other basic Revolutionary principles, one writer declared that America would become an "asylum for Liberty," in which aliens, whose intention it was to become permanent citizens, and "whose principles are congenial with our own," would find "equal liberty with ourselves." [1]

But Western democracy was quite sufficient unto itself, and the "holier than thou" attitude often came to the surface. Evidently there was a widespread suspicion among the Western patriots that the Eastern states had strayed somewhat from the paths of pure and undefiled democracy. Re-

[1] *Western Spy,* July 3, 1802.

mote from foreign influences, according to one writer, the Western States would prove to be "an asylum to the sons of freedom, even though liberty be banished from the Eastern states." Far stronger was the prejudice against the Old World, with its wars and its class distinctions. The "peaceful blessings" of America, according to one newspaper correspondent, were in strong contrast to the "pomp and desolation" that had overspread Europe. Other writers stressed the "calamities of War" which Napoleon had carried through the Continent in his campaigns.[2] The corruption of the English government served as another popular target for Western democrats, who thus renewed the execrations of Revolutionary days, and, at the same time, lauded the "purity" of the American brand of government. Others of them took up with great avidity any strictures upon the "tyrannical" King, or the English royal family, and dwelt on such matters at considerable length, doubtless much to the edification of their readers. The prejudice against foreigners also assumed the form of a strong nativism which protested against any favors to the "foreign born," and objected especially to them as officeholders.[3] From such statements it is quite evident that these Westerners were smugly assured that they alone held aloft the true torch of liberty, which elsewhere burned only dimly, if at all.

Another outward manifestation of this militant Western democracy was a strong opposition to class distinctions, a prejudice which the pioneers had doubtless brought with them from their old homes. One enthusiast hoped that the "genuine spirit of republicanism" would "totally annihilate the pernicious seeds of aristocracy," and certain inhabitants of the Illinois settlements carried this vindictive spirit to extreme lengths when they called down "destruction" upon "all combinations against the Rights of Man," and expressed the hope that, throughout the world, Liberty would "tread

[2] *Liberty Hall,* February 11, 1810; *The Supporter,* April 14, 1810; *Scioto Gazette,* May 15, 1811.
[3] *Liberty Hall,* November 15, 1809, and June 27, 1810.

beneath her foot the monarch and the despot." [4] Thomas Paine was, of course, held in great esteem in the Western country as the apostle of the Rights of Man, and one enthusiast, probably somewhat bibulously, described him as "the greatest political luminary of the eighteenth century, and the most distinguished advocate of the rights of man that ever wrote in any age or country." [5] But Jefferson, "the mild philosopher and man of the people," reigned as the high priest of Western democracy. His election as President was the occasion for much popular rejoicing, and his inaugural address was warmly commended for its moderation and sound democracy.[6] Nor did these Western settlers confine themselves to mere platitudes upon democracy, for they definitely pointed out certain ideals they expected Jeffersonian Republicans to realize. Civil and religious liberty, one representative statement read, must be preserved and "transmitted inviolate to the latest posterity." Another citizen expounded the true meaning of democracy as a "free and equal suffrage frequently exercised, talent and integrity the only qualifications for office, and submission to the will of the majority." Still another article pointedly reminded the members of Congress and other popular representatives that they should never forget they merely "represented" a "people jealous of their rights." [7]

These Western immigrants, with their origin chiefly from the Revolutionary masses, insisted that the theoretical liberalism of the period should be carried out in practice. Their most notable accomplishment in the early period up to 1812 was the constitution of Ohio, with its provisions for manhood suffrage, for complete separation of Church and State, for the removal of property qualifications for office, for the curbing of the executive power, and for other less significant

---

[4] *Western Spy*, July 9, 1800; *Missouri Gazette*, July 26, 1808; *Louisiana Gazette*, July 19, 1810.
[5] *Western Sun*, May 6, 1809.
[6] *Western Spy*, May 13, 1801.
[7] *Trump of Fame*, June 16, 1812; *Muskingum Messenger*, July 7, 1810; *Liberty Hall*, July 11, 1811.

reforms. All of these provisions had been included in the program of the Revolutionary liberals, but many of them had been ignored in the new constitutions of the Atlantic states. This same Revolutionary liberalism showed itself also in many issues that arose in actual administration in Ohio, and to a lesser degree in the territories. One of its striking manifestations in the Old Northwest was a definite policy to regulate, in the public interest, such monopolies as the public utilities, thus carrying out the anti-monopolistic theories which the American colonists had brought with them from England. The legislative assembly of the Northwest Territory set up this principle when it authorized the county courts of quarter sessions to fix ferry charges, and required ferry keepers to recognize their obligations to the public. This precedent was followed in the state of Ohio and in Indiana Territory, and in the former, the legislature in like fashion regulated the tolls to be charged on bridges built at private expense, and on turnpikes, with provision in each case for ultimate public ownership. This same modern principle was applied as well in a number of measures for the regulation of business. Thus, in 1799 the legislative assembly of the Northwest Territory fixed the charges to be made by millers, and drew up an act that would ensure accurate measures of their products. There were laws also, both in the Northwest Territory and in Indiana, for the careful inspection of exports, and acts were passed in Ohio and Indiana to secure standard measures. Essentially similar in principle to these acts was the Ohio law for the careful regulation of banks, and especially the provision that the state might purchase a part of the capital stock. These, and similar measures, represented a modern and liberal doctrine, which strongly asserted itself in the Old Northwest by enforcing a sense of obligation to the community on the part of those who performed public services, and was in contrast to the older theory of *laissez-faire*.

Another practical application of Revolutionary liberalism in the Western country was the strong support that was given to the principle of the freedom of the press, which was termed the "palladium of our rights," to be continued until "time is no more." [8] Doubtless the Alien and Sedition acts had greatly strengthened this attitude, and when they were repealed there was much outspoken rejoicing in the Old Northwest. One patriot bluntly maintained that the officers of the government should conduct themselves in such fashion that they would not fear newspaper criticism. Other enthusiasts declared that a free press was necessary for the continuance of a "genuine free Republican government," and that truth would always triumph, where there was freedom of investigation.[9] In a much similar spirit, Rev. John W. Browne, editor of *Liberty Hall,* insisted that, as the chief purpose of his paper was to give the truth, he would print communications that were written from any point of view, barring only those that were scurrilous or intentionally mean.[10] This offer, Browne, who was a strong supporter of the Republican administration, consistently carried out. The sentiment in the Old Northwest in favor of freedom of the press was also shown in frequent allusions to the satisfactory situation under Jefferson that evidently were purposely made to reflect upon the preceding Federalist administration. Indeed, the militant Republicanism of the West was constantly in evidence in efforts to check any possible reaction toward Federalism. Thus, in 1804 the *Indiana Gazette* warned its readers against the "indiscriminate abuse" of the federal administration in the Eastern papers, which in the writer's opinion merely represented the "effusions of party spirit or personal resentment." [11] In 1809, upon the eve of Madison's administration, another Republican partisan ironically called attention to the Federalist misstatements in the recent campaign. Now, he asserted, these same individuals were trying to forget their defeat by mock fu-

[8] *Scioto Gazette,* July 10, 1809.
[9] *Western Spy,* July 3, 1802; *Liberty Hall,* July 12, 1809; *Louisiana Gazette,* August 2, 1810.
[10] *Liberty Hall,* December 4, 1804.
[11] *Indiana Gazette,* October 23, 1804.

nerals for Liberty. This attempt he termed "a glorious display of aristocratic philanthropy to hang the dear lady *alive;* may she long live in the hearts of the Americans, and be tenderly nursed by the patriotic Madison." [12] Yet even this strongly Republican sentiment conceded the freedom of the press to the few Federalist supporters in the Old Northwest. This sense of fair play, so typical of the Western country, was occasionally in evidence when newspapers with Federalist leanings did not hesitate to criticize the national administration. As an illustration, an editorial in the *Commentator* published in Chillicothe, the hotbed of Western Republicanism, rather blamed the administration for the dismissal of Jackson, the British minister, and opposed an alliance with France under any circumstances.[13] Also, Western democracy, with its strict sense of justice, permitted the Federalist editor of the *Western Spectator* to criticize openly both the declaration and the conduct of the War of 1812. This point of view was well expressed in the motto which headed the columns of the *Indiana Gazette:* "Independence is my Happiness, and I state things as they are, without respect to Place or Persons." [14]

Their strong belief in the philosophic principles of the rights of man and the consent of the governed, and in democracy in general, inevitably led frontier settlers, who naturally were impatient of control, to protest when they felt the restraints of an outside power. This spirit showed itself in notable fashion in the strong opposition that gradually arose in the Northwest Territory to the autocratic régime of St. Clair and the judges. Harping upon the well-worn battle cry of Federalist class rule, as contrasted with Republican democracy, many of these critics played upon frontier prejudice by attempts to associate the territorial government with aristocracy and privilege. Later during the struggle for statehood in Ohio, one politician urged the in-

[12] *Liberty Hall,* March 2, 1809.
[13] *Commentator,* November 25, 1809.
[14] *Indiana Gazette,* August 7, 1805.

habitants not to cease their endeavors, and never to be satisfied, "short of a free government, and an equal participation of state and Federal privileges." After Congress had passed the enabling act for Ohio, *A Farmer,* writing in the *Western Spy,* was especially gleeful over the near prospect for the overthrow of an aristocracy, and an emergence from a colonial form of government, and there were many other similar expressions.[15] This desire for freedom from external control spread throughout the Old Northwest. In Indiana, likewise, soon after the territory was formed, the hope was expressed that it would quickly rival the "proudest of the states," and likewise in Illinois, even before the separation from Indiana, there was an openly expressed sentiment in favor of "free and independent state governments" in the neighboring territories.[16] Doubtless the author of this seemingly altruistic wish was not without hope that Illinois, too, would soon join the sisterhood of states. After the separation from Indiana, the Illinois settlers began openly to plan for statehood as a release from their "shackles," and as a means of giving them "a voice in the general government." [17]

The same opposition to any restraint which had been evident in the widespread hostility toward a territorial form of government, showed itself in the many expressions of prejudice against courts, judges, and lawyers. This attitude in the Old Northwest was comparable to the parallel one in the backwoods settlements of the older states, which came to a climax in Shays' Rebellion. A few typical examples will show how deep-seated this prejudice was among the Western pioneers. In 1805, a contributor to the *Scioto Gazette,* under the caption, *Common Law,* vigorously protested against the numerous statutes that had been passed in Ohio, since they made necessary so many judges, lawyers, clerks, and the like whom the people must support.[18] Closely related to this op-

---

[15] *Western Spy,* July 8, 1801, and July 24, 1803.
[16] *Western Sun,* July 11, 1807; *Missouri Gazette,* July 26, 1808.
[17] *Louisiana Gazette,* August 2, 1810.
[18] *Scioto Gazette,* December 12, 1805.

position to judges and lawyers was the struggle in Ohio over the right of the judiciary to interpret the state constitution, which reached a climax in the Sweeping Resolution. Undoubtedly General Worthington voiced a sentiment that was characteristic of the frontier, when he publicly intimated that the Ohio judiciary were endeavoring to lift themselves above their normal position as servants of the people.[19] Especially significant was a toast to the state of Ohio, at the Fourth of July banquet in Cincinnati in 1809: "No slavery —may judges, lawyers, and the preposterous unwritten law yield to the written law and good sense of her virtuous citizens," and two years later, also in Cincinnati, there was a somewhat more moderate toast to the judiciary, "Unbiased by party spirit, may they administer justice in mercy." [20] In an article in *Liberty Hall, A Farmer* included lawyers, traders, and clergy in a general denunciation.[21] Most striking of all these evidences of pioneer hostility toward the legal fraternity was the toast given at a Fourth of July banquet in Cahokia, in 1812: "May the bones of the judge bleach upon the surface of the earth without burial, who courts the favor of the rich—May the tongue be cut out that can usurp the province of a jury—May the hand wither that can directly or indirectly take a bribe." [22]

Another marked characteristic of the pioneers of the Old Northwest was their strong support of the Federal government. This nationalist, in preference to a state's rights point of view was the natural result of the circumstances under which American institutions had been established in this region. Unlike the original states, the territories and the states of the Old Northwest had been carved out of the national domain, while both the land system and the political institutions had been set up by Federal action, rather than by state laws, as was the case for so large a part of the Old

[19] *Scioto Gazette,* July 10, 1809.
[20] *Liberty Hall,* July 12, 1809, and July 10, 1811.
[21] *Ibid.,* December 21, 1809.
[22] *Missouri Gazette,* July 18, 1811.

Southwest. As a consequence, from the very beginning the inhabitants of the Old Northwest were accustomed to look to their creator, the Federal government, for the necessary aid in crises. Moreover, the common origin of the different administrative units tended to break down artificial barriers between them, and the necessary coöperation to meet the Indian peril hastened this process, until there was no such gulf between the citizens of Ohio and those of Indiana as existed between New Yorkers and Virginians. Within the Old Northwest there was bound to be a certain degree of sectionalism in view of the diverse origin of the early settlers, and it showed itself especially in those regions where either Southern or New England emigrants predominated. But as a whole the Old Northwest tended to develop into an amalgamated region that was eventually known as the Middle West. The many mutual problems of the different sections made a considerable degree of solidarity inevitable, and it frequently came to the surface, notably during the agitation over the opening of the Mississippi, and afterward in the popular approval of the Louisiana Purchase Treaty. It was evident, too, in the well-nigh hysterical wave of apprehension that swept through the Western country when the intrigues of Burr were noised abroad. This same spirit was often shown in exaggerated form at patriotic celebrations. Thus, at the Fourth of July banquet of the Republican Societies of Cincinnati in 1810, a toast to roads and canals proclaimed that: "Neither mountains 4,000 feet high, nor the discharge of our rivers into distant oceans can dissolve the union of the States." [23]

The strong support of the national government in the Old Northwest was shown in rather forceful fashion in the attitude of the Ohio legislature toward a number of amendments to the Federal constitution that were referred to it during this early period. In 1811 the legislature unanimously ratified an amendment which provided that any American citizen who accepted a pension, a title, or the like from a

[23] *Liberty Hall*, July 11, 1810.

foreign prince, should lose his citizenship and be incapable of holding office.[24] But this rather extreme Americanism was exceptional, for this same legislature displayed a moderation that was unusual in so new a state toward at least three rather important amendments that were brought before it during its third session, 1804–1805.[25] One of them, from the Massachusetts legislature, proposed to apportion representation according to population, thus greatly reducing the influence of the Southern states. Although the anti-slavery party had recently won a complete victory in Ohio, the legislature refused to accept this amendment, upon the ground that it was inexpedient, and would, in their opinion, excite jealousies and "destroy that confidence and good understanding which now prevails, and endanger the Union of the States." This stand seems to have had considerable local support, and one correspondent of a local paper aptly pointed out that, if the amendment were put into effect, it would strengthen Massachusetts at the expense of Virginia, and would destroy a "sacred compact of the union." [26] At this same session the Ohio legislature showed its regard for the interests of other sections when it withheld its consent to a second amendment, proposed by North Carolina, that would have prevented the further importation of slaves. This time the ground of its refusal was, that the proposed amendment was contrary to the mutual agreements between the different sections of the Union. This conservative decision was the more remarkable in view of a declaration in this same resolution, that the existence of slavery in the United States was "an evil of the most alarming nature" which seriously threatened the country's prosperity. This same broad-minded regard for the interests of the country as a whole was shown in response to a third proposed amendment, this one from the Kentucky legislature, to restrict the Federal judiciary power to cases in which the United States was a

[24] *Laws of Ohio,* Ninth General Assembly, pp. 98-99.
[25] *Ibid.,* Third General Assembly, pp. 466-472.
[26] *Scioto Gazette,* December 24, 1804.

party, or else to controversies between the states. The joint resolution by which the Ohio legislature rejected this proposal showed an especially sound view of the nature of the Federal Constitution, holding that while the states had surrendered certain rights for the general good, the Constitution had guaranteed citizens a trial "before a court entirely independent, and wholly free from the influence of any particular state." Furthermore, the legislature felt that "too frequent alterations" might tend to "unhinge" the principles upon which the Constitution rested.

The broad nationalism that the Ohio legislature displayed in dealing with proposed constitutional amendments was to have been expected in view of the distinctive civilization that had arisen in the Old Northwest. In the twenty-four years from the first settlement in 1788, pioneers from New England, from the Middle and Southern states, and from the backwoods, had mingled on this frontier, to establish a society which, combining the characteristics of all the important sections of the United States, was typically American. The political origin of the Old Northwest as a Federal domain, which at the outset Federal officials administered, had greatly influenced this nationalistic development. Moreover, the very antecedents of settlers, many of whom were Revolutionary veterans and most of them from the masses, ensured a thoroughgoing democracy in this Western country. In Ohio especially, the first state to be carved out of the Old Northwest, liberal precedents were set up that were followed as a matter of course, partly in the territories and wholly in the states that were formed from the remaining sections of the Old Northwest. Perhaps it is no exaggeration to say that the liberal constitution of Ohio represented the definite triumph of Western democracy over Eastern conservatism. But it was a democracy that in the end allied itself with the liberal elements of the North. In its economic and cultural development also, this civilization of the Old Northwest definitely ranged itself with the Northern, rather than with the Southern system. When the final contest came between the two, the inhabitants of the Old Northwest and the many settlers west of the Mississippi who had patterned their own civilization upon the one that prevailed east of the Mississippi and north of the Ohio, exercised a deciding influence upon the final victory of the North.

INDEX

INDEX